AMERICAN HEADLINES

Year by Year

M, A. Clover
207 N Clinton
Dwight
Ill.

AMERICAN HEADLINES

Year by Year

Editor-in-Chief
Calvin D. Linton, Ph.D.
Dean, Columbian College of Arts and Sciences
The George Washington University

Introductory Text
Walter A. Payne, Ph.D.
Chairman, History Department
University of the Pacific

THOMAS NELSON PUBLISHERS
Nashville • Camden • New York

Managing Editor
Secular Reference Books
MARY BRAY WHEELER

Updating Contributors
James Crutchfield
Alice Ewing

Editorial Assistants
Teri Mitchell
Genon Neblett

Research Assistants
Mary Jane Lunn
Henry McGuffey
Kristie McGuffey
Mary Anne McNeese
Julie Smithson

Creation and Production Staff
STRAVON EDUCATIONAL PRESS

Editor-in-Chief
Calvin D. Linton

Associate Editor
Elvin Albeles

Writers
Betty Brinkerhoff
William Jaber
Ronald G. Kirchem
Paulette S. Lee
Walter A. Payne
Robert M. Segal

Editorial Assistant
Diane Pearson

Artists
George Geygan
Morton Garchik
Charles Handler
James Roth
William Green

Index
Celia S. Greed

Picture Research
Norma Lloyd

Library of Congress Cataloging in Publication data
Main entry under title:

American headlines, year by year.

   Updated ed. of : The American almanac. c1977.
   Includes index.
   1. United States—History—Chronology. I. Linton,
Calvin Darlington, 1914–   . II. American almanac.
E174.5.A48 1985   973'.02'02   85-4888
ISBN 0-8407-7515-6

AMERICAN HEADLINES: YEAR BY YEAR was formerly published as THE BICENTENNIAL ALMANAC and then as THE AMERICAN ALMANAC. The present volume contains more pages and is updated with new text and photographs for years, 1977 through 1984. The present tense is used throughout the Almanac, both in the introductory and in the chronological entries, just as such an account would be presented by a contemporary journalist. In order to clarify or amplify certain entries, information that would not be available to a contemporary is sometimes added [in brackets]. The Almanac may therefore be read as a continuous journal, with useful insertions by a helpful editor—in a sense, the annotated diary of the American people.

Printed in the United States of America

1 2 3 4 5 6 7 8 9 10 — 89 88 87 86 85

CONTENTS

COLOR ILLUSTRATIONS
Portraits of the Presidents

The portraits of the Presidents of the United States appearing in the *American Almanac* are the official White House portraits by the artists whose names are printed in italic type on the list below. The pictures of Presidents Richard M. Nixon, Gerald R. Ford, Jimmy Carter, and Ronald Reagan are the authorized White House color photographs.

OTHER COLOR ILLUSTRATIONS

BLACK AND WHITE ILLUSTRATIONS
Signers of the Declaration of Independence

Portraits of the signers of the Declaration of Independence appear in the book *Signers of the Declaration,* published by the U. S. Department of the Interior in connection with the celebration of the Bicentennial. Photographs of 42 of the 56 portraits of the signers were supplied by the Independence National Historical Park of the U. S. Department of the Interior. Sources of the remaining 14 signers are given in the Acknowledgements.

ACKNOWLEDGMENTS

Color illustrations: The White House Historical Association, for portraits of the Presidents of the United States from George Washington to Lyndon B. Johnson; The White House Historical Association, for the photograph of Richard M. Nixon; The White House, for the photograph of Gerald R. Ford; The National Gallery of Art, for George Washington's Family, Salute to George Washington in New York Harbor, The White Cloud, Chief of the Iowas, See-non-ty-a, an Iowa Medicine Man; New-York Historical Society, for Benjamin Franklin, Ki-on-twog-ky, a Seneca Chief; The Corcoran Gallery, for Robert E. Lee, and Thomas J. Jackson; The United States Navy, for Sailors of the Air, The Battle of Midway, D Day; The United States Army, for the John F. Kennedy funeral cortege; United Press International, Commercial Division, for the Martin Luther King, Jr. funeral cortege, and for Martin Luther King, Jr. at Birmingham, Alabama; The United States Army, for the Vietnam photographs; and NASA, for the space-exploration photographs.

Black and white illustrations: Independence National Historical Park, for the signers of the Declaration of Independence, except the following: New-York Historical Society, for Benjamin Franklin; The R. W. Norton Art Gallery, Shreveport, Louisiana, for Philip Livingston, John Morton, John Penn, and James Smith; The Henry Francis du Pont Winterthur Museum for Benjamin Rush; Paul Geygan, for wash drawings of the following signers based upon portraits appearing in *Signers of the Declaration,* Button Gwinnett (this is a conjectural representation as no portrait or reliable likeness of Gwinnett is known to exist), Lyman Hall, Francis Lightfoot Lee, Lewis Morris, Caesar Rodney, Thomas Stone, Matthew Thornton, and William Whipple; New York Public Library, for pages 23, 25, 26, 31, 39, 71, 75, 92; *Harper's Weekly* (various issues), for pages 21, 34, 197, 216, 223, 227, 243, 245; United Press International, Commercial Division, for pages 139, 162, 179, 188, 190, 229, 259, 261, 263, 267, 271, 273, 275, 279, 281, 283, 285, 287, 289, 291, 292, 293, 297, 301, 305, 306, 307, 309, 310, 311, 313, 314, 315, 317, 319, 321, 323, 325, 327, 329, 331, 333, 335, 339, 341, 342, 343, 345, 347, 352, 359, 362, 363, 365, 367, 369, 371, 379, 383, 423, 425ff., 440ff.; Library of Congress, for pages 19, 87, 121, 135, 137, 145, 157, 159, 172, 177, 182, 184-5, 192, 193, 201, 203, 211, 221, 224, 225, 232, 233, 235, 241, 247, 248, 249, 252, 253, 255, 257; *Nashville Banner,* for pages 444-459; New-York Historical Society, for pages 33, 37, 43, 56, 73, 77, 81, 92, 93, 101, 107, 110, 111, 128, 129, 133, 147, 183, 303; Argosy Gallery, for pages 29, 45, 83, 91, 95, 119, 161, 163, 166, 173, 175, 176, 178, 184, 187, 207, 209, 214, 216; U.S. Army, for pages 164, 171, 177, 215, 295, 299, 355, 357, 359, 362, 379, 380; U.S. Navy, for pages 59, 87, 277, 352; U.S. Marines, for page 257; U.S. Army Signal Corps, for pages 239, 369, 375; NASA, for pages 415, 417, 420; Minnesota Historical Society, for pages 142, 151, 154, 265; Wells Fargo Bank, for pages 138, 205, 269; Union Pacific Railroad, for pages 199, 230; Texas State Library, for page 109.

Special thanks are gratefully offered to the following people for their assistance in gathering the hundreds of portraits and photographs appearing in the Almanac. W. Boer, II, Lieutenant Commander, U.S. Navy, Head Media Services Division, Public Information Division; Major Richard A. Gardner, U.S. Army; Glen Thomas, Corcoran Gallery of Art; Jerry M. Bloomer, Secretary-Registrar, The R. W. Norton Art Gallery; Carol J. Carefoot, Archivist, Texas State Library; Hillory A. Tolson, Executive Director, White House Historical Association; Mercedes Brown, The Museum of the Confederacy; Bonnie Wilson, Reference Librarian, Minnesota Historical Society; John J. Fletcher, Manager, United Press International, Commercial Photography Division.

Apprenticeship for Nationhood
1492-1775

As the year 1775 draws to a close, the American colonies are in a state of active rebellion. The colonies have finally formed a confederation. Their delegates, meeting in Philadelphia as the Second Continental Congress, continue to deny any intention of separating from the English connection, although their expressions of loyalty to George III lack conviction. While offering their Olive Branch Petition they are busy organizing a defense of their liberties on the field of battle. They have chosen General George Washington to lead their armed forces and he has taken command in the field, where the colonials are besieging Boston. Elsewhere Colonel Ethan Allen has captured Fort Ticonderoga; General Richard Montgomery has taken Montreal and joined forces with Colonel Benedict Arnold, who has completed an arduous march through the Maine wilderness to the plain before Quebec. Throughout the colonies, sides are being taken and British intransigence is breeding American revolution. The editor of *Pennsylvania Magazine,* Thomas Paine, is preparing for publication early in 1776 a pamphlet, *Common Sense,* to persuade the hesitant: "Everything that is right or reasonable pleads for separation. . .our present numbers are sufficient to repel the force of all the world."

How has it happened that the far-flung, disunited, hitherto incompatible settlers in America, who came to these shores for a variety of reasons and who still cherish the traditions of their English homeland, have reached this mood of no return? Even a Franklin or Jefferson could not have foretold this climax to a history of a century and a half of settlement, this unanticipated birth of a new nation.

Europeans were relative latecomers to the New World. When Christopher Columbus, a navigator for Spain, reached the Caribbean island of San Salvador on Oct. 12, 1492, the Indians—having migrated from Asia at least 20,000 years earlier—were well settled in the Western Hemisphere. They used the land in great numbers and in varying degrees of cultural achievement. Two highly developed and thickly populated areas were the Valley of Mexico, where the Aztec civilization was centered, and the central Andean area held by the Incas. But north of the Caribbean Sea and of Mexico there were no highly civilized or populous Indian communities or rich resources in gold or silver to attract conquest by Europeans.

A series of exploratory seafaring expeditions probed the North American Coast. John Cabot, sailing for the English in 1497, was the first. But he and the navigators in the French service who followed in the 16th century, Giovanni da Verrazano and Jacques Cartier, failed to establish settlements. Contact with North America was maintained by seasonal fishermen and by explorers who sporadically traded for fur with the Indians—the French in the St. Lawrence River, where Samuel de Champlain founded the trading post of Quebec in 1608; Henry Hudson sailing the Hudson River for the Dutch in 1609; the Dutch on the Delaware River in 1623 and the Connecticut River ten years later; and the Swedes on the Delaware after 1638. Spain was more energetic and intensive in the incorporation of new regions and new peoples within its vast domains from California to Florida to the Straits of Magellan, but only at isolated posts, such as Santa Fe and St. Augustine and Monterey, did Spain organize stable settlements north of Mexico.

England participated only modestly in this 16th-century expansion toward America. Sir Humphrey Gilbert was authorized by Queen Elizabeth to discover and colonize in unclaimed regions of North America; in 1578 and again in 1583 he led expeditions to the American coast, but he failed to colonize, and his exploits only furnished incentive to others. His half-brother, Sir Walter Raleigh, under a charter of 1584, sent expeditions that named the Virginia coast in honor of the Queen, and put a colony on Roanoke Island in 1585-1586, and another in 1587, but none endured until the lure of wealth in America attracted the support of merchants. A new way to employ private funds, the joint-stock company, enabled Englishmen, through the combined contributions of many investors, to engage in successful overseas enterprise. Of two such companies chartered in 1606, the Virginia Company of Plymouth and the Virginia Company of London, the latter (usually called the London Company) founded the first successful English colony at Jamestown in 1607.

Failing in their attempt to find gold or silver, and staving off starvation under John Smith's leadership, by 1612 these Virginians began to cultivate a species of tobacco from the West Indies that soon became their major source of income. In order to make colonization attractive, the London Company offered grants of land and brought in craftsmen to broaden the economy. Under the terms of the charter, colonists were assured of the rights of English law, and in 1619 the company initiated a plan of administration that resulted in the first elected colonial assembly, the House of Burgesses. This remained even after James I revoked the company's charter in 1624 and made Virginia a royal colony.

The Virginia Company of Plymouth (the Plymouth Company) founded a short-lived colony in 1607-1608 in Maine, and in 1620 a new company was chartered as the Council for New England under a former member of the Plymouth Company, Sir Ferdinando Gorges. Meanwhile, also in 1620, another group of settlers actually left Plymouth, England, in the *Mayflower,* landed at Cape Cod, and late in December began a settlement they named Plymouth. This group, known historically as the Pilgrims, had been given permission to settle on the territory of the London Company, but the area where they landed was outside the jurisdiction of that company, so they created their own local government in the *Mayflower* Compact, and they succeeded in maintaining their Plymouth colony until it was merged with the neighboring Massachusetts Bay colony in 1691. Their courageous survival taught Englishmen that colonization was possible in New England.

A larger colonial venture emerged in the form of the Massachusetts Bay Company, under patent from the Council for New England and chartered by Charles I in 1629. Its stockholders transferred the company to Massachusetts where many thousands of Puritans followed. The freemen of the company annually elected officers and representatives, called the General Court, to govern the company and the colony. Massachusetts gave rise to other colonies. Roger Williams led a dissident group to Rhode Island in 1636, and this group was granted a charter in 1644 as the colony of Providence Plantations. Thomas Hooker led a group to the Connecticut Valley in 1636 to form a government under their Fundamental Orders, and this group was given a royal charter in 1662. Another offshoot from Massachusetts was the colony of New Hampshire, which received a royal charter in 1679.

All the northern colonies were peopled mainly by Puritans who sought governments that would ensure obedience to God and that derived its authority from the people. They believed this was better done in New England than amidst the corruption of old England. While they directed public policy to fulfill the Scriptures, they also sought to improve their lives economically. Without mineral wealth or any single commodity comparable to Virginia's tobacco, New Englanders harvested the land and the sea. They planted corn and wheat, tended cattle, and produced lumber; they fished, constructed ships, and sailed them in Atlantic and Caribbean commerce.

Another noteworthy colony was founded out of the efforts of George Calvert, Lord Baltimore, also a member of the Council for New England. In 1632, Calvert died while a charter was being prepared for a grant on Chesapeake Bay. His son Cecilius was given this grant, and the resulting colony, to be governed by the Calvert family, was called Maryland. The Calverts were Catholic, and from its settlement in 1634 Maryland became a religious refuge for other Catholics. The Maryland Toleration Act of 1649, passed in the colonial assembly, established freedom of worship for all Christians, Catholic or Protestant, who believed in the Trinity. Tobacco culture suited this Chesapeake Bay colony just as it did the adjacent Virginia colony.

I n these settlements, down to the mid-17th century, the English monarchs not only permitted significant liberties in terms of self-government and religious practices, but also in terms of economic organization. By 1650, however, England, in response to contemporary economic doctrines, accepted the premise of mercantilism: that the state should dominate and prevail over private or colonial interests. In a series of Navigation Acts, England, under Cromwell, tried to prevent its rival, Holland, from engaging in trade with English colonies. Under Charles II new Navigation Acts were passed to limit colonial trade to ships built in England or in the colonies, and manned by Englishmen or colonials; and to deter the colonies from importing goods from outside England; and to prevent specific ("enumerated") colonial products—cotton, dyewood, ginger, indigo, sugar, and tobacco—from being exported anywhere except to England or other English colonies. Items were continually added to the list—rice, naval stores, furs, wood, molasses, and hats—as England sought to bring trade benefits to the mother country and to increase tax revenues from duties collected in England. But the policy was difficult to enforce, because of the great distance to America, the activities of competing nations such as Holland, and the attitudes of the colonists, who were in no way benefited by mercantilist laws.

Economic control became even more difficult as a number of other proprietors (such as the Calverts of Maryland) were granted charters by the Crown. In 1663, a royal charter was issued to eight influential Englishmen to develop the Carolinas, a vast region south of Virginia. Tobacco cultivation and small farming created a prosperous colony on Albemarle Sound, while another concentration of settlers grew within a decade near Charles Town [called Charleston after 1783]. Rice and other products grew well here, and Charles Town served a large back country and grew to be the only large city in the South. In 1729, proprietary control failed and royal governments were established in the colonies of North Carolina and South Carolina.

C harles II gave a charter to his brother, James, Duke of York, who proposed to seize a colony that had been established by the Dutch on the Hudson River. From the port of New Amsterdam at its mouth the Dutch settlers had profited from trade with English colonials, but Robert Nicholls seized New Amsterdam for the Duke of York in 1664, and the name of the city and the colony was changed to New York. At first the colonists were governed under a rigid law code, but in 1683 they also were granted a representative elected assembly.

In 1665 the Duke of York transferred part of the former Dutch colony to two friends, Lord John Berkeley and Sir George Carteret, and the colony of New Jersey emerged. It became a royal colony in 1702. In 1681 a charter was granted to a friend of Charles II, William Penn, who had tried, with other Quakers, to find a haven in New Jersey. The fertile lands along the west bank of the Delaware River appeared more promising, however, and these were accepted in payment of a debt owed by the King to Penn's father; the settlement was named Pennsylvania by Charles himself. William Penn was a remarkable proprietor. Under his Frame of Government the people made their own rules through an elected council and assembly, the council to initiate legislation. However, in 1701, Penn approved a charter that eliminated the powers of the council and made Pennsylvania the only colony with a unicameral law-making body. Penn believed that if men were good, their form of government would be good. The society that emerged in Pennsylvania was prosperous, based on farming, the fur trade, and commerce. Religious peace prevailed because all sects were tolerated, but political life was factious.

The policy of the Crown after 1663 to create new colonies under proprietors ran counter to the mercantilist requirement that the state should control economic policy, as was intended by the Navigation Acts. Royal charters gave authority to proprietors and companies, while elected colonial assemblies assumed important powers in determining local legislation. When Charles II empowered a royal commission in 1664 to visit the colonies and determine the effectiveness of the Navigation Acts, Massachusetts fell back on its charter of 1629 and refused to cooperate with the royal commission. As a result, the Crown revoked the charter in 1684.

The Duke of York succeeded to the throne as James II in 1685, and New York thereby became a royal colony. The Lords of Trade, a commission created in 1675 by Charles II to regulate the colonies, now tried to solve a number of problems by organizing a new Dominion of New England in 1686, to include Massachusetts, New York, New Jersey, Connecticut, Rhode Island, Plymouth, New Hampshire, and Maine. All assemblies were eliminated, and advisors to Governor Edmund Andros were royal appointees. Andros enforced the Navigation Acts, levied taxes, invalidated Massachusetts land titles, and was thoroughly opposed in the colonies.

When James II was banished by the Glorious Revolution of 1688 and replaced by William and Mary, the people of Massachusetts deposed and jailed Andros (who eventually reached England and governed Virginia). Massachusetts, Maine, and Plymouth were united under a new charter in 1691, but William kept the right to appoint a governor to represent him and to exercise royal control. In actual practice, however, assemblies retained the right to levy taxes and, with that right, a great deal of political power. Other colonies resumed their separate status, too.

In 1696, the Lords of Trade were replaced by the Lords Commissioners of Trade and Plantations (the Board of Trade). This board advised the Crown in matters of trade, and under their administration the enforcement of the Navigation Acts and similar mercantilist policies was relatively lax. The colonists accepted a system in which the interests of the king were defended by royal governors, admiralty courts and a customs service, and they resumed a measure of self-government in their cherished assemblies, all working for the mutual benefit of the colonies and the mother country. Gradually more colonies reverted to Crown control; New Jersey in 1702 and North and South Carolina in 1729.

Different patterns of economic and social organization appeared in the colonies as they adapted to varying environments. Tobacco, rice, indigo, and sugar culture dominated the plantations of Maryland, Virginia, and South Carolina. African slaves, imported into Virginia as early as 1619, were an inexpensive labor force that served for life and bore children to perpetuate the system. Although every colony accepted slavery as a legal institution, it flourished in the South. The large plantations were virtually self-contained, providing most of their own goods and services, and their educational and religious requirements.

New Englanders lived in close proximity to one another and, grouped mainly in towns, centered their daily lives on work, church, and political activities. In town meetings they solved local problems, elected preachers, and chose their representatives. Their militia defended them against Indians. In the Atlantic coastal settlements, south or north, perhaps one in 20 colonists lived in a city rather than on a plantation or in a small town. In the colonies, Philadelphia became the largest city (with some 40,000 people in 1775), second only to London among all English-speaking cities. Boston, New York, Charles Town, and Newport were the remaining cities with substantial populations comparable to English cities. Trade built such centers, and merchants provided income and employment for their inhabitants on a scale far more elegant than that of the town and rural dwellers. Their political power, their cultural facilities, including schools and newspapers, and direct and frequent contact with England and foreign parts offered excitement, enlightenment of the mind, and opportunities for corruption to some American colonists.

Farms prevailed in the relative isolation of the hinterlands at a distance from the coastal communities. Individual owners and, in a few cases, tenant farmers cleared the land, produced their own livelihood through their harvests, faced hostile Indians, and fought illness and disease. Religious observance, schooling, medical care, and entertainment were necessarily limited to their own devices, except for the occasional and unpredictable appearance of itinerant preachers, limited contact with county courts, militia activities, and elections. Even more isolated than the farmers were explorers and fur traders who expanded the habitable perimeter westward, constantly moving ahead of the settled areas and making possible further settlement. Inevitably this led to clashes with the Indians, the Spaniards, and the Frenchmen, all of whom claimed the lands on the periphery of the English settlements and beyond the Appalachian Mountains.

The Indians often sold land or invited Europeans to share the land for hunting. Resistance to encroachment was hopeless, for the Indians were usually outnumbered, lacked discipline and allies, and possessed inferior weapons. Nevertheless, occasionally the Indians were driven to wage what the colonists considered to be war—for example the Powhatan conflict in Virginia in 1622 and in New England the Pequot War in 1637 and the devastating King Philip's War in 1675-1677. The areas east of the Appalachians were free of Indians after 1676, and the southwest was safe for Europeans by the early 1700's. Indians often won victories—called "massacres"—but they lost the wars and the land. Indians with European allies represented a more formidable opponent, particularly in the trans-Appalachian regions, where France had established claims before 1700. Each of the nearly continuous European wars between England and France had its counterpart colonial conflict. The War of the League of Augsburg (1689-1697) was called King William's War in America; the War of the Spanish Succession (1702-1713) became Queen Anne's War. Americans were drawn into border raids, campaigns, and hostilities with the Indians. Colonial lives and property were lost, with little aid from England.

It was a threat from Spain and its Indian allies that led to the organization of the last colony, Georgia, in 1732. George II granted a charter to General James Oglethorpe and 20 others as trustees for 21 years, after which the colony would revert to royal control. Its purpose was twofold: to defend the area against Spain; and to provide English paupers, debtors, and the indigent unemployed a haven for rehabilitation. With land, tools, supplies, and the exhortation of missionary preachers such as John Wesley, the colony got under way. During the War of Jenkin's Ear (1739-1742) between England and Spain, Georgia proved its value as a buffer to Spanish activity on the southern flank of the colonies.

Another European conflict, the War of the Austrian Succession (1740-1748), called King George's War in America, resulted in a French invasion of Nova Scotia. This prompted New England colonists to seize Louisbourg on Cape Breton Island in 1745. Their victory was canceled by the treaty of Aix-la-Chapelle between England and France, but it taught some colonists that it might be wise to take a more active role in their own self-defense. A meeting was organized at Albany, New York, by the Board of Trade in 1754, attended by delegates from Massachusetts, Pennsylvania, New Hampshire, Connecticut, Rhode Island, Maryland, and New York. Benjamin Franklin, journeying from Philadelphia, proposed a colonial union to deal with Indian matters, giving the colonists the power of taxation to support their activities for their "general welfare." But this Albany Plan was met with indifference by both the Crown and all the colonial assemblies, except that of Massachusetts. England feared intercolonial union; and the colonists themselves were not ready to unite.

While the Albany Congress was in session, the colony of Virginia sent Colonel George Washington to the Ohio country, to drive the French out of Fort Duquesne [the present site of Pittsburgh]. He was unsuccessful, but the Virginians still believed that their charter extended to the western lands which the French held on the far side of the Appalachian range. England supported Virginia in this effort, and sent General Edward Braddock with troops in 1755. Washington, who served as aide to Braddock, was present at his defeat and death near Fort Duquesne. That same year the French in the north defeated English expeditions at Crown Point and Fort Niagara. Most Indian tribes decided to ally themselves with the victorious French.

At this point, England initiated a great war to extend English power around the world. In America this conflict was called the French and Indian War (1755-1770). Initially it went badly for the disunited 200,000 English colonists; the 55,000 Frenchmen with their Indian allies were superior wilderness fighters. But in 1758, when William Pitt came to power in England, adequate finances and the leadership of capable commanders changed the course of the war. Lieutenant Colonel Jeffrey Amherst and Brigadier James Wolfe recaptured Louisbourg on Cape Breton Island in July 1758, giving England control of the mouth of the St. Lawrence River. Fort Frontenac, guarding the other end of the river [the present site of Kingston, Ontario], fell to Lieutenant Colonel John Bradstreet in August, severing French ties with the Mississippi Valley and allowing John Forbes to capture Fort Duquesne in November. The war ended in America with the conquest of Quebec in 1759 by Major General Wolfe (who lost his life in the battle) and with the surrender of Montreal to Amherst in September 1760. All of Canada thus fell to England. The American colonists, who had joined fully in provisioning and fighting during the war, gained confidence in their own fighting ability as compared with that of the English troops.

In 1763 English troops stationed in America were confronted by a widespread Indian uprising led by Pontiac, an Ottawa leader, who had united several tribes in the northwest. Pontiac's Rebellion threatened the settlers from Pennsylvania to Detroit. In order to keep the colonists from encountering the bellicose Indians, George III issued a proclamation that forbade settlement beyond the crest of the mountain system. Such an order conflicted with the heightened expectation, after the victory in the French and Indian War, that no obstacle would remain the prevent westward expansion.

In the same year, George Grenville, First Lord of the Treasury, began to impose new policies to diminish English debts and the costs of an expanded empire. Among other actions, he ordered the strict collection of duties on molasses coming from the West Indies, and in 1764 he forbade the issuance of paper money in the colonies. He also lowered the duties on molasses, as a concession to the colonists, but added duties on sugar and indigo, along with textiles, coffee, wine, and pimento. Moreover, violators were to be tried in admiralty courts, not in civil courts with local juries. In 1765, a Stamp Act was passed, requiring a paid stamp to be affixed to all legal documents, almanacs, newspapers, playing cards, and dice—a new and harassing type of tax. Also a Quartering Act required colonists to furnish barracks or living quarters, utensils, fires, candles, salt, vinegar, beer, cider, and rum to English troops in their area. All these steps were supposedly to ensure a proper colonial contribution to the defense of the colonies.

Colonists petitioned to Parliament that the Sugar and Stamp Acts should be repealed. They were willing to be taxed by their own elected representatives, but the proposed taxes were enacted by a Parliament in which they were not represented. The Virginia House of Burgesses led in opposing the new acts. Massachusetts proposed a Stamp Act Congress, which met in New York in October 1765 and agreed that colonists should pay only those taxes raised by their own consent and representatives. The Sons of Liberty were organized to resist the Stamp Act; colonists refused to obey it; by March 1766, Parliament and the Crown repealed the Act. Colonial resistance won out, but Parliament passed the face-saving Declaratory Act to affirm its right to make laws for the American colonies.

In 1766, an Exchecquer official, Charles Townshend, took over direction of the colonies and initiated a new series of inflammatory acts. The Revenue Act of 1767 taxed imports of glass, tea, silk, lead, paper, and paints from England, but specified that the income was to remain in America. The American customs system was reorganized to collect the new duties. Townshend also met general resistance to the Quartering Act, which most colonists considered another kind of tax.

On Mar. 5, 1770, English troops, provoked by boys in front of the Boston customhouse, fired on them and killed five persons. The troops had to be moved out of Boston to an island in the harbor, where they remained for four years. On that same day of violence (the so-called Boston Massacre), Lord North's suggestion to repeal all the Townshend duties except the one on tea was passed by Parliament, and North soon let the Quartering Act die without being renewed. The North policy brought a period of good relations that were disturbed only by minor irritations. Then, in 1772, at the proposal of Samuel Adams, Boston and other Massachusetts towns set up Committees of Correspondence to formulate American rights and grievances and to communicate them to other towns and the world. The consequences of the burning near Providence of a British naval vessel, the *Gaspee,* gave Adams and the Committees of Correspondence fuel for their proceedings. The ship had harassed the colonists, but the English Commission of Inquiry in its unsuccessful investigation of the *Gaspee* affair bypassed Rhode Island courts. Concern spread to the Virginia assembly, which formed its own Committee of Correspondence and urged all other colonies to do the same in 1773. Such incidents formed a basis for union of the colonists.

Meanwhile, Parliament passed the Tea Act of 1773. Its purpose was to help the East India Company to sell more tea in America, at cheaper prices. Colonists reacted negatively, and when the next shipment of London tea arrived in December 1773, a "Boston Tea Party" was organized to throw it into Boston harbor. The English reaction was to assert their authority, and under the Boston Port Bill of 1774 no ships could enter the port until the tea was paid for. The colonists were outraged, and their anger was fanned as three more bills were passed by Parliament: the Massachusetts Government Act, which altered the charter of 1691; the Administration of Justice Act, which provided for trial in England of any customs or government officer charged with murder; and, finally, a new Quartering Act. Colonials labeled these the Intolerable Acts. At the same time, the Quebec Act was passed. Intended primarily to give a civil government to Canada, it attached to Canada western lands that were claimed by Virginia, Connecticut, and Massachusetts under their charters, and was interpreted as coercive of colonial interests.

General Thomas Gage, commander in chief of English colonial troops, was sent to Boston to govern Massachusetts. To deal with the emergency, an intercolonial congress was arranged by the Committees of Correspondence. This First Continental Congress convened in Philadelphia on Sept. 5, 1774, and by Oct. 26 it expressed the colonial position in a number of decisions. The Suffolk Resolves declared resistance to the Intolerable Acts. Joseph Galloway's moderate Plan of a Proposed Union between Great Britain and the Colonies was rejected. An important Declaration of Rights and Resolves was approved; it called for rights of assembly and petition, trial by peers (unlike admiralty courts or trial in England), freedom from a standing army, and the right to choose councils when the power to tax is involved. It was resolved to form an "Association" in each colony to oppose trade and consumption of British goods through nonimportation and nonconsumption agreements. Finally, it was decided to meet in Philadelphia again in May 1775 unless grievances were redressed.

In February 1775, Lord North secures passage of a conciliatory measure: the colonists could tax themselves for costs of common defense. But England generally regards the colonies to be in a state of rebellion. General Gage sends word that the Massachusetts militia are gathering arms and ammunition, and he sends 700 men to Concord on April 18, 1775, on a mission to seize military stores there.

Paul Revere, William Dawes, and Samuel Prescott ride out to warn the countryside that the British are coming. On April 19 the British kill eight Minute Men at Lexington. Militiamen fire on the British troops on their way back to Boston. The city is brought under a siege by a force that grew to 16,000 militiamen. American assemblies begin to arm for a general war.

By the time the Second Continental Congress gathers at Philadelphia on May 10, 1775, the delegates are committed to common action. They turn to problems of defense and create a Continental Army of 20,000 troops, with George Washington the unanimous choice for commander in chief. Each colony is urged to establish supplementary Committees of Safety.

The Congress continues to petition the king to redress colonial grievances. On July 5, Congress adopts the Olive Branch Petition (written by John Dickinson), beseeching George III to end hostilities. The next day they adopt a Declaration of the Causes and Necessities of Taking Up Arms (by Dickinson and Thomas Jefferson), which does not demand independence, but claims that the colonies' cause is just and their union perfect. It expresses their resolve to die freemen rather than slaves. This Congress sets the course of military action. Already, at Boston, on June 17, 1775, the British have won a hard-fought battle at Breed's Hill [later called Bunker Hill]; it was a battle that showed how well the colonials could fight. In September Congress sets up a committee to plan naval operations as well. On Nov. 9 Congress learns that George III has refused the Olive Branch Petition and is sending 20,000 troops instead. There is no turning back.

AMERICAN HEADLINES

Year by Year

1776

The year begins with the publication of Thomas Paine's pamphlet *Common Sense,* the first effective presentation of the American cause against the colonial status imposed by England. Thousands are converted to that cause within a few weeks following its publication. Colonial assemblies and the Continental Congress in Philadelphia begin considering declarations of independence. In July the draft prepared by Thomas Jefferson becomes the official Declaration of Independence. After that declaration is proclaimed, the war moves into a more relentless and aggressive stage.

Military operations, only in their ninth month as the year opens, find a defeat in the making in Canada. An American army, after capturing Montreal, is virtually destroyed at the walls of Quebec City in the last hours of 1775, and its leader, General Richard Montgomery, is killed. At about this time British naval units raid and burn the town of Norfolk, Virginia, and bombard Falmouth [Portland], Maine, destroying most of that town. Despite these disasters and despite the military actions at Lexington, Concord, and Bunker Hill earlier in 1775, a significant part of the American population remains uncommitted, either to war or independence. Massachusetts affords a major exception—it has been virtually independent since October 1774. But early in 1776 the American mood swiftly changes to one of greater belligerence, and to a more favorable attitude toward independence.

The British evacuate Boston in March, and prepare to launch their first major offensive, an attack on New York City. The Continental Army, beginning its second year under the command of General George Washington, spends most of the remainder of the year in an unsuccessful defense of New York City. Finding the effort hopeless, in October, the army abandons the city and the whole surrounding region to the British. The Continental Army retreats westward across New Jersey, and crosses the Delaware River into eastern Pennsylvania.

Late in the year some hope is rekindled by French and Spanish decisions to give some aid to the American cause. But the condition of the Continental Army continues to deteriorate owing to desertions, lack of clothing, and to shortages of food, and munitions and weapons. By the end of the year the Continental Army consists of only 5,000 poorly equipped troops, many of whom do not even have shoes or rifles. The year ends in a blaze of glory when, on the day after Christmas, the Americans carry out a surprise attack against a British-Hessian garrison at Trenton, New Jersey. This action lifts the morale of the American people and helps the army to survive the winter.

Jan. 9. Thomas Paine publishes *Common Sense,* attacking George III and presenting the Colonists with the first clear and popular statement of their cause.

Jan. 24 Colonel Henry Knox, under Washington's direction, reaches Cambridge, Massachusetts, with 43 cannons and 16 mortars that were captured several months ago by Ethan Allen. The weapons have been hauled overland from Fort Ticonderoga, New York.

Feb. 27 An American force in North Carolina defeats a Loyalist detachment at Moore's Creek, near Wilmington.

Mar. 4-5 General John Thomas seizes Dorchester Heights overlooking Boston Harbor from the British, thus placing that harbor within the range of Colonel Knox's artillery.

Mar. 7-17 The British evacuate Boston and sail for Halifax, Nova Scotia.

April 6 Congress passes a resolution permitting ports of the colonies to trade with all nations except Great Britain.

April 9 Congress passes a resolution calling for an end to the importation of slaves into the colonies.

April 12 A North Carolina convention empowers its delegates in the Continental Congress to vote for independence.

May 1-July 5 American forces retreat from Canada after ending their hopeless siege of Quebec. General Benedict Arnold makes his way with part of the depleted forces to Lake Champlain, while the British commander, General Guy Carleton, plans to invade the colonies from the north.

May 2 One million dollars worth of muni-

IN CONGRESS, JULY 4, 1776.

The unanimous Declaration of the thirteen united States of America.

THE DECLARATION OF INDEPENDENCE

tions are consigned to the Americans through a secret agent by order of Louis XVI, King of France.

May 9-16   Admiral Esek Hopkins, commanding the first squadron of the United Colonies, raids English naval installations in the Bahamas. He captures the city of Nassau and seizes large stores of military supplies.

May 10   Congress passes a resolution advising all the colonies to form new governments.

May 15   Virginia authorizes its delegation in the Continental Congress to vote for independence.

June 1-28   British naval units move against Charles Town [in 1783 renamed Charleston], South Carolina, harbor defenses. Fort Moultrie on Sullivan's Island repulses the attack and in counterbombardment seriously damages many of the British ships. The British abandon the attack after suffering more than 200 casualties. At the fort 10 men are dead and 21 wounded.

June 2   General John Sullivan, in charge of the last colonial troops in Canada, unsuccessfully attempts a counterattack and evacuates his forces across the St. Lawrence.

June 7   Richard Henry Lee of Virginia offers a resolution in Congress for a Declaration of Independence, but the resolution is tabled until a sufficient number of delegates arrive at a firm opinion concerning independence.

June 10   Supplies for the Americans are offered by Charles III, King of Spain, under an arrangement similar to that made by the French.

June 11   A committee to prepare a possible Declaration of Independence is formed in Congress. Headed by Jefferson, it also includes Robert Livingston, John Adams, Benjamin Franklin, and Roger Sherman. The committee selects Jefferson to draft the document.

June 12   The Virginia House of Burgesses becomes the first colonial legislature to adopt a Bill of Rights.

June 28   Jefferson's draft of the Declaration of Independence, with changes proposed by Franklin and Adams, is submitted to Congress.

June 29   Virginia, the first colony to change its form of government pursuant to the resolution adopted by Congress on May 10, adopts a new constitution for an independent Commonwealth of Virginia.

June 29   General Sir William Howe and his brother Admiral Lord Richard Howe appear in New York Harbor with a huge fleet, including transport ships, signaling the beginning of a full-scale British invasion effort. The appearance of the fleet is no surprise to the Americans.

July 2   General Howe, having sailed from Halifax, lands an army of 10,000 men, unopposed, on Staten Island.

July 2   Twelve of the 13 delegations in Congress (New York abstaining) vote for the principle of independence.

July 4   Congress adopts the Jefferson draft of the Declaration of Independence.

July 9   The Declaration of Independence, with the concurrence of New York, is proclaimed in Philadelphia.

July 12   Admiral Howe arrives with 150 transports carrying reinforcements for Staten Island, bringing the total number of men there to 32,000 including 9,000 German mercenaries.

July 20-21   Cherokee Indians attack Eaton's Station, a settlement on the Holston River in western North Carolina. North Carolina troops retaliate against the Indians by wiping out a nearby Cherokee town.

Aug. 12   Congress passes a bill to grant free land as bounty to British deserters.

Aug. 22-25   General Howe moves 20,000 troops from Staten Island across the Narrows to Flatbush, and moves by way of the unguarded Jamaica Pass against General Washington's positions on Brooklyn Heights.

Aug. 27-28   The Battle of Long Island rages.

Aug. 29   Long Island is evacuated by American troops in a quiet nighttime action that surprises the British.

Sept. 6   A peace conference on Staten Island fails. Howe demands revocation of the Declaration of Independence, and the Americans refuse.

Sept. 12   The lower part of Manhattan Island is evacuated by Washington.

Sept. 16   The Battle of Harlem Heights stings the British and delays their advance.

Sept. 21   A great fire destroys much of New York City, a town of almost 22,000 inhabitants, after Philadelphia the most populous in the colonies.

Sept. 21-22   Nathan Hale, an American agent, is captured by the British. The next day Hale is hanged without a trial. His last words are, "I only regret that I have but one life to lose for my country."

Oct. 5   British warships force the Hudson River passage between Fort Lee (in New Jersey) and Fort Washington (in New York), weakening Washington's hold on Manhattan Island.

Oct. 9   Spanish missionaries found a settlement on the coast of California. Officially named the Mission San Francisco de Asis, it is popu-

THE FIRST PUBLIC READING OF THE DECLARATION OF INDEPENDENCE
(Members of Congress leave Independence Hall.)

larly known as Yerba Buena. [In 1849 it becomes San Francisco.]

Oct. 11   General Arnold's small flotilla, built to help hold back the British on Lake Champlain, is destroyed in Valcour Bay. General Carleton's 87-gun fleet, manned by experienced sailors, cripples the improvised American fleet, but his plan to invade the colonies from Canada is frustrated.

Oct. 18   The Battle of Pell's Point delays the British advance northward out of New York City, and gives the Americans time to withdraw in order.

Oct. 23   Washington completes an evacuation northward from Manhattan Island.

Oct. 28   The Battle of White Plains inflicts heavy casualties on General Howe, and Washington slips away to the west, forming a new line at North Castle.

Nov. 16   Howe captures Fort Washington, but has to use 13,000 troops to do it.

Nov. 18   Washington decides to abandon the New York region, and moves across the Hudson River and westward across New Jersey. [On Dec. 1 he reaches the Delaware River.]

Dec. 6   A British force occupies the naval base of Newport, Rhode Island.

Dec. 11   Washington crosses the Delaware into Pennsylvania.

Dec. 12   Congress, fearing a British attack, flees from Philadelphia and meets temporarily in Baltimore.

Dec. 13   General Charles Lee is captured at Basking Ridge, New Jersey, by a British patrol.

Dec. 21   Silas Deane, Benjamin Franklin, Arthur Lee, and Thomas Jefferson meet in Paris, on authorization from Congress, to borrow money.

Dec. 26   Washington carries out a surprise assault on Trenton, New Jersey. His force of 2,400 captures nearly a thousand Hessians and huge supplies, while losing only five men.

Dec. 31   George Rogers Clark, in a move to prevent Daniel Boone from organizing Kentucky as a separate state, petitions Virginia for annexation of the settlements threatened by hostile Indians. The area is organized as a county of Virginia. [Kentucky County becomes the state of Kentucky in 1792.]

1777 **General Washington quickly follows up his surprise attack on** Trenton with a victory near Princeton. He then retires his army into winter quarters in the hills around Morristown, New Jersey. The recovery of most of New Jersey during the dead of winter is an impressive feat. It heartens the American cause and unnerves the British, whose officers are appalled at the thought of having to fight during the winter. Nevertheless, General Sir William Howe continues to hold New York City.

Meanwhile, in Canada, General John Burgoyne plans a vigorous campaign designed to cut the states into two parts by invading southward through Canada and upper New York State to link up with General Howe in New York City. Burgoyne's plans fall apart, one by one. First, his supporting forces under General Barry St. Leger, moving eastward along the Mohawk Valley, cannot bypass Fort Stanwix [Schuyler], and have to turn back. Secondly, Burgoyne himself wastes valuable summer fighting time by moving too slowly through the densely wooded, lake-strewn country of upper New York. He also leaves his flanks open, inviting attacks from American forces in New England. General John Stark, Colonel Daniel Morgan and General Horatio Gates peck away at his supply lines, finally stopping his advance altogether. Burgoyne is forced to surrender at Saratoga.

This American victory leads to the initial steps toward French alliance with America, and raises the morale of the American people. As the year ends, General Howe captures Philadelphia, driving Congress out of the city, and General Washington takes his tattered army into winter quarters at Valley Forge, Pennsylvania.

Jan. 3   Washington again crosses the Delaware River. Outmarching Lord Charles Cornwallis, who has been summoned by General Howe from New York, Washington meets the British at Princeton. The British are defeated and driven toward New Brunswick.

Jan. 6   Washington leads his tired army into the hills around Morristown, New Jersey, and establishes winter quarters.

Jan. 15   Settlers of the New Hampshire Grants—a former part of New Hampshire colony west of the Connecticut River, now claimed by New York—declare their independence and establish a ''republic'' under the name of New Connecticut.

Jan. 19   A highly effective issue of Thomas Paine's latest pamphlet, *American Crisis,* is published. It helps to raise American morale.

Mar. 12   Congress reconvenes in Philadelphia, after holding its sessions for three months in Baltimore.

May 20   The Cherokee Indians cede all their lands in the state of South Carolina by terms of the Treaty of DeWitts Corner.

June 14   Captain John Paul Jones, already a veteran in harrying British merchant ships, is appointed by Congress to command the 18-gun *Ranger,* with which he can raid the coast of England.

June 14   Congress passes a bill creating a flag of the ''United States.'' It contains 13 white stars in a blue field, with 13 alternating red and white stripes.

June 17-Oct. 17   General John Burgoyne leads an invasion from Canada, designed to cut the states into two parts along the line of Lake Champlain and Hudson Valley. Burgoyne plans to link up with General Howe in New York City.

July 6   Burgoyne reaches Fort Ticonderoga, captures it from General Arthur St. Clair, and continues on to reach the Hudson River at Fort Edward.

July 12   New Connecticut renames itself Vermont and adopts a constitution that includes manhood suffrage and the prohibition of slavery.

July 20   By terms of the Treaty of Long Island, the Overhill Cherokee Indians surrender all their lands east of the Blue Ridge Mountains and the Nolichucky River, western North Carolina.

July 27   Marquis de Lafayette, a French nobleman less than 20 years of age, arrives in Philadelphia and volunteers to serve the American cause without pay.

Aug. 3-6   Troops under General St. Leger, moving eastward from the Great Lakes, lay siege to Fort Stanwix, in the Mohawk Valley, but are unable to capture it.

Aug. 6   An American relief force under General Nicholas Herkimer reaches Fort Stanwix, but is ambushed at Oriskany by St. Leger. Although the Americans are defeated and Herkimer is killed, St. Leger fails to take Fort Stanwix.

THE SURRENDER OF BURGOYNE.

Aug. 16 General John Stark and his Vermont militiamen encounter a detachment of Burgoyne's troops near Bennington, Vermont, and annihilate them.

Aug. 25 General Howe launches a campaign to capture Philadelphia. He arrives at the head of Chesapeake Bay with an army of 10,000 men.

Sept. 9-11 Howe meets Washington's forward units at Brandywine Creek, Pennsylvania. While feinting an attack at Chadd's Ford, Howe strikes at Washington's right and drives the army back on Philadelphia.

Sept. 19 Congress once again flees from Philadelphia, this time to Lancaster, Pennsylvania.

Sept. 19 General Burgoyne is defeated at Freeman's Farm, near Saratoga, New York, by Colonel Morgan and a captain of militia, Henry Dearborn.

Sept. 21 Howe's troops ambush part of General Anthony Wayne's command, at Paoli, Pennsylvania, and inflict heavy casualties in bayonet attacks.

Sept. 25-Dec. 23 A group of army officers and some members of Congress plot to remove Washington from his command. A letter from Thomas Conway, an Irish adventurer, to General Gates, whom the plotters hoped to place in command of the American forces, is leaked to Washington, and the plot is exposed. The intrigue is popularly known as Conway's Cabal, although Conway had little part in it.

Sept. 30 Congress moves to York, Pennsylvania.

Oct. 3 General Sir Henry Clinton moves north out of New York City, and captures two forts on the Hudson River.

Oct. 4-5 The Battle of Germantown begins as a brilliant American assault, but it loses momentum. The British both exact and suffer heavy casualties.

Oct. 7 Washington disengages and moves his army to nearby Valley Forge, Pennsylvania, where he prepares winter camp.

Oct. 16 Burgoyne makes a plea to Clinton in New York for aid. Clinton moves up the Hudson River as far as Esopus [Kingston], which he burns, but then he turns back, abandoning any attempt to reach Burgoyne as too dangerous.

Oct. 17 Burgoyne surrenders his entire army at Saratoga. [News of Burgoyne's surrender electrifies Europe and gives an enormous boost to the American cause.]

Nov. 15 Articles of Confederation are passed by Congress, and presented to the states for ratification.

Dec. 17 France recognizes the independence of the United States.

1778

French recognition of American independence is followed by treaties of commerce and alliance, symbolizing the turning point in the war. The British respond to the treaties by sending a Peace Commission with generous terms, but the commission fails to accomplish its mission. General Sir William Howe is relieved of his command, and replaced by Sir Henry Clinton. After Burgoyne's defeat, which shocks all of Europe, Clinton is ordered to organize a new offensive. When he decides to abandon Philadelphia and attempt to reach New York City, Washington dashes out of Valley Forge in pursuit, and the armies meet at Monmouth. In the ensuing battle, the American General Charles Lee initiates a retreat which Washington manages to halt, but not before Clinton extricates his army from battle and continues on to New York. A suspicion of treason on the part of General Lee is current.

The British stir up Indians and Loyalists all along the frontier. The Americans, on the other hand, extend their holdings as a result of the expedition conducted by George Rogers Clark. British naval units launch a series of attacks and raids on American coastal cities. By the end of the year it appears that British strategy calls for a new offensive in the southern states.

Feb. 6   France and the United States sign two separate treaties, one of alliance and one of amity and commerce. [The treaty of alliance is the only one ever to be made in U.S. history.] The United States is to be given a free hand in conquering Bermuda and Canada, while the French are to be given a free hand in the West Indies.

Mar. 12-13   The state government of Vermont comes into effect, with Thomas Chittenden as governor. It functions independently of the United States.

Mar. 16   A British Peace Commission is authorized and given wide powers to negotiate with the Americans.

May 4   Congress ratifies both treaties with France.

May 8   General Clinton replaces General Howe in command of British forces in America. Clinton plans to evacuate Philadelphia.

May 15   George Rogers Clark begins a campaign to take control of the American West and Northwest from the British. He captures Cahokia, a base on the Mississippi River [near the present East St. Louis, Illinois].

May 30   British instigators encourage Loyalists and Indians to launch a campaign of terror along the American frontier, resulting in the burning of Cobleskill, New York, by 300 Iroquois Indians.

June 6   The British Peace Commission arrives at Philadelphia.

June 18   The British abandon Philadelphia and cross northeastern New Jersey.

June 19   General Washington breaks camp at Valley Forge, and sends General Charles Lee ahead to intercept Clinton's army, which is heading for New York City.

June 27-28   At Monmouth, New Jersey, Lee catches up with Clinton and engages in combat, then suddenly orders a retreat. Washington is furious, and rides in to take control, narrowly averting a serious defeat. The battle rages on in a disorderly fashion, because the British are also making tactical errors. Clinton finally manages to disengage, and continues on to New York. [Lee is dismissed from the Army in 1780.]

July 3   Indians and British Loyalists raid the

Philip Livingston
(1716-1778)
Signer of the Declaration of Independence

John Morton
(1725-1777)
Signer of the Declaration of Independence

lush Wyoming Valley of northern Pennsylvania, defeating a makeshift army of settlers, and massacring nearly everyone.

July 4   In the West, George Rogers Clark, on a mission for Governor Patrick Henry of Virginia, captures an important British post at Kaskaskia, at the confluence of the Kaskaskia and Mississippi rivers.

July 8   Washington establishes headquarters at West Point, New York.

July 9   Fairfield, Connecticut, is raided and burned by British naval units.

July 10   A large French fleet arrives in American waters. British sea raiders manage to burn Norwalk, Connecticut, before scurrying to various ports as the French fleet approaches.

July 20   George Rogers Clark captures Vincennes, a British post on the Wabash River.

July 21   North Carolina ratifies the Articles of Confederation.

July 22   Pennsylvania ratifies the Articles of Confederation.

July 24   Georgia ratifies the Articles of Confederation.

Aug. 8   A combined French-American siege of Newport, Rhode Island, fails. The French fleet of 17 ships under command of Count Jean Baptiste d'Estaing is in position and is prepared, but American land forces under General John Sullivan are delayed. By the time they arrive, the French are forced to turn about and face a large British fleet which is approaching Newport. A storm drives the fleets apart before a showdown battle can occur. Sullivan attacks the garrison at Newport but is unsuccessful, and withdraws.

Aug. 8   New Hampshire ratifies the Articles of Confederation.

Aug. 26   D'Estaing disengages and takes his storm-damaged fleet to Boston for repairs.

Aug. 26   The British Peace Commission is snubbed. Some of its members try to bribe members of Congress and are exposed.

Sept. 7-16   Shawnee Indians lay siege to Boonesborough, Kentucky, but fail to take it.

Nov. 11   Loyalists and Indians attack Cherry Valley, New York. Their leaders, Sir John Butler and the Mohawk Indian Joseph Brant, permit the massacre of more than 40 persons.

Nov. 26   New Jersey ratifies the Articles of Confederation.

Nov. 27   The British Peace Commission sails for England with its mission a complete failure.

Dec. 9   All the territory recently won by George Rogers Clark is annexed by Virginia, as the county of Illinois, with Captain John Todd as governor.

Dec. 10   John Jay of New York is elected president of the Continental Congress.

Dec. 29   Savannah, the capital of Georgia, is attacked from the sea by a force of 3,500 men. A delaying action by the American, General Robert Howe, fails and the town is taken. The fall of Savannah marks the opening action of a powerful British southern campaign.

THE BATTLE OF MONMOUTH.

1779

The war reaches a stalemate in the North. Although the British occupy New York City, it is nearly surrounded by American forces. General Sir Henry Clinton, under orders not to risk a major battle, organizes a number of nuisance raids. On the other hand, Washington cannot dislodge the British without seapower. The French possess the needed seapower, but their fleet always seems to be sailing on some kind of urgent schedule, plying between France, the American coast, and the West Indies. In reality, France and Great Britain are at war on a worldwide scale, and the American colonies are only one theater of war.

Slowly the British move the war to the southern states, where substantial Loyalist sympathy is known to prevail. While British troops and Loyalists strike hard in the south, Washington's army in the north deteriorates badly. The winter at Morristown is worse than that at Valley Forge, and a deep gloom prevails throughout the states. Haphazard, ineffective military operations on both sides, often amounting to no more than desultory raids, breed bitterness and hatred but achieve nothing useful. The British Navy supports the land operations by bombarding or burning coastal towns.

Jan. 6 Fort Sunbury, Georgia, falls, and Augusta is attacked.

Jan. 10 In France, John Paul Jones is presented with a battered old hulk, which he overhauls, refits and renames the *Bonhomme Richard*, in honor of Benjamin Franklin.

Jan. 29 Augusta, Georgia, is taken by a British force under General Augustine Prevost, who attacks from a base in Florida.

Feb. 3 Prevost moves on Port Royal, South Carolina, but the defenses of that town hold and the attack is repulsed.

Feb. 14 Colonel Andrew Pickens defeats a Loyalist group at Kettle Creek, Georgia, but he fails in his main objective to recapture Augusta.

April 1-30 Colonel Evan Shelby destroys a group of Chickamauga settlements in Tennessee, in retaliation for raids by the Indians. All raiding in the region thereupon ceases.

May 1 A British attempt to retake Cahokia is repulsed with heavy losses.

May 5 Delaware ratifies the Articles of Confederation.

May 10 A British squadron raids and burns Portmouth and Norfolk, Virginia.

May 31 General Sir Henry Clinton sends a large force up the Hudson River to capture West Point, but it reaches only as far as two unfinished redoubts south of West Point, one of which is Stony Point.

July 10 The entire navy of Massachusetts is destroyed in a mismanaged project to capture a Loyalist base at Castine, in the district of Maine. After failing to take a fort, the American ships allow themselves to be bottled up by a British squadron in the Penobscot River.

July 15 General Anthony Wayne leads a surprise bayonet attack on Stony Point and recaptures the post, making prisoners of the entire garrison.

Aug. 14 Congress issues a peace plan that includes the demand for complete independence, British evacuation of territory of the former colonies, and certain definite boundaries.

Aug. 19 The British are forced out of Paulus Hook, their last post in New Jersey.

Aug. 29 Generals John Sullivan and James Clinton defeat the Loyalist commander, Sir John Johnson, and his Indian ally, Joseph Brant, near Elmira, New York. This victory removes from New York the last organized Loyalist and Indian force.

The battle of the *Bonhomme Richard* and the *Seraphis*

Sept. 1-15 General Sullivan destroys more than 40 Seneca and Cayuga villages in retaliation for their part in the campaigns of terror against American settlers.

Sept. 3-28 General Benjamin Lincoln and Count Casimir Pulaski, in cooperation with the French fleet, lay siege to Savannah in a strong but unsuccessful effort to recapture it. Count Pulaski is killed, Admiral d'Estaing is wounded, and casualties to the French and Americans are heavy.

Sept. 23 John Paul Jones, commanding the *Bonhomme Richard,* encounters the British *Serapis,* a 44-gun frigate, convoying over 30 merchant ships. Jones attacks the big ship, and defeats it, but loses the *Bonhomme Richard* in the battle. He transfers his crew to the *Serapis* and sails for France.

Sept. 27 John Adams is named by Congress to represent the United States if and when peace negotiations take place.

Oct. 11 General Sir Henry Clinton abandons the naval base at Newport, Rhode Island, and prepares to lead a huge expedition to lay siege to Charles Town [Charleston], South Carolina.

Oct. 17 Washington returns his army to Morristown, New Jersey, winter quarters, where conditions are worse than in the previous ordeal at Valley Forge. Morale and strength reach an all-time low. Desertions soar and signs of mutiny appear.

Joseph Hewes
(1730-1779)
Signer of the Declaration of Independence

Thomas Lynch, Jr.
(1749-1779)
Signer of the Declaration of Independence

John Hart
(1711-1779)
Signer of the Declaration of Independence

George Ross
(1730-1779)
Signer of the Declaration of Independence

1780

American prospects are at their lowest point, with Georgia virtually under British control at the beginning of the year and most of South Carolina soon added. General Sir Henry Clinton personally leads a successful assault on Charles Town, South Carolina. The fall of that city costs the Americans 5,000 men captured, the loss of the South Carolina fleet, plus stores of weapons and supplies. As the British continue to advance, Congress cannot find a competent leader for the southern front; supplies are lower than ever; inflation is rampant; and many of the states add to the hardship by withholding food and supplies from troops of other states passing through. General Washington's army cannot move for fear that the British will break out of New York.

On the other hand, the southern Loyalists are neither as numerous nor as eager to fight as Clinton supposes them to be. Also, Washington discovers a brilliant leader in Nathanael Greene. Greene often loses skirmishes but he wins his campaigns, and he badgers Cornwallis into making some serious tactical errors. By the end of the year American strength and fighting ability have recovered while British control in the South becomes illusory.

Jan. 1   Daring guerrilla warfare continues, especially around Augusta, Georgia, and across the Savannah River in South Carolina.

Jan. 28   Fort Nashborough [in 1782 renamed Nashville] is established on the Cumberland River in North Carolina's trans-Appalachian territory to help secure the region from Indian attacks.

Feb. 1   A huge British fleet, including transport ships, arrives off the Carolina coast in preparation for a planned assault on Charles Town, South Carolina.

Feb. 1   New York cedes to Congress all its claims to western lands.

Mar. 1   Pennsylvania passes a law providing for the gradual abolition of slavery.

April 8   British frigates open the attack on Charles Town by running past the guns of Fort Moultrie, at the entrance to the harbor.

April 8   General Washington dispatches Maryland and Delaware troops to the Carolinas.

May 6   Fort Moultrie falls.

May 12   General Benjamin Lincoln hands over the city of Charles Town to the British. American losses include Lincoln's garrison of 5,000 men, four naval vessels which constitute most of the South Carolina navy, plus 300 cannons and stores of military supplies. The loss of Charles Town is a severe blow to American morale, and is followed by a considerable increase in the number of Loyalists.

May 25   Conditions in Washington's camp at Morristown are so bad as to generate mutiny. The first outbreak occurs when Connecticut regiments parade under arms to demand full rations and immediate payment of salaries. The mutiny is quelled by Pennsylvania troops. Two leaders are hanged.

May 29   A Virginia regiment is defeated and destroyed by Banastre Tarleton's British raiders at Waxhaw Creek, South Carolina.

June 8   General Sir Henry Clinton returns to New York from his victory at Charles Town, leaving Lord Charles Cornwallis in charge of the southern campaign.

June 11   Massachusetts adopts a constitution.

June 22   American reinforcements from Washington arrive in the Carolinas, despite hardships partly caused when supplies and food are refused the troops by some states through which they pass.

July 11   A French army of 7,500 arrives at Newport, Rhode Island. General Washington plans to use this army in cooperation with his own to recapture New York City.

July 12   A British fleet arrives at Newport and blockades the French, frustrating Washington's plan to retake New York.

Aug. 16   General Horatio Gates is soundly beaten at the Battle of Camden, South Carolina, by Lord Cornwallis. Only 700 of 3,000 American troops survive the campaign. One of the casualties is a German enthusiast for the American cause, General Baron Johann de Kalb.

Aug. 18   General Thomas Sumter is defeated by Tarleton in a short battle at Fishing Creek, South Carolina.

Aug. 25   Transylvania Seminary is chartered to be established in Kentucky County, Virginia, the first institution of higher learning west of the Appalachian Mountains.

Sept. 23   Major John André, an adjutant of General Clinton, is caught by New York militiamen with plans for the fort at West Point in his pockets.

Sept. 25   Benedict Arnold, who has been

negotiating with the British for more than a year, flees to British protection when he learns of André's capture and the failure of his plan to deliver his command, West Point, to the British.

Sept. 30 Major André is executed. Like Nathan Hale, the American spy whom the British executed in 1776, André was caught in civilian clothing, and the Americans refuse to treat him as a prisoner of war.

Oct. 7 Appalachian riflemen defeat a Loyalist contingent at Kings Mountain, North Carolina, killing or capturing everyone in sight. The Loyalists were on their way to support an invasion of North Carolina led by Lord Cornwallis. [When Cornwallis hears about Kings Mountain, he returns to his base in Camden.]

Dec. 1 Congress, having failed three times to pick a winning leader for the southern front, allows Washington to choose a successor to Gates, disgraced through his defeat at Camden. Washington selects Nathanael Greene, a brilliant strategist. Greene reorganizes his army, dividing it into two columns, one headed by Daniel Morgan and the other by himself. His strategy is to harass Cornwallis and live off the countryside.

Charles Town, 1780

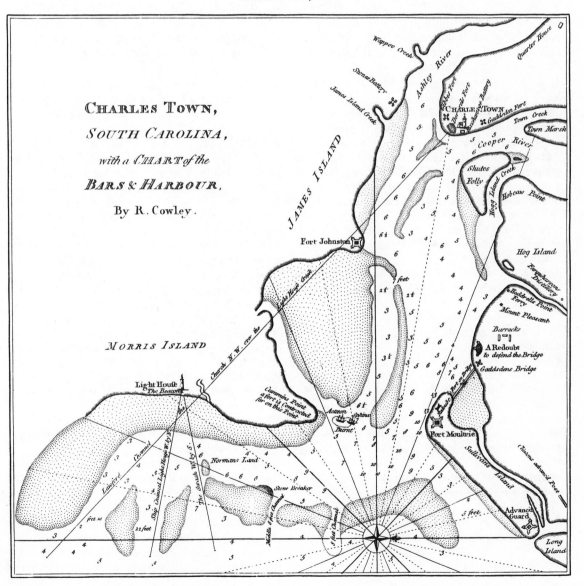

1781 An American victory this year appears remote. Britain controls the seas, blockades or possesses every major American port except Boston and Newport; Congress is unable to raise troops or money; the French alliance has been a disappointment. The recapture of New York is impossible for lack of naval support, although a French army is lingering on at Newport, Rhode Island, ready to fight. Washington's own army is destitute. Mutiny and desertion are common occurrences. Washington sums up his situation on May 1, 1781: ". . . instead of having everything in readiness to take the field, we have nothing and instead of having the prospect of a glorious offensive campaign before us, we have a bewildered and gloomy defensive one. . ."

Much to Washington's surprise and delight the situation has changed by August. Two powerful French fleets appear, one of them carrying another army. Cornwallis, after reaching Virginia, finds he cannot secure any of the states through which he has traveled. Washington tricks General Clinton into thinking he is about to strike at New York, and shows up at Yorktown, Virginia, instead, with a 16,000-man French-American army. Cornwallis has no alternative but to surrender his army of 7,000 troops. This event marks the end of British hopes to retrieve its rebellious American colonies. By this time the former colonies have adopted their first written constitution, the Articles of Confederation.

Jan. 1 Congress issues $191,000,000 in paper currency (Continentals).

Jan. 3 A mutiny breaks out among Pennsylvania troops. Negotiations restore order, but most of the mutineers prepare to desert the army.

Jan. 14 Virginia agrees to cede its claims to lands north of the Ohio River, removing the last barrier to ratification by Maryland (the sole holdout) of the Articles of Confederation. [The cession is not effective until 1784.]

Jan. 17 General Daniel Morgan wins a smashing victory over Tarleton at Cowpens, South Carolina.

Jan. 20 A mutiny of New Jersey troops is quelled by General Robert Howe, who hangs two of the leaders.

Feb. 6 Congress establishes a Department of Finance, and appoints Robert Morris as superintendent.

Feb. 9 In North Carolina, Generals Morgan and Nathanael Greene join forces as Cornwallis is enticed to pursue them. Crossing the Dan River into Virginia, they await reinforcements from Washington.

Mar. 1 Maryland ratifies the Articles of Confederation. The Articles of Confederation are declared in force.

Mar. 15 Cornwallis wins a technical encounter with Generals Greene and Morgan at the Battle of Guilford Courthouse, North Carolina, but Cornwallis suffers heavy casualties and fails in his attempt to subjugate the Carolinas.

Mar. 18 Cornwallis marches to Wilmington, North Carolina, to await reinforcements.

April 2 Commander John Barry on the American frigate *Alliance* is attacked by the British *Mars* and *Minerva,* and forces both to surrender.

April 25 Cornwallis, against the instructions of his superior, General Clinton, strikes out northward into Virginia, believing that the conquest of Virginia is essential in order to control the South.

May 20 Cornwallis reaches Petersburg, Virginia.

May 20 France makes a large loan available to the United States.

May 21 Washington and French General Rochambeau meet at Wethersfield, Connecticut, to decide on objectives. Rochambeau talks Washington out of his plan to attack New York.

May 22-June 19 Greene again loses, failing to take Ninety-Six, South Carolina, a heavily fortified town.

May 29 John Barry again captures two British ships, but this time they are men-of-war. Barry is wounded and his crew is nearly in mutiny before he wins the fight.

June 4 Tarleton almost captures Jefferson at Charlottesville, Virginia.

June 10 Benedict Arnold, now in British uniform, appears at Richmond, Virginia, leading raiding parties.

June 14 Congress amends its law of Sept. 27, 1779, in which John Adams is selected as sole negotiator for a peace; he now becomes one member in an American peace commission.

June 19 Generals Anthony Wayne, the Mar-

THE SURRENDER OF CORNWALLIS

quis de Lafayette, and Baron Friedrich Wilhelm von Steuben join forces to prevent raids by Arnold and Cornwallis. Arnold leaves Virginia, and Cornwallis moves toward Yorktown.

July 20   Slaves at Williamsburg, Virginia, set fire to several buildings, including Virginia's capitol.

Aug. 1   Cornwallis reaches Yorktown and sets up a base for operations.

Aug. 12   Rochambeau breaks camp at Newport and sets out to join Washington at White Plains.

Aug. 21   Washington sends out false data to convince General Clinton that New York is about to be attacked. Instead, the combined French-American army moves quickly toward Philadelphia, on its way to Virginia.

Aug. 30   French Admiral Count François de Grasse arrives off the Virginia coast with 28 ships and another French army. He moves into Chesapeake Bay near Lynnhaven, east of Norfolk, Virginia.

Aug. 31   De Grasse lands a French army near Jamestown, Virginia. These troops join those of Lafayette, while de Grasse sets up a blockade of Chesapeake Bay

Sept. 1   Washington and Rochambeau, marching southward, enter Pennsylvania.

Sept. 4   Spanish Franciscan Fathers in southern California found the mission village of El Pueblo Nuestra Señora la Reina de los Angeles de Porciuncula [Los Angeles].

Sept. 5-8   De Grasse is confronted with the British fleet under Admiral Thomas Graves. The two fleets meet in Chesapeake Bay. A sharp fight occurs, followed by three days of maneuvering.

Sept. 8   General Greene is defeated at Eutaw Springs, South Carolina. Despite this and earlier defeats, Greene has managed to push the British back into Charles Town, and to restore most of South Carolina to American control.

Sept. 9   Another French fleet arrives from Newport, Rhode Island. Graves withdraws toward New York. This action seals the fate of Cornwallis, who is now penned in on Yorktown Peninsula.

Sept. 14-24   The combined army of Washington and Rochambeau is transported down Chesapeake Bay and reaches Williamsburg, Virginia.

Sept. 28   The huge Allied force marches the nine miles from Williamsburg to Yorktown and besieges Cornwallis' forces.

Sept. 30   Cornwallis abandons the outer defenses of Yorktown.

Oct. 19   Cornwallis surrenders.

Oct. 24   Washington urges an attack on New York, but the French fleet is in a hurry to leave American waters.

Nov. 5   A large loan from the Netherlands is made available to the United States.

Dec. 31   With adequate funds on hand, an agency is needed to undertake their management, and the Bank of North America is chartered.

31

1782

Although the victory at Yorktown puts an end to British hopes of reconquering her rebellious American colonies, it does not end the war. Fighting along the eastern seaboard ends on Aug. 27, but warfare continues in the American West and Northwest. George Rogers Clark remains in the field throughout most of the year, finally winning a decisive victory over British-supported Indians in early November. Formal negotiations for peace begin in April, but the full American negotiating team is not available until October. By the end of November, a preliminary treaty is signed, more than 13 months after the surrender of Cornwallis.

Jan. 1 Loyalists, especially those who face charges of collaboration or treason, and many whose property is marked for confiscation, begin to leave from all of the states. Those from New England and New York are among the first to emigrate, mainly to Nova Scotia and New Brunswick.

Jan. 5 Wilmington, North Carolina, is evacuated by the British, as part of concerted plans to withdraw from all the ports and cities they have occupied during the war.

Mar. 7 In the Ohio country 96 Christian Indians of the Delaware (Leni-Lenape) tribe are massacred at Gnadenhutten by American militiamen in retaliation for the terrorism committed by other tribes.

Mar. 22 The British decide to open direct negotiations with the American peace commission.

April 12 Peace talks begin, but Benjamin Franklin is the only American commissioner present. Of the other commissioners, Henry Laurens has been a prisoner since he was captured in 1780. John Adams is negotiating a loan and recognition for the United States in the Netherlands. John Jay is on a mission in Spain.

April 16 Washington establishes army headquarters at Newburgh, New York.

April 19 The Netherlands recognizes the independence of the United States.

May 19 Sir Guy Carleton replaces Sir Henry Clinton as commander of all British forces in America, with headquarters in New York City.

June 4 Colonel William Crawford, a former associate of Washington, is ambushed and killed by a combined Indian-Loyalist force near Lake Erie in the Ohio country. The Indian part of the force is especially aroused because some of Crawford's men were participants in the massacre at Gnadenhutten in March.

June 11 Dutch bankers agree to lend $2,000,000 to the United States.

June 11 Savannah, Georgia, is abandoned by the British.

June 20 The Great Seal of the United States is adopted.

June 23 John Jay and Benjamin Franklin, American peace commissioners, confer in Paris.

Aug. 19 Encouraged by the defeat of Crawford and by other minor victories along the frontier, Indians and Loyalists conduct many more raids, some of which penetrate deeply into settled areas. Moving south of the Ohio, a combined force defeats frontiersmen at Blue Licks, near Lexington, in Fayette County, Virginia [Kentucky].

Aug. 20 Joseph Brant, the British-educated Mohawk chief, operating out of British-held Detroit, raids deeply into Pennsylvania and western Virginia [Kentucky].

Aug. 25 Brant burns the village of Hannastown, Pennsylvania.

Aug. 27 A minor skirmish between American and British troops on the banks of the Combahee River, in South Carolina, is the [last] action of the American Revolution in the East.

Sept. 27 Formal negotiations for peace begin in Paris, although Adams has not yet arrived, and Laurens is still in prison.

Oct. 8 A treaty of commerce and friendship is signed between the United States and the Netherlands.

Nov. 1 The U.S. peace commissioners decide against consulting with the French during the negotiations, and to proceed on their own initiative. This decision is contrary to their instructions from Congress [and later causes bad feelings on the part of the French].

Nov. 10 George Rogers Clark collects a force of riflemen and, in retaliation for the Blue Licks action in August, attacks the Shawnee Indian village of Chillicothe in the Ohio country. [This might be considered the last battle of the American Revolution.]

Nov. 30 A preliminary peace treaty is signed. The most important provisions relate to the establishment of boundaries and British recognition of American independence. The New

George Washington
FIRST PRESIDENT   1789-1797

The Washington Family

Salute to General Washington in New York Harbor.

Benjamin Franklin

John Adams
SECOND PRESIDENT   **1797-1801**

England and New York boundary with Canada is defined as the St. Croix River and the 45th parallel of latitude. This leaves the northern boundary of the District of Maine in Massachusetts unsettled. The British agree to abandon fortifications in the American Northwest, and accept the Mississippi River as the western boundary of the United States. A line through the Great Lakes and their connecting waterways is established as the northern boundary between the United States and British Upper Canada [Ontario]. All debts that are due to creditors of either country are accepted as valid debts. The British are to evacuate with "all convenient speed."

Dec. 14   Charles Town, South Carolina, is evacuated by the British.

Dec. 15   The French express anger with the U.S. peace commissioners for having negotiated without prior consultation with the French Government. A tactful handling of the situation by Benjamin Franklin prevents serious discord.

Dec. 24   French troops sail for home from Boston.

The Balance of Power. (A British view of the military and political situation: the United States is a dupe of France and Spain; Britain will triumph over her enemies; and America will reunite with Britain.)

1783

Although free, the United States is not "united." It is a loose confederation consisting of 13 states containing differing nationalities, differing religions, competing economic activities with strong tariff barriers, deep suspicions of any form of centralized control, and with sovereignty jealously guarded within each state. Despite all these factors and conditions, and despite weaknesses inherent in the Articles of Confederation, a sense of national unity is slowly materializing.

By the end of 1783 the army has disbanded. During the year several countries recognize the independence of the United States. American leaders are beginning to assess the results of the war, and are planning how to meet some of the more urgent problems that face the new country.

Feb. 3   Spain recognizes the independence of the United States.

Feb. 4   Great Britain proclaims cessation of hostilities.

Mar. 10   The Newburgh Addresses are issued by a group of anonymous dissident officers protesting lack of payment on salaries. The group threatens to defy Congress if their demands are not met.

Mar. 11   General Washington forbids unauthorized meetings by his officers; he views the Newburgh Addresses with disfavor.

Mar. 12   Washington calls his own meeting and condemns the tone of the Newburgh Addresses; he calls for patience and counsels his officers not to take any action that will contaminate their brilliant war records.

April 11   Congress proclaims cessation of hostilities.

April 26   About 7,000 Loyalists sail from the port of New York, heading for Canada.

May 13   The Society of the Cincinnati is established at a meeting in the headquarters of Baron von Steuben in Newburgh, New York. It is open to officers of the American Revolutionary Army and their eldest male descendants. More than 2,000 officers enroll, and Washington is chosen for the first president-general.

June 13   Washington's army is disbanded.

June 24   Congress flees from Philadelphia to Princeton, New Jersey, to avoid confrontation with a group of protesting veterans who march in from Lancaster, Pennsylvania.

July 8   A Massachusetts Supreme Court decision declares slavery in that state to have been abolished by Article I of the Massachusetts Declaration of Rights of 1780.

Sept. 3   The Treaty of Paris, ending the war, is signed in Paris by Great Britain and the United States.

Oct. 7   The Virginia House of Burgesses passes a law giving freedom to slaves who have served in the Continental Army.

Nov. 3   Congress discharges all its remaining soldiers who have signed up for the duration.

Nov. 25   New York City is evacuated by the British.

Nov. 26   Congress reconvenes at Annapolis, Maryland.

Dec. 4   Washington takes leave of his officers at Fraunces' Tavern in New York City. Staten Island and Long Island are evacuated by the British.

Dec. 19   General Washington resigns his commission before Congress at Annapolis, Maryland.

Dec. 31   The African slave trade is prohibited by all the northern states, plus Maryland, Delaware, and Virginia.

Members of the Continental Army march down Old Bowery, New York City.

The central Government of the United States proves ineffective. During the entire year, Congress is rarely able to assemble a quorum of nine states in order to do business. Moreover, Congress is driven out of Philadelphia by its own unpaid army. There is no money and no means to get it from the states, because Congress, under the Articles of Confederation, has no power to levy or collect taxes. Superintendent of Finances Robert Morris proposes a land tax, a poll tax, a tax on liquor, and a national tariff, but all are rejected by Congress. Morris resigns in dismay, but is talked into remaining at least until the army is paid. Later in the year a loan, provided by the Netherlands, brings some relief. Tension along the frontier mounts as the Government is unable to enforce its treaty obligations and ordinances, and movements appear for the creation of new states on the frontier. Restlessness is abetted as Spain and Great Britain stir up discontent among settlers in the West.

Jan. 14   The Treaty of Paris is ratified by Congress.

Feb. 22   The *Empress of China,* in search of new markets in the Far East, sails from New York.

Mar. 1   Virginia's offer to cede its western lands. [His proposal to create 10 states is adopted but never put into effect.]

April 23   Jefferson introduces a program to Congress for organizing the western cession lands. [His proposal to create 10 states is adopted but never put into effect.]

May 7   John Jay replaces Robert Livingston as Secretary of Foreign Affairs.

May-July   After Congress (in the Trenton Decree) awards disputed Wyoming Valley lands to Pennsylvania, Connecticut settlers who have settled there in previous years are ejected. The Pennsylvania Council of Censors condemns this action, but evictions and violence continue sporadically.

May 28   A Treasury Board is created to replace the Office of Superintendent of Finance.

June 2   North Carolina offers to cede all its western lands to the United States.

Aug. 23   Settlers of the western lands of North Carolina, disturbed by the possible lack of government pending acceptance of the cession offered by the state to the United States, meet at Jonesboro to plan the organization of a separate state.

Aug. 30   The *Empress of China* reaches Canton, China.

Sept. 21   The Pennsylvania *Packet and Daily Advertiser,* begins publication. [It is the first successful daily newspaper in America.]

Sept. 22   The first Russian settlement is established in Alaska, at Three Saints Bay on Kodiak Island.

Nov. 1   Congress meets at Trenton, New Jersey.

Dec. 5   Phillis Wheatley dies. Born in Africa and educated by the wife of her owner, a tailor in Boston, she wrote poetry that won recognition during her lifetime, and earned her freedom. One of her last poems celebrates both her own emancipation and that of the country in *Liberty and Peace* (1784).

Dec. 14   Delegates from three western counties of North Carolina—Washington, Sullivan, and Greene counties—propose to establish a separate state of Frankland, and choose John Sevier to be its governor. [Sevier takes office before the end of February 1785; on Nov. 14, 1785, the state is officially called Franklin.]

Dec. 24   Madison issues his *Remonstrance Against Religious Assessments,* one of the most eloquent statements ever made in America for the separation of state and church. [His argument results in the defeat of a bill in the Virginia House of Delegates designed to support all churches equally through taxation.]

Caesar Rodney
(1728-1784)
Signer of the Declaration of Independence

1785   **The United States searches for new opportunities in trade,** for ways to finance government, for a workable way to distribute and govern the western lands, for some means to put an end to chaotic relations between states, and finally to arrest the erosion of respect with which other nations hold the United States. Speculation and investment reach new highs, but so does inflation. A postwar migration is taking place. People begin to cross the Appalachian Mountains, going northward into Vermont and Maine and westward into New York and Pennsylvania. Because supplies of British manufactured goods are no longer available, Americans are impelled to make what they require. Many expect the Confederation Government and the state governments to participate in these activities, but these governments lack funds. Competing tariff systems, divergent economic aims, conflicting laws prevent any unified legislative or regulating effort. However, a series of conferences, mainly between the states of Maryland, Pennsylvania, Virginia, and Delaware, are proposed or scheduled.

Jan. 11   Congress moves to the newly designated capital, New York City, meeting in the City Hall.

Jan. 15   Davidson Academy is founded in Nashville in the state of Frankland. [It becomes successively Cumberland College in 1806, the University of Nashville in 1826, Peabody Normal College for Teachers in 1889, and George Peabody College for Teachers in 1905.]

Jan. 21   Wyandot, Chippewa, Delaware, and Ottawa Indians cede land in the Ohio country.

Feb. 7   The state of Georgia establishes Bourbon County [most of what is the present states of Alabama and Mississippi], although much of this territory is claimed by Spain as part of its Florida possessions.

Feb. 24   John Adams is appointed Minister to Great Britain.

Feb. 28   The British indicate that they will refuse to comply with the terms of the Treaty of Paris by giving up their posts in the Great Lakes region. The British refusal is based on grounds that Americans have failed to comply with the treaty—by having neither paid the debts owed to British merchants nor compensated the Loyalists.

Mar. 8   Henry Knox is appointed Secretary of War, succeeding Benjamin Lincoln.

Mar. 10   Thomas Jefferson is appointed Minister to France, succeeding Benjamin Franklin, who leaves France to take up a position in the Executive Council of Pennsylvania.

Mar. 25   Maryland and Virginia commissioners hold a conference at Alexandria, Virginia. The purpose of the meeting is to resolve conflicting laws and regulations for the navigation of the Potomac River and Chesapeake Bay.

Mar. 28   The Maryland-Virginia conference adjourns to meet at Mount Vernon with General Washington. As a result of full discussions, the Commissioners make recommendations to their own state legislatures embodying agreements on imports, a uniform currency, and uniform regulations. Before adjourning, they invite Pennsylvania to join in a pact.

April 30   The University of Georgia is chartered, becoming the oldest state-chartered institution of learning in the United States. [Classes begin in 1801.]

May 5   The Treaty of Dumpling Creek is signed between the state of Frankland and Cherokee Indians, in which the latter give up much of their lands.

May 15   The *Empress of China* returns to New York with a rich cargo.

Richard Henry Lee
(1732-1794)
Signer of the Declaration of Independence

Lewis Morris
(1726-1798)
Signer of the Declaration of Independence

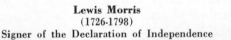

May 20 The land Ordinance of 1785 is passed by Congress, dividing the Northwest Territory into townships, which are, in turn, divided into 36 sections of 640 acres each. One section in each township is set aside for the support of public education.

June 23 Massachusetts bans the export of its goods in British ships, and also doubles tonnage duties.

July 20 Congress authorizes John Jay to negotiate with Spain for the free navigation of the Mississippi River. [He is unable to come to an agreement with Spain.]

Sept. 10 John Adams negotiates a treaty with Russia, endorsing the principle of free ships–free goods, and outlawing privateering.

Sept. 20 Pennsylvania passes a law levying heavy tonnage duties on ships of nations that do not have a treaty with the United States.

Oct. 10 Spanish authorities order Georgia to relinquish its claim to land which it annexed on Feb. 7.

Nov. 28 The treaty of Hopewell between the United States and the Cherokees disallows the Dumpling Creek cession of May 5.

Nov. 30 John Adams, U.S. Minister to Great Britain, demands that the British evacuate military posts in the West.

Dec. 5 The Maryland legislature endorses the agreements of the Mount Vernon Conference, and proposes to invite Delaware to sign the pact.

The Loss of Eden and Eden Lost. (A British caricaturist views with sadness the loss of America.)

1786 **The movement to reform Government gains momentum. On the** one hand, a successful agreement between Maryland and Virginia to regulate navigation on the Potomac River and in Chesapeake Bay is an encouragement, leading many to hope that agreements far larger in scope can be obtained this year. On the other hand, Shays's Rebellion points up the weaknesses of the Confederation Government. It is appalling to many to note that a state militia is needed to protect the Confederation's arsenal at Springfield, Massachusetts. Moreover, Washington and many of the major leaders of the American Revolution have made known their belief that the Confederation can never become a strong central government without the power to tax, and Congress can obtain this power only by amendment to the Articles of Confederation. Commercial war, a postwar depression, rival state tariff systems, debtor protests, the open defiance of the Treaty of Paris by Great Britain, and many other critical conditions and events have the combined effect of galvanizing national leadership into calling for a convention in Philadelphia "for the sole and express purpose of revising the Articles of Confederation."

January Losses from piracy mount since the removal of the protection of the British fleet. Pirates of Algiers, Tripoli, Tunis, and Morocco, infesting the Mediterranean Sea, demand money (tribute) from American ships.

Jan. 19 A *Bill for Establishing Religious Freedom* is enacted by Virginia. The work of James Madison and Thomas Jefferson, it affirms in essence that the state shall not establish, favor, or support any religion; and that all persons shall be free to profess their opinions in matters of religion without endangering any of their civil rights.

Jan. 21 Virginia invites all the states to a commercial conference to be held in September.

Feb. 20 New Jersey refuses flatly to pay its quota of funds requisitioned by Congress.

Feb. 22 John Adams initiates negotiations with the pirate state of Tripoli, which has demanded a tribute.

Feb. 28 The British refuse openly to abandon their military posts along the American northwestern frontier. These include forts at Oswego, New York (on Lake Ontario), at Niagara (western New York), at Detroit, and at Michilimackinac, at the entrance to Lake Michigan.

Mar. 1 The Ohio Company of Associates is founded in Boston. The leaders are Rufus Putnam, Benjamin Tupper, Samuel Parsons, and Manasseh Cutler. The company proposes to purchase 1,500,000 acres of land north of the Ohio River, at 66½¢ per acre, with the intention of establishing permanent settlements.

June-September A major depression reaches its most severe extent. Currency is unstable, prices are falling, the shipping industry, espe-

cially in New England is stagnant, and the lack of central control discourages cooperative nationwide improvements or investments across state lines. Several factors act to improve conditions by the end of September. Shipping is slowly recovering and manufacturing is beginning to revive, stimulated by a rise in prices as a result of growing shortages in some commodities.

June 28 Direct negotiations with the pirate state of Morocco result in a treaty. This is actually obtained in exchange for gifts, which many Americans view as tribute.

Aug. 7 Proposed amendments to the Articles of Confederation are submitted to Congress. These tend to show that the delegates are acutely aware of the weaknesses in the Confederation, especially in regard to fiscal matters.

Aug. 22-25 Over 50 communities hold a joint meeting at Hatfield, Massachusetts, protesting judicial practices, lawyers' fees, and taxes.

Aug. 29 John Jay is instructed to seek a commercial treaty with Spain. [The terms he brings back are rejected by Congress because they include denial of free navigation for Americans of the Spanish-controlled lower Mississippi River.]

Aug. 31 Armed insurgents prevent the sitting of court at Northampton, Massachusetts. They are farmers, many of them veterans of the revolutionary war, who have no means of paying high taxes or court costs, because even paper money is no longer available and payment in kind is not accepted.

Sept. 5 State Supreme Court sessions at Worcester, Massachusetts, are broken up by armed insurgents.

Sept. 11-14 In response to Virginia's invitation in January, a convention is held at Annapolis, Maryland, with 12 delegates from New York, New Jersey, Delaware, Pennsylvania, and Virginia, to consider commercial reforms. The delegates conclude that these cannot be separated from the question of political reforms, and for a full discussion of the latter representatives from at least nine states are needed. They decide to issue a call for a larger convention to meet in Philadelphia in May 1787, to consider what steps appear "necessary to render the Constitution of the Federal Government adequate to the exigencies of the Union."

Sept. 25 The Rhode Island Supreme Court hands down a decision that an act forcing a creditor to accept paper money violates the property guarantees of the Rhode Island Charter, which serves as the constitution of that state.

Sept. 26 About 500 insurgents appear in Springfield, Massachusetts, forcing the Supreme Court there to adjourn. Because there is a Federal arsenal in Springfield, Congress authorizes Secretary of War Henry Knox to raise a force to protect the arsenal. This force is never used because the insurgent band dissolves.

Dec. 26 A new insurgent band is gathered under the leadership of Daniel Shays, a former army captain. They march toward Springfield to join another unit led by Luke Day. Knox immediately calls for a new militia, to defend the arsenal. General Benjamin Lincoln is given command of this force.

A proclamation by Governor James Bowdoin of Massachusetts, calling for the suppression of [Shays] rebellion

Commonwealth of Maſſachuſetts.

By His EXCELLENCY

JAMES BOWDOIN, Eſquire,

Governour of the Commonwealth of Maſſachuſetts.

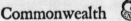

A Proclamation.

WHEREAS information has been given to the Supreme Executive of this Commonwealth, that on Tueſday laſt, the 29th of Auguſt, being the day appointed by law for the ſitting of the Court of Common Pleas and Court of General Seſſions of the Peace, at *Northampton*, in the county of *Hampſhire*, within this Commonwealth, a large concourſe of people, from ſeveral parts of that county, aſſembled at the Court-Houſe in *Northampton*, many of whom were armed with guns, ſwords and other deadly weapons, and with drums beating and fifes playing, in contempt and open defiance of the authority of this Government, did, by their threats of violence and keeping poſſeſſion of the Court-Houſe until twelve o'clock on the night of the ſame day, prevent the ſitting of the Court, and the orderly adminiſtration of juſtice in that county :

AND WHEREAS this high-handed offence is fraught with the moſt fatal and pernicious conſequences, muſt tend to ſubvert all law and government ; to diſſolve our excellent Conſtitution, and introduce univerſal riot, anarchy and confuſion, which would probably terminate in abſolute deſpotiſm, and conſequently deſtroy the faireſt proſpects of political happineſs, that any people was ever favoured with :

I HAVE therefore thought fit, by and with the advice of the Council, to iſſue this Proclamation, calling upon all Judges, Juſtices, Sheriffs, Conſtables, and other officers, civil and military, within this Commonwealth, to prevent and ſuppreſs all ſuch violent and riotous proceedings, if they ſhould be attempted in their ſeveral counties.

AND I DO hereby, purſuant to the indiſpenſible duty I owe to the good people of this Commonwealth, moſt ſolemnly call upon them, as they value the bleſſings of freedom and independence, which at the expence of ſo much blood and treaſure they have purchaſed—as they regard their faith, which in the ſight of GOD and the world, they pledged to one another, and to the people of the United States, when they adopted the preſent Conſtitution of Government—as they would not diſappoint the hopes, and thereby become contemptible in the eyes of other nations, in the view of whom they have riſen to glory and empire—as they would not deprive themſelves of the ſecurity derived from well-regulated Society, to their lives, liberties and property ; and as they would not devolve upon their children, inſtead of peace, freedom and ſafety, a ſtate of anarchy, confuſion and ſlavery,—I do moſt earneſtly and moſt ſolemnly call upon them to aid and aſſiſt with their utmoſt efforts the aforeſaid officers, and to unite in preventing and ſuppreſſing all ſuch treaſonable proceedings, and every meaſure that has a tendency to encourage them.

GIVEN *at the* COUNCIL-CHAMBER, *in* BOSTON, *this ſecond day of* September, *in the year of our* LORD, *one thouſand ſeven hundred and eighty-ſix, and in the eleventh year of the Independence of the United States of* AMERICA.

JAMES BOWDOIN.

By his Excellency's command.

JOHN AVERY, jun. Secretary.

1787

By the time the convention to consider political reforms meets in May, the "rebellion" in New England has been quelled. Many leading Americans have become convinced that the Articles of Confederation are unworkable. Although they may be appropriate for a league of independent states, most Americans feel that a strong and competent government is essential to meet the crises that are appearing everywhere. Fiscal problems, commercial rivalry, and lack of uniformity in action by all the states have led to a situation in which Congress has been able to muster a quorum for necessary action only during a few days in the year; for the remaining time, there is no central government at all.

One group of delegates proposes to dispense with the Articles of Confederation and start with a new form of union. Opposition to this plan comes from the smaller states, who fear domination by the larger states. Nevertheless, agreement is reached by September, and three states immediately signify their approval by ratifying the proposed Constitution.

Jan. 5 A decision of the North Carolina Supreme Court upholds the right of a court to void an act of a state legislature.

Jan. 27-Feb. 4 The Shays "rebellion" is quelled at Springfield, Massachusetts, by units of a militia hastily collected and led by General William Shepherd under the over-all command of General Benjamin Lincoln. The Shays forces are chased from Springfield toward Amherst and Petersham, where 150 rebels are captured and the rest are scattered.

Feb. 21 Congress adopts a resolution calling for a Constitutional Convention to meet on May 14 at Philadelphia.

May 14 Five states send delegates to the convention site; six others have selected delegates, but these have not arrived.

May 25 With the arrival in Philadelphia of delegates from seven states, a quorum for work is achieved. [New Hampshire's delegates do not arrive until July. Rhode Island decides not to attend.] George Mason, James Madison, Gouverneur Morris, Roger Sherman, James Wilson, and Elbridge Gerry are "floor" leaders; Washington is chosen chairman; William Jackson is secretary.

May 29 The "Virginia Plan" is presented by Edmund Randolph. Its provision of a two-house legislature, with seats in both houses apportioned by wealth or by population, favors the states having larger populations. Another feature, veto power by the central government, is also strongly opposed by smaller states.

June 15 William Paterson of New Jersey submits a rival plan. This would also add substantially to federal power, but it favors a single-house legislature in which all states are equally represented.

July 13 Congress passes another Northwest Ordinance bill, establishing a government for the Northwest Territory. The new ordinance is based on the Ordinance of 1784 which never went into effect. The prime interests behind the drive to institute a government for the Northwest Territory are the Ohio Company of Associates, a land-speculating group, and the Society of Cincinnati, a veteran's group. Both these groups plan to move settlers in great numbers into the Northwest Territory.

July 16-23 The Philadelphia convention accepts a Connecticut Compromise offered by Roger Sherman. It provides for a lower house with representation by population and an upper house in which each state has one vote. This overcomes the last major obstacle to the formulation of a rough draft of a new constitution.

Aug. 6-29 A draft of 23 articles is submitted, and a period of "Great Debates" follows.

Aug. 22 John Fitch demonstrates his steamboat on the Delaware River in the presence of members of the Constitutional Convention.

Sept. 17 Thirty-nine delegates of the 12 attending states at the convention in Philadelphia vote to approve the constitution, the final draft of which was written by Gouverneur Morris.

Sept. 28 Congress passes a resolution to send the new constitution to the nine states for ratification, and defeats motions to censure itself for having exceeded its authority.

Oct. 27 An essay [first of a series] advocating ratification appears in a New York newspaper, *The Independent Journal*.

Nov. 6 The African Methodist Episcopal Church is founded in Philadelphia by Richard Allen, in protest over the segregation practices of the St. George Methodist Episcopal Church, from which the new church gets its first adherents.

Dec. 7 Delaware becomes the first state to ratify the proposed Constitution. It does so by a unanimous vote of its legislature.

Dec. 12 Pennsylvania becomes the second state to ratify the Constitution, in a 46-to-23 vote.

Dec. 18 New Jersey ratifies the Constitution by a unanimous vote.

Dec. 20 Shakers or Shaking Quakers (United Society of Believers in Christ's Second Appearing) initiate a revival movement [that ignites religious fervor among other denominations, especially in Kentucky and other frontier regions].

Arthur Middleton
(1742-1787)
Signer of the Declaration of Independence

Richard Stockton
(1730-1781)
Signer of the Declaration of Independence

Thomas Stone
(1748-1787)
Signer of the Declaration of Independence

George Taylor
(1716-1781)
Signer of the Declaration of Independence

1788

Three states have ratified the new Constitution. Under its own terms, six more ratifications are needed to enact it. Throughout the year contests are waged on the pros and cons of the Constitution in the popularly elected state ratification conventions. Heated arguments take place between Antifederalists, who oppose adoption of the new Constitution, and Federalists, who support its ratification. As the roll of the states is called, and the Federalist argument is sustained, it becomes clear by midsummer that New York and Virginia are the critical states; rejection by either state could doom the efforts of the framers. The most prominent Federalists—Hamilton, Jay and Madison, generally using the single pseudonym of Publius—publish 85 brilliant letters in the New York *Independent Journal,* and other newspapers. These are almost immediately published in a brochure entitled *The Federalist* [*The Federalist Papers* in later years]. They are instrumental in swinging New York to ratification, more than a month after New Hampshire votes the ninth and nominally deciding ratification. Soon thereafter the states begin to choose electors who are to vote for the first President of the United States.

Jan. 2   Georgia ratifies the Constitution unanimously, becoming the fourth state to ratify.

Jan. 9   Connecticut ratifies the Constitution, 128 to 40, becoming the fifth state.

Feb. 7   Massachusetts is the sixth state to ratify the Constitution, after the chief Antifederalist leaders, John Hancock and Samuel Adams, receive promise of amendments guaranteeing civil liberties.

Feb. 27-Mar. 26   A petition by free Negroes, under the leadership of Prince Hall, is presented to the Massachusetts legislature protesting the kidnapping and selling into slavery of free Negroes. They refer specifically to a case in Boston in which the Negroes were beaten and transported to Martinique. The legislature takes up the case and passes a strong bill to prohibit the slave trade, with provisions for recovery of damages by any victim of kidnapping.

Mar. 24   Rhode Island refuses to call a ratifying convention, and instead conducts a referendum, in which the proposed Constitution is rejected.

April 7   Under authority of the Northwest Ordinance of 1787, Rufus Putnam of the Ohio Company of Associates leads a group of settlers to the mouth of the Muskingum River in the Ohio country, calling the village Muskingum. [They soon change its name to Marietta, in honor of Queen Marie Antoinette, and set up a local government.]

April 28   Maryland ratifies the Constitution, 63 to 11, becoming the seventh state to do so.

May 23   South Carolina becomes the eighth state to ratify the Constitution by a vote of 149 to 73.

June 21   New Hampshire's ratification, 57 to 46, brings the Constitution into operation.

June 26   In Virginia, opposition to the Constitution, led by Patrick Henry and George Mason, nearly destroys its effectiveness. Although the document is in effect technically, no one believes that the Union can exist without Virginia and New York. The influence of Washington saves the Constitution in Virginia, winning over Edmund Randolph, who requires and obtains a promise of a Bill of Rights to be added later. Virginia then ratifies, 87 to 79.

July 2   Congress declares the Constitution of the United States to be in effect, and issues instructions for choosing the members of the first bicameral Congress and electors for the first President.

July 15   Arthur St. Clair is installed as the first governor of the Northwest Territory at its capital, Marietta.

July 26   Opposition to the Constitution in New York, led by George Clinton, melts away with the news of Virginia's vote. New Yorkers, even after obtaining a promise of a Bill of Rights, ratify by the close vote of 30 to 27.

July 27   The Scioto Company purchases 1,781,760 acres in the Ohio country and plans to settle the region north of the 1,000,000 acres owned by the Ohio Company.

Aug. 17   The town of Losantiville is founded near the confluence of the Ohio and Great Miami Rivers. [The town is renamed Cincinnati, after the Society of the Cincinnati, in 1790.]

Sept. 13   New York City is declared to be temporary capital of the United States.

October-December   A serious drop in commodity prices is halted.

Oct. 2   The Confederation Congress is removed from Federal Hall in New York City to permit its renovation for its new role.

Nov. 1   The Congress adjourns.
Dec. 23   The state of Maryland offers to cede an area on the Potomac River to the United States for a Federal District.

John Penn
(1741?-1788)
Signer of the Declaration of Independence

William Hooper
(1742-1790)
Signer of the Declaration of Independence

William Whipple
(1730-1785)
Signer of the Declaration of Independence

Stephen Hopkins
(1707-1785)
Signer of the Declaration of Independence

1789

There is no central Government of the United States after Nov. 1, 1788, until the new Congress achieves its first quorum the first week of April. However, ballots have been counted earlier and the electors have cast their votes. The inauguration of President George Washington sets the first of many precedents.

One of the very first duties of Congress is to make good the promise of Federalist leaders to pass a Bill of Rights. Twelve amendments are proposed and are sent to the states for ratification. Ten of these are ratified by New Jersey, North Carolina, and Maryland before the end of the year. This Bill of Rights cannot become law until it has been approved by nine states.

By midyear Congress passes a tariff to obtain money for the daily expenses of Government. In its very first months Congress accomplishes what the Continental Congress and Confederation Congress could not do: it acquires funds with which to operate the machinery of Government. Congress spends the last half of 1789 in setting up a judiciary, including the Supreme Court provided in the Constitution, and executive departments, the heads (secretaries) of which are appointed by President Washington.

Jan. 7 Electors are chosen for the first Presidential election in United States history. In some states the citizens who are entitled to vote for state officials also vote for electors; in others the electors are chosen by the state legislature. In Massachusetts two are chosen by the people while eight others are appointed by the legislature from a list of 24 candidates. The electors, once chosen, are free to cast their ballots for whomever they please.

Feb. 4 The electors cast their ballots; 69 votes go the Washington; 34 go to John Adams, who therefore becomes Vice President. [This mode of selecting a Vice President is changed by the 12th Amendment in 1804.]

April 1 The House of Representatives is organized, with 30 of the 59 members present. Frederick A. Muhlenburg is elected Speaker of the House.

April 6 The Senate is organized with 9 of its 22 members being present. John Langdon is chosen temporary presiding officer.

April 6 The ballots for President and Vice President are counted in the Senate.

April 15 The *Gazette of the United States* begins publication as a Federalist newspaper, with John Fenno as editor.

April 16-23 George Washington is informed that he is elected, and he makes the journey to New York.

April 16 *The Contrast* is staged in New York City. It is the first comedy produced by a native American playwright, Royall Tyler, who served under General Lincoln in suppressing Shays's Rebellion.

April 30 Washington is inaugurated in the Senate Chamber of Federal Hall, New York City.

May 7 The Church of England in the United States is reorganized and renamed the Protestant Episcopal Church.

May 12 The Society of Saint Tammany is founded in New York City. It is a fraternal organization in vague opposition to the Federalists. Tammany was a Delaware Indian whose elevation to "sainthood" was made in jest, to parody the patron saints of royalist societies.

July 4 A tariff of 8½ per cent on the value of certain listed goods is passed by Congress. Goods imported into the United States in American ships are to be taxed at a rate 10 per cent lower than goods arriving in foreign ships.

Sept. 11 President Washington appoints Alexander Hamilton as Secretary of the Treasury Department, an office which was created by Congress on Sept. 2.

Sept. 12 General Henry Knox is appointed Secretary of War; he heads a department established by Congress on Aug. 7.

Sept. 20 The office of Postmaster General is created under the Treasury Department.

Sept. 24 The Federal Judiciary Act is passed, creating a six-member Supreme Court (a Chief Justice and five Associate Justices), 13 district courts, and three circuit courts; the act also establishes the office of Attorney General.

Sept. 25 Congress submits 12 amendments to the Constitution (the proposed Bill of Rights) to the states of ratification.

Sept. 26 Edmund Randolph is appointed the Attorney General, and Thomas Jefferson is appointed Secretary of State, heading the department that was designated as Foreign Affairs when it was created on July 27. John Jay is appointed Chief Justice of the U.S. Supreme Court.

Sept. 29　The United States Army is created, consisting of the forces already on hand during the final months of the Confederation Government. It comprises one regiment of eight companies of infantry, and one battalion of four companies of artillery, a total of 1,000 men.

Nov. 20　New Jersey is the first state to ratify the Bill of Rights.

Nov. 20　North Carolina becomes the 12th state to ratify the United States Constitution.

Nov. 26　Washington proclaims the nation's first Thanksgiving Day.

Francis Hopkinson
(1737-1791)
Signer of the Declaration of Independence

Benjamin Franklin
(1706-1790)
Signer of the Declaration of Independence

Lyman Hall
(1724-1790)
Signer of the Declaration of Independence

Thomas Nelson, Jr.
(1738-1789)
Signer of the Declaration of Independence

1790 The first census of the United States shows a population of almost 4,000,000. Virginia is the giant among states, with more than 820,000 inhabitants. Massachusetts, Pennsylvania, and North Carolina each have more than 400,000; New York and Maryland have more than 300,000; South Carolina, Connecticut, and New Hampshire have more than 200,000, with New Jersey approaching that level; the states with less than 100,000 inhabitants each are Georgia, Rhode Island, and Delaware. The Negro population, almost entirely enslaved, accounts for 19.3 per cent of the total, but Negroes are not counted as whole individuals for purposes of apportionment; the Constitution itself in this respect estimates each Negro as only three fifths of a person. For purposes of voting, only free, white males with a specific tax-paying capability (varying from state to state) are counted. The census fails to record the fact that almost the entire population is rural, living off the soil; there is no significant industrial activity. By far the majority of the white population were themselves born or descended from forebears born in Great Britain.

These original states—more precisely, 12 out of the 13, until Rhode Island accedes to the Union in May—now have a functioning central Government. In its House of Representatives, 54 out of the 59 members have indicated their approval of the new system; they are Federalists. They face important issues in their first session: fiscal problems, including that of the national debt; foreign affairs, including the troublesome occupation of American military posts by foreign troops as well as occasional incursions across the frontiers; and of course the problem of dealing with the Indians. For the solution of the fiscal problem they have the advantage of the power to tax and they have a brilliant administrator in the Treasury Secretary, Alexander Hamilton, who makes it clear that only a nation willing to pay its debts can establish credit. Because he is willing to horse-trade in Congress, he wins votes for his plan, with the incidental result that a site is chosen for the future capital of the nation on the bank of the Potomac.

Jan. 14 Treasury Secretary Alexander Hamilton presents a report on public credit, in which he argues that the United States should pay its debts at par value, even though many speculators would profit thereby. He also proposes that the Federal Government should assume all state debts incurred during the war.

April 4 The United States Coast Guard is created, under the Treasury Department, as a means of suppressing contraband trade and smuggling.

April 10 The first law is enacted by Congress to protect patents.

April 17 Benjamin Franklin, 84, dies in Philadelphia.

May 26 Congress accepts the cession from North Carolina of its western lands, which governed themselves from 1785 to 1788 as the State of Franklin without being recognized either by North Carolina or by Congress. The lands are redesignated officially as the Territory South of the River Ohio, and William Blount is appointed governor.

May 29 Rhode Island ratifies the Constitution, becoming the 13th state to do so.

June 20 Hamilton convinces Congress to pass the Assumption Act, under which the Federal Government is to assume the states' debts. He accomplishes this by winning Southern votes through a compromise: the capital is to be moved from New York to a Southern location.

July 31 The first patent is issued to Samuel Hopkins of Vermont, for a "process for making pot and pearl ashes" (potassium carbonate compounds) used in manufacturing glass.

Aug. 10 The *Columbia* sails into Boston harbor, the first American ship to circumnavigate the world. Leaving Boston three years ago, it carried furs from the northwest coast of North America to Canton, China, and tea from China to New England.

Aug. 12 Philadelphia is designated the temporary capital of the United States.

Dec. 6 Congress moves from New York to Philadelphia.

Dec. 14 Alexander Hamilton submits a plan for a Bank of the United States, mainly as a vehicle for the funding of debts under the Assumption Act and to establish credit.

Dec. 20 Samuel Slater installs the first cotton cording and spindle mill machinery at Pawtucket, Rhode Island.

1791 **Two major philosophies of government begin to polarize around** Hamilton and Jefferson. Hamilton supports the idea of an industrial society, copying that of Great Britain. Jefferson hates the British, admires France, and advocates a democratic agrarian society. Hamilton's Federalists support a strong central Government while Jefferson's followers favor a weaker central Government and stronger local Government. The two differing philosophies begin to compete directly, and one or the other is reflected in the various executive and legislative decisions that are made to solve the most urgent problems of the new nation. Among these are the consequences of renewed Indian attacks, the harassment of American shipping by Algerian pirates, the continuing British occupations of key frontier posts, and the debates surrounding the emerging Hamilton-Jefferson feud. Major vehicles for these debates are the rival journals sponsored as openly partisan organs: the *National Gazette,* edited by poet Philip Freneau, and the Federalist *Gazette of the United States,* founded two years ago under the editorship of John Fenno.

Jan. 5   Free Negroes of Charleston, South Carolina, present to that state's legislature a protest against the practice of preventing Negroes from instituting law suits or from testifying in court. The protesting document is rejected by the legislature.

Feb. 23   Hamilton's opinion on his proposed national bank is submitted. It is one of his most notable papers. In it he originates the doctrine of "implied powers."

Feb. 25   The Bank of the United States is chartered.

Mar. 3   An excise tax on distilled liquors and stills is passed by Congress.

Mar. 4   The independent state of Vermont, having adopted the Constitution of the United States, enters the Union as the 14th state. It has a population of about 85,000.

Mar. 30   A road is begun to connect the existing Wilderness Road of Virginia with White's Fort [Knoxville] in the Territory South of the River Ohio.

April 15   Ceremonies are held near Alexandria, Virginia, marking a 10-square-mile site for the future Federal District, including the existing communities of Alexandria and Georgetown, Maryland. The cessions of this land originated on the part of Maryland in December 1788 and on the part of Virginia in December 1789.

April 21   Work begins on a hard-surfaced 61-mile-long turnpike between Philadelphia and Lancaster. [It is completed in 1794.]

April 26   In the Treaty of Holston River, the Cherokee Indians cede most of the upper Tennessee River watershed, in return for the assurance that the remainder of their lands will be left to them with no further harassment.

June 12   The revolt of slaves in Haiti inspires a revolt of slaves in the Spanish colony of Louisiana. [The revolt fails, and 23 slaves are hanged.]

July 16   Benjamin Banneker, a notable Negro mathematician and scientist, is appointed one of three commissioners to survey the site for the new national capital. Banneker is the author of a popular almanac, the first issue of which is published this year.

Sept. 6   The state University of Vermont is founded in Burlington.

Sept. 10   General Arthur St. Clair, governor of the Northwest Territory, leaves Fort Washington, near Cincinnati, and marches northward to establish Forts Hamilton, St. Clair, Jefferson, Greenville, and Recovery [in western Ohio], all designed to protect settlers, and to prepare for defense against Miami Indian attacks.

November-December   President Washington adopts gradually the practice of consulting the department secretaries at regular intervals, giving rise to the concept of a "Cabinet."

Dec. 15   The first 10 of 12 amendments (Bill of Rights) proposed in 1789, having been ratified by three quarters of the states (the 10th state is Virginia), are declared to be in force.

The first Presidential Mansion, New York City

1792

During Washington's first administration, party lines have become drawn over domestic, mostly financial, issues. Beginning in 1792 more deep-seated philosophical differences between the contending "factions" begin to appear. While the Federalists retain their label, antifederalism becomes less significant than an affirmation of "republicanism" (in contrast to the alleged monarchical tendencies of Hamilton), and the followers of Jefferson and Madison adopt the label of Republican or Democratic-Republican. They continue to defend states' rights against excessive centralism, and therefore they insist on strict construction of the Constitution; but in foreign affairs they tend to support the ongoing French Revolution, whereas the Federalists distrust the French Republic proclaimed in September. Thus events abroad begin to intensify American political factionalism. In the election of 1792 President Washington is again returned to office, and John Adams is returned to the Vice Presidency, but not without a challenge from a Democratic-Republican candidate.

January The publication of Paine's *Rights of Man* is completed with the appearance of a second part. It is a political tract defending revolution, and maintaining that sovereignty resides in the will of the majority.

Jan. 12 The first U.S. Minister to Great Britain under the Constitution is Thomas Pinckney, a South Carolina Federalist.

Feb. 21 The Presidential Succession Act is passed providing that, if both the President and the Vice President are removed, resign, or die in office, the President pro tempore of the Senate (followed by the Speaker of the House) should succeed for the sole purpose of arranging for a Presidential election.

Mar. 5 General Arthur St. Clair is replaced as top army commander by General Anthony Wayne.

April 2 Congress passes the Coinage Act, which authorizes establishment of a mint, and prescribes a decimal system of coinage: dollars, dismes, cents, and milles. The U.S. dollar is to contain 24.75 grains of gold or 371.25 grains of silver, in a fixed legal-tender ratio of 15 to 1.

May 8 Congress passes a Militia Act authorizing the states to enroll into brigades and divisions all free, white males between the ages of 18 and 45.

June 1 With the approval of Virginia, of which it has been a part, Kentucky is admitted to the Union as the 15th State. Its constitution provides for male suffrage, toleration of slavery, and a bill of rights. Its population is about 75,000.

July 18 John Paul Jones, 45, hero of naval warfare, dies in Paris.

Aug. 21 Western Pennsylvanians register a strong protest at a meeting in Pittsburgh against the excise tax of 1791 which is levied on whiskey and on stills.

Oct. 12 The Society of St. Tammany celebrates Columbus Day in New York City, the first recorded major celebration of the discovery of America. [It is declared a legal holiday in 1892.]

Oct. 13 The cornerstone is laid for the President's Palace [White House] in Washington, Territory [District] of Columbia.

Dec. 5 In the election of 1792, President Washington receives 132 electoral votes, Vice President John Adams receives 77 electoral votes, and the Democratic-Republican candidate, George Clinton of New York, receives 50 electoral votes. Washington and Adams therefore retain their offices.

Benjamin Harrison
(1726-1791)
Signer of the Declaration of Independence

1793

The European war continues to cut deeply into American unity and tranquility. Jeffersonians eagerly side with the French and receive with enthusiasm news of the French decree of "war of all peoples against all kings." The news that France has declared war on Great Britain and has guillotined King Louis XVI, who is known widely as a friend of the Americans, cools the ardor of many Antifederalists. The President makes his own decision to issue a proclamation of neutrality. The behavior of Citizen Genêt, the Minister of France, strains neutrality and his recall is demanded. In return, the French Republic sends home the pro-royalist U.S. Minister to Paris, Gouverneur Morris.

January   In the case of *Chisholm* v. *Georgia* the U.S. Supreme Court upholds the right of a citizen of one state to sue another state, as granted in Article III Section 2 of the Constitution. [The 11th Amendment in 1798 repeals this section.]

Jan. 9   Jean Pierre Francois Blanchard, a French aeronaut who (with the American Dr. John Jeffries) crossed the English Channel in a balloon eight years ago, makes the first such flight in the United States, from Philadelphia to New Jersey, in the presence of President Washington.

Feb. 12   A Fugitive Slave Act is signed to implement the provisions of Article IV Section 2 of the Constitution, which explicitly authorizes the right of a slaveowner to recover an escaped slave. The act merely establishes the mechanism for recovery.

Mar. 1-2   Congress debates the propriety of Hamilton's conduct of his office as Secretary of the Treasury. Nothing irregular is discovered.

April 16   Eli Whitney demonstrates his cotton gin.

April 16-18   French Minister Edmond Charles Genêt, who arrived a week ago in Charleston, South Carolina, is feted and given a large welcoming ovation.

April 18   Washington studies the possibility of declaring American neutrality in the war that has broken out between the French Republic and Great Britain in February. He consults in a Cabinet session with Hamilton and Jefferson. Hamilton favors neutrality, but Jefferson espouses the French cause.

April 22   President Washington issues a Proclamation of Neutrality, based on his own assessment of the situation.

July 31   Captain Robert Gray aboard the *Columbia* sails into Boston after circumnavigating the world for the second time.

July 31   Jefferson submits his resignation as Secretary of State to assume leadership of the Democratic-Republicans. [He does not leave office until December.]

August   An epidemic outbreak of yellow fever strikes Philadelphia, killing more than 4,000 people, or about one seventh of the population.

Aug. 1   The President and his Cabinet discuss Genêt's conduct. He is regarded as exceeding his diplomatic privileges by commissioning privateer ships, and attempting to organize land expeditions against the British and Spanish. [On Aug. 16 Jefferson sends a request for Genêt's recall to Paris. The French accede, but Genêt remains in the United States as a private citizen.]

Sept. 18   President Washington lays the cornerstone for the Congress House [Capitol] in Washington city.

Nov. 25   An insurrection of slaves occurs in Albany. They set a number of fires which cause extensive damage in the town.

Roger Sherman
(1721-1793)
Signer of the Declaration of Independence

John Hancock
(1737-1793)
Signer of the Declaration of Independence

1794

The United States has a troubled year. The Supreme Court suffers a setback, a rebellion has to be quelled, a military expedition is launched against the Indians in the Ohio country. In addition, sectional conflict is generated by partisan differences over basic policies ranging from the troubles in Europe to economic problems. In New England Democratic-Republicans are accused of preferring to read Voltaire rather than the Bible. Southerners are bitter at Hamilton and the Federalists, whose policies favor the seaport cities and Eastern industry over the Southern agrarian society. Westerners protest vehemently against both factions, accusing the Federal Government of failing to protect the frontier or to provide for its development.

Jan. 2 Edmund Randolph of Virginia succeeds Thomas Jefferson as Secretary of State. [Randolph officially supports Washington's policies, but it is later discovered that he is secretly working against the Administration.]

Jan. 13 Congress approves a measure adding two stripes and two stars to the national flag, in recognition of the admission of Vermont and Kentucky.

Mar. 5 Congress passes and sends to the states the 11th Amendment, which repudiates the Court's decision in the case of *Chisholm* v. *Georgia,* and repeals a section in the Constitution. The law removes from the jurisdiction of Federal courts all cases in which citizens of one state are plaintiffs and the Government of another state is defendant.

Mar. 14 Eli Whitney obtains a patent to his cotton gin.

Mar. 27 Congress authorizes the formation of the U.S. Navy.

May 1 The Federal Society of Journeymen Cordwainers [shoemakers] is founded in Philadelphia.

May 6 John Hewett (of England) and four other mechanics set up the first steam engine to be constructed in the United States. It is built for the Belleville, New Jersey, waterworks.

June 1 Admiral Sir Richard Howe intercepts an enormous convoy of American ships, carrying provisions to relieve a famine in France, and protected by a French fleet. Howe's fleet defeats the

French but, during the battle, the convoy slips safely away.

June 5 A Neutrality Act is passed, forbidding United States citizens from enlisting in the service of any foreign power, and prohibiting the fitting out of foreign vessels in American ports.

July-Nov. 13 Farmers in western Pennsylvania, provoked by a Federal excise tax on liquor and stills, resist the collection of the tax, resorting to such violent acts as burning the home of the excise collector and tarring and feathering revenue officers. Much of their income is derived from the sale of grain in its easily transportable form: whiskey. Hamilton insists on making a test of the power of the Federal Government. At his urging, Washington orders 15,000 volunteers to help quell the revolt, which is dubbed the Whiskey Rebellion. Finally, in mid-November, 200 insurgents are arrested, ending the rebellion. [Later, 25 persons are tried, and all are pardoned.]

Aug. 20 General Anthony Wayne soundly defeats a large Indian army at the Battle of Fallen Timbers in the northwestern Ohio country. This action breaks all Indian resistance in the area.

Nov. 1 A ban on stage drama in Boston (in effect since 1750) is lifted, and the Boston Theater opens for the performance of plays.

Nov. 19 John Jay, as a special envoy of the United States to negotiate an agreement with Britain, and Baron Grenville for George III sign in London a treaty settling some, but not all, of the remaining differences between the recent enemies. Britain agrees to turn over no later than June 1, 1796, the border posts still occupied by its troops. The United States agrees to a settlement of prewar debts to British subjects, and to join in commissions to settle boundary disputes. The United States fails to raise sharply the question of British seizure of American merchant ships.

John Witherspoon
(1723-1794)
Signer of the Declaration of Independence

1795

Treaties become of overwhelming concern to the American people, in their first adventure in foreign relations outside of war. The terms of the Jay Treaty signed last year in London become known and arouse protest from all parts of the country, but the Senate barely ratifies it, and trade rather than quarrels with Britain become paramount. In the West, General Anthony Wayne, having decisively defeated an alliance of Indians, summons all the tribal chiefs to a forest clearing and exacts from them the Treaty of Greenville, with its usual aftermath of cessions by the Indians, a rush of white settlers into the "vacant" lands, and the ensuing frictions with the Indians still in occupancy. Finally, the western lands of Georgia, long in dispute with Spain, are redefined in the Treaty of San Lorenzo, to the advantage of the United States, and navigational and port rights along the Mississippi decrease the friction between this country and neighboring Spain.

Jan. 2   Timothy Pickering is appointed Secretary of War to succeed Henry Knox.

Jan. 29   The Naturalization Act is passed, making it mandatory to be a five-year resident of the United States before citizenship can be granted.

Feb. 2   Following Alexander Hamilton's resignation as Secretary of the Treasury, Oliver Wolcott is appointed to that post.

May 22   The first American Negro to play a dramatic part on the stage plays the character "Sambo" in *The Triumphs of Love*, by John Murdock.

June 1   A five-cent piece is minted in silver. This "half-disme" and the ten-dollar gold "eagle," minted in 1794, are among the first American coins.

June 25   The U.S. Senate ratifies the Jay Treaty with Britain by a narrow margin, and despite vigorous Democratic-Republican objection.

July 19   The Connecticut Land Company purchases a large tract on Lake Erie, in the Northwest Territory [northeastern Ohio]. Moses Cleaveland, the company agent, prepares to bring in settlers.

Aug. 3   The Treaty of Greenville is signed between General Anthony Wayne and the Indians defeated in 1794 at Fallen Timber. The Indians cede a large part of their lands in the eastern part of the Northwest Territory.

Aug. 20   Pickering is appointed *ad interim* to head the State Department, following the discovery that Secretary of State Edmund Randolph has been engaging in intrigues with France against the Jay Treaty and the Washington Administration. [The Pickering appointment is made official Dec. 10. In January 1796, James McHenry replaces Pickering as head of the War Department.]

Sept. 5   Congress agrees to pay to the Dey of Algiers about $1,000,000 as overdue tribute to ransom 115 seamen captured in previous years by the Barbary pirates, and to continue payment on an annual basis.

Oct. 27   The Treaty of San Lorenzo is signed between Spain and the United States. The U.S. signatory is Thomas Pinckney, previously Minister to Great Britain. The treaty defines the border between Spanish West Florida and western Georgia [in 1798 Mississippi Territory] at 31°N. lat. instead of 32°28′ N. lat. It also grants free navigation of the Mississippi River to Americans, along with the right to deposit cargo at New Orleans port.

Nov. 25   Georgia sells a huge area of land along the Mississippi River to four land companies. [The sale is tainted with fraud and is later rescinded.]

Josiah Bartlett
(1729-1795)
Signer of the Declaration of Independence

Abraham Clark
(1726-1794)
Signer of the Declaration of Independence

1796

Despite strong public pressure on President Washington to remain in office for a third term, he refuses. [This is the origin of the two-term tradition that remains intact until the election of Franklin Delano Roosevelt to a third term in 1940]. The country now undergoes its first transfer of political power, and bitter factional dispute makes its first appearance in American political history. Perceiving the rising mood of anxiety in the electorate, Washington, in his Farewell Address, makes an eloquent plea for union against party strife and against other disruptive forces. The election, which produces a Federalist President and a Democratic-Republican Vice President, proves that reverence for Washington will not transcend his term.

Jan. 1   Oliver Ellsworth, author of the Connecticut Resolutions at the Constitutional Convention, is appointed Chief Justice of the U.S. Supreme Court. He succeeds John Rutledge, whose brief tenure, following Jay's mission to London, failed to receive Senate confirmation.

Jan. 27   James McHenry of Maryland, army surgeon, former aide to Washington, and one of the signers of the Constitution, is appointed Secretary of War.

Samuel Huntington
(1731-1796)
Signer of the Declaration of Independence

Button Gwinnett
(1735-1777)
Signer of the Declaration of Independence

Feb. 29   Washington declares the Jay Treaty with Britain in effect.

Mar. 8   The U.S. Supreme Court rules that a Federal tax on carriages is an indirect tax, and hence is permissible under the Constitution. The significance of the decision lies in its assumption that the Court may pass judgment on the constitutionality of an act of Congress.

Mar. 15   The Treaty of San Lorenzo (also called Pinckney's Treaty) wins unanimous Senate approval, and thus becomes binding between Spain and the United States.

April 22   The U.S. Supreme Court rules that all treaties made under the Constitution are Federal law and take precedence over any conflicting state law.

May 18   Congress passes the Land Act of 1796, providing for surveys of all public domain lands within the old Northwest Territory. The law also provides for public auction sales of public domain land, establishing a minimum of $2.00 per acre, payable in one year, and minimum sales of 640 acres. Few private citizens have $1,280 to pay for land, and the main beneficiaries are speculators. Land offices are authorized for Cincinnati and Pittsburgh.

June 1   After six years as the Southwest Territory, many months after a census shows that its population is well over the prescribed 60,000, after a constitution has been framed providing for manhood suffrage and accepting slavery, after a general assembly has been elected and John Sevier (remembered fondly as governor of Franklin) is chosen as its first governor, Tennessee is admitted to the Union as the 16th state. However, only one member may be sent to the U.S. House of Representatives until 1800—a move generally interpreted as partisanly Federalist.

July 11   Captain Moses Porter with a force of 65 occupies the fort at Detroit, recovering it from British occupation.

Aug. 17   The Boston African Society is

52

Carter Braxton
(1736-1797)
Signer of the Declaration of Independence

crease in Antifederalist strength throughout the nation. Democratic-Republican strength derives from their unity behind Thomas Jefferson and from a general dissatisfaction with the Jay Treaty, which many consider too favorable to the British. With 13 candidates running, and with the Federalists unable to unite behind a single candidate, the electorate reflects its confusion by scattering its votes. John Adams wins the Presidency by 3 electoral votes, with a total of 71. Thomas Pinckney, whom the Federalists expected to become Vice President, wins only 59 votes to 68 for Jefferson; Aaron Burr, a dissident Jeffersonian, gets 30 electoral votes; Samuel Adams, 15; Oliver Ellsworth, 11; and 22 votes are split among seven other candidates. The Adams-Jefferson Administration has a Federalist Congress to cope with.

founded as a benevolent group for Negroes.

Aug. 29   As the result of discreetly conciliatory statements made to the French by the U.S. Minister in Paris, James Monroe, and following weeks of discussion in Washington's Cabinet, Secretary of State Pickering notifies Monroe that he is being superseded by Charles C. Pinckney. [When Pinckney is presented by Monroe on Dec. 7 to offer his credentials, the French Foreign Minister announces that the Directory will not accept a successor to Monroe until French grievances have been redressed, Pinckney is forced to leave France, and Monroe returns to the United States determined to justify his actions.]

Sept. 19   President Washington, in a valedictory to the American people, announces his intended withdrawal from politics and from public life. But the Farewell Address also includes a detailed description of his Administration's achievements, a plea for unity against divisive forces, and a warning against an overgrown military establishment and against geographical factions and parties.

Dec. 7   The election shows clearly an in-

Oliver Wolcott
(1726-1797)
Signer of the Declaration of Independence

1797

French-American relations, having become somewhat cooler after the Genêt incident of 1793, now deteriorate more rapidly, in the wake of the Jay Treaty, continued French naval aggressions, and a brazen insult to commissioners sent over by President Adams. Numerous defense measures are taken by Adams and his Congress. Democratic-Republicans, who have heretofore taken a pro-French stand, begin to line up behind the Federalists and the President to demand resistance against French aggressions. The commission in France is called home. Adams asks Congress to repeal the French-American Treaty of Alliance. But when Federalists in Adams' Cabinet ask for a declaration of war, the President steadfastly rejects this extreme.

Jan. 1 The capital of the state of New York is moved from New York City to Albany.

Jan. 23-30 Congress receives the earliest known petition by fugitive slaves. The petition is rejected after vigorous argument.

Feb. 8 The first glass-making plant to use coal for fuel is established in Pittsburgh, Pennsylvania.

Mar. 4 John Adams is inaugurated as the second President of the United States. He retains the Cabinet from the preceding Administration.

May 15 Adams calls a special session of Congress to debate the French-American crisis.

May 31 The President appoints a commission to France consisting of Charles C. Pinckney, John Marshall, and Elbridge Gerry. They are instructed to negotiate a treaty of amity.

June 1 Secretary of State Timothy Pickering reports that 300 U.S. ships have been seized at sea by the French.

June 26 Charles Newbold obtains a patent for his iron plow.

July 7 The House of Representatives (resort-ing to this power for the first time) impeaches Senator William Blount of Tennessee for conspiring to wage war on Spain and for stirring up the Cherokee Indians to war on Spain and the United States. [He is not convicted by the U.S. Senate, which dismisses the charges on Jan. 14, 1799.]

Oct. 21 The frigate *Constitution* ("Old Ironsides") is launched. This is the third war vessel launched this year. She has 44 guns and weighs 1,576 tons, as does the frigate *United States*. The third ship launched is the 36-gun *Constellation*.

Oct. 4-18 The three United States commissioners to France arrive in Paris and on Oct. 18 are visited by three agents of Foreign Minister Talleyrand. These three agents named Hottinguer, Bellamy, and Hauteval [identified later only as X, Y, and Z], suggest a $240,000 bribe to Talleyrand and a U.S. loan to France, in return for French concessions and French respect of the American flag. [The commissioners refuse the terms; Pinckney and Marshall leave Paris; Gerry remains to continue negotiations.]

Francis Lightfoot Lee
1737-1797
Signer of the Declaration of Independence

James Wilson
(1742-1798)
Signer of the Declaration of Independence

1798

The Federalists win a strong majority in the Congressional elections of 1798. However, the crisis in French-American relations causes the Federalist Party to split apart. Hamilton, the leading Federalist although he holds no office, breaks sharply with President Adams over the latter's willingness to continue to negotiate with France, despite the fact that the President pursues a vigorous policy to place the nation on a war footing. Many leading Federalists side with Adams in the dispute, and Federalist "hot-heads" in Congress secure the enactment, with no encouragement from Adams, of the four Alien and Sedition Acts. A remarkable counterattack by the Democratic-Republicans is embodied in the Kentucky and Virginia Resolutions, which constitute a repudiation of the whole Federalist philosophy. In the meantime, all treaties with France are suspended and an undeclared war begins between the United States and France.

Jan. 8 The 11th Amendment, prohibiting any citizen of one state from suing another state, is ratified. It supersedes the Supreme Court decision of 1793 in the case of *Chisholm* v. *Georgia*.

Jan. 17 John Marshall, speaking for the U.S. Commission to France, rejects all the proposed bribe terms and the accompanying bids for American concessions.

April 3 President Adams, two weeks after having reported to Congress the failure of the commission to France, releases the full correspondence between his commissioners and Talleyrand's agents, whom he identifies merely as X, Y, and Z—for which reason it is called the "XYZ Correspondence." [This is the first intimation that the public has of how cavalierly the Directory governing France is behaving toward the United States, and indignation is widespread.

April 30 The Department of the Navy is established by an act of Congress, with Benjamin Stoddert as its first Secretary. Prior to this law, all naval affairs have been conducted under Department of War authority.

June 6 Congress passes legislation abolishing imprisonment for debt, thus ending this practice in the United States.

June 18-July 14 Congress passes the first of four acts, collectively called the Alien and Sedition laws, [all of which quickly become highly unpopular]. These bills represent a Federalist campaign to take advantage of war fears in order to pass legislation designed to strengthen the national Government, partly by forcibly silencing political opposition. The first act is in the form of an amendment to the Naturalization Act of 1795, requiring 14 years of residence instead of 5 years as a prerequisite for obtaining citizenship. On June 25 the Alien Act is passed, giving the President deportation powers. On July 6 the Alien Enemies Act is passed, authorizing the President to arrest and imprison aliens in time of war, and on July 14 the Sedition Act is passed, providing for the arrest and imprisonment of anyone who writes or speaks against the President, Congress, or Government.

Sept. 12 Benjamin Franklin Bache, grandson of Benjamin Franklin, and vigorous editor of *Aurora,* is arrested for violation of the Sedition Act. He is accused of libeling President Adams. His arrest generates an enormous amount of protest against all the Alien and Sedition laws.

Oct. 12 Mississippi Territory is organized, with its capital at Natchez. It includes the strip of land between the Mississippi and Chattahoochee rivers and between West Florida and the pre-1795 border of West Florida, i.e., 31° and 32°28′ N. lat. [the southern part of the present states of Mississippi and Alabama. In 1804 the territory is extended north to the 35th parallel.]

Nov. 16 A set of resolutions drafted by Thomas Jefferson are sponsored by the Kentucky state legislature. They strongly protest against what is thought to be a dangerous usurping of power by the Federal Government, as for example the adoption of the Alien and Sedition laws. In formulating an abstract theory for this point of view, the so-called "compact theory" of government emerges: The Union is, in effect, a compact among sovereign states.

Dec. 24 Another set of resolutions, these drafted by James Madison, are sponsored by the Virginia legislature. These have the same purpose as those of Kentucky, and have very nearly the same effect.

Dec. 31 *Calder* v. *Bull* is handed down by the U.S. Supreme Court, ruling that a prohibition against laws that are enacted after the commission of a crime (ex post facto laws) apply only to criminal law, not to civil laws.

1799

Hamilton's objective is to build up a huge offensive capability and strike at both French and Spanish territory in the Western Hemisphere, hoping to divide the spoils with Great Britain. Hamilton sees himself as champion of an American nationalism. But Adams frustrates these bold designs by negotiating with France, which appears to be more conciliatory. Talleyrand's assurance that a minister will be received in Paris with respect is followed by the appointment of a new Minister, supported (at Hamilton's insistence) by two Federalist colleagues. Negotiations continue throughout the year. Adams is now faced with the hopeless duty of reuniting his party. Meanwhile the Democratic-Republican Kentucky and Virginia resolutions are widely circulating, and reaction sets in against the Federalist Alien and Sedition laws.

Feb. 7 Federal marshals arrest John Fries, the leader of a "rebellion" against the direct Federal tax on property levied last July. [Fries, accused of resisting the marshal, is twice tried and convicted of treason and sentenced to death, but he is pardoned by President Adams.]

Feb. 9 In the undeclared war with France, the American frigate *Constellation* forces *L'Insurgente* to surrender off the coast of Nevis Island in the Caribbean Sea.

Feb. 22 The Kentucky legislature issues another resolution, designed to rebut unfavorable replies to its resolution of the previous year. This time the document includes a statement asserting a state's right to nullify Federal laws.

Feb. 23 The first national quarantine act is passed, requiring Federal officials to give aid to municipalities which are seeking to enforce quarantine regulations.

April 1 The *American Review and Literary Journal* is published, becoming the first quarterly review in the United States. Its editor is Charles Brockden Brown, author of the esteemed novel *Wieland*.

June 6 Patrick Henry, 66, Revolutionary War leader who in 1775 spoke the words, "Give me liberty or give me death,"dies in Charlotte County, Virginia.

June 15 The New Hampshire Resolution is issued by the Federalist legislature of that state. It constitutes a notable rebuttal to the Virginia and Kentucky Resolutions.

Dec. 2 The Sixth Congress convenes its first session. [With 19 Federalists to 13 Democratic-Republicans in the Senate, and with 64 Federalists to 42 Democratic-Republicans in the House, it is the last Congress to have a Federalist majority.]

Dec. 14 Former President Washington, 67, dies two days after falling ill as a result of riding horseback in snow and sleet.

Dec. 26 General Henry "Light Horse Harry" Lee [father of Robert E. Lee], veteran of the American Revolution, and a close personal friend of Washington, delivers a eulogy, in which he describes Washington as "first in war, first in peace, first in the hearts of his countrymen."

George Read
(1733-1798)
Signer of the Declaration of Independence

William Paca
(1740-1799)
Signer of the Declaration of Independence

In the last years of the Administration of John Adams it becomes clear that the Federalist Party is doomed as a national political influence, a condition that is attributable to the antipathy between Adams and Hamilton. The operation of the Alien and Sedition acts only add to the appeal of the Jeffersonians, who begin to call themselves Republicans. A number of minor but significant events occur: the rise in prestige of John Marshall, despite his Federalism; the moving of the central Government to the District of Columbia; the fact [not yet revealed] that France rather than Spain is the nation's new neighbor across the Mississippi. The census of 1800 shows a healthy 35-per-cent increase in the population, to about 5,300,000, of whom more than 1,000,000 are Negroes (nine tenths of these enslaved). Virginia, with 900,000 inhabitants, retains first place despite the loss of Kentucky. Within a narrow range just above or below 600,000 each are Pennsylvania, New York, and Massachusetts; North Carolina slips to fifth rank with the loss of Tennessee. Newcomers to statehood are, of course, Vermont, Kentucky, and Tennessee.

Jan. 2   Free Negroes of Philadelphia present to Congress a petition against slavery, slave trade and the Fugitive Slave Act of 1793. [The petition dies in committee.]

April 4   The First Federal bankruptcy law is passed. [It is repealed in 1802.]

April 24   The Library of Congress is established, using a fund of $5,000, and a donation by Jefferson of his entire private library.

May 7   A bill is passed in Congress to divide the nine counties of the Northwest Territory into two parts divided by a line running due north from the Kentucky River confluence with the Ohio River. The sparsely populated west part becomes the Territory of Indiana, with its capital at Vincennes and William Henry Harrison as governor. The east part, the Territory Northwest of the River Ohio (usually also called the Northwest Territory), has Chillicothe as its capital.

May 10   The Land Act of 1800 (Harrison Act) is passed, establishing liberal credit terms and a new lower minimum acreage for purchasing public lands. This stimulates a surge of new land purchases, mostly by speculators.

May 12   President Adams dismisses Secretary of State Timothy Pickering.

June 6   John Marshall becomes Secretary of State.

June 12   Samuel Dexter of Massachusetts takes office as Secretary of War.

July 9   The first summer theater, Mount Vernon Gardens, is opened on Broadway in New York City.

Aug. 30   A planned insurrection in Virginia, led by a slave named Gabriel, is betrayed, and Gabriel and 35 other slaves are apprehended. [Trials and executions end Oct. 30 with the hanging of Gabriel.]

Sept. 30   The Convention of 1800 with the Consulate that has replaced the Directory in France results in the establishment of normal diplomatic relations between France and the United States.

Oct. 1   The secret Treaty of San Idlefonso, signed between France and Spain, provides for the cession of all of the Louisiana region to France. [Spain retains administrative control; the region is turned over to France in November 1803.] The American-Spanish dispute over navigation rights on the Mississippi River and related problems is now a French-American issue.

Nov. 17   Congress opens its first session in the new capital city of Washington.

Dec. 3   In the Presidential election the Federalists run John Adams and Charles C. Pinckney against Republicans Thomas Jefferson and Aaron Burr.

Edward Rutledge
(1749-1800)
Signer of the Declaration of Independence

1801

In the election of 1800 the Democratic-Republicans score striking gains. Jefferson and Burr each receives 73 electoral votes, while Adams and C.C. Pinckney receive 65 and 64 votes respectively, and John Jay receives 1. The tie for first place, which prevents a decision between the front runners for the posts of President and Vice President, throws the election into the House of Representatives, which in the end votes the Presidency to Jefferson. A few Federalists are turned out of office. The Federalists lose the legislative branch of Government as well as the executive branch, but retain the judiciary.

Jefferson becomes the first President to be inaugurated in the new capital city of Washington, D.C. His most urgent task is to deal with the Barbary Pirate states, one of which has just declared war on the United States. By dispatching a naval force to the Mediterranean Sea, Jefferson initiates American participation in the Tripolitan War.

Jan. 1   Samuel Dexter becomes Secretary of the Treasury.

January   Eleuthère Irénée Du Pont establishes a gunpowder plant at Wilmington, Delaware, and founds the E. I. DuPont de Nemours & Co. The New York *Evening Post* is founded as a Federalist newspaper.

Feb. 4   John Marshall takes his oath as Chief Justice of the Supreme Court. He continues to serve as Secretary of State.

Feb. 11-17   The electoral votes in the election of 1800 are counted. Because of a tie between Jefferson and Burr, each with 73 votes, the decision is constitutionally in the hands of the House of Representatives. After an all-night session during which 36 ballots are cast, Jefferson is finally chosen as President on Feb. 17 when three Federalist electors cast blank ballots, upon Hamilton's advice. Burr becomes Vice President.

Feb. 27-Mar. 3   Congress assumes jurisdiction over the District of Columbia. The Judiciary Act is passed, under the terms of which Adams makes several last-minute appointments in order to insure Federalist control of the Court.

Mar. 4   Thomas Jefferson is inaugurated as third President of the United States. It is the first inauguration to be held in Washington, D.C. His address stresses conciliation and the need for economy and limited powers in the Government.

Mar. 5   Henry Dearborn of Massachusetts becomes Secretary of War, and Levi Lincoln of Massachusetts is Attorney General.

May 2   James Madison takes office as Secretary of State.

May 14   Pasha Yusuf Karamanli of Tripolitania declares war on the United States, symbolizing his action by cutting down the flagpole at the U.S. Consulate in Tripoli city.

May 14   The Treasury Department is headed by Albert Gallatin of Pennsylvania.

Aug. 26   Robert Morris is released from debtor's prison under the Bankruptcy Act after more than three years. Morris was a major fund raiser for the Government during the Revolutionary War and was Superintendent of Finances under the Articles of Confederation, but he speculated in land imprudently and, while a U.S. Senator from Pennsylvania, was arrested for debt.

Oct. 19   Benjamin Latrobe designs and builds a new water supply system for Philadelphia. It is the first aqueduct water system in the nation.

Dec. 7   The Seventh Congress convenes, with 18 Democratic-Republicans and 14 Federalists in the Senate, and with 69 Democratic-Republicans and 36 Federalists in the House. Thus, the Federalists have lost control of Congress.

Francis Lewis
(1713-1802)
Signer of the Declaration of Independence

1802

Jefferson's announced policy of financial retrenchment is implemented by his new Secretary of the Treasury, Albert Gallatin. Gallatin vows to undo most of Hamilton's work. Jefferson promises to cut back the national debt, dismantle the Navy, reduce the Army, and repeal all internal taxes. The economy expands rapidly, stimulated by new westward migrations and the return of normal shipping and trade in the absence of war. Late in the year the Spanish rescind the treaty rights of Americans to ship through New Orleans, evoking an anger that causes the West to simmer. Jefferson, hearing that the Spanish have already secretly ceded New Orleans to France, warns General Napoleon Bonaparte, the apparent head of the ruling Consulate, that any hostile action will drive the United States to negotiate with his enemy, Great Britain. At the same time he instructs the U.S. Minister to France to recover the use of the Mississippi and its port by purchase, if possible.

Jan. 7   Western University, the first in the Northwest Territory, is chartered at the tiny community of Athens, belonging to the Ohio Company of Associates. [It is renamed Ohio University, a state institution, in 1804.]

Feb. 6   Congress passes a measure intended to aid and permit the arming of merchant ships in preparation for the Tripolitan War.

Mar. 8   The Judiciary Act of 1801 is repealed.

Mar. 16   Congress passes a bill establishing the United States Military Academy at West Point, New York, a site selected by George Washington.

April 29   A new Judiciary Act is passed, reducing to six from 16 the number of circuit courts, and provides that each is to be headed by a Supreme Court Justice.

April 30   President Jefferson signs the first Enabling Act, a bill that permits a territory organized under the Ordinance of 1787 to convert itself into a state. The present bill permits the inhabitants of the Northwest Territory to prepare for and apply for statehood.

May 1   President Jefferson, learning that Spain may have ceded its lands in America to France, instructs Robert R. Livingston, U.S. Minister in Paris, to find out if France might be willing to sell New Orleans and West Florida.

May 3   The city of Washington, D.C., is incorporated, with a mayor-and-council form of government. The mayor is to be appointed by the President and the council is to be elected by local property owners.

June   Lands along the Yazoo River are ceded by Georgia to the United States. About 50,000,000 acres of these lands, Georgia declares, were fraudulently sold to speculators in 1795 and the sales were rescinded in 1796. The original buyers of the lands want compensation. [The U.S. Supreme Court grants this in 1810.]

Aug. 25   Spanish officials withdraw the right of deposit that was granted to U.S. citizens at the port of New Orleans under the treaty of 1795. This act increases the anxiety of Jefferson and Minister Livingston to arrange a deal with France, the presumptive owner of New Orleans.

Oct. 2   The United States Patent Office is created as a bureau in the Department of State.

Nov. 1-26   The authorized constitutional convention of the Northwest Territory, meeting at Chillicothe, prepares its application for statehood.

Matthew Thornton
(1714?-1803)
Signer of the Declaration of Independence

1803 **Jefferson as President begins to alter some of the** concepts of Jefferson the political philosopher. In the course of trying to solve real problems, in the daily routine of executing his duties, he adopts measures and diplomatic moves worthy of a Federalist. In particular, he seeks to buy one town from France, because that town is a port essential to American traders, and he finds himself committed to purchasing an empire. This offends his strict constructionist views of the Constitution, but when the Democratic-Republican Senate confirms the treaty, he signs it. Meanwhile, he has already made plans to have the region explored; a party of experts to be led by the President's friend and secretary, Meriwether Lewis (and at Lewis' insistence by a brother of George Rogers Clark) is already gathered near St. Louis, ready for an expedition into the wilderness.

Jan. 12   President Jefferson appoints James Monroe Minister Plenipotentiary to assist Livingston in negotiations for rights of deposit at New Orleans or for the purchase of the city.

Feb. 24   The U.S. Supreme Court, in the case of *Marbury* v. *Madison,* decides that the plantiff, William Marbury, may not avail himself of an act of Congress against Secretary of State James Madison in order to receive an appointment as justice of the peace. The appointment was signed by President Adams just before his term ended, but was not delivered to Marbury; Madison refused to make the delivery; an act of Congress directed the Supreme Court to enjoin a member of the executive branch to carry out his official duties, in this case delivery of the appointment. The Court rules against Marbury on the grounds that Congress has no constitutional authority to prescribe this injunction. The decision is important, not because it voids an act of Congress for the first time, but because it affirms for the first time that it is the Court, not the legislature, that must rule on constitutional issues affecting any branch of the Government.

Mar. 1   Ohio is admitted to the Union as the 17th state. The state is bounded on the west by Indiana Territory, along a north-south line about 18 miles east of the previous border; and on the north by an east-west line at the latitude of the tip of Lake Michigan. The land north of this line [now Michigan] also goes to Indiana Territory. However, through oversight, Congress fails to pass a bill of formal admission. [This is corrected in 1953.]

Mar. 3   An act is passed providing for the sale of all ungranted lands in the Territory of Mississippi.

April 12   James Monroe arrives in Paris to assist Livingston in the negotiations with Talleyrand, the French foreign minister. Monroe learns that on the previous day Livingston was asked how much the United States would pay for the entire region of Louisiana.

April 19   Spain restores the right of deposit at New Orleans to Americans.

April 30-May 2   France cedes all of Louisiana to the United States for 80,000,000 francs, or about $15,000,000. Its boundaries to the west and south are not specified, but they are generally considered to extend west to the Stony [Rocky] Mountains and to follow the Sabine or Red Rivers northwest from the Gulf area. The purchase doubles the area of the United States. It includes the entire western half of the Mississippi-Missouri river system's drainage basin, about 820,000 square miles. The treaty of cession, signed on May 2 between France and the United States, is retrodated to April 30.

August-September   Negroes in New York City plot to set fire to the city. Eleven houses are burned before the plot is exposed. Eventually 20 persons are convicted of arson.

Oct. 17   The Eighth Congress convenes, with 25 Democratic-Republicans and 9 Federalists in the Senate, and 102 Democratic-Republicans to 39 Federalists in the House.

Oct. 20   The U.S. Senate approves the treaty of April 30 by a vote of 24 to 7.

Nov. 30   Spanish authorities complete their cession of Louisiana to France, formalizing the terms of the Treaty of San Ildefonso of Oct. 1, 1800.

Dec. 9   The 12th Amendment is passed by Congress and is sent to the states for ratification. The amendment provides for separate voting by electors for President and Vice President, a change prompted by the tie vote in the election of 1800.

Dec. 20   The United States takes formal possession of Louisiana region at New Orleans. William C. Claiborne, governor of Mississippi Territory, and Army Commander in Chief James Wilkinson accept control of the region on behalf of President Jefferson.

1804

A short interval of peace in Europe ends as France and Great Britain renew their fierce naval warfare. Both nations resume harassment of neutral shipping. American feelings begin to run higher against the British than against the French. The Barbary Pirates continue to demand tribute.

Federalists begin to consider the Louisiana Purchase as a menace to them, because the annexation of this region could upset the balance of power. Some New England Federalists, called the Essex Junto (because they have been meeting at Essex, Massachusetts, since the Adams Administration), go so far as to declare that the original states are thereby absolved from allegiance to the Union. The principal Federalist leader is still Alexander Hamilton, whose enmity toward Vice President Aaron Burr has tragic consequences. Hamilton helps assure Burr's defeat in elections in New York State, and thereby becomes involved in a duel that ends his life. The election of 1804 reflects the impotence of the Federalist Party.

Feb. 16 Lieutenant Stephen Decatur sails the ketch *Intrepid* into Tripoli harbor, where her crew boards and burns the captured 38-gun U.S. frigate *Philadelphia,* thus depriving the Tripolitanians of their prize. (Decatur's father, the commodore, recently used the *Philadelphia* as his flagship.) [For his bold action, the lieutenant wins a promotion to captain.]

Mar. 12 The U.S. Senate convicts the impeached Federal District Judge (of New Hampshire), John Pickering. He is found guilty of unlawful decisions, drunkenness, and profanity and is removed from his post.

Mar. 26 The Land Act of 1804 reduces minimum payment per acre for public land to $1.64 per acre, and authorizes the sale of quarter sections (160 acres).

Mar. 26 The Louisiana Purchase area is divided into the Territory of Orleans [approximately the area of the present state of Louisiana west of the Mississippi River] and the District of Louisiana.

April 25 Aaron Burr, having decided not to run for reelection to the Vice Presidency, fails to win the governorship of New York State in an election contest. Hamilton is most instrumental in securing Burr's defeat.

May 14 The Lewis and Clark Expedition to explore the Louisiana Purchase region leaves St. Louis, heading up the Missouri River. The party has two pirogue boats and a keelboat, with a total crew of 33 men.

June 7 Burr writes to Hamilton demanding a retraction of what he terms slurs on his character that are reported in the New York press. [Burr challenges Hamilton to a duel.]

July 11 Hamilton is mortally wounded in the duel, which takes place at Weehawken, New Jersey. [Hamilton dies in New York City ten hours later, on July 12.]

Sept. 25 The 12th Amendment to the United States Constitution is ratified.

Oct. 1 William C. Claiborne becomes governor of the Territory of Orleans.

Nov. 2 The Lewis and Clark Expedition establishes winter camp on the Missouri River shore at the village of the Mandan Indians [near Bismarck, North Dakota].

Nov. 29 The New York Historical Society is founded by jurist Egbert Benson, New York City Mayor De Witt Clinton, merchant John Pintard, and botanist Dr. David Hosack.

Dec. 5 In the first Presidential election under the 12th Amendment, the Electoral College casts 162 votes for President Jefferson to 14 for Charles C. Pinckney, the Federalist candidate for President. By an identical vote Democratic-Republican George Clinton becomes Vice President defeating Rufus King.

George Walton
(1741-1804)
Signer of the Declaration of Independence

The Napoleonic Wars continue to hurt American trade, and disrupt American politics. Each of the warring powers forbids neutral vessels to touch at the port of an enemy or the ally of an enemy. President Jefferson continues to steer a course of strict neutrality. British frigates operate with impunity, stopping American ships and searching for any British-born seamen, who are seized ("impressed") regardless of American naturalization. One encouraging development is a truce with Tripolitania. The Lewis and Clark Expedition completes the first organized land crossing of the continent.

January British Orders in Council and the French Berlin and Milan decrees each forbid a neutral vessel to touch at an enemy port, or at the port of an ally of the enemy. These measures imperil American shipping everywhere on the high seas.

Jan. 11 Michigan Territory is created out of part of Indiana Territory. It includes all of the lower peninsula and the eastern part of the upper peninsula. Its capital is Detroit. General William Hull is governor of the territory.

Feb. 11 Meriwether Lewis, co-leader of the Lewis and Clark expedition, acts as midwife in the birth of a child in Fort Mandan to Sacagawea, a 16-year-old Shoshone girl, wife of a French adventurer. [Both she and her husband are hired as official guides to the party. She is eventually restored to her people and lives to the age of 100.]

Mar. 1 Associate Justice of the U.S. Supreme Court Samuel Chase, in his capacity of circuit court justice, having been impeached on six

James Smith
(1719?-1806)
Signer of the Declaration of Independence

counts by the House of Representatives, is found innocent of all charges by the Senate. He was charged mainly with partisan behavior as a judge.

Mar. 2 An act of Congress provides for confirmation of French and Spanish land grants in Louisiana.

Mar. 4 Thomas Jefferson is inaugurated to a second term. He retains his Cabinet.

April 7 Lewis and Clark renew their journey northwestward on the Missouri River.

April 26-27 The city of Derna in Tripolitania is captured by an American-led land invasion force. The brother of Pasha Yusuf is put on the throne.

May 25 The Federal Society of Journeyman Cordwainers [shoemakers], the oldest labor union in the country (1794), conducts an unsuccessful strike. Its leaders are arrested.

May 26 The Lewis and Clark Expedition sights the Stony [Rocky] Mountains.

June 4 Pasha Yusuf, to regain his throne in Tripolitania, signs a treaty of noninterference and accepts ransom for American captives.

June 11 The Lewis and Clark Expedition reaches the Great Falls of the Missouri.

July 23 American trade with the French West Indies is threatened as Great Britain invokes its rule of 1756, which forbids a neutral nation to trade in a port in wartime if such trade has not been normally conducted at that port during peacetime.

Aug. 9 Zebulon M. Pike leaves St. Louis on an expedition northward to find the headwaters of the Mississippi River. [He fails.]

Oct. 10 The Lewis and Clark Expedition reaches a west-flowing river [the Snake].

Nov. 8-Dec. 30 The Lewis and Clark Expedition reaches the Pacific Ocean near the mouth of the Columbia, where the explorers remain for the winter and build Fort Clatsop.

Dec. 2 The Ninth Congress convenes, with 27 Democratic-Republicans and 7 Federalists in the Senate, and 116 Democratic-Republicans and 25 Federalists in the House.

1806

During the year the British escalate their disagreeable practice of impressment. In addition, both they and the French search and seize American vessels engaged in trade with either nation. These practices threaten to ruin the American shipping industry. President Jefferson loses much of his earlier popularity during several vain efforts to secure a change in the attitude of the belligerents with regard to American commerce. Congress passes a non-importation act, issues condemnations of impressment and seizure actions, and even threatens to withhold all American trade from either power, all to no avail. Finally, Jefferson tries to secure a treaty with Great Britain in order to ease the crisis. But the treaty provisions offered by Great Britain, and accepted by U.S. plenipotentiaries William Pinkney and James Monroe embarrass Jefferson, who does not even submit the treaty to the Senate for approval.

While the maritime crisis grows, former Vice President Aaron Burr, Harman Blennerhassett, and General James Wilkinson apparently plot to detach Mississippi Territory and the Territory of Orleans from the United States, occupy the Spanish province of Mexico, and out of these acquisitions create an empire for themselves. Wilkinson decides to change his allegiance once more (he is capable of holding the top commission in the U.S. Army while accepting fees from Spain) and reveals the plot to Jefferson. The President is infuriated, and offers an award for the arrest of Aaron Burr.

January Noah Webster, a grammarian and author of spelling books, publishes his *Compendious Dictionary of the English Language,* a modest compendium for use in schools, remarkable for its effort to distinguish between American and English usage. [This work is not to be confused with Webster's large two-volume dictionary published 22 years later.]

January-March Lewis and Clark spend the winter at Fort Clatsop in the Oregon country, mapping their major discoveries, and working over extensive notes on geography, Indians, plants, animals, and climate.

Jan. 25 Secretary of State James Madison issues a full report on the illegal actions of the belligerents in the European conflict. The report is effective in generating anti-British sentiment.

Mar. 9 Congress authorizes a commission to direct the construction of a national road, to run from Cumberland, Maryland, to the Virginia village of Zanesburg on the Ohio River. Zanesburg is given a new charter and renamed Wheeling. [It becomes the capital of a pro-Unionist government of Virginia in 1861 and of West Virginia in 1863.]

April 18 Congress passes the Non-Importation Act, banning the entry into the United States of specific British goods, but its effective date is delayed by order of the President.

May 30 Andrew Jackson, a popular former judge in Nashville, Tennessee, kills Charles Dickenson, a lawyer, in a duel. [The event becomes a political liability even when Jackson becomes President 22 years later.]

July 20 Aaron Burr begins recruiting men for a scheme to set up a government in Spanish Mexico and in adjacent parts of the U.S. Southwest. Harman Blennerhassett, an English adventurer who owns an island in the Ohio River, joins the conspiracy.

Sept. 23 The Lewis and Clark Expedition reaches St. Louis, where the exploratory journey began two years and four months earlier.

Nov. 15 Zebulon Pike, on a mission in Spanish territory for General James Wilkinson, one of Burr's friends, sights a landmark peak near the spot where a great stream issues from the Stony Mountains. [He is soon arrested by the Spaniards, then released; but the mountain is named, in his honor, Pike's Peak and is the goal of many west-bound migrants.]

Dec. 10 The Burr-Blennerhassett scheme is exposed by its former participant, James Wilkinson, to President Jefferson.

Robert Morris
(1734-1806)
Signer of the Declaration of Independence

1807 **It is becoming clear to most Americans that Great Britain** and France do not intend to abandon their practices of search and seizure. The British arouse the most profound resentment, for they commit the additional offense of impressing American seamen. In June an incident occurs that drives even the Federalists to support President Jefferson in his plans to apply economic sanctions. The U.S. Navy ship *Chesapeake* is shelled and forcibly boarded by H.M.S. *Leopard,* and four men are removed from the Chesapeake's crew. [Only one of the four men taken off is later proven to be a British deserter, and he is hanged.] The incident humiliates American pride. President Jefferson demands an apology. Receiving none, he obtains appropriations for new naval equipment and ships, and begins to regret having dismantled the American Navy shortly after the Barbary Pirate conflicts. Now Jefferson firmly believes that economic sanctions, properly applied, will force the British to stop their harassment of American shipping. His remedy, which Congress translates into law, is the complete closing down of U.S. ports to vessels from overseas and the restriction of commerce on the part of U.S. merchant ships to domestic operations.

Jan. 17   Aaron Burr is arrested in Mississippi Territory [Alabama] on charges of treason.

Feb. 10   A survey of the U.S. coast is authorized by Congress and delegated to the Coast Survey under the Treasury Department. [The work begins in 1816. The bureau is redesignated the Coast and Geodetic Survey in 1878.]

Mar. 2   Congress passes an act prohibiting the trade in the importing of any slaves.

June 22   The U.S.S. *Chesapeake,* a 38-gun frigate, is fired upon by H.M.S. *Leopard,* a 52-gun frigate, off Cape Henry. After taking three broadsides, with 21 casualties (including 3 dead), Captain James Barron of the *Chesapeake* strikes his colors. The ship is forcibly boarded and four men are taken off on the grounds that they are British deserters.

June 24   Aaron Burr is indicted at Richmond, Virginia, on charges of treason.

July   John Colter explores the Bighorn and Yellowstone basins in the Louisiana Territory [now southern Montana and northern Wyoming].

July 2   President Jefferson orders all British warships to leave American waters.

Aug. 3-Sept. 14   The trial of Aaron Burr on charges of treason ends in an acquittal on Sept. 1. The trial continues on a misdemeanor charge, but on Sept. 14 he is acquitted on this charge also. [Expected to stand trial on other charges, including one for the murder of Hamilton, Burr elects to jump bail instead, and flees to Europe.]

Aug. 17   The 140-foot-long flat-bottomed steam-driven ship *Clermont,* designed by Robert Fulton, proceeds with considerable noise and billows of smoke up the Hudson River from a New York City wharf in the direction of Albany. [It reaches Albany in 32 hours of sailing time, turns around, and in another 30 hours is back in New York. The *Clermont* is not the first steamship to run; but unlike its predecessor, built by John Fitch on the Delaware in 1790, it is reliable and proves an economic success.]

Oct. 1   New Yorkers read an essay in the manner of the *Spectator Papers* of 18th-century London. The American disciples of Addison and Steele are a 24-year-old lawyer, Washington Irving, his brother William, and James K. Paulding. The new essays are entitled *Salmagundi; or, the Whim-Whams and Opinions of Launcelot Langstaff, Esq., and Others.* [These essays, the first of a series, possess not only literary value, but also offer social and political information about New York at the time.]

Oct. 17   In response to Jefferson's note of July 2, the British announce that they will pursue the practice of impressment even more vigorously.

Oct. 26   The 10th Congress convenes, with 28 Democratic-Republicans and 6 Federalists in the Senate, and 118 Democratic-Republicans and 24 Federalists in the House.

Dec. 14   The American Non-Importation Act of April, 1806, is declared to be in force.

Dec. 18   President Jefferson asks Congress to formulate an Act of Embargo.

Dec. 22   Congress passes the Embargo Act, whereby all foreign trade into or out of the United States is prohibited, and U.S. ships are restricted to coastal trade. [This drastic application of the constitutional right invested in Congress to control foreign commerce proves disastrous and is repealed in March 1809.]

Thomas Jefferson
THIRD PRESIDENT   1801-1809

Alexander Hamilton

John Jay

John Randolph

James Madison
FOURTH PRESIDENT   **1809-1817**

James Monroe
FIFTH PRESIDENT   1817-1825

George Clymer
(1740-1813)
Signer of the Declaration of Independence

Samuel Adams
(1722-1803)
Signer of the Declaration of Independence

Samuel Chase
(1741-1811)
Signer of the Declaration of Independence

Benjamin Rush
1745-1813)
Signer of the Declaration of Independence

George Wythe
(1726-1806)
Signer of the Declaration of Independence

1808 **The Embargo Act remains in force throughout Jefferson's term.** It achieves the reverse of what the President hopes. By the end of the year the American shipping industry is nearly ruined, and several small seaports in New England such as Newburyport, Massachusetts, and New Haven, Connecticut, never recover from the effects of the embargo. These effects are especially severe for the New England states, which export and import large amounts of perishable goods and manufactured products. The Southern states, on the other hand, are not affected to the same extent, because Southern staple products of export, such as cotton, tobacco, and wheat, can be stored over long periods of time. The British are inconvenienced by the embargo, but remain unchanged in their attitudes. The French experience shortages in their West Indies colonies, but the embargo has little adverse effect in France itself. Napoleon makes a handsome profit by confiscating all American ships that arrive in French ports; he pretends to support Jefferson in seizing these ships, because, after all, he is helping Jefferson to enforce the embargo.

By the end of the year the Federalists begin to see an opportunity to take political advantage of the widespread disaffection relating to the embargo issue. However, only in New England do the Federalists score some minor successes. The Federalist candidates increase the proportion of electoral votes given to their candidates in the Presidential election, but James Madison and incumbent Vice President George Clinton easily defeat the Federalist team that ran four years ago and appears to be the best the Federalists can muster.

Jan. 1 The law prohibiting the African slave trade, passed last March, goes into effect.
April 17 The Bayonne Decrees, issued by Napoleon, order the seizure of any American ships in French, Italian, and Hanseatic League ports. Such seizure is justified on either of two bases: (1) if they are in truth U.S. ships, they are violating their own country's Embargo Act; or (2) they are really British ships, masquerading in false registry, and are therefore fair game.
July 8 John Jacob Astor incorporates the American Fur Company in New York City, with the object of competing against such Canadian fur traders as the North West Company for the very lucrative trade in skins and hides opened up as a result of the Lewis and Clark Expedition.
July 16 Another competitor for the anticipated fur trade appears when the Missouri Fur Company is incorporated by Manuel Lisa, William Clark (of the Lewis and Clark Expedition), Pierre Chouteau, and others, at St. Louis, Louisiana Territory. Lisa already has a post operating in western Louisiana Territory, where the Bighorn River flows into the Yellowstone.
Sept. 8 The large tribe of Osage Indians cede most of their lands in the Louisiana Territory [roughly, most of Missouri and northern Arkansas] to the Federal Government. They move to a reservation along the Arkansas River [in what is now Oklahoma].
Dec. 7 The national election, the second in which Presidential and Vice-Presidential candidates are selected separately, is a victory for the Democratic-Republicans. James Madison is picked for the Presidency with 122 electoral votes to 47 for Charles C. Pinckney, the Federalist candidate. George Clinton of New York retains the Vice Presidency, defeating Rufus King, also of New York, 113 to 47.
Dec. 12 A Bible Society is founded at Philadelphia, following an example set in London four years ago. Its purpose is to promote the use of the Scriptures.

Thomas Heyward, Jr.
(1746-1809)
Signer of the Declaration of Independence

1809

The Embargo Act of 1807 has to be repealed. It has virtually destroyed the shipping industry and all industrial activities related to that industry. Even more serious, it has provoked the anger of certain sections of the country against the Government, which is penalizing its own citizens, whereas before the French or, to a greater extent, the British could be blamed for the obvious results of their intolerable activities. The act and to some degree the Non-Intercourse Acts that follow have no influence on either the British or the French. Britain appears to be toying with the Americans by making and then breaking promises, just as the French invented the pretext last year of helping the Americans enforce their own laws. The sense of frustration is sharpened by the reappearance of resistance among the Indians whose lands have been absorbed over the past decade by white settlers and speculators. At least some Indians are aware that Britain might be willing to give them a hand against the more immediate evil (from their point of view), the Americans.

Jan. 9   The Enforcement Act is passed in an attempt to stop smuggling and other forms of evasion of the Embargo Act.

Feb. 1   A nullification of the Embargo Act is proposed by Senator Timothy Pickering of Massachusetts, former member of the Essex Junto, ardent Federalist, vigorous opponent of Democratic-Republican policies, and staunch friend of Britain.

Feb. 17   Miami University is chartered at Oxford (north of Cincinnati), Ohio. [Classes do not begin until 1824.]

Mar. 1   Illinois Territory is formed from that part of Indiana Territory lying west of the Wabash River and a line drawn north from Vincennes to Canada. [It includes the present states of Wisconsin and Illinois, and the eastern part of Minnesota.]

Mar. 1   The Embargo Act of 1807 is formally repealed, largely because of Senator Pickering's activity, and in its place the Non-Intercourse Act is passed, prohibiting trade with France and Great Britain, and authorizing resumption of trade with either belligerent whenever such belligerent respects the rights of the United States.

Mar. 4   President Jefferson retires to Monticello, his home near Charlottesville, Virginia, and James Madison is inaugurated as the fourth President.

Mar. 6   Robert Smith, former Secretary of the Navy, replaces Madison as Secretary of State.

April 19   The Non-Intercourse Act is suspended and trade with Great Britain is resumed on assurances from British Minister David Erskine that the British Orders in Council of 1807 are to be repealed.

May 15   The British Parliament refuses to ratify the informal undertaking proffered to Madison by Minister Erskine in April.

May 22   The 11th Congress convenes, with 28 Democratic-Republicans and 6 Federalists in the Senate, and 94 Democratic-Republicans and 48 Federalists in the House. The Senate has the same composition as that of the 10th Congress, but the Federalist delegation to the House is doubled at the expense of the Democratic-Republicans.

July 2   Tecumseh, chief of the Shawnee tribe, and his brother, the Prophet, begin a campaign to organize an Indian Confederacy of tribes to oppose the further incursion of white settlers on their lands. In the past seven years more than 30,000,000 acres have been acquired by white settlers north of the Ohio River.

Aug. 9   As a consequence of the British repudiation of the Erskine statement of April, the Non-Intercourse Act of Mar. 1 is reinstituted.

Aug. 17   Thomas Campbell, a dissident Presbyterian from Scotland, and a group of followers form the Christian Association of Washington (Pennsylvania). [After the arrival in September of Campbell's son Alexander, the sect grows and is popularly known as the Campbellite Movement. In 1832 it unites with other groups and thrives as the "Christian Churches (Disciples of Christ)" or, in its current terminology, merely the "Disciples of Christ."]

Sept. 12   The *Phoenix*, a steamboat with a screw propeller, designed by Colonel John Stevens, makes the first successful sea voyage by a steamship, sailing from New York to Philadelphia. The sea route is forced on the vessel because Robert Livingston, Fulton's patron and partner, refuses access to the Hudson. [The *Phoenix* operates successfully on the Delaware River for six years.]

1810

Madison's disappointment over the British refusal to ratify agreements worked out last year leads to the enactment of Macon's Bill No. 2 which restores trade with both England and France but provides for penalizing whichever nation refuses to recognize American neutral rights. Napoleon sees this law as a chance to bring the United States into his "Continental System" (Napoleon's master plan to blockade and to wage economic war against Great Britain). He deceives Madison into believing that all the French decrees against American shipping are to be lifted in November. Madison, acting on Napoleon's word, restores trade with France. But in August Napoleon issues an additional decree against American shipping. It is more than six months before Madison becomes aware of the deception, and in the meantime British-American conflict looms nearer. By the end of the year war appears inevitable.

New England is seething with secessionism, the British are discovered to be encouraging the Indian uprisings along the Western frontier, the British continue their practices of seizure and impressment, and finally a group of young Congressmen (dubbed "War Hawks") begin to articulate the wave of national pride that sweeps over the country.

The United States census shows a population of 7,239,881, a gain of nearly 2,000,000, or 36.4 per cent, in 10 years. The black population is 1,378,110, of which all but 186,746 are slaves. The number of states reaches 17 during the decade, with the admission of Ohio in 1803, and the center of population moves from northeast of Washington to northwest of Washington.

January   In a decision determining whether the rights of claimants against a state are to be respected, regardless of whether fraud is involved or whether the state decides to revoke the contract, the U.S. Supreme Court upholds the sanctity of contract and denies a state the privilege of committing an unconstitutional act (breaking the contract). The case in question, *Fletcher* v. *Peck,* makes it possible for private citizens benefiting from the Yazoo frauds of 1795 to recover more than $4,000,000, even though the state of Georgia tries to break its contract on discovering the fraud and then to cede the land to the Federal Government.

Mar. 23   Napoleon issues his Rambouillet Decree, ordering the seizure of all American shipping in any French port.

May 1   Macon's Bill No. 2 is passed, designed to replace the Non-Intercourse Act of 1809. It authorizes the restoration of all trade with Britain and France, but stipulates that trade will be broken with either nation that refuses to recognize American neutral rights.

July 12   The New York City Journeyman Cordwainers, who are striking for higher wages, are tried and convicted of conspiracy. The Court declares that an act lawful in itself may be unlawful if done by conspiracy. A similar decision had been handed down in a trial of Philadelphia Cordwainers in 1806. [This interpretation of strikes as conspiracies is reversed in 1842 by the Massachusetts Supreme Court.]

Aug. 5   Napoleon issues his Decree of Trianon, imposing drastic duties on goods made in the colonies and brought to French ports——another element of his "Continental System."

Sept. 26   An uprising occurs in Spanish West Florida, accompanied by demands for annexation to the United States. [The area exists as the Republic of West Florida for about a month.]

Oct. 27   President Madison proclaims that part of West Florida between New Orleans and the Pearl River to be part of the United States, and he attaches it to the Territory of Orleans [the later state of Louisiana].

Nov. 2   President Madison revives the Non-Intercourse Act against Great Britain, in the mistaken belief that Napoleon has lifted his various decrees against American shipping.

William Williams
(1731-1811)
Signer of the Declaration of Independence

1811   **The midterm elections held late in 1810 have a** drastic effect upon the course of events. Many old-line appeasers and peace advocates are defeated and replaced by young nationalists. Among the latter are freshman Representative John C. Calhoun of South Carolina; his colleague from South Carolina, Langdon Cheves; Peter B. Porter, Congressman from New York; Felix Grundy, Richard M. Johnson, and Henry Clay, Congressman from Kentucky. These are the famous "War Hawks" who bring an end to the period of diplomacy and economic sanctions. They are disgusted with diplomacy and feel that the national honor demands war. They openly advocate war with both France and Great Britain. A bill is pushed through raising a regular army, but they are not yet prepared to scrap the Jeffersonian prejudice against navies.

The Indian crisis spreads this year. The U.S. policy of obtaining land by "treaty" is beginning to be resisted by some Indian leaders, who plan to end the selling of their heritage. But the Indians have so decreased in number that they can put in the field only about 4,000 warriors, who would be opposed by at least 100,000 white men of fighting age in the Ohio Valley alone.

Jan. 15   Congress passes a resolution to annex East Florida [but does not make it public until 1818].

Jan 24-Feb. 20   Congress debates renewal of the charter for the Bank of the United States. After a prolonged contest, renewal is defeated.

Feb. 11   For the third time in four years the United States prohibits trade with Great Britain, in a further attempt to persuade the British to change their oppressive policies against U.S. merchant ships.

Mar. 4   The Bank of the United States is closed permanently.

Mar. 5   A pioneer group sets out from St. Louis to establish a fur-trading settlement on the Pacific Ocean by an overland route. [They succeed after a journey lasting nearly a year.]

April 12   Another group of pioneers, after sailing around Cape Horn, reach the Pacific Coast for the purpose of fur trading. John Jacob Astor finances the voyage, and the outpost is named Fort Astoria.

May 1   The British 38-gun frigate *Guerrière* stops an American vessel off Sandy Hook and impresses an American seaman into British naval service. The incident causes an angry outburst. A search for the *Guerrière* is initiated by the U.S. 44-gun frigate *President*.

May 16   The *President* overtakes a ship which is thought to be the *Guerrière*, but is later discovered to be the British corvette *Little Belt*. The *President* shells the British ship disabling it and inflicting casualties.

July 8   Tecumseh, Shawnee chief and leader of an Indian Confederacy, travels south to enlist the aid of Creek tribes.

Sept. 26   General William Henry Harrison, governor of Indiana Territory, leaves Vincennes with a large force and marches toward Tippecanoe Creek, where Tecumseh has his headquarters.

Oct. 31   Robert Fulton's side-wheeler, *New Orleans,* begins regular steamboat traffic on the Mississippi River.

Nov. 1   The United States offers compensation for the *Little Belt* affair, on condition that the British repeal their Orders in Council. The offer is refused.

Nov. 4   The 12th Congress convenes, led by "War Hawks." It is composed of 30 Democratic-Republicans and 6 Federalists in the Senate, and 108 Democratic-Republicans and 36 Federalists in the House.

Nov. 7   What begins as a surprise attack by the Indians ends in a modest but costly victory for General Harrison. About 185 casualties are recorded for Harrison's force of some 6,000. [This Battle of Tippecanoe is exaggerated into a "great victory," and is the basis for Harrison's military reputation and political triumphs.]

Nov. 18   *Niles Weekly Register* [one of the most notable of early papers] is founded at Baltimore by Hezekiah Niles.

Nov. 20   Construction of the Cumberland (or National) Road is begun, running toward the Ohio River from Cumberland, Maryland. [It reaches the Ohio River at Wheeling in 1818, and by 1840 reaches its western terminus in Illinois. It is now part of U.S. Route 40.]

Dec. 16   An earthquake at New Madrid [Missouri] causes the Mississippi River to flow backwards for a time, and results in huge floods. [Reelfoot Lake in Tennessee is formed by the overflow. The lake still exists.]

1812

The hostilities of several years are precipitated by the articulate War Hawks into a state of active belligerency. The specifications in the request for a declaration of war by President Madison or in the actual declaration by Congress are not the true "causes" of this war. Those most stridently championing the cause of free trade and seamen's rights are not from the maritime parts of the country, where the demand for war is inaudible. They are from the Southwest, where there is a need for expansion across West Florida to the Gulf, and the Northwest, where Canada appears to be a likely acquisition once war is under way. Actually, this year finds the West Florida drive partially satisfied, but very little enthusiasm and absolutely no sinews of war are supplied to conquer Canada. The Northeastern states refuse to commit their militias (New York's militia stops cold at the border), and Michigan actually returns temporarily to British hands. Sporadic victories at sea bring out the bonfires. But the war, not popular at the outset (witness the vote for it in Congress), becomes a burden as the year wears on.

Feb. 11 Governor Elbridge Gerry of Massachusetts signs a state law redistricting Essex County in that state in a manner suitable to the interests of the Democratic-Republican Party. The districts are shaped without concern for local geography, as is customary. [A clever map of the county with its grotesque shape has the appearance of a salamander, which a local wit derisively calls a "Gerrymander." The name becomes popular and is applied thereafter to all such artfully devised political map-making.]

Mar. 14 Congress authorizes an issue of bonds to provide funds for the possible undertaking of military action.

April 10 President Madison is empowered to call up 100,000 men for six months' service.

April 30 Orleans Territory enters the Union as Louisiana, the 18th state. Its population already exceeds 75,000 and New Orleans is the fifth most populous city in the United States.

May 14 The so-called Florida Parishes—that part of West Florida that was recently constituted the Republic of West Florida, lying between the Mississippi and Pearl rivers south of the 31st parallel—are formally annexed to the new state of Louisiana. The eastern part of West Florida, from the Pearl to the Perdido, along the Gulf coast, is annexed to the Territory of Mississippi.

June 1 President Madison asks Congress to declare war on Great Britain. He cites, as the principal points of irreconcilability with the British, their policy of impressing seamen, their disregard of normal trading relationships between sovereign powers, and evidence that they are encouraging the Indians to warlike acts.

June 3 Sir George Prevost, governor general of Canada, having concluded that war is inevitable, invites the Shawnee chief Tecumseh to meet with him at Amherstburg, Upper Canada [Ontario], opposite the city of Detroit.

June 4 Inasmuch as the name "Louisiana" is now used for a state, the Territory of Louisiana changes its name to Missouri Territory. It includes all of the original Louisiana Purchase except the state of Louisiana.

June 16 British Foreign Minister Lord Castlereagh announces suspension of the Orders in Council.

June 18 Congress declares war, generally accepting President Madison's statement of causes. The vote is 79 to 49 in the House and 19 to 13 in the Senate.

July 1 Congress enacts a new high tariff on imports as a means to raise money for the war.

July 12-Aug. 16 General William Hull, governor of Michigan Territory, crosses the Detroit River into Canada. His movements are known to the British because his personal papers were captured by the British a few days ago. He occupies the town of Sandwich [now part of Windsor], but upon learning that Michilimackinac [Mackinac Island] has fallen to the British without a shot, Hull retreats to Detroit for fear that General Brock will cut his lines of communication. On Aug. 16 he surrenders Detroit and its garrison to Brock without resistance.

July 19 A British attack on the new U.S. naval base on Lake Ontario at Sackets Harbor, New York, is repelled by the gunfire of a single ship, the *Oneida,* commanded by Lieutenant Melancthon T. Woolsey.

Aug. 15-16 An evacuation of U.S. occupants of Fort Dearborn at the southern end of Lake Michigan [Chicago] is ordered. During the evacuation the garrison is attacked and massacred. On the following day the fort is burned.

Aug. 19 Captain Isaac Hull (nephew of General William Hull), in command of the 44-gun

The battle between the _Constitution_ and the _Guerriere_

frigate _Constitution,_ meets the _Guerrière,_ a 38-gun frigate, off the coast of Nova Scotia. After one-half hour the _Guerrière_ strikes her colors, and has to be abandoned and blown up because she can no longer remain afloat. [Hull returns to Boston with the English prisoners of the _Guerrière,_ the first hero of the war.]

Aug. 23 General Brock reaches Fort George at the mouth of the Niagara River, facing American forces occupying Fort Niagara.

Oct. 9 Lieutenant Jesse Duncan Elliott, commanding a Lake Erie flotilla, surprises and captures two British brigs, the _Detroit_ and the _Caledonia._

Oct. 13 General Brock's army is attacked at Queenston Heights, [Ontario], by a force of 600 Americans. Brock is killed in the engagement, which, however, is lost by the Americans because the New York State militia refuses to cross into Canada, on the grounds that their military service does not require them to leave the state.

Oct. 18 The sloop _Wasp_ defeats the British brig _Frolic_ off the coast of Virginia.

Oct. 25 The 44-gun frigate _United States,_ commanded by Captain Stephen Decatur, encounters the 38-gun frigate _Macedonian,_ commanded by Captain John S. Carden. After a fierce and costly battle of 90 minutes, in which 104 casualties are suffered on the British ship and 12 on the _United States,_ the _Macedonian_ is captured and towed into New London. [This is the only British prize to reach an American port intact.]

Nov. 19 General Henry Dearborn, commanding the largest American army in the field, starts from Plattsburg toward Montreal, but at the Canadian frontier his militia refuses to cross, and he returns to Plattsburg.

Nov. 27 Congress authorizes the construction of six new heavy frigates. [These ships are not completed in time to be used in the war.]

December James Madison, in the nation's first wartime election, is elected to a second term as President, defeating De Witt Clinton of New York by 128 electoral votes to 89. Elbridge Gerry wins over Jared Ingersoll for Vice President, 131 to 86.

Dec. 29 The 44-gun frigate _Constitution,_ commanded by Captain William Bainbridge, destroys the 38-gun frigate _Java_ in a vicious fight off the coast of Brazil. Bainbridge is wounded twice in the battle.

71

1813 This war, in its second year, is shapeless, without justification, plan, purpose. Seamen are no longer being impressed, if anybody cares; there is no maritime commerce, for the entire coast is under effective blockade. As for expansion: Canada still belongs to the British, although they are driven out of Michigan Territory. Those who predicted Indian rampages are proven to have had some grounds. According to their custom, Indians when threatened try to kill those who threaten them. Tecumseh pays with his own life in Upper Canada; the Creeks are being subjugated by Andrew Jackson, the only important hero of land operations. Most of the heroes are sailors—Perry and Lawrence, not only daring in combat, but also speakers of memorable words, around whom legends begin to form. Aside from occasional bursts of glory, the war appears purposeless and unrewarding.

January General William Henry Harrison, hero of Tippecanoe, is given charge of all land troops in the West, about 10,000 men, and is ordered to recover Detroit from the British. An advance force under General James Winchester seizes the nearby settlement of Frenchtown [after 1815, Monroe], at the mouth of the Raisin River. Four days later, a combined British and Indian force under Colonel Henry A. Procter surprises Winchester and captures the entire force. Procter leaves the scene, allowing his Indian allies to loot, burn, and scalp in their manner. Some 900 Americans are killed in the battle of Frenchtown and the ensuing Raisin River Massacre.

Jan. 13 John Armstong, former Minister to France and now known to have been an author of the Newburgh Addresses of 1783, is appointed Secretary of War, replacing William Eustis.

Feb. 20 Lewis Cass is appointed governor of Michigan Territory.

Feb. 24 The 18-gun sloop *Hornet,* commanded by Master Commandant James Lawrence, sinks the 20-gun sloop *Peacock* in a hot fight off the coast of Guiana, South America.

Mar. 4 President James Madison is inaugurated to his second term.

April 15 U.S. forces under General James Wilkinson capture the Spanish fort at Mobile, which is being used by the British, and occupy the remainder of West Florida between the Pearl and Perdido rivers.

April 27 General Dearborn leads a raid on York [after 1834, Toronto], capital of Upper Canada, burning the town's public buildings. General Zebulon M. Pike is killed during this raid when a large powder magazine explodes. [The burning of Washington, D.C., in 1814 may be to some extent in retaliation for this action.]

May 1-9 Tecumseh and the British lay siege to Fort Meigs [near Toledo, Ohio] on the Maumee River, but fail to take it.

May 8 President Madison sends Secretary of the Treasury Albert Gallatin and Senator James A. Bayard of Delaware to join John Quincy Adams, the Minister to Russia, in St. Petersburg, on invitation of Tsar Alexander I, who has offered to mediate between Britain and the United States. [The British refuse the services of any mediator.]

May 24 The 13th Congress convenes. The Senate comprises 27 Democratic-Republicans and 9 Federalists, while the House has 112 Democratic-Republicans and 68 Federalists. It is worth noting that of the 36 members added to the lower House as a result of the new census figures, 32 are Federalists.

May 27 Lieutenant Colonel Winfield Scott leads a raid on Fort George, near the mouth of the Niagara River, and forces its abandonment by the British. [This, in turn, forces the British to withdraw from Fort Erie, on the Canadian side of the Niagara, opposite Buffalo, New York.]

June 1 Captain James Lawrence (having been promoted after his Hornet victory) is mortally wounded in battle between his ship, the 50-gun frigate *Chesapeake,* and the British 52-gun frigate *Shannon* just off Boston. Although the dying Lawrence commands, "Don't give up the ship," the disabled *Chesapeake* is captured and towed as prize to Halifax.

June 6-9 A British attack at Stony Creek [Hamilton, Ontario] pushes the Americans back toward Fort George. The Americans are now forced to abandon the recently won Fort Erie.

August Lieutenant Oliver Hazard Perry has constructed and equipped, in the past eight or nine weeks, a small flotilla of four ships at Presque Isle [Erie], Pennsylvania, on Lake Erie. He is also able to move five ships from the base at Black Rock, near Buffalo, New York, and bring them to Presque Isle. Altogether, his flotilla comprises two 20-gun brigs (the *Lawrence* and *Niagara*), a 3-gun brig (the *Caledonia*); five

A British caricaturist's view of the battle between the *Chesapeake* and the *Shannon*

schooners with a maximum of 4 guns, and a sloop. He intends to seek out the British sea force on Lake Erie.

Aug. 2   A British attack on Fort Stephenson, on the Sandusky River, northern Ohio, is repulsed by Major George Groghan's force, with heavy British losses.

Aug. 14   The British 21-gun ship *Pelican* captures the American 20-gun sloop *Argus* off the English coast. Before her own defeat, the *Argus* had a record of capturing 27 British merchant ships.

Aug. 30   The Creek Indians of Mississippi Territory, led by William Weatherford (also known as Chief Red Eagle), attacks Fort Mims, north of Mobile. The Indians kill 400 Americans and capture 500. [The conflict that follows, ending with the Battle of Horseshoe Bend in 1814, is sometimes called the Creek War.]

Sept. 5   Secretary of War John Armstrong sets up headquarters at Sackets Harbor, New York, in preparation for a major assault on Canada, with Montreal as the goal.

Sept. 10   Lieutenant Perry, seeking the British Lake Erie squadron, discovers it at Put-In-Bay, South Bass Island. The British flotilla of six ships—two brigs, two ships, a schooner, and a sloop, as Perry describes it—is commanded by Captain Robert Barclay, who has fought with Admiral Nelson. For an unknown reason, most of Perry's squadron keeps its distance, while the *Lawrence,* in the midst of the action, is virtually destroyed and suffers 80-per-cent casualties.

Perry shifts to the *Niagara* and the British fleet is forced to surrender with almost 70-per-cent casualties. This is the first time any British naval unit has been forced to yield. Perry sends a message to William Henry Harrison, "We have met the enemy, and they are ours." [Perry is promoted to captain. Lake Erie is under U.S. control.]

Sept. 18-Oct. 5   Without Lake Erie fleet protection, General Procter evacuates Detroit. General Harrison, free to cross Lake Erie, transports his entire army of 4,000 men across the lake in pursuit of Procter, who is retreating eastward from Detroit. After occupying Detroit, on Sept. 29, Harrison resumes his march to pin down the British. He catches up with Procter at the Thames River deep in Upper Canada. The British are soundly defeated, with the number killed, wounded, and captured totaling more than 500. Tecumseh is killed, ending all Indian hopes for building their confederacy.

Oct. 7   General Andrew Jackson takes command in the Creek War.

Nov. 9   Jackson defeats a Creek force in a major battle in Mississippi Territory [on the site of Talladega, Alabama].

Dec. 10-29   The Americans are forced out of Fort George, and burn the town of Newark [Niagara-on-the-Lake] before crossing the river. The British continue to advance, taking Fort Niagara, while their Indian allies plunder the town of Lewiston, New York. By Dec. 29 the British reach and burn Buffalo, after which they capture the nearby Black Rock Navy Yard.

1814   The collapse of Napoleon's military capability, following his invasion of Russia and his defeat later at Leipzig, leaves the British free to pursue a more aggressive war in America, including a proposed attack from Canadian bases and an assault on New Orleans. The raids on Washington and Baltimore in August and September are diversionary, meant to sap American morale, and to draw attention away from the real objectives. After the burning of Washington, Americans begin to stiffen their resistance; one sign is the defense of Fort McHenry in Baltimore Harbor. There are a number of victories: the American capture of Fort Erie in July, and Macdonough's action on Lake Champlain that ended the British Champlain invasion. In the South, the costly ambush at Fort Sims by the Creeks produces the leading hero of the war in Andrew Jackson. After destroying Indian power in Mississippi Territory, and beginning the long-anticipated conquest of East Florida, he turns to the defense of New Orleans. Information concerning the event that should provide the climax of the year, the signing of the peace at Ghent, is still en route across the Atlantic as the year ends.

January   Secretary of War John Armstrong reorganizes the Army, establishes a system of military districts, and removes a number of leaders of questionable competence, including James Wilkinson and Wade Hampton, whose projected campaign against Montreal dissipates in minor skirmishes.

Jan. 3   President Madison receives a British proposal for direct negotiations, and immediately accepts.

Mar. 24   General James Wilkinson is cleared in a court of inquiry into his conduct of operations on the north of Lake Champlain, but he is forced to resign and is replaced by General Jacob Brown.

Mar. 27   General Andrew Jackson leads the Tennessee militia in an attack in force against the Creeks at the Horseshoe Bend of the Tallapoosa River in Mississippi Territory. This battle destroys all Creek resistance, along with that of their Cherokee allies.

Mar. 28   The American frigate *Essex,* commanded by Captain David Porter, is trapped by two British ships, the *Phoebe* and the *Cherub,* in Chilean coastal waters off Valparaíso. A fight of three hours duration ends with the surrender of the *Essex,* after two-thirds of its crew are killed or wounded. [One survivor is David Farragut, 11 years old, a member of Porter's crew.]

April 1   The Flemish town of Ghent is designated the place where negotiations to end the war are to be carried on.

May 22   Andrew Jackson, having been given command of military activities in the South, is promoted to major general in the U.S. Army. (He was until now a major general in the Tennessee militia.)

July 3   General Jacob Brown recaptures Fort Erie, on the Canadian side of the Niagara River.

July 5   General Winfield Scott's brigade of 1,300 defeats a British force of 1,500 at Chippawa, north of Fort Erie.

July 25   The British, reinforced after their defeat at Chippawa, hold fast at nearby Lundy's Lane. The Americans retire, leaving the British in possession of the battlefield.

Aug. 8   Negotiations to end the war begin at Ghent.

Aug. 9   General Jackson's campaign against the Creeks ends as the Creeks cede over 20,000,000 acres of land—virtually all the land they claim—to the United States. [By 1840, all Creeks have been forced to move west of the Mississippi.]

Aug. 19-25   A British raiding expedition under General Robert Ross lands at Benedict, Maryland, where the Patuxent River enters Chesapeake Bay, southeast of Washington, D.C. By Aug. 22 it reaches Marlboro, a U.S. gunboat base, where Joshua Barney, the commander, blows up all the boats to prevent their being captured. On Aug. 24, the British win an easy fight at Bladensburg and proceed unopposed to enter Washington the next day. They burn the Capitol, the White House, and all the department buildings except the Patent Office. A storm then occurs, and the British board their ships and retire.

Aug. 30   John Armstrong resigns as Secretary of War and Secretary of State James Monroe, takes over his office [temporarily until Sept. 27, thereafter permanently].

Aug. 31   Sir George Prevost begins a campaign to invade the United States by way of Lake Champlain and the Hudson Valley.

Sept. 1   A British expedition lands at Castine, Maine, and advances as far as Bangor.

Sept. 11   Lieutenant Thomas Macdonough's

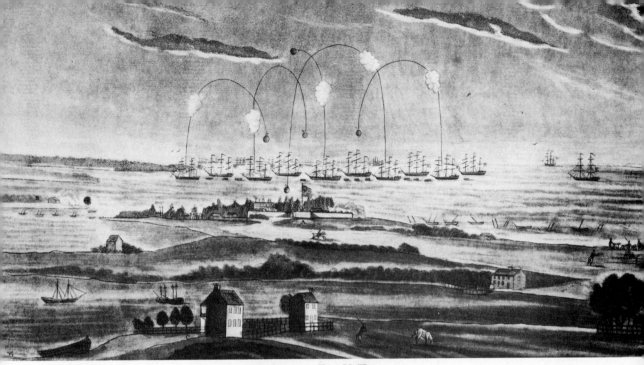

Bombardment of Fort McHenry

makeshift Lake Champlain flotilla of 4 ships and 10 gunboats destroys a British flotilla of 4 ships and 12 gunboats near Plattsburg. [This deprives General Prevost of naval support, and Prevost abandons his invasion and returns to Canada.]

Sept. 12-14 A British army under General Ross disembarks at North Point, at the Patapsco River mouth, in preparation for an assault on Baltimore. It is supported by a fleet under Admiral Sir Alexander Cochrane, which then prepares to bombard Fort McHenry, the only remaining barrier. The land operation meets heavy resistance within six miles of the city, suffers heavy casualties, including the death of General Ross, and falls back. When the bombardment of Fort McHenry also fails, the assault against Baltimore is abandoned. [Francis Scott Key, detained aboard one of the British ships, records the British failure in verse, providing the lyrics for *The Star-Spangled Banner*.]

Oct. 18 A convention of delegates from the New England states, hard hit by the war, is convoked by the Massachusetts legislature to meet at Hartford, Connecticut, for the purpose of preparing "a radical reform in the national compact."

Nov. 7 General Andrew Jackson invades Spanish Florida and captures Pensacola. [The occupation is brief; the city is permanently acquired in 1818.]

Nov. 26-Dec. 18 A British army of 7,500 embarks at Jamaica, in the West Indies, and sails for the Mississippi River. On Dec. 13 the fleet enters Lake Borgne, an inlet of the Gulf of Mex-

ico 40 miles east of New Orleans. By Dec. 18 the land forces are deployed within 5 miles of the city.

Dec. 15 The convention of New England antiwar Federalists meets at Hartford, Connecticut, to begin a secret session for the consideration of the grievances that prompted the call for their assemblage. There are 26 delegates: 12 from Massachusetts, 7 from Connecticut, 4 from Rhode Island, 2 from New Hampshire, and 1 from Vermont. [Maine is still a district within Massachusetts.] A former U.S. Senator from Massachusetts and member of the Essex Junto, George Cabot, presides.

Dec. 23-31 Jackson, having grouped his forces around New Orleans throughout December, stages a furious stalling action that stops the British advance and allows him time to complete his fortifications and breastworks along an old dry canal bed between a swamp and the Mississippi River.

Dec. 24 The British and U.S. negotiators meeting in Ghent reach an agreement, which is embodied in the Treaty of Ghent, settling none of the issues that brought on the war. Certain boundary commissions are set up to resolve outstanding border disputes; otherwise, it is proposed to resume relationships as they were at the outbreak of the hostilities. [News of the Treaty of Ghent reaches the United States in February 1815, after the Battle of New Orleans. The treaty is ratified on Feb. 16, 1815.]

1815

The Battle of New Orleans, fought two weeks after the Treaty of Ghent is signed, is the last action of the war. (It is doubtful whether the treaty would have been ratified if the British had taken New Orleans, so it is not accurate to assert—as many have done—that the war's most bitter battle settled nothing.) As soon as hostilities cease, a number of significant changes in the United States become apparent: a strong current of nationalism forged during the war; renewal of close relations between the United States and Great Britain; and a dramatic movement of people westward. The Democratic-Republican Party adopts many of the previous Federalist positions. President Madison's Administration supports many former Federalist proposals: a second Bank of the United States, a national university, protective tariffs, a uniform national currency, and a system of national roads and other so-called internal improvements. But the Federalist Party never recovers from a stigma of treasonable activity that is attributed by many to the leading Federalists who were seeking a fundamental change in direction at Hartford just as peace was in sight.

Jan. 1 The new year begins with a furious artillery duel at New Orleans. The Americans win, forcing the British to mark time until they can acquire reinforcements and more munitions.

Jan. 5 The Hartford Convention winds up its deliberations and prepares its resolutions for the consideration of the Congress. These include several changes in the U.S. Constitution, notably a slowing down of the admission of new states from the Western territories by requiring a two-thirds vote; a cancellation of the special privilege granted to the South whereby each slave is reck-

Elbridge Gerry
(1744-1814)
Signer of the Declaration of Independence

oned as three-fifths of a person for purposes of representation in Congress; the requirement in the future of a two-thirds vote for bills authorizing embargoes and similar restrictions on trade, including declarations of war. The apparent purpose is to strengthen the commercial and industrial interests, paramount in New England, as against the agrarian interests of the West and South, for whom the War Hawks have been spokesmen. There is no word of secession, although the posing of an extreme states'-rights program carries the intimation that the states continue to wield this degree of sovereignty, all else failing. [By the time the resolutions reach Washington, the reality of peace appears to make the grievances moot, and the entire convention is popularly tainted with intimations of near-treason. This is the impression that prevails historically.]

Jan. 8 The British launch a savage frontal attack on the nearly impregnable American entrenchments and breastworks at New Orleans. After this is repulsed with heavy losses, the whole action is repeated, with the same devastating results. In a third assault, the British commander, General Sir Edward Pakenham, is killed in action. British casualties total more than 2,000 men, while the Americans lose about 70, killed and wounded. [On Jan. 27 the British retire to their ships and leave the field of battle. Jackson emerges as the greatest hero of the war.]

Jan. 30 Former President Thomas Jefferson's personal library of 7,000 volumes is sold to the Government to become the nucleus of another library of Congress, replacing that burned by the British last year.

Feb. 6 The first charter for a railroad is issued, by the state of New Jersey, to John Stevens, who plans to build a railroad from Trenton

76

General Jackson in New Orleans

to New Brunswick. [It is never built.]

Feb. 27 Congress orders the gunboat flotilla to be disbanded and the boats put up for sale; and it orders all armed vessels to be taken off the Great Lakes.

Mar. 3 President Madison requests Congress to authorize a standing army of 20,000 men. [Congress gives assent, but restricts the army to a strength of about 10,000.]

May 10 Commodore Stephen Decatur sails from New York with 10 ships, bound for the Mediterranean Sea with instructions to end the depradations of the Barbary pirate states, Algiers, Tunis, and Tripoli.

June 17-30 Decatur seizes the Algerian 44-gun frigate *Mashouda* on the high seas. Two days later he captures the Algerian 22-gun brig *Estido*. He tows both into Algiers Harbor and threatens to bombard the city. The Dey of Algiers capitulates, signs a treaty of non-interference, and renounces all demands for tribute. [The same pattern is followed successfully against the Dey of Tunis on July 26 and against the Dey of Tripoli on Aug. 6.]

July 3 A commercial agreement is signed with Great Britain permitting the United States to trade with the British East Indies. The agreement also ends discriminatory duties.

Dec. 4 The 14th Congress convenes, with 25 Democratic-Republicans and 11 Federalists in the Senate, and 117 Democratic-Republicans and 65 Federalists in the House. Henry Clay is re-elected Speaker of the House.

Dec. 5 President Madison proposes a second Bank of the United States to succeed the first bank that failed to be rechartered in 1811.

1816

An era of nationalism is initiated by the programs and guided by the philosophy of Henry Clay of Kentucky and John C. Calhoun of South Carolina, whose combined formula for American progress [later dubbed by Clay the "American System"] includes the building of canals and roads, and the levy of tariffs for the protection of infant industries. The latter program largely favors the development of industrial centers outside New England: Pittsburgh's iron, competing with British iron; Kentucky's hemp and cotton-bagging industry, competing with Scottish jute; the woolen industries of Vermont and Ohio, competing with English wool.

For the postwar United States not only "feels like" a nation: it has become a nation economically, capable of providing for itself and, indeed, capable of supplying materials, such as cotton, much in demand in Europe. Only poor transportation stands in the way of the rapid development that is inevitable as the populations spills over the Appalachian barrier into the Northwest and the Southwest and even across the Mississippi. Thus, the combination of internal improvements plus protection for new manufactures is indeed a national system, and the nation surges into a spate of feverish activity.

Jan. 1   The newly laid-out town of Columbus, Ohio, replaces Chillicothe as the capital of Ohio.

Jan. 21   The African Methodist Episcopal Church is founded. It is the first Negro church in America to be jurisdictionally and denominationally free of all-white churches.

Mar. 14   A bill to create the second Bank of the United States, proposed by John C. Calhoun, passes in the House by a vote of 80 to 71, and in the Senate by 22 to 12. It authorizes capitalization of $35,000,000 of which the Federal Government is to subscribe one-fifth. In return, the bank is to pay a bonus of $1,500,000 to the Federal Government. It is hoped that the financial chaos brought about by the proliferation of private banks lacking the backing of specie, and the resulting inflation, will be stemmed as a responsible fiscal organization is available. The bank is authorized to open early next year.

Mar. 20   The U.S. Supreme Court hands down a decision, *Martin* v. *Hunter's Lessee,* which affirms its right to review the decisions of state courts, thus upholding the constitutionality of the Judiciary Act of 1789.

April 27   A tariff is passed that, for the first time, is specifically framed to protect new industries, rather than to raise revenues. Textiles and iron products are the chief beneficiaries, both industries that were developed during the war and are now facing competition from abroad.

June 11   The city of Baltimore becomes the first in the United States to use gas for street lighting.

Dec. 4   Secretary of State James Monroe of Virginia, the Democratic-Republican choice for the Presidency, and his running mate Daniel D. Tompkins of New York, defeat the Federalist candidates, Rufus King of New York and John E. Howard of Maryland, by 183 to 34 electoral votes. Only Massachusetts, Connecticut, and Delaware favor the Federalists.

Dec. 11   Indiana is admitted to the Union as the 19th state. The state capital is at Corydon, which replaced Vincennes as territorial capital in 1813.

Dec. 20   Calhoun introduces a bill that would set aside the $1,500,000 bonus paid by the Bank of the United States to the U.S. Treasury, creating from it a permanent fund to be used only for internal improvements. The bill is strongly opposed by President Madison.

Dec. 28   The American Colonization Society is founded by Robert Finley, a Presbyterian minister in Washington, D.C. Its purpose is to recolonize free Negroes in Africa. [Its activities result eventually in the foundation of the Republic of Liberia.]

Robert Treat Paine
(1731-1814)
Signer of the Declaration of Independence

1817

The phrase "Era of Good Feelings," in some ways a misnomer, is used in a Boston newspaper to emphasize the decline in partisan politics and political controversy. But even though the Federalist Party is disappearing, the nation is not a one-party state. New factions and conflicting philosophies are taking form. Debt and inflation are beginning to produce a cleavage between the established commercial and industrial East, and the growing West and changing South. A hint of sectional difference is apparent in the contrasts between the Calhoun-Clay and Madison attitudes toward internal improvements. This is a year of transition, of marking time, as steamships begin regularly to ply the Mississippi, the first canal between the Hudson and Great Lakes begins to be constructed, and the National Road approaches the Ohio River from the east.

January Jean Laffite establishes a base on an island off the coast of Spanish Mexico [Galveston], abandoning his base on the Baratarian coast near New Orleans. He resumes his practice of piracy, for which he has been pardoned by President Monroe in recognition of his services to the American side during the recent war. [Laffite loses control of his Galveston following and in 1821 sails away on his favorite ship, *Pride,* and disappears from history.]

Jan. 7 The second Bank of the United States opens under William Jones. [After Jones's disastrous administration of two years, the second president, Langdon Cheves, puts the bank on a sound financial basis.]

Feb. 8 Calhoun's bill to set aside a permanent fund for internal improvements is passed by Congress.

Mar. 3 President Madison's last official act is to veto the internal improvements bill.

Mar. 3 Alabama Territory is formed from the eastern part of Mississippi Territory, with its capital at St. Stephens, near Mobile.

Mar. 4 James Monroe is inaugurated as the fifth President of the United States.

April 28 Acting Secretary of State Richard Rush and British Minister in Washington Charles Bagot sign an agreement ending the presence of armed vessels on the Great Lakes, except for specified units. The agreement also provides for the gradual demilitarization of the frontier between Canada and the United States. [The agreement is later given the status of a treaty when ratified by the U.S. Senate.]

May 16 The steamship *Washington,* designed by the famous river engineer Henry Miller Shreve, makes a historic voyage from New Orleans to Louisville in 25 days, inaugurating regular steamboat service on the Mississippi. Ships can now carry a payload upstream as well as downstream, opening up significant commercial advantages.

July 4 De Witt Clinton, governor of New York State, breaks ground at Rome, New York, for the building of a canal [Erie Canal] between the Hudson Valley and Lake Erie. (This is New York's answer to the Cumberland Road.)

July 12 The Boston *Columbian Centinel* uses the expression "Era of Good Feelings" to describe the political climate of President Monroe's Administration.

Nov. 20 The Seminole Indians invade southern Georgia from their refuge in the swamps of Spanish East Florida.

Dec. 1 The 15th Congress convenes, with 34 Democratic-Republicans and 14 Federalists in the Senate, and 141 Democratic-Republicans and 42 Federalists in the House.

Dec. 10 Mississippi enters the Union as the 20th State, with its capital at Washington, a small town east of Natchez.

Dec. 26 General Andrew Jackson takes command of an American force organized to pursue the Seminole Indians and their runaway-slave allies from the Georgia border into Spanish East Florida, if necessary.

Thomas McKean
(1734-1817)
Signer of the Declaration of Independence

1818

The postwar economic upsurge, with its increase in industrial and agricultural productivity, its territorial expansion accompanied by liberal land and credit policies, is succeeded by a speculative boom and an overextension of credit. The Bank of the United States does little to hold back this inflationary process until late in the year, and it is too late. Branch banks are ordered to accept only their own bills, and to demand immediate payment in specie of all state bank notes. This procedure is particularly threatening to the new settlements in the South and West, where farmers and speculators alike have exhausted their credit. Meanwhile, responding to the pressure of migrating populations, the building of roads and canals and the improvement of river navigation continue.

The United States settles almost all of its outstanding disputes with British Canada in a convention that is more significant that the Treaty of Ghent. By the end of the year, the efforts of Secretary of State John Quincy Adams and General Andrew Jackson result in an ultimatum to Spain that can only be resolved by the acquisition of Florida, rounding out the territorial integrity of the Gulf and Atlantic seaboard. The shape of the United States, south of Canada and east of Spanish Mexico, is now well defined.

Jan. 1   The *American Journal of Science and Arts* ("Silliman's Journal") is founded at New Haven, Connecticut, by Professor Benjamin Silliman, who in 1802 became the first professor of chemistry and natural history at Yale University. [Silliman edits the journal for 26 years, and the magazine itself outlasts all its contemporaries.]

Jan. 6   General Andrew Jackson sends a letter through Representative John Rhea of Tennessee to President Monroe, proposing to take possession of Spanish Florida in a campaign that would occupy less than 60 days to execute. [Jackson regards failure to answer this letter as a tacit approval (a view not taken by President Monroe) and begins an invasion of Spanish Florida.]

March   A resolution in the House of Representatives, to grant recognition to certain revolutionary governments in South America that have been established in the course of achieving independence from Spain, is defeated because the Government prefers to concentrate on acquiring Florida from Spain.

April 7   Jackson seizes the Spanish fort at St. Marks on Apalachee Bay.

April 16   The Rush-Bagot Agreement of 1817 receives Senate approval.

April 18   By an act of Congress, the United States flag is to retain 13 stripes as a permanent part of its design, but a star is to be added for each state at the time of admission to the Union.

May 24   Jackson again captures the Spanish base of Pensacola. During this action Alexander Arbuthnot and Robert Ambrister, who are British subjects, are captured. [They are charged with aiding the Seminoles, runaway-slaves, and the Spanish.]

May 30   Scheduled packet sailing ship service begins between New York City and Liverpool. An improvement in ship design allows the packet ships to reduce the Atlantic Ocean crossing to 33 days from a previous 39 days.

June 3   Arbuthnot and Ambrister are executed. [This incident causes an outburst of indignation in Great Britain and a campaign to censure Jackson in the United States. But Jackson's conduct is popular, and is supported by Secretary of State John Quincy Adams. British Foreign Secretary Castlereagh takes the position that the two British subjects had placed themselves outside of the royal protection.]

Aug. 23   The *Walk-in-the-Water*, launched on April 28, becomes the first steamboat to ply the Great Lakes. It makes its first voyage from Black Rock, near Buffalo, bound for Detroit. [It is wrecked and lost in a storm in 1821.]

Oct. 20   A convention is signed between the United States and Great Britain. Its main provisions are: (1) American seamen are granted fishing rights off the coast of Newfoundland; (2) the 49th parallel of latitude is the boundary between the two countries from the Lake of the Woods to the crest of the Rocky Mountains; (3) Astoria, renamed Fort George by the British when their North West Company bought it from Astor in 1813, is returned to U.S. control, but the ownership of the Oregon country remains undecided.

Nov. 28   Secretary of State John Quincy Adams sends an ultimatum to Spain demanding that effective control of Florida be assumed by that country and that aggressive actions on the part of the Indians and runaway slaves be stopped. If this is not done, Adams warns, the entire region will have to be turned over to the United States.

December A request for the granting of statehood is received from a portion of the Territory of Missouri. The proposed area runs generally from latitude 40° 35' in the north (except for a wedge between the Des Moines and Mississippi rivers) to 36° 30' in the south (but extending to 36° between the St. Francis and Mississippi rivers) and from longitude 94° 42' in the west to the Mississippi River in the east. It is worth noting that the 36° 30' line is an extension westward of the boundary between Kentucky and Tennessee.

Dec. 3 Illinois Territory south of 42° 31' N. lat. is admitted to the Union as the 21st State. The northern part of Illinois Territory is added to Michigan Territory. Now Michigan Territory extends west to the Mississippi. The capital of the state of Illinois is Kaskaskia, on the Mississippi River. [The capital is transferred to Vandalia in 1820.]

Democracy Against the Unnatural Union. (A commentary on the political situation in Pennsylvania)

1819 America's first serious financial panic, occurring early in the year, is followed by a depression. Many state banks collapse, and enormous amounts of Western real estate are foreclosed by the Bank of the United States.

But there are more fundamental causes for the crisis, of which the credit collapse is only a consequence and a symptom. The swollen demand for the products of American farms and factories, resulting from scant supply of such goods at home and abroad during the war, is now satisfied; the market is declining. As prices fall, money becomes difficult to come by, but the habit of borrowing, formed in the expansive years, cannot be shaken. Those who insist on a return to specie—hard money——are seen as turning the clock back.

The outstanding change that is occurring in the country is the physical and territorial growth which increases the relative importance and influence of the frontier, and sends new spokesmen—Calhoun, Clay, and Jackson—to expound a diversity of programs. The needs of the several sections of the nation—the West, the South, and of course the East—begin to transcend those of the nation as a whole and the concept of states' rights again finds champions. The territories are straining to acquire statehood. The post-Revolutionary generation is ready to assume responsibility. But Marshall's Supreme Court continues to issue Federalist decisions; and President Monroe continues to represent the Virginia Dynasty with dignity and respect from all parts of the nation.

Jan. 12 A Congressional report, sponsored by Henry Clay, condemns Jackson's conduct in Florida. [It fails of adoption.]

Jan. 26 In view of the pending application for statehood on the part of Missouri, a resolution to reorganize Arkansas County of Missouri Territory as Arkansas Territory, extending south of the proposed Missouri boundary and west from the Mississippi River to 100° W. long., is introduced into Congress. An amendment to this resolution by Congressman John W. Taylor of New York, forbidding the introduction of slavery into the proposed Arkansas Territory, is defeated.

Feb. 2 In the case of *Trustees of Dartmouth College* v. *Woodward,* the U.S. Supreme Court prohibits a state from "impairing an obligation of contract." It declares a private corporate charter—in this instance, one granted by George III to Dartmouth College—to be a contract, which cannot be revised or impaired by a state.

Feb. 13 Congressman James Tallmadge of New York proposes two antislavery amendments to the legislation introduced last December to grant statehood to Missouri. [The amendments are adopted by the House of Representatives after fierce debate, but in the Senate, where the South retains a majority, the amendments are defeated.]

Feb. 22 A treaty is signed between Secretary of State Adams and the Spanish Minister to Washington, Luis de Onis, by which Spain cedes Florida to the United States, renounces all claims

to the Oregon country (the land west of the Rockies and north of the 42d parallel), and establishes a joint commission to define the borders between the Spanish and United States dominions from the 42d parallel southwest to the Sabine River, accepted as the western border of Louisiana. [The treaty is ratified by the U.S. Senate in 1821.]

Feb. 28 The University of Virginia is founded at Charlottesville by Thomas Jefferson, who designs the first buildings of the university. [The first classes are held in 1825.]

Mar. 2 Arkansas County of Missouri Territory is reorganized as Arkansas Territory, with its capital at Arkansas Post on the Mississippi River. [The territorial capital is moved to Little Rock in 1821.]

Mar. 3 A law is passed granting a $50 bounty to informers who report illegal importation of slaves into the United States. With the increasing enforcement of the Federal law against such importation, the price of slaves has risen, and smuggling has become profitable.

Mar. 6 The U.S. Supreme Court in *McCulloch* v. *Maryland,* reaffirms the authority of the Court to rule on the constitutionality of state law. In this case, denying Maryland's attempt to force an official of the Bank of the United States to pay a state tax for the bank; the Court enunciates the principle that "the power to tax involves the power to destroy," and on this ground forbids the state to tax the bank. The decision also upholds the "implied-powers" clause of the Constitution; in affirming the right of Congress to create a national bank, it lays the basis for Congressional authority not explicitly described in the Constitution.

May 24-June 20   The steam-assisted sailing packet *Savannah,* 300 tons register, leaves the port of Savannah, Georgia, and heads for Liverpool. She arrives at Liverpool 26 days later, beating the average packet sailing ship time by several days. She had used her engine to help her sails for only 80 hours before exhausting her coal supply. This is the first time steam power is used in an Atlantic crossing.

June   Major Stephen Long, an engineer, commissioned by Secretary of War John C. Calhoun to explore the territory south of the Missouri River, sets out with a group of scientists and soldiers from Pittsburgh. [He camps for the winter at Council Bluffs, explores the eastern Rocky Mountains (discovering the peak named for him), and returns with a map and valuable botanical and geological information late in 1820. He is so unimpressed by the region, that he calls it "The Great American Desert."]

Dec. 6   The 16th Congress convenes, with 156 Democratic-Republicans and 27 Federalists in the House, and 35 Democratic-Republicans and 7 Federalists in the Senate.

Dec. 14   Alabama enters the Union as the 22d state, with its capital at Huntsville. [The capital is transferred to Cahaba in 1820, to Tuscaloosa in 1826, and to Montgomery in 1847.]

Broadway and Grand Streets, New York City

In this election year, the continued "good feelings" that mark President Monroe's Administration ensure his reelection. Partisan activity reaches the vanishing point, and the electoral vote is virtually unanimous. As a national party, the Federalist Party no longer exists.

1820

The first serious controversy based on sectional differences becomes manifest this year. It is brought about by the realization of Southern politicians that the population of the North is increasing at a rate that assures Northern dominance in the House of Representatives; and that the control in the Senate (where each state has equal power) has already reached an equilibrium, 11 states favoring the Southern point of view (especially on such questions as the concessions afforded slavery under the Constitution) and 11 states favoring the Northern point of view. The proposed admission of Missouri, potentially a pro-slavery state, is under challenge from the North. In order to assure the admission of a 12th "slave state," the South must accept the admission of a 12th "free state." It happens that the District of Maine, in Massachusetts, is a likely candidate; but the North bargains shrewdly, and in the end a compromise [the Missouri Compromise] is arranged through the good offices of Henry Clay, whereby both Missouri and Maine are admitted, providing the institution of slavery in banned from most of the remaining states to be carved out of Missouri Territory. This is, in effect, a defeat for the South, because only Arkansas Territory is within the area in which slavery will be permitted.

The census results this year clearly show the population trend. Of the total population of 9,638,453, more than 54 per cent live in the North (compared with an even division in 1800). The rate of increase nationwide continues 33.5 per cent per decade, but the Old Northwest has almost doubled in population. It is worth noting that Ohio has advanced in rank to fifth place, followed closely by Kentucky. Almost 90 per cent of the Negro population of 1,771,656 are enslaved. The number of states has increased to 22 during the decade, with the addition of Louisiana, Indiana, Mississippi, Illinois, and Alabama.

Jan. 25 The state capital of Illinois is moved from Kaskaskia to Vandalia.

Feb. 6 The *Mayflower of Liberia* sails from New York, heading for Sierra Leone, West Africa, carrying 86 free Negroes who have elected to emigrate to that British colony, where freed and refugee slaves have been welcomed for 30 years.

Mar. 6 The Missouri statehood bill, including an amendment proposed by Senator Jesse B. Thomas of Illinois, is passed by Congress. (The compromise amendment passed the Senate on Feb. 17 by a vote of 34 to 10 and was accepted by the House of Representatives on Mar. 3 by a vote of 134 to 42.) The bill authorizes the people of Missouri to draw up a constitution under which they will decide whether or not to permit slavery to exist within the state, but it also prohibits slavery in any part of the Territory of Missouri north of the southern boundary of the state of Missouri (36° 30' N. lat.). [The state is finally admitted in 1821.]

Mar. 15 Maine is admitted as the 23d state, as part of the agreement under which Missouri is to be admitted [the Missouri Compromise]. The separation of the District of Maine was authorized by Massachusetts in 1816, and has been demanded by an increasing proportion of Maine's population of almost 300,000 since the end of the war [of 1812]. Portland is the capital.

Mar. 30 A group of Protestant missionaries from New England arrives in the Hawaiian Islands and is welcomed by King Kamehameha II.

April 24 A Public Land Act is passed by Congress, abolishing credit for land purchases from the public domain, but reducing the minimum price per acre from $2.00 to $1.25; the minimum purchase is reduced from 160 to 80 acres. In this year of depression the act is intended to help settlers purchase land, but it chiefly benefits land speculators.

July 5 The capital of Alabama is moved from Huntsville to Cahaba, in the south, closer to the main population centers.

July 14-15 Edwin James and two other members of the Stephen Long expedition climb the mountain at the eastern fringe of the Rockies that was first observed in 1806 by Lieutenant Zebulon Pike, who was unable to make the ascent. [The mountain is named for James by Long, but popular usage continues to call it "Pike's Peak."]

William Ellery
(1727-1820)
Signer of the Declaration of Independence

William Floyd
(1734-1821)
Signer of the Declaration of Independence

July 19   At the Missouri constitutional convention in session in St. Louis a provision is introduced to exclude all free Negroes and mulattoes from the state. [This proposal provokes heated arguments, not only in the Territory but throughout the country. In the end, Henry Clay persuades the convention to accept a provision that the state will never impair the rights of the citizens of any other state.]

Sept. 26   Daniel Boone, 85, the great explorer, pioneer, and trail blazer of Kentucky, dies in St. Charles County, Missouri.

Nov. 18   Nathaniel B. Palmer of Stonington, Connecticut, 21-year-old commander of the sloop *Hero* on a sealing expedition headed by Captain Benjamin Pendleton, reports the existence of land south of Cape Horn. [The land he sights is a peninsula of Antarctica, named the Palmer Peninsula in his honor by the Russian Admiral Fabian Bellingshausen. It is later renamed the Antarctic Peninsula.]

December   A political faction appears in Kentucky, called the "Relief Party," that advocates relief for delinquent debtors. This movement is an outgrowth of bank failures, foreclosures on credit, and a contest in the Kentucky courts as to whether relevant statutes are constitutional. [The contest is resolved in favor of the debtors, but a more lasting result is the division of the state Democratic-Republicans into two factions, one led by Henry Clay in opposition to the "Relief Party," the other led by Andrew Jackson in support of that party. The Clay group becomes known as the Whig Party, and the members of the Jackson group are called simply Democrats.]

Dec. 6   In the election of 1820 James Monroe is almost unanimously elected, with only a single electoral vote (out of 232) going to John Quincy Adams. Daniel D. Tompkins is reelected Vice President.

In 1821 events in Latin America attract considerable attention in the United States. A series of independence movements and wars for independence have been in progress there since 1810. Now nearly all of Spain's Latin American colonies have gained independence. The United States has adopted a cautious policy concerning the formation of new states in Latin America, at least until the Adams-Onis Treaty of 1819, settled the issues between the United States and Spain. But now Congress appropriates funds to defray the expenses of several missions to the newly independent countries, and preparations are made to open diplomatic relations with at least five of them: Peru, Colombia [including the later Venezuela and Ecuador], Mexico, Chile, and La Plata [Argentina].

January The U.S. Supreme Court, in *Cohens* v. *Virginia,* reaffirms its decision of 1816 in *Martin* v. *Hunter's Lessee,* that the Court has a right to review decisions of state courts. In this instance, the state court is supported, but the significant judicial point involved is the jurisdiction of the U.S. Supreme Court.

Jan. 17 Moses Austin, a Missouri lead-mine operator who has been ruined in the crisis of 1819, receives the grant of a large tract of land in northeastern Mexico (province of Texas) from the Spanish Government. He also receives permission to bring in 300 settlers for his colony. [His death in June prevents Moses Austin from reaching Texas; but after Agustín de Iturbide establishes Mexican independence in August, Moses' son Stephen, a member of the Missouri territorial legislature, obtains permission from the Mexican Government to inherit the grants, and leads the American settlers into Texas.]

Feb. 6 Columbian College is chartered in Washington, D.C. [In 1904 it changes its name to George Washington University. The name "Columbian" is retained for the College of Arts and Sciences.]

Feb. 19 The Adams-Onis Treaty with Spain is ratified by the U.S. Senate.

Mar. 5 President James Monroe is inaugurated for a second term.

May 31 The Cathedral of the Assumption of the Blessed Virgin Mary, the construction of which was begun in 1806, is dedicated in Baltimore, Maryland. It is the first Roman Catholic cathedral in the United States, and was designed by Benjamin Latrobe.

June 1 Emma Hart Willard, educator and author, founds a woman's school at Waterford, New York. [This Waterford Academy for Young Ladies is soon moved to Troy, New York, where it becomes the Troy Female Seminary, and is later known as the Emma Willard School. It is the first woman's collegiate-level school in the United States.]

Aug. 10 Missouri is admitted to the Union as the 24th state by Presidential proclamation, in accordance with the agreement [Missouri Compromise] arrived at in 1820. The population is just over 65,000. The village of Jefferson City is chosen as the state capital.

Sept. 4 Tsar Alexander I of Russia claims that the southern boundary of Alaska, Russia's territory in North America, is the 51st parallel [the northern end of Vancouver Island, British Columbia], in the Oregon country claimed by both Britain and the United States.

Sept. 18 Amherst College, after having had its first building opened last Aug. 9 with the benefit of an address by Noah Webster, begins to operate with a president, a faculty of 2, and a student body of 47 (15 of them brought over from Williams College by the president). [The college is not chartered by Massachusetts until Feb. 21, 1825, and it is the first to accept a Negro student, who graduates in 1826.]

Nov. 1 The *Walk-in-the-Water,* the first steamboat to ply the Great Lakes, is wrecked and lost in a storm.

Nov. 10 The New York State constitutional convention, under the leadership of the so-called Albany Regency (a radical faction of the Democratic-Republican Party led by Martin Van Buren), abolishes nearly all property qualifications for the right to vote. Free Negroes are not included among the newly enfranchised.

December The Supreme Court of Maryland decides, in the case of *Hall* v. *Mullin,* that a bequest of property to a slave by his owner entitles the slave to freedom by implication, since a slave, by law, cannot own property.

Dec. 3 The 17th Congress convenes with 44 Democratic-Republicans and 4 Federalists in the Senate, and 158 Democratic-Republicans and 25 Federalists in the House.

Dec. 18 A charter is issued to the University of Alabama at Tuscaloosa. [It opens for instruction in 1831.]

1822

Two years before the next Presidential election, state legislatures nominate three candidates, and a total of four are campaigning by the end of the year.

These events are significant in a number of ways. First, the nonexistence of partisan politics, with the demise of the Federalist Party, renders obsolete the traditional selection of Presidential candidates by the party caucuses in Congress. To fill the gap, state legislatures begin to assume the prerogative, and their candidates are likely to be chosen on the basis of personal popularity or as sectional champions. [The device of the party convention has not yet been developed.] Secondly, for the first time in 20 years there is actual doubt as to who will be the next President. Such competition encourages the trend toward relatively universal manhood suffrage and the organization of active local politics. Much of this expansion of "democratic" practice results from the growth in population along the frontier, where there is less reverence for tradition.

January Nicholas Biddle is elected president of the Bank of the United States, succeeding Langdon Cheves.

Jan. 23 The Mississippi state legislature holds its first meeting in the state house at Le Fleur's Bluff, which is re-named Jackson, after the popular general from Tennessee, and has been designated the new state capital, replacing the small town of Washington, east of Natchez.

Mar. 30 Congress approves territorial status for Florida in place of the military organization under General Jackson. [The first territorial legislature decides to move the capital from Pensacola to the site of Tallahassee in 1824. The first elected territorial legislature meets in 1827.]

May 4 President Monroe vetoes a bill authorizing Congress to impose tolls on the Cumberland Road. [The bill fails to pass over his veto.] The President claims that Congress does not have jurisdiction over public improvements, but he recommends passage of a constitutional amendment that would give Congress such authority.

May 30 An informer reveals a plan by slaves in Charleston, South Carolina, to revolt against their masters. [As a result, 134 Negroes are arrested, and 35 are hanged, including the leader, Denmark Vesey, a ship's carpenter who bought his freedom with money won in a lottery.]

June 19 The republic of Colombia, of which the South American hero Simón Bolívar is president, is recognized by the United States. [It comprises the territory in the countries of Colombia, Venezuela, Ecuador, and Panama, and is often called Gran (Greater) Colombia to distinguish it from the present smaller country.]

July 7 William Becknell, a Missouri trader, reaches Santa Fe in Mexico, with three wagonloads of merchandise. The route [the Santa Fe Trail] is 800 miles long, and runs from Independence Rock on the Kansas River westward along the Kansas and Arkansas rivers toward the Rocky Mountains, then south [through Raton Pass] to Santa Fe.

July 20 Andrew Jackson is nominated for President by the legislature of Tennessee. This attempt by a state legislature to perform a function (nomination of a President) hitherto undertaken by a national party caucus is seen by many as a usurpation or radical innovation. [Actually, it heralds the end of the national caucus method of choosing Presidents, and is part of the approaching "Jacksonian democracy."]

Sept. 15 William Henry Ashley and Andrew Henry organize a group of trappers [the "Mountain Men," including Jedediah Smith, Jim Bridger, and the Sublette brothers] systematically to take over the fur operations of the northern Rocky Mountain area. [The resulting Rocky Mountain Fur Company dominates the industry until 1834, when it is superseded by Astor's American Fur Company.

Oct. 27 A 280-mile section of the Erie Canal is opened between Rochester and Albany, New York.

Dec. 12 The United States recognizes the independent Government of Mexico, headed by Agustin de Iturbide, who calls himself "Emperor."

U.S. seaman's uniform, 1810-1830

1823 **Internal commerce and trade are stimulated by a growing** road-building and canal-building fever. This, in turn, helps the country to pull out of a depression that has impeded the economy since 1819. By the end of the year full economic growth has resumed, aided by a phenomenal burst of new industrial activity, which sparks a prodigious rise in foreign trade.

The revolutions in Latin America open up the first foreign markets to American manufactures. By 1822, nearly all of Spain's colonies and Portuguese Brazil have declared and won their independence. But during 1823 it begins to appear probable that France and perhaps other European nations, which have formed a league (the Holy Alliance) to oppose revolutionary movements, will seek to restore to Spain or conquer for themselves the insurgent possessions in Latin America. The United States views these probabilities with alarm. After according recognition to the new countries, the United States begins to formulate a policy aimed at discouraging Europeans from making any attempt to reconquer any land or to establish any more colonies in the New World. A British offer to associate itself with such policy is rejected in favor of independent action based on decisions worked out by Secretary of State John Quincy Adams and President Monroe. The policy is summarized and publicized in the President's annual message to Congress.

February The U.S. Supreme Court decides, in *Green* v. *Biddle,* that a contract clause applies between two states in the same manner as between two persons.

May 8 John Howard Payne's song "Home Sweet Home," composed for his play *Clari, or, the Maid of Milan,* is presented on stage at the Covent Garden Theatre in London. [It is soon to become the most popular song in America.]

June 20 The General Assembly of Tennessee protests that the traditional Congressional caucus to select the candidate for President of the United States is against the spirit of the Constitution for several reasons, chief among them being that it violates the equality secured to smaller states.

July 17 Secretary of State John Quincy Adams, aware that Russia, as a member (along with other European powers) of the Holy Alliance, is committed to the Spanish determination to recover its American colonies, and in delayed response to the ukase of 1821 concerning Alaska, summons the Russian Minister to Washington and informs him that "the American continents are no longer subjects for any new European colonial establishments."

Aug. 16 British Foreign Secretary George Canning, whose Government has recognized a number of the newly independent Latin American republics, suggests joint British-United States resistance against European (Holy Alliance) intervention in the New World.

Sept. 10 New York's Champlain Canal is opened, connecting the Hudson River and Lake Champlain.

Nov. 7 At a Cabinet meeting, President Monroe at first supports the idea of cooperation with Great Britain, as suggested by Canning. But Secretary of State Adams strongly opposes working with the British to prevent further European colonization or conquests in the New World, a policy he describes as "to come in as a cockboat in the wake of the British man-of-war." Monroe accepts Adams' principle of independent action.

Dec. 1 The 18th Congress convenes. It contains 44 Democratic-Republicans and 4 Federalists in the Senate, and 187 Democratic-Republicans and 26 Federalists in the House. Henry Clay is elected Speaker of the House.

Dec. 2 In President Monroe's annual message to Congress, the policy proposed by Secretary of State Adams [the Monroe Doctrine] is formally presented. Its four major points are: (1) "The American continents. . .are henceforth not to be considered as subjects for future colonization by any European powers"; (2) American systems are essentially different from those in Europe; (3) the United States opposes any attempt to extend a European system to any part of the New World; and (4) the United States will not interfere with existing colonies or dependencies, and will not interfere in the internal affairs of European states.

Dec. 23 An anonymous poem appears in the Troy (New York) *Sentinel,* "*A Visit from St. Nicholas.*" [Better known as *"Twas the Night Before Christmas,"* the poem is discovered to be by a professor of Greek and Oriental literature, Clement Clarke Moore, and appeared without his permission. It is included in a collection of his poems published in 1847.]

Boatswain's Mate   Lieutenant, Undress   Boatswain, Full Dress

Midshipman, Full Dress   Purser, Full Dress   Captain, Full Dress

U.S. Navy full dress uniforms (*ca.*) 1830's

1824

Henry Clay introduces his American System, a miscellaneous collection of projects and programs designed to develop the American economy. Some of the specific goals of the system include the building of a network of canals and roads, the creating of a domestic market for American-made goods, and the instituting of protective tariffs for the benefit of American industry. The goals are to be reached through cooperation between Government and private industry. Federalists and Democratic-Republicans can still be identified in Congress: 26 of the former, 187 of the latter. But the Democratic-Republicans are beginning to split into two factions. [These factions are to become new parties—the Democrats and the Whigs—while the Federalists disappear as a national party.] The election is calm, but it is an unusual election, because for the first time purely sectional candidates are nominated and because it cannot be decided in the Electoral College.

January In the case of *Osborn* v. *Bank of the United States,* the U.S. Supreme Court rules that the state of Ohio cannot tax the Bank of the United States. The Court further holds state officials responsible for damages caused by enforcing the Ohio statute (now ruled unconstitutional), and denies these officials the protection of the 11th Amendment.

Feb. 14 Although suffering from the effects of a stroke, William H. Crawford of Georgia is nominated for President by a "rump" Congressional caucus, attended by 66 members out of a total of 187 Democratic-Republicans in Congress. [This is the last time a Congressional caucus nominates a Presidential candidate.]

Feb. 15 John Quincy Adams is nominated for President by the legislature of his home state of Massachusetts.

Mar. 1 Construction begins on New Jersey's Morris County Canal, intended to connect New York City with the Delaware River at its confluence with the Lehigh River.

Mar. 2 The U.S. Supreme Court rules, in the case of *Gibbons* v. *Ogden,* that a monopoly permitted to a steamboat company by a New York State law is unconstitutional, because only the Federal Government has exclusive control over interstate commerce, including navigation on waterways.

Mar. 30 Henry Clay, in a speech before Congress defending his proposed protective tariff, defines his program as "the American System." He indicates that protective tariffs and internal improvements would secure expanding home markets and so decrease American dependence upon foreign goods.

April 17 Russia abandons its claim to the southern portion of Alaska (which includes part of the disputed Oregon country) and accepts, in a treaty, the parallel of 54° 40' as the southern limit of Alaska. [This settlement leaves the ownership of the land west of the Rockies, between 54° 40' and 42°, in dispute between the United States and Great Britain.]

April 30 Congress passes the General Survey Act, which authorizes Federal surveys of routes that have been proposed as national roads. This legislation supports President Monroe's suggestion in 1822 that Congress establish its authority in the field of internal improvements.

May 7 The state of Texas and Coahuila is formed under the new constitution of Mexico. A few thousand Americans have already entered Texas, some (including those in the Austin colony) with official permission, many as squatters. [No attempt to discourage American immigration is made until 1830, when the number of American settlers exceeds 30,000.]

May 22 A tariff is passed that raises the rates on certain items, such as cotton goods, raw wool, and iron. Woolen goods are excluded. Northern and Western producers have for several years sought for such a law against Southern opposition. The South is especially indignant that finished cotton is given an artificially high price, because this is used to clothe slaves and is an important factor in the Southern economy. The passage of this act seems a threat to the South, because it unites the North and West against the South.

May 25 The city of Tallahassee becomes the capital of Florida Territory.

May 26 The United States extends recognition to Brazil.

June 17 The Bureau of Indian Affairs is organized within the War Department. [It is transferred to the Department of the Interior in 1849.]

June 26 In the case of *Bank of United States* v. *Planter's Bank of Georgia,* the U.S. Supreme Court rules that if a state becomes a party to any banking or commercial business, it can be sued as a part of that business.

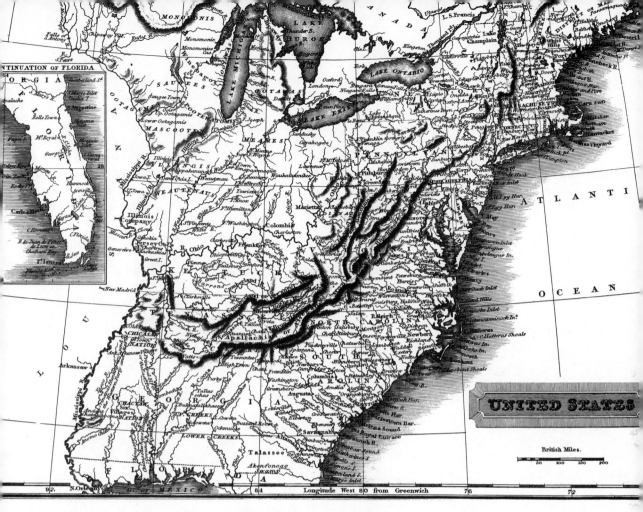

The United States (*ca.*) 1823

Aug. 1   At a convention in Utica, New York, electors to select the state governor and lieutenant governor are chosen by popular vote. [This is one of the first nominating conventions to be held at local government level.]

Aug. 4   The United States extends recognition to the new Central American Union [a short-lived state that includes what are now Costa Rica, Honduras, Guatemala, Nicaragua, and El Salvador].

Aug. 18   Fur trappers Jedediah Smith and William Sublette rediscover (12 years after it was first crossed but unreported by white men) South Pass, a wide gap in the Wind River Range of the northern Rockies. [The pass affords one of the best routes for getting through the Rocky Mountains and over the Continental Divide, and becomes a key section of the Oregon Trail.]

Sept. 20   Jim Bridger, trapper and scout, discovers Great Salt Lake.

Oct. 3   The Rensselaer School of Theoretical and Practical Science is founded at Troy, New York. Its innovative course of studies includes science and engineering rather than the customary classical curriculum. [In 1835 the Rensselaer Institute, as it is then called, produces the first graduates in the United States with degrees in engineering. The name Rensselaer Polytechnic Institute is adopted in 1861.]

December   Indiana enacts a fugitive slave act, empowering any justice of the peace to render decisions on claims for apprehended fugitives. Both fugitive and claimant have the right of a jury trial. [This act is declared unconstitutional in 1850.]

Dec. 1   In the national election, no electoral majority is achieved. Andrew Jackson has 99 votes, followed by John Quincy Adams with 84, William H. Crawford (the "official" Democratic-Republican candidate) with 41, and Henry Clay with 37. The Presidential election has to be decided in the House of Representatives next year. John C. Calhoun, originally a Presidential candidate, easily wins the Vice-Presidential election with 182 electoral votes.

1825

When Congress convenes in January it is faced with the responsibility of choosing a President from the three leading candidates—Jackson, Adams and Crawford—none of whom had gained an electoral majority in the election last year. Backers of the three candidates hope to build up enough votes for their favorite to form a majority within each of state delegations in Congress, and then within Congress itself. (In the election, each state has a single vote.) Jackson eventually secures 11 states, but he needs 13. Adams has 7 states and needs 6 more. Clay, who is out of the running, throws his support to Adams, who acquires more votes as a result of defections from Jackson's followers. (Jackson claims that they were "bought" by Adams.) Adams thus becomes President of the United States.

When it becomes known that Adams has appointed Clay Secretary of State, Jackson charges that a "corrupt bargain" has been made—that Clay traded his support for the promise of appointment. As a consequence, Jackson vigorously opposes Adams at every opportunity during the President's term of office.

One major consequence of the election is the split in the Democratic-Republican Party. The Adams-Clay faction becomes known as the National Republican [in the 1830's, Whig] Party, while the pro-Jackson group retains the name Democratic-Republican [after 1828, Democratic] Party. [These factions are visible in the 19th Congress, where the Adams-Clay group prevails, and in the 20th Congress, dominated by the opposition Jacksonians.]

January The capital of Indiana is transferred from Corydon to Indianapolis.

Jan. 3 Robert Owens, a Scottish mill owner and advocate of model communities for his workers, buys the colony of Harmonie in Indiana, a 20,000-acre estate previously used by George Rapp for a similar social experiment (which failed). [Owens' colony, called New Harmony, lasts three years and costs Owens most of his fortune. Its influence, however, is considerable, giving rise to numerous similar attempts at "Utopian Socialism."]

The keg from which Governor DeWitt Clinton of New York poured Lake Erie water into the Atlantic Ocean to commemorate completion of the Erie Canal.

Feb. 9 John Quincy Adams is chosen President by Congress, winning the votes of 13 of the 24 states. Jackson, who received a plurality of popular votes and of electoral votes, charges corruption.

Feb. 12 A chief of the Creek Indians, William McIntosh, agrees to cede all Creek lands in Georgia and to move his people out of the state. [McIntosh is regarded as a traitor by other Creeks and is killed by them. This Treaty of Indian Springs is repudiated.]

Mar. 4 John Quincy Adams is inaugurated as sixth President of the United States.

Mar. 7 Henry Clay is appointed Secretary of State by Adams.

July 19 The American Unitarian Association is founded by members of the liberal wing of the Congregational community in New England, inspired largely by the sermon preached in 1819 by William Ellery Channing at the ordination of Jarod Sparks of Boston. [It becomes known as the Unitarian Universalist Association in 1961, after combining with Universalists.]

Sept. 6 The city of Akron, Ohio, is laid out by General Simon Perkins at the highest point of the projected Ohio and Erie Canal [completed in 1832], connecting the cities of Portsmouth on the Ohio River and Cleveland on Lake Erie. [The name Akron is derived from a Greek word meaning "high."]

Oct. 26 The Erie Canal is officially opened at Buffalo, New York. It connects the Hudson River with Lake Erie by way of the canalized

Architect Stedman Whitwell's drawing of Robert Owen's model community at New Harmony

Mohawk River, channels in Lake Oneida, and short stretches of various other rivers. The length of the canal is 363 miles; the voyage by water from New York City to the Great Lakes is 550 miles long. [The completion of the canal initiates an era of enormous growth for New York City and other communities all along the route.]

Nov. 4 The New York Drawing Association is founded in New York City by a group of dissatisfied members of the Academy of Arts (founded in 1802), including Samuel F.B. Morse, who becomes its first president. [In 1828 the society is renamed the National Academy of Design.]

Dec. 1 Queen's College at New Brunswick, New Jersey, which was chartered by King George III and founded in 1766, changes its name in honor of Colonel Henry Rutgers, a principal benefactor of the school, to Rutgers College. [In 1924 it becomes Rutgers University.]

Dec. 5 The 19th Congress convenes. Because the Federalist Party does not exist at the national level, and the Democratic-Republican Party has split into two factions, the membership of this Congress can be described only as pro-Administration or anti-Administration. The Administration has 26 members out of the 46 Senators; while in the House 105 favor the Administration and 97 oppose it.

Dec. 6 President Adams outlines a sweeping program of national improvements and reforms in his annual message to Congress. Among his proposals are the foundation of a national university and government support for the arts and sciences.

Dec. 26 President Adams urges Congress to permit the United States to attend, in a consultative capacity, the Panama Congress called by Simón Bolívar to consider a Latin American general confederation. [Congress votes to permit envoys to attend the Panama Congress as observers only.]

1826

In one of the most remarkable coincidences in history, former Presidents Thomas Jefferson and John Adams both die on July 4, 1826, the 50th anniversary of the Declaration of Independence, which they both signed.

Sometime during the night before his death at Monticello, his home in Virginia, Jefferson asks "Is it the Fourth?" Assured that it is, he murmurs "Ah" and peacefully rests. He dies at 12:50 the next afternoon. Far away in Quincy, Massachusetts, John Adams, Jefferson's friend and sometime foe, dies at 5:30. His last words are "Thomas Jefferson still survives."

The revolutionary epoch is at an end. Americans, drawn together by their common grief, mingle with their sense of loss a feeling of triumph. They realize that they have a heritage; Jefferson and Adams, models of civic virtue, symbolize this legacy. To many the incredible conjunction of their deaths with the 50th anniversary of the birth of the nation indicates that God Himself approves of the United States and the beliefs of its people.

Ironically, the unity created by the great event is the last reflection of the Era of Good Feelings. The Founding Fathers, particularly Jefferson, are transformed into symbols of parties and causes. Thomas Jefferson, a man of contradictions, is uniquely fitted to this role. John Adams is more correct than he knows when he says that Jefferson still survives.

Jan. 6   The first number of the *United States Telegraph,* a newspaper edited by Duff Green and opposed to the administration of President John Quincy Adams, appears in Washington.

Jan. 24   The Creek Indians sign the Treaty of Washington, which cedes to the United States a large area, though less territory than an earlier treaty.

Feb. 13   The American Temperance Society, the first national organization to advocate the prohibition of alcoholic beverages, is founded.

Mar. 14   In the first great controversy of the Adams administration, the Senate approves the sending of two delegates to the Congress of the newly independent Latin American republics, scheduled to open at Panama, in the Republic of Colombia, on June 22. [Neither delegate ever reaches the conference.]

Mar. 30   John Randolph of Roanoke, in the course of the Senate debate over the Panama Congress, refers to the coalition of President Adams and Secretary of State Henry Clay as "the combination of the puritan with the blackleg."

April 8   Clay having challenged Randolph as a result of his insult, the two men fight a duel (in which neither is harmed) on the Virginia bank of the Potomac River.

April 26   A treaty of friendship, commerce, and navigation between the United States and Denmark is signed in Washington.

July 4   Former Presidents Thomas Jefferson and John Adams die on the 50th anniversary of American independence.

Aug. 2   Daniel Webster delivers a eulogy on Adams and Jefferson at Faneuil Hall in Boston.

Aug. 22-October   Jedediah Smith, explorer and discoverer of the South Pass in Wyoming, leads the first overland expedition from Utah to California.

Sept. 12   William Morgan, a renegade Freemason, is abducted in Canandaigua , New York. [His supposed murder, ascribed to aggrieved Masons, leads to the formation of the Antimasonic Party.]

Oct. 7   The first railroad in the United States is opened from the quarries at Quincy, Massachusetts, to the Neponset River. The road has metal tracks and the wagons are pulled by horses.

John Adams
(1735-1826)
Signer of the Declaration of Independence

Thomas Jefferson
(1743-1826)
Signer of the Declaration of Independence

1827

The tariff of 1824 having failed to end competition from Britain, the Northeastern wool and woolen interests seek higher duties on wool products. A bill is introduced into Congress placing minimum valuations of woolen goods so high that their importation is practically prohibited. The bill passes in the House of Representatives, but is defeated in the Senate by the tie-breaking vote of Vice President John C. Calhoun of South Carolina. The bill's rejection arouses protectionist forces in the manufacturing centers of the North. A convention attended by 100 delegates from 13 of the 24 states meets at Harrisburg, Pennsylvania, and demands higher tariffs on a variety of goods. The memorial of the convention is presented to Congress. Meanwhile, at a meeting in Columbia, South Carolina, Thomas Cooper, who had gone to jail in defense of civil liberties and has become a university president, defines the tariff issue in sectional terms.

Jan. 10   A tariff bill placing such high minimum valuations on woolens as to prohibit their importation is introduced in Congress.

Feb. 2   In *Martin* v. *Mott*, the Supreme Court declares that the President is the sole judge of the conditions under which he is authorized to call out the militia.

Feb. 7   Mme. Francisque Hutin makes her ballet debut at the Bowery Theater in New York City, introducing the new technique of toe dancing.

Feb. 10   The woolens bill, favored by Northern manufacturers and opposed in the South, passes in the House of Representatives.

Feb. 17   Governor George M. Troup of Georgia calls out the state militia to resist U.S. troops, who are on the scene to prevent the premature surveying of the Creek Indian lands. Although the Creeks ceded these lands in 1826, their transfer has not been completed.

Feb. 28   The woolens bill is killed in the Senate by the casting vote of Vice President Calhoun.

Feb. 28   The Baltimore and Ohio Railroad Company is incorporated in Maryland. It is the first railroad to receive a charter in the United States to carry passengers and freight.

Mar. 13   The Supreme Court decides, in *Ogden* v. *Saunders*, that a contract made after the passage of a bankruptcy law is limited by the provisions of such a law.

July 2   Thomas Cooper, the president of South Carolina College and a militant Jeffersonian, condemns protective tariffs at a meeting in Columbia, South Carolina.

July 30   A convention of 100 protectionists from 13 states convenes in Harrisburg, Pennsylvania.

Aug. 6   The United States and Great Britain conclude a treaty in which they renew their commercial agreements of 1818 and agree to continue their joint occupation of Oregon.

Aug. 14   Journeymen tailors strike in Philadelphia.

Nov. 15   The Creek Indians cede to the Federal Government all their lands in Georgia that were not surrendered by the treaty of 1826.

Dec. 3   The anti-Administration faction controls the 20th Congress, with 26 Senators and 119 Representatives; the Administration has only 20 Senators and 94 members of the House of Representatives.

Geological map of the United States (ca) 1830's

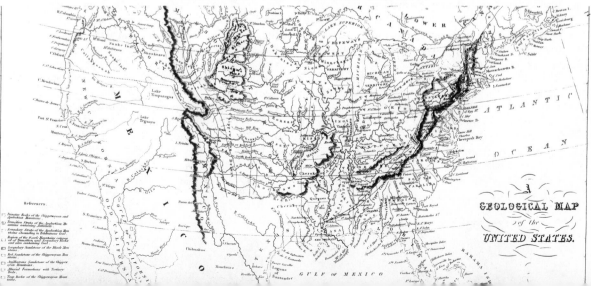

1828 The 20th Congress is dominated by the "Jackson men," supporters of Andrew Jackson and opponents of President John Quincy Adams. The Jacksonians may be attempting to use the tariff issue to discredit Adams. In any event, the Committee on Manufactures of the House of Representatives frames a bill that raises the duties on raw materials, iron, hemp, and flax and reduces the protection against imported woolens. The House passes this measure without amending it. The Senate modifies the provisions concerning woolen goods, making the bill acceptable to New England. Consequently, it passes in the Senate and is again approved in the House. President Adams signs what is labeled by some as the "Tariff of Abominations." The legislature of South Carolina adopts a set of eight resolutions declaring that the tariff is unconstitutional, oppressive, and unjust. The Georgia legislature also protests against the tariff. Accompanying the South Carolina resolves is the *South Carolina Exposition and Protest,* anonymously written by John C. Calhoun. In this lengthy essay Calhoun expounds the doctrine of nullification. He argues that a single state may interpose its authority to block the enforcement of a national law it considers to be unconstitutional. It is clear that Calhoun has abandoned his earlier nationalism and become a sectionalist.

Jan. 12   A treaty is signed between Mexico and the United States reaffirming the transcontinental boundary as established in the treaty with Spain of 1819.

Jan. 30   The South Carolina Canal and Railroad Company is incorporated. [This company is to construct the line known as the Charleston and Hamburg Railroad.]

Jan. 31   A tariff bill is introduced into the House of Representatives.

Feb. 11   Governor De Witt Clinton of New York, 58, dies in Albany.

Feb. 21   The Cherokee Indians of northern Georgia publish the first newspaper ever to appear in an Indian language, the *Cherokee Phoenix.*

Mar. 4-April 23   Debate on the tariff bill begins in the House, and on April 23 is passed by a vote of 105 to 94. [On May 13 the Senate passes the bill by a vote of 26 to 21.]

Mar. 24   The Pennsylvania legislature agrees to grant money for the construction of a railroad between Philadelphia and Columbia, said to be the first such undertaking by a government.

April 21   Noah Webster's *American Dictionary of the English Language* is published.

May 19   President John Quincy Adams signs the "Tariff of Abominations."

May 24   The Reciprocity Act, which offers the abolition of all discriminatory trade duties to reciprocating nations, is approved.

July 4   Charles Carroll, the last surviving signer of the Declaration of Independence, inaugurates construction on the Baltimore and Ohio Railroad, chartered in 1827. [When its initial section is opened in 1830 it is the first passenger railroad in the United States.]

Oct. 16   The Delaware and Hudson Canal is opened, connecting Honesdale, Pennsylvania, with Rondout, New York. This canal taps the anthracite coal region of northeastern Pennsylvania and makes this fuel available to the cities of New York and New England.

Dec. 3   Andrew Jackson of Tennessee, a Democrat, is elected President over the incumbent President, John Quincy Adams of Massachusetts, a National Republican. Jackson receives 648,286 popular votes and 178 electoral votes. Adams wins 508,064 popular and 83 electoral votes. Jackson captures New York, Pennsylvania, and the South and West. Adams carries New England, New Jersey, Delaware, and Maryland. The crucial state of New York goes for Jackson under the influence of Governor-elect Martin Van Buren, whose power is maintained by exercise of the "spoils system." Democrat John C. Calhoun of South Carolina is reelected Vice President, defeating the National Republican candidate, Richard Rush of Pennsylvania. Calhoun wins 171 electoral votes, Rush receives 83, and 7 are cast for William Smith of South Carolina, like Calhoun a Democrat.

Dec. 19   The South Carolina legislature adopts eight resolutions calling the "Tariff of Abominations" unconstitutional, oppressive, and unjust. The legislature orders the publication of the *South Carolina Exposition and Protest,* anonymously written by Calhoun. This document expounds the doctrine of nullification.

Dec. 20   A state law is approved in Georgia declaring that the laws of the Cherokee nation will be null and void after June 1, 1830.

Dec. 30   The legislature of Georgia condemns the tariff.

John Quincy Adams
SIXTH PRESIDENT   **1825-1829**

Ki-on-twog-ky, a Seneca chief

See-non-ty-a. An Iowa medicine man

The White Cloud, chief of the Iowa's

Andrew Jackson
SEVENTH PRESIDENT   1829-1837

Martin Van Buren
EIGHTH PRESIDENT   1837-1841

1829

Andrew Jackson of Tennessee becomes the seventh President of the United States. His victory is seen as a vindication of the common man. In his virtually inaudible inaugural address, Jackson promises governmental economy, the protection of the rights of the states, a "just and liberal" Indian policy, and civil service reform. After the ceremony, so many people follow the President to the reception at the White House that refreshments are placed on the lawn to keep part of the crowd outside. Secretary of State Martin Van Buren of New York is the most important figure in Jackson's Cabinet. The other members are Samuel D. Ingham of Pennsylvania, the Secretary of the Treasury; John Branch of North Carolina, the Secretary of the Navy; John M. Berrien of Georgia, the Attorney General; William T. Barry of Kentucky, the Postmaster General; and John H. Eaton of Tennessee, the Secretary of War. More influential than the official Cabinet is a group of unofficial advisors, called the "Kitchen Cabinet" by Jackson's opponents. These men include Van Buren, Amos Kendall, Isaac Hill, Francis Preston Blair, and William B. Lewis. Jackson is a believer in rotation in office. In practice this means the introduction of the "spoils system," whereby appointments are given to political partisans. Nevertheless, Jackson does not make wholesale removals of officeholders.

Jan. 9 A bill proposing the establishment of a territorial government for Oregon and the erection of a fort there is defeated in the House of Representatives.

Feb. 5 The Mississippi legislature declares that the "Tariff of Abominations" is "contrary to the spirit of the Constitution."

Feb. 24 The legislature of Virginia declares the tariff of 1828 unconstitutional.

Mar. 2 The first school for the blind in the United States, the New England Asylum for the Blind, founded by Dr. John Dix Fisher, is incorporated in Boston.

Mar. 4 Andrew Jackson is inaugurated as the seventh President of the United States and John C. Calhoun of South Carolina begins his second term as Vice President. Jackson delivers his address in a low voice. A boisterous reception in the White House follows.

Mar. 23 In a message to the Creek Indians, President Jackson tells them to accept subjection to the laws of Alabama or to move across the Mississippi River.

April 18 Secretary of War Eaton tells the Cherokee Indians to subject themselves to the laws of Georgia or to move to the area beyond the Mississippi River.

May 17 John Jay, 84, the first Chief Justice of the United States and a former governor of New York, dies in Bedford, New York.

May 29 The cornerstone of the first lock of the Chesapeake and Ohio Canal is laid near Georgetown.

June 4 The *Fulton the First,* a steamship, blows up in New York Harbor.

July 29 The Chippewa, Ottawa, and Potawatomi Indians cede land in Michigan Territory.

Aug. 8 The first self-propelled steam engine [locomotive] in the United States, the English-built *Stourbridge Lion,* is run on the Delaware and Hudson Canal Company's railroad from Carbondale to Honesdale in Pennsylvania.

Aug. 25 On the instructions of President Jackson, Secretary of State Van Buren directs Joel R. Poinsett, the U.S. Minister in Mexico, to open negotiations for the purchase of the department of Texas, in the state of Texas and Coahuila. Thousands of American settlers, led by Stephen Austin, hold land on the Brazos River in that area.

Oct. 16 Poinsett is recalled from Mexico at the request of the Mexican Government.

Oct. 16 The Tremont House opens in Boston, Massachusetts. It has 170 bedrooms, a few with water closets, a recently imported accommodation not generally found in buildings.

Oct. 17 Anthony Butler is instructed to continue negotiations with Mexico and to act as chargé d'affaires.

Oct. 17 A 14-mile-long canal connecting Chesapeake Bay with the Delaware River is formally opened. The construction costs are shared by private citizens and the Governments of the United States and neighboring states.

Dec. 8 In his first annual message to Congress, President Jackson questions the constitutionality of the Bank of the United States and proposes the distribution of surplus Federal revenues among the states.

The Senate debates the expediency of temporarily restricting the sale of public lands. Senator Thomas Hart Benton of Missouri charges that this is an attempt to check the settlement of the West so that the Northeast may keep a supply of cheap labor for its factories. He is supported by Senator Robert Y. Hayne of South Carolina, who argues for a cheap land policy. He warns that great revenues from land sales will breed corruption and undermine the independence of the states, and condemns the consolidation of the national Government. Senator Daniel Webster of Massachusetts answers Benton and Hayne. He defends his section, proposes low land prices, denies that the revenue is corrupting, and rejoices in the potential of the Federal Government. Hayne then advances the doctrines of state sovereignty and nullification and recalls the sectionalism of New England at the time of the War of 1812. In the course of an eloquent speech, Webster rejects nullification and declares that state sovereignty is limited. Attacking disunionist tendencies, he concludes with the words, "Liberty *and* Union, now and forever, one and inseparable!" This debate reveals the growing alliance between the South and the West against the East, and the shift of the advocacy for states' as against national rights from New England to the South and the West.

Jan. 13   A resolution introduced two weeks ago by Senator Samuel A. Foot of Connecticut, inquiring into the expediency of temporarily restricting the sale of public lands, is taken up in the Senate.

Jan. 18-27   Full-scale debate on the public lands question occupies the Senate. Senator Thomas Hart Benton of Missouri charges that the East is attempting to check the settlement of the West. The next day Senator Robert Y. Hayne of South Carolina comes to the support of Benton and the West; Senator Daniel Webster of Massachusetts answers Benton and Hayne, defending the East. Hayne, in his first reply to Webster, supports states' rights and nullification, whereupon Webster eloquently defends a national view of the Constitution. In rebuttal, Hayne maintains that the Federal government began as a compact between the states, but Webster argues that it originated as a popular government, and must prevail. The question of public lands is almost forgotten in the heat of the constitutional dispute.

Jan. 19   A law is passed in Mississippi that extends the jurisdiction of the state over the Indians within its borders.

Feb. 4   The first railroad in New Jersey, the Camden and Amboy, receives a charter.

Mar. 12   In *Craig* v. *Missouri,* the U.S. Supreme Court declares that state loan certificates receivable in discharge of taxes and debts due the state are bills of credit and are therefore unconstitutional.

Mar. 15   By a joint resolution, the Louisiana legislature supports the protective tariff.

Mar. 28   A treaty providing for the adjustment of indemnity claims is signed by the United States and Denmark.

April 6   The Mexican Government approves laws to keep U.S. settlers from further colonizing or introducing traffic in Negro slaves in its territory.

April 6   The Church of Jesus Christ of Latter-day Saints, the Mormon Church, is organized by Joseph Smith in Fayette, New York.

April 13   At a Jefferson Day dinner in Washington, President Jackson delivers this toast: "Our Federal Union. It must be preserved." Vice President Calhoun replies: "The Union—next to our liberty the most dear. . . ."

May 7   A treaty of commerce and navigation between the United States and the Ottoman Empire [Turkey] is signed, opening the Black Sea to American ships.

May 20   Congress reduces the duties on tea, coffee, and cocoa.

May 21   The Foot resolution is tabled in the Senate.

May 24   The first section of about 13 miles is opened on the Baltimore and Ohio Railroad between Baltimore and Ellicott's Mills.

May 27   President Jackson issues his first veto, against a bill that authorizes a Goverment subscription to the stock of the Maysville, Washington, Paris and Lexington Turnpike Road Company in Kentucky. Jackson declares that, because the road is within one state and is not connected to a system, it is local rather than national in character and therefore cannot be constitutionally supported by Federal funds.

May 28   President Jackson signs an act providing for the compulsory resettlement of all Indians west of the Mississippi River.

May 29   Congress reduces the duties on molasses and salt.

A contemporary cartoonist's view of the consequences of
Jackson's financial policies

May 29 The President is authorized to open American ports to British ships whenever British colonial ports are opened to American vessels without discrimination.

May 31 Jackson vetoes a bill authorizing a Federal subscription to the stock of the Washington Turnpike Road Company, calling it a local project. He approves a bill extending the Cumberland Road, terming this a national project.

July 15 The Sac and Fox Indians of the central Mississippi Valley, despite the objections of their chief, Black Hawk, cede all their lands east of the river to the United States.

Aug. 28 Peter Cooper's *Tom Thumb,* the first American-built locomotive, is used on the Baltimore and Ohio Railroad from Baltimore to Ellicott's Mills.

Sept. 11 The Antimasonic Party acquires national status by holding a convention in Philadelphia, following its successes in drawing votes in New York State.

Sept. 15 The Choctaw Indians, in a treaty at Dancing Rabbit Creek, cede their lands east of the Mississippi River to the United States.

Sept. 18 Returning to Baltimore, the *Tom Thumb* races a horse and loses.

Oct. 5 President Jackson proclaims the reestablishment of trade with the British West Indies.

Nov. 2 The *Best Friend of Charleston,* the first locomotive built for actual service in the United States, makes a trip on the Charleston and Hamburg Railroad in South Carolina.

Dec. 6 In his annual message to Congress, President Jackson opposes all Federal grants for local internal improvements, attacks the Bank of the United States, confirms his support for the principle of protection, and proposes the distribution of the surplus revenue among the states so that they may fund internal improvements.

Dec. 7 The first number of the *Washington Globe* appears. It is an Administration paper edited by Francis Preston Blair of Kentucky.

1831

The breach between President Andrew Jackson and Vice President John C. Calhoun, made evident by their dramatic confrontation at the Jefferson Day dinner in 1830, results in a reorganization of the Cabinet. Secretary of State Martin Van Buren and his supporters have encouraged the rift so that Van Buren rather than Calhoun might succeed Jackson. Contributing to the split was the Eaton affair. James H. Eaton, before becoming Secretary of War, had married the beautiful Margaret (Peggy) O'Neale Timberlake, the daughter of a Washington tavern keeper and widow of a navy purser. Gossip concerning Mrs. Eaton's background influenced Mrs. Floride Calhoun, a South Carolina aristocrat, and the wives of the Cabinet members to snub Mrs. Eaton. Jackson, who is sensitive because the late Mrs. Jackson had been the victim of similar spite, attempts unsuccessfully to compel the social acceptance of Peggy Eaton. Van Buren supports the President in his effort, thereby further improving his relationship with Jackson, while Calhoun is alienated from the President. At the opportune moment, Van Buren precipitates a reorganization of the Cabinet by indicating his intention to resign. Eaton submits his own resignation, and Jackson then requests and receives the resignations of other Cabinet members, all followers of Calhoun. [Van Buren is named Minister to Great Britain later in the year. His followers soon dominate the Democratic leadership, and Calhoun loses his role as a national figure.]

Jan. 1 The first issue of the *Liberator,* a militant abolitionist newspaper edited and published by William Lloyd Garrison and Isaac Knapp, appears in Boston, Massachusetts. Its motto is "Our Country Is the World—Our Countrymen Are Mankind."

Feb. 2 Senator Thomas Hart Benton of Missouri calls the Bank of the United States an institution "too great and powerful to be tolerated in a Government of free and equal laws," and opens the debate over the question of renewing the bank's charter in 1836.

Feb. 3 Congress amends the copyright law, extending the term from 14 to 28 years, allowing renewal for 14 additional years, and permitting renewal by an author's wife and children in case of his death.

Mar. 18 The U.S. Supreme Court, in *Cherokee Nation* v. *Georgia,* denies an injunction against Georgia on behalf of the Indian nation under the terms of a treaty of 1791, on the grounds that the Cherokees are not a foreign nation and therefore the Court lacks jurisdiction.

April 5 A treaty of amity, commerce, and navigation between the United States and Mexico is signed.

April 7 Secretary of War John H. Eaton resigns after finding his Cabinet position untenable because of the hostility of Vice President Calhoun toward Mrs. Eaton. [On April 11, in a related gesture, Secretary of State Martin Van Buren also resigns, precipitating a Cabinet shakeup.]

April 18 The University of the City of New York is chartered. [In 1896 it is renamed New York University.]

April 26 New York State abolishes imprisonment for debt, effective Mar. 1, 1832.

June 21 The colossal statue of George Washington by the celebrated Italian sculptor, Antonio Canova, an ornament of the State House at Raleigh, North Carolina, since 1821, is destroyed by fire.

July 4 "America," by Samuel Francis Smith, is first sung in Boston, Massachusetts.

July 4 Former President James Monroe, 73, dies in New York City. His last public service was as president of the state constitutional convention of 1828-1829, in which he took a conservative position against the extension of voting rights.

July 20 Roger B. Taney of Maryland is appointed Attorney General.

July 26 Vice President Calhoun reaffirms and elaborates the doctrine of nullification in the "Fort Hill Letter," taking the position that the same right which had empowered the states to set up the Federal Government for their own collective and individual best interests likewise empowers the states to declare invalid any action taken by the Federal Government inimical to their best interests.

Aug. 1 Lewis Cass of Ohio is appointed Secretary of War.

Aug. 8 Louis McLane of Delaware is appointed Secretary of the Treasury.

Aug. 9 The *De Witt Clinton,* the first steam locomotive operated in New York State, is placed in service on the Mohawk and Hudson Railroad between Albany and Schenectady.

Aug. 13-23   Nat Turner, a Negro preacher, leads a slave insurrection in Southampton County, Virginia. About 60 whites are killed during the revolt, possibly 100 Negroes are killed during the ensuing manhunt, and 20 Negroes, including Turner, are executed after trial.

Sept. 26   The Anti-Masonic Party holds a national convention at Baltimore, nominating former Attorney General William Wirt of Maryland for President and Amos Ellmaker of Pennsylvania for Vice President. [This national nominating convention sets a precedent soon adopted by the new major parties.]

Nov. 12   The English-built locomotive *John Bull* enters regular passenger service on the Camden and Amboy Railroad [later part of the Pennsylvania Railroad] in New Jersey.

Dec. 5   In the 22d Congress, the Democrats retain control, with a continuing narrow margin in the Senate of 25 Democrats and 21 National Republicans, but an even larger majority in the House of Representatives, which has 141 Democrats and 58 National Republicans. (Minority or independent members hold 14 seats in the lower House.)

Dec. 12   The National Republican Party meets in convention at Baltimore. Henry Clay of Kentucky is nominated for President and John Sergeant of Pennsylvania for Vice President. The party platform attacks President Jackson for abusing patronage and the veto power, endorses Henry Clay's "American System" of protective tariffs and federally aided internal improvements, and demands the rechartering of the Bank of the United States.

Dec. 12   Former President John Quincy Adams, now a Congressman from Massachusetts, presents in the House 15 petitions from Pennsylvania calling for the abolition of slavery in the District of Columbia.

The Cabinet Maker

1832

President Andrew Jackson is challenged by nullification in South Carolina, and he himself challenges the Bank of the United States by vetoing the bill renewing its charter. This veto becomes the major issue in a campaign for the Presidency that ends in Jackson's overwhelming reelection.

The nullification controversy has its origin in a tariff bill which, although it is milder than the Tariff of Abominations of 1828, is still protective. South Carolina, particularly, objects to protective tariffs in principle, and a special state convention adopts an ordinance nullifying both tariff acts, that of 1828 and that of 1832.

President Jackson is at once conciliatory and firm. He calls for a substantial reduction of tariff duties in his annual message to Congress. Then he issues a "Proclamation to the People of South Carolina," in which he rejects nullification and secession, asserting that the Federal Government is sovereign and indivisible. He warns: "Disunion by armed force is *treason.*" The South Carolina legislature adopts a series of defiant resolutions replying to Jackson's proclamation, and the new governor, Robert Y. Hayne (who bequeaths his Senate seat to Calhoun), issues a counterproclamation. Calhoun resigns as Vice President to become more effective as a Senator.

Meanwhile, the question of rechartering the Bank of the United States has become a great political issue, although the charter will not expire until 1836. The bank's president, Nicholas Biddle, takes the advice of Henry Clay and Daniel Webster and applies for renewal; authority to renew passes the House and the Senate; the President vetoes the bill, creating thereby the chief issue in the Presidential election campaign.

The National Republican and Anti-Masonic parties have already held their conventions in 1831. The Democratic Republicans—now officially the Democratic Party—hold their first national convention and endorse Andrew Jackson for a second term. In place of Calhoun they nominate Martin Van Buren as Jackson's running mate; Calhoun is no longer in their ranks. The Jackson-Van Buren ticket wins overwhelming victory at the polls.

Jan. 6   The New England Anti-Slavery Society is formed, with a program largely based on the thinking of William Lloyd Garrison, who opposes the resettlement of Negroes in Africa.

Jan. 25   In the U.S. Senate, William Learned Marcy of New York, in the course of defending the nomination of Martin Van Buren to be Minister to Great Britain, originates the phrase, "to the victors belong the spoils."

Jan. 25   The Senate rejects President Jackson's nomination of Van Buren as Minister to Great Britain. Vice President Calhoun casts the deciding ballot, breaking a tie vote, in the hope that the rejection will end Van Buren's political career. [It has the opposite effect.]

Mar. 3   In *Worcester* v. *Georgia,* the U.S. Supreme Court declares that the Federal Government has exclusive jurisdiction over Indian tribes and their lands within a state. [Georgia ignores the Court, and is supported by President Jackson, who is reported to exclaim: "(Chief Justice) John Marshall has made his decision: now let him enforce it!"]

April 6   Chief Black Hawk of the Sac and Fox Indians leads his tribes back across the Mississippi River into Illinois, in violation of a treaty of 1830 (to which he never agreed).

May 1   An expedition under Captain Benjamin L.E. Bonneville leaves Fort Osage on the Missouri River, beginning a three-year exploration of the West.

May 9   In the Treaty of Payne's Landing, some chiefs of the Seminole Indians agree to cede their tribe's lands in Florida and to move across the Mississippi River.

May 16   A treaty of peace, amity, commerce, and navigation between the United States and Chile is concluded in Santiago.

May 21-22   The first national nominating convention of the Democratic Party (as the Jacksonian faction of the Democratic-Republicans is now formally called) is held in Baltimore. President Jackson is unanimously endorsed for a second term. Martin Van Buren is named to run as Vice President. No party platform is adopted, but the party decides that all votes at its convention must receive a two-thirds majority to be accepted. [This "two-thirds rule" is retained by the Democratic Party until 1936.]

May 23   John Quincy Adams, chairman of the Committee on Manufactures of the House of Representatives, reports a tariff bill that lowers duties from the level of the Tariff of Abmonations of 1828, but retains the protective principle.

June 11 A bill to renew the charter of the Bank of the United States, which is due to expire in 1836, passes in the Senate by a vote of 28 to 20.

June 23 The U.S. Senate, by a vote of 21 to 20, rejects the award recommended by the King of the Netherlands in the matter of the border between Maine and Canada, which he was asked to arbitrate in 1828. King William I reported last year that about 8,000 square miles (of a total 12,000 square miles) should be allotted to the United States. [The continued dispute results in minor armed conflict on the Maine border in 1838-1839 and is not settled until 1842.]

July 3 The bank bill is approved in the House of Representatives by a vote of 107 to 85.

July 10 President Jackson vetoes the bill renewing the charter of the Bank of the United States. [The Senate fails, by a vote of 22 to 19, to override Jackson's veto of the bank bill.]

July 13 Henry R. Schoolcraft and an exploring party discover that the true source of the Mississippi River is Lake Itasca in the extreme western part of Michigan Territory [Minnesota].

July 14 The tariff act of 1832 is signed by President Jackson. [South Carolina's Congressmen publish an address to their constituents urging resistance to the tariff.]

Aug. 2 The Sac and Fox Indians are defeated by the Illinois militia after having been ambushed and massacred at the mouth of the Bad Axe River in Michigan Territory north of the Illinois line. [On Aug. 27 Chief Black Hawk is surrendered to the militia by the Winnebago Indians, with whom he took refuge. On Sept. 21 the Sac and Fox agree by treaty to remain west of the Mississippi River.]

Oct. 14 The Chickasaw Indians cede to the United States all their remaining lands east of the Mississippi River.

Oct. 26 A convention in Mississippi adopts a new state constitution that makes many offices elective.

Nov. 14 Charles Carroll, 95, the last surviving signer of the Declaration of Independence, dies in Baltimore.

Nov. 19-27 A state convention meets at Columbia, South Carolina, and on Nov. 24 adopts an ordinance nullifying the tariff acts of 1828 and 1832. Specifically, the tariff of 1832 is declared null and void as of Feb. 1, 1833, and the right to secede from the Union is invoked if the authority of the state should be challenged by the use of force on the part of the Federal Government. The South Carolina legislature then passes laws to enforce the ordinance.

Nov. 26 The world's first streetcar is placed in service by the New York and Harlem Railroad in New York City.

Dec. 4 In his annual message to Congress, President Jackson calls for the reduction of the tariff. Many assume that he is trying to placate the South Carolina firebrands.

Dec. 5 President Jackson is reelected over Senator Henry Clay of Kentucky, the National Republican candidate, and William Wirt of Maryland, the Anti-Masonic nominee. Jackson wins 687,502 popular and 219 electoral votes, Clay receives 530,189 popular and 49 electoral votes, and 33,108 popular and 7 electoral votes (those of Vermont) are cast for Wirt. The South Carolina legislature, in protest against Jackson's position on the tariff and nullification issues, casts its 11 electoral votes for John Floyd of Virginia for President.

Dec. 20 Governor Robert Y. Hayne of South Carolina, who has resigned from the U.S. Senate to open a vacancy for Calhoun, issues a statement that defies President Jackson's proclamation.

Dec. 28 John C. Calhoun resigns as Vice President to take Hayne's seat in the U.S. Senate.

Dec. 28 St. Louis College, in St. Louis, Missouri, founded as St. Louis Academy in 1818 and known as a college since 1820, is granted a charter as St. Louis University. It was originally a French-language institution, but its courses are now conducted in English, and it is the only Roman Catholic university west of the Appalachian Mountains.

Charles Carroll
(1737-1832)
Signer of the Declaration of Independence

In the face of the nullification of the tariff laws by South Carolina, President Andrew Jackson asks Congress for the authority to enforce the collection of duties. The statute authorizing the requested powers is popularly called the "Force Bill." Meanwhile, Senator Henry Clay of Kentucky introduces a compromise tariff bill, which he has devised after consultation with Senator John C. Calhoun of South Carolina and others. The Force Bill and the compromise tariff are signed by President Jackson on the same day.

As the nullification crisis recedes, renewed controversy occurs concerning the Bank of the United States. President Jackson asks his Cabinet for their opinions concerning the disposition of Federal deposits. Attorney General Roger B. Taney, who favors removal of the deposits from the Bank of the United States and their distribution among various state banks, finally is appointed to head the Treasury Department after two successive Secretaries of the Treasury, Louis McLane and William J. Duane, refuse to follow the President's orders. When Taney begins to remove the deposits to state banks, popularly called "pet banks," the Senate requests a copy of the paper Jackson read to the Cabinet. [The President refuses to supply it.]

Jan. 16   President Jackson asks Congress for the power to enforce the tariff law in the face of the South Carolina nullification ordinance.

Feb. 12   Henry Clay introduces a compromise tariff bill in the Senate. This bill [often called by historians the Compromise of 1833] proposes to decrease tariffs over a 10-year period to a maximum of 20 per cent. The compromise is acceptable to most Southern states and leaves South Carolina isolated.

Feb. 16   In *Barron* v. *Baltimore,* the U.S. Supreme Court rules that the provisions of the first 10 Ammendments to the Constitution (the Bill of Rights) are not binding on state governments.

Feb. 20   The Force Bill, granting the President the powers he needs to enforce the tariff statute, passes the Senate by a vote of 32 to 1. The sole negative vote is cast by John Tyler of Virginia.

Feb. 26   The Clay compromise tariff bill is approved in the House of Representatives, 119 to 85.

Mar. 1   The House passes the Force Bill, 149 to 47.

Mar. 1   The Senate approves the compromise tariff bill, 29 to 16.

Mar. 2   President Jackson signs both the Force Bill and the tariff bill.

Mar. 4   President Jackson is inaugurated for a second term; Martin Van Buren becomes Vice President.

Mar. 11-18   The state convention in South Carolina reconvenes. On Mar. 15 it rescinds its Ordinance of Nullification concerning the tariff. Before it adjourns, however, it adopts an ordinance nullifying the Force Bill.

Mar. 20   A treaty of amity and commerce is signed between the United States and Siam in Bangkok.

June 1   Secretary of the Treasury Louis McLane, having refused to follow the President's orders concerning the depositing of Federal funds in state banks, is appointed Secretary of State, and William J. Duane of Pennsylvania is appointed Secretary of the Treasury.

Sept. 3   The first issue of the New York *Sun,* a novel kind of newspaper, appears in New York City. Selling for only one penny, it is smaller than its six-cent competitors and tries to print news of interest to a larger segment of the population. Benjamin H. Day, a 23 year-old journalist from Worcester, Massachusetts, is the publisher.

Sept. 18   President Jackson reads to his Cabinet a paper drafted by Attorney General Roger B. Taney that lists the reasons for removing Federal deposits from the Bank of the United States.

Sept. 21   A treaty of amity and commerce between the United States and the Sultan of Muscat is signed in Muscat.

Sept. 23   Secretary of the Treasury Duane, who also refuses to remove the deposits from the Bank of the United States, is replaced by Attorney General Taney. [On Sept. 26, Taney issues the first order for their removal, which begins on Oct. 1.]

Nov. 15   Benjamin F. Butler of New York is appointed Attorney General.

Dec. 26   Henry Clay offers two resolutions of censure against Jackson for his plan to remove deposits from the Bank of the United States.

1834

Henry Clay, looking forward to the next opportunity to challenge President Jackson, sponsors two resolutions of censure against the President in the Senate. One declares that the stated reasons for removing the Federal deposits from the Bank of the United States are "unsatisfactory and insufficient." The other maintains that, by dismissing Secretary of the Treasury William J. Duane and appointing Attorney General Roger B. Taney in his place in order to effect the removal of the deposits, "the President. . .has assumed upon himself authority and power not conferred by the Constitution and laws, but in derogation of both." However, Jackson's supporters manage to put the House of Representatives on record in favor of the Administration's bank policy. President Jackson protests to the Senate concerning its vote to censure him, but the Senate refuses to enter the protest in its journals. In addition, the Senate rejects the nomination of Taney to be Secretary of the Treasury. The opposition to Jackson, exemplified by the censuring resolution, results in the formation of a new political party. Opposed to "King Andrew I," the members of the new party make a point of their anti-Tory position by calling themselves "Whigs." The loose coalition that comprises the Whig Party includes such diverse groups as the National Republicans, led by Henry Clay and Daniel Webster, and the advocates of States' Rights, led by John C. Calhoun.

Jan. 3   Stephen F. Austin is arrested at Saltillo in Mexico after presenting to President Antonio López de Santa Anna the demands of American colonists that Texas be made a separate state of Mexico. The arrest is based on interception of a letter written by Austin, urging that preparations be made to accomplish the separation of Texas despite Santa Anna's rejection of the proposal.

Feb. 17   Claims against Spain for the illegal capture of American ships during the revolt of the Spanish colonies are settled by a convention signed in Madrid.

Mar. 28   The U.S. Senate approves, by votes of 28 to 18 and 26 to 20, two censuring resolutions introduced by Henry Clay criticizing President Jackson for the removal of Federal deposits from the Bank of the United States. [The resolution is expunged from the Senate journal on Jan. 16, 1837.]

April 4   The House of Representatives passes four resolutions sustaining the bank policy of the Jackson Administration.

April 15   President Jackson makes a formal protest to the Senate concerning its resolution of censure.

May 7   By a vote of 27 to 16 the Senate refuses to enter Jackson's protest in its journals.

June 21   Cyrus Hall McCormick receives a patent for a mechanical mower and reaper, a machine that cuts grain as it advances across the field and then ejects the cut grain in quantities sufficient to be tied into a sheaf.

June 24   The Senate refuses to approve the appointment of Roger B. Taney as Secretary of the Treasury.

June 27   Navy Secretary Levi Woodbury is appointed Secretary of the Treasury, and John Forsyth of Georgia is appointed Secretary of State.

June 28   The Second Coinage Act establishes the ratio of 16 to 1 between silver and gold.

June 30   Congress redefines the duties of the Bureau of Indian Affairs, and sets aside as an unorganized Indian Territory the western part of Arkansas Territory [most of the present state of Oklahoma]. This Indian Territory is to be reserved for Indians to be removed from the East.

July 15   Fur trader Nathaniel J. Wyeth begins to build Fort Hall, on the Snake River in the Oregon country [Idaho]. [The outpost soon becomes the property of the Hudson's Bay Company, and later is a shelter on the Oregon Trail.]

Aug. 30   A new constitution for Tennessee is adopted by a convention at Nashville.

Oct. 1   In a letter to the Workingmen (a radical political party of Massachusetts), George Bancroft writes: "The feud between the capitalist and the laborer, the house of Have and the house of Want, is as old as social union, and can never be entirely quited." [The first of 10 volumes of Bancroft's *History of the United States,* the first full-length and authoritative treatment of the subject, appears this year; the last volume is published in 1874.]

Oct. 28   The Federal Government orders the Seminole Indians to leave Florida under the terms of the Treaty of Payne's Landing of 1832.

Dec. 1   In his annual message to Congress, President Jackson announces that the national debt will be paid off by Jan. 1, 1835.

As the "reign" of Andrew Jackson approaches its end, a confused political scene emerges. Jackson's domination of the Democratic Party ensures the nomination of his heir, and there is no doubt that Vice President Van Buren has successfully maneuvered himself to the succession. In the opposition camp, however, diversity prevails. The leader of the opposition, Henry Clay, is aware of the amorphous character of the new Whig Party, and chooses to distribute the variety of its appeal behind several nominees in the expectation that Van Buren will draw a mere plurality and Congress may pick one of the hopeful Whigs. The legendary military hero, William Henry Harrison, is placed in nomination at public gatherings in several states, and is the official Anti-Masonic candidate at the convention of that party in Harrisburg. (It must be remembered that this year the Anti-Masonic Party is virtually a major party, second only to the Democrats in the House of Representatives.) Harrison is expected to garner the Western vote. In the East, Daniel Webster is chosen (by a caucus in the Massachusetts legislature), and the Southern vote is to be attracted to Hugh Lawson White (named by a legislative caucus in Tennessee).

The political waters are further muddied by the turbulence occasioned by abolitionist activities. The American Anti-Slavery Society issues quantities of propaganda, and their fervor provokes Southern legislatures to enact laws prohibiting the circulation of antislavery material. Even in New York the postmaster announces he will not permit the transmission of such material if the addressee is Southern. Finally, President Jackson lends his support to this effort to protect the South from harsh criticism, justifying his recommendation of Congressional action to interfere with the mail by citing the danger of servile insurrection.

Jan. 30   In an attempt to assassinate President Jackson, Richard Lawrence, a painter, fires two pistols at the President, but both miss fire. [Lawrence is later judged to be insane.]

Mar. 3   By act of Congress, branch U.S. mints are established at New Orleans, at Charlotte, North Carolina, and at Dahlonega, Georgia.

May 6   The New York *Herald,* a penny newspaper, is founded by James Gordon Bennett, who promises in the first issue: "We shall support no party—be the agent of no faction or coterie, and care nothing for any election, or any candidate from President down to constable."

May 11-June 29   A convention held in Detroit formulates a constitution for Michigan that includes a clause prohibiting slavery in the state.

May 20   The nominating convention of the Democratic Party meets in Baltimore and selects Martin Van Buren of New York as its candidate for President, and Richard M. Johnson of Kentucky as the Vice-Presidential nominee.

June 30   A group of Texas colonists led by William B. Travis seizes Fort Anahuac at the mouth of the Trinity River, and captures its Mexican garrison.

July 6   John Marshall, 79, Chief Justice of the United States since 1801, dies in Philadelphia.

July 8   While tolling for the death of Chief Justice Marshall, the Liberty Bell develops a crack.

July 29   Abolitionist materials are taken from the post office in Charleston, South Carolina, by a mob and burned on the parade ground.

Oct. 2   The American settlers of Gonzales, near the Guadalupe River in central Texas, defeat a troop of Mexican cavalry. [This is considered the first battle of the Texas Revolution.]

Oct. 21   William Lloyd Garrison, the abolitionist, narrowly escapes from a mob in Boston. He is lodged for the night in the city jail for his own safety.

Oct. 29   At a primary meeting at Tammany Hall in New York City, the regular Democrats, over the protests of the radical Equal Rights faction, declare their ticket approved and the meeting adjourned. The radicals remain in the hall. In order to oust them, the regulars turn out the gas lights. The radicals then produce candles, which they light with the new self-igniting friction matches called locofocos. They proceed to formulate their platform and nominate their own ticket. [Thenceforth radical Democrats of this era are known as "Locofocos."]

Nov. 1   The Seminole Indians in Florida resist the attempt of authorities to move them west of the Mississippi River. They are led by the young chief Osceola and are supported by many runaway slaves.

Dec. 2 In his annual message to Congress, President Jackson recommends a law to prohibit the circulation of antislavery publications through the mails.

Dec. 7 The Whigs make their debut in Congress—the 24th Congress—as a vigorous minority, with 25 seats in the Senate, compared to 27 for the Democratic majority, and 98 seats in the House of Representatives, which the Democrats control with 145 members. James K. Polk of Tennessee is the new Speaker of the House.

Dec. 16 A convention of the Anti-Masonic Party, meeting in Harrisburg, Pennsylvania, nominates William Henry Harrison of Ohio for President and Francis Granger of New York for Vice President.

Dec. 16-18 A great fire in New York City destroys more than 600 buildings, causing more than $20,000,000 in damage.

Dec. 28 General Wiley Thompson and his soldiers are massacred by Seminole Indians at Fort King in Florida. On the same day, Major Dade and 100 men are killed at Fort Brooke.

Dec. 29 By the Treaty of New Echota, the Cherokee Indians surrender to the United States all their lands east of the Mississippi River in return for $5,000,000 transportation costs and for land in Indian Territory.

Attempted assassination of Andrew Jackson

1836

President Jackson has the satisfaction, in his last year in office, of seeing the demise of the Bank of the United States and the transfer of Federal deposits to the state banks. But he also foresees the long-range results of his triumph. In an effort to avoid the inflationary consequences of unrestrained printing of paper money by uncontrolled state banks (now that the Bank of the United States no longer exists), the President, always an advocate of "hard money," issues the Specie Circular, requiring that public lands be paid for in gold or silver. It is not successful. Land sales and prices drop; those who have specie hoard it; speculators thrive.

Southern sensitivity concerning the institution of slavery is outraged by a new tactic of the abolitionists—the flooding of Congress with petitions demanding the abolition of slavery. In the Senate, the petitions are accepted and filed. The House of Representatives is affronted, however, and refuses even to accept antislavery petitions. Only former President John Quincy Adams, now a Representative from Massachusetts, denounces as unconstitutional what he describes as a "gag rule."

The entire country is absorbed by events in neighboring Mexico, where a simmering dispute between the dictatorial Government of President Antonio López de Santa Anna and a rather large American colony in the department of Texas (part of the state of Coahuila and Texas) has erupted into insurgency. The climax comes in March, when a heroic band of "Texans" (as the Americans call themselves) defend the Alamo, a mission fort in the village of San Antonio, to the last man while a few miles away a convention prepares to declare the independence of the colony and an army gathers to consummate that independence. Out of the glorious defeat at the Alamo and the slaughter, a few days later, at Goliad, comes the Texan victory at San Jacinto, with the capture of President General Santa Anna himself. Even before General Sam Houston is elected president of the new republic, the U.S. Senate proposes the recognition of Texas.

The election of Martin Van Buren as President, at the end of the year, comes as an anticlimax.

Jan. 4   A constitutional convention at Little Rock adopts a constitution for Arkansas. Under the terms of the Missouri Compromise, slavery is permitted within the proposed state.

Jan. 11   James Buchanan of Pennsylvania presents in the Senate petitions calling for the abolition of slavery in the District of Columbia. [These and other antislavery petitions anger Southerners and result in a move by Senator Calhoun of South Carolina to bar such matters in the future. On Mar. 9 Calhoun's motion is defeated by a vote of 36 to 10. However, two days later the Senate approves, 34 to 6, a motion offered by Buchanan rejecting the antislavery petitions.]

Jan. 20   A treaty of peace, amity, commerce, and navigation is concluded between the United States and Venezuela in Caracas.

Feb. 18   The Bank of the United States, its national charter having expired, receives a state charter in Pennsylvania.

Feb. 23-Mar. 6   A Mexican army of less than 4,000 men besieges a small Texan garrison commanded by Colonel William B. Travis in the Alamo in San Antonio. Although there are opportunities for some of the Texans to escape, all choose to fight to the end. By Mar. 6, all 187 Texans, among them the famous Davy Crockett and Jim Bowie, are killed in the hand-to-hand fighting to which the Mexicans have to resort.

Mar. 2   A convention of Texans meeting at Washington, Texas, adopts a declaration of independence. [On Mar. 4 Sam Houston is named commander of the Texan army.]

Mar. 15   The U.S. Senate confirms President Andrew Jackson's appointment of Roger B. Taney as Chief Justice of the Supreme Court.

Mar. 16   The Texas convention adopts a constitution for the independent Republic of Texas.

Mar. 27   At Goliad General Santa Anna massacres a force of about 350 Texans led by Captain James W. Fannin, Jr.

April 20   Wisconsin Territory is organized, comprising all of Michigan Territory from the Great Lakes west to the Missouri, north of the

proudly from the walls — I
shall never surrender or retreat.
Then, I call on you in the
name of Liberty, of patriotism &
everything dear to the American
Character to come to our aid,
with all despatch — The enemy is
receiving reinforcements daily &
will no doubt increase to three or
four thousand in four or five days.
If this call is neglected, I am deter
mined to sustain myself as long as
possible & die like a soldier
who never forgets what is due to
his own honor & that of his
country —

Victory or Death

William Barret Travis
Lt. Col. comdt

Facsimile of part of the message written by Colonel Travis just before he and his men are killed at the Alamo. The message requesting reinforcements affirms Travis' decision to die rather than to surrender or retreat.

states of Illinois and Missouri. [In 1838 the western boundary is moved to the Mississippi.]

April 21   General Santa Anna's force of about 1,200 Mexicans is defeated near the San Jacinto River by an army of less than 1,000 Texans under Sam Houston. The Texans go into battle yelling "Remember the Alamo." They kill 630 of the Mexicans and capture the remainder, including Santa Anna himself. Only 9 Texans are killed.

May 14   Santa Anna signs treaties at Velasco, Texas, pledging peace and recognition. [The treaties are later repudiated by the Mexican Congress.]

May 18   A House committee headed by Representative Henry L. Pinckney of South Carolina recommends the "gag resolution" providing for the tabling (i.e., ignoring) of all petitions relating to slavery. [On May 26 the House adopts this resolution by a vote of 117 to 68, as well as resolutions declaring that Congress has no power over slavery in the states and that interfering with slavery in the District of Columbia is inexpedient.]

May 31   The fashionable Astor Hotel, built by the wealthy fur trader and merchant John Jacob Astor, opens near City Hall in New York City.

June 15   Arkansas becomes the 25th state to be admitted to the Union.

June 23   The Deposit Act is approved by Congress. It requires the Secretary of the Treasury to designate as a place of public deposit at least one bank in every state. In addition, beginning on Jan. 1, 1837, all surplus revenue over $5,000,000 must be distributed as a loan among the states in proportion to their population.

June 28   James Madison, 85, one of the authors of the Constitution and the Bill of Rights and the fourth President of the United States, dies at Montpelier, his estate in Virginia.

July 1   The U.S. Senate adopts a resolution calling for the recognition of Texas by the United States.

July 2   Congress passes an act that provides for the punishment of postmasters who deliberately withhold mail from any person. This provision of the act results from the controversy over the mailing and delivery of antislavery propaganda.

July 4   A resolution calling for the recognition of Texas is approved in the House of Representatives.

July 11   President Jackson directs Secretary of the Treasury Levi Woodbury to issue the Specie Circular, a document that prohibits the acceptance of anything (with minor exceptions) but gold and silver in payment for public lands

Aaron Burr
(1756-1836)

Antonio López de Santa Anna, Mexican general
who seized the Alamo

The Celeste-A1 Cabinet. (A satirical view of the Eaton-Timberlake marriage. President Jackson surrounded by his Cabinet puts his approval on the marriage by granting an audience to the bride.)

after Aug. 15. [Although its purpose is to deprive speculators of their financial power, its effect is to place all credit in their hands, resulting eventually in the panic of 1837.]

September   Missionaries Marcus Whitman and Henry Harmon Spaulding reach Fort Vancouver, a Hudson's Bay Company post on the Columbia River. With them are their brides, the first white women to cross the continent.

Sept. 5   Sam Houston is elected president of the Republic of Texas over Stephen F. Austin, receiving more than three fourths of the vote. Mirabeau B. Lamar is chosen vice president. Most of the voters favor the annexation of Texas to the United States.

Sept. 14   Former Vice President Aaron Burr, 80, long a controversial figure as a result of his involvement in an alleged conspiracy in 1807, dies in Port Richmond, New York.

Sept. 16   A treaty of peace and friendship is signed between the United States and Morocco.

Oct. 22   Sam Houston is inaugurated at Columbia as the first president of the Republic of Texas.

Nov. 30   A convention of peace, friendship, commerce, and navigation between the United States and the Peru-Bolivian Confederation is signed in Lima.

Dec. 5   President Jackson defends the issuance of the Specie Circular in his annual message to Congress.

Dec. 7   Democrat Martin Van Buren of New York is elected President, receiving 765,483 popular and 170 electoral votes and carrying 15 of the 26 states. The total popular vote of the Whig candidates is 739,795. William Henry Harrison of Ohio wins 73 electoral votes; 26 electoral votes are cast for Hugh L. White of Tennessee; Daniel Webster of Massachusetts receives 14 electoral votes. The South Carolina legislature gives that state's 11 electoral votes to Willie P. Mangum of North Carolina.

Dec. 12   The Whigs offer a resolution in the U.S. Senate calling for the repeal of the Specie Circular.

Dec. 15   The post office and patent building are destroyed by fire in Washington, D.C.

Dec. 27   Stephen Fuller Austin, 43, the founder of the American colony in Texas and the secretary of state of the Republic of Texas in the administration of President Sam Houston, dies in Columbia.

1837

The economic harvest of the Jackson years is the Panic of 1837, with an ensuing depression. During these years cotton production increased in the South, agriculture expanded in the West, cities grew, manufacturing replaced trade as the economic base in the North. These phenomena were accompanied by a rise in the sales of land, and also in the price paid for land. There was a need for internal improvements—roads, canals, etc.—and these had to be financed by states and private companies. Inevitably, speculation and inflation accompanied such activities, and President Jackson hoped to curb the unhealthy aspects of a growing economy by extirpating the central bank, which he considered the root of the evil. But with Federal funds distributed widely in "pet banks" and surplus revenues distributed among the states, the control exercised by the Bank of the United States is replaced by financial anarchy: the number of banks and the number of bank notes increase. In response to the President's Specie Circular issued last year, the local banks are faced with a critical situation, and call in their loans. (At the same time, a depression in Great Britain results in withdrawals of British investments and a decline in the demand for cotton.) First the New York City banks suspend specie payment; then others follow suit. Lacking sufficient hard money, banks fail, enterprises go bankrupt, unemployment spreads. As the depression deepens, President Van Buren continues to follow Jackson's policy, with the ill-advised codicil of a plan to fragment the single treasury into a system of "subtreasuries."

Jan. 26   Michigan is admitted to the Union as the 26th state. Its admission in 1836 as a free-soil state, to balance the admission of Arkansas, was delayed because of a dispute over the southern boundary of the proposed state, which in turn was the result of a surveyor's error. Of the two possible versions of that boundary, the more northerly is finally accepted by Michigan, although this awards the city of Toledo to Ohio. In compensation, Michigan receives from Wisconsin Territory the entire peninsula between Lakes Superior and Michigan [the present Upper Peninsula].

Feb. 11   In *Briscoe* v. *Bank of Kentucky,* the U.S. Supreme Court holds that a state-owned bank may issue notes for public circulation. This decision, one of the first made by the Court since Taney became Chief Justice, upholds state laws in a manner that provokes bitter dissent from the sole Federalist survivor on the Court, Associate Justice Joseph Story.

Feb. 14   In a second case left over from the docket at the death of Chief Justice Marshall, *Charles River Bridge* v. *Warren Bridge,* the U.S. Supreme Court under Taney rules that the rights of corporations are subordinate to the interests of the community.

Mar. 3   President Jackson recognizes Texas by nominating Alcée La Branche of Louisiana as chargé d'affaires to the new republic.

Mar. 4   By an act of Congress the number of Supreme Court justices is increased from 7 to 9.

Mar. 4   Martin Van Buren, the eighth President of the United States and the first born after the Declaration of Independence was signed, is inaugurated. Richard M. Johnson becomes Vice President.

Sept. 4   When the 25th Congress convenes in special session, the Democrats have only a plurality in the House of Representatives, with 108 members; the Whigs have 107 seats, and 24 seats are held by unaffiliated members. The Senate, however, is solidly Democratic.

Oct. 12   The issuance of $10,000,000 in Treasury notes is authorized.

Oct. 21   American troops treacherously seize the Seminole chief Osceola during a parley under a flag of truce.

Nov. 7   Abolitionist newspaper editor Elijah P. Lovejoy is murdered by a proslavery mob in Alton, Illinois. [The slaying provokes a wave of antislavery sentiment and strengthens the abolitionist cause.]

Nov. 8   Mount Holyoke Seminary, founded by Mary Lyon, is opened in South Hadley, Massachusetts. Its purpose is to afford to women the kind of education available to men in contemporary "academies," and 80 women enroll the first year. [In 1888 it becomes Mount Holyoke Seminary and College.]

Dec. 29   Canadian militiamen cross to the American side of the Niagara River and destroy the *Caroline,* an American-owned steamboat used to transport supplies to Canadian rebels. In the course of the action they kill Amos Durfee, an American citizen, on New York soil.

1838

The *"Caroline* **Affair," which began in the last week** of 1837, inflames Anglo-American relations. After an unsuccessful revolt in Canada, the insurgents whose goal is to win the independence of Canada from England established a base on Navy Island, a Canadian possession in the Niagara River. The *Caroline,* a small American steamer, was used to transport supplies from the New York shore to the rebel outpost. Canadian soldiers crossed to the American side of the river and set the ship ablaze and adrift, after which it sank. In the course of their raid, the Canadians killed an American citizen. Anti-Canadian feeling follows the destruction of the *Caroline.* A Canadian steamship in the St. Lawrence River is the object of a retaliatory attack. Secret "Hunters' Lodges" are organized to struggle for the "independence" of Canada. President Martin Van Buren issues proclamations of neutrality and sends General Winfield Scott to take command of American forces along the frontier. The protests of the United States are ignored by the British Government.

Jan. 5-13   President Martin Van Buren warns U.S. citizens not to take hostile actions against Great Britain by aiding the Canadian insurgents who have occupied an island on the Canadian side of the Niagara River. About a week later the rebels abandon their base and surrender their arms to a force of American militia.

Feb. 14   In the House of Representatives John Quincy Adams of Massachusetts presents 350 petitions opposing slavery and the annexation of Texas.

April 23   Steamship service is established on the Atlantic Ocean by two British vessels. Early in the day the *Sirius,* a small steamer owned by the British and American Steam Navigation Company, arrives at New York City from London after a trip of 17 days. Later on the same day, the *Great Western,* owned by a group connected with the Great Western Railway, arrives in New York from Bristol, England. The *Great Western,* a huge ship of 1,340 tons, takes 15 days to make the crossing.

May 21   Congress rescinds the Specie Circular by joint resolution.

May 29   Americans seize and burn the *Sir Robert Peel,* a Canadian steamship, in the St. Lawrence River.

June 12   The entire western part of Wisconsin Territory, between the Mississippi and Missouri rivers and between the Canadian border and Missouri, is reorganized as Iowa Territory.

July 7   All railroads in the United States are designated postal routes by Congress.

Aug. 18   An expedition under the command of Lieutenant Charles Wilkes leaves Hampton Roads in Virginia to explore the Pacific Ocean and the South Seas. The expedition is under government auspices, and is the first such venture authorized by Congress.

Oct. 30   Following the declaration of Governor Lilburn Boggs, that "the Mormons must be treated as enemies and must be exterminated or driven from the state, if necessary," mobs in northwestern Missouri attack the members of that sect, killing 17 and wounding many others. [About 15,000 Mormons flee eastward into Illinois.]

Nov. 12   President Van Buren issues a second proclamation of neutrality in reference to Canada.

Nov. 26   A treaty of commerce and navigation between the United States and the Kingdom of Sardinia is concluded at Genoa.

Dec. 11   A new "gag resolution," introduced by Representative Charles G. Atherton of New Hampshire, is approved in the House of Representatives by a vote of 126 to 73. Like previous resolutions, it provides for the tabling of all antislavery petitions.

State Street, Boston

113

1839

With the *Caroline* **affair yet to be settled, another** problem arises to ruffle British-American relations. The background for this dispute is traced to the vague definition of the northeastern boundary of the United States in the Treaty of 1783 with Great Britain. The nub of the difficulty is the determination of the "highlands" that are said, in this treaty, to mark the frontier; the local topography offers several possibilities. After the U.S. Senate, by a single vote, rejected the award of the impartial arbitrator, the King of the Netherlands, in 1832, the lumbermen and farmers of New Brunswick and Maine took matters into their own hands. Now the brawling stage is giving way to hostility on a more official scale. The legislature of Maine appropriates money for defense against trespassing Canadian woodsmen. The governor of Maine calls out the state militia, seizes most of the disputed area, and begins to erect forts in the region. The U.S. Congress authorizes the President to activate the Army. President Van Buren sends General Winfield Scott to Maine. Scott succeeds in arranging a truce [in what historians call the Aroostook War] between the authorities of Maine and New Brunswick.

The country is beginning to recover from the economic slump, but the Whigs are aware that President Van Buren has lost whatever popularity he had, and that a Whig Presidency is not an impossible dream. Nevertheless, Clay and Webster, the most prestigious Whigs, also know that the party is actually a coalition. The tactic of multiple candidates, tried four years ago, cannot be repeated; yet a single candidate with a positive program is likely to drive some part of the coalition to vote for a Democrat. Of the 1836 candidates, William Henry Harrison made the best showing, and he has a Western following. To win Southern votes, a Virginian who has been a Democratic Congressman, Senator, and governor may prove an attractive running mate. No platform is adopted.

Jan. 19   In Washington the United States and the Netherlands sign a treaty of commerce and navigation.

Feb. 7   Senator Henry Clay of Kentucky, an aspirant to the Presidential nomination of the Whig Party, denounces the abolitionists and denies that Congress has any power to interfere with the institution of slavery where it has already been established.

Feb. 12   Canadian lumberjacks in the valley of the Aroostook River, a region disputed between Maine and New Brunswick, arrest Rufus McIntire, a land agent appointed by Governor John Fairfield of Maine to help expel the lumberjacks.

Feb. 20   An act of Congress forbids duels in the District of Columbia.

Mar. 3   The events on the Aroostook border lead Congress to pass an act authorizing the President to call out the militia and enroll 50,000 volunteers in the Army.

Mar. 23-25   General Winfield Scott, sent to Maine by President Van Buren, persuades Lieutenant Governor Sir John Harvey of New Brunswick to agree not to use force to occupy the Aroostook region. Governor Fairfield, in turn, agrees to allow the British to retain possession of the Madawaska settlements on the St.

John River in the northern part of the region.

Aug. 26   Off Long Island an American ship captures the *Amistad,* a Spanish ship seized by Negroes [who, it later develops, were enslaved illegally under Spanish law].

Sept. 25   A commercial treaty is signed by the Republic of Texas and France, the first European country to recognize the independence of Texas.

Nov. 13   A state convention of abolitionists is held at Warsaw, New York, and nominates James G. Birney of Kentucky, secretary of the American Anti-Slavery Society and a former slaveholder, for President.

Dec. 2   The 26th Congress is more balanced than its predecessors. There are 28 Democrats in the Senate, and 22 Whigs. In the House of Representatives 124 seats are held by Democrats, 118 by Whigs.

Dec. 4-7   The nominating convention of the Whig Party meets at Harrisburg, Pennsylvania. On Dec. 6 this "union and harmony" convention chooses William Henry Harrison of Ohio as its Presidential nominee instead of the more conspicuous contenders, Henry Clay and General Winfield Scott. John Tyler of Virginia, a conservative defender of states' rights, is nominated for Vice President.

114

1840 **When the Democrats assemble in national convention in Baltimore,** President Martin Van Buren is unanimously renominated. As a result of strong opposition to the incumbent Vice President, Richard M. Johnson, no running mate is named. The Democratic platform endorses the principles of the Declaration of Independence, strict construction, and the independent treasury; it opposes Federal funding of internal improvements, the assumption of state debts, a national bank, a protective tariff, restrictions on naturalization, and Congressional interference with slavery.

A Democratic newspaper unwittingly gives the Whigs the theme of their campaign when it says that their nominee, General Harrison, would probably prefer modest retirement to the Presidency. In the "log cabin and cider" campaign that follows, the Whigs use Jacksonian techniques against the Democrats. Harrison himself is, like Jackson, a military hero, who defeated the Indians at the Battle of Tippecanoe and the British and the Indians at the Battle of the Thames. Thus do the Whigs use the campaign slogan "Tippecanoe and Tyler too." In the election Harrison wins a small popular and an overwhelming electoral majority.

With the admission of Arkansas and Michigan during the decade just ended, the roster of states now numbers 26—just double the Original Thirteen. But the national population of 17,069,453 is four times that of 1790, the year of the first census, and the rate of increase, 32.9 per cent, is maintained. It is doubtful if anyone has noticed that the center of population has moved across the Appalachians to the Monongahela Valley of western Virginia [now West Virginia]. The population of Virginia, indeed, has remained stationary during the decade, and the state, first in 1790, now ranks fourth in the nation, behind Ohio.

Jan. 8 By a vote of 114 to 108, the House of Representatives makes it a standing rule that no antislavery petitions or resolutions be received. It is noteworthy that the margin favoring this position is diminishing and a reversal appears possible.

Jan. 23 A bill establishing an independent treasury, the system proposed in 1837 whereby the Government keeps its own funds, passes in the Senate, 24 to 18.

Mar. 23 The Baltimore *Republican,* a Democratic newspaper, inadvertently supplies the theme of the Whig Presidential campaign by stating "that upon condition of his receiving a pension of $2,000 and a barrel of cider, General Harrison would no doubt consent to withdraw his pretensions, and spend his days in a log cabin on the banks of the Ohio."

Mar. 31 President Van Buren issues an Executive order establishing a 10-hour workday for Federal employees.

April 1 The first "national" convention of abolitionists, with delegates from six states, takes the names of the Liberty Party and confirms the nomination by the New York State convention of Nov. 13, 1839, of James G. Birney of Kentucky for President.

May 5-6 The Democratic national convention meeting in Baltimore, nominates President Van Buren for a second term, but fails to agree on a Vice Presidential candidate.

June 30 The Independent Treasury bill passes in the House of Representatives by a vote of 124 to 107. On July 4 it is signed by President Van Buren. [It is repealed by the Whig Congress in 1841.]

Aug. 26 At Lisbon the United States and Portugal conclude a treaty of commerce and navigation.

Nov. 13 Great Britain signs a commercial treaty with Texas, recognizing the independence of the new republic.

Dec. 2 Whig William Henry Harrison of Ohio is elected President, carrying 19 of the 26 states, winning 1,274,624 popular and 234 electoral votes. John Tyler is elected Vice President. The Whigs also win a majority in Congress. Van Buren receives 1,127,781 and 60 electoral votes. About 7,000 votes are cast for James G. Birney of the Liberty Party.

Dec. 13 The British Minister to the United States, Henry Stephen Fox, demands that Alexander McLeod, a Canadian deputy sheriff arrested in New York State and charged with participating in the destruction of the *Caroline* and murdering Amos Durfee in 1837, be released.

Dec. 26 British Minister Fox is informed by Secretary of State John Forsyth that the courts of New York State have exclusive jurisdiction over the McLeod case.

William Henry Harrison of Ohio becomes the first Whig President of the United States. In his inaugural address, he criticizes the expansion of Executive power, the independent treasury, the spoils system, and abolitionism. Daniel Webster of Massachusetts is appointed Secretary of State in the new Administration; most of the other Cabinet members, however, are followers of Senator Henry Clay of Kentucky, the actual leader of the Whigs. Only a month after taking office, President Harrison dies of pneumonia, and John Tyler becomes the first Vice President to succeed to the Presidency. He sets an important precedent by insisting, against some pressure to treat him as an Acting President, that he is indeed the Chief Executive. Henry Clay attempts to dominate a special session of Congress, announcing what he considers to be the Whig program. Under his leadership Whigs repeal the Independent Treasury Act; then they pass a bill providing for the establishment of a national bank. Tyler vetoes the bank bill. Congress fails to understand the signal and, unable to muster a two-thirds vote to override the veto, passes a second bank bill for a national bank. This bill is also vetoed by the President. All of the Cabinet members except Webster (who is involved in negotiations with Great Britain) resign forthwith. The new Cabinet appointments make it clear that the breach between the President and Clay is complete. Clay and his men refer to Tyler as "His Accidency" and to the President's few Whig supporters as the "Corporal's Guard."

Mar. 4-6   William Henry Harrison is inaugurated as the ninth President of the United States. John Tyler of Virginia becomes Vice President. President Harrison's Cabinet is chosen: Daniel Webster of Massachusetts, Secretary of State; Thomas Ewing of Ohio, Secretary of the Treasury; John Bell of Tennessee, Secretary of War; George E. Badger of North Carolina, Secretary of the Navy, John C. Crittenden of Kentucky, Attorney General; and Francis Granger of New York, Postmaster General.

Mar. 9   The U.S. Supreme Court upholds the lower courts and frees the Negro slaves who had taken over the Spanish ship *Amistad* in 1839.

Mar. 17   A claims convention between the United States and Peru is signed in Lima.

April 4   President William Henry Harrison, 68, dies of pneumonia. John Tyler becomes the 10th President of the United States and the first to succeed to the office because of the death of the incumbent. [On April 6 he takes the oath of office.]

April 6   The cornerstone of a temple is laid at Nauvoo, Illinois, by Mormons who were driven last year out of northwestern Missouri.

April 10   The New York *Tribune,* edited by Horace Greeley, begins publication. It is a penny newspaper dedicated to the Whig cause.

May 19   In a church in South Boston, Massachusetts, Theodore Parker, a Unitarian clergyman, preaches a sermon, "A Discourse of the Transient and Permanent in Christianity," that shocks many of his contemporaries. In it he rejects the concepts that Christ is supernatural and that the Scriptures deserve special reverence.

May 31   The 27th Congress, meeting in special session, has a Senate composed of 28 Whigs and 22 Democrats, with 2 independents; the House of Representatives has 133 Whigs and 102 Denocrats, with 6 unaffiliated.

June 7   Whig leader Henry Clay, during the special session called by the late President Harrison, introduces resolutions in the Senate embodying the Whig program. He calls for the repeal of the Independent Treasury Act, the reestablishment of a national bank, increased tariff revenues, and the distribution among the states of the proceeds from the sale of the public lands. President Tyler considers Clay's presentation an attempt to assert party leadership that belongs ex officio to the Chief Executive.

July 28   A bill reestablishing a national bank passes in the Senate by a vote of 26 to 23.

Aug. 6   The bank bill is approved in the House of Representatives, 128 to 97.

Aug. 13   The Independent Treasury Act of 1840 is repealed.

Aug. 16   President Tyler vetoes the bank bill. [On Aug. 19 the U.S. Senate fails to override Tyler's veto.]

Aug. 23   By a vote of 125 to 94, the House of Representatives passes a second bank bill, providing for the establishment of a national bank under another name.

Sept. 3   The U.S. Senate approves, 27 to 22, the second bank bill.

Sept. 4 Congress passes the Distribution-Preemption Act, which allows settlers to purchase ("preempt") up to 160 acres of public land at $1.25 an acre. In addition, it provides for the distribution of the revenues from land sales among the states. However, the act also stipulates that distribution will be suspended if the tariff rate exceeds 20 per cent. [A tariff increase in 1842 voids this section of the act.]

Sept. 9 The second bill to reestablish a national bank is vetoed by President Tyler. [The next day this veto is sustained in the Senate.]

Sept. 11 All the members of the Cabinet, except Webster, resign because of President Tyler's veto of the bank bills. [On Sept. 13 the President makes new Cabinet appointments.]

Oct. 4-Nov. 18 In Rhode Island, the People's Party, a group organized by Thomas Dorr, meets in Providence to frame a new state constitution. They consider this necessary be-cause the existing constitution, based on a charter issued in 1663 by Charles II, allows less than half of the male population to vote, and elects a state legislature representing less than 4,000 voters out of a population of more than 100,000.

Oct. 12 Alexander McLeod, a Canadian deputy sheriff, is acquitted in Utica, New York, of charges of participation in the *Caroline* affair.

Nov. 17 The brig *Creole* is captured by slaves during a voyage from Virginia to New Orleans. [They sail for the British islands in the West Indies, where slavery is illegal.]

Dec. 16 Lewis F. Linn of Missouri introduces a bill in the Senate that provides for forts along the route to Oregon and for grants of land to the immigrants.

Dec. 27-29 In Rhode Island, the "People's Constitution," adopted by the Providence convention, is ratified by a majority of those voting on it in a statewide referendum.

Horace Greeley, Charles Dana, Bayard Taylor, and other journalists

1842

The struggle for control of the Whig Party, resulting from the essential differences between President Tyler and party leader Henry Clay, dominates the domestic scene this year. Both Whig leaders hope to become the party nominee for the Presidency in 1844. President Harrison had publicly declared that he would not run for a second term, but Tyler did not follow this example, and last year demonstrated his resentment at Clay's effort to overshadow him. Now the rivalry assumes the form of a contest between the Presidency and the Congress; four vetoes by Tyler, which the Whig legislature cannot override, demonstrate both that Tyler is independent and even rigid and that Clay's blustering tactic will not pass laws. Clay resigns from the Senate, and Congress in the end passes bank and tariff statutes in the versions preferred by the President.

Webster provides Tyler with a foreign-policy victory by settling the major border disputes between Britain and the United States. This is made possible partly because the fall of Prime Minister Lord Melbourne and the consequent resignation of Foreign Minister Lord Palmerston brings forward as a negotiator Alexander Baring, Baron Ashburton. The new Foreign Minister is a personal friend of Webster and inclined to conciliation. The treaty they work out provides final boundaries between Maine and New Brunswick, between New Hampshire and Canada, between New York and Canada, and between Wisconsin Territory and Canada. These settlements, together with a better understanding concerning the festering *Caroline, Creole,* and McLeod affairs—which in combination almost brought the two countries to a state of belligerency—not only improve relations between Britain and the United States, but also make it possible for the question of Texas to receive proper attention.

Mar. 1 In *Prigg* v. *Pennsylvania,* the U.S. Supreme Court rules that the owner of a slave may recover him or her under the provisions of the Federal fugitive slave law of 1793, but that state authorities need not assist such retrieval.

Mar. 3 A law is approved in Massachusetts limiting the factory workday of children under 12 to 10 hours.

Mar. 21-23 Joshua R. Giddings, a Whig Representative from Ohio, offers resolutions concerning the *Creole* case. This case relates to slaves who, having captured the ship on which they were the cargo and having sailed it to Nassau, were being reclaimed by Secretary of State Daniel Webster from the British authorities there. Giddings, an ardent abolitionist, takes the position that the Negroes on the high seas were under Federal, not slave-state, jurisdiction and that the United States is not justified in demanding their return from British soil as property. The House of Representatives censures Giddings, who resigns his seat. [His constituents immediately reelect him, and he serves in the House until 1859.]

Mar. 30 Dr. Crawford W. Long of Jefferson, Georgia, becomes the first phsycian to use an agent to kill pain [ether] during an operation, other than a dental operation, on a human being.

Mar. 31 Senator Henry Clay of Kentucky resigns his seat. [For the next two years he prepares to become the Whig Presidential candidate.]

April 4 The British special commissioner, Alexander Baring, Baron Ashburton, arrives in Washington to begin diplomatic negotiations with U.S. Secretary of State Daniel Webster.

April 18 Thomas W. Dorr is elected governor of Rhode Island by a majority of the citizens newly franchised under the "People's Constitution."

May 3 Dorr is inaugurated governor of Rhode Island in Providence. [The incumbent governor, Samuel W. King, is declared reelected by the adherents of the old constitution.]

May 18 Dorr's supporters make an unsuccessful attempt to seize the state arsenal in Providence. [Governor King's supporters declare a state of insurrection, and Dorr leaves the state.]

June 10 The Wilkes expedition returns to New York after a four-year exploration of the Pacific. [His account of the work of the expedition, which included the surveying of 1,600 miles of the Antarctic coast and hundreds of islands, is published in five volumes in 1844.]

June 13 Secretary Webster and Lord Ashburton begin their discussions.

June 29 President Tyler vetoes a tariff bill that would maintain duties above the 20-per-cent

Fanueil Hall, Boston, 1839

level mandated (as of July 1, 1842) by the Compromise Tariff of 1833. Tyler opposes the bill because it also in effect repeals the 1841 statute that requires the distribution among the states of the surplus revenue from the sale of public lands to be suspended whenever the level of duties exceeds 20 per cent. [On July 1, the 20-per-cent level is reached, seriously reducing revenues.]

Aug. 9　In Washington a treaty is signed between the United States and Great Britain that provides for adjustments in the borders between the United States and the British possessions to the north. The most important territorial provision gives Maine about 7,000 of the 12,000 square miles in the disputed Aroostook region, which is less than the area awarded in 1831 by the King of the Netherlands and rejected by the U.S. Senate in 1832. On the other hand, Rouses Point, with its fort, now known to lie north of the 45th parallel (the accepted boundary), is conceded to New York State. Adjustments are made in the Vermont border, involving the true source of the Connecticut River, and in the area between the Lake of the Woods and Lake Superior. There are also provisions concerning navigation, extradition, and the suppression of the slave trade.

Aug. 9　Tyler vetoes a second tariff bill that would combine higher duties with distribution of revenues to the states, contrary to last year's legislation.

Aug. 20　The Senate ratifies the Webster-Ashburton Treaty by a vote of 39 to 9.

Aug. 26　Congress changes the beginning of the fiscal year from January 1 to July 1.

Aug. 29　An act is approved giving Federal courts the authority to grant habeas corpus writs when states have accused foreigners of deeds performed under the orders of their own nation.

Aug. 30　Tyler signs a third tariff bill which restores duties to higher levels in effect in 1832, but which simultaneously would end the distribution of revenues.

Oct. 20-21　Commodore Thomas ap Catesby Jones, in command of a U.S. naval squadron in the Pacific Ocean, hears that Mexico and the United States are at war and, fearing that the British will capture California, seizes the capital of that Mexican province, Monterey. Advised by the American consul, Thomas O. Larkin, that he is in error, he restores the post to Mexican control on the following day. [Tyler disavows Jones's action; reparation and apologies are made.]

Dec. 30　Tyler, under the advice of Secretary of State Webster, declares that the United States would be "dissatisfied" to see any foreign power take possession of the Hawaiian Islands.

1843

The issue of Texas has been dormant in American politics for five years. In 1837 the Republic of Texas had sought annexation in the United States, only to be rebuffed by President Van Buren, and the offer was withdrawn. The young republic had negotiated recognition from various European countries, including Britain and France, both of which, for a number of reasons have preferred to help Texas remain independent. (Among the reasons are a reluctance to see the United States expand; a recognition that it would be easier to negotiate more favorable economic relationships with a minor than with a major power; and a continuing antislavery sentiment, which had supported the Mexican antislavery position when Texas was a Mexican possession and which continues to hope to extirpate slavery in the new republic.)

The Tyler Administration, having reestablished amicable relations with Britain, is now free to reconsider the possibility of annexing Texas. Both the President and his new Secretary of State, Abel Upshur, favor doing so. Mexican President Antonio López de Santa Anna declares that the United States faces war if it attempts to annex Texas, and even Texas President Sam Houston is not enthusiastic about relinquishing independence. The deciding factor, however, will be public opinion in the United States. The gamut runs from anti-annexationist sentiment among Northern abolitionists to enthusiasm for potential increases in slave territory in the South.

Feb. 3 A bill introduced in 1841 by Lewis F. Linn of Missouri, providing for the fortification of the Oregon Trail and for land grants to those settling in Oregon, is passed in the U.S. Senate.

Mar. 3 The bankruptcy act of 1841 is repealed.

May 8 Secretary of State Daniel Webster resigns. He is the only Cabinet member who failed to resign in 1841, ostensibly because of his pending negotiation of a treaty with Great Britain. He is known to be displeased by President Tyler's intention to annex Texas.

May 22 The first wagon in a party of about 1,000 persons bound for Oregon pulls away from Elm Grove near Independence, Missouri.

May 28 Lexicographer Noah Webster, 84, dies in New Haven, Connecticut. He was founder of Amherst College, and in 1828 published his *An American Dictionary of the English Language.*

May 29 John C. Frémont sets out from near Kansas City, Missouri, on an exploratory expedition to the regions between the Rocky Mountains and Pacific Ocean. His guide on this trip [which takes more than 14 months] is Kit Carson, who accompanied Frémont on an expedition last year to the South Pass.

June 15 A truce is declared between Mexico and the Republic of Texas.

June 17 The Bunker Hill Monument is dedicated in Massachusetts. President Tyler attends the ceremony.

July 5 At a meeting at Champeog, on the Willamette River, the American settlers in Oregon adopt an "Organic Law," providing for a simple Government to function until the United States extends its jurisdiction over the Oregon country.

July 24 Abel P. Upshur of Virginia is appointed Secretary of State.

Aug. 23 President Santa Anna of Mexico informs the United States that his Government would "consider equivalent to a declaration of war against the Mexican Republic the passage of an act of the incorporation of Texas in the territory of the United States; the certainty of the fact being sufficient for the immediate proclamation of war."

Aug. 30 At a national convention held in Buffalo, New York, the Liberty Party unanimously renominates James G. Birney for President. The party platform condemns further expansion of slave territory.

Oct. 16 Secretary of State Upshur notifies Isaac Van Zandt, the Minister of the Republic of Texas in Washington, that the United States is willing to resume negotiations aimed at the American annexation of Texas.

Nov. 9 An extraditiion convention between the United States and France is concluded at Washington, D.C.

Dec. 4 The 28th Congress convenes, and the Whigs retain marginal control, with 28 members in the Senate and 115 in the House. The Democrats have 25 Senators and 108 Representatives.

Pennsylvania Avenue, Washington, D.C. as seen from the U.S. Capitol

Webster, Clay, and Calhoun

1844

In this election year Texas remains the prime issue. The third Secretary of State in the Tyler Cabinet, John C. Calhoun, ardently proslavery, concludes a treaty of annexation with the republic, but the U.S. Senate rejects it. Every political figure in the country now must take a stand.

Former President Andrew Jackson comes out for annexation, Former President Martin Van Buren finds it expedient to publish a letter opposing annexation, and simultaneously Whig leader Henry Clay takes an identical position. The publication of letters from these opposing aspirants for the Presidential nominations of the major parties arouses some suspicion; Van Buren's loss of the Democratic nomination and the substitution of pro-annexation James K. Polk is ascribed to their positions on this issue. Clay secures the Whig nomination, probably despite the stand he takes toward Texas (which he softens considerably during the course of the campaign), but he loses the election.

The nation as a whole is not enthusiastic about expanding the slave power by absorbing a vast territory where slavery will thrive, but those who favor annexation are united behind Polk and make him President. Clay's indecisive stand costs him the electoral votes of New York State, where a minor abolitionist candidate attracts enough votes to throw the state to Polk. Tyler, having himself withdrawn from the Presidential race, urges that Congress vote Texas into the Union by a simple majority.

Jan. 15   The University of Notre Dame, founded two years ago by brothers of the Congregation of the Holy Cross near South Bend, Indiana, receives its charter from the state legislature.

Feb. 24   The University of Mississippi in Oxford, Mississippi, is chartered. [It opens for instruction in 1848.]

Feb. 27   Nicholas Biddle, 58, former president of the Bank of the United States, dies near Philadelphia.

Feb. 28   Secretary of State Abel P. Upshur and Secretary of the Navy Thomas Gilmer are killed when a gun explodes aboard the U.S.S. *Princeton*.

Mar. 6   President Tyler appoints John C. Calhoun of South Carolina Secretary of State.

Mar. 22   A letter from ex-President Andrew Jackson, expressing support for the annexation of Texas by the United States, is published in the Richmond *Enquirer*.

April 12   A treaty is signed by the United States and the Republic of Texas providing for the annexation of Texas as an American territory, the cession of Texas' public lands to the United States, and the assumption by the United States of up to $10,000,000 of the Texan public debt.

April 18   In a note to the British Minister at Washington, Sir Richard Pakenham, Secretary of State Calhoun strongly defends the institution of slavery.

April 27   Letters are published from Martin Van Buren and Henry Clay, considered the likely candidates for the Presidency of the Democratic and Whig parties, concerning the annexation of Texas, an issue submitted to the Senate five days ago. In a letter printed in the Washington *Globe,* Van Buren warns that annexation might mean war with Mexico. Clay, in a letter sent from Raleigh, North Carolina, to Senator John J. Crittenden on April 17, and published in the *National Intelligencer* at Clay's request, declares that a Mexican war would be the inevitable result of annexation "at this time".

May 1   The national convention of the Whig Party meets at Baltimore and unanimously nominates Henry Clay of Kentucky for President. The Vice-Presidential candidate is Theodore Frelinghuysen of New Jersey.

May 24   Samuel F.B. Morse, the inventor of the telegraph, sends the first telegraphic message ("What hath God wrought!") from Washington to Baltimore, Maryland.

May 27-29   The Democratic national convention is held in Baltimore, the first convention to be reported over the telegraph. Van Buren is the clear favorite on the first ballot, but fails to attain a two-thirds majority; he is passed by Lewis Cass, on the fifth ballot; on May 29, on the ninth ballot, James K. Polk of Tennessee is unanimously nominated for President. For the Vice-Presidential nomination, George M. Dallas of Pennsylvania is selected. The platform calls for "the reoccupation of Oregon and the reannexation of Texas."

May 27   In Baltimore the Tyler Democrats nominate President Tyler for a second term.

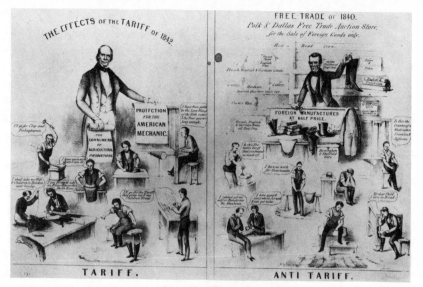

A pro-tariff cartoon

June 8 The Senate rejects the Texas treaty by a vote of 35 to 16.

June 25 Thomas W. Dorr, the unsuccessful leader of the disfranchised citizens of Rhode Island, is sentenced to life imprisonment for treason.

June 26 President John Tyler marries Miss Julia Gardiner in the Church of the Ascension in New York City. Tyler becomes the first President to marry while in office.

June 27 Mormon leader Joseph Smith, 38, is killed by a mob in Carthage, Illinois. Smith was in jail at the time for having destroyed the press of a dissident Mormon faction.

July 1 In a letter [the first of the "Alabama letters"] addressed to Stephen F. Miller of Tuscaloosa, Alabama, Henry Clay appears to modify his opposition to annexation, in an attempt to attract Southern votes. [He loses Northern votes instead.]

July 3 The first treaty between the United States and China is signed, giving Americans trading privileges in that country.

July 27 In the second of the "Alabama letters," Clay further qualifies his position on annexation.

Aug. 7 John Charles Frémont and his party reach St. Louis after an extended exploration of the Far West, which took him from South Pass to the Great Salt Lake, to Fort Vancouver in the Oregon country, along the slopes of the mountains that separate the desert from California [the Sierra Nevada], and back east around the southern end of the mountains. [In his extremely popular report of the expedition, with maps and charts of unexplored regions that are used by a generation of West-bound migrants, Frémont describes the intermontane desert as a "Great Basin," a term that continues to be used.]

Aug. 8 The Mormons in Nauvoo, Illinois, choose Brigham Young as presiding officer of their church.

Aug. 13 A revised constitution that ends property qualifications as a requisite for the suffrage and provides for direct election of the governor is ratified in New Jersey.

Aug. 20 Tyler withdraws from the Presidential race.

Nov. 1 In anticipation of possible statehood, a constitution for Iowa is adopted by a convention in Iowa City.

Dec. 3 In his annual message to Congress, Tyler recommends the annexation of Texas by joint resolution rather than by treaty. (Only a simple majority vote is needed to pass a joint resolution, whereas a two-thirds majority is required to ratify a treaty.)

Dec. 3 The motion of John Quincy Adams for the repeal of the "gag rule" on antislavery petitions is adopted by the House of Representatives.

Dec. 7 James K. Polk of Tennessee, a Democrat, is elected President over the Whig candidate, Henry Clay of Kentucky. Polk receives 1,338,464 popular and 170 electoral votes, carrying 15 of the 26 states. Clay wins 1,300,097 popular and 105 electoral votes. Some 62,300 votes are cast for James G. Birney, the nominee of the Liberty Party.

Dec. 12 Texas Secretary of State Anson Jones succeeds Sam Houston as president of the Republic of Texas.

In the last days of the Tyler Administration, the Republic of Texas is offered annexation to the United States by a joint resolution of Congress. The new President, James K. Polk, enthusiastically supports annexation. In Texas, annexation is accepted by Congress, a special convention, and the people. At the end of the year, the U.S. Congress admits the Lone Star State to the Union.

Soon after the annexation resolution passes Congress the Mexican Minister leaves Washington and the Government of Mexico breaks off diplomatic relations with the United States. General Zachary Taylor is ordered to ready his troops, then to move into Texas. Informed that Mexico will receive a commissioner to discuss the Texas question, the U.S. Government sends John Slidell to Mexico City to negotiate, but the Mexican government refuses to receive him because his rank as a Minister is inconsistent with international protocol. (Only friendly countries exchange ministers.)

President Polk also enters into a confrontation with Great Britain over the Oregon country. He first offers, then withdraws, the 49th parallel as the boundary between the two countries in this region. In his annual message, the President reaffirms the Monroe Doctrine and calls for the termination of the joint occupation of Oregon. Polk's Texas and Oregon policies suggest that he is inspired by the idea of "Manifest Destiny," a term coined in this year of expansionism.

Jan. 23   An act of Congress designates the Tuesday after the first Monday in November of election years as the uniform day for the election of Presidential electors.

Jan. 25   A joint resolution for the annexation of Texas to the United States is approved in the House of Representatives by a vote of 120 to 98.

Feb. 1   The Texas Baptist Educational Society receives a charter from the Congress of the Republic of Texas, for the purpose of opening a college at Independence. [This institution merges in 1886 with the University of Waco under the name of Baylor University.]

Feb. 20   President Tyler vetoes a bill forbidding payment for some naval vessels he had ordered constructed.

Feb. 27   The U.S. Senate passes an amended version of the Texas annexation resolution by the narrow vote of 27 to 25. The amendment, proposed by Thomas Hart Benton of Missouri, provides for negotiation with the Republic of Texas.

Feb. 28   By a vote of 132 to 76, the House of Representatives approves the annexation resolution as amended by the Senate.

Mar. 1   Tyler signs the joint resolution of Congress for the annexation of the Republic of Texas to the United States, the first use of this device in the acquisition of territory or the acceptance of a treaty. According to the resolution, Texas is to be admitted as a state, not a territory; up to four more states can be formed from Texas' area, with slavery banned north of the Missouri Compromise line of 36° 30'; and Texas is to reserve its public domain but pay its own public debts.

Mar. 3   Florida is admitted to the Union as the 27th state, with a constitution permitting the institution of slavery. [The "paired" state, Iowa, is admitted in 1846.]

Mar. 3   On the last day of the Tyler Administration, Congress overrides the President's veto of the bill prohibiting payment for some naval vessels. This is the first time Congress fails to sustain a Presidential veto.

Mar. 3   A postal act is approved that reduces the postal rates and grants subsidies to transatlantic steamship lines for carrying the mail.

Mar. 4   James K. Polk of Tennessee is inaugurated as the 11th President of the United States. George M. Dallas of Pennsylvania becomes Vice President. In his address, Polk endorses the American claim to the Oregon country and the annexation of Texas.

Mar. 6   Polk appoints James Buchanan of Pennsylvania as Secretary of State, Robert J. Walker of Mississippi as Secretary of the Treasury, William L. Marcy of New York as Secretary of War, Cave Johnson of Tennessee as Postmaster General, and John Y. Mason of Virginia as Attorney General.

Mar. 6   General Juan Almonte, the Mexican Minister in Washington, protests the proposed annexation of Texas and demands his passports to leave the United States.

Mar. 10   George Bancroft of Massachusetts is appointed Secretary of the Navy.

Mar. 28   The Mexican Government notifies Wilson Shannon, the U.S. Minister, that diplomatic relations between the two countries are severed.

May 14   A convention adopts a new constitution for Louisiana that ends property qualifications for voting and provides for the direct election of the governor.

June 8   Andrew Jackson, 78, the seventh President of the United States, dies near Nashville, Tennessee.

June 15   General Zachary Taylor is ordered to move his troops from Fort Jesup, Louisiana, to a point "on or near the Rio Grande" in order to defend Texas from invasion. [He leads 1,500 troops to the south bank of the Nueces River, which he reaches by July 31; by November he has a force of 4,500 men. The Nueces was the southern border of the Mexican department of Texas.]

June 23   In a special session, the Texas Congress approves annexation.

June 27   Thomas W. Dorr, leader of the Dorr Rebellion in 1842, is released under the terms of an act of amnesty by the Rhode Island legislature.

July 4   A convention summoned by President Anson Jones of Texas accepts the terms of annexation.

July 5-7   The first national convention of the Native American Party is held in Philadelphia. The party, which is represented in the 29th Congress by 6 members (4 from New York, 2 from Pennsylvania), opposes liberal immigration. It was founded in June, 1843, as the American Republican Party. [It develops into the American (or Know-Nothing) Party in 1849.]

July 12   Secretary of State James Buchanan informs Sir Richard Pakenham, the British Minister in Washington, that the United States is willing to divide the Oregon country along the 49th parallel.

July 19   A great fire in New York City destroys $6,000,000 worth of property.

July 29   Pakenham refuses the American offer of the 49th parallel for the boundary of Oregon without referring it to the British Government.

Aug. 27   A convention adopts a proposed constitution for Texas when it becomes a state.

Aug. 30   Polk instructs Secretary of State Buchanan to withdraw the offer of the 49th parallel as the Oregon boundary.

Sept. 16   John Slidell of Louisiana is chosen to go to Mexico and offer up to $40,000,000 for New Mexico, California, and the Rio Grande boundary for Texas.

Oct. 10   The Naval School, established by Secretary of the Navy Bancroft, officially opens at Fort Severn in Annapolis, Maryland.

Oct. 13   Annexation and the state constitution are approved by the Texas electorate.

Oct. 17   John Black, the U.S. consul in Mexico City, reports that the Mexican Government is willing to receive a commissioner to discuss the Texas question if U.S. naval forces off Veracruz are withdrawn.

Oct. 17   Thomas O. Larkin, the U.S. consul at Monterey, California, is instructed to block any foreign designs on California and to promote sentiment for annexation to the United States. [He receives his instructions as confidential agent April 17, 1846.]

Nov. 10   Slidell is appointed Minister to Mexico, and is instructed to offer U.S. assumption of American claims against Mexico (amounting to at least $6,000,000) in return for all Mexican territory north and east of the entire course of the Rio Grande, east of a line from its source north to the 42d parallel, and north of the 42d parallel. In addition, New Mexico west of the Rio Grande would be worth another $5,000,000, and the purchase of California for $25,000,000 would be acceptable.

Nov. 10   At Brussels the United States and Belgium sign a treaty of commerce and navigation.

Dec. 2   In his first annual message to Congress, President Polk reaffirms the Monroe Doctrine, opposing any European colonization of North America and any European attempts to maintain a balance of power there. The President also calls for the end of the joint occupation of Oregon. In addition, he expresses support for tariff revision and an independent treasury system. It is a Democratic 29th Congress that convenes to hear the Democratic President. In the Senate, 31 Democrats sit opposite 25 Whigs. The House of Representatives contains 143 Democrats, 77 Whigs, and 6 members of the ephemeral Native American Party.

Dec. 16   The Mexican Government refuses to receive Slidell, on the grounds that it agreed to receive only a commissioner, not a Minister.

Dec. 27   Pakenham asks that the U.S. Government reiterate its offer of the 49th parallel as the boundary for Oregon.

Dec. 29   Texas becomes the 28th state to be admitted to the Union.

1846 The general belief that it is the "Manifest Destiny" of the United States "to overspread the continent allotted by Providence for the free development of our yearly multiplying millions" (as editor John O'Sullivan wrote) leads to two confrontations this year, of which only one ends in war.

Relations between the United States and Mexico were broken last year, and as this year opens General Zachary Taylor is on the Nueces River, which Mexico considers the southern border of Texas; Minister John Slidell waits for a Government with which his country has no diplomatic relations to receive him nevertheless; and Captain John Frémont, disguised as an explorer, enters Monterey (the capital of Mexican California) with an intent that is not entirely peaceful. At year's end the Mexican cities of Monterrey (the capital of Nuevo León), Saltillo, and Tampico are in American hands, and Mexican California is in American hands.

The other potential trouble spot, the Oregon country, is the subject of unspectacular negotiations that result in the extension to the Pacific of the boundary (along the 49th parallel) that already separates Canada from the United States as far west as the Rocky Mountains. With the area south of that line now comprising the new Northwest, the last major controversy with Britain has been laid to rest.

Jan. 3 The phrase "Manifest Destiny" is first used in Congress by Representative Robert C. Winthrop of Massachusetts. It earlier appeared in an article by John L. O'Sullivan in the July-August, 1845, issue of *The United States Magazine and Democratic Review,* and in an editorial on the Oregon question in the New York *Morning News* on Dec. 27, 1845.

Jan. 12-13 The report of John Slidell, Minister to Mexico, that the Government of President José Joaquín Herrera has refused to receive him, reaches Washington, D.C. (By this time Mariano Paredes y Arrillaga has replaced Herrera as President.) Upon receipt of Slidell's report, General Zachary Taylor is ordered to advance from the Nueces River to the Rio Grande.

Jan. 27 Captain John Charles Frémont reaches Monterey in Mexican California in the course of his "exploratory" expedition to the West. (In fact, Frémont is under orders to prepare the way for the acquisition of California.)

Feb. 3 General Taylor receives his instructions to advance to the Rio Grande.

Feb. 6 Slidell reports to the U.S. Government that the Mexicans are stiffened in their resolve to fight by a belief that the United States and Great Britain will go to war over Oregon.

Feb. 10 The westward exodus of the Mormons from Nauvoo, Illinois, begins.

Feb. 19 A state government for Texas is formally installed at Austin.

Feb. 26 Secretary of State James Buchanan notifies U.S. Minister to Great Britain Louis McLane that the Oregon question will be reopened if the British make the first move to negotiate the joint occupation of Oregon.

Mar. 3 General José Castro, the Mexican military commander at Monterey, California, warns Frémont to leave. [Before the week is out, Frémont withdraws to a nearby mountain retreat to await developments.]

Mar. 8 General Taylor, having been forced by heavy rains to remain at the Nueces, begins his advance to the Rio Grande.

Mar. 12 President Paredes of Mexico declines to receive Slidell.

Mar. 24 Taylor reaches the Rio Grande opposite the Mexican town of Matamoros.

April 12 The Mexican commander at Matamoros, General Pedro de Ampudia, warns General Taylor to retreat beyond the Nueces River.

April 13 The Pennsylvania Railroad Company is incorporated for the purpose of linking the existing railroad from Lancaster to Harrisburg with Pittsburgh. [The first segment, as far as Lewistown, is in operation by Sept. 1, 1849.]

April 23 The resolution for terminating the joint occupation of Oregon is approved in the Senate by a vote of 42 to 10 and in the House of Representatives by a vote of 142 to 46. It includes a conciliatory expression of the possibility of compromise.

April 25 A reconnoitering party of 63 soldiers is surrounded and attacked by a force of 1,600 Mexican cavalry; 11 Americans are killed, 5 are wounded, and the rest are captured.

April 26 The U.S. Government is informed by General Taylor that "hostilities may now be considered as commenced." [The news reaches

Washington in 13 days.]

April 27 Polk signs the joint resolution of Congress authorizing the termination of the Anglo-American occupation of Oregon.

April 30-May 1 The Mexican army crosses the Rio Grande in force. Taylor retreats about 10 miles to Point Isabel in order to protect his base of supply.

May 3-9 The Mexicans lay siege to Fort Taylor, opposite Matamoros, commanded by Major Jacob Brown. Taylor sets out from Point Isabel for the fort to relieve the besieged garrison. The Mexican force, under General Mariano Arista, with three times the strength of Taylor's army, attempts to intercept the U.S. troops, and at Palo Alto an artillery duel occurs, the first real battle of the war. The Mexican casualties are high, and Arista retreats southward to Resaca de la Palma, where the Americans prevail in hand-to-hand combat. When Taylor reaches the fort, Major Brown is found to have been killed. Taylor renames the post Fort Brown and the nearby community Brownsville.

May 9 In a morning meeting of the Cabinet, President Polk proposes sending a war message to Congress. Then the news of the April 25 skirmish arrives. The Cabinet reconvenes and unanimously supports the declaration of war.

May 11-13 Polk tells Congress on May 11 that "Mexico has passed the boundary of the United States, has invaded our territory and shed American blood upon the American soil." By a vote of 174 to 14, the House of Representatives declares that "by act of the Republic of Mexico, a state of war exists between that Government and the United States." The House also authorizes the raising of $10,000,000 and 50,000 volunteers for the purpose of prosecuting the war. The next day the war declaration passes in the Senate, 40 to 2. On May 13 Polk signs the declaration of war against Mexico.

May 17-18 The Mexicans evacuate Matamoros, and General Taylor's forces cross the Rio Grande and occupy the town.

May 21 Polk gives the required one year's notice for the termination of the joint occupation of Oregon with Great Britain.

June 3 General Stephen Watts Kearny, commander of the Army of the West, is ordered to occupy California with the support of the naval forces commanded by Commodore John D. Sloat that are off the Mexican West-coast port of Mazatlán. [On June 8 Commodore Sloat sails for California.]

June 10 The United States and the Kingdom of Hanover sign a treaty of commerce and navigation at Hanover.

June 14 A group of American settlers led by William B. Ide seize the town of Sonoma and declare California independent. [They are given assistance by Captain Frémont, and raise a flag on which appears the emblem of a bear. For this reason the event is called the Bear Flag Revolt.]

June 15 Secretary of State James Buchanan and British Minister in Washington Richard Pakenham sign an agreement that finally terminates the dispute between the two countries concerning Oregon. The 49th parallel is accepted as the boundary between Canada and the United States westward from the Rocky Mountains to Puget Sound, an inlet of the Pacific Ocean; the precise boundary in the Strait of Juan de Fuca, around the southern end of Vancouver Island, is left for more precise determination.

June 18 The U.S. Senate ratifies the Oregon agreement by a vote of 41 to 14.

June 19 At Elysian Fields, in Hoboken, New Jersey, the first known baseball game is played under rules established by Alexander Cartwright. In this game the New York Nine defeat the Knickerbockers, 23-0.

July 7-9 Commodore Sloat seizes Monterey, raises the American flag, and declares California part of the United States. Acting under Sloat's orders, Commander John B. Montgomery occupies San Francisco and Lieutenant James W. Revere takes possession of Sonoma, seat of the "Bear Flag Republic."

July 22-25 The Army of the West, under General Kearny, arrives at Bent's Fort, its rendezvous point at the junction of the Santa Fe Trail and the Arkansas River.

July 23 Commodore Sloat relinquishes command to Commodore Robert F. Stockton.

July 24 The California Battalion is formed and Frémont is placed in command, with the rank of major.

July 31 Polk signs the Walker tariff bill, approved the previous day although its passage in the Senate required the vote of Vice President Dallas. It reverses the trend toward protectionism (as compared with tariff for revenue), somewhat lowering duties, particularly on nonluxury items.

Aug. 2 Kearny's Army of the West begins its march southward through the desert toward New Mexico.

Aug. 6 The Independent Treasury Act is approved, reestablishing government-run sub-treasuries, in the manner established by an 1840 law (revoked in 1841).

Aug. 8   A bill providing the $2,000,000 requested by President Polk to "facilitate negotiations" with the Mexicans is passed by the House of Representatives, amended by a provision [the Wilmot Proviso] introduced by Representative David Wilmot of Pennsylvania that requires the exclusion of slavery from any territory acquired from Mexico.

Aug. 10   The U.S. Senate adjourns without having considered the "Two Million Bill" and the Wilmot Proviso.

Aug. 10   The Smithsonian Institution is chartered. It is named for an English scientist, James Smithson, whose bequest of slightly over $500,000 made it possible and who prescribed in his will that the funds be used "for the increase and diffusion of knowledge among men."

Aug. 13   Commodore Stockton takes possession of Los Angeles.

Aug. 15   The first newspaper in California, the *Californian,* appears at Monterey.

Aug. 15   General Kearny arrives at Las Vegas [New Mexico] and declares New Mexico part of the United States.

Aug. 16   General Santa Anna, having reached an understanding with President Polk that the two might negotiate acceptable terms if Santa Anna were to regain the presidency of Mexico, lands at Veracruz after passing through the American blockade.

Aug. 17   Stockton proclaims the annexation of California to the United States and establishes a local Government with himself as governor.

Aug. 18   Kearny's forces occupy Santa Fe, ending a grueling march of over 800 miles that began at Leavenworth, Kansas.

Aug. 19   Taylor's forces set out for Monterrey, not to be confused with Monterey in California, capital of the state of Nuevo León. He also declares an armistice for the next eight weeks.

Sept. 10   Elias Howe patents a sewing machine.

Sept. 19-25   General Taylor's troops approach Monterrey on Sept. 19, and enter the city itself on Sept. 21. General Pedro de Ampudia surrenders on Sept. 24, and the capitulation is effected the next day.

Sept. 22   Kearny promulgates laws for New Mexico and appoints Charles Bent governor.

Sept. 22-30   The Mexicans in California rebel under the leadership of Captain José Maria Flores and recapture Los Angeles, Santa Barbara, and San Diego from the Americans.

Sept. 25   General Kearny sets out from Santa Fe for California with 300 men, after having directed Colonel Alexander W. Doniphan to lead an expedition in support of General John E. Wool's planned attack on the city of Chihuahua, in northern Mexico.

Oct. 6   Enroute to California, General Kearny meets Kit Carson, who informs him about the success of the U.S. forces in California. Kearny sends 200 of his 300 men back to New Mexico before proceeding on his way.

Oct. 8   General Santa Anna, reaching San Luis Potosí, abandons his deal with Polk and begins to prepare for an attack on the U.S. invaders of Mexico.

Oct. 13   The War Department notifies General Taylor that the eight-week armistice that he concluded with the Mexicans after the capture of

An anti-Mexican War cartoon

OUR MEXICAN RELATIONS.

Zachary Taylor
TWELFTH PRESIDENT   1849-1850

James K. Polk
ELEVENTH PRESIDENT   **1845-1849**

John Tyler
TENTH PRESIDENT   **1841-1845**

William Henry Harrison
NINTH PRESIDENT 1841

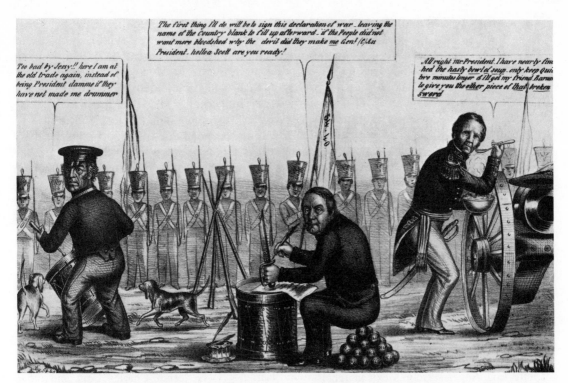

The first thing I'll do will be to sign this declaration of war _ leaving the name of the Country blank to fill up afterward _ if the People did not want more bloodshed why the devil did they make me Gen! (G)Ass President _ hollea Scott are you ready!

Too bad by Jessy!! here I am at the old trade again, instead of being President damme if they have not made me drummer

All right mr President. I have nearly finished the hasty bowl of soup _ only keep Quiet two minutes longer & I'll get my friend Barnum to give you the other piece of that broken Sword

President (C) ass Beginning Operations. (As seen by this caricaturist the Mexican war is being run by Senator Cass from Michigan and President Polk is merely the drummer boy.)

Monterrey has been disapproved.

Oct. 16   Dr. William Thomas Morton, a dentist, makes the first public use of letheon [ether] to kill pain in an operation at Massachusetts General Hospital in Boston. This event brings to the attention of physicians the application of the gas for medicine, although it was first used four years earlier by Dr. Crawford Long. [In November, Oliver Wendell Holmes suggests that the medical use of such agents be described as "anesthesia."]

Nov. 5   The Navy Department orders Commodore Stockton to recognize General Kearny as governor and commander-in-chief in California.

Nov. 15   Commodore David Conner captures Tampico on the Gulf coast of Mexico.

Nov. 16   Saltillo, the capital of the state of Coahuila, is occupied by Taylor's forces.

Nov. 23   General Winfield Scott is ordered to command an expedition against Veracruz, another city on Mexico's Gulf Coast, and the historic approach to Mexico City from the sea.

Dec. 12   American Minister Benjamin A. Bidlack signs a treaty of peace, amity, navigation, and commerce with New Granada [Colombia], at Bogotá. The treaty grants to the

United States the right of way across the isthmus of Panama. The United States in turn guarantees the neutrality of the isthmus and Granadan sovereignty over it.

Dec. 14   Colonel Doniphan and about 1,000 of his volunteers leave Santa Fe for a rendezvous with General Wool in Chihuahua. [Although Wool fails to appear at the rendezvous, Doniphan's contingent not only reaches the city and captures it, but continues its march of more than 3,600 miles miles to make contact with General Taylor in Monterrey and eventually to sail for New Orleans and return to Missouri.]

Dec. 27   El Paso is occupied by Doniphan's force, after defeating the Mexicans in the Battle of El Brazito, just north of El Paso.

Dec. 28   Iowa becomes the 29th state. The territorial capital, Iowa City, becomes the state capital [until 1857, when it is moved to Des Moines], and Ansel Briggs, a Democrat, is the first governor.

Dec. 29   Forces under Kearny and Stockton advance northward from San Diego toward Los Angeles.

Dec. 29   Victoria, the capital of the state of Tamaulipas, is occupied by Taylor's forces.

In 1847 Americans spend almost as much energy in conflict with each other as they do in combat against the Mexicans. These quarrels within the camp of approaching victory are potentially more ominous than the bloodletting about to be concluded along the front from Veracruz to Monterey. Eventual peace between Mexico and the United States is possible, after the soldiers are interred and the price of the land is determined and paid. The use to which the conquered territory will be put—whether slaves or free men will determine the base of its economy—is not so easily resolvable. Relations between the Whig generals Zachary Taylor and Winfield Scott are hostile, and there is friction between General Taylor and the Administration. In California, American leaders General Kearny and Commodore Stockton dispute the right to govern that province. Back home, antislavery forces in Congress continue their effort to enact into law the Wilmot Proviso, which proposes to exclude slavery from any territory acquired from Mexico. Whigs and antislavery Democrats attack the war policy of the Polk Administration.

Jan. 3 General Scott reaches Camargo. Without consulting General Taylor, Scott orders that 9,000 of Taylor's best troops be transferred to the expedition against Veracruz. Scott also directs Taylor to stay on the defensive on the line of Monterrey.

Jan. 10 Forces under Commodore Robert F. Stockton and General Stephen Watts Kearny recapture Los Angeles from Mexican rebels two days after clashing with them near the San Gabriel River.

Jan. 12 General Taylor withdraws his troops from Victoria.

Jan. 13 The Mexican forces commanded by Andres Pico surrender to Frémont, acting under Stockton's orders. The treaty of Cahuenga, by which the Mexicans are granted generous terms of capitulation, is signed.

Jan. 15 In the House of Representatives, Robert Barnwell Rhett of South Carolina declares that the states are the joint owners of the territories and the Federal Government is merely their agent.

Jan. 16 Stockton elevates Frémont to the rank of lieutenant colonel and appoints him governor of California.

Jan. 16 A bill establishing a territorial government for Oregon that includes the restrictions of the Northwest Ordinance concerning slavery passes in the House of Representatives by a vote of 133 to 35.

Jan. 19 Governor Charles Bent and other Americans are killed by Mexican insurgents at Taos, New Mexico.

Jan. 22 Taylor, in a letter to General Edmund P. Gaines that is published in the New York *Morning Express,* defends his grant of an armistice to the Mexicans and criticizes the Polk Administration. [On Jan. 27 Secretary of War William L. Marcy reprimands General Taylor for the letter to Gaines.]

Feb. 4 Troops under Colonel Sterling Price recapture Taos from the Mexican rebels.

Feb. 5-14 Disobeying orders to communicate with General Scott, General Taylor goes on the offensive, advancing west of Saltillo.

Feb. 8 In the House of Representatives, supporters of President Polk introduce a bill to provide $3,000,000 to the President to facilitate negotiations with the Mexicans concerning the acquisition of territory.

Feb. 13 General Stephen Watts Kearny receives instructions from Washington to establish a new government for California.

Feb. 15 The "Three Million Bill," including a stronger Wilmot Proviso, passes in the House of Representatives by a vote of 115 to 105.

Feb. 18-19 General Scott sets up headquarters at Tampico and establishes a civil administration for the occupied Mexican territory (the first such system in U.S. history) that leaves

General Scott enters Mexico City.

local affairs in the hands of Mexican officials.

Feb. 22-23   In the hard-fought Battle of Buena Vista, west of Saltillo, Taylor's troops defeat a Mexican army under Santa Anna, forcing the Mexicans to withdraw and ending the struggle in northern Mexico.

Feb. 28-Mar. 1   Colonel Doniphan's force wins the Battle of Sacramento and occupies Chihuahua.

Mar. 1-3   The Senate, by a vote of 29 to 24, approves the "Three Million Bill," but it deletes the Wilmot Proviso. The House of Representatives accepts the Senate version by a vote of 115 to 81.

Mar. 3   By a vote of 26 to 18, the Senate tables the Oregon bill, passed by the House, that excludes slavery from that region.

Mar. 3   An act of Congress authorizes the issuance of postage stamps. Previously postage was usually paid on delivery. The practice of printing a small official label that could be attached to mail, indicating that postage was paid (by purchase of the label), is already under way in England and several other countries. The first U.S. stamps, one for 5 cents with a portrait of Benjamin Franklin and another for 10 cents with a portrait of George Washington, are authorized for use beginning July 1.

Mar. 3   Congress provides for the introduction of gas lighting into the Capitol and its grounds.

Mar. 9   The first large-scale amphibious landings in U.S. military history are made on the beaches south of Veracruz by Scott's troops.

Mar. 22-29   Following the refusal by the Mexican commander at Veracruz to surrender, a bombardment of the city and the castle of San Juan de Ulúa begins. The Mexicans capitulate on Mar. 27, and the occupation of the city by Scott's troops takes place two days later.

April 8   Scott's troops advance toward Mexico City along the National Road.

April 15   Nicholas P. Trist, the chief clerk of the Department of State, is appointed peace commissioner to Mexico. He is authorized to offer alternative payments depending on the amount of territory ceded by Mexico.

April 26   The legislature of Massachusetts describes the war as "wanton, unjust, and unconstitutional."

May 31   Colonel Richard B. Mason becomes governor of California and Kearny, Stockton, and Frémont depart for Washington. [It is important to note that California does not become a territory before it is admitted as a state; all gov-

ernors are administrators of a province of Mexico that has been conquered.]

July 22   An advance party of Mormons enters the valley of the Great Salt Lake. Brigham Young and the rest of the Pioneer Band arrive two days later.

Aug. 6-11   Reinforcements for General Scott's army under General Franklin Pierce reach Puebla, which was occupied by Scott on May 15. Scott's forces now begin the last phase of their advance toward Mexico City, and headquarters are set up at Ayotla in the Valley of Mexico.

Aug. 19-24   U.S. troops rout the Mexicans at Contreras and at Churubusco. On Aug. 24 an armistice goes into effect.

Aug. 27-Sept. 14   Trist and the Mexican commissioners conduct negotiations that end with a rejection of the American terms by the Mexicans. The armistice is terminated. On Sept. 8 troops commanded by General William J. Worth defeat the Mexicans in the Battle of Molino del Rey. On Sept. 12 the hill of Chapultepec is bombarded by artillery. The next day the hill and the San Cosme and Belén gates to Mexico City are captured by Scott's forces, which now enter Mexico City. The U.S. flag is raised over the National Palace; U.S. marines guard the "halls of Montezuma."

Nov. 22   The new Mexican Government of Manuel de la Peña y Peña informs Trist that it has appointed commissioners to discuss peace on the basis of the original American offer.

Nov. 26   General Taylor departs for the United States. [On Dec. 3 he arrives in New Orleans, where he receives a tremendous reception.]

Dec. 4   Trist ignores instructions to return home and proceeds with peace negotiations.

Dec. 29   In a letter to A.O.P. Nicholson of Nashville, Senator Lewis Cass of Michigan, former governor of Michigan Territory, promulgates the doctrine of popular sovereignty as an argument against legislation such as the Wilmot Proviso, which would have the Federal Government decide whether or not slavery would be permitted in the states to be formed from the territory acquired from Mexico. (Earlier, such legislation, embodied in the Missouri Compromise, was applied to the territory of the Louisiana Purchase.) Cass proposes that those who settle in the territories in question should have the sole right to determine their institutions. [Later John C. Calhoun disdainfully refers to the doctrine as one of "squatter sovereignty."]

1848

From one point of view, the Treaty of Guadalupe Hidalgo comes just in time, for it is signed just nine days after gold is discovered at Sutter's mill in what is still a Mexican province. The treaty not only extends the American empire in a wide zone across the continent. It also brings an increase in acrimony as proslavery and antislavery factions apply their differences to the new lands and even to slightly earlier acquisitions, such as Oregon.

The political scene reflects the circumstances. As Presidential nominating time approaches, candidates are measured, at least in part, in terms of their position on the great issue (inasmuch as the controversies concerning the annexation of Texas and the war with Mexico are no longer available). The Whigs, associated more with the North than with the South, and having two competing leaders (Clay and Webster), neither of whom can muster a winning constituency, select as their candidate a slaveholding Southerner. This is the war hero, Zachary Taylor, considered safely nonpolitical. The Democrats, with their Southern tinge, pick Lewis Cass of Michigan, who has developed the idea of popular sovereignty (let the settler decide), to head their ticket. Antislavery Whigs ("Conscience Whigs," they call themselves) and antislavery Democrats (Barnburners) join with the Free-Soil Party to support ex-President Martin Van Buren. As it happens, they muster enough strength in one state to make Taylor the next President.

Jan. 2   Nicholas P. Trist, the U.S. commissioner who is no longer authorized to negotiate, nevertheless begins to discuss peace terms with the Mexican commissioners.

Jan. 3   Girard College opens in Philadelphia; under the terms of its endowment by financier Stephen Girard, only white boys who are orphans may study there.

Jan. 10   Senator Stephen A. Douglas of Illinois introduces a bill providing that the provisional laws of Oregon, which exclude slavery from that territory, shall remain valid until changed by the territorial legislature.

Jan. 24   Gold is discovered in California by James W. Marshall while he is supervising the erection of a sawmill on the American River for Johann A. Sutter.

Jan. 31   In the aftermath of the Kearny-Stockton Affair, a court-martial finds John C. Frémont guilty of mutiny, disobedience, and prejudicial conduct, and dismisses him from the Army. [President Polk grants him clemency, but Frémont resigns and resumes his activities as an explorer, with some gold prospecting on the side.]

Feb. 2   Trist and the Mexican commissioners sign a treaty in the village of Guadalupe Hidalgo, near Mexico City, which provides for the cession of Texas, New Mexico, and California to the United States in return for $15,000,000 and the assumption by the U.S. Government of claims against Mexico (valued at $3,250,000). The territory that becomes part of the United States as a result of the treaty includes the entire Southwest from the 42d parallel south to the Gila and Rio Grande rivers. [Within this area, comparable in size to the Louisiana Purchase, are the present states of Texas (claimed by the United States as of 1845), California, Utah, Nevada, and New Mexico; most of Arizona; the Oklahoma panhandle; most of Colorado; southwestern Kansas; and southwestern Wyoming. The treaty, despite its questionable origin, is submitted by Polk to the Senate for ratification on Feb. 22, and after ratification by the Senate and the Mexican Congress becomes effective on July 4.]

Feb. 9   The Oregon bill excluding slavery, that was passed by the House of Representatives in 1847 but tabled by the Senate, is reintroduced in the House.

Feb. 18   General Winfield Scott relinquishes command of the American army in Mexico.

Feb. 23   Former President John Quincy Adams, 80, dies in the House of Representatives, where he has served since 1831.

Feb. 29   A military armistice suspends formal hostilities between the United States and Mexico.

Mar. 29   John Jacob Astor, 84, the foremost entrepreneur of his generation, dies in New York City. Worth more than $20,000,000, he is the richest man in the United States at the time of his death.

May 22-26   The Democratic national convention, held in Baltimore, nominates Senator Lewis Cass of Michigan for President and General William O. Butler of Kentucky for Vice President.

May 29   Wisconsin becomes the 30th state,

restoring the balance between free and slave states. The St. Croix River becomes the northwestern border of the state.

May 31 Congress authorizes the purchase of the papers of James Madison.

June 7-9 In Philadelphia, General Zachary Taylor of Louisiana and Millard Fillmore of New York are nominated for President and Vice President by the Whig national convention.

June 12 Mexico City is evacuated by the American army.

June 22 The antislavery (Barnburner) faction of the Democratic Party meets at Utica, New York, and nominates Martin Van Buren of New York for President and Henry Dodge of Wisconsin for Vice President. They are called Barnburners because their alleged willingness to endanger the Union by antagonizing the slave interests is compared to the willingness of a farmer to burn down his barn to get rid of the rats.

June 27 Senator Jesse D. Bright of Indiana introduces an amendment to the Oregon bill extending the Missouri Compromise line to the Pacific; Senator John C. Calhoun of South Carolina opposes the amendment.

July 4 The cornerstone of the Washington monument is laid in Washington, D.C.

July 12 The question of the extension of slavery is referred to a Senate committee chaired by John M. Clayton of Delaware.

July 19 The first Woman's Rights Convention is held at Seneca Falls, New York.

July 27-28 The Senate approves, 33 to 22, a bill proposed by John Middleton Clayton, a Whig from Delaware, that would exclude slavery from Oregon and forbid New Mexico and California from passing laws on the slavery question. The Clayton Compromise bill is tabled in the House of Representatives.

Aug. 9 In Buffalo, New York, the national convention of the Free-Soil Party nominates Van Buren for President and Charles Francis Adams of Massachusetts for Vice President.

Aug. 14 Polk signs a bill, passed by the House on Aug. 2 and by the Senate on Aug. 13, that establishes a territorial Government and prohibits slavery in Oregon.

Aug. 19 The discovery of gold in California is announced in the New York *Herald.*

Nov. 7 In the first Presidential election to be held on the same day in every state, Whigs Zachary Taylor and Millard Fillmore defeat Democrats Lewis Cass and William O. Butler and Free-Soilers Martin Van Buren and Charles Francis Adams. Taylor receives 1,360,967 popu-

AN AVAILABLE CANDIDATE.
THE ONE QUALIFICATION FOR A WHIG PRESIDENT.

An anti-Zachary Taylor cartoon

lar and 163 electoral votes, and Cass wins 1,222,342 popular and 127 electoral votes. Although 291,263 votes are cast for Van Buren, he carries no state, but his popular vote in New York gives that state and the election to Taylor.

Dec. 5 In his annual message to Congress, President Polk confirms the discovery of gold in California.

Dec. 15 In London a postal treaty is concluded between the United States and Great Britain.

Dec. 22 A caucus of 69 Southerners in Congress is held to consider the slavery question.

1849 The Whig Administration takes office in Washington. President Zachary Taylor's victory over the Democratic candidate, Lewis Cass, was close, and Taylor does not have a Whig Congress to work with. At the beginning of the year an address attacking the attitudes and actions of the North in the controversy over slavery is signed by 48 Southerners in the 30th Congress. When the 31st Congress convenes in December, the House of Representatives is deadlocked. The seats are almost evenly divided between the Democrats and the Whigs, and a small group of Free-Soilers hold the balance of power.

Meanwhile, territorial governments have not been established in California and New Mexico because of a dispute over the status of slavery in these areas. The discovery of gold in California last year and the subsequent massive influx of settlers [the Forty-Niners] have made the organization of a territory imperative. President Taylor sends messengers to the people of California and New Mexico to urge them to form governments. In California a constitution prohibiting slavery is adopted and ratified, and a state Government begins to operate. Taylor proposes that Congress immediately admit California to the Union. But Southerners oppose such a move, because the admission of a free state would upset the even balance between free and slave states.

Jan. 15 The second meeting of a Congressional caucus called to discuss the slavery question draws about 80 Southerners.

Jan. 22 An "Address of the Southern Delegates," written by Senator John C. Calhoun of South Carolina, is signed by 48 out of about 80 Southerners present at a third caucus on slavery. The address condemns the North's "systematic agitation" against slavery and charges that the North is attempting to destroy the institution through emancipation or war. Northern "acts of aggression" against the rights of the South specified in the address include the exclusion of slavery from the territories, opposition to slavery in the District of Columbia, and resistance to the return of fugitive slaves.

Feb. 12 A temporary government for San Francisco in California is established by a mass meeting.

Feb. 28 The first shipload of gold seekers arrives at San Francisco.

Mar. 3 The Department of the Interior, at first called the Home Department, is created. The department is given responsibility for matters involving the census, Indians, public lands, and patents. [On Mar. 8 Thomas Ewing becomes the first Secretary of the new department. He had been Secretary of the Treasury for Presidents Harrison and Tyler, and had resigned with the Tyler Cabinet in 1841.]

Mar. 3 Minnesota Territory is organized. It is bounded, south of Canada, by Lake Superior and the new state of Wisconsin (east of the St. Croix River) on the east; by the new state of Iowa on the south; and by the Missouri River on the west. Its population of about 5,000 is mostly concentrated around St. Paul, near Fort Snelling at the Falls of St. Anthony on the upper Mississippi. Alexander Ramsey is the first governor.

Mar. 3 The coinage of the gold dollar and the double eagle ($20) are authorized.

Mar. 5 General Zachary Taylor of Louisiana is inaugurated as the 12th President of the United States. Millard Fillmore of New York becomes Vice President.

Mar. 7 Senator John M. Clayton of Delaware is named Secretary of State.

Mar. 10 The legislature of Missouri asserts that only the people of a territory, not Congress, can prohibit slavery—an official endorsement of Cass's "popular sovereignty."

May 10 A riot outside the Astor Place Opera House in New York City, growing out of a feud between British actor George Macready and American actor Edwin Forrest, results in about 20 deaths.

May 17 A great fire devastates the waterfront of St. Louis as the wharfs are ignited by steamships burning alongside.

June 15 James Knox Polk, 53, the 11th President of the United States, dies in Nashville, Tennessee.

Aug. 11 President Taylor issues a proclamation disapproving of the López expedition to win Cuba's independence from Spain. The expedition is being organized by Narciso López, a former officer in the Spanish army and a native of Venezuela, who has made the liberation of Cuba his prime objective.

Aug. 12 Albert Gallatin, 88, Secretary of the

Treasury under Presidents Jefferson and Madison, dies in Astoria, Long Island, New York.

Sept. 1-Oct. 13 A convention meets at Monterey and adopts a constitution for California that prohibits slavery.

Oct. 1 A convention in Mississippi calls for a convention of the slave states to meet in Nashville, Tennessee.

Nov. 13 The California constitution is ratified by the voters.

Nov. 14 A bridge across the Ohio River at Wheeling, Virginia, is formally opened. It is the longest suspension bridge in the world.

Dec. 3 The first session of the 31st Congress convenes in Washington. The Senate is under Democratic control, with 35 members to 25 for the Whigs. But the division of the House of Representatives into 112 Democrats, 109 Whigs, and 9 Free-Soilers results in a lengthy organizational contest.

Dec. 4 In his annual message to Congress, President Taylor advocates that California be immediately admitted into the Union.

Dec. 20 The state Government begins to operate in California. The lack of a territorial Government and an increasing and turbulent population have resulted in an intolerable situation, which is not always improved by the formation of vigilance committees ("Vigilantes") to substitute for official law-enforcement agencies.

Dec. 20 A treaty of amity, commerce, and navigation is concluded between the United States and the Hawaiian Islands in Washington.

Dec. 22 Democrat Howell Cobb of Georgia is elected Speaker of the House of Representatives after three weeks of acrimony and 63 ballots.

Edgar Allan Poe
(1809-1849)

In the 7th decennial census, the total population of the United States is recorded at 23,191,876. The rate of increase in population, 35.9 per cent over the decade, is the highest so far attained. [It is not surpassed in later decades.] Since 1840, four new states have entered the Union: Florida, Texas, Iowa, and Wisconsin. This has maintained the equilibrium between free and slave states in the Senate, but the admission this year of California, credited to the next decade, will end that balance. In the House of Representatives the influence of slavery has receded so completely that this year, of the 234 members, 144 represent free soil and 90 represent states in which slavery is permitted.

It is therefore obvious that the United States, victorious only two years ago in the war with Mexico, may be rent asunder by sectional antagonisms arising out of the controversies over slavery and its possible extension into the territories acquired from Mexico. Early in the year the venerable Henry Clay of Kentucky returns to the Senate and offers a set of eight resolutions in an attempt to resolve the basic disputes between the North and the South. For the North, Clay offers the admission of California to the Union as a free state and the prohibition of the slave trade in the District of Columbia. For the South, he proposes that Congress not interfere with slavery in the District of Columbia or with interstate slave trading, and that a stronger fugitive-slave law be enacted. For both, he suggests that territorial governments be organized in New Mexico and Utah without any provisions regarding slavery. In addition, Clay advocates settling the Texas question by adjusting that state's boundaries in return for the assumption of its debts by the U.S. Government.

Clay's proposals set the stage for a great debate. Clay argues for his resolutions. The dying Senator John C. Calhoun of South Carolina opposes Clay's measures in a speech read by one of his colleagues. However, Massachusetts Senator Daniel Webster supports Clay with an eloquent defense of the Union. Compromise is rejected by New York Senator William H. Seward and Ohio Senator Salmon P. Chase on one side, and Senator Jefferson Davis of Mississippi on the other. Clay's resolutions are soon referred to a select committee of 13 Senators, of which the Kentuckian serves as the chairman. This committee reports out an "Omnibus Bill" containing all the territorial provisions and separate bills concerning fugitive slaves and the District of Columbia slave trade. President Zachary Taylor does not support Clay's moves, but after his death in July the New President, Millard Fillmore, backs the compromise proposals. Gradually, the series of acts comprising the "Compromise of 1850" are approved by both Houses of Congress and signed by President Fillmore.

At the same time that the United States barely survives a major sectional crisis, it acts boldly in foreign affairs. Secretary of State John M. Clayton negotiates a treaty with British Minister Sir Henry Bulwer, in which the United States and Great Britain mutually renounce exclusive control over a Central American canal. Daniel Webster, Clayton's successor at the State Department, rejects Austria's protest concerning American actions during the 1848 revolution in Hungary. The ardor for expansion continues to appear, particularly among those who see no other way to maintain the influence of the slave power, in Southern support for the expeditions of General Narciso López against Cuba, a territory seen as potentially within the American orbit.

Jan. 2   A treaty of amity, navigation, and commerce is signed by representatives of the United States and El Salvador in León.

Jan. 29   Senator Henry Clay of Kentucky proposes eight resolutions designed to settle the controversies between the North and the South over slavery. The resolutions call for the admission of California to the Union as a free state, the establishment of territorial governments for New Mexico and Utah without reference to slavery, the adjustment of the boundaries of Texas, the assumption of the Texas debt by the Federal Government, no interference with slavery in the District of Columbia, (the abolition of the slave trade in the District of Columbia,) and the enactment of a more effective fugitive-slave law. The final resolution asserts that Congress has no power over the slave trade between the states.

Feb. 12 A Congressional resolution is approved that provides for the purchase of the manuscript of George Washington's "Farewell Address."

Mar. 4 The speech of Senator John C. Calhoun of South Carolina against the compromise resolutions is read by Senator James M. Mason of Virginia, Calhoun being too ill to deliver it.

Mar. 6 The Mississippi legislature calls for a convention of the slave states to meet in Nashville, Tennessee, on June 3.

Mar. 7 Daniel Webster of Massachusetts supports Clay's resolutions in a speech in the Senate. In his concern for the preservation of the Union, he concedes more to the proslavery faction that is acceptable to many of his constituents. [The Seventh of March oration, noted for its eloquence, arouses a storm of vilification and possibly accounts for the failure to consider Webster as a Presidential candidate in 1852.

Mar. 11 Senator William H. Seward of New York speaks against compromise.

Mar. 12 California requests admission to the Union.

Mar. 13-14 Clay's proposed compromise is opposed by Jefferson Davis of Mississippi in a Senate speech.

Mar. 26-27 Ohio Senator Salmon P. Chase rejects the compromise.

Mar. 31 John Caldwell Calhoun, 68, a spokesman for the South since the War of 1812, Vice President of the United States under John Quincy Adams and Andrew Jackson, Senator, and political philosopher, dies in Washington, D.C.

April 18 Clay's resolutions are referred to a select committee of 13 Senators, with Clay himself as chairman.

April 19 Secretary of State John M. Clayton and the British Minister to the United States, Sir Henry Lytton Bulwer, sign a treaty in Washington delineating the role of the two countries in Central America. The treaty provides that neither nation will exclusively control or fortify a Central American ship canal, when such a canal is constructed; and that the nationals of both countries will have equal rights and pay equal charges to use such a canal. The treaty also guarantees the neutrality of such a canal, and affirms that neither country will colonize America.

April 27 The *Atlantic* sails from New York for Liverpool, inaugurating regular steamship service between those two cities by the Collins Line, an American-owned enterprise which is in competition with the British Cunard Line.

May 8 The Senate select committee headed by Henry Clay reports three bills to the floor of the Senate: an "Omnibus Bill" concerned with California, the two territorial governments, and the Texas boundary and debt; a fugitive-slave measure; and a bill to abolish the slave trade in the District of Columbia.

May 19 The second expedition led by General Narciso López lands at Cárdenas in Cuba.

May 22 An expedition financed by Henry Grinnell, a New York merchant, and led by Lieutenant Edwin Jesse De Haven, sails from New York for the Arctic to search for Sir John Franklin, who disappeared while exploring the polar region in 1845.

May 25 A convention in New Mexico adopts a constitution that establishes boundaries for the proposed state and prohibits slavery.

June 3-10 A convention with representatives from nine slaves states meets in Nashville, Tennessee, advocating resolutions opposing Clay's compromise, and advocating that the Missouri Compromise line be extended to the Pacific. This would include the Southwest and California south of Monterey in the area open to slavery.

Jenny Lind

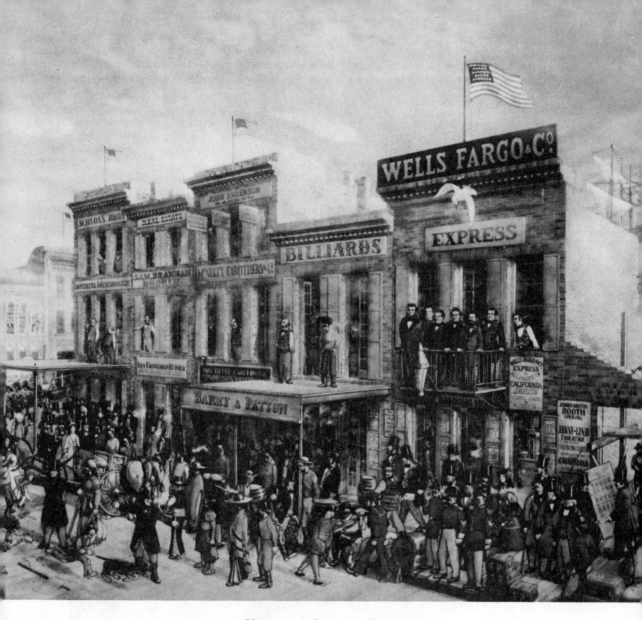

Montgomery Street, San Francisco

July 1 The first overland mail service west of the Missouri River is established on a monthly basis between Independence and Salt Lake City.

July 9 President Zachary Taylor, 65, dies of cholera morbus [gastroenteritis] in the White House.

July 10 Millard Fillmore of New York takes the oath of office as the 13th President.

July 22 President Fillmore appoints Daniel Webster of Massachusetts Secretary of State

July 31 The Senate passes, 32 to 18, a bill establishing a territorial Government for Utah with no restriction on slavery. Utah Territory would extend from the Rocky Mountains to the California border at the crest of the range [the Sierra Nevada] on the west edge of the desert, and between Oregon Territory on the north and New Mexico Territory on the south. This area, when it was still Mexican territory, was part of the "State of Deseret" proclaimed by the Mormons in 1847.

Aug. 9 The Senate approves, 30 to 20, a bill that adjusts the boundary between Texas and New Mexico and provides for the payment of $10,000,000 to Texas. The area added to New Mexico is north of the 32d parallel and west of the 103d meridian.

Aug. 13 A bill providing for the admission of California to the Union as a free state passes in the Senate by a vote of 34 to 18.

Aug. 15   The Senate approves, 27 to 10, a bill that establishes the Territory of New Mexico with no restriction on slavery. The territory runs west to the Colorado River. [It includes the area of the present state of Arizona, the southern tip of Nevada, and Colorado south of the Arkansas River.]

Aug. 23   The fugitive-slave bill passes in the Senate, 27 to 12.

Sept. 6-9   By a vote of 108 to 97, the House of Representatives approves the combined Texas and New Mexico bills; the California statehood bill, 150 to 56; and the Utah bill, 97 to 85. On Sept. 9, with Fillmore's signature, New Mexico and Utah become organized territories, and California enters the Union as the 31st state.

Sept. 11   Jenny Lind, Swedish soprano making a tour of the United States under the auspices of P. T. Barnum, gives her first U.S. performance in New York City.

Sept. 12   The fugitive-slave bill is approved in the House, 109 to 76.

Sept. 16   By a vote of 33 to 19, the Senate passes a bill that abolishes the slave trade in the District of Columbia.

Sept. 17   The House approves the District of Columbia slave-trade bill, 124 to 47.

Sept. 18   Fillmore signs the fugitive-slave act. An amendment to the 1793 fugitive-slave law, this measure removes fugitive-slave cases from state to Federal jurisdiction. Special Federal commissioners are to be appointed who will conduct hearings and issue warrants of arrest and certificates of return. Although a mere affidavit from a master is to be accepted as proof of ownership, those accused of being slaves are not permitted jury trials or allowed to testify in their own defense. The commissioners are to receive $10 for granting a certificate of return and $5 for denying one. They are authorized to summon aid or a posse. Those evading or obstructing the law are to suffer severe penalties.

Sept. 20   The District of Columbia slave-trade act is signed by Fillmore.

Sept. 20   The first Federal land grants for railroads are approved. Land is given to Illinois, Mississippi, and Alabama to aid in the construction of a railroad from Illinois to Mobile, Alabama.[Within the next 21 years, about 130,000,000 acres of public lands, valued at the time at about $125,000,000 are granted to the railroads.]

Sept. 28   President Fillmore appoints Brigham Young governor of Utah Territory.

Sept. 28   By act of Congress, flogging is prohibited in the U.S. Navy and merchant marine.

Nov. 25   A treaty of friendship and commerce between the United States and the Swiss Confederation is signed in Berne.

Dec. 13-14   The Georgia Platform, which accepts Clay's compromise, is adopted by a state convention at Milledgeville.

Dec. 21   In a communication to the Austrian Foreign Minister [the Hulsemann Letter] Secretary of State Webster defends American recognition of revolutions in Erurope. [Webster, along with many Americans, demonstrates his sympathy with the Hungarian Revolution when its leader, Louis Kossuth, visits the United States in 1851.]

Henry Clay addressing the U.S. Senate

1851 **In the year following the momentous Compromise of 1850,** the slavery issue and sectionalist conflict appear to become less of a national political burden. But the public is not allowed to forget that these problems exist, because orators, newspapermen, writers, composers, and reformers in general continue to articulate their opinions concerning the institution of slavery and many other controversial questions—women's rights, education for women and blacks, temperance, and suffrage. The possible expansion of the Southern economic system to the Spanish colony of Cuba is a particularly attractive idea to some, but it is officially discouraged. The real national concerns are for production, railroad expansion, inventions, and public tranquillity.

Jan. 27 John James Audubon, 65, after a life of writing and achievement as an artist, naturalist, and ornithologist, dies in New York City.

Feb. 10 Illinois Governor Augustus C. French, as authorized by Congress, signs the charter of the Illinois Central Railroad, granting it 2,700,000 acres of land in alternate sections (each one mile square) on each side of its proposed route, from Cairo to Galena. [Such a gift of public domain is known as a land grant and becomes the usual technique for funding railroad construction.]

April 25 President Fillmore issues a proclamation ordering U.S. citizens not to participate in expeditions against Cuba. He labels such actions as "palpable violations" of U.S. neutrality laws.

May 4 A large part of the city of St. Louis is destroyed by fire.

May 29 Sojourner Truth, a free Negro born as a slave named Isabella, attends the Second Woman's Rights Convention for Ohio at Akron, and is acclaimed for her moving presentation.

June 2 The Quaker mayor of Portland, Maine, Neal Dow, signs the so-called "Maine Law," which drives liquor traffic out of his city.

Aug. 3 Despite the proclamation by President Fillmore in April, Narciso López, a Venezuelan revolutionist, sails from New Orleans with some 400 armed followers, Spanish refugees and some Southern Americans, in a third attempt to overthrow Spain's power in its Cuban colony.

Aug. 16 Colonel William L. Crittenden of Kentucky and about 50 other American volunteers with the López expedition are sentenced by a Spanish military court and executed in Havana after their capture three days earlier.

Aug. 21 Riots in New Orleans protest the execution of Americans by Spain, and the crowd wrecks the Spanish consulate.

Aug. 26 A song called *Old Folks at Home* [later shortened to *Swanee River*] is copyrighted in the name of Edwin P. Christy. It is actually the work of Stephen C. Foster, the well-known composer of *O Susanna,* who has written this "Ethiopian song" for Christy's minstrels to sing in New York City.

Sept. 1 López is garroted publicly in Havana after his capture on August 28, and nearly half his supporters who are Americans are sent to prison in Spain. [They are released after Congress votes a $25,000 indemnity for damage to the New Orleans consulate.]

Sept. 12 Francis Parkman sends copies of the American edition of his *History of The Conspiracy of Pontiac* to friends.

Sept. 14 James Fenimore Cooper, 62, dies at Cooperstown, New York, where he lived and wrote after 1834.

Sept. 18 The *New York Daily Times* is founded by Henry J. Raymond with George Jones, as a Whig Republican newspaper. [It becomes the *New York Times* in 1857.]

Oct. 15-16 The Second National Woman's Rights Convention is held at Worcester, Massachusetts, attended by such nationally prominent women as Lucy Stone, Mrs. Lucretia Mott, Mrs. Paula Wright Davis, Angelina Grimké, and Sojourner Truth.

Nov. 14 Herman Melville publishes the first American edition of his novel, *Moby-Dick or, The Whale.*

Dec. 24 More than 30,000 volumes in the Library of Congress are burned as a great fire sweeps its wing of the Capitol.

Dec. 20 Captain T. V. Sullivan opens a branch of the Young Men's Christian Association in Boston. The organization was founded in London in 1844.

Dec. 29 Lola Montez (Marie Dolores Eliza Rosanna Gilbert), an Irish dancer and adventuress, opens her American tour in *Betley, The Tyrolean* at the Broadway Theater in the city of New York.

The Presidential election shows that most Americans prefer to avoid the slavery issue. Both Democrats and Whigs accept the Compromise of 1850 as final; indeed, the Whigs decry further agitation concerning slavery and affirm states' rights. The Free-Soil Party, however, attacks both the Compromise and the slave system, and proposes to provide free homestead lands and encourage open immigration. The voters give a decisive victory to the Democrats, now a conservative and a Southern-directed party; the Whigs disintegrate; and the Free-Soilers are out of the running. With the deaths of the last two giant politicans of the War of 1812 era, the generation of John Quincy Adams, Andrew Jackson, John C. Calhoun, Henry Clay, and Daniel Webster is ended. It would appear that the nation could turn to the expansion it craves, with the unpleasant matter of slavery neutralized for a while. Yet the sensational reception of Mrs. Stowe's *Uncle Tom's Cabin* does not square with the notion of social apathy.

Jan. 5   President Fillmore informs Congress that the Americans captured in the Narciso López expedition to Cuba have been released and pardoned by the Spanish Government, and he recommends prompt authorization for the indemnity payment for damages to Spanish subjects in the New Orleans riots.

Feb. 10   Congress votes funds for the relief and return of American citizens lately pardoned by Spain.

Mar. 20   Harriet Beecher Stowe publishes *Uncle Tom's Cabin; or, Life Among the Lowly,* a two-volume sentimental novel depicting black slavery with its injustice and abuse. The author is especially angered by the Fugitive Slave law of 1850. [The work is a best-seller with both a national and international impact.]

Mar. 29   The state of Ohio passes a law setting a 10-hour day as the standard maximum for the employment of women. Those who are willing to work longer may do so.

April 20-21   The New York State Temperance Society is formed at Rochester, with Elizabeth Cady Stanton as president.

May   The American Women's Educational Association is organized in New York City by Catharine E. Beecher, who aims to further public interest in the liberal education of wives, mothers, and housekeepers for entrance into the professions.

June 1-5   The Democratic national convention meets in Baltimore and nominates Franklin Pierce of New Hampshire for President on the 49th ballot. For Vice President it names William R. D. King of Alabama, a distinguished leader of the Senate.

June 17-20   The Whig Party, gathering at Baltimore, nominates war-hero General Winfield Scott of Virginia on the 53d ballot; his running mate is William A. Graham of North Carolina.

June 29   Henry Clay, 75, ill since 1850, dies of tuberculosis in a Washington, D.C., hotel and is buried in Lexington, Kentucky.

July 4   Frederick Douglass, Negro lecturer, newspaperman, and abolitionist, raises at Rochester, New York, the question of why the black people should celebrate the Fourth of July.

Aug. 11   The Free-Soil Party convenes at Pittsburgh to nominate John P. Hale of New Hampshire for President and George W. Julian of Indiana for Vice President.

Aug. 23   *Uncle Tom's Cabin,* with a dramatization by George L. Aiken, is performed as a stage play at the National Theater in New York City.

Oct. 1   The offer by Joshua Bates of $50,000 to the city of Boston for the purchase of books is instrumental in the founding of the Boston Public Library. [It opens in 1854.]

Oct. 24   Daniel Webster, 70, Secretary of State under President Fillmore until illness forces his retirement, dies at his home in Marshfield, Massachusetts. He expected to be the Whig candidate for President, and after failing to be nominated, supported Franklin Pierce.

Oct. 25   President Fillmore writes on Webster's death to his executive department heads: "He has bequeathed to posterity the richest fruits of the experience and judgment of a great mind conversant with the greatest national concerns. In these his memory will endure as long as our country shall continue to be the home and guardian of freedom."

Nov. 2   Franklin Pierce wins election as the 14th President of the United States with 1,601,117 votes; William R. D. King is elected Vice President. Pierce carries 27 states with 254 electoral votes to Scott's 4 states with 42 electoral votes in a strong victory over the Whigs. The Free-Soilers get 5 per cent of the vote.

Nov. 24   Commodore Matthew C. Perry sails for Japan on the steam frigate, *Susquehanna,* flagship of a small naval squadron. He has instructions to seek to end Japanese exclusion of contact with the Western world, to ameliorate or end ill treatment of marooned and shipwrecked American seamen in that country, and to open the Pacific to expanding United States trade.

Dec. 6   In his third annual message to Congress, President Fillmore reviews the peace and prosperity of his Administration and states that "the United States entertains no designs against Cuba. . .its incorporation into the Union at the present time [is] fraught with serious peril" because it could revive sectional conflicts over the slave system.

The riverboat *New St. Paul* at Galena, Illinois, 1852

1853

In his first year in the Presidency, Franklin Pierce makes it clear that territorial expansion—Manifest Destiny, as a journalist termed it in 1845—is a national policy. Pierce himself is dominated and aided by Southern expansionists, and in his inaugural address he states that his Administration does not intend to shirk further territorial acquisitions. Concrete evidence of this spirit is found in the Gadsden Purchase and in Pierce's support for the Japanese venture under Commodore Perry that was initiated by Daniel Webster, President Fillmore's Secretary of State. The question of what to do with national territories already acquired begins to revive tensions and rivalries incompatible with the general belief that the Compromise of 1850 really ended sectional strife.

Feb. 21　The Coinage Act reduces the amount of silver in all coins smaller than a dollar. It also authorizes the minting of $3 gold pieces.

Mar. 2　Washington Territory is organized out of Oregon Territory, to include the Pacific Northwest north of the Columbia River and the 46th parallel east to the Rocky Mountains. One task for the new territory is to negotiate treaties with the Indians to relinquish their lands.

Mar. 4　Franklin Pierce is inaugurated as the 14th President of the United States. Delivering the first inaugural address to be spoken from memory, Pierce supports the Compromise of 1850 and advocates the peaceful acquisition of new territory.

Mar. 7　Jefferson Davis reenters politics as Secretary of War in the Pierce Cabinet. He had resigned two years ago as Senator from Mississippi in protest against the Compromise of 1850.

Mar. 16　Isaac Ingalls Stevens resigns from the Army to accept appointment as governor of Washington Territory.

Mar. 24　William R. D. King takes the oath of office as Vice President at an estate near Matanzas, Cuba, where he is staying for his health. The unusual ceremony is authorized by an act of Congress passed on Mar. 2.

April 8　Based on Congressional instructions to pursue four main rail routes to the Pacific, Governor Isaac Stevens begins a survey of a possible northern route between the 47th and 49th parallels.

April 18　Vice President King, fatally weakened by tuberculosis, returns to his plantation, "King's Bend," near Cahaba, Alabama, where he dies without having taken up his duties.

April 25　William Beaumont, 65, army surgeon who has won lasting fame for his studies on the physiology of the stomach and the chemistry of gastric digestion, dies in St. Louis. His studies were based on observation over many years of the stomach of a young man that had been opened by a close-range musket shot.

May 31　The first Negro YMCA is organized in Washington, D.C., by Anthony Bower.

July 4　Mrs. Amelia Jenks Bloomer, a publisher and reformer for women's causes, delivers a Fourth of July address at Hartford, and draws great public attention for her "Turkish" style in short skirt and full trousers [to which the name of "bloomers" is later applied].

July 6-8　A National Negro Convention is held in Rochester, New York.

July 7　A merger of ten small railroads establishes the New York Central Railroad Company, which connects New York City with Buffalo.

July 8-14　The naval squadron under Commodore Matthew C. Perry reaches Yedo [Tokyo] Bay. Perry presents letters from President Fillmore to representatives of the Japanese emperor, who requires time for reply.

Oct. 8　William Walker of Yuba County, California, sails with 45 other California adventurers in the brig *Carolina* for Guaymas, Sonora, on the Mexican mainland in the Gulf of California. Their ostensible purpose is to stop Apache raids against California.

Oct. 22　Secretary Marcy instructs Minister Gadsden in Mexico City to seek a larger natural boundary with Mexico, including all of Lower California.

Nov. 3　The Walker expedition lands at La Paz, Lower California, captures the Mexican governor, and declares the "Republic of Lower California."

Nov. 12　The first novel by an American Negro, William Wells Brown, is published in London, England, as *Clotel; or, the President's Daughter: A Narrative of Slave Life in the United States.*

Dec. 30　James Gadsden secures the cession from Mexico of a 29,640-square-mile strip of desert land south of the Gila River for $10,000,000.

1854

The major political events of 1854 are associated with the Kansas-Nebraska Bill initiated by Senator Stephen A. Douglas. The notion that the Compromise of 1850 had ended sectionalism appears to have been wishful thinking; the slavery issue is still paramount. With the effective repeal of the Missouri Compromise, political parties now realign. A new Republican Party emerges to challenge the Democrats. Debate gives way to action in the new territories, particularly in Kansas, where "popular sovereignty" is practiced in the form of increasing combat between Southern proslavery raiders from Missouri and resentful, indignant volunteers from the Northern states.

Expansionist activities abroad appear in relation to Cuba, Mexico, Hawaii, and Japan. The imperialistic Ostend Manifesto, which appears to shock the nation, expresses a mood developing in certain high quarters.

Jan. 18   William Walker, by proclamation, adds the Mexican state of Sonora to his "republic" of Lower California.

Jan. 23   Illinois Senator Stephen A. Douglas, chairman of the Senate Committee on Territories, introduces a bill aimed at organizing the country west of the Missouri River and north of 37° N. lat. into the territories of Kansas and Nebraska. Under the bill, each territorial government would decide whether to permit or prohibit slavery within its jurisdiction. This policy is referred to as "popular sovereignty." The passage of this bill would be an equivalent to an outright repeal of the Missouri Compromise.

Jan. 24   An *Appeal to Independent Democrats* is published by Northern opponents of the bill. They describe it as a slaveholders' plot and a violation of the Missouri Compromise and the Compromise of 1850, since both proposed territories are situated north of the 36°30′ parallel.

Feb. 28   A meeting of 50 opponents of the Douglas proposal, held in a schoolhouse at Ripon, Wisconsin, urges the formation of a new political organization, which would take the name of Republican Party.

Feb. 28   The *Black Warrior,* a United States merchant steamer, is seized at Havana, in Spain's colony of Cuba. Her cargo of cotton is confiscated and she is fined over a technical matter of her papers.

Mar. 8   Walker and 34 of his supporters cross back into California and surrender to the U.S. military commander at San Diego. The hostility of the inhabitants of Sonora and Lower California and their own logistical ineptness have frustrated their adventure.

Mar. 15   In the *Black Warrior* affair, Secretary of State William L. Marcy instructs Minister to Spain Pierre Soulé to seek an indemnity of $300,000 and a Spanish disavowal of the incident.

Mar. 31   The Treaty of Kanagawa is signed with Japan, declaring peace and friendship, permitting U.S. ships to purchase supplies at the ports of Shimoda and Hakodate, providing for protection of American nationals shipwrecked in Japan, and allowing a U.S. agent to remain at Shimoda. It is the first time Japan has treated with a foreign government as with an equal.

April 3   Secretary Marcy instructs Minister Soulé that, should circumstances permit, he may offer Spain as much as $130,000,000 for Cuba. If this is not feasible, he is to endeavor to "detach that Island from the Spanish dominion. . . ."

April 4   Secretary Marcy instructs the American commissioner to Hawaii, David L. Gregg, to determine whether King Kamehameha III would accept annexation by the United States.

April 26   The Massachusetts Emigrant Aid Society [after 1855, the New England Emigrant Aid Company] is organized to provide antislavery settlers to go to Kansas if and when the proposed territories are established. Their objective would be to ensure that Kansas would not become a slave state.

April 29   The Ashmun Institute receives a charter from the Commonwealth of Pennsylvania. It is the first United States institution of higher education dedicated mainly to educating Negro youths. [The name is changed to Lincoln University in 1866.]

May 22   The House of Representatives passes the Kansas-Nebraska Bill, 113 to 100.

May 25   The Kansas-Nebraska Act is approved by the Senate, 37 to 14, and goes to President Pierce for his signature. Kansas Territory extends south of 40° N. lat. [Kansas and most of Colorado], Nebraska Territory includes the territory between that parallel and Canada west of the Missouri [Nebraska and parts of Montana, South Dakota, North Dakota, and

Wyoming, and a strip of Colorado]. Existing Federal treaties with Indians, confirming most of these territories to them in perpetuity, are ignored.

May 26 Federal and state military forces collaborate in returning Anthony Burns, a fugitive slave apprehended in Boston, to his master.

June 17 The Order of the Star-Spangled Banner holds its second national convention in New York City. Basically "native American" and anti-Catholic, its members answer questions about the group with "I know nothing about it." As a political organization it is known, therefore, as the Know-Nothing or Native-American Party.

June 29 Andrew H. Reeder, a Pennsylvania lawyer and a popular-sovereignty Democrat, is appointed as the first territorial governor of Kansas.

July 6 Citizens at Jackson, Michigan, form the first Republican Party unit. Their program is repeal of the Fugitive Slave Law and the Kansas-Nebraska Act and the abolition of slavery in the District of Columbia.

July 13 Republican groups are formed at meetings in the states of Indiana, Ohio, Vermont, and Wisconsin.

Aug. 3 The Graduation Act is passed, providing for the disposal through sale of public lands unsold for periods of 10 to 30 years. Sale prices range from $1 per acre for 10-year land down to 12½ cents per acre for land unsold in 30 years, with supporters of the act mainly from the North and West.

Aug. 9 After a two-year isolated sojourn at Walden Pond, near Concord, Massachusetts, Henry David Thoreau publishes *Walden, or Life in the Woods*. Its philosophy is that of an individual gaining freedom by relating to nature and by the rediscovery of himself.

Aug. 16 Secretary Marcy instructs the U.S. Ministers to Spain, Great Britain, and France —Pierre Soulé, James Buchanan, and John Y. Mason—to meet at Ostend, Belgium, to discuss the acquisition of the island of Cuba.

Aug. 24 Dr. John V. De Grasse, a black physician graduated from Bowdoin College in Maine, is admitted to the Massachusetts Medical Society.

Oct. 16 Abraham Lincoln, local lawyer and political speaker in Peoria, Illinois, during the election campaign, denies that the Kansas-Nebraska act is a proslavery plot, but calls for opposition to slavery and gradual emancipation of the slaves.

Oct. 18 Ministers Soulé, Buchanan, and Mason end their conversations at Ostend by sending a confidential diplomatic dispatch aggressively recommending the purchase of Cuba or, if purchase is refused, the seizure of the island from Spain by force.

Nov. 11 A draft of a proposed treaty to annex the Hawaiian Islands, providing for immediate statehood and a $300,000 annual payment to the king and chiefs, is received in Washington.

Nov. 13 The nature of the communication from Ostend, called the Ostend Manifesto, becomes known to the public. Secretary Marcy is shocked by the unexpected opposition to it and bluntly disavows the plan.

Nov. 29 John W. Whitfield is elected as a proslavery candidate for delegate to Congress from Kansas Territory. His election is marked by fraud and violence, mainly on the part of armed men from western Missouri.

Dec. 17 Pierre Soulé resigns as Minister to Spain.

Dec. 28 William H. Russell joins with Alexander Majors and W. B. Waddell in a partnership to establish regular overland freight service from a center at Fort Leavenworth, Kansas, to California, with the help of government subsidies.

Visitors at Niagara Falls (ca.) 1854

1855

The question of the extension of the institution of slavery dominates and focuses national attention. Nebraska remains calm and proceeds in an orderly way to establish a free-soil Government; but Nebraska has only free-soil neighbors, and its natural setting is suited to free labor. Kansas, adjacent to slaveholding states, becomes a tragic symbol for those who would spread slavery and a target for abolitionists. President Pierce withholds Federal intervention, and political conflict drifts into civil conflict in "bleeding Kansas."

In a more indirect way, the efforts of the American filibuster wars in Nicaragua are "symbolic" of the hopes of some to extend slave culture overseas.

Jan. 16 Nebraska Territory organizes peacefully and successfully under acting Governor Thomas B. Cuming, who convenes the first legislature at Omaha. There are few slaves in Nebraska [15 when slavery is outlawed by territorial law in 1861].

Jan. 28 William Henry Aspinwall and other American associates complete the first transcontinental water-rail route connecting New York and California. The rail section is the 47-mile track, from Manzanillo on the Caribbean to Panama City on the Pacific, of the Panama Railroad in the Panama Province of New Granada [Colombia], which has conceded the franchise to Aspinwall's New York Corporation. The crossing takes only four hours.

Jan. 31 Secretary of State William L. Marcy sends instructions to Hawaii rejecting a draft treaty of annexation to the United States. He asserts that U.S. policy is not to cause important changes in the Government of Hawaii. The death on last Dec. 15 of King Kamehameha III may have influenced the change in policy.

Feb. 6 Ralph Waldo Emerson proposes to the Anti-Slavery Society of New York that slavery can be ended by offering full payment to slaveholders at his estimated cost of $200,000,000. The proposal is not seconded.

Feb. 20 The second territorial governor of Nebraska, Mark W. Izard, reaches Omaha.

Mar. 3 The text of the Ostend Manifesto is published. Northerners resent the Administration's willingness to add slave territory in Cuba.

Mar. 3 Congress authorizes the appointment of a consul general to Japan.

Mar. 30 The election of a legislative assembly in Kansas Territory brings a struggle between proslavery and free-soil factions. Some 5,000 armed "border ruffians" from Missouri establish a proslavery legislature through fraud and intimidation; 6,300 ballots are cast out of a registration of less than 3,000 voters.

May 4 William Walker sails from San Fran-

cisco on the brig *Vesta* with the "Immortal Fifty-six," a band of filibusters (freebooters). They propose to intervene in a civil war in Nicaragua at the invitation of Nicaraguan liberals.

May 9 John Mercer Langston, educator, diplomat, and public official, addresses the 22d anniversary meeting of the American Anti-Slavery Society at New York City, having just won election as clerk of Brownhelm Township, Ohio, the first Negro to win elective office in the United States.

May 21 Massachusetts passes a stringent personal liberty law. It in effect negates the Fugitive Slave Act of 1850 by guaranteeing full protection to all citizens, including blacks such as Anthony Burns, whose spiriting out of Boston last year still rankles antislavery elements.

June 6 The Native-American (Know-Nothing) Party holds a national council and adopts a proslavery plank. This reduces the movement to a Southern party.

June 16 Walker's filibusters land at Realejo, Nicaragua. He is commissioned a colonel in the Nicaraguan liberal forces.

June 22 The Treaty of Kanagawa is officially promulgated.

July 4 The first edition of Walt Whitman's *Leaves of Grass* goes on sale.

July 16 The Kansas legislature, after meeting for two weeks at Pawnee City, moves to Shawnee Mission and enacts statutes for severe penalties for antislavery agitation, as well as a test oath for office holding.

July 31 Governor Reeder of Kansas Territory, charged with land speculation and disliked for his opposition to the proslavery legislative assembly, is removed from office.

Aug. 4 Townsend Harris of New York, a trader and briefly attached to the U.S. mission in China, is appointed Consul General to Japan.

Sept. 3 Wilson Shannon, commissioned governor of Kansas Territory, arrives to succeed Reeder.

Sept. 5 Kansas antislavery colonists meet at Big Springs to repudiate the proslavery legislature and to seek admission to the Union as a free state.

Oct. 1 John W. Whitfield is reelected to be the congressional delegate of the proslavery forces in Kansas.

Oct. 9 Ex-Governor Reeder is elected congressional delegate from Kansas by the free-soil elements.

Oct. 23-Nov. 2 Antislavery forces in Topeka, Kansas, create a Free-State party and draw up a constitution prohibiting slavery in the territory.

Nov. 8 William Walker, after winning several important military engagements, is made general and commander-in-chief of the army of a Nicaraguan coalition government under President Patricio Rivas. Walker is actually in control of Nicaragua.

Nov. 10 Henry Wadsworth Longfellow publishes *The Song of Hiawatha*.

Nov. 14 Governor Shannon of Kansas Territory organizes a "Law and Order" Party at a proslavery meeting at Leavenworth.

Nov. 26 Public order continues to decline in Kansas as shootings and brawls break out along the Wakarusa River near Lawrence [the "Warakusa War"]. About 1,500 "border ruffians" enter Kansas but do not attack Lawrence, which is heavily guarded by free-soil settlers.

Dec. 3 The 34th Congress, at its first session, has a membership in the House of 108 Republicans, 83 Democrats, and 43 members of the new Know-Nothing Party. The Senate consists of 42 Democrats, 15 Republicans, and 5 Know-Nothings.

Dec. 8 The participation of Walker and the filibusters in military operations in Nicaragua is condemned in a proclamation by President Pierce.

Dec. 11 Matthew Fontaine Maury, naval officer and oceanographer, reads the final proof and publishes the first textbook on modern oceanography, *The Physical Geography of the Sea*.

Dec. 15 The Topeka Constitution with its accompanying ordinances is adopted.

Dec. 15 Frank Leslie's *Illustrated Newspaper* [later *Leslie's Weekly*] is issued in New York.

Broadway, from Anthony to Franklin Streets, New York City

1856

The Kansas question remains the dominant issue. The forces supporting and those attacking slavery contend for advantage, in this case centered on the role of slavery in the constitution of Kansas as the territory becomes a state. No solution is reached by the time Congress adjourns at the end of August. The Republicans charge that the Democrats are leaving "Bleeding Kansas" in a condition of chaos in order to exploit the issues in the national elections. These elections are closely fought, and the results indicate a hardening of sectional voting patterns between the Democrats and Republicans. The American or Know-Nothing Party polls about one fourth of the popular votes, but it has so few electoral votes that, because of the slavery issue, it has no future.

Manifest Destiny, or the extention of U.S. influence into new territory, has a bizarre manifestation in Central America, where the adventurer William Walker succeeds in establishing himself as president of Nicaragua and achieves recognition of a sort from the United States Government.

Jan. 15   The Free-State party in Kansas elects a legislature at Topeka, which gives the territory two governments.

Jan. 24   President Pierce directs a special message to Congress condemning the acts of the Topeka legislature as rebellious. He supports the proslavery legislative assembly and his appointee, Governor Wilson Shannon.

Feb. 11   Pierce issues a proclamation commanding "all persons engaged in unlawful combinations against the constituted authority of the Territory of Kansas or of the United States to disperse and retire peaceably to their respective abodes," thereby committing his Administration to the support of the proslavery Government.

Feb. 22   Meeting at Philadelphia, the national convention of the Know-Nothing Party (officially the American Party and formerly the Native-American Party) nominates former President Millard Fillmore and Andrew J. Donelson of Tennessee (a nephew of Andrew Jackson) for Vice President. The party stresses the preservation of the Union as a compromise between the Democrats and the Republicans.

March   John Greenleaf Whittier publishes a volume called *The Panorama and Other Poems,* in which are included "The Barefoot Boy" and "Maud Muller."

Mar. 4   The Topeka legislature passes a request for statehood and elects Andrew H. Reeder and James H. Lane to serve as U.S. Senators from Kansas.

Mar. 17   Senator Stephen A. Douglas of Illinois, introducing a bill authorizing Kansas to elect a constitutional convention and establish a state government, denounces as lawless the Topeka legislature and the New England Emigrant Aid Company.

Mar. 19   An investigative committee is established by the House of Representatives to review the Kansas elections. [It discloses evidence of fraud and violence. For example, more than 6,000 people voted although a census in February recorded 2,905 as eligible to vote.]

Mar. 23   It is reported that, at a meeting in New Haven, Connecticut, to aid members of the Kansas Emigrant Aid Society, clergyman Henry Ward Beecher observed that a Sharp's rifle is a greater argument against slavery than a Bible. [This introduces the term "Beecher's Bibles" into the language of the day.]

April 21   The first bridge across the Mississippi River, between Davenport, Iowa, and Rock Island, Illinois, is completed and open to railroad traffic.

May 15   Following the murder of James King, editor of the San Francisco *Daily Evening Bulletin,* citizens unite to establish a "Committee of Vigilance, for the protection of the ballot-box, the lives, liberty, and property of the citizens and residents of the City of San Francisco."

May 19-22   Charles Sumner of Massachusetts, an organizer of the Republican Party, in the course of polemics in the Senate against proslavery action in Kansas, includes intemperate remarks about Andrew P. Butler of South Carolina, who is absent. Two days later South Carolina Representative Preston S. Brooks, a nephew of Senator Butler, enters the Senate chamber and attacks and canes Senator Sumner at his desk. [This event greatly adds to national tensions over slavery and Kansas. Brooks retains his House seat without censure. Sumner, severely injured, is unable to resume his Senate seat until December 1859.]

May 21   Proslavery forces attack and sack Lawrence, Kansas, killing one man, destroying buildings and presses, and looting homes.

May 24-25   John Brown, an abolitionist who has come to Kansas to prevent it from becoming a slave state, leads a group that includes four of his sons to retaliate for the violence at Lawrence. The band slaughters five proslavery colonists living near Dutch Henry's Crossing at Pottawatomie Creek.

June 2-6   Holding its national convention at Cincinnati, the Democratic Party nominates James Buchanan, Minister to Great Britain and former Secretary of State, for President on the 17th ballot. For Vice President it selects John C. Breckinridge, a Kentucky Congressman. Democrats reaffirm the Compromise of 1850, offer the Kansas-Nebraska Act as the only safe compromise to solve the slavery question, and urge the annexation of Cuba.

June 4   Governor Shannon of Kansas Territory orders all irregular armed units to disperse.

June 17-19   The Republican Party holds its first national convention at Philadelphia and nominates Colonel John C. Frémont, a former U.S. Senator from California, for President and William L. Dayton of New Jersey for Vice President. The party platform supports Congressional authority to deal with slavery in territories and favors the admission of Kansas as a free state.

June 29   Nicaraguan "elections" give General William Walker 15,835 votes (out of 23,236 cast), and the 32-year-old American adventurer becomes President of Nicaragua.

July 3   The House of Representatives passes a bill to admit Kansas as a free state under the Topeka Government. [It fails in the Senate.]

July 12   U.S. Minister to Nicaragua Colonel John H. Wheeler takes it upon himself to recognize the Walker Government in the name of the United States. [Secretary of State William L. Marcy soon recalls Wheeler.]

July 17   A disastrous railway accident near Philadelphia takes the lives of 66 children during a Sunday school outing.

Aug. 13   A proslavery stronghold, Franklin, Kansas, is seized by forces of the Free-State Party.

Aug. 16   Gail Borden receives a patent for the "concentration of milk" [condensed milk].

Aug. 18   Territorial Governor Shannon of Kansas resigns and is replaced by acting Governor Daniel Woodson.

Aug. 18   Congress passes an act to give American citizens the right to discover and exploit guano fertilizer resources on unclaimed islands in the Atlantic and Pacific oceans and the Caribbean Sea.

Aug. 25   Governor Woodson proclaims Kansas Territory to be in a state of insurrection and calls out the militia.

Aug. 30   Osawatomie, Kansas, defended by 40 of John Brown's men, is attacked and pillaged by some 300 proslavery men.

Aug. 30   Wilberforce College in western Ohio, founded through the Methodist Episcopal Church, is the second institution for higher learning for Negroes. (Ashmun Institute, founded in 1854, was the first.)

Sept. 9   John W. Geary, former mayor of San Francisco, arrives in Kansas as the new Presidential appointee to govern the territory.

Sept. 15   Governor Geary uses Federal troops to intercept and disband some 2,500 "border ruffians" who are marching to attack the free-soilers at Lawrence. [Geary reports that "Peace now reigns in Kansas."]

Sept. 17   The Whig Party assembles in a national convention at Baltimore and endorses the Know-Nothing candidates.

October   William Ferrel, in "An Essay on the Winds and Currents of the Ocean" in the *Nashville Journal,* introduces his theory [Ferrel's law] that the force of the earth's rotation deflects bodies to the right in the northern hemisphere and to the left in the southern.

Nov. 4   In the national elections, Democrat James Buchanan is elected President with 1,832,955 popular votes and 174 electoral votes from 14 slave and 5 free states. Frémont, the first Republican candidate, gets 1,339,932 popular votes and 114 electoral votes from 11 free states. Fillmore receives 871,731 popular votes and Maryland's 8 electoral votes.

Nov. 16   Laura Keene, British actress and theatre manager, opens her own Laura Keene's Theatre in New York City, continuing a career as a pioneer woman theatre manager.

Nov. 25-26   Lucy Stone, presiding at the Seventh National Woman's Rights Convention at New York City, reviews the gains made by women in seven years in legal status, industrial employment, the founding of "female" colleges, and the acceptance of women in higher education on "nearly equal" terms.

Dec. 2   President Franklin Pierce directs his fourth and final annual message to Congress, lamenting that Kansas Territory "was made the battlefield, not so much of opposing factions or interests within itself as of the conflicting passions of the whole people of the United States."

Dec. 13   Walker is driven from the important city of Granada by Central American troops.

1857

The slavery issue intensifies. It divides state and national legislatures, and even religious bodies such as the Presbyterian Church; the Presbyterian United Synod of the South breaks away to form six synods and 21 presbyteries in which slavery may not be discussed. The Dred Scott decision deepens the controversy. It declares an act of Congress unconstitutional for the first time since *Marbury* v. *Madison* in 1803. Even more important, it makes slavery theoretically legal and ineradicable in every state and territory. To abolitionists it seems to end all hope for solutions under the law; to black men it guarantees permanent servitude. Kansas continues with a dual government, and the "Mormon War" in Utah threatens violence in another territory. Territorial expansion continues to be a goal of the Administration, and progress is made in transportation and communications, including a feasible route to California by way of the Panamanian isthmus.

Jan. 12 The Kansas proslavery territorial legislature assembles at Lecompton to begin its deliberations, in defiance of Governor John W. Geary's directions.

Feb. 19 The Kansas territorial legislature calls for the election in June of delegates to draw up a constitution under which statehood may be achieved.

March 3 To meet the needs of the South, the tariff is reduced to a general level of 20 per cent, the lowest rate since 1850; and the free list of articles is enlarged.

Mar. 3 Congress passes a bill that authorizes the Postmaster General to accept bids for overland stage-coach service for mail and passengers from the Missouri River to San Francisco.

Mar. 4 President James Buchanan is inaugurated as the 15th President. In his brief inaugural address he supports the Democratic policy of popular sovereignty in Kansas.

Mar. 4 Governor Geary resigns in Kansas when he fails to get the support of the Buchanan Administration.

Mar. 6 The U.S. Supreme Court, in the case of *Dred Scott* v. *Sandford,* as read by Chief Justice Roger B. Taney, denies the suit of Dred Scott, a Negro, for his freedom. Scott bases his claim on the fact that he was transported from the slave state of Missouri to free territory (Illinois and Wisconsin Territory) by his master, then returned to Missouri; his sojourn in free territory, he asserts, made him free. The Court denies this claim on the grounds that a slave is property; a property right is protected from dissolution, except through the due process of law, under the Constitution; no such process occurred in the case of Scott. Then the Court adds the opinion (which becomes the law of the land) that no act of Congress (or, it follows, of a territorial legislature) can constitutionally deprive a slavemaster of his property. Therefore, the Mis-

souri Compromise was unconstitutional and any territorial statute banning slavery would also be unconstitutional. The concept of popular sovereignty, as envisaged in the Kansas-Nebraska Act, is invalid and indeed statutory relief becomes unavailable to free-soil advocates.

Mar. 26 President Buchanan appoints Robert J. Walker, a former Secretary of the Treasury, governor of Kansas Territory to replace Geary.

Mar. 26 An allied force of Central American troops lays siege to William Walker's filibusters at Rivas, Nicaragua.

April 4 The Army orders General William S. Harney to move from Florida to Fort Leavenworth in case further lawlessness should erupt in Kansas Territory.

May 1 William Walker surrenders to Commander Charles H. Davis of the American Navy in the face of certain defeat by Central American siege forces.

May 20 President Buchanan decides to send an army force to Utah, which is declared to be in a state of rebellion because of its treatment of migrants passing through the territory on the way to California.

May 26 Governor Walker is inaugurated in Kansas and pledges a fair vote for a constitution.

June 15 The Kansas proslavery legislature, meeting in Lecompton, calls an election for delegates to a constitutional convention, but free-state opponents do not recognize the legitamacy of the call.

June 17 Townsend Harris, Consul General to Japan, negotiates a commercial agreement with that empire.

July 13 Alfred Cumming is commissioned governor of Utah Territory in place of Brigham Young, the founder of the "State of Deseret." Cumming is authorized to use a civil posse or, if this fails, to call upon Federal troops to enforce obedience to national laws.

150

July 15   Governor Walker persuades the Free State convention, meeting in Topeka, to participate in a new election.

July 18   Federal troops from Kansas leave for Utah Territory.

Sept. 7   The proslavery territorial legislature convenes its delegates at Lecompton to frame a constitution for Kansas.

Sept. 11   Colonel Albert S. Johnston takes command of the Utah Expedition from General Harney.

Sept. 11   A group of migrants crossing the southern part of Utah Territory and bound for California are ambushed by Indians and whites led by Mormon elder John D. Lee, who had promised protection to the travelers. Of about 150 in the camp, only 17 children survive. [Lee is executed for the crime in 1877. The incident is known as the Mountain Meadows Massacre.]

Sept. 15   Brigham Young issues a proclamation forbidding any armed force to enter Utah and ordering his people to mobilize under martial law.

Sept. 16   The Butterfield Overland Mail Company gets a government contract to provide service from St. Louis and Memphis to Fort Smith, Arkansas, and from there to El Paso, Fort Yuma, Los Angeles, and San Francisco. The company offers semiweekly service in a 25-day run for an annual mail subsidy of $600,000.

Oct. 4   Major Lot Smith leads a mounted Mormon attack that destroys 72 Federal wagons with several months of troop provisions. No casualties occur.

Oct. 13   Residents of Minnesota Territory vote to adopt a constitution and apply for statehood. The population of the territory has increased from 6,000 in 1850 to 150,000.

Oct. 15   Under fairly strict supervision, Kansas elects a new legislature in which Free-State members win a sizeable majority.

Nov. 5   The Utah Expedition unit is ordered to winter at Fort Bridger in the northeastern corner of Utah Territory [now southwestern Wyoming].

Nov. 7   The Kansas constitutional convention adjourns, having adopted the Lecompton constitution, which provides for slavery in Kansas. Only one article is to be submitted for popular vote, and it is for the "constitution with slavery" or for the "constitution without slavery," the property in slaves already in Kansas not being subject to change.

Nov. 10   Federal marshals arrest William Walker. [He is charged in a New Orleans court

with outfitting a steamship with arms and men for a return to Nicaragua; bail is set at $2,000 pending trial. He jumps bail and on Nov. 24 he reaches Greytown, Nicaragua, to resume his presidency.]

Dec. 7   Commodore Hiram Paulding exceeds instructions and lands on Nicaraguan soil to apprehend Walker and return him to Federal marshals.

Dec. 8   President Buchanan opens his first annual message to Congress with regrets for the current monetary crisis [the "Panic of 1857"], and for the need to request funds for the campaign to supress rebellion in Utah.

A family in Sherburne County, Minnesota, 1857

Dec. 9   Senator Stephen A. Douglas opposes the Lecompton constitution.

Dec. 17   Governor Walker of Kansas Territory resigns because President Buchanan decides to uphold the Lecompton constituion. Frederick P. Stanton becomes acting governor.

Dec. 21   The election is held on the Lecompton constitution. Free State men refuse to participate; 6,226 votes are cast for the "constitution with slavery" and 569 votes for the "constitution without slavery."

Dec. 29   William Walker is taken by a Federal marshal to Washington, where he is told that he is not charged by the Executive Branch as a lawbreaker.

1858 The Lincoln-Douglas debates that occur during the Congressional elections this year are among the great confrontations in American history. The language and the philosophies of the two candidates for a U.S. Senate seat from Illinois offer clear, compelling formulations of sensitive national political and cultural positions. The challenger (and loser), Abraham Lincoln, gains a countrywide reputation that paves the way to a Presidential nomination. Stephen A. Douglas, an able and inspired Senator, retains his seat and his party leadership, but his dedication to "popular sovereignty" does not sit well with the Southern wing of his party, and serves to split the party until it is hopelessly fractured.

The territorial questions become less ominous when disturbances virtually end in Kansas by August. Although the Dred Scott decision theoretically supports slavery in the territory, Free-Soilers win the elections, to a degree proving Douglas' point at Freeport, which is merely "popular sovereignty" in practice: let the settlers decide. In Utah, by year's end, a compromise leaves a Federally appointed governor in charge but allows the Mormons to govern themselves in most matters. Of the so-called Mormon war of 1857-1858, an observer comments: "Wounded, none; killed, none; fooled, everybody."

Jan. 4 Kansas voters elect a governor, a delegate to Congress, state officers, and a state legislature. On the same day they defeat the entire proslavery Lecompton constitution, by a vote of 10,226 to 162.

Jan. 7 President Buchanan communicates to the Senate his disapproval of William Walker's activities in Nicaragua, on the grounds that they interfere with larger considerations of isthmian transit and turn Central Americans against the United States.

Jan. 10 The Japanese diplomatic post is upgraded with the appointment of Townsend Harris as Minister Resident and Consul General.

Jan. 25 William Walker, speaking at Mobile, Alabama, attacks the Buchanan isthmian policy and seeks Southern support for his Nicaraguan activities and for his plans to "Americanize" Central America.

Feb. 2 President Buchanan recommends the admission of Kansas to statehood, but he submits the unpopular Lecompton constitution to Congress.

Feb. 3 Senator Stephen A. Douglas condemns the Lecompton constitution as a violation of "popular sovereignty." In the Senate debate, James H. Hammond of South Carolina declares that "cotton is king" and that the South is strong enough to get along without the North.

Mar. 4 Captain Matthew Calbraith Perry, 64, after a distinguished career in the U.S. Navy, dies at Tarrytown, New York. He is remembered chiefly for having conducted the negotiations that persuaded Japan to sign treaties with the United States.

Mar. 18 The Mormons decide to abandon Salt Lake City and avoid a war with Federal troops by a "Move South" policy.

Mar. 23 The Senate approves the admission of Kansas under the Lecompton constitution by a vote of 33 to 25.

April 1 The House votes, 120 to 112, to resubmit the Lecompton constitution to another popular vote in Kansas.

April 6 President Buchanan proclaims to the Mormons that they are in rebellion and are "levying war against the United States," and calls on Utah Territory to respect the Federal law.

May 4 Congress approves a "compromise" bill sponsored by William H. English of Indiana, which provides for another popular vote on the Lecompton constitution. If the constitution is approved and slavery is accepted, land grants and revenues will be available to Kansas along with statehood. Otherwise, statehood will be deferred until Kansas has a population of 93,420.

May 8-9 John Brown, with a party of 12 white men, is joined by 34 American and Canadian blacks in secret convention at Chatham, Canada West [Ontario]. Brown outlines a plan to raise a general slave insurrection in the South; a "Provisional Constitution and Ordinance for the People of the United States" is adopted with a preamble stating that the Dred Scott decision leaves blacks without protection.

May 11 The eastern part of Minnesota Territory, with a population of about 150,000, is admitted to the Union as the 32d state (and the 17th free state). Its first governor is Henry H. Sibley of Michigan, a Democrat. The western part, between the Red and Missouri rivers, remains Minnesota Territory.

May 13-14 The Eighth National Woman's Rights Convention meets in New York City at Mozart Hall with Susan B. Anthony presiding, and with constant interruptions due to the "rowdyism" of a number of men present.

May 21 Governor Cumming of Utah Territory informs Colonel Albert Johnston, commander of the Utah Expedition, that no organized military force exists in the territory and that hostilities are ended. [Federal troop occupation continues, however, in accordance with Johnston's military orders.]

June 14 Governor Cumming of Utah issues a proclamation that "peace is restored to our Territory."

June 17 Abraham Lincoln opens his campaign as the Republican candidate for the seat of incumbent Democratic Senator Stephen A. Douglas of Illinois by a speech at the Republican state convention in Springfield. Lincoln attacks slavery, but not slaveholders, and borrows from Scripture (Matthew xii, 25) the warning that "A house divided against itself cannot stand." He adds that "this Government cannot endure permanently half slave and half free."

June 18 The United States signs a treaty at Tientsin to bring about closer relations with the empire of China.

June 26 Colonel Johnston marches his Federal troops through Salt Lake City, which is nearly empty because most Mormons have heeded a call to "Move South." [The troops establish their center at Camp Floyd, midway between Salt Lake City and Provo.]

July 1 Mormon administrators return to Salt Lake City from Provo; they invite their followers to do the same.

July 6 A party of prospectors led by William Green Russell and John Beck finds gold washings along the South Platte River near Cherry Creek in the extreme northwestern part of Kansas Territory. [Rumors of this and other "finds" cause a gold rush to that area, which becomes part of Colorado Territory in 1861.]

July 8 Stephen A. Douglas opens his campaign for reelection to the Senate at Chicago, Illinois; Abraham Lincoln is in the audience.

July 24 Lincoln challenges Douglas to a series of joint debates. The challenge is accepted, and debates are arranged for seven different cities in Illinois.

July 29 Townsend Harris, Minister Resident to Japan, negotiates a treaty of amity and commerce, with the purpose of opening several ports to American trade and of bringing about an exchange of ministers and consuls.

Aug. 2 The Kansas electorate again rejects the Lecompton constitution, this time by a vote of 11,812 to 1,926. Kansas, therefore, in accordance with the act of Congress passed May 4, remains a territory.

Aug. 21 The first of seven joint statewide debates on slavery and the territories between Lincoln and Douglas takes place at Ottawa, Illinois.

Aug. 23 A play based on the best-seller temperance novel by Timothy Shay Arthur, *Ten Nights on a Bar-room Floor,* as adapted for the stage by William W. Pratt, opens at the National Theatre in New York City.

Aug. 27 At Freeport, Lincoln and Douglas meet for their second debate. When Lincoln asks whether there is a legal way to keep slavery out of a territory, Douglas responds that, although the Dred Scott decision prohibits the outlawing of slavery, the effect of such outlawing could result if there were no local police black codes to protect slavery; in such a situation, no slaveholder would bring his property into the territory. [This suggestion becomes known as the Freeport Doctrine.]

Sept. 15 Lincoln and Douglas hold their third joint debate at Jonesboro.

Sept. 16 John Butterfield, accompanied by a newspaperman, Waterman L. Ormsby, begins the first run of the Butterfield Overland Mail Company from St. Louis to San Francisco. [The mail reaches San Francisco on Oct. 10, after a run of 23 days 23 hours over nearly 3,000 miles.]

Sept. 18 The fourth Lincoln-Douglas debate takes place at Charleston, where Lincoln rejects the concept of Negro equality with whites.

October The last three debates between Lincoln and Douglas are held at Galesburg, on Oct. 7; Quincy, on Oct. 13; and at Alton, on Oct. 15. At the final confrontation Lincoln states that the "real issue" of the debates "is the sentiment on the part of one class that looks upon the institution of slavery *as a wrong,* and of another class that *does not* look upon it as a wrong." Douglas asserts that the issue is that slavery can continue if each state answers the question for itself: "If the people of all the states will act on that great principle, and each state mind its own business, attend to its own affairs, take care of its own Negroes, and not meddle with its neighbors, then there will be peace . . . throughout the whole Union."

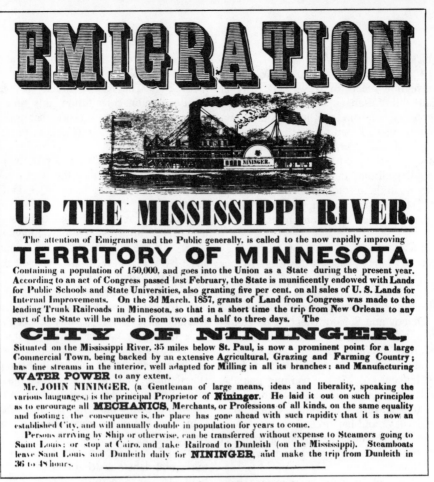

EMIGRATION

UP THE MISSISSIPPI RIVER.

The attention of Emigrants and the Public generally, is called to the now rapidly improving

TERRITORY OF MINNESOTA,

Containing a population of 150,000, and goes into the Union as a State during the present year. According to an act of Congress passed last February, the State is munificently endowed with Lands for Public Schools and State Universities, also granting five per cent. on all sales of U. S. Lands for Internal Improvements. On the 3d March, 1857, grants of Land from Congress was made to the leading Trunk Railroads in Minnesota, so that in a short time the trip from New Orleans to any part of the State will be made in from two and a half to three days. The

CITY OF NININGER,

Situated on the Mississippi River, 35 miles below St. Paul, is now a prominent point for a large Commercial Town, being backed by an extensive Agricultural, Grazing and Farming Country; has fine streams in the interior, well adapted for Milling in all its branches; and Manufacturing **WATER POWER** to any extent.

Mr. JOHN NININGER, (a Gentleman of large means, ideas and liberality, speaking the various languages,) is the principal Proprietor of **Nininger**. He laid it out on such principles as to encourage all **MECHANICS**, Merchants, or Professions of all kinds, on the same equality and footing; the consequence is, the place has gone ahead with such rapidity that it is now an established City, and will annually double in population for years to come.

Persons arriving by Ship or otherwise, can be transferred without expense to Steamers going to Saint Louis; or stop at Cairo, and take Railroad to Dunleith (on the Mississippi). Steamboats leave Saint Louis and Dunleith daily for **NININGER**, and make the trip from Dunleith in 36 to 48 hours.

A contemporary poster advertises the advantages
of settling in the Territory of Minnesota, and
specifically in the city of Nininger.

Oct. 16   Henry Wadsworth Longfellow published *The Courtship of Miles Standish,* a long narrative poem wth a theme of romance among the Massachusetts Pilgrims.

Oct. 25   Senator William H. Seward of New York delivers a speech at Rochester, New York, on the slavery issue in which he declares: "It is an irrepressible conflict between opposing and enduring forces, and it means that the United States must and will, sooner or later, become either entirely a slave-holding nation, or entirely a free-labor nation." [This radical antislavery position probably costs Seward the Presidential nomination for the Republican Party in 1860.]

Oct. 30   President Buchanan issues a warning to William Walker, who has been acquitted in New Orleans of charges of violating neutrality laws, not to sail back to Nicaragua.

Nov. 1   Oliver Wendell Holmes publishes *The Autocrat of the Breakfast-Table,* a series of essays that have been appearing for several years in the *Atlantic Monthly.*

Nov. 2   The election in Illinois gives the Republican candidates for state office a popular victory, but the Democrats win the state legislature. [The Illinois legislature reelects Douglas to the U. S. Senate on Jan. 5, 1859.]

Nov. 8   At Shanghai, China, two conventions are signed to satisfy claims of United States citizens and to fix tariff and duty rates.

Dec. 1   Walker's filibusters sail on the schooner *Susan* from Mobile without permission. [They are shipwrecked off British Honduras, where a British vessel of war picks them up.]

Dec. 6   President Buchanan, referring to Utah in his second annual message to Congress, states: "The authority of the Constitution and the laws has been fully restored and peace prevails throughout the territory."

Dec. 20   John Brow makes a raid from Kansas into Missouri to free 11 slaves. He murders one man in the course of this episode of his warfare on slavery.

1859

Widespread fear and alarm appear during the year. Northerners fear that the South will demand the extension of slavery into free states, based upon the logic of the Dred Scott decision that legitimizes its introduction into free territories. Southerners believe that abolitionists in the North must be silenced because they threaten the very existence of the slavocracy by their hostility in the political arena, in the courts, and even in refusing to respect the fugitive-slave laws. Some Southerners do cling to the hope of opening new territories to slavery; and a few even advocate that the United States reopen the traffic in African slaves.

The Kansas abolitionist, John Brown, finally justifies both fear and alarm in an electrifying incident at Harpers Ferry. Supported and financed in the North, this zealot proposes to lead a general slave rebellion to be centered in the Southern mountainous region. He believes that free blacks and slave blacks from the United States and even from Canada will join his rebellion. Abolitionist and antislavery sentiment in the North is vociferous in favor of an act that bases its legitimacy on a morality higher than the current laws. When the Virginia authorities hang this disturbed, courageous man, they create a martyr.

Jan. 1 The shipwrecked crew of the schooner *Susan* with filibusters who support William Walker's Nicaraguan campaigns, are returned to New Orleans by a British warship.

Feb. 1 John Brown leaves Kansas with slaves liberated in his Missouri invasion last December to take them to freedom in Canada.

Feb. 14 The Territory of Oregon is admitted to the Union as the 33d state and the 18th free state. (Its boundaries are modified: the section east of the Snake River and the 117th meridian are attached to Washington Territory.) The new state has about 50,000 inhabitants, and its first governor is a Democrat, John Whiteaker.

Mar. 3 The U.S. Senate ratifies the two conventions signed at Shanghai on Nov. 8, 1858.

Mar. 15 Washington Irving hands his publishers the final copy of the last volume of his five-volume biography, *The Life of George Washington.*

April 4 Bryant's Minstrels at Mechanic's Hall in New York City perform Dan Emmett's new plantation song and dance, "Dixie's Land." [The lively walk-around music gains wide popularity in both the North and the South and soon is generally called simply "Dixie."]

April 7 Robert M. McLane presents his credentials as Minister to the Mexican constitutional Government of Benito Juárez, which is engaged in a civil war as a result of an attempt to enforce liberal reforms in that country.

April 18 The Leavenworth and Pike's Peak Express Company dispatches a trial run in an attempt to establish stagecoach service between Leavenworth and the gold fields in northwestern Kansas. [On May 7, the run is completed; it is soon reduced to 10 days.]

May 6 John H. Gregory strikes a gold lode on the North Branch of Clear Creek, and the news of "Gregory Gulch" sets off a great rush to northwestern Kansas.

May 9 Governor Alfred Cumming of Utah, faced by a confrontation between Federal troops and armed Mormons, proclaims that any assemblage of armed men is unlawful.

May 9-19 A Southern commercial convention meets at Vicksburg, Mississippi, and, faced by the rising cost of field hands, advocates that "all laws, state or Federal, prohibiting the African slave trade, ought to be repealed."

May 12 Susan B. Anthony opens the Ninth National Woman's Rights Convention in New York City. The delegates petition the state legislatures to eliminate the word "male" in state constitutions and to legislate for all citizens, asking: "Where, under our Declaration of Independence, does the white Saxon man get his power to deprive all woman and Negroes of their inalienable rights?"

June 3 Abolitionist John Brown leaves Boston, in the course of a campaign in the North to raise funds through public appearances and from private antislavery donors.

June 10 Peter O'Riley and Patrick McLaughlin discover a rich vein of gold in the Washoe Mountains of western Utah Territory [Nevada]. [Henry T. P. Comstock claims a share because of his prospecting in the same area. The operation soon becomes the Ophir Mine; an assay of heavy bluish quartz proves to be one-fourth gold and three-fourths pure silver; and the Ophir Mine and so-called Comstock Lode becomes the richest in mining history.]

July 2 Stagecoach and mail service is established to Salt Lake City. [It is then linked to Placerville, California, by the Central Overland,

California & Pike's Peak Express Company.]

July 5-29   At a convention at Wyandotte [since 1886 a part of Kansas City, Kansas], the delegates frame another constitution for Kansas; in this constitution slavery is prohibited in the territory.

July 27   John E. Ward, the U.S. Envoy to China, reaches Peking.

Aug. 1-2   The New England Colored Citizens' Convention is held in Boston.

Aug. 2   Horace Mann, 63, pioneer in the field of education, dies at Yellow Springs, Ohio, where he has been president of Antioch College since 1853.

Aug. 12   F. H. Conway's play, *Pike's Peak, or, The Search for Riches* is presented as the first "novelty piece" of the season at the Old Bowery Theatre in New York City. (A "novelty piece" is a production based on contemporary events featured in newspaper or periodical articles.)

Aug. 25   Secretary of War John B. Ford receives an anonymous letter, warning that John Brown has a plan to begin a black insurrection and will enter Virginia at Harpers Ferry on the upper Potomac. The information is not considered reliable.

Aug. 27   Edwin L. Drake, president of the Seneca Oil Company, discovers petroleum while drilling near Titusville, Pennsylvania. This is the first successful find of "Seneca oil," which, it is hoped will prove (along with kerosene) to be a substitute for costly whale oil as an illuminant. [In the first year, oil wells, mostly in Pennsylvania, produce about 2,000 barrels; in 1860 about 500,000 barrels are produced.]

Oct. 4   The Wyandotte constitution is ratified by the people of Kansas Territory by a popular vote of 10,421 to 5,530.

Oct. 16   John Brown, with the intention of acquiring arms for his effort to liberate slaves on a grand scale, prepares to raid the U.S. arsenal at Harpers Ferry, Virginia. He enters the town with 18 men (including 5 blacks), murders 4 men, and takes hostages. One of the captives is Colonel Lewis W. Washington, a great-grandnephew of George Washington.

Oct. 18   Colonel Robert E. Lee, commanding a force of U.S. marines, captures John Brown and his men and finds Colonel Washington safe; Brown is wounded and 10 are killed, including two of Brown's sons.

Oct. 24   As a result of the increase in population in northwestern Kansas because of the gold rush, together with the lack of effective govern-ment, the inhabitants of the settlements around Cherry Creek convene to organize their own authority. Auraria and St. Charles (which has been renamed Denver for the governor of Kansas Territory) are the principal communities. At Denver a convention sets up the Territory of Jefferson, with an area extending from the 102d to the 110th meridian and from the 37th to the 43d parallel. [The territory is not recognized by Congress, which organizes the Territory of Colorado in 1861.]

Oct. 25-Nov. 2   Brown goes on trial at Charles Town, Virginia [now West Virginia]. The Richmond *Enquirer* states: "The Harpers Ferry invasion has advanced the cause of disunion more than any other event that has happened since the formation of the government. . . ." Brown tells the court that he only intended to free slaves and says "if it is deemed necessary that I should forfeit my life for the furthering of the ends of justice and mingle my blood further with the blood of my children and with the blood of millions in this slave country whose rights are disregarded by wicked, cruel, and unjust enactments, I say, let it be done." The Commonwealth of Virginia finds him guilty of murder, criminal conspiracy, and treason.

Nov. 8   Delivering a lecture on "Courage" at Boston, Ralph Waldo Emerson refers to John Brown as "that new saint."

Nov. 28   Washington Irving, 76, internationally renowned American man of letters, dies near Tarrytown, New York.

Dec. 2   John Brown is hanged at Charles Town. His last written message is: "I John Brown am now quite *certain* that the crimes of this *guilty, land:* will never be purged *away;* but with Blood. I had *as I now think: mainly* flattered myself that without *very much* bloodshed; it might be done."

Dec. 5   The Republicans in the House of Representatives propose John Sherman of Ohio as Speaker of the 36th Congress. They meet intense opposition because Sherman is among 68 Republicans who endorse and use as campaign literature *The Impending Crisis of the South,* a reasoned but passionate attack on slavery by a Southerner, Hinton R. Helper, published in 1857.

Dec. 5   Charles Sumner of Massachusetts returns to his Senate seat, having finally recovered from his beating by Representative Preston Brooks in 1856.

Dec. 5   *The Octoroon,* an original play by Dion Boucicault, opens at the Winter Garden in

President Buchanan and his Cabinet

New York City. The sensitive treatment of the theme of slavery as it affects Zoe, a beautiful girl with Negro blood, is well received by both proslavery and antislavery audiences.

Dec. 8   Helper's *The Impending Crisis,* and especially its inexpensive *Compendium,* quickly become best-sellers because of the House debate over the speakership.

Dec. 17   At the Old Bowery Theater in New York City, George C. Boniface, a well-known actor, plays John Brown in *The Insurrection, or, Kansas and Harpers Ferry,* another "novelty piece."

Dec. 19   President Buchanan opens his third annual message to Congress by noting that events at Harpers Ferry "are but symptoms of an incurable disease in the public mind, which may break out in still more dangerous outrages and terminate at last in an open war by the North to abolish slavery in the South."

Dec. 26   The New York *Tribune* is distributing Helper's *Compendium* at the rate of 500 copies a day in the North and West; in the South distributors are being arrested, and in many places it is a crime to possess the book.

Dec. 29   The national committees of the American and Whig parties agree to merge as the Constitutional Union Party for the forthcoming national election.

Dec. 31   *Harper's Weekly* announces that hundreds of Southern students are withdrawing from Northern medical colleges to return home.

1860

All the formal preparations are concluded this year for the confrontation that even the President realizes is inevitable, as he reveals with exceptional clarity in his final message to Congress. These events include the party nominating conventions, the election itself, and of course the first withdrawal from the Union by one of its states.

The parties who are to confront one another are eager, to the last, to reach an agreement. Such attempts are in a sense part of the prologue to combat, for they provide moral justification to each side as they indulge in fratricide. From Jefferson Davis and Abraham Lincoln—who are to lead the contending forces—to the Senators who form a committee in the last weeks of peace, gestures toward reconciliation are made. But it is probable that they all are aware of the fact that the North has the votes, the power, and the will to survive. The South has only a tradition and the personal courage of its defenders.

The split in the Democratic Party is inevitable and fatal. The Republicans are united because their platform reflects their origin as heir to the free-soil position. Only extreme abolitionists are more opposed to slavery than the Republicans, and they may find a voice in the Constitutional Union Party. It is worth noting, however, that this minor party has more electoral votes than the candidate (Douglas) of the party in power when the election takes place. It is also notable that Lincoln, although a minority President in terms of the popular vote (only 39.8 per cent, compared to a respectable 29.4 per cent for Douglas and 18.2 per cent for the other Democrat, Breckinridge), has a clear electoral majority. This suggests that he would probably have defeated any candidate the opposition might have agreed on, if they could have agreed; his votes are effectively distributed; in short, the North is politically dominant. Now the question must be answered: Is it militarily dominant?

Jan. 30-Feb. 1 Republican John Sherman withdraws as a candidate for Speaker of the House of Representatives. Although his party has 114 members to 92 belonging to the Democratic Party, he cannot overcome the opposition ascribed to his endorsement of an antislavery tract, Hinton R. Helper's *Compendium*. On the 44th ballot William F. Pennington of the American Party is elected Speaker.

Feb. 2 Jefferson Davis of Mississippi introduces a set of resolutions in the U.S. Senate on the political and constitutional aspects of slavery. These resolutions defend the legality of the institution in the states and the territories, and the legal right to recover fugitive slaves.

Feb. 22 Massachusetts shoemakers in Lynn and Natick strike for higher wages, and the strike spreads to 20,000 New England workers, including women.

Feb. 23 The Kansas territorial legislature passes the Wyandotte free-soil constitution into law over the veto of Governor Samuel Medary.

Feb. 27 Abraham Lincoln delivers his first major Eastern address at Cooper Union in New York City. He rejects "popular sovereignty," condemns Northern extremism as well as Southern secessionist threats, but holds that no compromise on the extension of slavery to the territories is possible.

April 3-13 The first run of the Pony Express is made from St. Joseph, Missouri to Sacramento, California; riders in relay carry 49 letters and some special newspaper editions in 10 days. The service was organized by William H. Russell and Alexander Majors, proprietors of an overland freight-carrying coach line.

April 23-May 3 The Democratic Party nominating convention meets in Charleston, South Carolina. Northern delegates dominate the meeting and reaffirm the 1856 platform planks. On April 30 the convention adopts the majority report of the Northern delegates as the party platform, and delegates from Alabama, Askansas, Florida, Georgia, Louisiana, and South Carolina withdraw from the convention. The delegates remaining in the convention, unable to muster a two-thirds majority for a candidate after 57 ballots, adjourn on May 3. [They reassmble on June 18.]

May 9-10 The Constitutional Union Party, comprising remnants of the Whig and American parties, is established in Baltimore and nominates for President John Bell of Tennessee and for Vice President Edward Everett of Massachusetts. The party denounces sectionalism and advocates enforcement of the Constitution and the Federal laws.

May 16-20 The Republican national conven-

Balloon view of Boston, 1860

tion gathers in Chicago, Illinois. William H. Seward is the favorite Presidential candidate on the first two ballots, but his radical antislavery position is too extreme for the delegates. They nominate Abraham Lincoln of Illinois on the third ballot. Hannibal Hamlin of Maine is selected to run for Vice President. A straight free-soil platform is adopted, with planks favoring a protective tariff and free land for homesteading.

May 24-25   The Davis resolutions of Feb. 2 are adopted in the U.S. Senate, which has 36 Democrats and 26 Republicans. However, a great debate on the resolutions widens the split between Southern and Northern Democrats.

June 9   Mrs. Ann Sophia Stevens, a best-selling author, publishes *Malaeska: The Indian Wife of the White Hunter*. It is the first offering of the Irwin P. Beadle Dime Novel Series, published in New York City and advertised as available "for only ten cents!!!!"

June 18-23   The Democratic Party majority reconvene in Baltimore and, after more Southern delegates withdraw, nominate Stephen A. Douglas for President on the second ballot; Herschel V. Johnson of Georgia is finally selected as his running mate. The platform advocates popular sovereignty in the territories.

June 22   President Buchanan vetoes a homestead act passed by both Houses.

June 28   Delegates from the eight Southern states who withdrew from the Democratic convention in Charleston convene in Baltimore and, calling themselves National Democrats, they nominate John C. Breckinridge of Kentucky for President and Joseph Lane of Oregon for Vice President. Their party platform supports slavery in the territories.

July 1   Charles Goodyear, 59, inventor, dies in New York City. Although he discovered and in 1844 patented the process of vulcanizing rubber, he did not profit from his invention and dies in poverty. [The company named after him (as a mark of respect) is not ever to be controlled by his family.]

Aug. 6   William Walker lands with a hundred men at Trujillo, Honduras, and seizes the town, including the customhouse whose revenues belong to the British Government.

Aug. 8   The ship *Erie,* Nathaniel Gordon skipper, sails for Cuba to pick up slaves. [With an illegal cargo of 890 slaves, the ship is captured by United States forces and returned to New York. On Nov. 8, 1861, Gordon is convicted of piracy (slave trading) under an act of 1820, and on Feb. 21, 1862, he is hanged.]

Aug. 20   The British war vessel *Icarus* enters the port of Trujillo, Honduras, and Captain Norvell Salmon demands that Walker surrender the customhouse he has seized to the British Government. [On Sept. 3 Honduran General Mariano Alvarez joins Captain Salmon, but Walker prefers to surrender to Salmon. Two days later, despite Walker's protestations, Salmon turns him over to Honduran authorities. On Sept. 11 Walker is tried in a court-martial by Honduran troops at Trujillo, and the next day he is shot by a firing squad.]

Sept. 8   The Lake Michigan excursion steamer *Lady Elgin* collides with a lumber ship; 300 passengers are killed.

Nov. 6   In the Presidential elections Republican Abraham Lincoln gets 1,865,593 popular votes with 180 electoral votes; Douglas wins 1,382,713 popular and 12 electoral votes; Breckinridge polls 848,356 popular and 72 electoral votes; and Bell has 592,906 popular and 39 electoral votes. Lincoln carries 18 free states, Breckinridge has 11 slave states, Bell wins 3 border states, and Douglas carries Missouri and three of New Jersey's electoral votes.

Nov. 7   Charleston, South Carolina, raises the palmetto flag at the news of the election of Lincoln; and city authorities arrest a Federal officer trying to transfer supplies from the Charleston arsenal to Fort Moultrie in the harbor.

Nov. 8   Stephen C. Foster, whose Negro minstrel songs are in decline, copyrights "Old Black Joe." The song is notable, not only for its music, but because its words abstain from the use of Negro dialect and express authentic feelings and memories.

Nov. 10   The South Carolina legislature convokes a special convention to meet at Columbia on Dec. 17 to discuss secession.

Nov. 12   A sharp drop in prices and heavy selling hit the financial market in New York City.

Nov. 14   Major Robert Anderson is ordered to take command of Fort Moultrie in Charleston Harbor.

Nov. 30   The legislature of the state of Mississippi draws up resolutions on secession.

Dec. 3   President Buchanan, in his fourth State of the Union message to Congress, observes: "The different sections of the Union are now arrayed against each other, and the time has arrived, so much dreaded by the Father of his Country, when hostile geographical parties have been formed."

Dec. 8   Secretary of the Treasury Howell

Millard Fillmore
THIRTEENTH PRESIDENT   **1850-1853**

Franklin Pierce
FOURTEENTH PRESIDENT   1853-1857

James Buchanan
FIFTEENTH PRESIDENT   1857-1861

Abraham Lincoln
SIXTEENTH PRESIDENT   1861-1865

Cobb of Georgia resigns.

Dec. 12   Secretary of State Lewis Cass of Michigan, no enemy of the South, resigns on the grounds that Buchanan refuses to reinforce the Federal forts in Charleston Harbor.

Dec. 14   The Georgia legislature calls on Alabama, Florida, Mississippi, and South Carolina to appoint delegates to a convention to consider confederacy in the South.

Dec. 18   Senator John J. Crittenden of Kentucky introduces a resolution before a special Congressional committee to conciliate Southerners by restoring the principle of the Missouri Compromise. He proposes to extend the 36°30′ line to separate free and slave soil to the California boundary, to protect slavery where it is established; and to compensate owners whose fugitive slaves are not recovered. [This resolution, known as the Crittenden Compromise, is not passed by Congress.]

Dec. 20   The special state convention at Columbia, South Carolina, on the third day of its session, passes by a unanimous vote an ordinance dissolving the union between South Carolina and the other states of the United States.

Dec. 20   In the U.S. Senate, a Committee of Thirteen is named to look into the state of affairs in the Union. It includes Senators William H. Seward of New York, Stephen A. Douglas of Illinois, Jefferson Davis of Mississippi, Ben Wade of Ohio, and Robert Toombs of Georgia.

Dec. 22-24   The South Carolina convention calls on the Federal Government to restore Forts Moultrie and Sumter, the Charleston Arsenal, and Castle Pinckney to the authority of the state of South Carolina. The convention then issues a "Declaration of Immediate Causes" for its secession. Governor Francis W. Pickens proclaims independence, freedom, and sovereignty for South Carolina.

Dec. 26   Major Robert Anderson transfers the garrison of Fort Moultrie to Fort Sumter, where he strengthens the facilities and mounts guns.

Dec. 27   Fort Moultrie and Castle Pinckney are occupied by troops of South Carolina, and a Federal revenue cutter, the *William Aiken,* is seized by state troops.

Dec. 30   South Carolina seizes the United States arsenal in Charleston. This completes the occupation by the state of all Federal facilities in the Charleston Harbor area except Fort Sumter.

Dec. 31   President Buchanan refuses a request by South Carolina officials that he withdraw Federal troops from Charleston.

Savannah, Georgia (looking east toward Fort Jackson) (*ca.*) 1860's

161

1861

Between January and early June, 10 slave states follow South Carolina along the path of secession. Southern Congressmen, politicians, and army and navy officers leave the North to stand with their own states. Southern states seize Northern facilities in their area—forts, arsenals, barracks, port facilities, custom houses, a mint office—most of which are unmanned or held by a few officials and caretakers. Churches, such as the Presbyterian, undergo schism between North and South. In any case, a new nation emerges: the Confederate States of America, with its constitution, President, armed forces, and foreign policy aspirations.

Abraham Lincoln insists, aside from the question of slavery, that a minority has no right to leave the Union; Jefferson Davis holds that the Southern states, *as* sovereign states, have the right of self-determination. The issues of the war are, therefore, clearly not solely the determination of which system of economy shall prevail, slave or free. The constitutional controversy raised by Jefferson and Madison in support of the Virginia and Kentucky resolutions in 1798, the positions of the Essex Junto and the Hartford Convention, the doctrine of states' rights most powerfully articulated by John C. Calhoun for decades—all these anticipated the contemporary poles of opinion for which Lincoln and Davis are now spokesmen.

The Civil War opens on April 12 with the Southern attack on Fort Sumter, South Carolina. Slowly hostilities get under way. Lincoln calls for 75,000 volunteers at first; then he calls for more and more manpower, of which the North has an abundance. Davis also asks for volunteers and is swamped with more men than he can arm. The Union moves to blockade the Atlantic Coast of the Confederacy. The Union navy is limited but purposeful, and is moderately successful in this first year of war. The Union army takes the offensive, but its first campaign against Richmond, Virginia, ends a few miles from Washington in a Confederate victory at the Battle of Bull Run (or Manassas) in July. Thereafter the Northern generals, Winfield Scott and George B. McClellan, fail to move to the offensive in spite of their greater strength, while Southern military leaders win local battles and hold back the Union troops.

Jan. 3   State troops from Georgia seize Fort Pulaski, near the mouth of the Savannah River.

Jan. 4-5   Alabama state forces seize the U.S. arsenal at Mount Vernon, near Mobile, and Fort Morgan and Fort Gaines, guarding the entrance to Mobile Bay.

Jan. 6-7   Facing no opposition, Florida troops occupy the Federal arsenal at Apalachicola, and capture Fort Marion at St. Augustine.

Jan. 8   The last Southerner in President Buchanan's Cabinet, Secretary of the Interior Jacob Thompson of Mississippi, resigns.

Jan. 9   The Mississippi legislature votes, 84 to 15, to secede from the Union.

Jan. 9   Buchanan's relief ship, *Star of the West,* bringing reinforcements to Federal troops at Fort Sumter, fails under fire in its attempt to enter Charleston Harbor.

Jan. 10   Florida secedes, by a vote of 62 to 7.

Jan. 10   Louisiana forces seize the Baton Rouge arsenal, and Fort Jackson and Fort St. Philip at strategic positions on the Mississippi River south of New Orleans.

Jan. 11   Alabama secedes, by a vote of 61 to 39.

Jan. 12   Florida troops take Fort Barrancas,

The interior of Fort Sumter after the bombardment

Fort McRee, and the Pensacola Navy Yard.

Jan. 14   Louisiana captures Fort Pike near New Orleans.

Jan. 14-18   Federal troops garrison Fort Taylor at Key West, Florida, making it a strategic Union coastal base, and garrison Fort Jefferson on the Dry Tortugas Islands, west of Key West. [Fort Jefferson becomes a Union prison for political prisoners.]

Jan. 19   The Georgia legislature votes to secede, 164 to 133.

Jan. 21   Five Southern U.S. Senators from secessionist states, including Jefferson Davis, leave Washington to return home.

Jan. 24-26   Georgia seizes the Federal arsenal at Augusta and Fort Jackson near Savannah.

Jan. 26   Louisiana votes, 113 to 17, for secession.

Jan. 28   Fort Macomb near New Orleans falls into the hands of Louisiana troops.

Jan. 29   Kansas, with a population exceeding 100,000 (more than is required under the law of May 4, 1858), is admitted to the Union as the 34th state under its Wyandotte constitution. That part of Kansas Territory west of the 102d meridian is not included in the state. The capital is Topeka.

Feb. 1-23   A Texas convention votes, 166 to 8, for secession, and calls for a popular vote to confirm it.

Feb. 4   In Montgomery, Alabama, the convention of the Confederate States of America, with delegates from the first six seceding states, assembles with Howell Cobb of Georgia presiding. [On Feb. 9 they elect Jefferson Davis of Mississippi provisional President and Alexander H. Stevens of Georgia Vice President.]

Feb. 7   The Choctaw Indian nation declares its allegiance to the South.

The battery at Charleston, South Carolina, during the bombardment of Fort Sumter

163

An ambulance evacuates wounded Civil War soldiers

Feb. 8   Arkansas troops seize the Federal arsenal at Little Rock.

Feb. 11   President-elect Abraham Lincoln departs from Springfield, Illinois, on his way to Washington, D.C.

Feb. 16   Texas troops take over the Federal arsenal at San Antonio.

Feb. 18   Jefferson Davis is inaugurated as provisional President of the Confederate States of America.

Feb. 21   The Confederate convention, in the role of a provisional Congress, declares the Mississippi River free and open to commerce.

Feb. 28   Congress organizes the western part of Kansas Territory as the Territory of Colorado; a strip of eastern Utah Territory and southern Nebraska Territory are included in Colorado. The capital is Colorado City, and William Gilpin is appointed governor.

Mar. 1   Confederate President Davis places General Pierre G. T. Beauregard in command in Charleston, South Carolina.

Mar. 2   Congress organizes two new territories. Nevada Territory is formed out of the extreme western part of Utah Territory. [Its area corresponds to that of the state as constituted in 1864, except that its western boundary is the 116th meridian and its southern boundary is the 37th parallel.] Dakota Territory is formed out of all of the vast Nebraska Territory north of the 43d parallel, together with the remaining part of Minnesota Territory; it extends from the Red River to the Rocky Mountains. [The western part of this new territory is detached in 1863 to form Idaho Territory.]

Mar. 2   Congress approves the Morrill Tariff Act with specific duties in place of ad valorem duties imposed by the tariff of 1846, while duties are raised from 5 to 10 per cent.

Mar. 4   Abraham Lincoln is inaugurated as 16th President of the United States.

Mar. 9   The Confederate Convention at Montgomery authorizes the organization of an army.

Mar. 11   The Constitution of the Confederacy is adopted unanimously by the convention at Montgomery, and it goes to the Confederate States for ratification. [All ratify it.] The constitution is similar to that of the United States, but the term of office for the President is set at six years (with no second term); the budgetary power of Congress is limited concerning tariffs and internal improvements; and Cabinet members may sit with members of Congress.

Mar. 16   The convention (provisional Congress) of the Confederacy adjourns.

Mar. 18   Lincoln appoints Charles Francis Adams as Minister to Great Britain and William

L. Dayton to France.

Mar. 18 In Texas, Governor Sam Houston refuses to accept secession and is forced to resign.

Mar. 29 Lincoln decides to send a relief expedition by sea to Fort Sumter, South Carolina, where Major Robert Anderson is holding out.

Mar. 31 Lincoln orders an expedition to relieve Fort Pickens at Pensacola Bay, Florida.

April 11-13 General Beauregard demands the evacuation of Fort Sumter, and Major Anderson refuses. At 4:30 A.M. of April 12, Confederate guns fire on the fort. The Union force of 85 officers and men with the help of 43 workmen face more than 4,000 Confederates. The fort surrenders at 2:30 P.M. on April 13. [This action marks the beginning of the Civil War.]

April 12 Union reinforcements land at Fort Pickens, Florida, to maintain Federal control.

April 15 Lincoln proclaims that a state of insurrection exists and calls for 75,000 militia; he also calls a special session of Congress for July 4.

April 17 Virginia secedes at a state convention by a vote of 88 to 55.

April 19 Lincoln proclaims a blockade of the Confederate States.

April 20 Colonel Robert E. Lee resigns his U.S. Army commission, and two days later, as a major general, he assumes command of the Virginia troops.

April 20 The Gosport Navy Yard near Norfolk, Virginia, is evacuated by Union forces.

April 29 The provisional Congress of the Confederacy reconvenes at Montgomery, Alabama, and hears President Davis ask for authority to prosecute the war. Congress gives him the power to raise volunteers, make loans, issue letters of marque and reprisal, and use all land and naval forces of the nation.

May 6 The Confederate Congress declares that a state of war exists with the United States.

May 6 The Arkansas legislature votes to secede, 69 to 1, and Tennessee announces its sympathy with the South and calls for a popular vote on the issue set for June 8. [The voters in the western and central parts of Tennessee favor secession, but in the eastern section there is enough Union sentiment to allow U.S. Senator Andrew Johnson to remain in Washington.]

May 13 Great Britain recognizes both sides in the war as belligerents.

May 13-15 A group of delegates to the Virginia convention from the western part of the state, in disagreement with secession, meet in Wheeling to prepare for defense of the Union in their region.

May 20 North Carolina becomes the 11th state to vote for secession.

May 20 The Confederate capital is moved from Montgomery to Richmond, Virginia.

May 24 Federal troops cross the Potomac River and occupy Alexandria, Virginia.

May 27 Chief Justice Roger B. Taney, sitting as a circuit judge, rules in *Ex Parte Merryman* that Lincoln's suspension of the writ of habeas corpus is unconstitutional on the grounds that such suspension is a legislative prerogative. [The President ignores the Court, indicating that preservation of the Union requires the suspension. Noting the doubtful legality of the President's actions, Congress passes an act on Mar. 3, 1863, giving the President the power to suspend the writ of habeas corpus in certain instances.]

June 3 Stephen A. Douglas, 48, recent Democratic candidate for the Presidency, dies in Chicago.

June 3 General George Brinton McClellan, acting on orders to clear Confederate forces out of western Virginia, defeats a small Confederate force at Philippi.

June 9 The Federal Government founds the Sanitary Commission, an organization that is responsible for "the sanitary condition of the United States forces": nursing, medical supplies, and advice (on such matters as their grievances and pay) to soldiers and their families.

June 10 Dorothea L. Dix is appointed Superintendent of Women Nurses to supervise Union hospital nursing during the war.

June 11-25 Pro-Union delegates, mostly from the western counties of Virginia, meet at Wheeling to continue the preparations initiated by the convention of May 13-15. They form an alternate "government" of the state of Virginia, including an assembly and a governor (Francis H. Pierpont), and they select two U.S. Senators [who are admitted to the Senate upon the withdrawal of the secessionist Senators].

June 16 A telegraph line is authorized from Missouri to San Francisco by the Pacific Telegraph Act.

June 17 Union troops under General Nathaniel Lyon take Boonville, Missouri, to insure control of the lower Missouri River.

June 28 The Central Pacific Railroad Company of California is incorporated at Sacramento to aid in completing a transcontinental rail line.

July 11-13 General George B. McClellan's

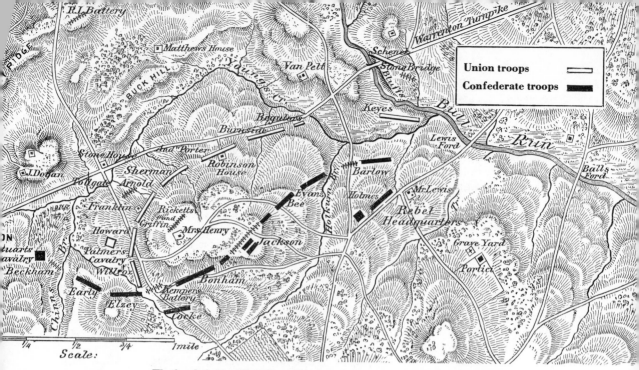

Union troops ▭
Confederate troops ▬

The battlefield of Bull Run, showing the positions of the opposing sides

Union forces under General William S. Rose-crans win several important skirmishes at Rich Mountain, and at Laurel Mountain in western Virginia. They pursue fleeing Confederates and defeat them again at Carrick's Ford.

July 16-21 Union General Irvin McDowell marches westward from the Potomac River opposite Washington, with his troops singing "John Brown's Body" and heading for Richmond. As they approach high land near Manassas, Virginia, on July 21, they clash with troops of General Beauregard's command under General Thomas J. Jackson. The Confederates stand like a stone wall (giving Jackson his nickname)until reinforcements under General E. Kirby Smith of General Joseph E. Johnston's command appear; the combined Confederate force sends the Union troops into a retreat that becomes a rout all the way back to the Potomac.[This Battle of Manassas, or (First) Battle of Bull Run, brings the seriousness of the war home to the citizens of Washington as the defeated troops appear.]

July 20 The term "copperhead" for a Northerner who opposes Lincoln's war policies first appears in the New York *Tribune*.

July 22 A resolution proposed by John J. Crittenden, now a member of the House of Representatives, having passed the House, is passed in the Senate. It declares that the war is being fought to uphold the Constitution and the Federal Government, not to attack slavery or established state constitutions.

July 26 Union forces retreat from Fort Fillmore, New Mexico, leaving most of this territory under Confederate control.

Aug. 5 Lincoln signs a measure to institute the first national income tax, which imposes a 3-per-cent tax on income over $800 (to go into effect Jan. 1, 1862).

Aug. 6 Lincoln signs a bill that frees slaves who are used by Confederates either in labor or in arms. [This is the first of two Confiscation Acts.]

Aug. 7 Construction of seven ironclad gunboats is authorized by Federal authorities.

Aug. 8 Secretary of War Simon Cameron states that the Federal policy which requires citizens to obey the fugitive slave law does not apply to those who help slaves avoid recapture by secessionist slaveholders.

Aug. 10 In a battle at Wilson's Creek, southwest of Springfield, Missouri, Union General Nathaniel Lyon loses his life and his outnumbered troops are forced to retreat by Confederate troops under General Benjamin McCulloch. However, the presence of the Union forces has brought about the resignation of the secessionist governor, Claiborne Jackson, allowing pro-Union influence to prevail in Missouri.

Aug. 16 Lincoln proclaims an end to commercial relations with inhabitants of the rebel states.

Aug. 18 Four New York newspapers are banned in the mails for disloyalty: the *Journal of*

166

Commerce, Daily News, Day Book, and *Freeman's Journal.*

Aug. 19   A proslavery group in Missouri joins the Confederacy, but the free-soil majority in the state expel the rebel "government." [The ambivalent situation in Missouri, a border state in which slavery is legal although free labor predominates, continues throughout the war, which is largely carried on in Missouri by guerrillas on both sides.]

Aug. 24   Confederate President Davis names James M. Mason of Virginia as commissioner to Great Britain, John Slidell of Louisiana to France, and Pierre A. Rost of Louisiana to Spain. All are instructed to obtain recognition of the Confederacy and to purchase arms, munitions, and supplies.

Aug. 28   Commodore Silas H. Stringham and General Benjamin F. Butler lead a land-and-sea attack on Cape Hatteras, North Carolina, seizing Forts Clark and Hatteras to aid the Union blockade.

Aug. 30   General John C. Frémont, from his headquarters in St. Louis, declares an unauthorized emancipation of slaves in Missouri. [Lincoln countermands it.]

Sept. 3   General Leonidas Polk orders the invasion of Kentucky by Confederate troops to force that border state to abandon its "neutrality."

Sept. 6   Federal forces under General Ulysses S. Grant move to Paducah, Kentucky, at the mouth of the Tennessee River, to establish Federal control in the state.

Sept. 15   General Robert E. Lee retreats from a five-day campaign to seize Cheat Mountain in western Virginia.

Oct. 4   Lincoln approves a contract for building ironclad warships.

Oct. 7   The 10-day Pony Express run is officially discontinued in anticipation of the telegraph service that will transmit information within seconds.

Oct. 12   James M. Mason and John Slidell, Confederate commissioners to Europe, evade a Union blockade to escape to Cuba.

Oct. 12   The *Manassas,* an ironclad Confederate ship previously used as a tug, attacks Union shipping on the Mississippi.

Oct. 24   The first transcontinental telegraph message is transmitted when the telegraph wires of the Overland and the Pacific telegraph companies are linked from Denver to Sacramento.

Nov. 1   President Lincoln names General George B. McClellan to replace ailing General Winfield Scott as General in Chief of the Union armies.

Nov. 2   President Lincoln removes General John C. Frémont from command in the Western Department at Springfield, Missouri.

Nov. 6   The provisional Government of the Confederate States is replaced by a permanent Government; President Jefferson Davis is elected for a six-year term.

Nov. 7   A Union squadron of 77 vessels and 12,000 troops under Flag Officer Samuel F. DuPont and General Thomas W. Sherman occupy Port Royal Sound, South Carolina, with the intention of organizing there a major Northern blockading base.

Nov. 8   The Union ship *San Jacinto,* under Captain Charles Wilkes, stops a British mail packet, the *Trent,* and apprehends by force Confederate commissioners James M. Mason and John Slidell, who are passengers en route to Europe from Havana. [On Nov. 24 the *San Jacinto* arrives at Boston, where Mason and Slidell are imprisoned at Fort Warren.]

Nov. 26   A constituent convention gathers at Wheeling, in western Virginia, to establish a separate state as mandated by a referendum held on Oct. 24. [The proposed constitution for the new state is approved in a popular election in April 1862.]

Dec. 4   Southern Presbyterians, meeting in Augusta, Georgia, organize the Assembly of the Presbyterian Church in the Confederate States of America, separating from the Northern Presbyterians.

Dec. 10   A group of Kentucky proslavery advocates set up a "government" that is admitted to the Confederacy. [The admission of both the Kentucky and the previously organized Missouri secessionist "governments" accounts for the 13 stars on the Confederate flag, although only 11 states belonged to the Confederate States.]

Dec. 19   The British Minister to the United States, Lord Lyons, tells Secretary of State William H. Seward that the two Southern commissioners taken off the British ship *Trent* must be released.

Dec. 20   A joint committee on conduct of the war is formed by Congress. [This committee, dominated by radical Republicans, monitors, and at times hampers, Executive decisions.]

Dec. 26   The *Trent* crisis ends when the Cabinet finds that the seizure of Mason and Slidell is illegal and informs Lord Lyons that the two captives will be released.

1862

During this second year of conflict the Union fares well in the West, but discovers that the Confederates can prove a redoubtable foe. In the Mississippi Valley, and to some extent, in Kentucky and Tennessee, Union forces under Generals Halleck, Grant, Thomas, Buell, and Pope win major battles that give the North control of all the Mississippi River except the stretch between the main Confederate center at Vicksburg, Mississippi, and Port Hudson (near Baton Rouge), Louisiana. Decisive victories include Grant's occupation of Fort Henry and Fort Donelson and the naval operation of Farragut in the capture of New Orleans.

Around Richmond and Washington the contest is less decisive. The Union Army of the Potomac under McClellan tests the Confederate Army of Northern Virginia under Lee. For the Union, the conquest of Richmond is a major goal; they try to take the capital of the Confederacy in a pincer movement between Yorktown and Washington. Southern Generals Lee, Johnston, Ewell, Jackson, and Stuart outfight and outmaneuver superior numbers of Union troops. Union forces cannot capture Richmond, but neither can the Confederates, despite a successful campaign in the Shenandoah Valley, carry the war north of the Potomac. In an effort to do so, Lee is turned back at Antietam in September. Antietam shows Northern strength and weakness. It costs McClellan his command, and the armies end the year facing each other across the Rappahannock.

Jan. 6 President Lincoln confers with General in Chief George B. McClellan in response to pressure from radical Senators, who are impatient with McClellan's inaction.

Jan. 10 Lincoln writes Secretary of War Simon Cameron that he is anxious over the lack of an offensive in the West.

Jan. 11 Sailing from Hampton Roads, Virginia, a Union fleet of about 100 vessels, carrying 15,000 troops under General Ambrose E. Burnside and Commodore Louis M. Goldsborough, heads for North Carolina.

Jan. 11 Lincoln accepts the resignation of Secretary of War Simon Cameron, who has been charged with incompetent leadership, contract frauds, and overactive politics. [On Jan. 15 he is replaced by Edwin M. Stanton.]

Jan. 13 General McClellan disagrees on war plans offered by Lincoln, which involve confronting the Confederacy "with superior forces at *different* points, at the *same* time."

Jan. 18 John Tyler, 62, 10th President of the United States, dies in Richmond, Virginia.

Jan. 19 A small but strategically important battle is won by Union General George H. Thomas at Mill Springs, central Kentucky, against Confederate troops commanded by General George B. Crittenden. It gives the Union control from the Cumberland Gap to the lower Cumberland River, and opens the way into eastern Tennessee.

Jan. 26 Confederate General P. G. T. Beauregard is ordered from the Potomac to the West to serve under General Albert S. Johnston.

Jan. 27 Lincoln issues General War Order No. 1, setting Feb. 22 as the day for Union army and navy advances against the Confederacy.

Jan. 30 The U.S.S. *Monitor,* a strange-looking ironclad warship, is launched at Green Point [now part of Brooklyn], New York. It was designed by John Ericsson for the specific purpose of challenging the Confederate ironclad *Virginia* (converted from the captured Union frigate *Merrimack*).

Jan. 30 The released Confederate commissioners, Mason and Slidell, reach Southampton, England.

Jan. 31 Lincoln's Special War Order No. 1 orders the Army of the Potomac to seize the Manassas Junction railhead, site of the Battle of Bull Run.

Feb. 5 Julia Ward Howe's popular patriotic poem, "Battle Hymn of the Republic," appears in the February issue of *Atlantic Monthly,* set to the tune of "John Brown's Body."

Feb. 6 Confederate Fort Henry is bombarded by a Union force of seven gunboats, which seizes this important position on the Tennessee River.

Feb. 8 General Ambrose E. Burnside defeats a Confederate force at Roanoke Island, North Carolina, gaining a key coastal base from which to launch an invasion of North Carolina.

Feb. 11-15 General Ulysses S. Grant captures Fort Donelson, Tennessee, on the lower Cumberland River. The Union gains control of western Kentucky and access to western Tennessee in this four-day battle. [On Feb. 17, Grant is promoted from brigadier general to major general of volunteers.]

Feb. 20   William Wallace Lincoln, 12, the President's youngest son, dies at the White House of typhoid fever.

Feb. 22   Jefferson Davis is inaugurated as President of the Confederate States of America in Richmond.

Feb. 25   General Don Carlos Buell's Union troops occupy Nashville, Tennessee, without bloodshed. This is the first Confederate state capital to fall to the Union.

Feb. 28   Confederate forces capture the town of Tucson in western New Mexico Territory. [The town becomes the capital of the ephemeral Territory of Arizona, which has a delegate in Richmond. The Union regains the area before the end of the year.]

Mar. 4   General Grant is ordered to remain at Fort Henry, Tennessee, losing his opportunity to advance; on this same day, the Senate confirms Andrew Johnson as brigadier general and military governor of Tennessee.

Mar. 6   Lincoln urges Congress to cooperate with any legal state which adopts the gradual abolition of slavery, by giving that state "pecuniary aid" to be used to compensate for the change of system.

Mar. 8   Union General Samuel R. Curtis routs Confederate General Earl Van Dorn at the Battle of Pea Ridge, or Elkhorn Tavern, Arkansas; most of the state of Missouri and control of the middle stretch of the Mississippi River are lost by the Confederacy.

Mar. 8   The Confederate ironclad C.S.S. *Virginia* (formerly the U.S.S. *Merrimack)* soundly defeats four Union wooden vessels at Hampton Roads, Virginia.

Mar. 8   President Lincoln issues General War Order No. 2 that provides for sufficient forces to defend Washington, while General McClellan's troops move south.

Mar. 9   The first modern battle of ironclads takes place at Hampton Roads between the U.S.S. *Monitor* and the C.S.S. *Virginia*; Lieutenant Samuel D. Green commands the *Monitor,* while the *Virginia* is under Lieutenant Catesby ap Roger Jones. The five-hour battle is a draw, but each vessel claims victory.

Mar. 11   In War Order No. 3, Lincoln removes General George B. McClellan as General in Chief of the Union armies, and all generals are to report temporarily to Secretary of War Stanton.

Mar. 14   Union General Burnside seizes New Berne, North Carolina, another strategic base. Burnside is immediately promoted to major general.

Mar. 14   Union troops capture New Madrid, Missouri; Confederate defenders flee to Island No. 10 in the channel of the Mississippi River [Island No. 10 is submerged early in the 20th century].

Mar. 23   General James Shields defeats Confederate General Thomas S. (Stonewall) Jackson's troops at Kernstown, Virginia, opening a campaign in the Shenandoah Valley.

April 5   General McClellan begins a Union siege of Yorktown, Virginia, against Southern forces under General Joseph E. Johnston.

April 6-7   A massive battle is fought at Shiloh, or Pittsburg Landing, Tennessee, with Union troops under General Grant driving back the attack of Confederate General Albert S. Johnston, who is killed in the two-day battle.

April 7   A major Confederate defeat occurs at Island No. 10 in the Mississippi River near New Madrid, Missouri, where Union General John Pope captures huge amounts of arms and supplies, and greatly weakens Southern control of the Lower Mississippi River.

April 10   President Lincoln approves a joint Congressional resolution to emancipate the slaves.

April 11   Fort Pulaski, on Cockspur Island, near Savannah, Georgia, falls to Union troops after a fierce bombardment from nearby Tybee Island, in which rifle-bore cannons are used for the first time. The victory menaces the city of Savannah.

April 16   President Jefferson Davis approves the conscription of every white male between ages 18 and 35 for three-year service.

April 16   Lincoln signs a bill ending slavery in the District of Columbia.

April 24-25   Captain David G. Farragut's fleet of 17 vessels runs under the guns of Fort Jackson and Fort St. Philip, on the Mississippi 70 miles below New Orleans, and into New Orleans, through the Confederate blockade. On April 25, New Orleans falls to Farragut. [For this victory in July he is elevated to the rank of rear admiral.]

May 3   Confederate General Joseph E. Johnston withdraws his army from Yorktown, Virginia, and retreats toward Richmond.

May 5   Congress passes an act establishing the Department of Agriculture, to be headed by a commissioner. [It receives Cabinet rank in 1889.]

May 6   Henry David Thoreau, 55, essayist,

dies in Concord, Massachusetts.

May 9   The major Confederate naval base at Hampton Roads falls to Union forces when the Southerners evacuate Norfolk, Virginia.

May 10   The Battle of Plum Run Bend on the Mississippi River in Tennessee is won by Union ironclad vessels against Confederate wooden boats.

May 11   The Confederacy scuttles the C.S.S. *Virginia (Merrimack)* after the evacuation of Norfolk, principally because no suitable port remains from which to operate.

May 15   Union gunboats steam up the James River toward Richmond, but Confederate artillery at Fort Darling, on Drewrys Bluff, turns the Union ships back, 8 miles short of the Confederate capital.

May 20   The Homestead Act is passed, providing for a free grant of 160 acres of land to any citizen over 21 years of age, or the head of a family, who occupies and improves land in the public domain for five continuous years.

May 23-25   Confederate General Jackson defeats Union forces at Front Royal, Virginia. On May 25 Jackson defeats Union General Nathaniel P. Banks at Winchester. The Confederacy now controls most of the Shenandoah Valley and threatens Washington, 50 miles to the east.

May 30   General Henry W. Halleck leads Union troops into Corinth, Mississippi, to find that outnumbered Confederate forces under General Beauregard have already withdrawn.

June 1   In a two-day battle at Seven Pines, or Fair Oaks, Virginia, Union forces under General McClellan turn back a Confederate attack by forces now commanded by General Robert E. Lee. The Army of Northern Virginia is the name now given by General Lee to all the forces under his direct command.

June 5   Liberia and Haiti become the first Negro nations to be recognized by the United States."Liberia was recognized by Great Britain in 1848, by France in 1852; Haiti was recognized by Great Britain in 1833, by France in 1825. The slave power in the Federal Government prevented earlier recognition by the United States."

June 6   Commodore Charles Davis, with nine Federal vessels, captures Memphis, Tennessee. [This is the last naval battle on the Mississippi River system.]

June 8-9   General Jackson continues his Shenandoah Valley campaign by defeating Union forces under General John C. Frémont at Cross Keys and those under General James Shields at Port Republic, Virginia.

June 16   A large Confederate cavalry unit under General James Ewell Brown (Jeb) Stuart returns to Richmond, Virginia, after a four-day reconnaissance around Federal forces under General McClellan. It is a spectacular morale-building action.

June 19   Lincoln signs a law prohibiting slavery in U.S. territories.

June 25-July 1   In an effort to capture Richmond, General McClellan attacks a few miles east of the city; Confederate troops are moved into position to counter the thrust. Confederate troops under General Ambrose P. Hill then attack at Mechanicsville, Virginia, but Union forces under General Fitz John Porter stops them. Lee's troops drive Porter's Union forces at Gaines' Mill back across the Chickahominy River. McClellan's Army of the Potomac withdraws toward Harrison's Landing on the James River, after winning a battle at Malvern Hill. The seven-day battle for Richmond ends, with heavy casualties on both sides.

July 1   Three important Congressional measures become law: the Federal income tax is revised to 3 per cent on incomes of $600 to $10,000 and to 5 per cent on incomes higher than $10,000; the Pacific Railroad Act provides for a railroad to be built by the Union Pacific and Central Pacific railroads from Nebraska to California; and the first of two antipolygamy laws is passed, directed against the Mormons in Utah Territory.

July 2   President Lincoln signs the Morrill Land-Grant College Act, providing each loyal state with 30,000 acres of land for each Senator and Representative, the land to be used for agricultural and mechanical schools under a measure proposed by Senator Justin S. Morrill of Vermont.

July 14   A law is signed to establish retroactive as well as future pensions for wounded and killed Union soldiers and their families.

July 17   Abraham Lincoln signs the second Confiscation Act, which authorizes the Government to free slaves in areas taken by Union arms, to employ Negroes to engage in combat against the rebellion, to confiscate rebel property, and to colonize in some "tropical country" outside the United States those liberated slaves who wish to emigrate.

July 22   Lincoln reads to his Cabinet the first draft of an Executive order [the Emancipation Proclamation] that would proclaim the freedom of all the slaves in the South. Secretary of State

Seward suggests that after a military victory the North might be better prepared for this drastic change in Federal policy.

July 24 Martin Van Buren, 80, eighth President of the United States, dies in Kinderhook, New York.

Aug. 6 Federal ironclad vessels destroy the C.S.S. *Arkansas* at Baton Rouge, Louisiana, eliminating the last major Confederate warship on the Mississippi.

Aug. 9 Union General John Pope's troops, moving southward in a major offensive, battle General Jackson's forces at Cedar Mountain, or Slaughter Mountain, Virginia.

Aug. 14 A group of free Negroes meets with the President at the White House, and he suggests Central American colonization for their people.

Aug. 17 Facing semistarvation, Sioux Indians begin an uprising in Minnesota by raiding settlers, towns, and troops; hundreds of lives are lost.

Aug. 30 A five-day Southern attack under General Robert E. Lee ends at Manassas, Virginia, with the defeat of John Pope's Federal forces. [This is usually called the Second Battle of Bull Run.]

Aug. 30 Confederate troops under General Edmund Kirby-Smith defeat Union forces at Richmond, Kentucky.

Sept. 2 Lincoln restores General McClellan to full command in Virginia and Washington, as Union armies withdraw to the Washington area.

Sept. 15 Confederate troops under General Jackson capture Harpers Ferry, Virginia, taking about 12,000 prisoners. This engagement is part of a joint effort, with General Lee, to invade the North.

Sept. 17-18 A battle is fought at Antietam Creek near Sharpsburg, Maryland, between more than 75,000 Union troops under General McClellan and about 40,000 Confederates under General Lee. The Confederates hold their ground before withdrawing on the second day; the Union has 2,010 dead, and the South loses about 2,700. The total number of casualties reaches 26,193 dead, wounded, and missing, which makes this battle one of the most costly engagements of the war. [It ends the proposed invasion of the North this year.]

Sept. 22 President Lincoln, following the victory at Antietam, announces that all slaves

President Lincoln visits Union forces after Antietam.

held in states in rebellion will be free, as of Jan. 1, 1863.

Sept. 23   The Sioux uprisings end in the defeat of Chief Little Crow's army at Wood Lake, Minnesota.

Sept. 27   President Davis is authorized by the second Conscription Act to call out men between 35 and 45 years of age.

Sept. 27   The "Chasseurs d'Afrique," the first Union regiment of free blacks, is formed at New Orleans.

Oct. 4   Union General William S. Rosecrans defends the important rail center at Corinth, Mississippi, defeating Confederates under General Earl Van Dorn and General Sterling Price and stopping their advance in Mississippi.

Oct. 8   The Confederacy loses the battle of Perryville, or Chaplin Hills, Kentucky, when General Don Carlos Buell's Federal forces stop the Confederate invasion of Kentucky under General Braxton Bragg.

Nov. 4   Richard J. Gatling receives a patent for a rapid-fire gun [the Gatling gun].

Nov. 5   After months of dissatisfaction with the leadership of General McClellan. who failed to make the most of his victory at Antietam, President Lincoln replaces him with General Ambrose E. Burnside as commander of the Army of the Potomac.

Dec. 1   President Lincoln sends his annual State of the Union message to Congress. The message recommends compensation for freed slaves and colonization outside the country for free Negroes who consent to this; he concludes

An aerial reconnaissance balloon being inflated at Gaines Hill, Virginia

by saying: "In *giving* freedom to the *slave* we assure freedom to the *free*—honorable alike in what we give and what we preserve."

Dec. 7   At Battle Grove, near Fayetteville, General James G. Blunt and General Francis J. Herron defeat Confederate General Thomas C. Hindman, thus maintaining Union control of northwestern Arkansas.

Dec. 11-15   General Burnside, determined to confront General Lee in a showdown battle, leads the Army of the Potomac across the Rappahannock River. He occupies Fredericksburg, Virginia, meeting with limited resistance. General Lee's Army of Northern Virginia withstands a massive assault at the heights behind Fred-

ericksburg and the Union forces withdraw across the Rappahannock. An estimated 114,000 Union troops are engaged in this battle, with Union losses put at 12,653 casualties, compared to 72,500 Confederate troops with 5,309 casualties. This defeat for the Union is as costly as the victory at Antietam.

Dec. 26   Thirty-eight leaders of the Sioux uprising are hanged at Mankato, Minnesota, by order of President Lincoln.

Dec. 29   Union troops under General William T. Sherman fail in an attack on Confederate troops at Chickasaw Bayou, north of Vicksburg, Mississippi.

Military of Charleston, South Carolina

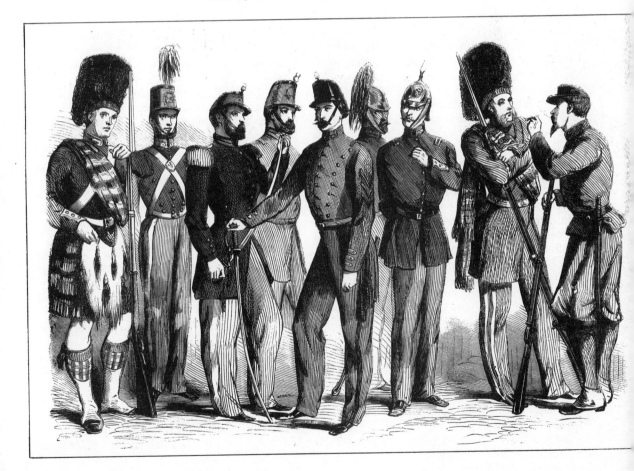

1863

This is the decisive year of the war, the year of the great battles. It begins with a Union army stalemated, taking heavy casualties, almost demoralized. Good news comes first from the West, where Rear Admiral Farragut and General Grant are bringing together the force that finally takes Vicksburg and denies the Mississippi to the Confederates. In the east the initiative is with the Confederates; General Lee decides to take the offensive and the Union does not seem to have the leadership to stop him. His crossing of the Potomac and then of the Mason-Dixon line shocks the North. Yet he is stopped at Gettysburg—stopped, but not routed, because Meade, the victor in the battle, refuses to pursue his foe. President Lincoln celebrates the turning point of the war with these words: "We had only to stretch forth our hands and they were ours. And nothing I could say or do could make the army move." McClellan, Burnside, Meade—the parade of commanders is enough to try even Lincoln's patience. Yet in the West another general seems to know how to fight. Grant does not rest on his victory at Vicksburg. When Rosecrans at Chattanooga is almost as sorely besieged by the Confederates as Pendleton was encircled at Vicksburg by the Union forces, it is Grant who organizes the plan of battle for victory. The taking of Chattanooga, despite the natural advantages of the terrain for the Confederate besiegers, is a brilliant feat; more than this, it opens up the South to penetration from the west. Now the task is to squeeze the Confederate forces, to break them into fragments that may be defeated one at a time. This is the possibility as the year ends.

Jan. 1   Abraham Lincoln signs the Emancipation Proclamation, a Presidential war measure. Its provisions apply only to the areas that are in rebellion against the Union. In these areas, all slaves are declared to be free. (The exercise of that freedom, of course, will be made effective when and if the Federal armies advance into the Confederacy.) Freed Negroes are invited to enlist in the Union armed service.

Jan. 3   At Murfreesboro, or Stone's River, Tennessee, southeast of Nashville, Union troops under General William S. Rosecrans hold back a Confederate attack led by General Bragg.

Jan. 7   The Richmond *Enquirer* calls the Emancipation Proclamation "the most startling political crime, the most stupid political blunder, yet known in American history."

Jan. 26   Lincoln removes General Burnside from command, following his defeat at Fredericksburg, and names General Joseph Hooker to command the Army of the Potomac.

Jan. 31   Confederate gunboats attack and damage Union blockaders at Charleston, South Carolina, interrupting the Northern blockade.

Feb. 10   P. T. Barnum intrudes upon the war with his spectacular and colorful staging of the marriage, at Grace Church, New York City, between two dwarfs who are part of his exhibitions: Charles S. Stratton ("General Tom Thumb"), 2 feet 5 inches tall, and equally small Mercy Lavinia Warren.

Feb. 24   The Union forms Arizona Territory out of the half of New Mexico Territory west of the 109th parallel.[When formal organization takes place in December, Prescott becomes the capital.]

Feb. 25   Congress establishes a national banking system, the member banks of which must have one third of their capital invested in U.S. securities. Those securities may then be used as the base support for issuing national bank notes as currency to the public. [By the end of the year, 400 banks are established.]

Feb. 26   The National Council of the Cherokee Indians rejoins the Union and abolishes slavery.

Mar. 3   Lincoln signs a Conscription Act, drafting all males between 20 and 46 years of age (with some exceptions), but allowing those drafted the alternatives of hiring a substitute to enlist for three years or purchasing exemption for $300.

Mar. 3   Idaho Territory is formed out of the eastern part of Washington Territory and the western part of Dakota Territory. [Its area comprises that of the present states of Idaho, Montana, and Wyoming.]

Mar. 3   Jay Cooke is named U.S. Government agent and given the responsibility of popularizing the sale of Union war bonds.

Mar. 3   Congress establishes the National Academy of Sciences.

Mar. 10   President Lincoln issues an amnesty order for soldiers who are absent without leave if they report before April 1.

Mar. 14   Rear Admiral David G. Farragut leads a Union flotilla up the Mississippi River past the armed Confederate base at Port Hudson, Louisiana.

April 2   An unsettling "bread riot" occurs in Richmond, Virginia, when a mob breaks into the city's shops. Police and militia are required to stop the looting.

April 7   Rear Admiral Samuel Francis Du Pont attacks Charleston Harbor, South Carolina, with nine *Monitor*-type ironclad steamships, but the Union vessels are driven back.[Du Pont later indicates that ships of this type are too vulnerable to be used against forts.]

April 14   William A. Bullock introduces the first web-fed printing press (a press that prints from a continuous roll) at Pittsburgh. [Bullock is killed four years later in an accident involving the installing of one of his presses.]

April 16-17   Rear Admiral David D. Porter sends a 12-vessel flotilla south past Vicksburg on the Mississippi River, as part of the campaign by General Ulysses S. Grant against that Southern stronghold.[On April 30, after moving on the west bank of the Mississippi to the south of Vicksburg, General Grant's forces are ferried across the river to attack Vicksburg from the south.]

April 20   The President announces that the state of West Virginia is to be formed out of the northwestern portion of Virginia as a war measure, effective June 20.

April 28-May 4   General Joseph Hooker's Army of the Potomac, with about 70,000 troops, begins an offensive, crossing the Rappahannock above Fredericksburg and outflanking Robert E. Lee's Army of Northern Virginia. Lee, with about 47,000 men in his command, drives back the superior Army of the Potomac on May 3 and captures Chancellorsville, west of Fredericksburg. The Union armies fall back across the Rappahannock on the following day. In the course of the battle of Chancellorsville, General Jackson is accidentally wounded by one of his own men.[He dies of complications following the amputation of an arm on May 10.]

May 14   General Grant captures Jackson, the capital of Mississippi, as his forces close in on encircled Vicksburg from the east.

May 18-23   General John C. Pemberton, in command at Vicksburg, decides to hold the city. The first Union assault on Vicksburg is launched on the next day, and are driven off with high casualties. On May 22 a second Union frontal assault on Vicksburg is decisively beaten off and

General Grant begins to prepare for a siege of attrition, rather than a series of costly attacks.

May 21-27   General Nathaniel Banks, leading Union troops from Alexandria, Louisiana, lays siege to Port Hudson (above Baton Rouge), one of the few remaining strong points of the Confederates along the Mississippi River. On May 27 the siege ends as Confederate General Franklin Gardner's forces inflict heavy casualities on the Northerners.

May 26   Gold is discovered at Alder Gulch in Idaho Territory. [The boom town of Virginia City, Montana, develops here from a camp of about 10,000 miners.]

May 28   The first black Northern regiment, the 54th Massachusetts Volunteers, leaves Boston for South Carolina, under Colonel Robert G. Shaw.

June 3   General Robert E. Lee begins a second invasion of the Union, starting from Fredericksburg, Virginia, with about 75,000 men.

June 14   Union General R. H. Milroy is attacked by Lee's army at Winchester, Virginia. The Union forces are surprised and withdraw.

June 14   A second assault by General Banks' forces against Port Hudson, Louisiana, is driven off with heavy casualities. Confederate losses are light.

June 16   Confederate troops begin to cross the upper Potomac River; panic breaks out in Washington as people crowd trains and prepare for evacuation.

June 20   In accordance with Lincoln's proclamation of April 20, West Virginia becomes the 35th state in the Union. Wheeling is the capital.

June 20   Jay Cooke organizes the first national bank in Philadelphia where he leads the campaign for the sale of Union war bonds.

The redoubt at McConihe, Virginia

GEORGIA CITIZEN

EXTRA.

Tuesday, July 23, 1861, 6 A. M.

GLORIOUS VICTORY!

The Federalists 80,000, routed by 40,000 Confederates.

GREAT SLAUGHTER ON BOTH SIDES!

FOUR BATTERIES TAKEN AND EIGHT RIFLE CANNON.

The Enemy in full retreat to Washington and the greatest Consternation Prevailing in Washington.

The following glorious news was received here last night at 12 o'clock First Dispatch by way of the West.

1ST DISPATCH.

Louisville, July 22.—The following news of the Confederate victory creates most intense excitement here, startling the public mind, the morning papers having published dispatches from Washington claiming brilliant victory for Federalists. There is the greatest rejoicing among southern rights men

NORTHERN REPORT.

On Monday noon, OUR troops after gaining a great victory, were eventually repulsed and commenced a retreat on Washington. After the latest information from Centreville, last night, a series of events took place in the highest degree disastrous. Many confused statements are prevalent, but enough is known to warrant the statement that we have suffered to a degree which casts gloom over the remains of the army and excites the deepest melancholy throughout Washington. The carnage was tremendously heavy on both sides, and on ours, it is represented as frightful.

We were advancing, taking masked batteries, gradually but surely driving the enemy towards Manassas, when the enemy seemed reinforced by Gen. Johnston.

We were immediately driven back and a panic among our troops suedenly occurred. A regular stampede took place.

It was understood that Gen. McDowell undertook a stand near Centreville, but the panic became so fearful that the whole army became demoralized and it was impossible to check them either at Centerville or at Fairfax Court House.

A large number of troops in retreat, fell on the wayside from exhaustion, and scattered along the route, all the way from Fairfax Court House. The road from Bull's Run was strewed with arms and knapsacks, discarded by the troops the better to facilitate retreat. General McDowell was in rear of retreat, endeavoring to rally the men, but with only partial success.

Only 200 Fire Zouaves left from the slaughter--69th and other N. York Regiment suffered

FRIGHTFULLY.

SHERMAN'S, CARLISLE'S, GRIFFIN'S AND WEST POINT BATTERIES WERE TAKEN BY CONFEDERATES!!

Also the 8 seige 32 pounder Rifle Cannon.

Col. Wilcox, of Michigan, commanded brigade.

Capt. M'Cook, of Ohio, killed.

Col. Heintzleman wounded.

Washington is a scene of the most intense excitement. Wagons are continually arriving bringing the dead and wounded.

The feeling in the city is awfully distressing. Both telegraph and steamboat communication with Alexandria is suspended to the public The greatest alarm prevails through out the city.

The fortifations are strongly reinforced by fresh troops.

It is supposed Gen. Mansfield will take charge of the fortifications on the other side of the river.

Large rifled cannon and mortars are being sent over.   LOOMIS.

2d Dispatch.

Dispatch from Pres't. Davis.

Richmond, July 22d.—President Davis sends an official dispatch to Secretary of War announcing complete and decisive victory over the enemy, who after ten hours battle, fled precipitately in the direction of Leesburg and Centreville, pursued by Cavalry and Light Infantry, till night put an end to the pursuit.

The enemy left on field, large stores, munitions, arms, vast piles of slain, every where in direction of flight. Dead bodies and wounded were scattered along the route. The neighboring farm houses on the road were crowded with the wounded enemy.

The Confederate force immediately engaged was 15,000, Federals estimated at 35,000. This refers to the left wing where the battle principally raged, and does not include right and center forces, which were only partially engaged.

The entire Confederate forces were about 40,000—Federals nearly 80,000. Enemy lost several batteries, field artillery, one regimental stand of colors.   PRITCHARD.

3d Dispatch.

Richmond, July 22d. Congress met at noon. After Prayer, Presi-

---

Facsimile of part of a page of the *Georgia Citizen*, July 23, 1861

Sam Houston
(1793-1863)

June 23-30 Union General William S. Rosecrans engages troops under General Braxton Bragg at Tullahoma, Tennessee, in order to prevent reinforcements from reaching the surrounded Confederates in Vicksburg. On June 30 Bragg's forces withdraw across the Tennessee River in the direction of Chattanooga.

June 28 Lincoln replaces General Hooker with General George Gordon Meade to command the Army of the Potomac; Meade is to engage Lee's advancing forces.

July 1-3 General Lee encounters Union forces of General Meade's army at Gettysburg, Pennsylvania, a few miles north of the Maryland border. Lee's forces, first with superior numbers, entrench themselves on the first day of battle; Union General John F. Reynolds is killed. Heavy fighting begins the next day with the Confederate attack failing and the Union defense holding. The battle ends with the retreat of General Lee. Union casualties are 23,049 out of over 85,000 troops; Lee loses 20,451 dead, wounded, and missing out of nearly 65,000 troops.

July 4-8 The Vicksburg siege ends on July 4, with the surrender of the Confederate troops under General John C. Pemberton to the army under General Grant. With the surrender of Port Hudson, Louisiana, to General Banks on July 8, the Union controls all of the Mississippi River, except for guerrilla raids.

July 4-20 General Meade fails to pursue his victory as General Lee retreats southward from Gettysburg, reaching the Potomac River on July 14, and the Rapidan River in Virginia a few days later.

July 10 Union troops under Rear Admiral John A. Dahlgren begin a second siege of Charleston Harbor.

July 11-18 With the appearance of the first draft lists in New York City, resentment over the unfairness of conscription to the poor (who cannot substitute for or purchase exemption) results in a week of rioting. Although draft offices are at first the object of the crowd's wrath, numbers of the city's discontented, including many Irish immigrants, form mobs that vent their hostility mainly on Negroes, who are scapegoats for the fact that there is a war. Among rioters and Negroes, hundreds are killed, and property destruction of some $2,000,000 value is incurred. In the end, soldiers from Meade's command at Gettysburg are brought in to quell the riot.

July 26 Sam Houston, 70, former President of Texas, dies at his farm at Huntsville.

July 26 General John Hunt Morgan is captured at Salineville, Ohio, with remnants of his Confederate cavalry after a spectacular, 25-day raid through Kentucky into Indiana and Ohio behind Union lines. [He is imprisoned at Columbus, Ohio, but escapes on Nov. 27.]

Aug. 3 Governor Horatio Seymour of New

Members of the 107th U.S. colored infantry

York, shocked by the draft riot, requests that President Lincoln suspend conscription in that state.

Aug. 17-23   The Union forces of Admiral Dahlgren bombard Fort Sumter in Charleston Harbor, now defended by General P. G. T. Beauregard. [The fort is reduced to rubble, and its guns are replaced by infantry; but the fort continues to hold out. It is abandoned in February 1865.]

Aug. 19   The Federal Government resumes the draft in New York City without difficulty.

Aug. 21   William Clarke Quantrill leads a Confederate guerrilla force into Lawrence, Kansas, looting, burning, and killing about 150 men and boys.

Sept. 2   Union General Burnside occupies Knoxville, Tennessee, cutting railroad lines to Chattanooga in preparation for an assault on the latter city.

Sept 9   The Army of the Cumberland under General Rosecrans occupies Chattanooga after General Braxton Bragg withdraws his Confederate army into Georgia. [Bragg awaits reinforcements commanded by General James Longstreet that are being sent by rail all the way from Virginia.]

Sept. 10   Confederate troops under General Sterling Price evacuate Little Rock, Arkansas, thus weakening the hold of the Confederacy in the region west of the Mississippi. [A Union Government is set up in Little Rock, and Confederate Governor Harris Flanigin moves to Washington, Arkansas, remaining there until 1865.]

Sept. 19-20   At West Chickamauga Creek, southeast of Chattanooga, the Federal Army of Rosecrans engages troops under Bragg, now reinforced by Longstreet's forces. The Confederate troops break through Union lines at Chickamauga and drive Rosecrans' troops into retreat toward Chattanooga after extremely heavy losses to both sides. [The Union troops hold Chattanooga while the Confederates deploy their troops south of the city from Missionary Ridge to Lookout Mountain.]

Oct. 9-Nov. 10   General Meade's Army of the Potomac and Lee's Army of Northern Virginia maneuver and parry thrusts against each other, with minor results. [The two armies gradually settle into winter quarters, parallel to each other—the Confederates along the Rapidan River, the Union army along the Rappahannock River, both in northern Virginia.]

Oct. 15   At Charleston, South Carolina, a

Jefferson Davis and his Cabinet with General Lee in the Council Chamber at Richmond

Wounded and dead lie in the field, following the battle at Gettysburg.

Confederate submersible boat, the *H. L. Hunley,* sinks during a practice dive, and the inventor, H.L. Hunley, dies in the action. [The ship is recovered for further use.]

Oct. 16 General Ulysses S. Grant is put in command of a new Military Division of the Mississippi, with three departments combined: the Ohio, the Cumberland, and the Tennessee.

Oct. 19 General Grant relieves General Rosecrans, who is under siege at Chattanooga, and puts General George H. Thomas in command of the Army of the Cumberland.[Grant reaches Chattanooga on Oct. 23.]

Oct. 29 Grant opens up a supply line by ferrying goods northeast, up the Tennessee River, from a Union base at Bridgeport, Alabama. The besieged forces in Chattanooga are no longer likely to be starved into surrender.

Nov. 2 Troops of Union General Nathaniel Banks seize Brazos Island, in extreme southern Texas.

Nov. 16 General Burnside withdraws to Knoxville, Tennessee, followed by Confederate troops under General Longstreet, who is attempting to prevent aid from reaching Grant and Thomas at Chattanooga.

Nov. 19 President Abraham Lincoln is at the battlefield at Gettysburg, Pennsylvania, to participate in the dedication of a National Cemetery. The principal speaker of the day, Edward Everett, a well known scholar and rhetorician, delivers a two-hour oration. This is followed by a brief address by President Lincoln, which is received politely.[The next day Everett sends a congratulatory note to Lincoln. Lincoln replies: ''I am pleased to know that, in your judgment, the little I did say was not entirely a failure.''

Lincoln's Gettysburg Address becomes one of the most admired speeches in modern times.]

Nov. 23-25 At Chattanooga, General Grant breaks out of the city to attack General Bragg's Confederate troops on a wide front. General Joseph Hooker captures Lookout Mountain south of the city by scaling it from the valley to its east, with light fighting. On Nov. 25 General William T. Sherman attacks the Confederates on Missionary Ridge southeast of Chattanooga; later that day General George H. Thomas' troops drive the Confederate forces off the mountain. The Union forces lose 5,824 out of 56,000 troops; the Confederate casualities are 6,667 out of 46,000 troops. Most of Bragg's army flees into Georgia.

Nov. 29 General Longstreet makes a futile attack on Fort Sanders near Knoxville, Tennessee, and, thrown back by Union forces, he retreats eastward. [He settles into winter camp at Greenville, Tennessee.]

Nov. 30 President Davis accepts the resignation of defeated General Bragg and names General William J. Hardee to replace him.

Dec. 8 Lincoln issues a Proclamation of Amnesty and Reconstruction, a moderate reconstruction plan to pardon all rebels (except high Confederate officials and military men who resigned to join the South) and to reinstate any seceded state where 10 per cent of the voters in the 1860 election would take an oath to the Federal Government and bar slavery.

Dec. 16 The Confederacy names General Joseph E. Johnston to command the Army of Tennessee, replacing General Hardee, and Johnston's command of the Army of Mississippi is given to General Leonidas Polk.

1864

Many of the great expectations of the North are realized during this years, in both the military and political arenas. Grant is given command of the Union armies. He assigns to Sherman the task of penetrating the Confederacy from the Tennessee Valley to the Atlantic Ocean, cutting a swath across the lower South. In a campaign of deliberate and efficient destruction of any resource of use to the Confederacy, Sherman drives to Atlanta by September and then to the sea at Savannah by Christmas. Confederate General Hood tries to divert him in Tennessee, only to be checked, and then beaten at Nashville by General Thomas, a Virginian remaining loyal to the Union.

In May, Grant takes charge of the Virginia campaign, and a series of battles are fought with Lee's Army of Northern Virginia: the Wilderness, Spotsylvania Court House, Cold Harbor, and Petersburg. Casualties run to the tens of thousands for both armies in the deadliest fighting—including the world's first trench warfare—of the war. By mid-June Grant settles into a nine-month siege that contains Lee in the Petersburg-Richmond area.

The public is becoming weary of destruction and casualties. Northerners wonder if their armies can defeat the Confederacy. Southerners are horrified at the tales they hear of the ruthless march through Georgia. Desperation pervades the South, but in the North a surge of peace sentiment complicates the political campaigns that precede the Presidential election of 1864. Lincoln's nomination in June is linked, on the National Union ticket, with that of lifelong Democrat Andrew Johnson at a time when Union forces are stalemated before Richmond. Even in August, when McClellan becomes the Democratic candidate, Lincoln feels his defeat is probable; the Confederates are at the outskirts of Washington, and Sherman has not yet entered Atlanta. However, military victories at Mobile Bay, in the Shenandoah Valley, and at Atlanta apparently reassure the electorate, for Lincoln has 350,000 more popular votes than he won four years ago; and McClellan, whose popular vote almost equals that of Lincoln's 1860 tally, has a geographically concentrated constituency and therefore only one tenth of the electoral votes cast.

Jan. 11   A constitutional amendment to abolish slavery in the United States is proposed in the U.S. Senate by John B. Henderson of Missouri.

Jan. 13   Composer Stephen C. Foster, 38, dies in poverty and obscurity in Bellevue Hospital in New York City.

Jan. 22   Isaac Murphy is inaugurated as provisional governor of the free-state Askansas government. He was the only member of the 1861 convention to vote against secession.

Feb. 1   President Lincoln orders a draft of 500,000 men for three years, or the duration of the war, to be effective Mar. 10.

Feb. 3   General William T. Sherman sets out from Vicksburg, Mississippi, against Confederate forces around Meridian. [His troops enter Meridian on Feb. 14 and destroy railroads, supplies, and buildings in the area.]

Feb. 17   The Confederate submersible ship *H.L. Hunley,* only partly submerged and using a pole extending from its prow with a bomb attached, attacks and sinks the U.S.S. *Housatonic* off Charleston, South Carolina; the *Hunley* sinks with its prey.

Feb. 20   In a battle near Olustee, or Ocean Pond, Florida, Union General Truman Seymour is repulsed by General Joseph Finegan and withdraws with heavy casualties to Jacksonville.

Feb. 22   The Union Government in control of eastern Louisiana and centered in New Orleans chooses Georg Michael Hahn as governor.

Feb. 24   Lincoln signs an act of Congress to compensate slave-owners in Union-controlled areas whose slaves volunteer to enlist in the Army. The sum is not to exceed $300 each, and the volunteer is to become a free man.

Mar. 2   Ulysses S. Grant, nominated by Lincoln, is confirmed by the U.S. Senate as a lieutenant general. (The grade is revived by an act of Congress on Feb. 29.) [Grant receives his commission at a White House ceremony on Mar. 9.]

Mar. 12   Grant is officially made General in Chief of the Union armies; General Henry W. Halleck is demoted to Chief of Staff.

Mar. 14   Lincoln orders a draft of 200,000 men for the military service (Army, Navy, and

Marine Corps) of the Union; this is to be filled by volunteers until April 15, and thereafter by draft.

Mar. 18   A constitution abolishing slavery is approved by Arkansas voters.

Mar. 28   Union soldiers on furlough in Charleston, Illinois, are attacked by about 100 Southern sympathizers (Copperheads). Five are killed and many are wounded.

April 4   The plan of France's Napoleon III to place Archduke Ferdinand Maximilian of Austria on a throne in Mexico is condemned in a joint resolution passed in the U.S. House of Representatives. [The United States continues to support the Government of Benito Juárez, although French troops occupy an increasing part of Mexico. On April 10 the Austrian archduke accepts the proffered throne, and he is installed as Emperor Maximilian on June 10.]

April 5   Industrialist George M. Pullman receives a patent on a folding upper berth for a railroad car.

April 6   In New Orleans, a constitutional convention under Union control adopts a new state constitution and abolishes slavery in Louisiana.

April 8   The U.S. Senate, by a vote of 38 to 6, approves the 13th Amendment to the Constitution.

April 9   Union General Nathaniel P. Banks, leading one of the two main forces in a campaign up the Red River to take Shreveport, Louisiana, is driven back by Confederate General Richard Taylor at Sabine Crossroads. A Confederate Government of Western Louisiana remains in control of Shreveport.

April 22   For the first time, U.S. coins are stamped with the motto, "In God We Trust."

April 30   Joe Davis, the five-year-old son of the Confederate President, dies after a fall at the Confederate White House in Richmond.

May 4-12   A two-day battle in the Wilderness area of Virginia, initiating a major campaign by the Army of the Potomac against the Army of Northern Virginia, ends in a draw between Grant and Lee, with casualties of 17,666 for the 100,000 Union troops and possibly 7,500 for the 60,000 Confederates. On May 8, Grant engages Lee's armies near Spotsylvania Court House. He fails to outflank the Confederates, but in a message to Halleck, Grant writes, "I propose to fight it out along this line if it takes all summer". On May 11, Union cavalry commanded by General Philip H. Sheridan meet Confederate cavalry led by General J. E. B.

Stuart at Yellow Tavern, about 6 miles north of Richmond; although Sheridan withdraws, Stuart is wounded. He dies the next day.

May 5   Swarthmore College is founded by a group of Quakers (Society of Friends), at Swarthmore, Pennsylvania, near Philadelphia.

May 7   General William T. Sherman, now commanding the Division of the Mississippi —which includes the armies of the Cumberland, of the Tennessee, and of the Ohio—sets out, under orders from Grant, from Chattanooga with a force of about 100,000 to invade Georgia, which is defended by Confederate forces under General Joseph E. Johnston, commander of the 60,000-strong Army of Tennessee.

May 15   Confederate General John C. Breckinridge wins an impressive battle at New Market, in the Shenandoah Valley of Virginia, with the participation of a small group of cadets from the Virginia Military Institute, which is holding the valley against Union forces under General Franz Sigel.

May 16   General Benjamin F. Butler and the Army of the James are driven off by Confederate troops under General Beauregard at Drewrys Bluff, Virginia, and the Union attack on Richmond stalls.

May 18-19   New England novelist Nathaniel Hawthorne, 60, dies in Plymouth, New Hampshire.

May 25   Confederate General Johnston holds the advancing Union forces at New Hope Church, Georgia, about 25 miles northeast of Atlanta; both sides move into entrenchments.

May 26   The territory of Montana is formed out of the northeastern part of Idaho Territory; the two territories are now separated by the High Bitterroot Mountains. Montana's first capital is Bannock [moved in 1865 to Virginia City] and the first governor is Sidney Edgerton.

May 31   Radical Republicans, unhappy with the policies of Lincoln, meet at Cleveland, Ohio, and nominate General John C. Frémont for President and Brigadier General John Cochrane of New York for Vice President in the forthcoming national election.

June 3   Lee holds against a three-day frontal attack by Grant at Cold Harbor, Virginia, 8 miles north of Richmond.

June 8   At Baltimore, the National Union Party nominates Abraham Lincoln for President and Governor Andrew Johnson of Tennessee for Vice President. The party adopts the name of National Union for this convention to indicate that it not only represents most Republicans, but also has in its ranks pro-Union Democrats, such as Andrew Johnson. Its platform calls for bringing an end to the rebellion and ratification of the 13th Amendment to end slavery.

June 10   Union General Samuel D. Sturgis, seeking to divert General Forrest's cavalry from attacking Sherman, is defeated in a surprise attack by the Confederates at Brices Crossroads in northeastern Mississippi.

June 14   Confederate General Leonidas Polk, observing enemy operations from Pine Mountain, Georgia, is killed by Federal artillery fire.

June 18   At Petersburg, Virginia, after a costly four-day battle, Grant's 100,000-man Army of the Potomac settles into a siege opposite Lee's army 20 miles south of Richmond.

June 19   In a major naval battle off Cherbourg, France, Captain John A. Winslow, commanding the U.S.S. *Kearsarge,* sinks the C.S.S. *Alabama,* a Confederate raider which has captured 65 Union merchant ships.

June 27   General Sherman attacks General Johnston's entrenched Confederate forces at Kennesaw Mountain, near Marietta, Georgia. The Union troops are defeated with high casualties.

June 29   Secretary of the Treasury Salmon P. Chase, having expressed serious disagreements with Lincoln, resigns from the Cabinet.

July 2   The U.S. Congress charters the Northern Pacific Railroad to build a route from Lake Superior to Portland, Oregon, and to open the land for settlement.

July 4   Congress passes an act legalizing the importation of contract laborers. By Presidential order, the Federal Office of Commissioner of Immigration is established to process contract laborers.

July 8   The Wade-Davis Act is passed by Congress. It embodies Congressional plans for Reconstruction. [It is strongly opposed by Lincoln, who refuses to sign it.]

July 9-12   General Jubal Early, after leading a corps of Confederate troops through the Shenandoah Valley with repeated successful skirmishes since June 28, defeats General Lew Wallace at Monocacy, Maryland, clearing the way for a direct assault upon Washington. On July 11, Early invades the suburbs of Washington, but on July 12 he is forced to withdraw to Leesburg, Virginia.

July 17   President Davis relieves General Joseph E. Johnston of command of the Army of Tennessee, which has retreated to the outskirts of Atlanta, Georgia, and General John B. Hood is placed in command to oppose General Sherman.

July 18   Union casualties are very high during Grant's campaign against Richmond but, in spite of Northern concern over manpower losses, President Lincoln calls for 500,000 more volunteers.

July 20-22   General Hood attacks Union forces under General George H. Thomas at Peachtree Creek near Atlanta and is defeated, at a cost of 4,796 casualties out of about 20,000 troops. He then sends General William Hardee

The Great Denver Flood, May 1864

A pro-Lincoln cartoon

against General James B. McPherson, who is in command between Atlanta and Decatur. McPherson is killed in the battle, but Hood's troops fail on their second attack on the Union forces, which surround Atlanta and begin a siege of the city.

July 30 General John McCausland of General Early's Confederate command, in a raiding operation, seizes Chambersburg, Pennsylvania. When the town's citizens do not meet his demand for $500,000 in currency or $100,000 in gold, he burns the town.

Aug. 1 General Philip H. Sheridan is named to command the Army of the Shenandoah, to check the operations of General Early, which are intended to relieve the Union pressure against Richmond.

Aug. 5 Admiral David G. Farragut leads a Union fleet of 18 ships against Mobile Bay, Alabama. His U.S.S. *Tecumseh* is torpedoed and sinks, but the Union forces disable the C.S.S. *Tennessee* and close the major port at Mobile, making it possible to invest the city by land. [On Aug. 23, Fort Morgan, in Mobile Bay, is taken by Union forces, closing Mobile to Confederate blockade runners.]

Aug. 5 Lincoln's pocket veto of the Wade-Davis bill draws a vindictive attack by the bill's authors, Benjamin Wade and Henry W. Davis, in the form of a manifesto printed first in the New York *Tribune*.

Aug. 29-31 The Democratic Party meets at Chicago, Illinois, nominating General George B. McClellan for President, and George H. Pendleton of Ohio, for Vice President. The platform supports a strong peace program.

Sept. 1-2 General Hood begins to evacuate Atlanta; at nearby Jonesborough, Union troops defeat General Hardee's forces. On Sept. 2 Sherman occupies the city, and reorganizes his forces there.

Sept. 4 A Union raiding party surprises General John Hunt Morgan in Greeneville, Tennessee, and the Confederate cavalry leader is killed.

Sept. 5 In Union-occupied Louisiana, voters ratify a new constitution that abolishes slavery.

Sept. 17 John C. Frémont, urging a united Republican election effort, withdraws as a Presidential candidate of the radical faction of the party.

Sept. 19-22 Sheridan's Union forces attack

and soundly defeat Early's army at Opequon Creek, north of Winchester, Virginia. Three days later, at Fisher's Hill, he inflicts high casualties on Early's troops.

Sept. 29   Grant, concerned lest an attempt may be made to relieve General Early, sends a Union division to seize Fort Harrison near Richmond.

Oct. 2   President Jefferson Davis places General Pierre G.T. Beauregard in overall command of the Division of the West to direct operations of General John B. Hood and General Richard Taylor as defenses appear to be deteriorating in areas under their command.

Oct. 7   The U.S.S. *Wachusett*, finding the raider, C.S.S. *Florida*, at Bahia, Brazil, forces the Confederate ship to surrender.

Oct. 12   Roger B. Taney, 87, Chief Justice of the U.S. Supreme Court since 1835, dies in Washington.

Oct. 13   Maryland voters adopt a new constitution and abolish slavery in that state.

Oct. 19   General Jubal Early launches a surprise attack on Union General Sheridan's forces at Cedar Creek, Virginia, and is defeated. [This last fight in the Shenandoah area is the occasion celebrated in the well-known poem by Thomas Buchanan Read, ''Sheridan's Ride.'']

Oct. 23   The defeat of General Stirling Price and his army by Union General Samuel R. Curtis' Army of the Border at Westport, Missouri, ends most Confederate power west of the Mississippi.

Oct. 31   President Lincoln proclaims the entry of Nevada into the Union as the 36th state. Its admission is facilitated by the need of two more votes in the Senate to pass the 13th Amendment.

Nov. 8   President Lincoln is reelected. Andrew Johnson wins the Vice Presidency. Lincoln and Johnson receive 212 electoral votes to 21 for General McClellan and George H. Pendleton; the tickets win 2,206,935 to 1,803,787 respectively in popular votes; the Republicans get strong support from soldiers (116,887 to 33,748), and they maintain strong majorities in both the House and the Senate. The uncast 81 electoral votes of the seceded states would not have affected the outcome.

Nov. 9   General Sherman's troops receive instructions to live off the land as they march through Georgia, but not to violate private property recklessly. [The general abuse of these instructions by personnel who may have acted without authorization results in enormous destruction along the route of the army and be-

A pontoon bridge on the James River above Jones' Landing

Confederate battery on the James River, Virginia, shelling the Federal *Monitors* and the laborers on the Dutch Gap Canal

comes a legend of Northern terror tactics in the South.]

Nov. 16　　After having destroyed the city, except for houses and churches, General Sherman sets out from Atlanta with 60,000 troops and 5,500 artillery on his march to the sea across Georgia.

Nov. 19　　Georgia Governor Joseph E. Brown calls for volunteers between the ages of 16 and 35 to oppose Sherman, but without much success.

Nov. 21　　The Confederate Army of Tennessee under General John B. Hood leaves Florence, Alabama, headed for Nashville and Pulaski, Tennessee.

Nov. 22　　Union troops occupy Milledgeville, the capital of Georgia.

Nov. 25　　A sensational, but ineffective, Confederate plot to burn New York City fails after fires are set in several hotels and in P.T. Barnum's "museum."

Nov. 29　　Colonel John M. Chivington, a U.S. cavalry commander, massacres more than 500 Arapaho and Cheyenne men, women and children in a raid on their camp at Sand Creek, Colorado Territory.

Nov. 30-Dec. 2　　General Hood's Army of Tennessee, advancing on Nashville, attacks Union General John M. Schofield's retreating forces at Franklin, Tennessee, but fails to defeat Schofield. Hood's losses include not only the lives of 1,750 men, but those of six Southern

generals. Three days later, Hood reaches Nashville, where General George H. Thomas is entrenched.

Dec. 6　　Salmon P. Chase, former Secretary of the Treasury and uncompromising enemy of the slave power, is named fifth Chief Justice of the U.S. Supreme Court.

Dec. 13　　Sherman captures the Confederate Fort McAllister on the Ogeechee River near Savannah, opening river communication with Union naval forces and ensuring needed supplies.

Dec. 16　　General Thomas' Army of the Cumberland defeats Confederate General Hood's Army of Tennessee in a two-day battle at Nashville, ending the main Confederate campaign in the West.

Dec. 20　　General William J. Hardee evacuates Confederate forces from Savannah, Georgia, and withdraws northward to South Carolina, leaving Sherman in control of the city. [Sherman sends the following telegram to Lincoln on Dec. 21: "I beg to present to you as a Christmas gift the city of Savannah with 150 heavy guns and plenty of ammunition and also about 25,000 bales of cotton."]

Dec. 25　　Union troops under General Benjamin F. Butler and a large fleet under Rear Admiral David D. Porter fail in a two-day sea-land attack on Fort Fisher south of Wilmington, North Carolina. Wilmington is now the only major Southern port still open.

1865 The Confederacy is reduced to a desperate, hopeless holding action, effective only in southern Virginia and the Carolinas. General Sherman's army moves northward until the total surrender of his Confederate opponents is achieved at Durham Station, North Carolina, late in April. Early in April, Lee after finally becoming General in Chief of the Confederacy, attempts to defend the capital of the Confederacy against Grant, but, lacking the means, surrenders the main Confederate army at Appomattox Court House. In May Jefferson Davis, in flight, is arrested. By early June, all Confederate resistance ceases.

The Union is clearly saved by force of arms, but in its hour of victory it loses its compassionate and beloved leader, who proposed, once the fighting was over, "to bind up the nation's wounds. . . ."

In any case, the nation is pledged by the 13th Amendment to abolish human servitude for black Americans. Abolition, not long ago a "radical" position even in the antislavery camp, has become the law of the land. Now the question of implementing such law arises. Nowhere in the South does the Negro vote. Some states go through the motions of constitutional conventions, but usually without basically repudiating secession. Such Southern recalcitrance is matched by the resentment of radical Republicans in the North. Southern Congressional delegates remain unseated in the Congress. Bitter political battles begin where military battles leave off.

Jan. 15 After a three-day bombardment by Rear Admiral David D. Porter with about 60 vessels and General Alfred Terry with land forces, Fort Fisher, south of Wilmington, North Carolina, is captured from Confederate defenders under Colonel William Lamb.

Jan. 15 Edward Everett, 71, former Senator, scholar, and orator, dies in Boston.

Jan. 31 The House of Representatives passes the 13th Amendment by 119 to 56, with 8 abstentions. The amendment now goes to the states for ratification. [Illinois is the first state to ratify, on Feb. 1.]

Jan. 31 General Robert E. Lee is named General in Chief of the Confederacy.

Feb. 3 Three peace commissioners for the Confederacy—Vice President Alexander H. Stephens, John A. Campbell, and Robert M.T. Hunter—meet with Abraham Lincoln and Secretary of State William H. Seward on board the *River Queen* in Hampton Roads off Fort Monroe, Virginia. Lincoln asks unconditional restoration of the Union; the Confederate delegation insists on retaining two independent nations.

Feb. 16-17 General Sherman takes Columbia, the capital of South Carolina, as General Beauregard leaves the city. During the night of Feb. 17 the city burns. Each side blames the other for starting the fire.

Feb. 17 All debts incurred by the Confederacy are repudiated in the U.S. Senate.

Feb. 17-18 Charleston, South Carolina is evacuated by General William J. Hardee, and the cradle of secession falls into Union hands on the following day.

Feb. 20 The House of Representatives of the Confederacy authorizes the use of slaves as soldiers. [The Senate concurs on Mar. 8.]

Feb. 22 General John M. Schofield enters Wilmington, North Carolina, as Confederate General Braxton Bragg evacuates the port without opposing the Union troops.

Feb. 22 A new state constitution is approved in Tennessee; slavery in the state is abolished.

Mar. 3 Congress creates a Bureau of Refugees, Freedmen, and Abandoned Lands [the Freedmen's Bureau], which is to provide food, clothing, fuel, and land for "refugees and freedmen from rebel states."

Mar. 3 Congress imposes a 10-per-cent tax on state bank notes. [This has the effect of driving such notes out of circulation. They are replaced by national bank notes, issued by the banks belonging to the national banking system. Some 700 state banks are chartered as national banks.]

Mar. 4 Lincoln concludes his second inaugural address: "With malice toward none, with charity for all, with firmness in the right as God gives us to see the right, let us strive on to finish the work we are in, to bind up the nation's wounds, to care for him who shall have borne the battle and for his widow and his orphan, to do all which may achieve and cherish a just and lasting peace among ourselves, and with all nations."

Castle Thunder, Richmond, Virginia, May, 1865

Mar. 11 General Sherman seizes Fayetteville, North Carolina.

Mar. 11 Lincoln proclaims a pardon for all military or naval deserters who return within 60 days; those who do not return within this period forfeit their citizenship and the rights of citizenship.

Mar. 13 President Davis signs the law to admit Negroes into the Confederate Army.

Mar. 27 President Lincoln discusses possible peace terms with Grant and Sherman, at City Point [now part of Hopewell, near Petersburg], Virginia.

April 1-2 Confederate General George E. Pickett attempts to hold the right side of the Confederate defensive line at Petersburg, but he is defeated at Five Forks by Union Generals Sheridan and G.K. Warren. On April 2, Lee orders the evacuation of Petersburg and a retreat through Richmond to Amelia Court House, Virginia.

April 2 Union General James H. Wilson seizes Selma, Alabama, defeating Confederate troops under General Nathan B. Forrest and General Richard Taylor; the Union force turns toward Montgomery, Alabama. [Montgomery is taken on April 12.]

April 2-3 President Davis and his Cabinet depart from Richmond as fire, looting, general disorder, and destruction afflict the capital of the Confederacy. On April 3 they reach Danville, Virginia, where Davis hopes to establish the next capital of the Confederacy.

April 3 Richmond and Petersburg are occupied by Union troops. Lincoln arrives at Petersburg to confer with Grant.

April 4 Lincoln inspects the captured Southern capital and confers with General Godfrey Weitzel, who is in charge of the Union occupation of Richmond.

April 4 Davis makes an appeal for continued resistance. [This is his last message as President.]

April 5   Secretary of State William H. Seward is seriously injured in a carriage accident in Washington.

April 6   At Sayler's Creek to the west of Petersburg, Virginia, the Confederate Army of Northern Virginia clashes with the Union Army of the Potomac. Lee loses about a third of his retreating army, and some 8,000 of the troops surrender.

April 9   General in Chief Robert E. Lee meets with General in Chief Ulysses S. Grant at Appomattox Court House, Virginia, and the Army of Northern Virginia surrenders to the Union forces.

April 11   Lincoln tells a crowd gathered in front of the White House that he hopes for the return of the Southern states to the Union as soon as possible. [This is his last public address.]

April 12   Mobile, Alabama, the only major city still in Confederate hands, is taken without a fight by troops under Union General Edward R.S. Canby.

April 14-15   While attending a comedy, *Our American Cousin,* at Ford's Theatre in Washington, President Abraham Lincoln is shot by actor John Wilkes Booth. (During the same night, Secretary of State William H. Seward is stabbed in his bed by an accomplice of Booth, but the wound is not fatal.) Lincoln dies on April 15 at the home of William Peterson, across the street from Ford's Theatre, the victim of a bullet that entered the back of his head and lodged near his right eye.

April 15   Vice President Andrew Johnson is administered the oath of office by Chief Justice Salmon P. Chase, becoming the 17th President of the United States.

April 19-21   The body of Abraham Lincoln is moved from the White House to the rotunda of the Capitol, and the public begins to file past the catafalque until the following day. On April 21 the funeral train bearing the body of Lincoln leaves Washington on its way to Springfield, Illinois. [Huge crowds view it along the rail route

Outside the Appomattox courthouse where Lee surrendered to Grant

through Harrisburg, Philadelphia, New York City, Albany, Rochester, Buffalo, Cleveland, Columbus, Indianapolis, and Chicago. Lincoln is interred at Springfield on May 4.]

April 19 Jefferson Davis reaches Charlotte, North Carolina, with his party.

April 26 General Sherman and General Johnston meet near Durham Station, North Carolina, where the second major Confederate army surrenders.

April 26 John Wilkes Booth is surrounded by Federal troops near Bowling Green, Virginia, and he is killed (probably by a Federal soldier).

April 27 Near Memphis, Tennessee, on the Mississippi River, the steamer *Sultana* explodes, killing an estimated 1,450 passengers, who are Union prisoners of war returning North.

May 1-2 President Andrew Johnson (under the advice of the Attorney General) orders a military commission of nine Army officers to try eight persons accused of implication in the Lincoln assassination. On May 2 Johnson issues a proclamation, based on "evidence in the Bureau of Military Justice," that names Jefferson Davis and five other persons as having "incited, concerted, and procured" the murder of Abraham Lincoln and the attack on Seward.

May 4 General Edward R.S. Canby takes the surrender of the Confederate Department of Alabama, Mississippi, and East Louisiana from General Richard Taylor at Citronelle, Alabama.

May 9 Trial begins for the eight accused of participating in the murder of Abraham Lincoln.

May 10 The Government of the Confederacy ceases to exist when Federal troops capture President Jefferson Davis, Mrs. Davis, and some officials near Irwinville, Georgia.

May 10 President Johnson declares that the armed resistance proclaimed by Lincoln on April 19, 1861, "may be regarded as virtually at an end. . . ."

May 12 President Johnson appoints General Oliver O. Howard to head the recently created Freedman's Bureau.

May 17 General Philip H. Sheridan is given general command over Federal forces west of the Mississippi and south of the Arkansas rivers, where scattered units under General E. Kirby Smith continue to resist.

May 22 Jefferson Davis is imprisoned at Fort Monroe, Virginia. [He remains in prison until May 13, 1867.]

May 23-24 The Army of the Potomac parades in a final review in Washington; a similar parade is held the following day by General Sherman's army.

May 26 The surrender of the Trans-Mississippi Department Army is arranged at New Orleans, where representatives of Generals Kirby and Canby meet to sign a convention. [Except for minor skirmishes and guerrilla activity in the West, the war is at an end.]

May 29 Citing the actions of Lincoln on and after Dec. 8, 1863, in regard to amnesty, President Johnson proclaims amnesty and pardon for members of the Confederacy who take an oath of allegiance (although many classes of officials, military leaders, and property owners are excluded). [Johnson later grants liberal pardons to persons in the excluded groups.]

June 2 "Copperhead" Lambdin P. Milligan, sentenced to be hanged, is reprieved by President Johnson.

June 6 Missouri voters approve a new constitution without slavery in that state.

June 6 Prisoners of war from the Confederacy are released by President Andrew Johnson.

June 13 Johnson appoints William L. Sharkey to be provisional governor of Mississippi in a continuing policy of trying to restore pro-Union state governments as quickly as possible.

June 23 Johnson ends the Federal blockade of Southern states.

June 30 The military commission trying the alleged accomplices in the assassination of Lincoln finds all eight guilty. David Herold, Lewis Payne, George A. Atzerodt, and Mary E. Surratt are sentenced to hang; Samuel Arnold, Samuel A. Mudd, and Michael O'Laughlin are sentenced to life imprisonment; and Edward Spangler is given six years' imprisonment.

July 3 General Patrick E. Connor reaches Fort Laramie in Idaho Territory [Wyoming] to oppose increasing Arapaho Indian attacks on the Overland Mail route, mail stations, and telegraph lines.

July 8 The four convicted Lincoln conspirators are hanged in Washington, and the four sentenced to imprisonment are taken to Fort Jefferson in the Dry Tortugas Islands off the Florida keys.

July 8 Writing to the Union League of Savannah, Georgia, radical Republican Charles Sumner states: "It is impossible to suppose that Congress will sanction any governments in rebel states which are not founded on 'the consent of the governed.' This is the cornerstone of republican institutions. Of course by the 'governed' is meant all the loyal citizens without distinction of color. Anything else is a mockery."

July 19 J. Madison Wells, governor of Louisiana, proclaims the need for Louisiana residents to take the oath of allegiance required by Lincoln on Dec. 8, 1863, or forfeit their right to vote.

Aug. 21 At Jackson, Mississippi, the state constitution is amended to abolish slavery by a vote of 86 to 11.

Aug. 24 Captain James M. Moore and party, including Clara Barton, end their search of Andersonville Prison, Georgia, seeking to identify Union war graves and register war dead.

Sept. 1 At Lexington, Virginia, trustees announce that General Robert E. Lee has accepted the presidency of Washington College.

Sept. 3 A unit of General Connor's command under Colonel Cole defeats about 3,000 Sioux, Cherokee, and Arapaho Indians in a three-day battle on the Powder River in Idaho.

Sept. 4 A *New York Times* editorial calls for a trial of Jefferson Davis for treason to show that "the attempted secession was not only a failure, but a crime."

Sept. 19 Inventor George M. Pullman receives a patent for both an upper and a lower berth sleeping car, to be featured in his first car, Pioneer.

Oct. 2 Robert E. Lee takes the standard amnesty oath of allegiance to support the United States, the Union, and the emancipation of slaves.

Oct. 11 President Johnson paroles Vice President Alexander H. Stephens and four other high Confederate officials who have been in Federal prisons.

Oct. 31 The public debt of the United States stands at $2,740,854,750, estimated at over $75 per capita.

Nov. 10 Captain Henry Wirz, the Confederate commandant of Andersonville Prison in Georgia, where atrocities against prisoners of war have been uncovered, is hanged after conviction in a military court. [This is the only execution of a Confederate official carried out by a Federal authority.]

Nov. 18 Samuel Clemens, a young reporter and correspondent of San Francisco, using the pseudonym of Mark Twain, publishes a story, "The Celebrated Jumping Frog of Calaveras County," in the New York *Saturday Press*. [The story is reprinted in other journals, and is the title piece of his first book, published in 1867.]

Nov. 24 The Mississippi state legislature adopts a code of laws dealing with the status of Negroes as a result of their emancipation. [This

Richmond in ruins

is the first of a series of "black codes" enacted in the South, ostensibly to protect certain Negro legal rights but intended to bind black labor to the land through apprenticeship and vagrancy laws.]

Dec. 6 Johnson opens his first annual message to Congress with an expression of "gratitude to God in the name of the people for the preservation of the United States," and ends with comments on the promise shown by the "throngs of emigrants that crowd to our shores [as] witnesses of the confidence of all peoples in our permanence."

Dec. 18 The 13th Amendment to the Constitution, which makes slavery illegal throughout the United States, is ratified by 27 states and the amendment is declared adopted by Secretary of State William H. Seward.

Dec. 18 The House votes $25,000 to Mrs. Mary Lincoln in lieu of Abraham Lincoln's final salary; a proposal by an Illinois representative to increase the sum to $100,000 is rejected.

Dec. 18 Reviewing the favorable public reaction to Johnson's annual message, the *New York Times* calls this an "approval . . . by the people, North and South, it is a popular ratification of the policy he has acted upon. Let Congress set itself against all attempts to contravene it."

The national stage is set for the Reconstruction of the Union after the bitter and costly years of civil strife. But the major participants find it difficult to adjust and to compromise their differences concerning the treatment of the 4,000,000 emancipated "freedmen." Andrew Johnson seeks a lenient return of the Southern states to the Union and statehood. In his stubborn dedication to his own course of action, his Democratic and limited Republican support slowly slips from him. Congressional Republicans, with a growing proportion of Radicals, demand reform of the former Confederate states and champion the freedom and the equality of the exslaves. The Southern states resist Reconstruction, resort to "black codes" to maintain their control over the exslaves, defy Congressional demands for meaningful changes in their way of life.

A confrontation between the President and Congress is under way in mid-February, when Johnson vetoes an amendment to the bill extending the term of the Freedmen's Bureau that would provide military force to protect blacks. He also vetoes a Civil Rights Act. The unprecedented overriding of his veto gives notice to the President that his version of Reconstruction does not have legislative support. The 14th Amendment embodies the will of Congress to establish civil rights for blacks, to deny full Congressional representation to states infringing male suffrage, to postpone the return of former Confederate leaders to politics, and to repudiate the Confederate war debt and deny payment for freed slaves.

In the South, only Tennessee is readmitted; the other 10 states resist Reconstruction; and race riots in Memphis and New Orleans reveal forces that still can be aroused in the South.

Jan. 2   In a New York newspaper, Elizabeth Cady Stanton informs women of a petition to Congress dealing with the proposed 14th Amendment, in which reference to "male inhabitants" and "male citizens" threatens the disenfranchisement of women on the basis of sex.

Jan. 8   Samuel Shellabarger of Ohio, speaking to the House of Representatives on Reconstruction, argues that the secessionist states have forfeited their rights within the Union and that Congress has the legal right to restore a Republican form of government. [This becomes the Congressional approach to Reconstruction.]

Jan. 9   In Nashville, Tennessee, Fisk School opens in an army barracks as a college for blacks; it is named for General Clinton B. Fisk, an official of the Freedmen's Bureau. [It is chartered in 1867 as Fisk University.]

Feb. 11   Robert E. Lee testifies in Washington, D.C., before a Congressional Reconstruction committee under Michigan Senator Jacob H. Howard. The two-hour interrogation on Southern conditions and public sentiments produces little result.

Feb. 19   President Johnson, preferring a modified version of Lincoln's moderate concept of Reconstruction for the South, vetoes a bill to extend the life and expand the functions of the Freedmen's Bureau. He explains that Congress is not entitled to legislate for the South when the latter is not represented there.

Feb. 22   In an unplanned speech to serenaders gathered at the White House, Andrew Johnson makes inflammatory statements against Congressional Reconstruction and describes Thaddeus Stevens, Charles Sumner, and Wendell Phillips as opponents in his growing disagreement with Congress.

Mar. 17   The Canadian Reciprocity Treaty of 1854, involving offshore fishing rights and duty-free commodity exchange, is abrogated by the United States.

Mar. 27   President Johnson vetoes a Civil Rights Bill that would guarantee equal protection of the laws to the freed Negroes, and would give the Federal courts jurisdiction over cases involving these rights. It is intended to nullify the state "black codes." Johnson states that "in all our experience as a people living under Federal and state law, no such system. . .has ever before been proposed or adopted." He says that its provisions interfere too greatly with the rights of states.

April 2   Johnson proclaims that "the insurrection which heretofore existed in the states of Georgia, South Carolina, Virginia, North Carolina, Tennessee, Alabama, Louisiana, Arkansas, Mississippi, and Florida is at an end. . . ," leaving only Texas unreconciled with the Union.

April 6   The Senate overrides Johnson's veto

of the Civil Rights Bill by a margin of only one vote.

April 9   The House repasses the Civil Rights Bill. This is the first time a major piece of legislation is passed over a Presidential veto.

April 17   Ex-Confederate official Clement C. Clay, Jr., in a Federal prison as one of the Southern conspirators in the murder of Lincoln and the assassination attempt on Seward, is released. Only Jefferson Davis, of all of the Confederate prisoners, remains in jail.

April 30   In Memphis, Tennessee, white residents, resenting the behavior of Federal black troops, join a dispute between local police and soldiers that leads to three days of rioting in which 47 blacks are killed and more than 80 Memphis residents are injured.

May 10   The 11th National Woman's Rights Convention opens in New York City and, with Susan B. Anthony presiding, pursues the argument that "the Negro and woman now hold the same civil and political *status,* alike needing only the ballot. . ."; and, with Lucretia Mott as president, the American Equal Rights Association is formed.

May 29   General Winfield Scott, 80, famed military leader, and commander of the United States Army until his retirement in 1861, dies in West Point, New York.

June 16   The proposed 14th Amendment to the Constitution, passed by both Houses of Congress, goes to the states for ratification. Its principal clause establishes the citizenship of all Negroes, and it also denies to any state that withholds the vote from any male over 21 a proportionate representation in Congress.

June 17   Lewis Cass, 83, soldier, diplomat, and Secretary of State under James Buchanan, dies in Detroit, Michigan.

June 20   The Joint Committee of Fifteen makes its report to Congress. The committee was set up by both Houses, comprising 6 Senators and 9 Representatives, both Radicals and Conservatives, to consider the manner in which Reconstruction of the South should be handled. Now it recommends that the Confederate states, as now constituted, are not entitled to be represented in Congress, and holds that Congress, rather than the President, has authority over Reconstruction.

July 4   In a disastrous fire at Portland, Maine, some 1,500 buildings are destroyed with a loss of $10,000,000 in property.

July 16   A second Freedmen's Bureau Bill, merely extending the life of the bureau until July 1868, is vetoed by President Johnson. [The bill is passed by both Houses over the veto.]

July 19   Tennessee, under control of Radical Republicans, ratifies the 14th Amendment.

July 24   Tennessee is restored to full participation in the Union by joint resolution of Congress and the signature of President Johnson.

July 30   Race riots break out in New Orleans, Louisiana, and some 200 blacks and whites are killed or wounded during a political rally.

Aug. 14   Andrew Johnson tries to line up political moderates behind his Reconstruction policies at a National Union Party meeting in a three-day national convention in Philadelphia.

Aug. 20   Johnson, proclaiming the end of insurrection in Texas, states "that peace, order, tranquillity, and civil authority now exist in and throughout the whole of the United States of America."

Aug. 20   The National Labor Union, a loosely knit federation of unions, is organized in Baltimore, seeking an "Eight Hour System" for its 60,000 workers (including women) in 13 states.

Photographers rest at Mammoth Caves, Kentucky (*ca.*) 1866)

General Robert E. Lee

General Thomas J. (Stonewall) Jackson

Andrew Johnson
SEVENTEENTH PRESIDENT   1865-1869

Ulysses S. Grant
EIGHTEENTH PRESIDENT   **1869-1877**

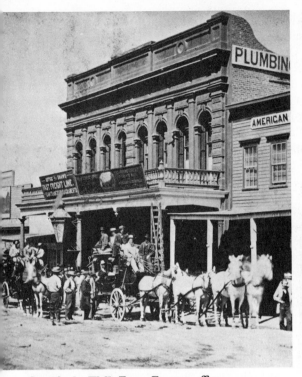

Outside the Wells Fargo Express office,
Virginia City, Nevada, (*ca.*) 1866

The directors of the Union Pacific
stand under a sign marking the 100th meridian
and the distance from Omaha.

Aug. 28-Sept. 15   President Johnson goes on
a campaign speaking tour, a "swing around the
circle" of cities such as Philadelphia, New York,
Chicago, Louisville, and Pittsburgh, but with
poor speeches and humiliating results in attacking Radical opponents.

Sept. 7   Cyrus W. Field succeeds in his second attempt to lay an Atlantic cable from Valen-
tia, Ireland, to Heart's Content, Newfoundland,
after an eight-year delay since the first attempt
failed in 1858.

Oct. 10   Elizabeth Cady Stanton, as a woman
denied the vote but legally eligible for office in
New York state, runs for the national House of
Representatives in the 8th Congressional District.
[She receives 24 votes.]

Oct. 13   The former Confederate state of
Texas rejects the 14th Amendment, unanimously
in the state senate and 67 to 5 in the lower
house; it is the first Southern state to vote against
the amendment. [All the other secessionist states
follow suit, leading a Radical Republican from
Ohio, Congressman James A. Garfield, to comment: "The last one of the sinful ten with scorn
and contempt has flung back into our teeth the
magnanimous offer of a generous nation."]

Dec. 3   Andrew Johnson directs his first annual message to Congress with regret that 10
states remain without Congressional representation (50 seats are vacant in the House and 20 in
the Senate). He states that the "interests of the
nation are best to be promoted by the revival of
fraternal relations, the complete obliteration of
our past differences, and the reinauguration of all
the pursuits of peace."

Dec. 17   The Supreme Court, in *Ex Parte
Milligan,* orders the release of Lambdin P. Milligan, a civilian Southern sympathizer, who was
arrested on Oct. 24, 1864, in Indiana, charged
with furthering the cause of insurrection, convicted by court martial, and sentenced to death.
The Court holds that neither the Executive
Branch nor the Supreme Court can order a military commission to try civilians outside the actual
theater of war.

Dec. 21   Captain William J. Fetterman and
80 men are ambushed by Sioux under Red Cloud
and slaughtered near Fort Phil Kearny on the
Powder River in Idaho Territory.   [In 1868 it
is decided to abandon the fort and the Bozeman
Trail, as the Sioux demand, and a temporary
peace is signed with Red Cloud.]

193

1867

Congress moves into greater and greater confrontation with President Andrew Johnson as the year wears on. Usurping a Presidential power, Congress calls itself into special session for March. Once in session, a whole series of controls are enacted to increase Congressional power and promote Congressional Reconstruction. On the assumption that no lawful government exists in 10 Southern states, Congress passes a Reconstruction Act and two supplementary statutes that impose military force to monitor civil, judicial, and police powers in the South. Negroes are given the vote, and over 700,000 are registered to some 625,000 whites, while former Confederate officials cannot vote on state matters. Johnson vetoes all such measures, which he considers harsh and unlawful.

Congress then moves against the constitutional authority of the President himself and passes a series of bills to thwart his power as Commander in Chief, to freeze his officers in their Cabinet positions, and to make him guilty of an impeachable offense (a "high misdemeanor") if he removes such office-holders without consulting the Senate. Johnson determines to test the constitutionality of the act.

January   In this month's issue of *Student and Schoolmaster* appears a story about a bootblack from Manhattan's back alleys, *Ragged Dick,* by Horatio Alger, Jr. [It is the first of a continuing series of stories and books that bring fame to the author and inspiration to children, parents, teachers, and preachers.]

Jan. 7   Representative James M. Ashley of Ohio offers a House resolution to empower the Judiciary Committee to consider the impeachment of Andrew Johnson, and it passes.

Jan. 8   Negro male residents of the District of Columbia are given the right to vote by national authority in a Congressional bill passed over Andrew Johnson's veto, a step toward universal manhood suffrage by Radical Republican initiative.

Jan. 22   The 40th Congress calls itself into special session for March 4, continuing its challenge to the power of the Presidency.

Jan. 31   Manhood suffrage becomes obligatory in Federal territories by act of Congress, a second step toward nation wide manhood suffrage.

Feb. 7   Frederick Douglass, an ex-slave, leads a Negro delegation to call on the President to urge the vote for former slaves.

Feb. 18   The Augusta Institute, a college for black students, is founded in Augusta, Georgia, in the basement of the Springfield Baptist Church. [It is moved to Atlanta in 1879 and is then called the Atlanta Baptist Seminary. In 1913 it becomes Morehouse College.]

Mar. 1   Nebraska, with a population that President Johnson says is "as high as 40,000" (it was 28,000 in 1860), is admitted to the Union as the 37th state; the capital is moved from Omaha to the village of Lancaster, which is now renamed Lincoln. [The population increases rapidly as the railroads attract settlers, reaching 123,000 in 1870.]

Mar. 2   The First Reconstruction Act is passed by Congress (over President Johnson's veto) and establishes martial law in five military districts in the South (outside of Tennessee). The 10 existing states in the area are to be readmitted after they call constitutional conventions elected by universal manhood suffrage, when they establish state governments that guarantee black suffrage, and after ratifying the 14th Amendment. On this day, also, Congress passes the Command of the Army Act, which requires Andrew Johnson to issue all military orders through the General of the Army, Ulysses S. Grant; this law virtually deprives Johnson of command of the Army. Finally, Congress passes the Tenure of Office Act, which prohibits the President from removing from office without Senatorial approval any official whom he has appointed with the advice and consent of the Senate.

Mar. 2   Howard Normal and Theological Institute for the Education of Teachers and Preachers is chartered in Washington, D.C., by the Freedmen's Bureau, whose director is General Oliver Otis Howard. [As Howard University, it becomes the most prestigious institution of higher learning with a predominantly black student body.]

Mar. 7   The Order of the Knights of St. Crispin, threatened by industrial development, is organized in Milwaukee, Wisconsin, as a labor union to protect shoemakers against the introduction of machinery and the competition of apprentices.

Mar. 23   When the Southern states fail to call conventions, Congress passes a supplementary Reconstruction Act that requires Federal military commanders to create procedures for registering voters.

Mar. 29 The editor of the Pulaski (Tennessee) *Citizen* publishes the first newspaper story of a mysterious new, secret organization in the South called the "Kuklux Klan," an "Invisible Empire of the South," whose rituals and activities support white supremacy and oppose Radical Reconstruction.

Mar. 30 Secretary of State William H. Seward signs a treaty with Russian Minister Edouard de Stoeckl to purchase Alaska for the sum of $7,200,000 and to expand U.S. boundaries to the Arctic Ocean.

April 9 The Senate ratifies the Alaska treaty by a vote of 37 to 2 when Seward convinces Senators of the value of Alaskan natural resources and the strategic gains for U.S. interests on the Pacific and the Arctic oceans.

May 9-10 A two-day national convention of the American Equal Rights Association, Lucretia Mott presiding, meets in New York City. A memorial to Congress from the convention declares: "Woman and the colored man are loyal, patriotic, property-holding, tax-paying, liberty-loving citizens; and we can not believe that sex or complexion should be any ground for civil or political degradation. . . . [but] one-half of the citizens are disfranchised by their sex, and about one-eighth by the color of their skin. . . ."

May 13 Jefferson Davis, after two years of imprisonment at Fort Monroe, Virginia, appears for a hearing in the U.S. Circuit Court at Richmond, where "the caged eagle" of the Confederacy is released on $100,000 bail pending trial.

July 6 Johnson submits the Alaska purchase treaty to the House of Representatives to secure the necessary appropriation for the purchase price and for the occupation and government of the territory.

July 19 Congress, in a second supplementary Reconstruction Act, gives military commanders in the Southern states the power to determine the elegibility of voters; Johnson vetoes it, and both Houses repass it this same day.

July 25 An important convention to amend the constitution of New York, strongly urged to give the vote to women, rejects the proposal 125 to 19.

Aug. 10 John H. Surratt, tried for implication in Lincoln's assassination, is kept in a Federal prison, although the jury votes 8 to 4 for acquittal. [He is released on June 22, 1868.]

Aug. 12 Secretary of War Edwin M. Stanton, who opposes Johnson's concept of Reconstruction, is "suspended," but not removed, from the Cabinet by the President, and General Ulysses S. Grant is named as Secretary to replace Stanton. This action is taken in spite of the Tenure of Office Act passed in March, which Johnson hopes to test in court through this maneuver, and through which Congress hopes to find grounds for impeaching Johnson.

Aug. 13 Augustin Daly, a rising playwright, presents the melodrama *Under the Gaslight* to audiences in New York City.

Aug. 28 Navy Captain William Reynolds occupies the two Midway Islands (west of Hawaii) for the United States, annexing them as a possible coaling station for Pacific commerce.

Sept. 5 At the "cow town" of Abilene, Kansas, southern drovers and northern meat dealers, headed by Joseph M. McCoy of Illinois, hold a banquet to celebrate the first shipment of cattle to the east on the Kansas Pacific Railroad, as herds begin to arrive over the Chisholm Trail on the "Long Drive" from Texas.

Oct. 3 Elias Howe, 48, famed and enriched by his invention of the sewing machine, dies in Brooklyn, New York, in the year when his machine wins the gold medal at the Paris Exhibition.

Oct. 21 Federal commissioners in Indian Territory meet with Kiowa and Comanche Indians on Medicine Lodge Creek. [The treaty that results is the first of a series that establishes separate reservations for Indians.]

Nov. 20 The House Judiciary Committee votes 5 to 4 to recommend the impeachment of Johnson.

Dec. 3 President Johnson, in his third annual message to Congress on the state of the Union, defies impeachment by saying that "cases may occur in which the Executive would be compelled to stand on its rights, and maintain them regardless of all consequences."

Dec. 4 The Order of the Patrons of Husbandry, or National Grange, a secret society for agriculturalists, is organized in Washington, D.C., by Oliver H. Kelley and others to further such interests of farmers as lower railroad rates, opposition to monopolies, founding of agricultural schools, and other social and educational ways to alleviate rural isolation and apathy.

Dec. 7 The House of Representatives defeats a vote on impeachment.

Dec. 19 At Angola, New York, a passenger train plunges off a bridge and burns, taking the lives of 44 persons in the two rear cars.

Popular sentiment in the North and Radical Republican resentment in the House of Representatives lead to the Covode Resolution to impeach Andrew Johnson in March. Radicals raise few specific issues in their debate, but, rather, levy random and virulent charges, including the violation of the Tenure of Office Act. (Inasmuch as Lincoln, not Johnson, appointed Stanton, technically Johnson could not be legitimately accused of dismissing an official he had appointed.) The margin of one vote, with the help of seven Republicans, spells the failure of a Congressional attempt to dominate the Presidency, and the concept of an independent Executive branch in the Federal Government is preserved.

Johnson survives the trial in the Senate, but he has lost his following; even the Democratic Party cannot envisage a victory with him as its standard-bearer, and they choose instead a former governor of New York who is not entirely hostile to the South; Horatio Seymour had certainly been no crusader for the abolition of slavery. Grant, ruffled at Johnson's attempt to use him in the Stanton affair, is willing to "wave the bloody shirt" (the current phrase for "bait the South") and accepts the radical position on Restoration. His election is virtually guaranteed.

Jan. 13-14   The U.S. Senate refuses to concur in Johnson's suspension of Secretary of State Stanton, and on the following day General Grant resigns as interim Secretary of War. Although Johnson expects Grant to place the office at his disposal in this situation, Grant allows Stanton to return to his office at the War Department.

Feb. 21-22   President Johnson, determined to exclude Stanton, names General Lorenzo Thomas as interim Secretary of War. Stanton obtains a warrant for his arrest and blocks Thomas from assuming the secretaryship.

Feb. 24   Representative John Covode of Pennsylvania offers a resolution to impeach Johnson for "high crimes and misdemeanors," and the House passes it, 126 to 47.

Mar. 11   Congress passes a third supplementary Reconstruction Act providing that a new state constitution may be ratified by a majority of the number actually voting.

Mar. 26   Jefferson Davis is charged with treason in the Richmond circuit court, but trial is postponed.

May   The first specialized American medical journal, *The American Journal of Obstetrics and Diseases of Women and Children,* appears in New York.

May 11-26   Chief Justice Salmon P. Chase presides in the Senate impeachment trial of *The United States* v. *Andrew Johnson, President.* On May 16 articles of impeachment—nine involving Johnson's alleged plot to violate the Tenure of Office Act, the 10th his "ridiculous harangues" in speeches against Radical Congressmen, and the 11th an omnibus article embracing all the charges—are submitted for Senate

vote. The last article is voted on first. With 35 voting "guilty" and 19 "not guilty," the vote lacks the necessary two-thirds majority to convict by a single vote. On May 26 an identical vote is reached on other articles. Johnson is acquitted.

May 20   Horatio Alger deposits *Ragged Dick; or, Street Life in New York* for copyright and sale in book form.

May 20-21   The Republican national convention, meeting in Chicago, nominates Ulysses S. Grant for President and Schuyler Colfax of Indiana for Vice President. Its platform supports Radical Reconstruction.

May 26   Secretary of War Stanton resigns.

June 1   James Buchanan, 77, 15th President of the United States, dies at Wheatland, near Lancaster, Pennsylvania.

June 22-25   Arkansas is readmitted to the Union when it provides civil and political equality for all men and civil rights without regard to race or color. Three days later Alabama, Florida, Georgia, Louisiana, North Carolina, and South Carolina are also admitted under the same conditions.

July 4-9   The Democratic national convention, meeting in New York City, opposes Radical Reconstruction. Horatio Seymour of New York is nominated for the Presidency and Francis P. Blair of Missouri for the Vice Presidency.

July 14   The House of Representatives votes, 113 to 43, to appropriate funds to purchase Alaska.

July 28   The 14th Amendment is declared ratified by 30 states and in effect.

July 28   Anson Burlingame, a former Minister to China from the United States, but now representing China, signs a treaty with Secretary of State Seward that deals with commercial matters and provides for unrestricted Chinese immigration to the United States as a source of labor on American railroads.

August *The Overland Monthly,* a San Francisco periodical, contains Bret Harte's *The Luck of Roaring Camp,* a story that gains him national fame.

Aug. 11 Thaddeus Stevens, 76, Radical Republican leader, dies in Washington, D.C. He arranged for his burial in a Negro cemetery at Lancaster, Pennsylvania, and provided for his stone an epitaph which reads: "I have chosen this that I might illustrate in my death The Principles which I advocated through a long Life: Equality of Man Before His Creator."

Aug. 26 Louisa May Alcott receives proof readings for her *Little Women: or, Meg, Jo, Beth, and Amy,* a book for girls. [On Oct. 30 she learns that *Little Women* is sold out in Boston as a best-seller.]

Nov. 3 Grant wins the Presidential election by 3,013,421 popular votes (including perhaps 500,000 Negro votes) and 214 electoral votes, to 2,706,829 popular votes and 80 electoral votes for Seymour. Mississippi, Texas, and Virginia are ineligible to cast their 23 electoral votes, and Grant loses only Georgia and Louisiana in the South.

Dec. 25 President Johnson proclaims unconditional pardon and amnesty without reservations for those accused of treason against the Union during the Civil War.

Formal notice of the impeachment of President Andrew Johnson is given the Senate by a member of the House of Representatives.

1869 **Ulysses S. Grant assumes the leadership of a nation** that continues to muddle through its Reconstruction. The readmission of most Southern states in 1868 brought passage of the important 14th Amendment, and now Congress moves toward its goal of Negro suffrage under the 15th Amendment, which includes authorization for Congress "to enforce this article by appropriate legislation." [As subsequent events show, Congress finds it necessary to pass a number of Force Bills to compel some degree of respect for the letter of the amendment, once its passage is ratified through a similar policy of compulsion.]

This may well be considered the year of unfinished business, for it introduces problems that can only be solved, or not solved, in the future. The competence of President Grant is such a problem, for he is a novice, or perhaps an innocent, whose very Cabinet reflects his inexperience; only one member, Secretary of State Hamilton Fish, is capable of handling his job. Entirely trusting in his Radical Republican friends, Grant is ready to give them a free hand; this involves not merely an attempt to tame the South and enfranchise the Negroes, but also the freedom to harness the resources of the nation to the needs of entrepreneurs, including business buccaneers. The building of the transcontinental railroads—the first of which is completed this year—is surely beneficial to the nation (although the problem of coping with the thousands of Chinese who built it remains to be solved). But the speculative attempt to buy up the nation's gold supply, connived in by Grant's own brother-in-law, A. E. Corbin, is sheer piracy. To Grant's credit, he frustrates the attempt by selling Federal gold as soon as he discovers the plot; but the perpetrators survive unpunished.

The year is also notable for the organizations that are founded: for woman's suffrage, for "temperance," and for the organization of workers. There is no lack of energy in the United States as it enters the fifth postwar year.

Jan. 19-20 The first National Woman's Suffrage Convention gathers in Washington, D.C. In view of the current movement for black male suffrage through a 15th Amendment, the convention resolves that "a *man's* government is worse that a *white* man's government, because, in proportion as you increase the tyrants, you make the condition of the disenfranchised class more hopeless and degraded."

Feb. 27 Congress passes the 15th Amendment to the Constitution to ensure black male suffrage in the North and in the South, and sends it to the states for ratification. [The readmission of the remaining three seceded states is conditioned on their ratification of the 14th and 15th Amendments.]

Mar. 4 Ulysses S. Grant becomes 18th President of the United States, and his brief inaugural address covers law and order, revenue collection, "civilizing" Indians, and paying the public debt in gold. Only 46 years of age, the youngest President ever elected, and completely unfamiliar with politics (having voted only once), he affirms: "The office has come to me unsought; I commence its duties untrammeled."

Mar. 18 Congress passes the Public Credit Act to pay the public debt in gold, leaving $356,000,000 in greenbacks (paper currency issued during the Civil War) and a bitter debate about redeeming them.

April 7 The first all-professional baseball team, the Cincinnati Red Stockings, opens its season; the shortstop is the highest paid player at $1,400 a year.

April 13 The National Grange holds its first annual session in Washington, D.C., with state organizations already founded in Iowa, Minnesota, and New York.

April 13 George Westinghouse receives a patent for the first air-brake, which is important for high speed and safety in railroading.

April 16 Ebenezer Don Carlos Bassett, named Minister Resident and Consul General to Haiti, is the first Negro appointed to the American diplomatic service.

May 10 The rails of the Union Pacific Railroad, with 1,086 miles of track from Omaha, Nebraska, and the Central Pacific, with 689 miles of track across mountain and desert from Sacramento, California, are joined with a golden spike at Promontory Point (near Ogden), Utah, to complete the first transcontinental railroad. [Trains begin to roll in October.]

June 1 Thomas Alva Edison patents his first major invention, an "electrographic vote recorder."

Aug. 11 Samuel Clemens receives the first printed copy of his *Innocents Abroad,* a work contrasting Europe and America, written under his pseudonym, Mark Twain. [The book is an immediate best-seller with 100,000 copies.]

Aug. 16 Augustin Daly, famed dramatist, enters the field of theater management, opening at the Fifth Avenue Theatre in New York City.

Sept. 1 The National Prohibition Party is founded at Chicago by some 500 men and women from 20 states.

Sept. 24 On this "Black Friday," a financial panic occurs after two stock gamblers, Jay Gould and James Fisk, try to organize a corner on the gold market. The Grant Administration dumps $4,000,000 in gold on the market, the price falls within fifteen minutes from 162 to 133, and many investors are ruined.

Oct. 8 Franklin Pierce, 65, the 14th President of the United States, dies at Concord, New Hampshire. Although he defended the institution of slavery on constitutional grounds during his Administration, he remained loyal to the Union during the Civil War.

Dec. 6 The first National Negro Labor Convention creates the Colored National Labor Union at Washington, D.C.

Dec. 9 The Noble Order of the Knights of Labor is founded by Uriah S. Stephens, a garment cutter in Philadelphia, as a "great brotherhood of toil." It is a secret order because the legal status of labor organizations is uncertain. [After ending its secrecy in 1881 the Knights of Labor becomes a major labor organization, reaching its greatest strength in 1886 with more than 700,000 members.]

Dec. 24 Edwin M. Stanton, 55, named to the Supreme Court four days earlier, dies in Washington, D.C.

The chief engineer of the Central Pacific, (left), and the chief engineer of the Union Pacific shake hands as their respective locomotives stand side by side, signifying the completion of the first transcontinental railroad line.

1870

During the last two decades the United States has not undergone major demographic change. Its population has increased from just over 23,000,000 to 38,358,371, at a rate of 35.6 per cent in the decade before the Civil War, slowing down to 22.5 per cent in the postwar decade. Before the war California, Minnesota, Oregon—all free-soil—joined the Union; during and after the war Kansas, Nevada, and Nebraska became states, and West Virginia was carved out of the Old Dominion, bringing the number of states to 37. The black population declined from 15.7 to 12.7 per cent of the total, and numbers about 4,000,000; the foreign-born component is about this size as well, including a number of north-European immigrants attracted to America primarily because of the availability of free land. They did not change the economic makeup of the population, because they are mainly farmers. In 1870 the nation remains four-fifths rural. There are still only 13 cities with populations exceeding 100,000. New York, Brooklyn, and Philadelphia remain the top three; Baltimore and Boston have fallen behind St. Louis and Chicago; the tenfold growth of Chicago symbolizes the westward shift of the population.

Reconstruction seems destined to continue for as many years as the civil conflict that brought it into being. However, by March, the 15th Amendment is approved, and the right of black males to vote is the law of the land. In May, Congress passes legislation to add military force at the state and local levels to see that the exercise of the black vote is respected, and by July, Virginia, Mississippi, Texas, and, last of all, Georgia conform to the will of Congress by ratifying the 14th and 15th Amendments and thereby qualify for readmission to the Union. It is an uneasy "union," however, in which Radical Republicans and local leaders under their tutelage and programs control Southern state governments. Southerners continue to resist real and imagined "Africanization" and Reconstruction governments; an increasing role in this resistance takes the form of violence and terror under such groups as the Ku Klux Klan. Blacks gain a few seats in Congress and in state legislatures and state and Federal offices, but none are elected as state governors.

At a Washington conference in January, Clara Barton makes an appeal to the soldiers whom she nursed in the Civil War: "Brothers, when you were weak and I was strong, I toiled for you. Now you are strong, and I am weak because of my work for you, I ask your aid. I ask the ballot for myself and my sex, and as I stood by you, I pray you stand by me and mine." But women are still unrepresented and politically unrecognized, except in the Territory of Wyoming.

Jan. 10 John D. Rockefeller and others organize the Standard Oil Company of Ohio, capitalized at $1,000,000. Its base is a refinery in Cleveland. Although there are 2,000 wells in the country, the price of oil fluctuates wildly and the 41-year-old ex-bookkeeper who heads the new company is one of a large number of speculators in the business world.

Feb. 25 The Senate seats Hiram R. Revels, a Republican of Mississippi, the first black Senator.

Mar. 30 The 15th Amendment to the Constitution, having been ratified by 29 states, is declared in effect. It assures that the "right of citizens of the United States to vote shall not be denied or abridged by the United States or by any state on account of race, color, or previous condition of servitude."

May 13 Countering Southern terrorist opposition to Radical reconstruction, Congress passes a Force Bill in accordance with the second section of the 15th Amendment. This bill gives jurisdiction to Federal courts and officers to enforce the amendment.

June 11 William Gilmore Simms, 66, leading man of letters for the Old South, dies in Charleston, South Carolina. His best-known novel is *The Yemassee, a Romance of Carolina,* published in 1835.

July 12 A patent for celluloid is granted to John W. Hyatt and his brother Isaiah. He is reported to have been trying to find a material to replace ivory in the making of billiard balls. [First produced commercially in 1872, the product opens an era of cheap synthetic materials (plastics) to replace costly natural products.]

The north side of the White House (ca.) 1870

July 14 A tariff bill is passed that partially reverses the decade-long trend toward higher duties under the Morrill Tariff. Some 160 articles, mainly raw materials, are placed on the free list, and rates on other commodities (coffee, sugar, tea, wines) are reduced, as is the income tax; but the products of Eastern mills and factories continue to be protected.

July 15 The state of Georgia is readmitted for a second time to the Union, the last Southern state to return. The second readmission is necessitated by the action of the state legislature, following its first readmission, of refusing to seat Negroes elected to that body. Georgia was then returned to military government until it made amends by ratifying the 15th Amendment.

Aug. 14 Admiral David Glasgow Farragut, 69, Civil War hero, dies at Portsmouth, New Hampshire.

Sept. 19 Christine Nilsson, a Swedish operatic singer, has her American debut at Steinway Hall in New York City.

Oct. 12 Robert E. Lee, 63, Confederate General in Chief, dies in Lexington, Virginia.

Dec. 10 Governor John Campbell of Wyoming signs a measure passed by the territorial legislature giving women the right to vote and hold office.

Dec. 12 Joseph H. Rainey, a Congressman from Georgetown, South Carolina, is sworn in as the first Negro in the House of Representatives.

Dec. 16 Black members of the Methodist Episcopal Church, South, organize the Colored Methodist Episcopal Church at Jackson, Tennessee.

Dec. 21 A major production of the 1870-1871 season, *Saratoga,* by Bronson Howard, is presented in New York City by Augustin Daly. This first major play by Howard is a comedy of manners in the French style.

The first passenger train crosses the Ohio River, (ca.) 1870.

1871

In his third year in the Presidency, General Grant presides over the formal Reconstruction of the disrupted Union when the Senators from Georgia are seated late in February. However, at the state and local levels, his Administration has to resort to more Force Bills to discipline Southerners who continue to flout the 15th Amendment. In the process, serious inroads continue to be made on the powers of the states.

The performance of Grant as President does little to recommend the leadership of military men in national politics. Civil service reform is initiated, but it gains no headway. Corruption occurs with great frequency; "Boss" Tweed, a notorious practitioner of graft and fraud, is only one among many other similar figures. The accomplishment of Secretary of State Hamilton Fish in settling Anglo-American differences in the Treaty of Washington is outstanding in an otherwise undistinguished year.

Jan. 11-12 Victoria Claflin Woodhull addresses a Memorial to the House Committee on the Judiciary to seek the right of suffrage for women. The National Suffrage Convention at Washington, D.C., receives a letter from Esther Morris, first woman justice of the peace in Wyoming Territory, in support of woman suffrage. [On Feb. 1 the House Committee on the Judiciary tables the Woodhull Memorial to end further discussion.]

Feb. 24 The Senators from Georgia are seated and the South has full representation in Congress for the first time in a decade.

Feb. 28 Congress passes a second Force Act, placing national elections under the control of Federal courts and marshals down to the state and local levels.

Mar. 3 Congress, in an effort to end political corruption, creates a Commission on Civil Service Reform. [On Mar. 4 Grant names George W. Curtis to head the commission.]

Mar. 4 The National Association of Professional Base-Ball Players, the first professional league, is formed in New York.

April 10 Phineas T. Barnum, promoter and showman, starts his "Great Travelling Museum, Menagerie, Caravan, and Hippodrome" in Brooklyn, New York.

April 20 Congress passes its third and broadest Force Act, which specifies court procedures and penalties for unlawful conspiracies and other violations of the 14th Amendment that infringe on the political and civil rights of blacks.

April 30 More than 100 Apaches under Federal military protection are massacred by a mob at Camp Grant, Arizona.

May 11 The National Woman's Suffrage Association convenes in New York City to organize and direct national efforts to correct the omission of consideration for women in the 14th and 15th Amendments.

May 24 The Senate, by a vote of 50 to 12, ratifies the Treaty of Washington, which establishes an international commission at Geneva to arbitrate the claims by the United States against Great Britain for damages done during the Civil War by British-built Confederate raiders such as the C.S. *Alabama*.

July 8 *The New York Times* intensifies an exposé of the fraudulent practices of William Marcy ("Boss") Tweed, whose "ring" arranges all bills against the city and county of New York to be overcharged, the excess being divided among its members. [On Oct. 26 Tweed is named in a civil suit to recover the millions of dollars said to be stolen from the city treasury. Bail is put at $2,000,000. On Dec. 16 he is arrested in a criminal action. Although he is released again on bail, Tweed spends much of the rest of his life in and out of jail.]

July 28 Writing from Brooklyn, New York, Walt Whitman, whose volume of poetry *Leaves of Grass* (published in 1855) has received little popular acclaim, sends a friend a copy of a "latest edition" of *Democratic Vistas,* a prose work appearing this year.

Sept. 5 In New York City, Augustin Daly presents another of his plays, *Divorce*. It becomes one of the hits of the American theater, running for 200 performances.

Sept. 30 Edward Eggleston publishes the first installment of a novel, *The Hoosier Schoolmaster,* in *Hearth and Home*. [It runs serially until Dec. 30, and becomes a best-seller when published as a book.]

Oct. 8-14 Disastrous fires break out in the central area of the city of Chicago and in the forests of Michigan and Wisconsin. The Chicago fire ends on Oct. 10, after a toll of more than 300 persons killed, nearly 90,000 homeless, and 17,450 buildings destroyed at a loss of about $196,000,000. More than 1,000 lives are lost before the Michigan and Wisconsin fires end on Oct. 14.

Nov. 10 Henry Morton Stanley, a naturalized American citizen and reporter for the New York *Herald,* locates the explorer David Livingstone at Ujiji in central Africa. Stanley is on a reportorial mission for his newspaper, and locates the explorer just in time to save his life. [Stanley's words of greeting, "Dr. Livingstone, I presume?", are reported in his account, published in 1872, and become legendary.]

The Powell Expedition, created in 1869 by the Smithsonian Institution to explore the Colorado River, rests in camp. (*ca.*) 1871.

1872

President Ulysses S. Grant is elected to a second term. His victory occurs despite a serious division in the Republican Party. The radical Republicans are dissatisfied with the administration of Reconstruction. Furthermore, when corruption in the Grant Administration surfaces shortly before the election, a group of prominent Republicans, including Charles Sumner and Carl Schurz, bolt the party to form the Liberal Republican Party and to nominate Horace Greeley for President. The Democratic Party, seeking to take maximum advantage of any weakness on the part of the still popular war hero, casts its support behind Greeley by making him their candidate for the Presidency. Although the Liberal Republicans reject a formal association with the Democrats, their platforms are basically similar, and both support an end to Reconstruction by the withdrawal of the Federal military from the South.

Stories of political corruption pervade the election year news. The Crédit Mobilier, a construction company owned by the Southern Pacific Railroad, is accused of bribing high Government officials, including Vice President Schuyler Colfax. Colfax is not renominated, but the new Vice Presidential candidate for 1872, Massachusetts Senator Henry Wilson, is also publicly associated with the Crédit Mobilier scandal. Corruption at the local level is also exposed, notably in the case of William Marcy ("Boss") Tweed, grand sachem of Tammany Hall, the Democratic organization in New York City. Tweed goes on trial for stealing millions of dollars in public funds.

Feb. 2 An act of Congress fixes Congressional elections on the first Tuesday after the first Monday in November, effective in 1876.

Feb. 22 The Prohibition Party holds its first nominating convention at Columbus, Ohio. James Black of Pennsylvania is nominated for President and the Reverend John Russell of Michigan for Vice President. [The ticket is given 5,607 votes on Election Day.]

Mar. 1 As a result of several recent expeditions in a previously unexplored part of the new Territory of Wyoming, an act of Congress is signed by President Grant designating as a "public park or pleasuring ground for the benefit and enjoyment of the people" a tract of land "lying near the headwaters of the Yellowstone River." [The tract becomes known subsequently as Yellowstone National Park and is the first Government program to preserve the national heritage for the entire population (for purposes other than education) rather than for a private interest.]

Mar. 5 President Grant appoints a commission to examine plans for an interoceanic canal across the Isthmus of Darien, Colombia.

April 2 Samuel Finley Breese Morse, 81, American painter, best known for his development of the telegraph and the invention of the Morse code, dies in New York City. He made telegraphy practical by a relay device placed at intervals along the wire.

May 1 Dissidents from the regular Republican Party, calling themselves the Liberal Republican Party, hold a national convention in Cincinnati. Horace Greeley is nominated for President and Benjamin Gratz Brown of Missouri for Vice President.

May 9-10 A group calling itself the Equal Rights Party meets in New York City to nominate the suffragette, Victoria Claflin Woodhull, for President and the Negro reformer, Frederick Douglass, for Vice President.

May 22 Congress passes an Amnesty Act restoring civil rights to all Southern citizens with the exception of approximately 600 former Confederate leaders.

June 5-6 The Republican Party meets in Philadelphia to nominate Ulysses S. Grant for President and Henry Wilson for Vice President. Negro delegates participate in the Republican Party's convention for the first time.

June 10 The Freedmen's Bureau, created by Congress as a bureau of the War Department in 1865 to supply the newly freed slaves with medical aid, food rations, and schools, is allowed to lapse by Congress.

July 9-10 The Democratic National Convention meets in Baltimore. Unable to agree on candidates from their own party, the Democrats decide to support the Liberal Republican ticket: Horace Greeley for President and Benjamin Gratz Brown for Vice President.

Sept. 3 The "Straight" Democratic National Convention meets in Louisville, Kentucky, to nominate Charles O'Conor of New York for President and John Quincy Adams II of Massachusetts for Vice President. [O'Conor does not accept the nomination.]

Sept. 4 The New York *Sun* accuses Vice President Schuyler Colfax, and the current Republican candidate for Vice President, Henry Wilson, along with several other political figures, of having accepted bribes in the form of stocks from the Crédit Mobilier of America, the construction arm of the Union Pacific Railroad.

Sept. 14 An international tribunal, set up by the United States and Great Britain under the Treaty of Washington of Feb. 27, 1871, to arbitrate serious differences outstanding between the two countries, awards the United States $15,500,000 in damages against England for the *Alabama* claims. These claims arise from the destruction of American ships by English-equipped Confederate cruisers during the Civil War. The tribunal, which meets in Geneva, is composed of Swiss, Italian, and Brazilian members acceptable to both parties. [The settlement is a major precedent for subsequent efforts at international arbitration.]

Oct. 2 Francis Lieber, 72, a political scientist, who wrote the first code of military law and procedure in the world, dies in New York City. He also edited, from 1829 to 1833, a work called *Encyclopedia Americana,* largely based on translations from a German encyclopedia. [This first significant American encyclopedia is reprinted until the eve of the Civil War, and has no direct connection with the work of the same name that begins publication in 1911.]

Oct. 10 William Henry Seward, 72, Secretary of State under Presidents Lincoln and Johnson, dies in Auburn, New York. He is best known for his purchase of Alaska from Russia (''Seward's Folly'') in 1867.

Oct. 21 The Islands of San Juan in Puget Sound (claimed both by the United States and England) are awarded to the United States by Emperor William I of Germany, who acted as arbitrator in the dispute.

Nov. 5 Susan B. Anthony and a group of women, testing the 14th Amendment by attempting to vote in the Presidential election, are arrested.

Nov. 5 Ulysses S. Grant is elected to a second term, defeating Horace Greeley. Henry Wilson is elected Vice President. The electoral vote is 286 to 66 and the popular vote is 3,596,745 to 2,843,446. The Republican Party also wins control by a two-thirds majority in both Houses of Congress. Incuded are seven Negroes. [The electoral votes cast for Grant are recorded, but Greeley's 63 votes are distributed to a number of candidates because he dies before the official tally is made.]

Nov. 9 A fire in Boston, Massachusetts, kills 13 people and destroys property over a large surrounding area.

Nov. 29 Horace Greeley, 61, dies at Pleasantville, New York, just 24 days after losing the Presidential election. Founder of the New York *Tribune,* he is best remembered for his radical stands on such political issues as antislavery, women's rights, and an end to Reconstruction. He popularized the slogan, ''Go West, young man!''

Dec. 2 The House of Representatives appoints a committee headed by Luke P. Poland of Vermont to investigate the Crédit Mobilier.

Dec. 11 Pinckney Benton Stewart Pinchback, a veteran of the Union Army, becomes acting governor of Louisiana. He is the first Negro to hold the office of governor in the United States. [He is also elected to the House of Representatives in 1872 and to the U.S. Senate in 1873, but is refused his seats.]

Stagecoach passing Mt. Shasta, California (*ca.*) 1870's

President Grant begins his second term confident of the public's endorsement. The Republican Party controls a two-thirds majority in both houses of Congress, and the Democrats have lost most of their political power. But problems are brewing for the President and the country. In his naiveté, the President is unable to give credence to the stories of scandal and corruption involving members of his Cabinet and close friends. His public popularity is not enhanced by his signing, just after his reelection, the "Salary Grab" act, substantially raising his own and all top government officials' salaries.

The nation's preoccupation with corruption in high places and acts of aggrandizement by political figures is suddenly diverted to more pressing problems. The country's seeming economic well-being is shattered by a major financial crash. The economy is in fact overexpanded, particularly in railroad construction, and the weak link turns out to be the banking house of Jay Cooke and Company, which helped the U.S. Government finance the Civil War and also underwrote the construction of the Northern Pacific Railroad. Cooke announces its failure in September. Investors in Europe, where a depression is already under way, begin to call in American loans. The New York Stock Exchange closes its doors for 10 days; other businesses fail; and railroad construction is curtailed, with some railroads defaulting on their bonds. The unemployed begin to move about the country seeking jobs, and bread lines appear in the cities.

Jan. 7-9   A blizzard sweeps over most of Minnesota, freezing unsheltered livestock and causing extensive property damage and loss of life.

Feb. 12   Congress terminates the coinage of silver, because the intrinsic value of bullion exceeds its face value. [In 1876, when abundant silver is discovered in the West, this act becomes known as "The Crime of '73."]

Feb. 18   The House of Representatives censures Congressmen Oakes Ames and James Brooks for their connection with the Crédit Mobilier, the railroad construction company that has been charged with bribing and attempting to bribe Congressmen to secure U.S. Government contracts.

Mar. 3   The lame-duck 42d Congress passes the "Salary Grab" act, doubling the President's salary and increasing that of others by 50 per cent. The provision that the increase be made retroactive to the beginning of the term further outrages the Democrats.

Mar. 3   Congress passes an act sponsored by Anthony Comstock, secretary of the Society for the Suppression of Vice, prohibiting the sending of obscene literature through the mails.

Mar. 3   Congress passes two land acts, one (the Timber Cultures Act) providing grants of 160 acres to anyone who will plant trees on one quarter of the granted acreage; the other (the Coal Lands Act) opening public lands for purchase by private individuals and groups (160 acres to individuals, 320 acres to groups) at prices ranging from $10 to $20 per acre.

Mar. 4   President Ulysses S. Grant is inaugurated for a second term, and Henry Wilson replaces Schuyler Colfax as Vice President.

April 14   The U.S. Supreme Court in the Slaughterhouse Cases decides, 5 to 4, that the 14th Amendment recognizes both state and Federal citizenship. The Court's action faces up to the fact that most civil rights derive from the state constitutions and consequently are not safeguarded by the 14th Amendment. [Although the cases deal with a monopoly given to a slaughterhouse by Louisiana, this interpretation has the effect of limiting the Federal protection of Negroes' civil rights and, more profoundly, of reaffirming and redefining the areas of state sovereignty.

May 1   The U.S. Post Office issues one-cent ("penny") postcards.

May 7   Salmon Portland Chase, 65, Chief Justice of the U.S. Supreme Court for eight years, staunch supporter of civil rights, and a founder of the Republican Party, dies in New York City.

July 3   President Grant issues a proclamation authorizing the Centennial Exposition of 1876 to be held in Philadelphia.

Aug. 18   John Lucas, Charles Begole, and A. H. Johnson are the first men to climb Mount Whitney, the highest mountain in the United States, 14,495 feet above sea level.

Sept. 8   Jay Cooke and Company, a large and respected banking house, declares itself bankrupt. [The bank's collapse precipitates the "Panic of 1873" and the ensuing three-year depression during which more than 10,000 businesses fail. The basic economic problems are overproduction, a declining market, and deflation.]

Oct. 18 Yale, Princeton, Rutgers, and Columbia hold the first football conference, drafting a code of rules.

Oct. 31-Nov. 8 The *Virginius*, fraudulently sailing under the U.S flag while bringing arms and men to Cuba (in revolt against Spain), is captured by the *Tornado,* a Spanish ship. Local authorities in Cuba shoot the captain, 36 of the crew, and 12 passengers. Public sentiment in the United States is aroused at what appears to be an act of hostility to the country.

Nov. 19 William "Boss" Tweed, who controlled Tammany Hall, the Democratic organization in New York, is convicted on 102 counts of fraud. [He is sentenced to 12 years' imprisonment; is freed after little more than a year; is rearrested on other charges; escapes from jail and finds asylum in Cuba; is returned to the United States by Spain; and spends two more years in jail, dying there.]

Nov. 27 The Hoosac Tunnel, the second longest railroad tunnel in the world, is completed. It is 4.7 miles long, 26 feet wide and between 23 and 26 feet high. It runs through a spur of the Green Mountains in Massachusetts. The tunnel for the first time provides access for trains crossing from the Connecticut Valley to the Hudson Valley.

Nov. 29 The *Virginius* affair is settled. The Spanish Government promises to return the ship to the United States and to pay $80,000 to American families whose members were executed. It is clear by now that the ship was under control of Cuban revolutionaries when attacked.

Dec. 23 Sara Moore Grimké, 81, who with her sister Angelina Emily Grimké crusaded against slavery and for women's rights, dies at Hyde Park near Boston.

The Presidential Inauguration Ball

1874

Mark Twain and Charles Dudley Warner in their novel *The Gilded Age,* published this year, characterize the era as one of political corruption and economic speculation. The depression that began last year begins to abate, but jobs and food are still scarce. Early in the year a grasshopper invasion in the Middle West and a potato-bug blight in the East destroy most of grain, corn, and potato crops, forcing farmers to leave their homesteads in search of work.

Frustrated by the inability of the political and industrial leaders to remedy their economic plight, some Americans turn to new forms of political and economic organizations for help. The Grange, originally formed as a social organization, is transformed into a center for political and economic action on behalf of farmers. It is most powerful in Illinois, Wisconsin, and Iowa, where it forces state legislatures to regulate the railroads and to control and reduce high intrastate freight rates, specifically on farm produce. The Grange also helps the farmers organize the first cooperatives. A new political party, the Greenback Party, issues a platform that advocates "cheap money"—that is, the free issuance of greenbacks rather than the minting of gold and silver—to help debtors, mainly farmers, repay their loans.

The mood of discontent and dissatisfaction with the status quo produces an upset in the November elections. The Democrats, who two years previously were practically discounted as a political force, win a majority of the seats in the House of Representatives. In the South, Reconstruction is ending, sometimes violently. Republican state governments struggling for survival are replaced by Democrats who at times physically battle the "carpetbaggers" to gain possession of the offices they win through the elective process. This process is left increasingly in the hands of the local white elements as the Federal Government reduces its "interference" in Southern political activity.

Jan. 20   With the exception of the increase in salaries for the President and the U.S. Supreme Court Justices, Congress repeals the "Salary Grab" Act passed in 1873.

Jan. 21   Morrison R. Waite is confirmed as Chief Justice of the U.S. Supreme Court, replacing Salmon P. Chase. Waite is President Grant's third appointment to this office, the Senate having found the first two, Attorney General George Henry Williams and diplomat Caleb Cushing, unacceptable.

Jan. 31-Mar. 2   The Minnesota legislature appropriates $5,000 to relieve destitute inhabitants on the frontier whose crops had been destroyed by a grasshopper invasion. Two months later the Minnesota legislature appropriates an additional $25,000 for the purchase of seed grain. [Iowa and other states ravaged by the grasshoppers, make similar appropriations.]

Mar. 8   Millard Fillmore, 74, the Vice President who became the 13th President at the death of Zachary Taylor, dies in Buffalo, New York.

Mar. 11   Charles Sumner, 63, militant anti-slavery partisan, and a founder of the Republican Party, dies in Washington, D.C.

Mar. 11   The Wisconsin legislature, influenced by the Grange, a farmers' organization, passes the Potter Law regulating intrastate freight rates. [Iowa passes a similar statute on Mar. 23.]

April 15-May 15   Joseph Brooks, a Republican, and Elijah Baxter, a Democrat, battle for recognition as governor of Arkansas. Brooks takes possession of the state capitol despite his apparent defeat by Baxter. Brooks appeals to President Grant for help, and supported by the two U.S. Senators from Arkansas, organizes armed support. Grant tells the state legislature to make the decision. They choose Baxter. In fights between the two sides, 20 men are slain.

April 22   President Grant vetoes a bill passed by Congress validating the issuance of greenbacks in 1873.

May 4   The U.S. Supreme Court declares, in *Bartemeyer* v. *Iowa,* that the right to sell liquor is not protected by the privileges and immunities clause of the 14th Amendment.

May 4   Secretary of the Treasury William A. Richardson resigns following the disclosure that he permitted a friend to receive exorbitant commissions for collecting taxes due the Federal Government.

May 8   Massachusetts passes the first 10-hour working day for minors (under 18 years old) and for women.

May 16   The Ashfield reservoir dam on the Mill River at Williamsburg, Massachusetts, collapses, drowning more than 100 people and causing extensive property damage.

May 21 President Grant's daughter, Nellie, marries Algernon Frederick Sartoris. It is the third wedding in the White House.

June 18 Congress passes an act permitting farmers in specified areas to be absent from their homesteads or preemption lands until May 1, 1875, without losing their rights under the residence requirement laws. This enables settlers whose crops have been destroyed by grasshoppers to seek work elsewhere without fear of losing their claims.

June 20 Congress passes a currency act fixing the maximum amount of greenbacks in circulation at $382,000,000.

June 20 The territorial government of the District of Columbia is abolished and is replaced by a government of three President-appointed commissioners. This completely disfranchises the citizens of the capital city.

July 4 The largest arch bridge in the world, and the first to use significant amounts of steel in its construction, spans the Mississippi River at St. Louis, the work for seven years of engineer Captain James B. Eads. All St. Louis watches as two locomotives cross the river on the new bridge. [This bridge assures the future of St. Louis; it is a milestone in bridge building; it still stands.]

Aug. 4-18 The Chautauqua Assembly is established by Methodist minister John Heyl Vincent and manufacturer Lewis Miller, who propose to combine summer recreation with the training of Sunday school teachers and church workers. The Assembly is held on the shore of Lake Chautauqua in northwestern New York State.

Sept. 18 The Nebraska Relief and Aid Soci-

ety organizes to collect money and supplies for distribution among the destitute settlers of the state. (This is one of the many relief organizations established throughout the West to bring aid to farmers whose crops are destroyed during the grasshopper invasion.)

Nov. 3 In the Congressional elections, the Democrats gain control of the House of Representatives for the first time since the Civil War. The Republicans lose 89 seats in the House and 4 in the Senate.

Nov. 7 A cartoon by Thomas Nast in *Harper's Weekly* uses the elephant to symbolize the Republican Party. [The symbol soon becomes as familiar as Nast's earlier Tammany Tiger.]

Nov. 18 The Woman's Christian Temperance Union is organized in Cleveland, Ohio.

Nov. 24 Joseph F. Glidden receives a patent for barbed wire. [The wire becomes the most popular fencing material to restrict cattlemen from grazing their stock on the farmers' land, and transforms the "wide open spaces." It also makes possible the breeding of superior cattle by controlling cattle to good grazing area. The number of pounds of barbed wire sold from 1874 to 1881 increases from 10,000 to 120,000,000.]

Nov. 25 A political convention in Indianapolis, consisting mostly of farmers from the South and West, organizes the Greenback Party. The party's platform calls for currency inflation and an end to specie payment (settling of debts in cash) so that farmers may repay debts and mortgages with "cheap" money.

Dec. 9 Ezra Cornell, 67, founder of Cornell University, dies in Ithaca, New York.

The Third-Term Panic. (The first use of the elephant as the symbol of the Republican Party)

1875

Rumors of gold in the Black Hills of Dakota Territory were substantiated in 1874 by General George A. Custer, head of a U.S. Government team of soldiers and scientists organized to look into the gold claims. This year prospectors enter the Black Hills, although they are temporarily restrained by U.S. military forces under General Sheridan, who tries to honor a pledge to the Sioux Indians not to permit trespassers on their Black Hills reservation. Federal agents in October finally open the Black Hills to any prospectors willing to chance an Indian attack.

Business, slowly recovering from the depression of 1873, begins to form pools [the precursor of the trust] to fix and maintain prices. Labor unions actively organize in industry and in coal mining. The "Molly Maguires," a secret coal miners' union in Pennsylvania, resort to terrorist tactics to fight mine owners.

For the beef-cattle industry on the Great Plains the year is a rewarding one, for by now—before the new barbed-wire fencing has been introduced—there is free pasturage from Texas to Canada, and the refrigerator car makes it possible to bring beef to the East and also to transship it as far away as Europe. It is the time of the cowboy and the long drive—the herding of thousands of head of cattle to the railheads from Abilene, Kansas, west to Dodge City. From these loading points the cattle are shipped to the slaughterhouses of Chicago and Kansas City.

Jan. 14　Congress passes the Specie Resumption Act, reducing the value of greenbacks in circulation from $382,000,000 to $300,000,000 and allowing the resumption of specie payment by Jan. 1, 1879. The bill, twice before recommended by President Grant, is an attempt to balance the inflation desired in the West with the "sound money" policy desired in the East.

Jan. 25　Congress passes a law permitting the Commissioner of Agriculture to distribute seed to areas devastated by grasshoppers, and appropriates $30,000 for this purpose, despite the objection of those who consider the appropriation unconstitutional. [Such distributions were made as early as 1839 by Commissioner of Patents Henry Leavitt Ellsworth, long before there was a Department of Agriculture.]

Jan. 30　The United States and King Kalakaua of Hawaii sign a treaty of commercial reciprocity. While favoring the export of sugar to the United States, the real intent of the treaty is to prevent the Islands from falling into hostile hands.

Feb. 10　Congress appropriates $150,000 more for the purchase and distribution of food in areas ravaged by the grasshopper plague.

Mar. 1　Congress passes a Civil Rights act, originally sponsored by the late Charles Sumner, guaranteeing equal rights to Negroes in public accommodations (theaters, inns, public amusements, and public conveyances on land and water). The act also prohibits excluding Negroes from jury duty. [This law is ruled unconstitu-tional by the U.S. Supreme Court in 1883.]

Mar. 3　The coining of silver 20-cent pieces is authorized by Congress.

Mar. 5　Blanche Kelso Bruce, a Negro from Mississippi, begins his term in the U.S. Senate. [He is the first Negro to serve a full term.]

Mar. 15　Archbishop John McCloskey of New York becomes the first American to be named a Cardinal by the Roman Catholic Church.

Mar. 30　The U.S. Supreme Court, in *Minor* v. *Happersett,* rules that the right to vote is not protected by the privileges and immunities section of the Constitution. The decision establishes that the 14th Amendment does not restrict a state from setting up suffrage requirements excluding women.

May 1　The St. Louis *Democrat* describes a so-called "Whiskey Ring," a conspiracy of distillery owners and U.S. Internal Revenue officers engaged in defrauding the U.S. Government by nonpayment of the Federal liquor tax.

May 3　The United States joins the General [after 1878, Universal] Postal Union, a multinational agreement among various national postal services.

May 10　Secretary of the Treasury Benjamin H. Bristow reveals that General Orville Babcock, President Grant's private secretary, and several close friends of the President are involved in the "Whiskey Ring." This scandal, though not directly involving the President, comes closer to incriminating him than any of the previous scandals in the Grant Administration.

May 17 Aristides, ridden by jockey O. Lewis, wins the first Kentucky Derby at Churchill Downs, Kentucky. The purse is $2,850. The race is limited to three-year-olds and takes place over a 1½-mile [after 1896, 1¼-mile] track.

May 17 John Cabell Breckinridge, 54, Vice President under James Buchanan, who served the Confederacy as a general officer and as Secretary of War during the Civil War, dies at Lexington, Kentucky.

May 29 President Grant announces that he has no intention of running for a third term.

July 23 Isaac Merrit Singer, 63, developer of the first efficient and practical sewing machine, dies in Torquay, England.

July 31 Former President Andrew Johnson, 66, dies at Carter's Station, Tennessee, a few months after making a bitter speech against President Grant in the U.S. Senate, to which he was elected from Tennessee in 1874.

Sept. 10 Dr. John A. Warder organizes the American Forestry Association in Chicago. It is dedicated to the purpose of conserving natural resources.

Nov. 22 Vice President Henry Wilson, 63, dies. He was a founder of the Republican Party and a U.S. Senator (1855-1873) from Massachusetts.

Dec. 6 The 44th Congress convenes, marking the first time since 1859 that the Democrats have a majority in the House, with 169 members to 109 for the Republicans. In the Senate, however, the Republicans still lead with 45 to 29 for the Democrats.

The court house in Greenville, Tennessee where former President Andrew Johnson lies in state.

211

1876 The most disputed Presidential election in U.S. history occurs as the nation celebrates its Centennial. Samuel J. Tilden, a Democrat, receives a clear popular majority assuring him 184 electoral votes to 163 for Rutherford B. Hayes, his Republican opponent. Not included in the electoral totals, however, are the disputed votes from Oregon, Florida, Louisiana, and South Carolina. Tilden only needs one more electoral vote to win the Presidency. The day following the election the New York *World* quotes Hayes as resigned to defeat, but his party refuses to concede because victory can still be achieved if Hayes is somehow credited with all the electoral votes from all four disputed states.

President Grant sends Federal troops and prominent men from both parties to the three Southern states to assure a "fair count" of the votes. Riots break out and there is concern that the country is on the verge of another civil war. When the electoral votes are counted, it is found that Oregon's total is faulty and that the three Southern states are sending in two sets of counts (a Republican and a Democratic set) for each candidate. Congress is confronted with the dilemma of validating the votes. Both Houses must be present at the official counting—a crucial point, because the Republicans control the Senate while the Democrats control the House. If either chooses not to attend, the count cannot be official. To avoid a conflict a joint Congressional committee is created to decide just how and by whom the disputed electoral votes are to be counted [in 1877].

In the West the war with the Indians appears to be winding up, although the Sioux warriors confront U.S. troops in Montana Territory. The resulting defeat of General George A. Custer is the worst the Army has known in all its battles with the Indians. The policy of breaking treaties is, for once, costly, and the Sioux chiefs Sitting Bull and Crazy Horse seem determined to protect what can only be a lost cause.

Feb. 1 The United States orders all Sioux to return to their reservation, despite the fact that prospectors are being permitted to settle at gold camps in the Black Hills portion of the reservation. [Sioux chiefs Sitting Bull and Crazy Horse continue to collect military supplies along the Little Bighorn River. The Sioux have been on a war footing since the United States broke its treaty of 1868. The U.S. Army prepares for war against the Sioux.]

Feb. 2 The National League of Professional Base Ball Clubs is organized in New York City, with Morgan G. Bulkeley as president. The eight teams comprise Boston, Chicago, Cincinnati, Hartford, Louisville, New York, Philadelphia, and St. Louis.

Feb. 24 President Grant's personal secretary, Orville E. Babcock, is found not guilty of complicity in the "Whiskey Ring."

Mar. 2 Secretary of War William W. Belknap resigns after the House of Representatives passes a resolution calling for his impeachment. He is accused of sharing in the profits of trading-post sales in the Indian territories. The award of Indian post-traderships are within the jurisdiction of the Secretary of War. It is charged that Belknap received as much as $6,000 in one year from a single trading post.

Mar. 7-10 Alexander Graham Bell receives a patent for a device that transmits sound over wire. Three days later he uses the device to call his assistant from an adjoining room: "Mr. Watson come here. I want you." This is the first known use of the device [the telephone] to transmit a human message.

April 18 President Grant vetoes a bill to reduce Presidential salaries. The bill is an attempt to repeal the provision of the "Salary Grab" act of 1873 that had not been previously repealed by Congress.

April 20 The American Chemical Society is organized in New York City. Its purpose is to promote research and advancement in chemistry.

April 24 The U.S. Supreme Court, in *Walker* v. *Sauvinet,* rules that provisions of the 6th and 7th Amendments to the Constitution that assure trial by jury in criminal and civil cases are not protected by the 14th Amendment, and consequently a state may modify or abolish trial by jury in its own proceedings.

May 10 The Centennial Exposition celebrating the 100th anniversary of the Declaration of Independence opens in Fairmont Park, Philadelphia. Fifty countries send exhibits. Many inventions, including the telephone, typewriter, and the refrigerator car, are displayed.

May 15   The House Judiciary Committee begins investigations of Minority Leader James G. Blaine, who is accused of having favored specific railroad interests in 1869 when he was Speaker of the House.

May 18   The first national convention of the Greenback Party, meeting in Indianapolis, nominates Peter Cooper of New York for President and Samuel F. Carey of Ohio for Vice President. The platform demands the creation of paper money and the repeal of the Specie Resumption Act.

June 5   James G. Blaine, defending himself before the House Judiciary Committee against charges of corruption in connection with the sale of bonds to the Union Pacific Railroad, reads passages from a series of letters he had written to a contractor, Warren Fisher. These letters were obtained from a witness, James Mulligan, Fisher's bookkeeper, who was testifying against Blaine. Although Blaine refuses to turn over the so-called Mulligan Letters to the committee, the passages he reads appear to exonerate him.

June 14-16   The Republican National Convention meets in Cincinnati, Ohio, and, after casting six ballots favoring James G. Blaine, nominates Rutherford B. Hayes, governor of Ohio, for President and William A. Wheeler of New York for Vice President. Blaine's defeat is largely attributed to the current investigation of his possible illegal connection with the Union Pacific Railroad. The Republican platform supports a "sound-money" policy.

June 25   General George A. Custer, ignoring the orders of his commanding officer, General Alfred H. Terry, decides not to wait for the main forces to arrive before attacking Sitting Bull and his Sioux warriors who are camped along the Little Bighorn River. General Custer splits his force into two columns, one for each side of the stream. He himself at the head of 265 men bivouacs on the right side of the river. The Indians, who number about 2,500, surround the soldiers. In the engagement every U.S. soldier including General Custer is killed. General Terry arrives in time to save the column on the left side of the stream.

June 27-29   The Democratic National Convention meets in St. Louis and nominates Samuel J. Tilden, governor of New York, for President, and Thomas A. Hendricks of Indiana for Vice President. Tilden is known for his part in the destruction of the powerful and corrupt "Tweed Ring" in New York. The Democratic platform supports the repeal of the Resumption Act of 1875, and economy in government.

July 4   Edward M. Bannister, a Negro, wins first prize for his painting "Under the Oaks" at the Centennial Exposition in Philadelphia.

July 25   A bill for the free and unlimited coining of silver is introduced into the House of Representatives by Richard P. Bland of Missouri, who coined the slogan "Crime of '73" in referring to the act in that year that terminated silver coinage.

Aug. 1   William Belknap is acquitted by the U.S. Senate of charges of accepting bribes for the sale of post-traderships. The vote, 37 to 25 against Belknap, is short of the two-thirds required to find him guilty. (Most of the Senators who vote for acquittal do so because, in their opinion, Belknap's previous resignation has made action by the Senate moot.)

Aug. 1   Colorado is admitted to the Union as the 38th state, and because of the year is known as the Centennial State. It has been a territory since 1861, and since 1870, by the time the Indians ceased to be a serious problem to the white settlers and the railroads entered the state, it has increased fivefold in population, approaching 200,000. Its first bid for statehood was vetoed by President Andrew Johnson in 1867. Its seat of government, for the time being, is at the eastern edge of the mountains, at Denver, on Cherry Creek.

Oct. 6   The American Library Association is established in Philadelphia by several prominent librarians including Melvil Dewey, the originator of the Dewey Decimal System. Dewey becomes the first secretary of the association.

Nov. 7   The Presidential election is held. Samuel Tilden receives 4,284,020 popular votes to 4,036,572 for Rutherford B. Hayes. The electoral vote immediately authenticated is 184 for Tilden (one short of a majority) and 163 for Hayes. The electoral votes for Florida, Louisiana, and South Carolina, and one vote for Oregon, are in doubt.

Nov. 23   William "Boss" Tweed, convicted of fraud in New York and a fugitive, having escaped from jail, is returned to the New York authorities after being apprehended in Spain.

Dec. 5   Almost 300 people die in a fire at Conway's Theatre in the city of Brooklyn, in New York.

Dec. 5   President Grant, in an address to Congress, apologizes for his mistakes, characterizing them as "errors of judgment not of intent."

Dec. 6   Florida, Louisiana, and South

Carolina submit two sets of electoral votes, while Oregon duplicates one of its three votes. In Oregon, where Hayes has won the popular vote, a Republican postmaster is disqualified as an elector. The secretary of state of Oregon, a Republican, nevertheless submits the disqualified elector's vote, while the Democratic governor sends in two votes for Hayes and one for Tilden. If Congress accepts the governor's version, Tilden wins the election. In the three Southern states, Tilden easily wins the popular vote, but the election boards, influenced by the presence of Federal troops, give the votes to Hayes. Congress must decide, first, which sets of electoral votes are to be accepted and, second, who is to count the electoral votes.

Dec. 14 Wade Hampton, a Democrat, takes the oath of office as governor of South Carolina despite the presence of Federal troops, who continue to police the state. This defiant act by Hampton symbolizes the end of Reconstruction, because the support by the Federal forces for the Republican claimant, hitherto a predictable factor, fails to materialize.

Dec. 29 The bridge over the gorge in Ashtabula, Ohio, collapses in a snowstorm as the Pacific Express is passing over it. Almost 90 persons die in the disaster.

**Celebrating the Centennial of the Declaration of Independence
(The Horticultural Hall contains the International Centennial Exhibition.)**

1877

After 12 years, Reconstruction is almost formally brought to an end. As part of the bargain between the restive white Southerners, who want to return to mastery in their own land, and a Republican leadership eager to take charge of a country on the brink of great economic development, the Southern Democrats allow Hayes to capture enough disputed electoral votes to become President. For his part, Hayes orders the remaining Federal troops out of the three Southern states in which they have power. Without Federal troops to protect them, the last "carpetbag" governments flee to the North, and the Democrats take over the state governments. Southerners expect that a return to home rule, aided by a President who owes no political favors to radical Republicans, will help the South regain its economic stability dislocated by years of Civil War and Reconstruction, return the Negroes to political impotence, and to some extent turn the clock back.

Jan. 2   George F. Drew, a Democrat, is inaugurated governor of Florida, ending the "carpetbag" government there.

Jan. 29   The bill forming the Electoral Commission is passed by Congress. The House selects 3 Democrats and 2 Republicans. The Senate selects 3 Republicans and 2 Democrats. Two of the Justices selected are Democrats; two are Republicans; the fifth is to be selected by the four Justices and it is tacitly understood that they will choose an independent. Justice David Davis is chosen but declines. (As he has just been elected U.S. Senator from Illinois, he deems himself ineligible.) The four Justices then pick Justice Joseph P. Bradley, a Republican.

February   Both Houses meet in a joint session to decide the electoral vote. Unable to agree on Florida's electoral votes, the decision is left to the Electoral Commission, which votes along party lines: 8 to 7 for Hayes. Precisely the same procedure and results decide Louisiana's votes. In the instance of Oregon's single disputed electoral vote and in the case of the entire South Carolina vote, the Commission unanimously picks the slate of electors favoring Hayes.

Mar. 1   The U.S. Supreme Court declares, in *Munn v. Illinois,* that a state can regulate private business if it is "affected with a public interest." This ruling opens the way for states to regulate private industry in many fields if it is for the social good.

Mar. 2   The Electoral Commission names Rutherford B. Hayes as President. The Republicans have gained the support of the Southern Democrats by promising to end Reconstruction in the South, especially by withdrawing all Federal troops; by promising to appropriate a substantial amount of money for local improvements; and by

The Lame Deer Fight

agreeing to appoint at least one Southerner to the Cabinet.

Mar. 3   President Hayes privately takes the oath of office.

Mar. 3   The Desert Land Act is passed, providing for the sale of 160 acres of land at 25 cents an acre to anyone agreeing to irrigate a portion of the land within three years and at the end of that time to pay an additional dollar an acre. This bill, ostensibly passed to help pioneers, is lobbied through by wealthy cattlemen as a means of acquiring large tracts of land cheaply.

Mar. 5   President Hayes is inaugurated in a public ceremony as the 19th President.

Mar. 5   President Hayes appoints a Southerner, David McKendree Key of Tennessee as his Postmaster General.

April 10   Federal troops leave Columbia, South Carolina. Democratic elected officials assume their offices.

April 24   The last of the Federal troops withdraw from the South as they depart New Orleans.

June 14   The United States commemorates the 100th anniversary of the flag by establishing Flag Day.

July 17   Workers on the Baltimore and Ohio Railroad at Martinsburg, West Virginia, strike against a management order for a 10-per-cent cut in wages combined with a simultaneous doubling of the number of cars on a train without an increase in the work crew. [The strike spreads spontaneously. Governor Henry M. Mathews of West Virginia orders in the militia, but the train carrying the troops is prevented by workers from leaving the station. The station is set on fire and 12 men are killed.]

Oct. 5   Chief Joseph of the Nez Percé Indians, with 200 braves and 600 women and children, surrenders to the United States forces after a four-month retreat stretching over 2,000 miles in an attempt to reach Canada. Chief Joseph is within a few miles of Canada when he gives up to save his women and children.

An anti-Tilden cartoon by Thomas Nast

A TRUCE—NOT A COMPROMISE, BUT A CHANCE FOR HIGH-TONED GENTLEMEN TO RETIRE GRACEFULLY FROM THEIR VERY CIVIL DECLARATIONS OF WAR.

1878

President Hayes continues a house-cleaning program designed to eliminate corruption in the Administration he inherited from Grant. His Cabinet comprises men selected for ability rather than for cronyism, as was often the case in the Grant Cabinet. Among his most capable department heads are John Sherman, Secretary of the Treasury, previously chairman of the Senate Finance Committee [and even better known subsequently for the Sherman Antitrust and Sherman Silver Purchase acts of 1890]; and Carl Schurz, friend of the Indian and promoter of a system of national parklands, who becomes Secretary of the Interior.

The grasshoppers which had ravaged the crops in the West are now under control, and settlers begin to farm their lands again. Industry is emerging from the depression that began in 1873. Employment increases. The strikes of the previous year spur many workers to join labor unions emphasizing higher wages and shorter working hours. Some flock to the Knights of Labor, the first significant national labor union, but despite swelled ranks the Knights fail to become an effective labor organization. They lack trained leadership and experience, and as they grow in numbers they fail to forge a program.

Jan. 10 Senator Aaron Augustus Sargent of California introduces in Congress the following proposed amendment to the Constitution: "The right of citizens of the United States to vote shall not be denied or abridged by the United States or by any state on account of sex." [This amendment is introduced regularly thereafter until passed in 1919.]

Jan. 14 The U.S. Supreme Court, in *Hall* v. *De Cuir*, rules that a Louisiana Reconstruction statute forbidding the segregation of the races on a Mississippi river boat is unconstitutional because a state cannot interfere with interstate commerce.

Feb. 19 Thomas A. Edison receives a patent for his invention of a sound-recording device, which he calls a "phonograph."

Feb. 22 The Greenback Labor Party with delegates from 28 states present, organizes in Toledo, Ohio. It is a fusion of the Greenback and the National parties, with a platform that advocates the free coinage of silver, the recalling of bank notes, a shorter work week, and a limitation on Chinese immigration.

Feb. 28 The Bland-Allison Act, requiring the Government to buy between $2,000,000 and $4,000,000 of silver each month to be coined into silver dollars, is passed by Congress over President Hayes's veto. This bill is a compromise with Western farmers and silver miners who had been lobbying for the free and unlimited coinage of silver since large deposits of the metal were discovered in the West in 1876.

April 16 The U.S. Supreme Court in *Reynolds* v. *United States* decides its first important case involving the First Amendment right to freedom of religion. The question at issue is whether the practice of polygamy by members of the Mormon Church may be prohibited in view of First Amendment guarantees. The Court holds that the free exercise of religion does not include toleration of "criminal" or "immoral" acts sanctioned by a particular religion.

June 11 Congress passes an Organic Act (constitution) for the District of Columbia, based on the temporary formula devised in 1874. Three commissioners, two civilian residents appointed by the President, and one member of the Corps of Army Engineers also appointed by the President, are to make recommendations to Congress on legislation. Residents do not have the vote in either local or national elections.

July 11 President Hayes, honoring his preelection campaign pledge to institute civil-service reform, to ferret out corruption, and to improve the reputation of the Republican Party, dismisses Chester A. Arthur, port collector of customs at the New York Customs House, and Alonzo B. Cornell, port naval officer, who have refused to carry out his orders to investigate corruption in their jurisdiction. Hayes waits until Congress adjourns to dismiss the two officials to avoid a violation of the Tenure of Office Act, which had been passed in 1867 to limit President Johnson's alleged abuse of executive privilege. [The act is repealed in 1887.]

Aug. 21 Lawyers meet in Saratoga, New York, to form the American Bar Association.

Nov. 5 For the first time since 1858, Republicans lose control of both houses of Congress. The 46th Congress will have 42 Democrats and 33 Republicans in the Senate, 149 Democrats and 130 Republicans in the House. A surprising development is the election to the House of members of the newly-formed Greenback Labor Party, which wins 14 seats.

Freedom of competition gives way to "big-business economy." As competition in industry and transportation grow, businessmen begin to fear the effect of competition on their profits, and devise ways of limiting it. The most successful device within the law is the "trust," a form of organized business in which corporations entrust their stocks to a board of trustees, who are authorized to act for the component corporations. This device, which several businesses adopt, circumvents many state laws that greatly restrict interstate corporations. The largest and most efficient trust is that organized by John D. Rockefeller, head of the Standard Oil Trust, comprised of the major corporations engaged in refining and transporting petroleum. The Hepburn Committee, set up by the New York State legislature, reveals that the Rockefeller interests totally dominate the oil industry, freezing out all competition throughout the entire world. The committee also reports on the chaotic situation in the railroads, revealing extensive price discrimination in different parts of the country. Small merchants and farmers begin to demand greater government regulation of private enterprise.

Jan. 1   The Government resumes specie payments authorized by the Specie Resumption Act of 1875. Despite the fact that greenbacks are now worth their equivalent in gold, Secretary of the Treasury John Sherman, with a gold reserve of over $200,000,000, expresses doubt that there will be a rush to redeem the greenbacks.

Jan. 25   Congress passes the Arrears of Pensions Act, providing that an eligible veteran may receive back pensions from the date of his discharge to the date of filing his claim.

Feb. 15   President Hayes signs an act allowing female attorneys to argue cases before the U.S. Supreme Court. To qualify, however, a female attorney must have argued before a state supreme court for at least three years.

Feb. 22   Frank W. Woolworth and his partner W. H. Moore open a "five-cent" store in Utica, New York. Their new idea is to have a single fixed price for all commodities.

Mar. 3   Congress establishes the United States Geological Survey. It is to be a bureau of the Department of the Interior. Clarence King is named its first director.

April 29   President Hayes vetoes the Army Appropriations bill because the Democratic Congress has inserted a rider making it illegal for a President to send in Federal troops during a Congressional election. President Hayes acts because the rider nullifies the Force Act and violates the constitutional guarantee of the equality of the three branches of the Government. The Republicans support the veto as they still want the option of military intervention in the South if it is needed.

May 1   President Hayes vetoes a bill restricting Chinese immigration as a violation of the Burlingame Treaty of 1868.

May 7   California adopts a state constitutional provision that forbids the employment of Chinese. The statute is in response to recent anti-Chinese sentiment caused by high unemployment in the depression of 1873, and the fear that jobs would be taken by Chinese immigrants. The movement is led by Denis Kearney, whose Workingmen's Party is the vehicle for militant anti-Chinese agitation limited to California.

May 8   George B. Seldon, an attorney of Rochester, New York, applies for a patent on his concept of a horseless carriage to be activated by a gasoline-fueled internal-combustion engine. [He receives the patent in 1895.]

May 24   William Lloyd Garrison, 73, a staunch abolitionist and proponent of women's rights, dies in New York City. He was the publisher of *The Liberator,* which carried in its first issue in 1831 Garrison's determination to fight for his principles: "I am in earnest—I will not equivocate—I will not excuse—I will not retreat a single inch—*and I will be heard.*"

June 16   A pirated version of *H.M.S. Pinafore* is performed at the Bowery Theater in New York City. It is the first Gilbert and Sullivan play produced in the United States.

June 28   Congress passes an act establishing the Mississippi River Commission, whose function it will be to improve navigation on the river.

Oct 21   Thomas A. Edison devises a practical incandescent lamp at his laboratory in Menlo Park, New Jersey. It consists of a carbonized thread inside a hollow glass sphere from which all air has been evacuated. [The patent for this lamp is issued on Jan. 27, 1880.]

Dec. 31   Despite the fact that a patent has not yet been granted, Thomas A. Edison publicly demonstrates his new incandescent lamp to several thousand people, who are brought to Menlo Park by special trains.

1880

With the South once more under the control of the conservative white portion of its population and the entrepreneurs and industrialists of the North ready and eager to proceed with the development of the country, the sectional issues fade into insignificance. Although the South is solidly Democratic and the Republicans are entrenched in the North, no issues that arouse popular enthusiasm or even interest mark the national elections this year. President Hayes has eliminated himself in advance. No conspicuous candidate has appeared for either party. The combatants in the political arena this year do not have outstanding qualifications. The electorate divides almost evenly, with only some 9,000 votes separating the winner from the loser.

The Republican Party is sharply split into factions: the Stalwarts, conservatives who support former President Ulysses S. Grant; and the Half-Breeds, relatively liberal, who back Senator James Gillespie Blaine of Pennsylvania. In the convention a deadlock develops, with no nominee able to garner the required number of votes. On the 36th ballot Blaine's followers throw their support to a dark horse, Congressman James Abram Garfield of Ohio. As a concession to the Stalwarts, the delegates choose Chester Alan Arthur of New York as the nominee for Vice President.

The Democratic Party convention nominates Major General Winfield Scott Hancock, a Civil War hero who is still on active duty and who is chosen largely because of his public popularity.

The 10th decennial census places the total number of inhabitants of the United States (including Alaska) at 50,189,209, an increase of 26 per cent over the tabulation of 1870. During the decade the number of states increased to 38 with the admission of Colorado. The geographical center of the United States has almost reached the Indiana-Ohio border. The census is for the first time handled by the Census Office in Washington, D.C., and the procedures of the count are markedly improved.

Jan. 27 Thomas Alva Edison is granted a patent for his incandescent electric lamp.

Feb. 4 *Hazel Kirke,* a realistic domestic drama by Steele MacKaye (in which he also appears as an actor) opens at his Madison Square Theatre in New York City, marking the beginning of a transition from the romantic era in theatrical productions.

Mar. 1 The U.S. Supreme Court rules that the practice of barring Negroes from service on juries is unconstitutional.

Mar. 24 The Salvation Army is founded in the United States when George Railton and seven women workers establish a command in Philadelphia. (First established in London in 1865, the organization was then called the Christian Mission.)

Mar. 31 Wabash, Indiana, introduces the innovation of lighting its streets by electric lamps.

June 2-8 At the national convention of the Republican Party, meeting in Chicago, it takes 36 ballots to nominate James A. Garfield, Congressman from Ohio. His running mate, Chester A. Arthur, is relatively unknown; he was removed from his only public office, as collector of the port of New York, for political reasons by President Hayes two years ago.

June 22-24 The Democratic Party, at its national convention in Cincinnati, nominates Winfield Scott Hancock, a distinguished Union general with no political experience or known views, as its candidate for the Presidency. His running mate is William H. English, of Indiana.

Nov. 2 James A. Garfield is elected President, receiving 4,453,295 popular votes and 214 electoral votes, to Winfield S. Hancock's 4,444,082 popular votes and 155 electoral votes. The Republicans gain control of the House of Representatives; in the Senate, however, power is nearly evenly divided, with two political independents holding the balance.

Nov. 8 After a successful season in London, French actress Sarah Bernhardt appears at Booth's Theatre in New York City to begin her American tour with a performance of *La Dame aux camélias,* a popular play by Alexandre Dumas *fils.*

Nov. 11 Lucretia Coffin Mott, 87, reformer and pioneer who helped to organize the first Woman's Rights Convention in 1848 in Seneca Falls, dies in Abington, near Philadelphia, Pennsylvania.

1881

Despite the Republican victory last year which elected James Abram Garfield President, the party remains divided. On the day after his inauguration, Garfield names James Gillespie Blaine, a member of the Half-Breed faction of the party, as Secretary of State, a move that widens the split between that group and the Stalwarts, the opposing faction. The Stalwarts, led by Senators Roscoe Conkling and Thomas Platt, both of New York State, succeed temporarily in blocking Garfield's appointment of William H. Robertson as collector of the Port of New York. But in May both Senators resign from the Senate in protest over the President's action. When the New York legislature fails to reelect either Senator, the power of the Stalwarts begins to decline.

The circumstances of the assassination of President Garfield—at the hands of an individual who was seeking public appointment and was frustrated by not having obtained it—contribute to the public indignation against the spoils system, and against the Stalwarts, whom some hold indirectly responsible for the President's death. The public's mood is reflected in the New York *Tribune* headline: "Killed by the spoils system?" The country is without a functioning President for 90 days, until Vice President Chester Alan Arthur takes the oath of office. Having been, during the 1870's, the collector of customs for the Port of New York, a post that carried with it extensive power to make political appointments under the spoils system, Arthur is considered by many as a Stalwart factionalist. However, he promises an Administration free from factionalism. As for his attitude toward the spoils system, in his first message to Congress Arthur calls for the removal of appointments to the Federal civil service from political party control.

Jan. 24   The U.S. Supreme Court, in the case of *Springer* v. *U.S.*, rules that an income tax imposed during the Civil War is constitutional because it is not a direct tax of the type that is prohibited by the Constitution.

Feb. 10   The Tuskegee Normal and Industrial Institute is chartered at Tuskegee, Alabama, as a vocational school for Negroes. [Booker T. Washington, becomes its principal. The institute initiates college-level classes in 1923 and changes its name to Tuskegee Institute in 1937.]

Mar. 4   James Abram Garfield is inaugurated as the 20th President of the United States.

May 21   The American Association of the Red Cross is founded through the efforts of Clara Barton, who is familiar with the work of the Red Cross in Europe. Barton is named its president [In 1893 the name is changed to the American National Red Cross Society. In 1905 the society receives a charter as a semi-official government agency.]

June 1   The play *The Professor,* written and produced by and starring the well-known actor William H. Gillette, opens in the Madison Square Theatre in New York City.

July 2   President Garfield, while waiting for a train in the Washington, D.C., railroad station, is shot by Charles J. Guiteau, a Stalwart supporter and disappointed seeker for a Federal office. [The President contracts blood poisoning from a bullet lodged against his spine, and suffers through the heat of a Washington summer, dying on Sept. 19.]

July 12   The United States, Great Britain, and Germany, all of which have commercial interests in the Samoan Islands, recognize Malietoa Laupepa as king of the islands.

July 20   The Indian leader, Sitting Bull, who has been a fugitive since the Battle of Little Bighorn, surrenders to Federal troops at Fort Buford in Dakota Territory.

Aug. 1   The University of Texas is organized at Austin. [Classes begin in 1883.]

Aug. 2   Samuel Gompers and other dissatisfied members of the Noble Order of the Knights of Labor meet at Pittsburgh and establish the Federation of Organized Trades and Labor Unions. [The latter is reorganized in 1886 as the American Federation of Labor.]

Sept. 7   Sidney Lanier, 39, the leading Southern poet, dies in Lynn, North Carolina, of tuberculosis resulting from his incarceration as a prisoner of war.

Sept. 13   Ambrose Everett Burnside, 57, Union commander at the Battles of Bull Run, Antietam, and Petersburg, dies in Bristol, Rhode Island. [His hair style of side-whiskers, called "burnsides," is the origin of the word sideburn.]

Sept. 19   President Garfield, 49, dies at his home in Elberon, New Jersey.

Sept. 20   Chester Alan Arthur is sworn in as 21st President of the United States.

Oct. 30   George Washington DeLong, 37, Arctic explorer whose ship *Jeannette* was crushed by ice on June 13 during an unsuccessful effort to traverse the Bering Strait to reach the North Pole, dies in the Siberian Arctic of starvation while trying to reach safety in a lifeboat. [His diary, *Voyage of the "Jeannette,"* is published in 1883.]

Nov. 14   The trial of Charles J. Guiteau for the assassination of President Garfield opens. [He is convicted on Jan. 25, 1882, and is executed on June 30 of that year.]

Nov. 22   Secretary of State James G. Blaine invites Latin American nations to a peace conference scheduled to convene in November 1882.

Dec. 5   The 47th Congress convenes with 37 Democrats and 37 Republicans in the Senate; there are 147 Republicans, 135 Democrats, and 11 others in the House.

Dec. 12   Blaine resigns, and is replaced by Senator Frederick T. Frelinghuysen of New Jersey. [The latter revokes Blaine's invitations to Latin American countries. However, Blaine becomes Secretary of State once more in 1889 and this time his Latin American policy is realized.]

The Garfield and Rudolph families in front of the Rudolph home in Hiram, Ohio (*ca.*) 1881

1882

An unprecedented surplus has accumulated in the Treasury of the United States. It exists because taxes and tariffs inaugurated to meet the nation's enormous need for funds during the Civil War have been imposed during the 17 years since the war. As a consequence, Government borrowing, which can be an important outlet for private investments, has been reduced, and idle resources and rising unemployment threaten the economy. In his message to Congress on Dec. 4, President Arthur states that "either the surplus must lie idle in the (Federal) Treasury or the Government will be forced to buy at market rates its bonds not then redeemable, and which under such circumstances cannot fail to command an enormous premium, or the swollen revenues will be devoted to extravagant expenditures, which, as experience has taught, is ever the bane of an overflowing treasury."

The President's fears are realized; swollen Federal funds begin to be tapped for "pork-barrel" bills, providing funds for wasteful and often useless projects. The surplus leads to increasing demands for a reduction in tariffs. The President appoints a commission to study the tariffs. Opposition to President Arthur's no-spending, tariff-reduction policies become loud and persistent, President Arthur also attempts to lessen the magnitude of the spoils system, but encounters stiff opposition from his own party. The Democrats gain control of the House of Representatives in the midterm elections.

Jan. 2 The Standard Oil Trust, founded in 1879, is reorganized to eliminate competition among the 40 companies that belong to it. The voting stock of member firms, which control nine tenths of the refining capacity of the United States, is now in the hands of nine persons.

Jan. 6 Richard Henry Dana, 67, author of *Two Years Before the Mast* and other works, dies in Rome, Italy.

Feb. 7 John L. Sullivan wins the bare-knuckle boxing championship of the world, knocking out Paddy Ryan in the 9th round of a bout in Mississippi City, Mississippi, under London Prize Ring rules.

Feb. 25 Congress passes a Reapportionment Act, enlarging the House of Representatives from 293 to 325 members.

Mar. 16 The U.S. Senate approves the provisions of the Geneva Convention of 1864, which prescribe the care of the wounded and the protection of hospitals and medical personnel in wartime.

Mar. 22 Congress passes a bill, proposed by Senator George F. Edmunds of Vermont, imposing penalties against the practice of polygamy.

Mar. 24 Henry Wadsworth Longfellow, 75, the most popular American poet of the 19th century, dies in Cambridge, Massachusetts.

Mar. 29 The Knights of Columbus, a lay Roman Catholic fraternal society, is established in New Haven, Connecticut. Its purposes are to promote benevolence, encourage religious and racial tolerance and patriotism, and to further the interests of the Roman Catholic Church.

Mar. 31 Congress votes to provide special pensions for the widows of Presidents John Tyler, James K. Polk, and James A. Garfield.

April 3 Jesse W. James, 36, head of a band of bank and railroad bandits, is killed by Robert Ford, a member of his own gang, in St. Joseph, Missouri.

April 26 President Arthur requests authority to act against the small group of terrorists called the "Cowboys" who have been harassing residents of the Territory of Arizona.

April 27 Ralph Waldo Emerson, 79, essayist, philospher, and poet, dies in Concord, Massachusetts.

May 6 A Chinese Exclusion Act, passed over President Arthur's veto, suspends for 10 years all immigration of Chinese laborers and denies citizenship to all foreign-born Chinese.

May 8 Pete J. Maguire, a New York City trade unionist, originates a proposal for a labor holiday. [The Knights of Labor celebrate with a parade in New York this year. In 1894 Congress enacts a statute declaring the first Monday in September a national holiday, Labor Day.]

May 15 A nine-man tariff commission is created by the U.S. Congress to suggest reforms in view of the accumulating surplus in the Treasury.

May 15 A team of Arctic explorers led by Lieutenant Adolphus W. Greely reaches 83° 24′ 30″ N. lat., near Ellesmere Island, Canada, less than 600 miles short of the North Pole.

May 22 The United States signs a treaty of commerce and amity with Korea and recognizes that country's independence.

Aug. 1   A rivers and harbors bill is vetoed by President Arthur on the grounds that, although it professes to meet his request for improvements of the Mississippi River and its tributaries, the bill actually includes $14,000,000 for special-interest projects favored by Congressmen from specific states. [The bill is passed over the President's veto the following day.]

Aug. 3   Congress passes an immigration act prohibiting entry to the United States of all "undesirables" such as the insane, criminals, and paupers, and establishing a head tax of 50 cents on each immigrant.

Sept. 4   The Pearl Street electric power sta-

tion, built by Thomas A. Edison, in New York City, begins operation. It is driven by steam, and serves some 60 buildings, supplying sufficient power for the use of about 400 incandescent lamps.

Nov. 6   Less than one year after her debut on the London stage, English socialite-turned-actress Lily Langtry appears in *As You Like It* at the Fifth Avenue Theatre in New York City.

Dec. 4   The tariff commission submits its report, recommending a reduction of tariffs averaging between 20 and 25 per cent. [The recommendations are rejected by Congress.]

A Thomas Nast cartoon reaffirms the durability of the Republican Party.

1883

Although a mild recession has beset the American economy, the questions of tariffs and civil service reform are the year's major topics of concern.

Political experts are surprised when the President, himself a recognized beneficiary (and supposed advocate) of machine politics and the spoils system, signs the Pendelton Act, also called the Civil Service Reform Act. The measure establishes the Civil Service Commission to set up and administer a system of competitive examinations for about 12 per cent of Federal office positions.

The controversy in Congress over tariff use and tariff reduction leads to the adoption of a revolutionary Congressional rule under which measures passed by the two Houses of Congress in different forms must be referred to a conference committee to produce a single bill acceptable to both Houses.

Jan. 16 An act introduced by Senator George H. Pendleton of Ohio is passed, establishing a civil service commission and providing for competitive examinations for some civil service jobs. [It does not abolish the spoils system but removes many jobs from its rolls.]

Feb. 16 A coal mine near Braidwood, Illinois, is flooded, costing the lives of about 70 miners.

Mar. 3 In a move to build up the strength of the U.S. Navy, which ranks 12th among the fleets of the world powers, Congress authorizes the building of three steel cruisers, the first to be constructed since the Civil War.

Mar. 4 Alexander Hamilton Stephens, 71, former Vice President of the Confederate States of America, dies in Atlanta.

Mar. 24 The first long-distance telephone service is inaugurated between New York City and Chicago.

May 17 Buffalo Bill (William F. Cody) opens his "Wild West" series of shows in Omaha, Nebraska.

May 25 President Arthur presides at ceremonies marking the opening of the Brooklyn Bridge, spanning the East River and linking the cities of Brooklyn and New York. The bridge, designed by John Roebling, has a record span of 1,595 feet; it is the first suspension bridge to use steel wire for cables and steel for the structure suspended from the cables.

Calamity Jane (Martha Jane Burke) (ca.) 1880's

June 9 At an exposition in Chicago, a 15-hp electric locomotive moves trains along a 3-foot-gauge track elevated above the ground. [This is the first elevated railway in the United States.]

Sept. 4 Peter Cooper, 92, designer of the first American steam locomotive, and founder of the Cooper Union for the Advancement of Science and Art, dies in New York City.

Sept. 8 The Northern Pacific Railroad completes its line from Ashland, Wisconsin, to Portland, Oregon, becoming the nation's second transcontinental line.

Oct. 15 The U.S. Supreme Court declares unconstitutional the Civil Rights Act of 1875, under which the rights of Negroes to equal accommodations in public facilities is guaranteed. The Court (Justice John Marshall Harlan dissenting) maintains that Congress may concern itself only with state actions, not individual actions that violate the rights of citizens.

Oct. 22 The Metropolitan Opera House, occupying an entire block between 39th and 40th streets on Broadway in New York City, opens with a performance of *Faust,* by Charles François Gounod. The "Met" replaces the Academy of Music on 14th Street as the center of operatic production in the United States. [On Sept. 16, 1966, the "Met" company is rehoused in the Lincoln Center for the Performing Arts on the west side of New York City.]

Nov. 18 Under an international agreement, designed to avoid the complications caused by differences in railroad schedules, the United States is divided into four standard time zones: Eastern, Central, Mountain, and Pacific, as measured west from Greenwich (England) mean time.

Dec. 3 The 48th Congress convenes, with 38 Republicans, 36 Democrats, and 2 others in the Senate; 197 Democrats, 118 Republicans, and 10 others in the House.

Rutherford B. Hayes
NINETEENTH PRESIDENT   1877-1881

James A. Garfield
TWENTIETH PRESIDENT   1881

Chester A. Arthur
TWENTY-FIRST PRESIDENT   1881-1885

Grover Cleveland
TWENTY-SECOND PRESIDENT 1885-1889
TWENTY-FOURTH PRESIDENT 1893-1897

1884

The Presidential campaign of 1884 is waged on the basis of personalities rather than on political issues. Slurs, slander, and scandal make the campaign politically one of the dirtiest in the history of the United States. During the campaign the satirical cartoon comes into wide use and has significant influence. President Arthur lacks the support needed to be nominated for a full term by the Republican Party, which chooses James Gillespie Blaine. (Nomination was denied to Blaine in 1876 and 1880 because it was revealed that he had used his influence as a Congressman to do favors for certain business firms.) Blaine's candidacy causes a group of dissident delegates to bolt the convention. Termed by the New York *Sun* "Mugwumps," they adopt the nickname and hold their own convention, pledging their support for the Democratic candidate if he is of a liberal character.

The Democratic Party nominates Governor Grover Cleveland of New York, who has built a formidable reputation as a reformer and antimachine politician. On July 21, however, Cleveland's candidacy is rocked by the revelation that he is the father of an illegitimate child—a fact that Cleveland freely admits. Blaine, on the other hand, loses Roman Catholic support when he fails to repudiate a remark by Protestant clergyman Samuel Dickinson Burchard, who calls the Democrats "the party whose antecedents are rum, Romanism, and rebellion."

Jan. 1   Mark Twain's *The Adventures of Huckleberry Finn* is published.

Jan. 18   The steamer *City of Columbus* is wrecked off Gay Head Light, Massachusetts, with a loss of 103 lives.

Feb. 2   Wendell Phillips, 73, abolitionist leader and notable orator, dies in Boston.

Mar. 6   Susan B. Anthony and about 100 demonstrators from a suffragist convention call on President Arthur at the White House and urge him to include in his next inaugural address a recommendation for woman suffrage.

Mar. 13   A coal mine disaster in Pocahontas, Virginia, takes 112 lives.

Mar. 21   George Fuller, 62, an artist widely known for his haunting, introspective paintings of figures, dies in Brookline, Massachusetts.

May 17   The U.S. Congress changes Alaska from an unorganized territory to the organized District of Alaska, subject to the laws of the state of Oregon, administered by an appointed governor. [Alaska is divided into judicial districts in 1900, is given nonvoting representation in Congress in 1906, and becomes an organized territory with an elected legislature in 1912.]

June 3-6   The Republican Party national convention, meeting in Chicago, chooses James G. Blaine as its Presidential candidate, with John A. Logan as his running mate.

June 22   A rescue expedition commanded by Captain Winfield Scott Schley locates survivors of the heroic A.W. Greely Arctic expedition. Only 7 men, including Lieutenant Greely, are left alive from 26 who started out in 1881.

June 27   The Bureau of Labor Statistics is established as part of the Department of the Interior, to collect statistics on labor in the United States. [The bureau becomes part of the Department of Labor in 1913.]

July 8-11   The Democratic convention meets in Chicago and nominates Grover Cleveland as its Presidential candidate. The Vice-Presidential nominee is Thomas B. Hendricks, a former U.S. Senator from Indiana, who was Samuel Tilden's running mate in 1876.

Aug. 5   The cornerstone of the pedestal for the Statue of Liberty is laid on Bedloe's Island in New York Harbor.

Oct. 6   The Naval War College is founded at Newport, Rhode Island.

Nov. 4   Grover Cleveland is elected President, the first Democratic President in nearly 25 years. The popular vote is very close: 4,879,507 for Cleveland to 4,850,293 for Blaine. In the electoral college Cleveland receives 219 votes and Blaine receives 182 votes.

Nov. 8   McClure's Syndicate, the first press syndicate, is founded by Samuel Sidney McClure.

The "Great Flood" of 1884 at Lawrenceburg, Indiana

1885

Grover Cleveland, the first Democratic President in a quarter of a century, takes office with a Democratic House of Representatives but a Senate controlled by the Republican Party. He also finds a Treasury surplus of nearly $500,000,000, and agriculture in a slump. Cleveland's businesslike solutions and independence of action begin to make enemies for him from the beginning of his term. In addition, despite the passage of the Civil Service Reform Act in 1883, the President still has the responsibility for appointing 88 per cent of all Federal employees. The years of Republican ascendancy have entrenched hundreds of high-level Federal officials. Cleveland begins by replacing thousands of postmasters and all but a few revenue collectors. His own supporters accuse him of violating the Tenure of Office Act, under which the President may not remove officials without consent of the Senate. He makes many other enemies by vetoing hundreds of private pension bills, by trying to stop the free coinage of silver, and finally be being rude to the press because of their interest in the President's private life.

Cleveland's extensive personnel changes dismay the "Mugwumps" and others who bolted their own parties to vote for the President. Indicative of his predicament is the comment made by the noted reformist, Carl Schurz, with whom Cleveland split during the year: "Your attempt to please both reformers and spoilsmen has failed. I warned you more than once that your principal danger was to sit down between two chairs. . . .".

When the newly elected House of Representatives convenes in December, it authorizes the appointment of a five-man bipartisan committee on rules to prepare an outline of action for the 49th Congress. The House adopts the majority report of the committee, which advises that the jurisdiction of the House Appropriations Committee be limited.

Jan 13   Schuyler Colfax, 62, Vice President of the United States during the first term of President Ulysses S. Grant, dies in Mankato, Minnesota.

Feb. 11   President Cleveland vetoes a bill "for the relief of dependent parents and honorably discharged soldiers and sailors who are now disabled and dependent upon their own labor for support." The President notes that, despite his support for generous provision for veterans, the bill puts "a further premium on dishonesty and mendacity." [An effort to pass the measure over the President's veto fails on Feb. 24.]

Feb. 21   The Washington Monument is dedicated, 26 years after the laying of its cornerstone.

Feb. 25   Congress passes an act forbidding unauthorized fencing of public lands in the West. [On Aug. 17 President Cleveland reinforces the measure by ordering the removal of illegal enclosures.]

Feb. 26   Congress passes the Contract Labor Act, forbidding immigration of laborers who have agreed to work for the cost of their passage.

Mar. 3   Congress passes a measure providing for the establishment of a Board of Fortifications and Coast Defenses to investigate the defensive position of the United States.

Mar. 3   The U.S. Post Office inaugurates special delivery service for first-class mail.

Mar. 3   Congress passes a bill creating the rank of General of the Army.

Mar. 4   Grover Cleveland is inaugurated as the 22d President of the United States.

Mar. 18   Bryn Mawr College, chartered in 1880, is opened at Bryn Mawr, near Philadelphia.

April 3   Land Commissioner William A.J. Sparks suspends official entry of all titles to land that are under suspicion of being fraudulent, thus making available to bona fide settlers some 2,750,000 acres of Western land that are currently controlled by speculators.

June 19   The Statue of Liberty, a gift of the French people, arrives in New York City. The pedestal where the statue will stand is under construction on Bedloe's Island, New York Harbor.

July 1   The United States notifies Canada that its agreements on fishing rights contained in the Treaty of Washington of 1871 are now terminated, thus renewing a longstanding dispute. Canada immediately declares that American fishing vessels trespassing in Canadian waters will be seized after this date.

July 23   Ulysses S. Grant, 63, 18th President of the United States, dies in Saratoga, New York. [His remains are later interred in a magnificent mausoleum, Grant's Tomb, in New York City, dedicated by President McKinley in 1897.]

Aug. 10   The first electric street railway in the United States, a 3-mile line in Baltimore, is opened by Leo Daft, owner of an electric power company. The power reaches the car through a pole that is in contact with overhead wires; the current is collected by a moving carriage or trolley attached to the end of the pole.

Oct. 14   Josh Billings (pseudonym of H.W. Shaw), 67, "cracker-barrel" humorist, dies in Monterey, California.

Oct. 29   George B. McClellan, 59, Union general in the Civil War, dies in Orange, New Jersey.

Nov. 25   Vice President Thomas A. Hendricks, 66, dies in Indianapolis, after serving less than one year in office.

Dec. 7   The 49th Congress convenes, with 43 Republicans and 34 Democrats in the Senate; there are 183 Democrats, 140 Republicans, and 2 others in the House.

Dec. 8   President Cleveland, in his annual message to Congress, calls for suspension of mandatory coinage of silver dollars, asserting that the continued coinage of silver will result in its replacement for all the gold owned by the Government. In the same message, the President calls for the establishment of a commission to meet with a counterpart British commission on the question of fishery rights off the coast of North America. [The Senate rejects the proposal in 1886, but Cleveland reaches agreements with Great Britain to handle the matter unofficially.]

Dec. 18   The House of Representatives adopts the majority report of a committe recommending that the jurisdiction of the Appropriations Committee be curtailed; a minority report contends that such an action would weaken the control over appropriations and impede the proper management of Treasury funds.

U.S. Senators in action. Sketched in the Senate by E. W. Kemble, (*ca.*) 1886.

227

1886 The conflict between the President and the Senate over application of the Tenure of Office Act of 1867, raised in the closing months of 1885, comes to a climax in 1886. The Senate challenges the President's authority to remove anyone from office who has been appointed with the approval of the Senate. The Senate uses as a test case the removal of a minor official in Alabama. Attorney General Augustus H. Garland is directed by the Senate to forward all papers concerning that office. Garland, acting under orders from the President, refuses, and the Republican majority then recommends to the Senate resolutions censuring the Attorney General. The President sends the Senate a special message in which he insists that he alone has the power to remove officials or to suspend them from office. Cleveland also refuses to concede the right of the Senate to inquire into his motives or his actions. The President questions the constitutionality of the Tenure of Office Act—the statute used to impeach President Johnson in 1867—and the Judiciary Committee reports out a bill calling for its repeal. By winning on this issue, the President strengthens the power of the Executive Branch of the Federal Government.

The question of special pension bills continues to plague President Cleveland, who remarks that in a single day nearly 240 such bills have been presented to him for signature.

The Haymarket Riot, occurring in May, results in a major setback for labor. Fear and anger over the events in Chicago, which are widely attributed to "anarchists," sweep through the country.

Midterm elections reflect a growing popular dissatisfaction with the Cleveland Administration. The Republicans gain 12 seats in the House.

Jan. 18 Congress passes the Presidential Succession Law, providing that "in case of removal, death, resignation, or inability of both the President and Vice President," the Secretary of State succeeds to the high office, followed by other members of the Cabinet in order of seniority. The fact that there is no Vice President (because of the death of Hendricks last November), together with the experience of President Garfield's long period of disability after he was shot, thus brings about the first action to implement the provisions in the Second Article of the Constitution.

Feb. 15 Representative William R. Morrison of Illinois introduces in the House a tariff bill calling for a reduction in duty rates. [The measure, after discussion and amendment in the Ways and Means Committee, is defeated.]

April 13 Senator Orville H. Platt of Connecticut proposes to the Senate that the rule of secrecy in executive sessions is not sanctioned in the Constitution or by the practice of the Founding Fathers. [The bill is opposed by both major political parties, and on Dec. 15 the matter is tabled in order to avoid any party responsibility for such action.]

April 22 President Cleveland breaks precedent by sending Congress a special message advocating establishment of a labor commission to settle labor disputes.

May 1-4 Some 340,000 union members stage a nationwide work stoppage in support of a campaign to obtain the eight-hour day. At one of the strike locations, the McCormick reaper plant in Chicago, a group of pickets is fired upon by police on May 3, resulting in the death of one picket and injuries to many others. On the evening of May 4 union members (including socialists and anarchists) stage a mass meeting to protest the shootings under the eyes of nearly 200 policemen, who move in to disperse the crowd as the meeting is about to break up. Suddenly a bomb is thrown, killing seven policemen and injuring many others. Police and rioters then begin shooting. About 10 civilians are killed and nearly 50 wounded. [Eight anarchists are arrested as accessories to the crime, tried, and found guilty; seven are sentenced to death and one to imprisonment. On Nov. 17, 1887, four of the seven are hanged. It is never discovered who threw the bomb.]

May 10 The U.S. Supreme Court, in *Santa Clara County* v. *Southern Pacific Railroad,* rules that the 14th Amendment to the Constitution applies to corporations as well as to individuals, thus protecting corporations from discriminatory taxation by the states.

May 15 Emily Dickinson, 56, prolific and original poet, dies in Amherst, Massachusetts. [Her works, first published after 1890, are unknown to most contemporaries.]

June 3 President Cleveland marries Frances Folsom, 24-year-old daughter of his former law partner.

June 7 Richard March Hoe, 74, inventor of the rotary and the web-fed printing presses, dies in Florence, Italy.

June 30 James Gibbons of Baltimore becomes the second American cardinal of the Roman Catholic Church.

July 1 The U.S. Supreme Court rules, in *Wabash, St. Louis & Pacific Railroad* v. *Illinois,* that a state law controlling railroad rates is unconstitutional on the grounds that it infringes on the Federal Government's exclusive right to control interstate commerce.

July 10 Henry Kirke Brown, 72, sculptor known for his equestrian statues, notably that of George Washington in Union Square, New York City, dies in Newburgh, New York.

Aug. 4 Samuel Jones Tilden, 72, Democratic Presidential candidate in the election of 1876, dies near Yonkers, New York.

Sept. 4 Geronimo, Apache Indian leader, surrenders to U.S. General Nelson A. Miles in Arizona, after years of raiding white settlements.

Sept. 17 Asher Brown Durand, 90, painter and engraver, a founder of the Hudson River school of painting and of the National Academy of Design, dies in South Orange, New Jersey.

Oct. 28 The Statue of Liberty, the work of Frédéric Auguste Bartholdi and a gift of the French people to the United States, is dedicated by President Cleveland.

Nov. 18 Chester Alan Arthur, 56, 21st President of the United States, dies in New York City.

Nov. 21 Charles Francis Adams, 79, diplomat and editor, grandson of John Adams and son of John Quincy Adams, dies in Boston.

Dec. 7-8 The American Federation of Labor is founded by the Federation of Organized Trades and Labor Unions and several unaffiliated unions; Samuel Gompers, president of the founding federation and of the International Union of Cigarmakers, is elected president of the new organization.

Dec. 26 John Alexander Logan, 60, Union general in the Civil War, founder of the Grand Army of the Republic, and U.S. Senator from Illinois, dies in Washington, D.C.

Geronimo (center) and his braves shortly before surrendering

1887

The tariffs, the question of minting silver coins, and administrative reform issues all remain as perennial and tough problems to plague President Cleveland. Disillusionment with Cleveland's Administration grows rapidly as the President continues doggedly to exercise his veto powers and to act independently of those who supported his election. On the sensitive major issue of civil service reform, for example, a special committee of the National Civil Service Reform League asserts that, "tried by the standard of absolute fidelity to the reform as it is understood by this League, it is not to be denied that this Administration has left much to be desired."

In December the President's annual message is devoted to tariff reform. With a surplus in the Treasury of more than $100,000,000, Cleveland considers the existing tariff schedules illogical. He makes low tariff a basic demand. This is challenged immediately by the Republicans, led by James G. Blaine. Cleveland's stand on tariffs provides the Republican Party with its main election issue for the next Presidential campaign.

Jan. 20 The U.S.-Hawaiian Treaty for reciprocal trade is renewed with a modification that permits the United States to build a naval base at Pearl Harbor.

Feb. 2 Congress passes the Electoral Count Act, under which each state is made responsible for enumerating its electoral returns and Congress is deprived of any power over the electoral vote unless a state is unable to decide the matter or unless a fraud is committed.

Feb. 4 The Interstate Commerce Act is passed by Congress. It is the first important Federal law regulating big business. An antimonopoly measure, it declares that railroads must make reasonable and just charges, that pooling and rebates are illegal, and it regulates charges for long- and short-haul runs. The act also creates the Interstate Commerce Commission, with power to inquire into the management of the carriers, summon witnesses, and invoke the aid of the Federal courts.

Feb. 8 The Dawes Severalty Act is passed by Congress, empowering the President to terminate Indian tribal government and communal ownership and to divide Indian lands at the rate of one-quarter section (160 acres) for each head of a family.

Feb. 11 President Cleveland vetoes the Dependent Pension bill, the first general bill passed by Congress since the Civil War that would permit pensions to servicemen for non-service-related disabilities.

Mar. 3 Congress passes the Hatch Act, which provides for subsidies to states for the establishment and support of agricultural experiment stations, for educational extension programs for farmers, and for agricultural research.

Mar. 3 Congress passes an act giving the Government power to seize and administer the property of the Mormon Church. [The property seized under the act is not returned until 1896, when the church renounces the practice of polygamy.]

Mar. 8 James Buchanan Eads, 67, engineer known for his work in improving the channel of the Mississippi River and for building the steel-arch bridge across the river at St. Louis, dies in Nassau, Bahamas.

Mar. 8 Henry Ward Beecher, 74, clergyman, orator, and advocate of abolition and women's rights, dies in Brooklyn, New York.

June 7 President Cleveland signs a routine order authorizing the return to the Southern states of captured Confederate flags. [On June 15, as a result of protests by Union army veterans and Republican politicians, the order is canceled.]

Aug. 1 President Cleveland refuses to sign a rivers and harbors act that he considers extravagant. This "pocket veto" kills the bill.

Nov. 19 Emma Lazarus, 38, the poet whose sonnet, "The New Colossus," is inscribed on the base of the Statue of Liberty in New York Harbor, dies in New York City.

Dec. 5 The 50th Congress convenes, with 39 Republicans and 37 Democrats in the Senate, and 169 Democrats, 152 Republicans, and 4 others in the House.

Dec. 6 President Cleveland devotes his entire annual message to Congress to the implications of the huge Treasury surplus and the need for reduction of tariffs.

Railroad workers stand in front of a Union Pacific work train in Denver.

230

1888

The stage was set for the Presidential election campaign this year by President Cleveland's annual message to Congress last December. The odds against Cleveland are suggested in the fate of the tariff bill proposed by Democratic Representative Roger Mills. Providing for lower rates for manufactured goods, the bill is passed by the lower House but fails in the Republican Senate. The protectionists who are hostile to Cleveland are a powerful bloc; other blocs are alienated from the President for other reasons. Many of his past official acts have angered large numbers of former supporters. These acts include his 1887 veto of a big pension bill for veterans, a suggestion to governors that the Confederate flags should be returned to the Southern states, and his opposition to turning over surplus funds to the states, as advocated by many leading Republicans.

The Democratic Party renominates President Cleveland as its candidate. The Republicans nominate Senator Benjamin Harrison of Indiana, grandson of a former President and a Civil War general. The Republican cause, stressing the principle of high protective tariffs, receives lavish support from major industries and manufacturers. But if this is not enough, the style of the times offers other modes of attack. Late in the campaign the Republicans publish a false letter from an ostensibly confused naturalized citizen to the British Minister, Sir Lionel Sackville-West, asking for advice on how to vote. The Minister's innocent reply favors Cleveland. The public uproar over foreign "intervention" in American politics loses many votes for the Democrats, and costs Sackville-West his job. In the election Cleveland wins a popular plurality of 5,540,050 votes to 5,444,327 for Harrison; the latter, however, carries 233 electoral votes to 168 for Cleveland. The Republicans gain control of both Houses of Congress.

Jan. 30 Asa Gray, 78, one of the world's leading botanic scientists, dies in Cambridge, Massachusetts. [Gray's *Manual of Botany* remains a standard text in the 20th century.]

Feb. 15 U.S. Secretary of State Thomas F. Bayard and the British representative, Joseph Chamberlain, sign a treaty designed to end the long-standing conflict over American and Canadian fishing rights in the North Atlantic Ocean.

Mar. 11-14 A major snowstorm [the "blizzard of '88"] strikes the eastern United States, killing 400 persons. New York and other cities are cut off by a disruption of transportation and communications.

Mar. 16 Louisa May Alcott, 56, author of *Little Women* and other juvenile classics, dies in Concord, Massachusetts.

Mar. 23 Chief Justice Morrison Remick Waite of the U.S. Supreme Court, 71, dies in Washington.

April 18 Roscoe Conkling, 59, New York State Republican leader, U.S. Senator, and opponent of civil service reform, dies in New York City.

May 15 Belva Ann Lockwood, woman attorney, and first woman to argue a case before the U.S. Supreme Court, becomes the first woman to run for President when she is nominated by the Equal Rights Party at its national convention in Des Moines, Iowa.

June 5-7 The Democratic Party national convention meets in St. Louis and nominates President Cleveland for reelection. Allen G. Thurman is chosen to be his running mate.

June 13 Congress passes an act transforming the National Bureau of Labor (created in 1884 in the Department of the Interior) into the independent Department of Labor, but without Cabinet rank [achieved in 1913].

June 19-25 The Republican Party national convention meets in Chicago. Senator Benjamin Harrison is named the Presidential candidate on the eighth ballot. The Vice-Presidential nominee is Levi P. Morton, a New York Congressman.

Aug. 21 The Republican-dominated Senate rejects the fishing rights treaty of Feb. 15, but the practical terms of the document enable the U.S. and Canadian fishing industries to maintain amicable operations.

Oct. 1 Congress passes a bill providing for voluntary arbitration in railroad-labor conflicts and empowers the President to name an investigatory commission with power to act as a board of conciliation.

Nov. 6 Benjamin Harrison and Levi P. Morton win in the National elections, defeating Cleveland and his running mate, Allen G. Thurman.

1889

With the inauguration of Benjamin Harrison the Republican Party is in control of all branches of the Federal Government. However, its majorities in the 51st Congress are narrow enough to enable the Democrats, particularly in the House of Representatives, to engage in obstructive tactics. It is partly because of these tactics that Harrison's term begins to be called "The Period of No Decisions." The President and leaders of both political parties become deeply committed to business interests, finances, and the spending of huge amounts of the public's money. But agrarian unrest and labor protests seem to evade the notice of the Administration.

While Congress is becoming known as the "Billion Dollar Congress," farm and labor organizations are sprouting up and growing powerful everywhere in the nation. In the Middle West and South a huge farmers' alliance group is formed by the end of 1888. An attempt at unification of the two largest farmer-labor groups, at a conference in St. Louis, in 1889, almost succeeds. Despite its failure, a new and large social protest movement, supported by farmers' alliances, the National Grange, and the Knights of Labor, is reaching out for political power, especially in the South and Middle West. These agrarian and labor groups are attracting huge and enthusiastic crowds. Political meetings among them begin to take on the feel of revival meetings. By the end of 1889 a tidal wave of unrest is unleashed and is preparing to make itself felt in the coming midterm elections.

Feb. 9   The Department of Agriculture, created by Congress in 1862, is raised to Cabinet rank. President Cleveland appoints the incumbent Commissioner of Agriculture, Norman J. Colman, as the first Secretary of Agriculture.

Mar. 2   Kansas passes the first antitrust law to be enacted by a state. [During the year North Carolina, Tennessee, and Michigan adopt similar legislation.]

Mar. 4   Benjamin Harrison is inaugurated as the 23d President of the United States.

Mar. 8   John Ericsson, 86, Swedish-born American naval engineer, designer of the *Monitor,* the first armored turret ship, dies in New York City.

April 22-23   A central tract within the western part of Indian Territory [the future Oklahoma Territory] is opened to white settlement by proclamation of President Benjamin Harrison, after pressure by homesteaders to be permitted to buy Indian lands. Within the two days thousands of settlers arrive, and Guthrie and Oklahoma City are laid out as tent cities.

April 29-June 14   The United States, Great Britain, and Germany hold a conference in Berlin on the future of the Samoan Islands. The three powers sign a treaty recognizing Malietoa as king and providing for joint supervision and administration of the islands.

May 31   The city of Johnstown, Pennsylvania, the leading steel-making center in the United States, is virtually destroyed by flood following the failure of the South Fork Dam on the Conemaugh River, about 10 miles east of the city, after a storm. Johnstown is inundated by some 30 feet of water; the death toll is estimated at more than 2,000 and property damage at about $10,000,000.

July 23   John L. Sullivan defeats Jake Kilrain in a 75-round bare-knuckle fight at Richburg, Mississippi, for a stake of $20,000 and the title of World Champion. [This is the last professional heavyweight match in the United States under the London rules (bare-knuckle.)]

Sept. 9   The play *Shenandoah* by Bronson Crocker Howard, treating the theme of conflicting loyalties to the Union and the Confederacy during the Civil War, opens in New York City. [It is the first successful production of Charles Frohman.]

Football teams in action: Cornell v. Rochester, Oct. 19, 1889

Oct. 2   At the invitation of the United States, delegates from all Latin American nations except the Dominican Republic convene in Washington. The conference, officially called the first International Conference of American States, is presided over by Secretary of State James G. Blaine. [The conference remains in session until April 19, 1890.]

Nov. 2   After frequent petitions to Congress for the admission of Dakota Territory as a single state or as two separate states, the Territory is admitted to the Union as two states, North Dakota (the 39th state) and South Dakota (the 40th state). The capitals are respectively Bismarck and Pierre.

Nov. 8   Five years after application to Congress for admission, the Territory of Montana is admitted as the 41st state of the Union. Helena, which replaced Virginia City as territorial capital in 1875, is the state capital.

Nov. 11   The Territory of Washington is admitted as the 42d state of the Union. The territorial capital, Olympia, becomes the state capital.

Nov. 14   Nellie Bly, a reporter for the New York *World,* sets out to better the fictional feat of Phileas Fogg in Jules Verne's *Around the World in Eighty Days.* [Traveling by train and ship, she completes her globe-circling journey on Jan 25, 1890, in 72 days 6 hours 11 minutes.]

December   A meeting of farm and labor organizations in St. Louis offers a platform of proposals for its members that include free coinage of silver; the abolition of national banks; ownership of railroads and the telegraph system by the Federal Government; the use of the tariff only to provide necessary revenues; and the restriction of land ownership to American citizens. The organizations represented include the two major farm organizations, the Southern Alliance and the Northwestern Alliance, and the Knights of Labor. [This meeting is interpreted by some as a precursor of the Populist movement of the 1890's.]

Dec. 2   The 51st Congress convenes, with 39 Republicans and 37 Democrats in the Senate, and 166 Republicans and 159 Democrats in the House. It is the first Congress since the 43d (1873-1875) that is entirely controlled by the Republicans.

Dec. 6   Jefferson Davis, 81, President of the Confederate States of America during the Civil War, dies in New Orleans.

The Sullivan-Kilrain fight, 1889

1890 This is a watershed year. According to the director of the Census Bureau, the United States no longer has a settlement frontier; settled areas extend throughout almost the entire nation. The population as recorded in the 11th decennial census, 62,979,766, is double that at the beginning of the Civil War; each decade has seen a rate of increase of about 26 per cent. An extraordinary portion of the increase in the last decade has been from abroad—more than 5,000,000 out of the 12,800,000 added population are immigrants. More than one third of the population live in urban areas, compared with less than one fifth 30 years ago. The new states are being formed from the north-central and northwestern territories: Montana, the Dakotas, and Washington in 1889; this year, the mountain states of Wyoming and Idaho.

The West is won, vast areas are under cultivation and vast amounts of produce, especially wheat, are being harvested, but the American farmer finds little satisfaction as prices continue to fall and tenantry increases. Interest rates are prohibitive, but the farmers must borrow because they cannot afford to pay the prices charged for storing or marketing their crops or for the goods they need to keep alive and produce. They have suffered through years of drought. Their enemies are the railroads, the bankers, the Government. They seek an end to a tariff that protects—and so raises the prices of—manufactures; they want a currency they can live with, unlimited coins and paper. They have formed organizations which this year, for the first time, show political strength. Farmer-backed candidates in the West and in the South defeat old-line Democratic and Republican office-holders—in Kansas, where the People's Party takes control, in South Carolina and Georgia, where farm-backed Democrats are victorious. Congressmen and U.S. Senators owe their seats to organized farmers. Among the newly elected Congressmen are 30-year-old William Jennings Bryan in normally Republican Nebraska and 34-year-old Tom Watson in Georgia.

The major legislation this year is passed before the elections and the convention in Florida reveals the popular temper. It is ambivalent in its effect. The McKinley Tariff is thoroughly protectionist and the highest yet enacted, but it includes protection for certain farm products as well as for manufactures. (Inasmuch as few farm products are in need of protection, farmers are not impressed.) The antitrust act is normally against the monopolies, but its principal author—not Senator John Sherman, but Senator George Edmunds, chairman of the Judiciary Committee—knows that the unions, in their capacity to "restrain" trade, are the targets. The Silver Purchase Act is clearly a friendly gesture to mineowners and to "cheap money" advocates alike.

May 2   Oklahoma Territory is formed out of the western half of the unorganized Indian Territory. The new territory includes primarily that area not reserved to the Five Civilized Tribes (Cherokee, Creek, Seminole, Chickasaw, and Choctaw) plus a strip of public land west of the 100th meridian between 36°30′ and 37° N. lat. acquired from Texas in 1850 [the Oklahoma Panhandle]. Lands reserved to other Indian tribes are within the territory. [Not all the land within the territory, however, is immediately open to settlement by non-Indians. Runs such as that of April 22, 1889, are repeated until 1893, when the greatest occurs in the Cherokee Strip adjoining Kansas, east of the Panhandle.] Guthrie, founded in the run of 1889, is the territorial capital.

May 19   William Clyde Fitch produces his *Beau Brummell,* specially for the actor Richard Mansfield. [Like many of the 35 other Fitch social dramas, it is successful enough to become popular in both America and Europe.]

June 9   Composer and music critic Reginald deKoven produces one of his most successful works, the comic operetta *Robin Hood,* which contains the song "Oh Promise Me." It is produced in Chicago by a drama troupe called "The Bostonians."

June 27   Congress passes a Dependent Pension Act, providing funds to all poor or disabled veterans of the Civil War.

July 2   A Force Bill designed to obtain Federal supervision over the electoral process in order to protect the voting rights of minorities, especially Negroes, is passed by the House of Representatives. [It fails in the Senate, indicating that Congress is no longer primarily concerned with Reconstruction. This message is understood in the South, leading to a period of deliberate and open violation of the civil rights of Negroes, not only by terrorist groups but particularly by state governments.]

July 2 The Sherman Antitrust Act is passed, empowering the Federal Government to prosecute any corporation or person entering into contracts of restraint of interstate trade or commerce with foreign nations. [The act does not include a section proposed by Senator Sherman, exempting labor and farm organizations from prosecution under it. During its first years of enforcement, the unions are the principal defendants under the Sherman Act, and its use against monopolies or trusts is rare; the first notable instance of its use as an antitrust law against an industrial monopoly is in 1911, resulting in the U.S. Supreme Court decision of *Standard Oil Company* v. *United States*. The deficiencies of the Sherman Act as an antitrust vehicle results in the passage of the Clayton Act in 1914.]

July 3 Idaho is admitted to the Union as the 43d state. Boise, becomes the state capital.

July 10 Wyoming is admitted to the Union as the 44th state. Cheyenne, the capital of Wyoming Territory, remains as the state capital. This is the first state to grant the vote to women in its constitution.

July 14 Congress passes the Sherman Silver Purchase Act, requiring the Federal Government to purchase an amount of silver equal to the estimated total U.S. production, and providing for an increase by about 125 per cent in the amount of silver to be used to make coins.

Nov. 1 Mississippi includes in its constitution a clause making the right to vote dependent upon a voter's ability to understand certain parts of the state constitution. [Such "understanding" clauses, designed to disfranchise minority group voters, are adopted by many other states.]

Nov. 4 In the Congressional elections the Democrats win a landslide victory and gain control of the House of Representatives. The Republican defeat is considered to be a reaction against the high tariff recently passed.

Nov. 17-Dec. 29 Indian agents appointed by the Democratic Administration, unfamiliar with their responsibilities, learn of a wave of religious ceremonies, centered around a so-called Ghost Dance, that is activating the Plains Indians. Misinterpreting this religious revival as insurrection, they send troops to the Pine Ridge Agency in South Dakota, and the frightened Sioux are driven into the Badlands. On Dec. 15, at the Standing Rock Agency, a group of Sioux in government service, instructed to make some arrests, shoot Chief Sitting Bull, a prisoner at the agency, and a fight breaks out costing 12 Sioux lives, including that of Sitting Bull. In the hysteria that follows, other clashes occur, the most serious of which is on Wounded Knee Creek, northeast of Pine Ridge, where a convoy of 356 Sioux, who had surrendered to the troops, are attacked in their encampment, resulting in the slaughter of at least 200 Sioux (including women and children) and 60 U.S. cavalrymen. [Savage fighting continues for weeks; by Jan. 16, 1891, the Ghost Dance War is over. This is the last major Indian "outbreak."]

Nov. 29 The first Army-Navy football game is played, at West Point, New York. The score is Navy 24, Army 0.

Dec. 1 The Supreme Council of the Southern Alliance, a farm organization claiming 3,000,000 members, meets at Ocala, Florida. Its delegates are aware of victories in a number of states: the governor, most of the state legislators, and 60 per cent of the Congressmen from Georgia owe their seats to the Alliance; almost identical is the situation in South Carolina; and some 25 Democratic Congressmen in five other Southern states support the program of the Alliance. Its essential features are "cheap money," long-term credits from the Government, government control of the railroads and telegraph systems, an end to protective tariffs. Overtures from Knights of Labor members to form a political party are not accepted.

A tightrope walker crosses Niagara (*ca.*) 1890.

1891 **The word "Populist" is coined by a western Democrat** as a label for the political movement that already has seated nine independent Congressmen and two Senators in the 52d Congress. Farmers and workers in the West and South now begin to build a third national political party, based on the support of the various Farmers' Alliance and labor groups. The Populist Party takes shape at a convention of 1,400 delegates, called the National Union Conference, held in Cincinnati in May. [At first the party includes millions of Negro farmers and workers, but Tom Watson, a Southern leader, turns against the Negroes and reads them out of the movement. He is the most popular of a large number of politicians who begin to exploit the discontent of farmers in order to seize control of state governments in the South. Their success in accomplishing this is also based on their policy of removing blacks from political and social life—the whole system of "Jim Crow." From the beginning, the Southern Populist movement excludes the Negro and encourages racial hatred.] The national Populist planks are for the most part familiar: unlimited coinage of silver, government ownership of railroads, telegraphs, and telephones, a Federal parcel post system, a graduated income tax, an eight-hour day, the popular election of U.S. Senators, the secret ballot, and a law of initiative and referendum. [Many of these reforms are later taken up by the major parties and enacted into law.]

Jan. 31 An Indian agent friendly to the Sioux people takes over the agency on the Pine Ridge Reservation, South Dakota.

Mar. 3 Congress passes the Forest Reserve Act, permitting the President to close public forest lands so as to form national forests. [President Harrison immediately creates 13 national forest preserves comprising 21,000,000 acres. These become national forests in 1907.]

Mar. 3 Intermediate appellate courts, known as courts of appeal, are created to relieve the United States Supreme Court of considering all appeals that come to trial. The system is made up of 11 districts, each of which contains from 3 to 15 circuit judgeships [eventually totaling 97 judges].

Mar. 4 The International Copyright Act is passed, protecting British, French, Swiss, and Belgian authors who are published in the United States, and American authors who are published in those countries.

Mar. 14 Eleven Sicilian immigrants are lynched by a mob who storm a New Orleans jail. The incident generates an Italian-American diplomatic crisis, since three of the immigrants are Italian nationals. The lynching arises out of the murder last October of the New Orleans police chief who, at the time of his murder, was investigating Italian immigrant secret societies suspected of involvement in organized crime.

April 4 Edwin Booth makes his final appearance as an actor, performing in *Hamlet* at the Brooklyn Academy of Music.

April 7 Phineas Taylor Barnum, 81, showman and impresario, dies in Philadelphia. [He leaves $8,000,000 and a circus that becomes part of the Ringling Brothers circus in 1907.]

May 5 The Music Hall opens in New York City on 57th Street, with concerts conducted by the celebrated Russian composer, Peter Ilich Tchaikovsky. [The concert hall was financed mainly by steel magnate Andrew Carnegie, and is named in his honor Carnegie Hall in 1898.]

May 18 A convention in Cincinnati, dominated by the Northwestern Alliance, votes to found "what should be known as the People's Party of the United States of America."

July 31 Thomas Alva Edison applies for a patent on a moving-picture camera.

Nov. 9 The play *A Trip to Chinatown,* by Charles H. Hoyt, closes after establishing a record consecutive run of 650 performances. [The record stands until 1918.]

December James Naismith, a Canadian instructor at the School for Christian Workers at Springfield, Massachusetts [after 1910 called the International Young Men's Christian Association Training School, and after 1940 Springfield College], invents the game of basketball to involve his physical education students in "clean living through sports" during the winter.

Dec. 7 The 52d Congress convenes with 47 Republicans, 39 Democrats, and 2 independents in the Senate; and with 235 Democrats, 88 Republicans, and 9 independents in the House. Many of the Democrats and all the independents are sympathetic to the rising "people's" movement.

1892

Grover Cleveland is again chosen as the Presidential candidate of the Democratic Party to run against the incumbent Republican, Benjamin Harrison. Cleveland's principal supporters are those who favor a gold standard and who strongly oppose both the free coinage of silver and the issuing of any more paper money. The People's Party arouses enthusiasm for its reformist platform, and wins 8.5 per cent of the popular vote and 22 electoral votes; this is the first time since the Civil War that a third party is a contender in the Electoral College.

The great strike at the Homestead steel workers in Pennsylvania has a marked effect on the outcome of the election, principally because of the mill owners' campaign to destroy the striking union. Workers all across the country are angered at the success of Andrew Carnegie and his chief executive, Henry Clay Frick, in breaking the strike and at their refusal to recognize any union. Workers are left to express their anger at the ballot box, and they vote in large numbers for either the Democrats or the Populists. The possibility is voiced that the Populists may even replace the Democrats.

Feb. 12   Abraham Lincoln's birthday becomes an official holiday.

Feb. 22   The People's Party is formally organized in St. Louis. Every farm organization and many labor organizations send delegates, who number 860 in all and include U.S. Senators from Kansas and South Dakota, Representative Tom Watson, and General James B. Weaver, a former Representative from Iowa on the Greenback Party ticket and that party's candidate for President in 1880.

Mar. 26   Walt Whitman, 73, dies in Camden, New Jersey.

April 12   The United States offers an indemnity of $25,000 for the actions of a mob in New Orleans last March, when 11 Italian immigrants were lynched. [Italy accepts the offer.]

April 19   J. Frank Duryea, with the help of his brother Charles, constructs one of America's first successful automobiles. It is a horse-buggy powered by a single-cylinder, four-horsepower gasoline engine, with friction drive. [It runs for the first time on Sept. 21, 1893. The last Duryea model is built in 1917.]

May 5   The Chinese Exclusion Act of 1882 is extended for another 10 years.

June 7-10   The Republican Party, at its convention in Minneapolis, Minnesota, renominates President Harrison for the Presidency on the first ballot. Whitelaw Reid, editor in chief of the New York *Tribune,* is acclaimed as Harrison's running mate.

June 21-23   The Democratic national convention, meeting in Chicago, again nominates Cleveland as its Presidential candidate, with Adlai E. Stevenson as the Vice Presidential candidate. Stevenson is a former Congressman from Illinois.

June 29-July 1   The Prohibition Party holds its convention at Cincinnati, nominating John Bidwell for the Presidency.

July 1-9   The Carnegie Steel Company's contract with the Amalgamated Association of Iron and Steel Workers of America expires at the Homestead, Pennsylvania, steelworks. The company makes no effort to negotiate. The workers strike. Violence erupts on July 6 as the company attempts to land Pinkerton agents by boat at the struck plant. Two strikers and two guards are killed in the first encounter at the wharf. Two hours later another attempt to land is made, and this results in the wounding of hundreds of guards and strikers. Pennsylvania troops are sent to restore order on July 9.

July 2-5   The People's Party, at its first national convention in Omaha, nominates James B. Weaver to be its candidate for President.

Sept. 7   James J. Corbett knocks out John L. Sullivan in the 21st round of a heavyweight fight in New Orelans, becoming world champion. This is the first championship fight held following the rules of the Marquis of Queensberry, which require gloves and three-minute rounds.

Oct. 23   The World's Columbian Exposition is officially dedicated in Chicago by Vice President Levi Morton to celebrate the 400th anniversary of the discovery of America.

Nov. 8   The Democratic Party candidates, Grover Cleveland and Adlai Stevenson, defeat Benjamin Harrison and Whitelaw Reid, by a popular vote of 5,555,436 to 5,182,690, and by an electoral vote of 277 to 145. Weaver, the Populist candidate, wins the electoral votes of the states of Kansas, Colorado, Idaho, and Nevada. In addition, state and local Populists win numerous offices.

Nov. 20   The Homestead steel strike is ended with the complete defeat of the union.

1893

Even before Cleveland takes office an economic crisis is seen to be brewing. Ten days before the inauguration, the Philadelphia and Reading Railroad files bankruptcy proceedings. Later, prices of grain, cotton, steel, and timber fall steadily, while the stock market fluctuates wildly. Many financiers, including August Belmont, J. P. Morgan and Henry Villard, warn Cleveland that a panic is nearing, and add their pressure to get a repeal of the Sherman Silver Purchase Act of 1890, which they blame for the crisis. The chief fear among Eastern financiers and businessmen is that in a panic the United States could easily be forced off the gold standard. Early in May the panic begins. More railroads go broke; many of the great financial trusts begin to collapse; European banks begin selling their American stocks and bonds, and a huge run on banks ensues, until more than 500 banks have failed. A vigorous battle begins, with the goal of repealing the Sherman Act. Forces for and against repeal are lined up geographically: the West and South favor retention of the act, and the East favors immediate repeal. Despite the repeal of the act in October, the deepening depression is becoming worldwide, and is wiping out prosperity in all sections of the economy.

Jan. 5 Pope Leo XIII sends the first Apostolic Delegate to the United States from Vatican City, the political headquarters of Roman Catholicsm.

Jan. 17 Former President Rutherford B. Hayes, 71, dies in Fremont, Ohio.

Jan. 17 John L. Stevens, U.S. Envoy Extraordinary to the kingdom of Hawaii, without consulting the U.S. Government, lands U.S. marines ostensibly to protect the lives and property of Americans living in the islands. He is acting on behalf of a self-constituted Committee of Safety, headed by a Hawaiian-born son of a missionary, Sanford B. Dole. The committee was the power behind the throne of King Kalakaua; after the king was succeeded by his sister Liliuokalani in 1891, the committee prepared to seek annexation to the United States. Their first step, after the marines land, is to set up a provisional government headed by Dole, deposing Liliukolani. [On Feb. 1 Stevens declares Hawaii a U.S. protectorate. Envoys of the "provisional government" reach Washington on Feb. 14 and seek a treaty of annexation from the U.S. Senate; no action is taken, and on Mar. 9 President Cleveland, immediately after his inauguration, sends James H. Blount as a special commissioner to investigate the situation in Hawaii.]

Feb. 1 Thomas A. Edison establishes a motion-picture lot at his big plant and laboratories at West Orange, New Jersey.

Feb. 24 The Philadelphia and Reading Railroad files bankruptcy proceedings.

Mar. 1 Congress passes the Diplomatic Appropriations Act, under which certain envoys accredited to foreign countries as Ministers may receive the title of Ambassador. The first U.S. Ambassador is Thomas F. Bayard, appointed by President Cleveland to the Court of St. James's.

Mar. 4 Grover Cleveland is inaugurated for the second time, this time as the 24th President of the United States. [He is the only President whose terms of office are separated and who therefore is counted twice in the roll of the Presidents.]

April 13 U.S. troops are ordered by Commissioner Blount to withdraw from the Hawaiian Islands, ending the protectorate status declared on Jan. 17. [The "provisional government" remains in power.]

May 1 The World's Columbian Exposition in Chicago is officially opened to the public at ceremonies presided over by President Cleveland. The U.S. Post Office issues the first commemorative stamps in its history in honor of the exposition and the 400th anniversary of the first voyage of Columbus. [Before the exposition closes at the end of October, an attendance of about 27,500,000 is reported.]

May 5-June 27 Stock markets experience a frenzied period of sell-off and decline.

May 24 The Anti-Saloon league is founded at Oberlin, Ohio, as a state organization. [Two years later it is formally established nationwide.]

June 20 Eugene V. Debs founds the American Railway Union, an industrial union. [In less than one year it gains 150,000 members in 465 lodges.]

June 26 Governor John Peter Altgeld of Illinois pardons the three convicted conspirators in the Haymarket Riot of 1886 who were not hanged, upon the advice of Clarence Darrow and other reformists.

July 12 At the Columbian Exposition a group of historians hear a paper by Frederick Jackson Turner, a young professor at the Univer-

A group of excursionists wait at the railroad station at Winslow, Arizona. (*ca.*) 1890's

sity of Wisconsin, entitled "The Significance of the Frontier in American History." This is the first attempt to introduce this concept to historians. [It influences the writing of history for generations.]

Aug. 7　The 53d Congress convenes, with 44 Democrats, 38 Republicans, and 3 independents in the Senate; and 218 Democrats, 127 Republicans, and 11 independents in the House. The independents in both Houses are mainly Populists.

Aug. 7-Oct. 30　A legislative battle occurs in Congress over the highly controversial question of repealing the Sherman Silver Purchase Act of 1890. Cleveland urges its repeal, and he is suc-

cessful, but the issue splits the Democratic party.

Aug. 23-29　A tropical storm devastates a coastal area from Charleston, South Carolina, to Savannah, Georgia, killing nearly 1,000 persons.

Sept. 16　A 6,000,000-acre tract of land in the Cherokee Strip of Oklahoma Territory is opened to white settlers. More than 100,000 persons rush into the area to stake their claims.

Oct. 18　Lucy Stone, 75, a leader in the women's rights movement, dies in Boston.

Nov. 7　The state of Colorado, under the Populist Administration of Governor Davis H. Waite, enacts voting rights for women.

239

1894 **Contrary to the President's hopes, the repeal of the** Silver Purchase Act of 1890 does not alleviate the depression. Gold reserves shrink to about $60,000,000; during one 17-day period in January more than $11,000,000 in gold is paid out of the Federal treasury. The Populists clamor for silver and paper money, and a silver convention in Omaha in June is addressed by William Jennings Bryan, now editor of the Omaha *World-Herald*. Many of the "silver Democrats" at the convention, and thousands outside, have read the most popular pamphlet of the period, *Coin's Financial School,* written by "Coin," the pseudonym of William H. Harvey. Before the end of the year 642 banks have failed, one quarter of all heavy industry is idle, over 22,500 miles of railroads are in receivership.

The railroads are much in the news because of the strike conducted by the powerful American Railway Union, 150,000 strong and led by the foremost union organizer of his time, Eugene V. Debs. Starting out as a sympathy strike for a small group of Pullman employees, it is magnified by the aggressive performance of President Cleveland, who calls out Federal troops to quell the unusual violence of the desperate strikers. Debs ends up in jail, in contrast with the fate of Jacob Coxey, leader of one of the numerous bands or "armies" of unemployed (Coxey's Army numbers 500) who march to state capitals and to Washington this year with petitions for redress. The movement is made to appear ridiculous when Coxey is arrested for the misdemeanor of trespassing on Government property.

Great damage is done to the Democratic Party by the adamant defense of gold made by President Cleveland, by his conduct in the railway strike, by the mere fact of the economic situation. Bryan and the Populists look forward to 1896. So do many Republicans, who see an opportunity to exploit Democratic weakness and have no fear of Populism. The midterm elections are a test run. Both Houses of the 54th Congress are solidly Republican. The Populists show a 42-per-cent gain in the popular vote, with 6 Senators and 7 Representatives in the 54th Congress.

Jan. 17   The Federal Government offers a bond issue of $50,000,000 to make up for gold reserve losses.

Mar. 17   A treaty is signed with China under which Chinese laborers are to be excluded from entry into the United States. [It is ratified by the U.S. Senate on Aug. 13.]

Mar. 25-May 1   Jacob S. Coxey leads an "army" of unemployed people (most of them Populists) from Massilion, Ohio, in a protest march to Washington. By the time they reach Washington their number is about 500. Bearing a petition for relief, they parade down Pennsylvania Avenue to the Capitol, where Coxey and two others are arrested on the steps for trespassing. The "army" quickly disbands.

April 10   An arbitration settlement on Bering Sea pelagic sealing is made official by Congressional approval of a bill putting the terms into effect.

April 14   Thomas Alva Edison gives a public demonstration of a moving picture camera in a parlor at 1155 Broadway, New York City. The showing is of two men boxing, a dancing girl, and a child being bathed.

May 11-Aug. 6   A strike is declared at the plant of the Pullman Palace Car Company in the "model" town of Pullman, Illinois [now part of Chicago], where the workers have taken wage cuts of 25 per cent and where one third of them have been unemployed during the past year. On June 26 the American Railway Union adopts a boycott against Pullman; the railroad switchmen refuse to connect Pullman palace cars. When the railroads' General Managers Association threatens to punish any worker in the nation who observes the boycott, many American Railway Union workers walk out. An injunction is taken out on July 2 against Debs, ordering him to call off the strike. The next day, with freight traffic in and out of Chicago stalled by the strike, Cleveland orders Federal troops to that city without consulting Governor John Peter Altgeld of Illinois. Violence breaks out as crowds begin to detach Pullman cars from the trains. The troops thereupon escort the trains, a clash occurs on July 7 in Kensington [now part of Blue Island], a suburb south of Chicago, and 7 men are killed. In Chicago a mob sets fire to unoccupied buildings of the recent Columbian Exposition, smashes switches, and stops trains. Governor Altgeld protests the use of Federal troops in the strike. Debs

Members of Coxey's Army on their way to Washington, D.C.

is arrested on July 10. He is indicted for criminal conspiracy and for contempt of court. Finally, on July 20 the troops are withdrawn. By Aug. 6 the strikers at Pullman have run out of funds and give up the struggle. The Pullman Company refuses to rehire them unless they sign a no-union pledge; those who refuse are blacklisted.

July 4   The Republic of Hawaii, with Sanford Dole as President, is proclaimed. [It is recognized by the United States on Aug. 7.]

Aug. 18   The Carey Land Act is passed, authorizing the Secretary of the Interior to cede public lands to states where irrigation is planned. It is named for its sponsor, Senator Joseph Maull Carey of Wyoming.

Aug. 28   The Wilson-Gorman Tariff is passed. A Democratic measure, it reduces many rates and adds to the free list. It also contains a controversial clause permitting the Federal Government to levy an income tax on incomes in excess of $4,000 per year. Cleveland refuses to sign it, but it becomes law nevertheless.

Sept. 1   A huge forest fire, near Hickley, Minnesota, halfway between Minneapolis and Duluth, kills more than 400 persons and destroys more than 160,000 acres of forest before it burns out.

Nov. 13   Another Federal bond issue of $50,000,000 is offered. Because of poor public response, most of this loan is taken over by New York bankers.

Dec. 14   Eugene Debs is sentenced to six months in jail.

1895

The economy continues its erratic downward course, but President Cleveland struggles to maintain the nation on the gold standard despite widespread belief that both he and gold are responsible for the present depression. Cleveland floats a third bond issue, turning for aid to August Belmont and J. P. Morgan. With the help of the foreign Rothschild interests, these financiers provide 3,500,000 ounces of gold for $62,000,000. Such funding maneuvers outrage both the Populists and "silver Democrats."

In May the U.S. Supreme Court strikes down the income tax provision of the Wilson-Gorman tariff bill. This income tax would have applied only to incomes of more than $4,000 per year, and thus the Court is accused of joining Cleveland and the rich against the poor. By the end of the year prices and wages reach their lowest points. The Morgan-Belmont loan lasts to the end of the year; by this time there are definite signs that the depression may ease off. The supply of gold increases, but the improvement comes too late to save Cleveland. The silver movement is sweeping the nation, and the President is isolated and abandoned in office.

Jan. 22 Several hundred manufacturing companies send representatives to a convention in Cincinnati, Ohio, where it is decided to form a national organization. [On Jan. 21, 1896, the organization holds its first convention under the name of the National Association of Manufacturers of the United States.]

Feb. 11 Gettysburg National Military Park, a tract of almost 2,400 acres including the site of the Civil War battle and the national cemetery dedicated by Lincoln in 1863, is established by Congress. [The area is transferred from the War Department to the National Park Service on Aug. 10, 1933.]

Feb. 20 Frederick Douglass, 78, dies at Anacostia Heights, Washington, D.C. An escaped slave, he became an abolitionist leader, persuaded Lincoln to use Negro troops on the Union side, and was appointed U.S. Minister to Haiti by President Harrison.

Mar. 5 Democratic Congressmen who support the coinage of silver broaden their split with the regular wing of the party by issuing the "Appeal of the Silver Democrats." [This event is an early indication that the Democratic Party is turning against Cleveland and the gold standard.]

Mar. 20 A coal mine explosion at Red Canyon, Wyoming, kills 60 persons.

May 15 Advocates of the free coinage of silver from 17 states and territories meet in convention in Salt Lake City, Utah Territory.

May 20 The U.S. Supreme Court, in *Pollock* v. *Farmer's Loan and Trust Company,* by a 5-to-4 vote, voids the income tax clause of the Wilson-Gorman Tariff of 1894. [This decision leads to the enactment of the 16th Amendment in 1909.] In the case of *United States* v. *E. C. Knight Co.,* the Court removes all monopolistic

intrastate business from the control of the Federal Government's Sherman Antitrust Act, thereby greatly weakening the act's provisions.

May 27 In the case *In re Debs,* the U.S. Supreme Court holds that the Federal Government may regulate interstate commerce, and is thus justified in having issued an injunction against Eugene V. Debs to prevent interference with the movement of mail by the American Railway Union during the strike of 1894.

June 11 Charles E. Duryea receives a patent on an automobile. It is an improved version of one he and his brother Frank first completed in 1893.

July 20 Secretary of State Richard Olney takes notice of the fact that a dispute exists between Great Britain and Venezuela concerning the boundary between Venezuela and the British colony of British Guiana [now Guyana]. Olney invokes the Monroe Doctrine, declares U.S. interest in helping solve the dispute, and asserts in explanation: "Today the United States is practically sovereign on this continent, and its fiat is law upon the subjects to which it confines its interposition."

Aug. 31 The first professional football game is played between the Latrobe (Pennsylvania) Y.M.C.A. team and a team from nearby Jeannette. Latrobe defeats Jeannette, 12-0.

Sept. 9 The American Bowling Congress is organized in New York City. [This group soon establishes uniformity in rules and standard bowling equipment. Its headquarters is later moved to Milwaukee, Wisconsin.]

Sept. 18 Booker T. Washington, founder and president of the Tuskegee Institute, addresses the Cotton States Exposition in Atlanta. [This Atlanta Compromise Address gains for Washington

THE DEAD-HORSE PARTY.

UNCLE SAM. "To hear them boys talk, you'd think it was their nag was doin' the work."

A pro-gold cartoon by W. A. Rogers

a national reputation as a Negro leader.]

Oct. 12   The Westinghouse Electric Company completes the installation of ten big generators at Niagara Falls, forming the first large power grid.

Nov. 5   A patent (originally applied for in 1879), is issued to George B. Selden for a car that includes a clutch, but incorporates the carriage (wagon) body. Sedlen calls it the "Road Engine." [The Electric Vehicle Company and then the Association of Licensed Automobile Manufacturers collect royalties until 1911 from others who manufacture gasoline-powered cars.]

Nov. 26   Lord Salisbury, British Foreign Minister, replies to Olney's letter of July 20 concerning the dispute between his country and Venezuela. Salisbury refuses to accept Olney's invocation of the Monroe Doctrine; he says that unless the United States can control every action of every Latin American state, it can hardly "protect them from the consequences attaching to any misconduct of which they may be guilty towards other nations."

Nov. 28   On Thanksgiving day the first automobile race in the United States is run, from Chicago to Evanston, Illinois (54 miles). Frank Duryea's car and a late-model Benz of Germany are the only cars that manage to finish the run. The Duryea car is declared the winner, covering the distance in 7 hours 53 minutes.

Dec. 2   The 54th Congress convenes, with 43 Republicans, 39 Democrats, and 6 Populists in the Senate; and 244 Republicans, 105 Democrats, and 7 Populists in the House.

Dec. 17   President Cleveland recommends the creation of an independent commission to determine the boundary between Venezuela and British Guiana, after disclosing the correspondence on the subject between Secretary of State Olney and Lord Salisbury. [On Dec. 21 Congress approves the setting up of such a commission.]

Dec. 17   The Anti-Saloon League is officially organized as a national body in Washington, D.C., after its founding in Oberlin, Ohio.

1896

This year appears at first to be one of triumph for silver; it ends in a victory for gold. The Democratic party is split and is wrenched from the President's control, under the leadership of free-silver advocate William Jennings Bryan, who entered politics on the wave of Populism. The party's platform for the Presidential election—with Cleveland as a lame-duck gold defender—refers to the gold standard as un-American and anti-American. Cleveland's former supporters avoid him; members of Congress cease to visit him; only a small number of gold-standard Democrats and the Mugwumps (independent Republicans) remain loyal to the President. He finds himself in the predicament of Andrew Johnson after the impeachment trial in 1868, abandoned by his supporters for the remainder of his term. At the Democratic convention comes one of the most dramatic moments in the history of American politics: Cleveland is denounced from the podium, with suggestions of impeachment, and then William Jennings Bryan rises and makes his famous "cross-of-gold" speech, perhaps the most electrifying oration yet made at a convention. Bryan is nominated the next day by the enthusiastic Democrats. The Populists are impressed, and forsaking their independence they also select Bryan. (They find Bryan's banker running mate unacceptable, however). Even a group of Republicans, eschewing gold, support Bryan.

The Republican party is not unaffected by the silver movement and cheap-money campaigns. Presidential candidate William McKinley, best known for the protectionist tariff bearing his name, is equivocal in his support of the gold standard, and he at times talks as if he is a "bimetalist," favoring both gold and silver. Mark Hanna, McKinley's campaign manager, quietly proposes some solid appeals against both silver and cheap money. He solicits huge sums of money from bankers, corporations and industries (nearly $4,000,000). Hanna sells McKinley to the public like a commodity. While Bryan speaks to wild applause in 27 states, McKinley stays at home. In some companies employees are ordered to vote for McKinley or be fired; or it is indicated that the company will have to go out of business if McKinley should lose. There is even talk of the secession of New York City should Bryan be elected. By mid-October it becomes clear that Hanna's campaign is beating Bryan. In the election Bryan carries the South and some Western states, but McKinley carries the heavily populated and wealthier Eastern states, plus California, Oregon, and the industrial Middle West.

Jan. 1   An American investigating commission is appointed in accordance with the recommendations of President Cleveland to deal with the 82-year-old boundary dispute between Venezuela and Great Britain's Guiana colony. [The boundary commission convenes and meets with no unwillingness on the part of either of the disputing parties to provide it with information. A treaty between Great Britain and Venezuela on Feb. 2, 1897, makes its findings moot, and it disbands Feb. 27, 1897.]

Jan. 4   Utah is admitted to the Union as the 45th state, with its capital at Salt Lake City. During the 46 years between the formation of Utah Territory and statehood, the area was diminished by the formation of Colorado, Nevada, and Wyoming.

Jan. 6   The fourth bond issue in three years is floated, this time in public subscription totaling $100,000,000. The loan is made necessary

despite the signs of economic recovery, because Federal treasury reserves are down to about $79,000,000, which is considered so low as to endanger continuance of the gold standard.

Feb. 28   Belligerent rights are accorded to the Cuban insurrectionists by a concurrent resolution of the U.S. Congress, and Spain is offered United States cooperation if it chooses to negotiate with the Cuban rebels.

April 23   The new Edison "Vitascope" movie projector is publicly demonstrated, at Koster and Bial's Music Hall, in New York City.

May 22   Spain declines the offer of U.S. offices for negotiating with the rebel Cubans.

May 27   A tornado strikes St. Louis, Missouri, destroying much of the city, killing 306 persons, and doing $13,000,000 in damage. More than 5,000 are left homeless.

May 28   In *Plessy* v. *Ferguson,* the U. S. Supreme Court deals a heavy blow to civil rights

In and about Baltimore (*ca.*) 1890's

for Negroes, and legitimizes Jim Crow practices. The Court accepts as legal the "separate-but-equal" principle, stating that the reservation and assignment to Negroes of such public facilities as separate railroad cars (at issue in this case), toilets, parks, and other accommodations does not deprive Negroes of the civil rights guaranteed by the 14th Amendment to the Constitution. [This decision stands until it is explicitly overturned in *Brown* v. *Board of Education of Topeka* in 1954.]

June 11   The house where Lincoln died (on April 15, 1865) in Washington, D.C., becomes a national historic monument, and is refurnished as a typical home of the 1860's.

June 16-18   The Republican Party holds its national convention in St. Louis, where William McKinley of Ohio is nominated for President. Garret A. Hobart, with no political background outside of New Jersey, is nominated for Vice President. However, 34 Republicans bolt this convention in order to support "silver coinage" candidates of the Democratic party.

June 28   An anthracite coal mine at Pittston, Pennsylvania, caves in, leaving 58 persons dead.

July 7-11   The Democratic Party holds its national convention in Chicago, and like the Republican Party is split over the issue of silver coinage and the gold standard. A group of "gold Democrats" bolt the convention to form their own party, the National Democrats. On July 8 William Jennings Bryan, in the debate on the party platform, advocates the free coinage of silver, contrary to President Cleveland's gold policy. His audience remains spellbound for moments after the speech, which includes an eloquent reference to labor being crucified on a "cross of gold," then bursts into wild acclaim. Bryan is nominated for President on the 5th ballot. Arthur Sewall of Maine, a banker who nevertheless supports free coinage of silver, becomes the Vice Presidential candidate.

July 22   The "silver Republicans" hold their own convention in St. Louis. Under the leadership of the "bimetalist" Henry Moore Teller of Colorado, they nominate the Democratic Party candidates as their candidates in the coming election.

July 22-25   The People's Party national convention meets in St. Louis and nominates the Democrat William J. Bryan as its Presidential candidate. However, before nominating Bryan, they name Tom Watson for Vice President. Wat-

son by this time has made a complete reversal in his attitude toward Negroes, from a policy of bringing black voters into the Populist movement to one of complete exclusion.

July 30   An accident on the Atlantic City and West Jersey Seashore railroad, near Atlantic City, New Jersey, kills 60 persons.

Aug. 17   A discovery of gold is made on Rabbit Creek (now renamed Bonanza Creek), a tributary of Klondike River, in Yukon Territory, northwestern Canada, just east of the border with Alaska. [Access to the region is extremely difficult; the only passable route leads northward through wilderness passes from the port of Skagway, Alaska. News of the strike reaches the U.S. West Coast in the summer of 1897; in the next two years the Klondike gold rush courses through the passes to the Yukon, making a city of 20,000 where the town of Dawson remains. By 1900 a railway is built from Skagway to Whitehorse, in the Yukon, from which boats can use the navigable Lewes and Yukon rivers to reach the Klondike.]

Sept. 2-3   The "gold Democrats," also known as "sound-money Democrats," hold a convention at Indianapolis, Indiana, and nominate John M. Palmer and Simon Bolivar Buckner for President and Vice President respectively.

Oct. 1   A rural free delivery system is established by the U.S. Post Office Department, with the placing in operation of five routes in West Virginia. [This service is responsible for the phenomenal rise of mail-order houses during the next few years.]

Nov. 3   Despite the expensive Democratic campaign, and the brilliant oratory of Bryan, in the election McKinley receives 7,102,246 popular votes; Bryan gets 6,492,559. Republicans sweep the Electoral College with 271 votes, while Bryan gets 176. The Republicans maintain their control of both Houses of Congress. [This election ends the effort to establish a silver or bimetal (silver-gold) standard, and also ends the People's Party and Populism as a national movement.]

Dec. 15   The first American ice hockey league game is played, in a four-club circuit, made up of two clubs each from the neighboring cities of New York City and Brooklyn. The game, between the Brooklyn Skating Club and the St. Nicholas Skating Club, played at St. Nick's arena in New York City, is won by the St. Nicks, 15-0.

1897

During the year prosperity rapidly returns to all sectors of the economy. Because of an increasing supply of gold—partly through discoveries of gold—the gold base of American currency is expanding. Price declines are checked and a mild inflationary trend appears. Business interests concentrate on getting Congress to pass a higher tariff. As if to divert public attention from this effort, there is an obvious attempt to interest the American people in foreign affairs. The press arouses public sympathy for insurrection in Cuba, probably more for the purpose of increasing circulation than for any interests in the plight of the Cubans. However, that plight is verified by a horde of reporters and correspondents and even in Congress leading politicians exercise pressure both on outgoing Cleveland and on incoming McKinley to take a stand against the concentration camps set up by the Spanish administration in Cuba. Neither President is anxious to meddle in the Spanish-Cuban crisis; the American interest is to stabilize the island, whose economy is closely geared to important segments of American industry.

January The U.S. Supreme Court, in *United States* v. *Trans-Missouri Freight Association,* decides that the fixing of transportation rates by the 18 railroads in this association is a monopolistic action and is in violation of the Sherman Antitrust Law.

Jan. 12 A national monetary conference to discuss the gold standard meets in Indianapolis, Indiana. It appoints a commission to present Congress with a monetary reform plan.

Feb. 2 Great Britain and Venezuela formally agree to submit to arbitration their dispute concerning the boundary between Venezuela and British Guiana, thus avoiding a confrontation between Britain and the United States over a varying interpretation of the Monroe Doctrine. [The international arbitration commission makes the U.S. investigating commission unnecessary, and the latter ends its investigation on Feb. 27.]

Feb. 2 The capitol of Pennsylvania, in Harrisburg, is destroyed by fire. [In 1906 a new capitol is dedicated on the same site.]

Feb. 17 The National Congress of Mothers is founded in Washington, D. C., by Phoebe A. Hearst [the mother of William Randolph Hearst] and Alice M. Birney. [This organization becomes the National Congress of Parents and Teachers (PTA) in 1924.]

Mar. 2 A literacy test for immigrants, the product of lobbying of the Immigration Restriction League, passed by Congress, is vetoed by Cleveland. [It is the first of three such tests to be enacted and vetoed, the second rejected by Taft in 1909 and the third by Wilson in 1915.]

Mar. 4 President William McKinley is inaugurated as the 25th President of the United States. [On Mar. 5 former Senator John Sherman becomes Secretary of State and Lyman J. Gage becomes Secretary of the Treasury.]

Mar. 15 The 55th Congress convenes in special session, with 47 Republicans, 34 Democrats, and 7 others in the Senate; 204 Republicans, 113 Democrats, and 40 others in the House. (The "other" members are chiefly Populists.)

Mar. 17 James J. ("Gentleman Jim") Corbett loses his heavyweight championship in the 14th round of a fight with Bob Fitzsimmons at Carson City, Nevada.

April 22 The submarine *Argonaut* is built by Simon Lake. The first really manageable submersible craft, it is shaped like a cigar, has a 30-hp engine using gasoline, and is 36 feet long. A hose, held on the surface by a float, supplies air. [In 1898 the *Argonaut* makes an undersea voyage from Norfolk to New York.]

An organ-grinder and his wife, New York City (*ca.*) 1897

Gold seekers on the summit of Chilkoot Pass, Yukon Trail, Alaska, 1897

Actresses on the way to the Klondike mines, 1897

An Indian totem village and totem poles, Howkan, Alaska, 1897

June 15 At a meeting in Chicago, led by Victor L. Berger and Eugene V. Debs, the Social Democracy of America is formed from remnants of the American Railway Union and other socialist factions. [The majority of this organization takes the name of Social Democratic Party in 1898, and win two seats in the Massachusetts legislature.]

July 7 The Dingley Tariff is passed by a strict Republican Party vote in Congress. Despite McKinley's promise of a tariff for primarily revenue purposes, this tariff is the highest yet and is frankly protectionist. It reimposes higher duties on wool and hides, and raises the duties on linen, silk, and chinaware.

July 14 A shipment of $750,000 in gold arrives in San Francisco, from the Klondike gold fields. [Three days later another shipment, of $800,000 in gold, reaches Seattle.]

October 1 The 1½ mile Boston "subway" is completed. The first underground transportation system in the United States, it uses streetcars that are kept off the streets by following roadways prepared below the street level, then covered over. [This "cut-and-cover" method is later superseded by tunnels, and streetcars give way to trains.]

Oct. 29 Henry George, 58, economist and founder of the single-tax movement, dies in New York City. At the time of his death he is a candidate for mayor of New York City.

249

1898 **A violent explosion sinks the American battleship** *Maine* **in** the harbor of Havana, Cuba, in February. This event provides a justification for war—for some months jingoists, "yellow" journalists, and ardent patriots have been clamoring for war with Spain over the issue of Cuban independence and over charges that atrocities have been committed by the Spanish colonial authorities in Cuba. The Court of Inquiry in March determines that the *Maine* has been sunk by an underwater mine, and the nation is united in its belief in the culpability of Spain. [In later years most experts conclude that it seems highly improbable that the Spanish Government caused the explosion.] Although Spain makes concessions, and the U.S. Minister in Madrid knows that Spain would give up Cuba—and might even be willing to cede it to the United States—President McKinley fears that the Republican Party will suffer should he resist this clamor for war.

The Spanish-American War begins amid a festive atmosphere of enthusiasm, parades, and feverish patriotism. In reality, there are no urgent political goals in this war, and no strong economic motives for it. Officials disclaim any intention of seeking new territory or of exercising jurisdiction over Cuba. It is simply a war "to free Cuba." Old Civil War veterans, many rising political figures, and enthusiastic sons of wealthy families all flock to the colors, each hoping to make a name for himself in this "splendid little war." Those few who point out the needlessness of the war, who criticize jingoism and warmongering, are dismissed as unpatriotic cranks.

In early May a panic grips the Atlantic seaboard when news arrives that the Spanish fleet under Cervera has left the Cape Verde Islands and for 19 days cannot be located. Nervous calls for Federal protection of seaboard cities are heard, but after Cervera is discovered hiding in a Cuban harbor with his entire fleet, all fears of coastal invasion are dissipated. Dewey has by this time reduced the Spanish Pacific fleet to junk in Manila Bay, and Cervera's Atlantic fleet is soon demolished. The war on land is less dramatic and more difficult. The Spanish forces give a good account of themselves at El Caney and at San Juan Hill. American land forces contrast greatly with the efficient U.S. Navy. Spain has six weeks to prepare for the invasion of Cuba, and can muster 200,000 troops to oppose one tenth of that many Americans; yet the expeditionary force is allowed to land without a struggle. With 13,000 troops in Santiago, only 1,700 Spanish soldiers defend the city against 15,000 Americans. In 105 days of fighting (May 1-Aug. 13) the United States wrests a centuries-old empire from Spain.

Jan. 1   The amalgamation of various communities to form an enlarged New York City, authorized by the state legislature, becomes effective. The original city of New York, Manhattan Island, was enlarged in 1874 by acquisition of the southern part of Westchester County. Now other Westchester communities are annexed after a plebiscite, forming the new borough of the Bronx. Communities in Queens County are also constituted a borough, as is Manhattan. All of Staten Island is transformed into the borough of Richmond. Finally, the great city of Brooklyn, the fourth largest in the nation, becomes the fifth borough of the enlarged city of Greater New York.

Jan. 25   The U.S.S. *Maine* arrives in Havana to help insure the protection of American lives and property. It is welcomed by the Spanish administration and the Cuban public.

Feb. 9   A letter describing President McKinley as "weak" and "a cheap politician" is published by the *New York Journal*. Its author is Dupuy de Lôme, Spain's Minister to the United States, and it was only intended to be read by a private addressee in Cuba. [De Lôme is forced to resign but American hostility to Spain is aroused.]

Feb. 15   The U.S.S. *Maine* explodes, killing 260 of the crew of 350. [The war cry "Remember the Maine," becomes, like "Remember the Alamo," a patriot's call to action.]

Feb. 25   Commodore George Dewey at his Pacific base in Hong Kong receives secret orders from Assistant Secretary of the Navy Theodore Roosevelt to coal his ships and prepare to attack Admiral Patricio Montojo's Pacific Squadron in the Philippine Islands should war be declared.

Mar. 17   Blanche Kelso Bruce, 57, former Senator from Mississippi, and a registering official of the U.S. Treasury under Garfield, dies in Washington, D.C. A former slave, Bruce spent all of his adult life fighting for the civil rights of minority groups.

Mar. 19   The battleship *Oregon* begins an epic journey of 14,760 miles from San Francisco to Key West, Florida, by way of Cape Horn around the tip of South America. [This voyage, which takes 69 days, stimulates renewed interest in a canal across the Isthmus of Panama to shorten the journey from the Pacific to the Atlantic Ocean.]

Mar. 27   U.S. Minister to Spain Stewart L. Woodford is instructed to tell the Spanish Government that the United States has no intention of annexing Cuba, and that an armistice between Spain and the Cubans should be effected until Oct. 1, with an immediate end to the use of concentration camps.

Mar. 28   A court of Naval Inquiry, set up to determine the cause of the explosions that sank the *Maine,* concludes that an underwater mine attached to the ship's hull set off forward ammunition magazines aboard the ship. It is not known who set the mine.

April 5   President McKinley recalls U.S. consuls in Cuba.

April 9   Spain accepts the demands of Mar. 27 insofar as an armistice is concerned; as for the camps, the Spanish Government says they have already been closed.

April 11   McKinley ignores the Spanish concessions and asks Congress for authorization to use force in securing the freedom of Cuba from Spanish control.

April 19   Congress adopts a resolution declaring that Cuba should be free and sovereign and authorizing the President so to inform Spain and to use whatever force is required to accomplish this purpose, with the understanding that the United States does not intend to infringe on Cuban sovereignty once it is obtained. The House vote is 311 to 6; in the Senate 42 vote for the resolution, 35 oppose it. [On April 20 McKinley signs the resolution; war is formally declared on April 25.]

April 21   The passport of U.S. Minister to Spain Woodford is revoked before he can personally deliver an ultimatum from Washington embodying the resolution.

April 22   A U.S. blockade of Cuban ports is declared, and Admiral William T. Sampson is placed in command. On the same day the U.S. gunboat *Nashville* captures the war's first merchant marine prize, the Spanish ship *Buena Ventura*. Congress authorizes a volunteer army numbering 200,000 men. [No more than 87,000 of the 223,000 who enlist ever leave the United States.]

April 24   Spain officially rejects the ultimatum.

April 27   Commodore Dewey's fleet steams out of Hong Kong and heads for the Philippines. The fleet consists of the modern steel cruisers *Olympia* (the flagship), *Boston, Baltimore,* and *Raleigh,* and the gunboats *Petrel* and *Concord.*

April 29   Admiral Pascual Cervera's Atlantic fleet of 4 cruisers and 3 torpedo boats leaves Cape Verde Islands bound across the Atlantic. [Its size and whereabouts are unknown to the American public for the next 19 days, arousing fears of a possible Spanish assault on American port cities.]

May 1   Admiral Montojo's Pacific fleet of five nearly worthless cruisers and two small armored cruisers is anchored in Manila Bay as Commodore Dewey leads his fleet past the outer fortifications, bringing to bear ten 8-inch guns, twenty-three 6-inch guns, and twenty 5-inch guns. Montojo has only seven 6.30's, four obsolete 5.9's, and twenty 4.7's, and his land batteries consist of ineffective ancient smooth-bore guns. The Spanish fire is wild and erratic during the battle, which for the Americans is like target practice. The entire Spanish fleet is disabled or sunk by midday. Aboard the Spanish ships 381 men are killed; one overweight American engineer dies of heat prostration aboard an American vessel, the only U.S. casualty of the battle. The fleet prepares to invest the city of Manila.

May 8   General Nelson Miles is ordered to form an army of 70,000 to take Havana.

May 12   A new state constitution of Louisiana is ratified. It contains a clause that restricts the right to vote, in cases of doubtful literacy, to those whose fathers or grandfathers were voters before 1867. [This so-called "grandfather" clause has the effect of disfranchising Negroes of that state, reducing the number of black voters in Louisiana from 130,000 in 1896 to 5,000 in 1900. It is adopted by most Southern states.]

May 19   Cervera's fleet arrives at Santiago de Cuba. [When it is discovered to be there by Commodore Schley on May 28, the fear of raids on American coasts is ended.]

May 26   The battleship *Oregon* arrives at

U.S. troops in Porto Rico on their way to the front

Key West in time to catch up with the fleet moving toward Santiago.

May 29   The Spanish fleet is blockaded at Santiago. The American fleet consists of the battleships *Indiana, Oregon, Iowa, Massachusetts,* and *Texas,* and the cruisers *New York* and *Brooklyn.* On June 1 Admiral Sampson assumes command of the fleet. He attempts to block the harbor entrance by sinking an old ship at its narrows, but it drifts into deeper water within the harbor before sinking, and its crew is captured.

June   11   U.S.   marines   land   near Guantánamo, east of Santiago. On June 15 they defeat the Spanish in a small action.

June 20   The island of Guam in the Ladrones (Marianas) Islands is captured by the cruiser *Charleston.*

June 22   General Shafter with 17,000 troops land at Daiquirí, 15 miles east of Santiago. [They defeat a Spanish force at Las Guásimas on June 24.]

July 1-3   In further land actions near Santiago, 3,500 U.S. troops battle 600 defenders for a day before capturing the village of El Caney. Roosevelt's Rough Riders charge up San Juan Hill, overlooking the city, and suffer heavy casualties in two battles before taking the redoubts on top. U.S. troops now occupy the heights surrounding Santiago, after losing altogether 225 dead and about 1,400 wounded. On July 3 Cervera's fleet attempts to dash through the blockade, but in a four-hour chase it is destroyed, with a loss of 323 killed and 1,750 taken prisoner. U.S. casualties are one killed and one wounded.

July 7   In a bill of annexation signed by President McKinley, Hawaii becomes part of the United States.

July 17   Santiago surrenders to General William R. Shafter. [On July 21 the port of Nipe, on the northern coast of Cuba, is captured in the final action of the war in Cuba.]

July 25   General Miles invades Porto Rico [after 1932, Puerto Rico], fighting one sharp engagement at Guanica on the southern coast.

July 25   General Wesley Merritt arrives at Manila Bay with reinforcements. His force brings the total number of troops committed to the capture of Manila to 10,700, assisted by several thousand Filipino guerrilla rebels led by Emilio Aguinaldo.

July 26   The Spanish ask for peace terms through the French Embassy in Washington.

July 28   The city of Ponce, Porto Rico, surrenders to General Miles.

July 30   President McKinley dictates the

252

terms of surrender.

Aug. 1 The Cuban Expeditionary Force embarks for Long Island, New York, after survey shows serious weakening of troop strength and efficiency by yellow fever, and food poisoning. [Of about 5,000 lives lost during the entire war by U.S. forces, at least 4,600 were caused by disease or lack of sanitation.]

Aug. 9 Dewey and Merritt make a formal demand for Spanish surrender of the Manila garrison.

Aug. 9-12 Spain agrees to surrender. On Aug. 12 fighting stops, according to the terms of the protocol. These terms include the cession of Porto Rico and one of the Ladrones [Guam is chosen] to the United States, and the right of the United States to occupy Cuba and the Philippines pending final settlement under a treaty of peace.

Aug. 13 Filipino rebels and Americans fight to secure Manila, unaware that fighting has been halted by protocol. Manila is captured.

Sept. 15 The National Institute of Arts and Letters is founded by the American Social Science Association at New York City. [In 1904 the institute founds the American Academy of Arts and Letters.]

Oct. 6 *Cyrano de Bergerac,* a play by Edmond Rostand, is staged at the Garden Theater in New York City. [It becomes one of the most popular plays of the time.]

Oct. 12 A riot breaks out in a southern Illinois coal field when a company at Virden, Illinois, attempts to use Negro miners to break a strike. Thirteen persons are killed in the actions.

Nov. 8 Theodore Roosevelt, the lieutenant colonel who led the Rough Riders up San Juan Hill, is nominated by the Republican Party for governor of New York.

Dec. 10 The Treaty of Paris is signed, ending the Spanish American War. Under its provisions, the terms of the cease-fire are formalized, ceding Porto Rico and Guam to the United States, and establishing the sovereignty of Cuba. In addition, the Philippine Islands are formally ceded to the United States in return for the payment to Spain of $20,000,000.

Colonel Theodore Roosevelt and his Rough Riders on San Juan Hill

1899 The Spanish-American War turns America away from isolationism and establishes the nation as a world power. The presence of this power is immediately revealed in American strategic supremacy in the Caribbean Sea; in the possession of large territories (Hawaii, Guam, the Philippines) in the Pacific Ocean, and not contiguous to the United States mainland; in American leadership in considering plans for building a trans-Isthmian canal; in the growth of a powerful navy; and in the involvement of the United States in international politics, such as that relating to the Far East and China. The United States is now a major industrial nation with rapidly expanding foreign markets.

The most serious immediate postwar problem relates to the Philippines. The United States begins to set aside its sense of civilizing mission and views these islands as spoils of victory. But it is necessary first to suppress the national independence movement led by Emilio Aguinaldo, who has cooperated with the Americans in the liberation of the islands. The continuing arrival of American troops after the war makes it clear to Aguinaldo that the independence of the Philippine Republic, which he has proclaimed and struggled for, is not going to be recognized by the United States.

At home, an interesting phenomenon is the proliferation of the self-propelled vehicle, in a number of forms and styles, all being produced in significant numbers by at least 50 manufacturers. Among the important lines of motor files, autokinetics, mocoles, and motorigs [a few of the contemporary names for the automobile] are the "locomobiles," along with a regular series of Stanley steam cars invented in 1897 by Francis E. Stanley of Mechanic Falls, Maine; a large group of electric cars, including those of the Riker Electric Motor Company of Brooklyn, the American Electric Vehicle Company of Chicago, and three models of the Columbia Automobile Company of Hartford, Connecticut; 29 different models, all electric, and all by the Fisher Equipment Company of Chicago (including landaus, buses, cabs, wagons, and coupes); and finally a series of electrics by the Pope Manufacturing Company, also of Hartford. Cars in production that use the internal-combustion engine—the least usual mode of propulsion—include the Duryea buggies and three-wheelers, the big series of Winton cars by the Winton Motor Carriage Company of Cleveland, and the Packard Brothers' car, which is an improved version of the Winton.

January In a statement on U.S. policy in the Philippines, President McKinley declares: "The Philippines are ours, not to exploit but to develop, to civilize, to educate, to train in the science of self-government."

Jan. 5 Emilio Aguinaldo, leader of a movement for Philippine independence already in progress, calls for a convention of his revolutionary assembly at Malolos, 20 miles northwest of Manila, to be held on Jan. 20. Aguinaldo, who has cooperated with the Americans against the Spanish forces, is disturbed by the terms of the peace treaty, which ignore the independence movement.

Jan. 15 Edwin Markham's poem "Man With a Hoe" appears in the San Francisco *Examiner*. The poem was inspired by a painting by Jean François Millet.

Jan. 20 Filipino independence of U.S. rule is ratified by the revolutionary assembly. President McKinely appoints a commission to study

problems of civil order in the Philippines.

Feb. 1 The United States officially establishes jurisdiction over the island of Guam, ceded by Spain under the terms of the Treaty of Paris.

Feb. 4 Aguinaldo launches an attack against U.S. forces in Manila, and is repelled.

Feb. 6 The treaty of peace between the United States and Spain (the Treaty of Paris) is ratified by the Senate by a vote of 57 to 27, just one vote more than the two-thirds majority required.

Feb. 17 The Anti-Imperialist League is founded to oppose American expansion, including the conquest of the Philippines.

Mar. 2 Mount Rainier National Park is established, in the Cascade Range of the state of Washington.

Mar. 3 Congress establishes a code of criminal law for the District of Alaska.

Mar. 30 General Arthur MacArthur expels

Admiral Dewey with President McKinley and Cardinal Gibbons, 1899

the Filipinos from their capital at Malolos and forces them to retire to Tarlac.

May 18-July 29 The United States attends a world conference, held in The Hague, Netherlands. [The only result of the conference is the empaneling of justices to form an International Court of Arbitration, which could serve to arbitrate international disputes if requested to do so.]

June 9 James J. Jeffries knocks out world heavyweight champion Bob Fitzsimmons in the 11th round at Coney Island, New York.

July 18 Horatio Alger, 67, the author of popular juvenile fiction, dies in Natick, Massachusetts.

Aug. 17 The National Afro-American Council, organized on Sept. 15, 1898, holds its first annual conference in Chicago. Its main concern is the rise in the number of lynchings (now about 100 each year) taking place in the Southern states.

Sept. 6 An international trade doctrine with respect to China is proposed by Secretary of State John Hay. He urges the great powers with spheres of influence in China to keep the treaty ports open to all trade [hence it is called the Open Door Policy], without discrimination. Its intent is to secure the American trade position in China on an equal footing with the other leading nations involved in the China trade.

Nov. 24 General Elwell S. Otis reports that most of Luzon Island, the main island of the Philippines, has been taken from Aguinaldo's Filipino forces.

Dec. 2 An agreement is signed by the three signatories of the Berlin Treaty of 1889 relating to Samoa: the United States, Germany, and Great Britain. The new treaty abolishes the monarchy and divides the archipelago among the three great powers. [However, Great Britain decides to trade its portion with Germany for certain other islands, including Tonga, and part of the Solomons. The division that results leaves the eastern portion of the Samoan archipelago —the islands east of the 171st meridian, including Tutuila—in the hands of the United States. The U.S. Senate ratifies the treaty in 1900.]

Dec. 4 The 56th Congress convenes, with 53 Republicans, 26 Democrats, and 8 others in the Senate; 185 Republicans, 163 Democrats, and 9 others in the House. The third-party group in both houses is comprised mainly of Populists, who have lost most of the seats they held in the 55th Congress.

_1900_ As the 20th century opens, the United States is enjoying a period of general prosperity and public complacency, growing industrialism, and significant social change. The 12th decennial census puts the population at 76,212,168, an increase of almost 21 per cent over that of 1890. The number of states is now 45, with the addition during the decade of Idaho, Wyoming and Utah. The illiteracy rate of persons over the age of 10 is about half what is was 30 years ago. The eastern part of the country remains the center of industrialism and population; New York is the largest city, with a population of 3,437,202; followed by Chicago, with 1,698,575; and Philadelphia, with 1,293,697. More than one third of the nation is urban; manufacturing is replacing farming as a major source of income, and big business is absorbing small business. The public is becoming aware of the "trust." Railroad trackage totals about 193,000 miles. About 8,000 passenger automobiles share some 150,000 miles of surfaced roads with innumerable horse-drawn vehicles.

The Presidential election campaign is largely dominated by controversy growing out of the recently concluded war. Under the terms of the Treaty of Paris, Spain has given up its claim to Cuba and has ceded to the United States the Philippine Islands, Puerto Rico, and Guam. The United States is, however inadvertently, a world power.

President McKinley and Theodore Roosevelt (who views the Vice Presidency as a road going nowhere) run on a platform advocating the gold standard and stressing the need for a canal through the Isthmus of Panama. They also advocate prosperity under the symbol of the "full dinner pail." McKinley does no campaigning, but Roosevelt visits 24 states, travels 21,000 miles, and makes 700 speeches. The Democrats, headed again by William Jennings Bryan of the golden tongue, oppose as imperialism the policy of expansion of U.S. interests. McKinley's reelection, with 292 electoral votes against Bryan's 155 electoral votes, indicates that empire is acceptable to most Americans, if it means they will eat well. Virtually unnoticed is the election as governor of Wisconsin of the progressive Republican, Robert M. La Follette, who hopes to turn the Republican Party in a populist direction.

Jan. 25   The House of Representatives votes to unseat Congressman-elect Brigham Henry Roberts of Utah, on the grounds of polygamy. Roberts, a Democrat, helped frame Utah's constitution. [He serves in France as a chaplain during World War I.]

Jan. 29   The baseball American League is founded and demands recognition by the National League, which is denied. [Recognition is granted in 1903.]

Mar. 5   The Hall of Fame for noted Americans is founded at New York University in New York City.

Mar. 14   Congress passes the Gold Standard Act, under which other forms of money are made redeemable in gold on demand, a gold reserve of $150,000,000 is created, and the sale of bonds is authorized when necessary to maintain the reserve.

Mar. 20   Secretary of State John Hay announces that the Open Door policy toward China has been accepted by Germany, Russia, Great Britain, Italy, and Japan.

April 7   Congress passes the Foraker Act, establishing civil government for Puerto Rico. It also introduces free trade for the island with the United States; levies a two-year tariff on imports from the island, the proceeds to go to the island's treasury; and asserts that Puerto Ricans are not entitled to all rights of U.S. citizens.

April 30   John Luther (Casey) Jones, 36, an engineer on the Illinois Central Railroad, dies at the throttle of the Cannon Ball Express, while slowing down near Vaughan, Mississippi, to try to save his passengers from a collision. [Wallace Saunders, a black railroad worker, immortalizes Casey Jones in a popular ballad.]

May 1   A mine explosion in Scofield, Utah, costs the lives of more than 200 miners.

May 11   James J. Jeffries defends his heavyweight boxing championship, knocking out James J. Corbett in the 23d round, at Coney Island, New York.

May 14   Sanford Ballard Dole is appointed first governor of the U.S. territory of Hawaii. Dole has been president of the Republic of Hawaii since 1894.

June 5   A commission of four Americans,

Benjamin Harrison
TWENTY-THIRD PRESIDENT   **1889-1893**

William McKinley
TWENTY-FIFTH PRESIDENT   1897-1901

Theodore Roosevelt
TWENTY-SIXTH PRESIDENT   **1901-1909**

William Howard Taft
TWENTY-SEVENTH PRESIDENT   **1909-1913**

headed by Judge William Howard Taft, reaches Manila and begins to organize a Government of the Philippine Islands. Opposition by the self-proclaimed Government of Emilio Aguinaldo continues, however, as he leads an insurrection that engages some 60,000 American troops in guerrilla warfare.

June 19-21 The Republican national convention meets in Philadelphia and nominates President William McKinley unanimously for a second term on the first ballot. Theodore Roosevelt is enthusiastically endorsed as his running mate.

June 21 U.S. General Arthur MacArthur grants amnesty to Filipino insurgents.

June 30 Piers and German steamships burn at Hoboken, New Jersey, at a cost of 326 lives.

July 4-6 The Democratic national convention names William Jennings Bryan unanimously as its candidate for the Presidency on the first ballot. Adlai Stevenson, former President Cleveland's running mate, is picked to run with Bryan.

July 5 Henry Barnard, 89, educator and first U.S. Commissioner of Education, dies in Hartford, Connecticut.

Aug. 8-10 The first international lawn tennis competition for the Davis Cup is held in Longwood, Massachusetts. The United States wins, three matches to none.

Aug. 14 In accordance with the Open Door policy toward China, U.S. troops join an international relief expedition to relieve Peking during the Boxer Rebellion.

Sept. 8 A hurricane kills more than 6,000 persons and causes extensive property damage in Galveston, Texas.

Nov. 6 William McKinley is reelected President of the United States, and Theodore Roosevelt is elected Vice President. This time McKinley somewhat exceeds his previous percentage of victory, and greatly exceeds his margin of the popular vote: by some 860,000 over Bryan, as compared with 600,000 four years ago.

Nov. 15 Andrew Carnegie founds the Carnegie Institute of Technology, in Pittsburgh, thus proving by action the concept expressed in his recently published *The Gospel of Wealth* that donations should be made during the life of the donor.

The mast of the sunken *Maine*

1901 President William McKinley's assassination, six months after his second inauguration, catapults the nation into the era of Theodore Roosevelt. A military hero of the Spanish-American War, he perceives the demands of the American people for action to stabilize the economic forces that have dramatically confronted them. The industrialization of the country, and especially the growth of huge trusts in such fields as steel, railroads, banks, and financial institutions (despite the passage in 1890 of the Sherman Antitrust Act), require new approaches. Reformists, mostly Westerners, who call themselves Progressives, demand control of these economic titans. Roosevelt, whose tactic is to "speak softly and carry a big stick" and whose hands are largely tied by a Congress of conservative Republicans, moves slowly, principally by executive action, toward reform.

The growth of industrialization incidentally has given rise to new concepts of production, applying its "scientific management" to men as well as machines. When Frederick Winslow Taylor and Maunsel White, efficiency engineers, develop high-speed metal alloys for cutting tools, Taylor insists that workers match the speed of their tools. Thus is developed the system sometimes called "Taylorism," under which both machines and labor are specialized. For labor this often comes to mean a working existence of unprecedented monotony and fatigue.

Jan. 10   The Spindletop oil gusher blows in south of Beaumont, Texas, representing the first significant oil discovery in the state.

Jan. 21   Elisha Gray, 65, inventor who was involved in a noted legal battle with Alexander Graham Bell over credit for invention of the telephone, dies in Newtonville, Massachusetts.

Feb. 25   The United States Steel Corporation is formed by a merger of 10 companies. Capitalized at more than $1,000,000,000, it is the largest industrial corporation in the world.

Mar. 2   Congress attaches to an Army appropriations bill an amendment, proposed by Senator Orville Platt of Connecticut, establishing the conditions under which the United States would end its occupation of Cuba. The amendment would require Cuba to refrain from making treaties with foreign powers, keep its public debt within the limits of ordinary revenues, permit American intervention if necessary to protect Cuban independence, and provide the United States with land for naval or coaling stations.

Mar. 4   William McKinley is inagurated for a second term as President of the United States.

Mar. 13   Benjamin Harrison, 67, 23d President of the United States, and currently on the International Board of Arbitration at The Hague, dies in Indianapolis.

Mar. 23   Emilio Aguinaldo, Filipino rebel leader, is captured in an expedition planned and led by the U.S. General Frederick Funston. [On April 2 Aguinaldo takes an oath of allegiance to the United States and urges his people to submit to U.S. rule.]

May 27   The U.S. Supreme Court rules on the so-called Insular Cases growing out of the Spanish-American War. The Court holds that territories gained during the war are neither part of the United States nor foreign countries; that authorization by Congress is necessary to impose duties on goods shipped to the United States from Puerto Rico, but that goods shipped to Puerto Rico from the United States are duty-free; and that citizens of such territories do not automatically have the rights of U.S. citizens (thus upholding the Foraker Act of 1900).

June 12   The Cuban Constitutional Convention, assured that Cuban sovereignty would not be diminished, agrees to the Platt Amendment passed by the U.S. Congress in March.

July 4   William Howard Taft is made governor of the Philippines, ending military government.

Sept. 6   President William McKinley is shot by Leon Czolgosz, an American anarchist, at the Pan American Exposition in Buffalo, New York.

Sept. 7   The United States and other nations involved in the Boxer Rebellion in China in 1900 sign a treaty with China under which the Chinese agree to pay an indemnity of $333,000,000 over 40 years for deaths and losses suffered by foreign nationals in the uprising. [In 1908 the United States remits a large part of its share of the indemnity in the form of scholarships for Chinese students, and in 1924 cancels all further payments.]

Sept. 14   President McKinley, 58, dies from the assassin's bullet, and Theodore Roosevelt becomes the 25th President of the United States.

Nov. 18 The Hay-Pauncefote Treaty, concerning rights in the building of a canal across the Isthmus of Panama, is signed by the United States and Great Britain, whereby the United States receives the sole right to build, operate, and fortify the canal and agrees to guarantee its neutrality and permit passage by ships of any nation for peaceful purposes.

Nov. 27 The Army War College is established by Secretary of War Elihu Root, to pro-

vide advanced military training for officers. This training is considered necessary in view of criticism of Army performance in the Spanish-American War.

Dec. 3 Theodore Roosevelt delivers his first message to Congress, calling for broad social and economic reforms and regulation of the activities of large business interests, while conceding that "captains of industry. . .have on the whole done great good to our people. . . ."

A beach scene at Coney Island, New York (*ca.*) 1900's

1902 Beginning his first full year as President of the United States, Theodore Roosevelt emphasizes his determination to deal with the domestic problems of the country, and especially to curb the further growth of the trusts and to promote Federal regulation of private business. He also takes a major step to consummate his lifelong devotion to the conservation of natural resources by signing the Reclamation Act. The program is inaugurated as construction of the Roosevelt Dam is begun on the Salt River in Arizona [completed in 1911].

As the country faces a coal shortage because of a strike by the anthracite coal miners headed by John Mitchell, president of the United Mine Workers of America, Roosevelt takes the first Presidential step to settle, rather than break, a strike. The coal-mining industry is largely monopolized by eight coal-hauling railroads dominated by John Pierpont Morgan. It pays notably substandard wages, and safety precautions in the mines are virtually nonexistent. The strikers demand an eight-hour day, a 20-per-cent wage increase, and union recognition. George F. Baer, stating the operators' opinion, says, "The duty of the hour is not to waste time negotiating with the fomenters of this anarchy." When Roosevelt calls both sides to the White House and proposes mediation of the dispute, Mitchell agrees but Baer refuses. Baer's intransigent attitude evokes public sympathy for the strikers for perhaps the first time in a major labor dispute. When Roosevelt threatens to have the Army operate the mines, the owners begin to bend, and the President is able to persuade J. P. Morgan to arrange a settlement. This unprecedented Presidential initiative is attacked strongly by the conservative press, but its success gains him wide public support and considerable political leverage.

Jan. 1 The first postseason college football classic, the Rose Bowl, is inaugurated at Pasadena, California; the University of Michigan defeats Stanford University by a score of 49-0.

Feb. 18 The United States uses the Sherman Antitrust Act for the first time against the country's great financiers. Suit is brought for restraint of interstate commerce against the Northern Securities Company, a vast railroad complex including the Burlington, Northern Pacific, and Great Northern systems, built by J. P. Morgan, John D. Rockefeller, Edward H. Harriman, and James J. Hill.

Mar. 6 The Bureau of the Census is established in the Department of the Interior. Previous censuses were made under supervision of U.S. marshals with temporary staffs.

April 11 Wade Hampton, 84, Civil War Confederate general who raised Hampton's Legion and later served as governor of South Carolina and as U.S. Senator, dies in Charleston.

May 5 Bret Harte, 65, enormously popular writer of tales of the early West, such as "The Luck of Roaring Camp," and "The Outcasts of Poker Flat," dies in Albany, New York.

May 12 Anthracite coal miners strike, demanding union representation, an eight-hour work day, and a 20-per-cent wage increase.

May 20 The United States withdraws from Cuba as the Republic of Cuba is instituted under the presidency of Tomás Estrada Palma.

June 2 Oregon adopts the novel political devices of general initiative and referendum, under which the public can override actions of the legislature and initiate a popular vote on legislation.

June 17 Congress passes legislation providing for irrigation of arid lands in the Western states. Called the Reclamation Act or the Irrigation Bill, it is sponsored by Francis G. Newlands of Nevada.

June 28 The Isthmian Canal (or Spooner) Act is passed by Congress, authorizing construction of a canal across the Isthmus of Panama at a cost not to exceed $40,000,000, providing Colombia grants perpetual control to the United States of the strip of land through which the canal is to pass.

July 1 The Philippines Government Act is passed by the Congress, establishing civil government in the islands under the supervision of the United States. It provides for an 81-member Assembly to be elected by qualified voters for two-year terms, each member to represent a constituency on the basis of population.

Sept. 20 A fire in a church in Birmingham, Alabama, results in the death of 115 persons.

Sept. 23 John Wesley Powell, 68, geologist, pioneer in the classification of American Indian languages, and founder of the U.S. Bureau of

American Ethnology, dies in Haven, Maine. Although he lost an arm during the Civil War, Powell led the first expedition to explore the Colorado River through its 900-mile length from Utah to California by boat.

Oct. 16-21   President Roosevelt appoints a commission to make recommendations for settling the strike of anthracite coal miners. The strike ends when the miners accept a 10-per-cent pay increase but fail to win union recognition.

Oct. 26   Elizabeth Cady Stanton, 86, woman suffrage leader who organized the first women's rights convention in 1848 in Seneca Falls, New York, dies in New York City.

Nov. 23   Walter Reed, 49, U.S. Army bacteriologist who proved that yellow fever is carried by mosquitoes, dies in Washington, D.C.

Dec. 8   Oliver Wendell Holmes is appointed Associate Justice of the U.S. Supreme Court.

Dec. 19   After Great Britain, Germany, and Italy blockade five Venezuelan ports in an effort to obtain payment of financial claims by their nationals, the United States persuades the European powers to submit to arbitration in view of the agreement of Venezuelan President Cipriano Castro to such a solution.

U.S. Marines in China during the Boxer Rebellion

1903 **The United States acquires a 10-mile strip of land** across the Isthmus of Panama, to be used for construction of an Atlantic-Pacific canal. The manner of its acquisition, however, is unconventional and unprecedented. As an outcome of the Spooner Act of 1902, authorizing the President to acquire land from Colombia for the proposed canal site, the United States and Colombia negotiate the Hay-Herrán treaty. The U.S. Senate ratifies this treaty but the senate of Colombia is dissatisfied with its terms and rejects it. Leaders in Panama, which is part of Colombia, learn that the proposed canal may be built in Nicaragua if agreement cannot be reached with Colombia. They therefore plan a revolt and declaration of independence to avoid the loss of the canal. A request for U.S. aid is made and a U.S. naval force is dispatched to prevent Colombian interference with the planned insurrection. Panama proclaims its independence, under the leadership of Manuel Amador, and the United States promptly recognizes the new Government. A second canal treaty, the Hay-Bunau-Varilla Treaty, is signed with Panama within the month.

In President Theodore Roosevelt's continuing battle against the trusts, the U.S. Congress passes the Elkins Law, strengthening the Interstate Commerce Act of 1887 by requiring the railroads to abide by published rate schedules and by providing for penalties against railroads for the granting of secret rebates to certain shippers; it also makes the shipper who accepts a rebate guilty along with the carrier that grants it. Creation of the Federal Bureau of Corporations to carry on investigations also makes possible increased public awareness of the affairs of big-business operations.

Pursuing his conservation policies, President Roosevelt establishes the first National Wildlife Refuge at Pelican Island, in the Indian River in Florida. Meanwhile, specific legislation action to ameliorate or correct certain social ills begins to appear in the individual states, which pass laws limiting the hours of labor of children and establish state departments of labor or industrial boards. Public awareness of social problems is sparked by a new type of journalism, in which reporters dig out and publish the facts of life. Notable among these journalists, whose reports appear in the new mass-circulation periodicals, are Ida Minerva Tarbell, author of the two-volume *History of the Standard Oil Company,* and Lincoln Steffens, whose articles expose corruption in municipal government as well as in business. Absolutely no intention of improving the public weal is to be found in the production of *The Great Train Robbery* by Edwin Porter, the first motion picture to employ motion by the camera as well as by the actors and the first to have a full-blown plot.

Jan. 22   Colombian chargé d'affaires Tomás Herrán and Secretary of State John Hay agree on the provisions of the Spooner Act of 1902 concerning the building of a canal in Panama.
Jan. 24   The Alaskan boundary dispute between the United States and Canada is referred to a commission of three Americans, two Canadians, and one Briton.
Feb. 4   Congress passes the Elkins Act, which makes punishable by fine or imprisonment the act of giving or receiving rebates or special favors in interstate commerce transactions.
Feb. 11   The Expedition Act is passed by Congress and $500,000 is appropriated in a move to facilitate action on Federal antitrust suits by giving them precedence over other legal cases pending in the circuit courts.
Feb. 14   Congress establishes the U.S. Army

General Staff Corps to coordinate the activities of infantry, artillery, and other services and to act as liaison between the field soldiers and the Secretary of War and his civilian staff.
Feb. 14   President Roosevelt creates a Department of Commerce and Labor, with a Secretary of Cabinet rank; it is first headed by George B. Cortelyou of New York.
Feb. 23   The U.S. Supreme Court, in the case of *Champion* v. *Ames,* declares that Congress has the authority to bar the mailing of lottery tickets across state lines. The decision affirms the precedence of Federal police power over that of the states.
Mar. 17   The Senate ratifies the Hay-Herrán Treaty of Jan. 22.
May 23   Wisconsin adopts legislation providing for the first direct primary election system

for state candidates in the United States.

June 20   The senate of the Republic of Colombia rejects the Herrán-Hay Treaty.

July 17   James McNeill Whistler, 69, painter of *Portrait of My Mother,* dies in London.

Aug. 1   In the first transcontinental automobile journey, a Packard reaches New York City 52 days after leaving San Francisco.

Oct. 20   The dispute concerning the boundary between the District of Alaska and Canada is decided in favor of the American contention that the boundary follow the crest of the mountains. The British commissioner sides with the United States against Canada.

Nov. 2   Under orders from President Roosevelt, the U.S.S. *Nashville* drops anchor at Colón to protect the right of "free and uninterrupted transit across the Isthmus," but in reality to assist a Panamanian revolution against Colombian rule.

Nov. 6   The United States recognizes the Republic of Panama which was formed three days ago. Colombian troops are prevented from quelling the insurrection.

Nov. 18   A treaty is signed by Secretary of State John Hay for the United States and Philippe Jean Bunau-Varilla for Panama, granting the United States the use in perpetuity of a 10-mile zone on both sides of a proposed canal, in return for a U.S. guarantee of neutrality of the canal and payment of $10,000,000 down and annual rentals.

Dec. 17   Orville Wright becomes the first man to fly a heavier-than-air machine, remaining aloft for 12 seconds in the first of a series of tests at Kitty Hawk, North Carolina. Later the same day his brother, Wilbur Wright, makes a flight that lasts 59 seconds.

Dec. 20   The Iroquois Theater in Chicago is destroyed by fire, with a loss of 602 lives.

Flight of the *Kitty Hawk*

1904

The Presidential election campaign of 1904 tests whether the American electorate accepts the reformist policies of Theodore Roosevelt. Confident of his popularity among the people, Roosevelt assures his nomination by permitting the conservative Republicans to control the seating of delegations to the convention and the framing of a platform. The Democratic Party moves even further to the right. Wanting no more of Bryan, the delegates choose Judge Alton B. Parker of New York, a colorless conservative. Imperialism has become a relatively dead issue, both parties espouse an antitrust position, and the Democrats drop the issues of silver and the income tax.

Taking no chances on the actual election, and fearing that Wall Street is funding Parker's campaign chest, Roosevelt permits his campaign manager to seek contributions from the very trusts that he has been attacking. Personal contributions come from such men as Edward Harriman and J. P. Morgan. Roosevelt's doubts prove groundless; he is elected by a plurality of more than 2,500,000 votes, the highest percentage of the popular votes (56.4 per cent) since records were kept. State elections indicate that the trend toward reform is as strong as Roosevelt's personal popularity. Machine Republicans are defeated by reformist Democrats in several states.

In foreign affairs, Roosevelt displays his "big stick." When the Dominican Republic, refuses to pay financial claims of European countries, Roosevelt maintains that the United States will not countenance European intrusion into the Americas even to collect valid debts. He recognizes that the situation ". . .may finally require intervention by some civilized nation, and in the Western Hemisphere the United States cannot ignore this duty. . . ." In effect, this is a corollary that alters the Doctrine from barring intervention in the Americas by European countries to permitting the United States to intervene when necessary.

In the Far East, Roosevelt is concerned with the threat to the Open Door policy represented by Russian expansion in Manchuria. When Japan undertakes a surprise attack on the Russian fleet at Port Arthur, Roosevelt warns France and Germany against aiding Russia. He has reservations, however, about total victory for Japan, lest this might "possibly mean a struggle between them and us in the future."

Jan. 2 James Longstreet, 83, Confederate general in the Civil War who was called General Robert E. Lee's "war horse," dies in Gainesville, Georgia.

Jan. 4 The U.S. Supreme Court rules that Puerto Ricans, although not U.S. citizens, are nevertheless not aliens and thus may not be refused admission to the country.

Feb. 7-8 Fire sweeps the business center at Baltimore, destroying some 2,600 buildings in 80 blocks, but taking no lives.

Feb. 26 The Hay-Bunau-Varilla Treaty, providing the United States with land in Panama for a cross-isthmus canal, is ratified by the U.S. Senate.

Feb. 29 President Roosevelt names a seven-man Isthmian Canal Commission to supervise construction of the Panama Canal. [On March 8 he names Rear Admiral John G. Walker chairman of the commission.]

Mar. 14 The U.S. Supreme Court rules that the merger of the Northern Pacific, Great Northern, and Burlington railroad systems through the Northern Securities Company violates the Sherman Antitrust Act.

May 4 The Panama Canal Zone is legally transferred to the United States.

May 14 The third modern Olympiad, the first ever held in the United States, opens in St. Louis. With few contestants from other countries, the United States wins 21 events.

June 15 The excursion steamer *General Slocum* burns in the East River in New York City; 1,030 persons are killed.

June 21-23 The Republican national convention, meeting in Chicago, nominates Theodore Roosevelt for a full term as President. Charles W. Fairbanks is the nominee for Vice President.

July 4 Using a cable from San Francisco to Manila, President Roosevelt sends a message around the world that is returned in 12 minutes.

July 6-9   The Democratic convention, meeting in St. Louis, nominates Judge Alton B. Parker of New York as its candidate for the Presidency.

Sept. 26   Lafcadio Hearn, 54, journalist, writer, and translator, who lived in Japan and sought to interpret that country to the Western world, dies in Tokyo.

Oct. 8   The first Vanderbilt Cup automobile race, a 300-mile road event, is held; the winner is A. L. Campbell, driving a Mercedes. [The event is discontinued in 1917.]

Oct. 27   The first section of the New York City subway goes into operation between City Hall and West 145th Street.

Nov. 8   Theodore Roosevelt is elected President of the United States, receiving 7,629,461 popular and 336 electoral votes, defeating Alton B. Parker, the Democratic candidate, who receives 5,084,223 popular and 140 electoral votes. The Vice President is Charles W. Fairbanks, Senator from Indiana.

Dec. 6   President Roosevelt enunciates his corollary to the Monroe Doctrine, which states that the United States has the sole responsibility to police the Western Hemisphere.

An automobile cavalcade in Minneapolis

1905

President Roosevelt follows up his 1904 corollary to the Monroe Doctrine by signing a protocol with the Dominican Republic, under which the United States is empowered to take over Dominican financial affairs and settle its foreign and domestic debts. When the U.S. Senate refuses to ratify this protocol, President Roosevelt acts independently to appoint a customs receiver for Santo Domingo. The President also offers his services as mediator between Russia and Japan, at the request of the latter country, and sponsors a conference at Portsmouth, New Hampshire, that ends the Russo-Japanese War. Before the Portsmouth Conference opens, Roosevelt sends Secretary of War William Howard Taft to Tokyo, where he reaches an executive agreement under which Japan acknowledges U.S. rights in the Philippine Islands and the United States acknowledges Japan's rights in Korea.

On the domestic scene, in a period of active unionization, many state governments are enacting laws designed to aid the workingman in a paternalistic fashion. The U.S. Supreme Court, however, rules most such laws unconstitutional. A significant event in the evolution of the labor movement is the formation, in competition with the American Federation of Labor, of the Industrial Workers of the World. Unions representing 40 trades, most of them based in the West, formulate the more radical policy of the IWW, with the aim of organizing the entire industrial population. The IWW advocates the use of direct action by means of strikes, boycotts, and sabotage rather than collective bargaining or arbitration.

Feb. 15   Lew Wallace, 78, general in the Union Army in the Civil War and author of *Ben Hur,* dies in Crawfordsville, Indiana.

Feb. 20   The U.S. Supreme Court rules, in the case of *Jacobson* v. *Massachusetts,* that states have the right to enact laws requiring vaccination.

Feb. 23   A lawyer named Paul Harris founds a club in Chicago dedicated to the ideal of service for its members, who are to come from various professions or occupations. Because its offices are filled in rotation by various members each week, the organization is called the Rotary Club.

Mar. 4   Theodore Roosevelt is inaugurated for a full term as President.

Mar. 31   President Roosevelt appoints a customs receiver for the Dominican Republic to ease that country's financial difficulties with European creditors.

April 17   In the case of *Lochner* v. *New York,* the U.S. Supreme Court holds that a state cannot set the maximum number of hours an employee may work. The New York State law limiting the baker's day to 10 hours and his week to 60 hours is held to violate the 14th Amendment. Justice Holmes dissents.

May 31   Japan, financially exhausted although clearly gaining a military victory over Russia, asks President Roosevelt to mediate in the Russo-Japanese War.

June 27-July 8   The Industrial Workers of the World (IWW), nicknamed the "Wobblies," is founded in Chicago by Eugene V. Debs, William D. Haywood, and others, with the aim of uniting all workingmen and gaining union control of production.

July 1   John Milton Hay, 66, Secretary of State under Presidents McKinley and Roosevelt, dies in Newbury, New Hampshire.

July 5   James J. Jeffries having retired as heavyweight boxing champion, Marvin Hart gains the title by knocking out Jack Root in the 12th round at Reno, Nevada. Jeffries referees the bout and presents the title to Hart.

July 22-October   An epidemic of yellow fever breaks out in New Orleans. Some 400 deaths occur before the outbreak is controlled by an antimosquito campaign undertaken by the U.S. Government.

July 25   John F. Stevens, railroad builder and explorer, arrives in the Canal Zone to take over as chief engineer, with responsibility for providing housing and sanitary measures for employees and for recruiting competent supervisors. Work is hampered by failure to decide whether the canal is to be at sea level or of the lock type.

Sept. 5   The Treaty of Portsmouth, ending the Russo-Japanese War, is concluded through the mediation efforts of President Roosevelt.

Oct. 31   The play *Mrs. Warren's Profession,* by George Bernard Shaw, is closed by police after one performance in New York City. The action is taken at the instigation of Anthony Comstock, secretary of the Society for the Prevention of Vice.

A New York City elevated train after plunging to the street

1906

Continuing his role of mediator in foreign affairs, President Theodore Roosevelt is instrumental in bringing about the Algeciras Conference, during which the European powers reach agreement on the status of Morocco. This is an unusual departure for U.S. foreign policy, inasmuch as the issues involved in the conference are entirely European. In Cuba a revolt breaks out following the reelection of Tomás Estrada Palma. After an unsuccessful attempt to mediate, President Roosevelt, under the terms of the Platt Amendment, sends U.S. troops to the island and establishes a provisional Government. In October, strained relations with Japan result from the segregation of Japanese children in the schools of San Francisco—a symptom of the general opposition on the West Coast to Japanese immigration. Public opinion in Japan is outraged until President Roosevelt persuades San Francisco to desegregate its schools.

On the domestic front, the Railway Rate Regulation Act strengthens the Interstate Commerce Commission by extending its control over express and sleeping-car companies and pipeline, ferry, and terminal facilities. The ICC is empowered to fix future maximum rates and to establish divisions and through routes; stronger regulations against rebating are included; and passes are prohibited. The act makes some concessions to the railroad interests. Congress also passes a Pure Food and Drug Act and legislation requiring inspection of meat. Taking an early step toward territorial status, the District of Alaska is granted the right to elect a nonvoting delegate to the U.S. House of Representatives.

Jan. 16-April 7   A conference on the status of Morocco, with the participation of the United States, is held in Algeciras, Spain. The role of the United States in world affairs is apparently as a partisan of Britain and France against Germany.

Feb. 8   Paul Laurence Dunbar, 33, son of an escaped slave, author of verse and short stories in the dialect of his race, dies in Dayton, Ohio.

Feb. 23   Tommy Burns wins the heavyweight boxing championship, defeating Marvin Hart in the 20th round, at Los Angeles.

Mar. 12   The U.S. Supreme Court rules, in *Hale* v. *Henkel,* that witnesses in antitrust suits can be compelled to testify against their employers and to produce written evidence pertinent to the case.

Mar. 13   Susan Brownell Anthony, 86, pioneer of the woman suffrage movement and an organizer of the Woman's Rights Convention in Seneca Falls, New York, in 1848, dies in Rochester, New York.

April 18   Algernon Sidney Crapsey, a clergyman of the Protestant Episcopal Church, goes on trial for heresy in Batavia, New York, charged with having preached against the divinity of Christ. [He is found guilty and unfrocked on Dec. 5.]

April 18   The most damaging earthquake in U.S. history, followed by fire, destroys much of San Francisco. Loss of life is estimated at about 700, property damage totals about $400,000,000, and looting is widespread.

May 14   Carl Schurz, 77, statesman and reformer who unsuccessfully urged President Andrew Johnson to readmit the Confederate States immediately after the Civil War, dies in New York City. German-born, a refugee after the failure of the 1848 revolution, he was a Civil War general, a Senator from Missouri, Secretary of the Interior in the Hayes Administration, and editor of the New York *Evening Post.*

June 4   The Reynolds and Neill report is issued on conditions in the meat-packing industry. The reporting commissioners were appointed by President Roosevelt as a result of the adverse impression of the industry conveyed in Upton Sinclair's book, *The Jungle,* published this year.

June 29   Congress passes the Railway Rate Regulation Act, also called the Hepburn Act, authorizing the Federal Government to fix rates for interstate shipments. The provisions of the antirebate Elkins Act of 1903 are incorporated in the Hepburn Act.

June 29   President Roosevelt signs an act of Congress providing for a lock-type rather than sea-level canal in Panama.

June 30   The Pure Food and Drug Act, prohibiting the misbranding and adulteration of foods and medicines involved in interstate or foreign commerce, is passed by Congress; Dr. Harvey Wiley of the Department of Agriculture is named administrator. At the same time the Meat Inspection Act is passed, requiring Federal

Workmen clear debris at Post and Montgomery Streets following the San Francisco earthquake.

inspection of all meat involved in such commerce. (The Constitution reserves for the states the right to regulate goods not involved in interstate or foreign commerce.)

Aug. 23-Oct. 3 President Tomás Estrada Palma of Cuba requests assistance of the United States in putting down a rebellion. President Roosevelt, after attempting mediation, sends U.S. troops under Secretary of War William Howard Taft, who sets up a provisional Government on Sept. 29. On Oct. 3 Charles Edward Magoon is named governor of Cuba under the terms of the Platt Amendment, to rule ''long enough to restore order and peace and public confidence.''

Sept. 24 President Roosevelt names Devils Tower in Wyoming as the first National Monument. The tower, a natural rock formation 865 feet in height, rises above the Belle Fourche River. The category of National Monument derives from the Preservation of American Antiquities Act of June 8.

Nov. 4 Charles Evans Hughes is elected governor of New York State, narrowly defeating newspaper publisher William Randolph Hearst.

Nov. 9 President Roosevelt sails on the U.S.S. *Louisiana* to inspect the progress of work on the Panama Canal. He is the first President to leave the country while in office.

Dec. 10 President Roosevelt receives the Nobel Peace Prize for his efforts in ending the Russo-Japanese War of 1904-1905. He is the first American to win a Nobel Prize.

Dec. 12 Oscar S. Straus of New York City is appointed Secretary of Commerce and Labor by President Roosevelt. He is the first Jew to receive a Cabinet post.

269

1907

After years of business prosperity, the United States faces a serious financial panic, as big business becomes increasingly alarmed at the thrust of the "trust-busting" policies of President Roosevelt. The root of the difficulty is the weakness of the banking and credit system, but the overt beginnings of the panic are a steep decline in the stock market followed by a run on the Knickerbocker Trust Company of New York. Unemployment soars and wage cuts are widespread. The Government moves to ease the crisis by greatly increasing its deposits in the banks, and toward the end of the year J. P. Morgan persuades other capitalists to join him in making loans to preserve the solvency of threatened banks and corporations.

In foreign affairs, the second Hague Peace Conference, attended by 44 nations including the United States, meets from June to October. Like the first, held in 1899, the conference operates on the principle that war is inevitable and seeks merely to regulate acceptable methods of warfare. Proposals for a limitation of armaments are rejected, but a new convention providing for the limitation of the use of force for the recovery of foreign debts is adopted, thus reinforcing the Monroe Doctrine. Other conventions adopted revise the laws on war on land and apply the principles of the Geneva Convention to maritime war. A resolution is adopted recommending creation of a world judicial arbitration court, but it is not implemented.

Jan. 22   The first American performance of *Salome,* by Richard Strauss, adapted from a play by Oscar Wilde, is given at the Metropolitan Opera House. The theme, including the dance of the seven veils and the display of the prophet Jokanaan's head on a platter, is shocking to the public, and further performances are canceled.

Feb. 8   The United States and the Dominican Republic sign a treaty providing that the United States collect customs to pay foreign and domestic creditors of the Dominican Republic. This formalizes an arrangement already in operation since 1905 under Executive order, after the U.S. Senate refused to agree to such a treaty. [On Feb. 25 the Senate ratifies the Feb. 8 treaty.]

Feb. 12   The steamer *Larchmont* sinks in Long Island Sound, with a loss of 131 lives.

Feb. 26   The U.S. Congress passes a General Appropriations Act, including a provision increasing to $12,000 the annual salaries of Cabinet members, the Speaker of the U.S. House of Representatives, and the Vice President; and to $7,500 the salaries of members of Congress.

Mar. 13   A financial panic begins with a sharp drop of the stock markets.

Mar. 14   President Roosevelt, with the authorization of the U.S. Congress, concludes a "gentlemen's agreement" with Japan to exclude Japanese laborers from the United States.

Mar. 21   U.S. marines land in Honduras, which is in a state of revolution, to protect American lives and American-owned banana plantations.

April 1   The Panama Canal Commission is reorganized. Lieutenant Colonel George W. Goethals is named to direct construction.

June 15-Oct. 18   The second Hague Peace Conference is held with Joseph H. Choate representing the United States. Of particular interest to the United States is a new convention that prohibits the use of armed force to collect debts. The establishment of a world court, backed by the United States, fails.

Aug. 3   Augustus Saint Gaudens, 59, sculptor of monumental works such as *The Puritan,* dies in Cornish, New Hampshire.

Sept. 12   The *Lusitania,* the largest steamship in the world (gross tonnage almost 32,000), docks in New York harbor on her maiden voyage from Liverpool. [In November she sets a record of 4 days 18 hours 40 minutes from Ireland to New York.]

Oct. 16   Secretary of War William Howard Taft opens the first meeting of the Legislative Assembly of the Philippine Islands.

October-November   A run begins on Oct. 21 on the Knickerbocker Trust Company that wipes out that bank. Many other banks fail, unemployment rises, and food prices soar. Increased bank deposits infused by the U.S. Treasury restore confidence, supported by loans from such capitalist leaders as J. Pierpont Morgan.

Nov. 16   Oklahoma is admitted as the 46th State of the Union, after the Territory of Oklahoma and the Indian Territory agree to admission as a single state.

Dec. 6   A coal mine explosion in Monongah, West Virginia, takes the lives of 361 miners.

Dec. 10 Albert A. Michelson, physicist at the University of Chicago, receives the Nobel Prize in physics for his spectroscopic and meteorological studies. He is the first American to win a Nobel Prize in physics.

Dec. 16 The "Great White Fleet," comprising most of the ships of the U.S. Navy, sails from the West Coast for Australia on the first leg of a world cruise to demonstrate U.S. naval strength.

Dec. 19 A coal mine explosion in Jacobs Creek, Pennsylvania, costs the lives of 239 miners.

Ships of the Great White Fleet during the world cruise

1908 **President Theodore Roosevelt, having vowed upon his election in** 1904 that he would not again run for the Presidency, handpicks as his successor Secretary of War William Howard Taft, who has distinguished himself by his diplomatic successes in the Philippines, Latin America, and Japan. Taft fully supports Roosevelt's progressive policies at home. The Republican convention hammers out a platform designed to sound progressive without offending conservatives. Because tariff reduction is an urgent popular issue, the platform promises to call a special session of Congress to achieve it. The labor vote is wooed by a plank, drafted by Taft, condemning the use of injunctions to halt strikes. However, when this plank is attacked by the National Association of Manufacturers, Taft and Roosevelt offer a compromise that infuriates Samuel Gompers, president of the American Federation of Labor.

The Democrats, stung by Parker's sound defeat in 1904, nominate William Jennings Bryan for the third time. Their platform espouses the antitrust principle and also promises tariff reduction. It departs from such compatibility with the opposition by calling for an income tax, for a fund to be established by national banks to pay depositors of insolvent banks, and for the election of U.S. Senators by direct vote instead of by state legislatures.

Taft easily wins, with 7,675,320 popular votes and 321 electoral votes, while Bryan receives 6,412,294 popular and 162 electoral votes. Taft's plurality of almost 1,265,000, however, is only about half that of Roosevelt in 1904, and several Western states shift to Bryan.

The progressive movement among the states continues to be led by Oregon, which adopts the principle of recall of all elective officials. Also, the Oregon law limiting women workers in industry to a 10-hour work day is upheld by the U.S. Supreme Court.

American art attracts considerable interest when a group of painters calling themselves The Eight hold their first showings in New York City's Macbeth Gallery. Rejecting the traditional standards, they introduce a radical concept by portraying scenes of everyday life in realistic terms. The group comprises Arthur B. Davies, Maurice B. Prendergast, Robert Henri, John Sloan, George B. Luks, William J. Blackens, Everett Shinn, and Ernest Lawson. Their works, which share no common style, outrage critics, who dub the movement the "Ashcan School."

Jan. 23 Edward MacDowell, 46, composer, principally of piano pieces, dies in New York City. He is the first American composer to have won recognition abroad.

Feb. 3 The U.S. Supreme Court rules, in *Loewe* v. *Lawlor* (the so-called Danbury Hatters case), that the boycotting of industry by labor is conspiracy in restraint of trade within the meaning of the Sherman Antitrust Act.

Mar. 4 Fire destroys a grammar school in Collingwood, near Cleveland, Ohio; 175 children lose their lives.

April 12 About one-third of the city of Chelsea, Massachusetts, is wiped out by fire, with some 10,000 persons left homeless.

May 28 Congress passes legislation regulating child labor in the District of Columbia, with a view toward prodding the states to follow suit.

May 30 Under the impact of the financial panic of 1907, the Aldrich-Vreeland Currency Act is passed by Congress. It establishes a National Monetary Commission to study the banking and currency systems of the United States and foreign countries.

June 8 The National Conservation Commission is established, headed by Gifford Pinchot, chief of the U.S. Forest Service, with a mandate to submit reports on water, timber, soil, and mineral resources.

June 16-20 The Republican National Convention meets in Chicago and nominates William Howard Taft, President Roosevelt's choice, as candidate for the Presidency. James S. Sherman of New York is picked as his running mate.

June 23 The United States suspends diplomatic relations with Venezuela because of that country's refusal to pay compensation for injuries to American citizens during revolutionary activities.

June 24 Grover Cleveland, 71, the 22d and 24th President of the United States, dies in Princeton, New Jersey.

July 3 Joel Chandler Harris, 59, author of the Uncle Remus tales, dies in Atlanta.

July 7-10 The Democratic National Convention meets in Denver, Colorado, and nominates William Jennings Bryan as its candidate for the Presidency.

Oct. 1 The Ford Motor Company introduces the Model T, priced at $850.

Nov. 3 William Howard Taft is elected 27th President of the United States, with 51.6 per cent of the popular vote.

Dec. 2 The Federal Council of Churches of Christ in America, representing most Protestant denominations, is founded in Philadelphia.

Dec. 24 Motion-picture censorship is inaugurated by the Society for the Prevention of Vice, which persuades the mayor of New York City to revoke the licenses of theaters until and unless they agree to remain closed on Sundays and to present no immoral films.

Dec. 26 Jack Johnson wins the heavyweight boxing championship, stopping Tommy Burns in the 14th round, in Sydney, Australia.

The Model T Ford

273

As William Howard Taft assumes the Presidency of the United States, a deep split appears in the ranks of the Republican Party. The conservative wing, headed by Nelson W. Aldrich in the Senate and Speaker of the House of Representatives Joseph Gurney ("Uncle Joe") Cannon, fights vigorously against the "insurgents" or progessives of the party, who seek to continue and extend the policies of Theodore Roosevelt. Taft himself, although ostensibly espousing a continuation of Roosevelt's policies, ignores his pledge to retain any members of Roosevelt's Cabinet who might wish to remain, and instead surrounds himself with conservative advisers. The conflict is highlighted by the tariff question. The President calls Congress into special session on March 15 to consider tariff reduction, as he had promised before his election. The House bill sponsored by Representative Sereno Elisha Payne of New York contains substantial reductions from the Dingley tariff of 1897. But the bill reported by the Senate Committe on Finance, headed by Senator Aldrich, contains almost 850 amendments, the great majority of which represent increases. Despite a critical and thorough analysis of the bill by progressive leader Senator Robert M. La Follette and appeals by Midwestern progressives, the Payne-Aldrich Act is signed by President Taft. Moreover, he calls it ". . .the best tariff bill that the Republican Party has ever passed."

Jan. 27   The United States and Great Britain agree to refer to the international court of arbitration at The Hague their long-standing dispute over the Newfoundland fisheries. [The decision, rendered on Sept. 7, 1910, extends American privileges in the Newfoundland fishing areas and establishes a commission to settle individual disputes.]

Feb. 21-22   The "Great White Fleet" of American naval vessels arrives at Hampton Roads, Virginia, completing a world cruise begun in 1907 as a show of American naval strength. President Roosevelt reviews the fleet on the second day.

Mar. 4   William Howard Taft is inaugurated as the 27th President of the United States.

Mar. 4   Congress passes the Lacey Act, which protects bird life by supporting the state laws prohibiting indiscriminate killing of game birds and wildfowl. Such laws have been made necessary by the feather fashions of the time. The Lacey Act prohibits the importation of slaughtered birds or interstate commerce in this commodity.

Mar. 30   The cantilever-type Queensboro Bridge over the East River in New York City is opened to traffic.

April 1   Following the official termination of the provisional administration of Cuba by United States appointees, troops are withdrawn from the island, leaving it under the administration of President José Miguel Gómez.

April 6   Robert E. Peary, Matthew Henson, and four Eskimos become the first men to reach the North Pole. [On Sept. 6, when Peary announces his accomplishment, he is informed that

Frederick Albert Cook, another American explorer, claims to have reached the Pole five days earlier; the claim is later proved false.]

June 10   Edward Everett Hale, 87, clergyman, chaplain of the U.S. Senate, and author of *The Man Without a Country,* dies in Boston. His father, Nathan, was a nephew of the patriot Nathan Hale.

July 12   Congress passes an amendment to the Constitution, authorizing the imposition of a tax on incomes. The amendment must be ratified by three fourths of the states.

Aug. 5   President Taft signs the controversial Payne-Aldrich Tariff Act.

Sept. 9   Edward Henry Harriman, 61, railroad executive whose contest in 1901 with James J. Hill for control of the Northern Pacific Railroad led to a panic in Wall Street, dies in Tuxedo Park, New York.

Oct. 26   Lieutenant F. E. Humphreys, after instruction from Wilbur Wright, becomes the first Army officer to fly solo in the Army's first airplane from its airfield at College Park, Maryland.

Oct. 26   Oliver Otis Howard, 78, general in the Union Army in the Civil War, who later served as commissioner of the Freedmen's Bureau and was a founder and president of Howard University, dies in Burlington, Vermont.

Nov. 13   The St. Paul Mine at Cherry, Illinois, explodes, with a loss of more than 250 lives.

Nov. 18   United States ships and troops are dispatched to Nicaragua after reports that 500 revolutionaries, including two Americans, have been executed by President José Santos Zelaya, a

Liberal. [Prevented from suppressing the rebels, who belong to the Conservative Party favored by the United States, Zelaya resigns; the United States refuses to recognize his successor, José Madriz; in 1910 the Conservatives come to power.]

Dec. 26   Frederic Remington, 48, painter of studies of the American West such as *The Bronco Buster* and *The Last Stand,* dies in Ridgefield, Connecticut.

Dec. 31   The Manhattan Bridge, a suspension bridge over the East River in New York City, is opened to traffic.

Going around a hairpin turn in the first Vanderbilt Cup automobile race, 1909

1910

The 13th decennial census of the United States shows the population to be 92,228,496, including about 8,795,000 immigrants who have arrived since 1900. The center of population is in Bloomington, Indiana. Illiteracy has decreased to 7.7 per cent of persons over the age of 10, compared to 10.7 per cent in 1900. Only one new state, Oklahoma, was admitted during the preceding decade.

In the second year of President Taft's term, the split deepens between the conservatives and progressives in the Republican Party. A rift also appears in the relations between the President and his predecessor, Theodore Roosevelt, who comments on his return from a foreign tour that Taft "completely twisted around the policies I advocated and acted upon." In the Congressional elections, progressive Republicans win significant victories in the West, and Republicans are defeated by Democrats in many Eastern and Midwestern states. Theodore Roosevelt calls for "government supervision of capitalization, not only of public service companies, including, particularly, railways, but also all corporations doing an interstate business. . . ." His concept of a "square deal" would include a graduated income tax, the conservation of natural resources, and the maintenance of military strength.

The party split has repercussions in the House of Representatives, where the progressives, led by George W. Norris of Nebraska, revolt against the power of Speaker Joseph G. Cannon and amend the rules. Henceforth members of the Rules Committee are to be elected by the House rather than appointed by the Speaker, and the Speaker is ineligible for membership on that committee.

Feb. 8   The Boy Scouts of America organization is founded in the District of Columbia. It is based on a movement that originated in England in 1908 and rapidly spread to other countries. The United States is the 12th country to join the movement. [The organization is chartered by Congress in 1916.]

Mar. 17   The Camp Fire Girls Organization is formed at Lake Sebago, Maine. [It is chartered in 1912.]

Mar. 19   The House of Representatives amends the House rules to reduce the power of the Speaker and make him ineligible for membership on the Rules Committee.

Mar. 26   The Immigration Act of 1907 is amended by Congress to exclude from the United States paupers, criminals, anarchists, and diseased persons.

April 12   William Graham Sumner, 69, economist and sociologist, dies in Englewood, New Jersey. From his professor's chair at Yale University he had wide influence as an advocate of free trade and "big business" for more than 35 years.

April 21   Samuel Langhorne Clemens, 74, prolific author of novels, essays, and volumes on his travels, dies in Redding, Connecticut. He is known nationally and internationally as the beloved humorist Mark Twain, a name he invented from his brief career as a riverboat pilot.

April 25   Charles Evans Hughes, governor of New York, is appointed an Associate Justice of the U.S. Supreme Court by President Taft.

May 16   The Bureau of Mines is established in the Department of the Interior.

June 5   William Sidney Porter, 48, who developed the art of the short story under the name of O. Henry, dies in New York City.

June 18   The Mann-Elkins Railroad Act is passed by Congress, further strengthening the Interstate Commerce Commission by giving it jurisdiction over telephone, telegraph, and cable companies.

June 20   New Mexico Territory, with a population of more than 325,000, and Arizona Territory, with a population of more than 200,000, are authorized by Congress to form state governments and apply for admission to the Union.

June 24   Congress passes legislation requiring that [radio] equipment be carried on all passenger ships leaving the United States.

June 25   Congress establishes the Postal Savings Bank system, under which 2-per-cent interest is paid on savings accounts. [The system is abolished in 1967.]

June 25   Congress passes the Publicity Act, requiring that U.S. Representatives report on campaign contributions received by them.

June 25   The White Slave Traffic Act, commonly called the Mann Act, is passed by Congress, barring the transportation of women across state lines for immoral purposes.

July 4 Melville Weston Fuller, 77, Chief Justice of the U.S. Supreme Court since 1888, dies in Sorrento, Maine. [President Taft replaces Fuller with Edward Douglass White, an Associate Justice since 1894. White is the first Associate Justice promoted to Chief Justice.]

Oct. 17 Julia Ward Howe, 91, author and lecturer, writer in 1862 of "The Battle Hymn of the Republic," dies in Middletown, Rhode Island. She was a founder of the American Woman's Suffrage Association and president of the U.S. branch of the Women's International Peace Association, and the first woman to join the American Academy of Arts and Letters.

Oct. 26 William James, 68, psychologist and philosopher, author of *Varieties of Religious Experience,* dies in Chocorua; New Hampshire.

Nov. 8 In the midterm elections, the Democrats gain control of the House of Representatives for the first time since 1885, but the Republicans retain control of the Senate. Woodrow Wilson is elected governor of New Jersey.

Nov. 14 The first airplane to take off from the deck of a U.S. warship is a Curtiss biplane flown by Eugene Ely from the U.S.S. *Birmingham* riding at anchor at Hampton Roads, Virginia.

Dec. 3 Mary Baker Eddy, 89, founder of the Christian Science Church and author of *Science and Health with Key to the Scriptures,* passes in Newton, Massachusetts.

A Curtiss plane, piloted by Eugene Ely, makes the first aircraft takeoff from the deck of a ship.

1911 **In the third year of President Taft's Administration the** rift between Taft and Theodore Roosevelt widens as the latter openly sides with the progressives, and Taft allies himself with the conservatives. Senator Robert M. La Follette of Wisconsin organizes the progressive Republicans into a league to promote their goals: direct primary elections, direct election of U.S. Senators, reform of state constitutions to permit voter initiative, referendum, and recall, and above all, a major reduction in tariffs—views that coincide closely with those of Roosevelt. The Pinchot-Ballinger controversy of 1910, during which Gifford Pinchot, a staunch Roosevelt supporter and an ardent conservationist, was discharged by Taft as chief of the Forest Service, further alienated Roosevelt. However, at least one of his dreams comes true and he presides in person at the opening of a dam across the Salt River in Arizona Territory, the construction of which was begun in his Administration, and which bears his name. At the year's end it is Roosevelt, under the banner of the New Nationalism, who proposes to lead the progressives against conservatism despite the initiative taken by the Senator from Wisconsin.

Taft suffers a minor but humiliating defeat in foreign policy. He negotiates a reciprocal trade agreement between the United States and the Dominion of Canada, under which a group of articles produced in both countries would be duty-free and another group would carry common rates of duties. Despite opposition by progressives, favorable legislation is passed in Congress. But the Canadian people, still smarting over the definition of the Alaskan boundary that was settled by a British vote in favor of the United States in 1903, are further angered by rumors that the reciprocity agreement could lead toward ultimate annexation of Canada by the United States. The Canadian electorate votes out of office the Liberal Government of Sir Wilfrid Laurier that favors the agreement, and reciprocity in trade with the United States is defeated.

Jan. 21　The National Progressive Republican League, representing the progressive wing of the Republican Party, is organized by U.S. Senator Robert M. La Follette of Wisconsin.

Feb. 3　The electric self-starter for automobiles, for which Charles F. Kettering holds the patent, is demonstrated. [Kettering is a vice president of Dayton Engineering Laboratories Co. (Delco), which is acquired in 1916 by the General Motors Company.]

Mar. 7　Some 20,000 U.S. troops are ordered to the Mexican border to protect American interests during a revolution led by Francisco Madero. [The troops are recalled on June 24.]

Mar. 18　The Roosevelt Dam, built across the Salt River in Arizona, about 75 miles northeast of Phoenix, is opened by Theodore Roosevelt.

Mar. 25　Fire sweeps the Triangle shirtwaist factory in New York City; about 145 persons, most of them women, are trapped and killed.

May 1　The U.S. Supreme Court rules that the forest reserves of the United States are subject to Federal rather than state regulation.

May 15　The U.S. Supreme Court, in *Standard Oil Company (New Jersey)* v. *U.S.,* orders dissolution of the Standard Oil Company of New Jersey on the ground that it engages in "unreasonable" restraint of trade. The company controlled 33 subsidiaries and was the glaring example monopoly in its field. The ruling, expressing the principles of Chief Justice White, marks the first use of the rule of "reason" in interpretation of the Sherman Antitrust Act.

May 29　The U.S. Supreme Court, ruling in *U.S.* v. *American Tobacco Company,* finds the "tobacco trust" to be in violation of the Sherman Antitrust Act.

June 9　Carry (Amelia) Nation, 64, temperance activist famous for her hatchet-wielding forays into saloons, dies in Leavenworth, Kansas.

July 7　A treaty barring for 15 years pelagic sealing north of the 30th parallel, and regulating land sealing, is signed by the United States, Great Britain (for Canada), Russia, and Japan, in a move to protect the endangered animals and thus ensure continuance of the sealing industry.

July 24　The United States and Japan renew their commercial treaty, continuing the "gentlemen's agreement" under which Japan pledges not to issue passports to laborers wishing to emigrate to the United States, while still maintaining the Japanese right of immigration.

Aug. 22 Statehood for Arizona is vetoed by President Taft because he considers the proposed state constitution's provision for recall of judges a threat to the independence of the judiciary.

Sept. 12-Nov. 5 The first cross-country airplane flight is made by Calbraith R. Rodgers, flying from New York City to Long Beach, California, in a Wright biplane in 82 hours 4 minutes of flying time over a period of seven weeks.

Oct. 16 The Progressive Republicans meet in Chicago and nominate Robert M. La Follette as their candidate for the Presidency.

Oct. 29 Joseph Pulitzer, 64, founder of the St. Louis *Post-Dispatch* and of the Pulitzer prizes, dies in Charleston, South Carolina. Like his rival William Randolph Hearst, Pulitzer promoted the technique of sensational news coverage.

Dec. 18 The United States abrogates an 1832 treaty with Russia because of that country's refusal to honor passports of Jewish Americans and certain clergymen.

Dec. 23 Theodore Roosevelt announces in a private letter his availability as the Republican candidate for the Presidency.

The front page of the Chicago *Daily Tribune* describes the sinking of the *Titanic*.

1912 The year is dominated by national elections in which the split in the Republican Party brings to the Presidency a Democrat for the first time since 1892. The ultimate breach between President Taft and Theodore Roosevelt comes on Feb. 12, when Taft in a speech refers to the Progressives (clearly including Roosevelt) as "Extremists—not Progressives; they are political emotionaries or neurotics." Shortly thereafter, Roosevelt publicly announces his intention to seek the nomination. At the Republican national convention the conservative backers of President Taft hold close control and through machine politics succeed in barring 235 Roosevelt delegates chosen in direct primary elections. Roosevelt and his followers bolt the convention in a stormy scene, establish the Progressive ("Bull Moose") Party, hold a formal convention, and nominate Roosevelt as their candidate.

The Democratic national convention, meanwhile, has its own problems, and requires 46 ballots to nominate Governor Woodrow Wilson of New Jersey as its Presidential choice. For 29 ballots the lead is held by Champ Clark, Speaker of the House and Democratic hero by virtue of having dethroned the dictatorial Uncle Joe Cannon. It is the influence of William Jennings Bryan, the three-time loser, that turns the tide to Wilson.

The campaign, in these days of burgeoning progressivism, is obviously favorable to anyone but the conservative Taft. The popular vote proves this; even Eugene Victor Debs, the perennial candidate of the Socialist Party, receives an amazing 900,672 votes. Roosevelt, running on a ticket never before heard of, outstrips Taft in popular votes, 4,118,571 to 3,486,720. Electorally, he demolishes Taft, 88 to 8. Although in combination the Republicans could have defeated Wilson, who receives 6,301,254 votes (to their 7,605,291), in the electoral college Wilson, with his comfortable 435 votes, would nevertheless have emerged victorious. This is sometimes forgotten by those who point to Wilson's unimpressive 41.8 per cent (the lowest proportion of the popular vote since Lincoln). Roosevelt's defection helps Wilson, but does not in itself assure his triumph. It is noteworthy that the Democrats win both Houses of Congress; thus it is not unreasonable to conjecture that a substantial part of Roosevelt's vote would have gone to Wilson had the former President remained out of the race.

Jan. 6   New Mexico becomes the 47th state of the Union. With a capital city (Santa Fe) 300 years old, under territorial government for more than 60 years, and a population of more than 325,000, its statehood was overdue.

Jan. 7   In a message to Congress, President Taft recommends the adoption of an annual national budget, pointing out that the United States is the only major country operating without one.

Jan. 12   Textile workers in Lawrence, Massachusetts, go on strike to protest a reduction of wages following the enactment of a minimum-hours law. The action demonstrates the growing power of the Industrial Workers of the World in the Eastern states.

Jan. 22   The Florida East Coast Railroad opens a line between Key West and the mainland.

Feb. 14   Arizona, with a population exceeding 200,000, becomes the 48th state of the Union after having removed from its constitution a provision for recall of judges. [Upon achievement of statehood, the provision is restored.]

Feb. 25   Theodore Roosevelt announces that he is a candidate for the Republican nomination for President.

Mar. 7   The U.S. Senate is ready to approve the general arbitration treaty signed with France and Great Britain, providing for the referral of international disputes to the International Court of Arbitration at The Hague. However, amendments sponsored by Senator Henry Cabot Lodge, requiring consent of the Senate in cases involving the Monroe Doctrine and excluding Orientals from the United States, makes passage of the bill impossible.

Mar. 14   The Department of Justice begins an action to prevent the merger of the Southern Pacific and Union Pacific railroads.

April 14-15   The British liner *Titanic,* on her maiden voyage, sinks after striking an iceberg in the North Atlantic Ocean, taking the lives of more than 1,500 persons, many of them Americans.

May 13   Congress passes, and forwards to the states for ratification, an amendment to the

Constitution changing the manner in which U.S. Senators are elected. If ratified, Senators will be elected by direct popular vote, and vacancies may be temporarily filled by the chief executive of the state pending such election.

May 15   Clara Barton, 91, founder of the American Red Cross, dies in Glen Echo, Maryland.

May 30   Wilbur Wright, 45, inventor with his brother Orville of the practical airplane, dies in Dayton, Ohio.

June 1   Lieutenant Henry H. Arnold of the Signal Corps, flying a Burgess-Wright airplane, reaches a record altitude of 6,540 feet.

June 5   A force of U.S. marines lands in Cuba to protect American interests during political disorders.

June 18-22   President Taft and Vice President Sherman are renominated by the Republican national convention after hundreds of Roosevelt delegates are weeded out by the credentials committee. The remaining Roosevelt delegates abstain, and Taft is picked on the first ballot.

June 25-July 2   The Democratic national convention meets in Baltimore, Maryland, and nominates Governor Woodrow Wilson of New Jersey, on the 46th ballot, as its candidate for the Presidency. Thomas R. Marshall of Indiana is his running mate.

Aug. 2   The U.S. Senate passes a resolution called the Lodge Corollary to the Monroe Doctrine, broadening the scope of the doctrine to cover foreign corporations.

Aug. 5-7   The Progressive ("Bull Moose") Party meets in Chicago, Illinois, and nominates Theodore Roosevelt as its candidate for the Presidency, and Senator Hiram Johnson of California as the Vice-Presidential candidate.

Aug. 24   The delivery of small parcels by the U.S. Post Office is authorized effective Jan. 1, 1913.

Aug. 24   Congress passes the Panama Canal Act, providing toll-free passage for U.S. ships engaged in coastwise trade, although the Hay-Pauncefote Treaty with Great Britain provides for equal access for all nations. [After British protests, President Woodrow Wilson in 1914 asks repeal of the exemption, which Congress passes on June 11.]

Sept. 5   General Arthur MacArthur, 67, who served in the Civil War, in the Indian campaigns, in the Spanish-American War, and as military governor of the Philippines, dies in Milwaukee.

Oct. 14   Theodore Roosevelt, on a campaign

Theodore Roosevelt addresses a campaign rally of the Bull Moose Party at Morrisville, Vermont.

trip to Milwaukee, is shot by Joseph Schrank. The bullet strikes a thick manuscript and enters his chest, but he makes his scheduled speech before being taken to a hospital.

Oct. 30   James S. Sherman, Vice President and also candidate for reelection on the Taft ticket, dies in Utica, New York, during the campaign at the age of 57. [His candidacy is filled by Nicholas Murray Butler, president of Columbia University.]

Nov. 5   Woodrow Wilson is elected 28th President of the United States, defeating President Taft and Theodore Roosevelt. Wilson fails to win a majority of the votes cast, but his constituency is solid: he carries 40 of the 48 states. Taft carries only Vermont and Utah.

Dec. 10   Elihu Root, statesman and lawyer, president of the Carnegie Endowment for Peace, receives the Nobel Peace Prize. Alexis Carrel receives the Nobel Prize in medicine and physiology "in recognition of his works on vascular suture and the transplantation of blood vessels and organs."

281

1913

President Woodrow Wilson has an impressive background of political knowledge gained as professor and president of Princeton University, a highly liberal record as governor of New Jersey, and the support of progressives throughout the nation. He takes office supported by a Democratic Senate and House of Representatives and loses no time in putting into effect the program he calls the New Freedom in both domestic and foreign affairs.

The first foreign crisis he faces arises in Mexico even before his inauguration, when, on Feb. 18, the moderate Government of Francisco Madero is overthrown by General Victoriano Huerta. Wilson refuses to recognize the Huerta regime and, in effect, ends "dollar diplomacy" by stating that the United States will no longer support special business interests in foreign countries. When a new revolution breaks out and Huerta rejects Wilson's suggestion of an armistice, Wilson demands his resignation. Upon Huerta's refusal, Wilson announces U.S. support of the revolutionary movement under Venustiano Carranza.

The first domestic manifestation of the New Freedom is the businesslike implementation of the newly passed 16th Amendment, in the form of modest taxes on personal income, a new concept not easily accepted by all U.S. salary earners. [Wage earners are not initially affected.] The pledged reduction in taxes on imported goods is made part of the same act. Another landmark is the new banking system, long overdue. The President's custom of addressing Congress in person meets with general approval.

Feb. 17 An art exhibition opens at the 69th Regiment Armory in New York City, organized by the Association of Painters and Sculptors. Known as the Armory Show, it is the first presentation in the United States of European contemporary art, such as the controversial *Nude Descending a Staircase* by Marcel Duchamp.

Feb. 25-July William (Big Bill) Heywood personally leads the silk workers of Paterson, New Jersey, in a strike against the introduction of multiple looms. This strike fails to accomplish its purpose, but it indicates the influence of the Industrial Workers of the World.

Feb. 25 The 16th Amendment to the Constitution of the United States is declared in effect, having been ratified by 38 states. It gives Congress power to levy and collect taxes on income.

Mar. 4 Woodrow Wilson is inaugurated as the 28th President of the United States.

Mar. 4-5 Congress separates the Department of Commerce and Labor into two Cabinet-level departments and establishes the U.S. Board of Mediation and Conciliation. President Wilson appoints William B. Wilson of Pennsylvania as the first Secretary of Labor and William C. Redfield of New York as Secretary of Commerce. Secretary Wilson is a former miner, a leader of the United Mine Workers, and a Congressman. Redfield is a business executive and a Congressman.

Mar. 12-April 21 A strike of some 150,000 garment workers begins in New York City, protesting long hours, low wages, and refusal of union recognition. The strike spreads to Boston and is settled there, with the strikers winning on all points.

Mar. 21-26 Tributaries of the Ohio River flood in Indiana and Ohio, causing massive disaster over a wide area. About 700 lives are lost, 200,000 are made homeless, and more than $175,000,000 in damage is caused. The Miami River particularly devastates the city of Dayton, Ohio.

Mar. 31 John Pierpont Morgan, 76, financier and founding partner of J. P. Morgan and Company, one of the most powerful banking houses in the United States, dies in Rome, Italy.

April 8 President Wilson appears before Congress to deliver a message on tariff revision. He is the first President since John Adams to address Congress in person.

April 24 Secretary of State William Jennings Bryan achieves the last of 21 ratifications of arbitration treaties with foreign countries, providing that no signatory will wage war until a dispute has been submitted to arbitration by an international commission.

May 10 Congress designates the second Sunday in May as Mother's Day. The holiday developed from a similar celebration held in Philadephia five years earlier.

May 31 The 17th Amendment to the Constitution is declared in effect, having been ratified by 36 states. It provides for direct election of Senators rather than selection by state legislatures as in the present method.

Aug. 26 The Keokuk Dam across the Mississippi River at the mouth of the Des Moines River is opened. This was the head of navigation for steamships. Now a mile-long dam is creating a lake upstream, and will provide 200,000 horsepower of electricity for the area.

Oct. 3 The Underwood-Simmons Tariff Act is passed by Congress. One section of the bill fulfills the Democratic pledge to reduce tariffs: it lowers average duties to 30 per cent and admits some raw materials free. Another section implements the 16th Amendment by imposing the first personal income tax: a 1-per-cent income tax is levied on incomes of more than $3,000 for a single person and a maximum of 6 per cent on incomes exceeding $50,000.

Oct. 16 Governor General Francis Burton Harrison of the Philippines, appointed by President Wilson, announces a policy of filling the membership of the Philippine Commission, which governs the islands, with a majority of Filipinos. (Originally set up in 1900 with five U.S. members chaired by William Howard Taft, the commission received three Filipino members in 1901 and one more in 1908.)

Dec. 23 The Federal Reserve Bank Act is signed, dividing the country into 12 districts, each with a Federal Reserve Bank. The act also provides for an elastic currency based on commercial assets rather than bonded indebtedness, mobilization of bank reserves, public control of the banking system, and decentralization rather than centralization.

Dancing at the Breakers Hotel in Palm Beach, Florida

1914 The U.S.-Mexican crisis continues. In April, nine American sailors ashore for supplies are arrested in Tampico; although they are released with an apology, U.S. Admiral Henry T. Mayo demands the raising of the American flag on Mexican soil and a special 21-gun salute. A few days later President Wilson orders a U.S. naval force to Tampico Bay. Then word is received in the White House that a German ship is unloading munitions at Veracruz, and President Wilson orders the taking of the city. To forestall further hostilities, the ABC powers (Argentina, Brazil, and Chile) offer to mediate the dispute, and the offer is accepted by both the United States and Mexico. The arbitration commission, meeting in May and June, rejects U.S. claims for indemnity but suggests that President Huerta resign. Huerta declines, but he is expelled in mid-July and Venustiano Carranza assumes leadership.

The tide of European immigration to the United States in the decade 1905-1914 brought to these shores 10,500,000 Europeans, three-quarters of them from Slavic countries and southern Europe and about one sixth from western and northern Europe.

This is the year for which Americans have long waited—the year when it is possible to sail from the Atlantic to the Pacific oceans for the first time without rounding the Horn. As for the unhappy events in Europe, Americans are informed that they not only *can* be neutral—they *should* be neutral. Congress continues to make America safe for the people, by monitoring business in the progressive tradition. Two new bulwarks are raised to protect the public: a more stringent antitrust act and a commission to keep interstate business practices "fair." Mother's Day is semiofficially added to the calendar, as President Wilson authorizes its observance for the first time.

Feb. 13   The American Society of Composers, Authors, and Publishers (ASCAP) is organized in New York City under the leadership of composer Victor Herbert, to protect its members from copyright infringement and to work for improvement of the copyright laws.

Mar. 12   George Westinghouse, 67, founder of the Westinghouse Electric Company, inventor of the air brake and compressed-air railroad signals, and holder of more than 400 patents, dies in New York City.

April 1   A permanent civilian Government is established in the Panama Canal Zone, replacing the Isthmian Canal Commission. George W. Goethals, chief engineer of the commission, is appointed governor by the President.

May 30   Lassen Peak in California's Sierra Nevada range, long considered extinct, proves that it is the only active volcano in the continental United States.

July 29   The Cape Cod Canal is opened, connecting Cape Cod Bay and Buzzards Bay in Massachusetts. The canal is less than 8 miles long, but it cuts 75 miles from the New York-Boston run.

Aug. 1   Marcus Garvey founds the Universal Negro Improvement Association (UNIA) in Kingston, Jamaica. Its purpose is to increase Negro economic and political power in Africa, eventually forming a Negro Empire there. [The Garveyite Movement, based on UNIA, arouses the national consciousness of black Americans in the years after World War I, and is a major factor accounting for the urbanization of black Americans. It reaches its highest effectiveness in 1920.]

Aug. 4   President Wilson issues a proclamation of neutrality as war breaks out in Europe. [On Aug. 19 he calls on Americans to be neutral "in thought as well as action."]

Aug. 15   The Panama Canal is informally opened to commerce, 12 days after the first steamer makes the passage.

Sept. 26   The Federal Trade Commission Act is passed by Congress. It is designed to eliminate unfair business practices in interstate commerce.

Oct. 15   Congress passes the Clayton Antitrust Act, reinforcing and extending the Sherman Antitrust Act. The new act provides for prevention of unlawful price discrimination, tying contracts, stock acquisitions in competing corporations, and interlocking directorates. It also limits the use of the injunction in labor disputes, exempts labor organizations from the antitrust laws, and permits strikes, boycotts, and picketing by unions.

Nov. 23   U.S. marines sail from Veracruz, Mexico, their mission of preventing German infiltration into that country evidently successful. However, Venustiano Carranza, who has deposed Huerta and demanded U.S. evacuation of Veracruz, is himself busy in that city preparing to defend his revolution against his erstwhile colleagues, Emiliano Zapata and Francisco Villa.

Dec. 10   Theodore William Richards becomes the first American to receive the Nobel Prize in chemistry. The award is made for his accurate determinations of the atomic weights of various elements.

Dec. 24   John Muir, 76, explorer and naturalist, discoverer of the glacier in Alaska that bears his name, and a potent force in establishing forest conservation and national park policies, dies in Los Angeles.

A parade of the Ringling Brothers circus, 1914

1915

Despite its proclamation of neutrality, the United States becomes increasingly embroiled in the war in Europe. Following the German warning that merchant ships sailing in British waters will be sunk with no efforts to rescue passengers, and that neutral ships will enter the war zone at their own risk, the United States replies that any loss of American lives will be considered a "violation of neutrality," for which Germany will be held responsible. Shortly thereafter the British liner *Lusitania* is sunk by a German submarine off the coast of Ireland, with the loss of more than 100 American lives. In consequence three notes of protest are dispatched to Germany, Secretary of State William Jennings Bryan resigns his office in disagreement with the President's diminishing dedication to neutrality, and the nation is warned by Wilson to be "prepared."

Jan. 25　Alexander Graham Bell in New York City calls Dr. Thomas A. Watson in San Francisco, and repeats across 3,000 miles of wire the phone call between adjoining rooms that made history in 1876: "Mr. Watson, come here, I want you."

Jan. 25　The U. S. Supreme Court, in *Coppage* v. *Kansas,* rules that a state may not forbid an employer to refuse employment on grounds of union membership. Associate Justice Holmes dissents.

Jan. 26　The Rocky Mountain National Park in Colorado, containing 65 named peaks exceeding 10,000 feet in height, is established by Congress.

Jan. 28　The U. S. Coast Guard is created by Congress, combining the Revenue Cutter Service and the Life Saving Service. Although under the Treasury Department, the Coast Guard is specifically described as part of the military services, and must cooperate with the Navy whenever the President so directs.

Feb. 6-20　The San Francisco Panama-Pacific International Exposition is held to mark the opening of the Panama Canal. Some 13,000,000 visitors attend the exposition during its run, which features public airplane rides.

Feb. 8　*The Birth of a Nation,* a 12-reel motion picture produced by D. W. Griffith, has its first showing in Los Angeles. Based on the 1905 novel *The Clansman* by Thomas Dixon, it gives a new dimension to the "movie," transforming a novelty into an art form. [Its treatment of history, particularly its sympathetic depiction of the Ku Klux Klan during the Reconstruction period, arouses controversy in later years.]

Feb. 23　Governor Emmet D. Boyle of Nevada signs a law reducing the residence requirement for securing a divorce to six months.

April 5　Jess Willard wins the world heavyweight boxing championship, knocking out Jack Johnson in the 26th round, in Havana, Cuba.

April 16　Nelson Wilmarth Aldrich, 74, U.S. Senator from Rhode Island, who was chiefly responsible for the drafting and passage of the Payne-Aldrich Tariff Act of 1909, dies in New York City.

May 7　The British liner *Lusitania* is sunk by a German torpedo 10 miles off Kinsale, Ireland. The ship, one of the fastest afloat, with a crew of more than 600 and 1,250 passengers, sinks in less than 10 minutes, with a loss of nearly 1,200 lives, more than 100 of them American, including author Elbert Hubbard, producer Charles Frohman, and sportsman Alfred Gwynne Vanderbilt. The *Lusitania* was unarmed, carrying nothing more lethal than small arms cartridges.

May 13　Secretary of State William Jennings Bryan signs a note protesting the sinking of the *Lusitania,* and demanding reparations and an end to unrestricted submarine warfare.

June 7　Secretary Bryan, ordered to transmit a second protest note to Germany, considers this step too bellicose, and resigns his post. He is replaced by Robert Lansing.

June 21　President Wilson personally sends a third note to Germany in connection with the sinking of the *Lusitania,* warning that further violations of U. S. neutrality will be considered "deliberately unfriendly."

June 24　The excursion steamer *Eastland* explodes at her pier on the Chicago River and capsizes, causing the death of more than 800 persons.

July 28　U. S. marines are landed at Port-au-Prince, Haiti, from the U. S. S. *Washington* following the murder by outraged Haitians of President Guillaume Sam, who has just ordered the execution of 167 political prisoners. [Haiti becomes in effect a U. S. protectorate.]

Aug. 10　An experimental military training camp for civilians is opened at Plattsburg[h], New York.

Aug. 15　The New York *World* begins publication of papers exposing plans for sabotage, espionage, and propaganda involving many German-Americans and members of German embassies and consular staffs. [The German officials are recalled.]

Sept. 29 Theodore N. Vail, president of the American Telegraph and Telephone Company, makes the first transcontinental wireless telephone call.

Oct. 5 Germany apologizes for the *Lusitania* sinking and offers reparations.

Oct. 15 American bankers, organized by J. P. Morgan & Company, agree to lend Great Britain and France $500,000,000, the largest loan floated in any country.

Oct. 19 The United States recognizes Venustiano Carranza as President of Mexico.

Nov. 14 Booker Taliaferro Washington, 59, author of *Up from Slavery*, founder of Tuskegee Institute, and advocate of the economic independence of Negroes, dies in Tuskegee, Alabama.

Dec. 4 The "peace ship" *Oskar II* sails to Norway on a mission to negotiate an end to the war. Aboard are Henry Ford, who has chartered it, and a band of peace promoters.

Dec. 4 Georgia grants a charter to the "new" Ku Klux Klan, a revived version of the organization that was presumably dissolved in the 1870's. Colonel William Simmons is the organizer.

Dec. 7 President Wilson addresses Congress on the necessity of "preparedness" in view of the events in Europe.

Dec. 18 President Wilson, left a widower in August 1914, marries Edith Bolling Galt, a widow of 42, at her home in Washington, D. C.

John D. Rockefeller, Sr. strolls on Fifth Avenue, in New York City.

1916

Although this is an election year, President Wilson continues an active, if cautious, foreign policy. The European war seems to be inexorably involving the United States, and even in America military responses appear to be required in Mexico and the Dominican Republic. There may be some interrelationship between the trouble spots, for Germany is not likely to abstain from stirring up the waters of the Caribbean. This consideration hastens the conclusion of the long-negotiated purchase of Denmark's islands in that sea. The menacing situation also inspires a thorough reorganization of the U. S. defense organization.

As for the election itself, the Democratic claim that Wilson has kept the country out of the war cannot be gainsaid. Justice Hughes is a strong candidate for the Republicans, and the Wilson victory is narrow; only 3.14 percentage points separate the two candidates, and the results hang in the balance as the late California vote is counted over a three-day period.

Jan. 1   The postseason college football classic, the Rose Bowl, initiated in 1902, is resumed after a gap of 14 years. Washington State University defeats Brown University, 14 to 0.

Jan. 24   The U. S. Supreme Court, in *Brushaber* v. *Union Pacific,* rules that the Federal income tax is constitutional.

Jan. 28   Louis D. Brandeis is appointed an Associate Justice of the U. S. Supreme Court by President Wilson. He is the first Jew to sit on the Court.

Feb. 22   With the authorization of President Wilson, his personal advisor Colonel Edward House meets with British Foreign Secretary Sir Edward Grey. The two draw up a memorandum agreeing that, if requested by France and Great Britain, the United States will call for a negotiated peace; and if Germany rejects the offer, the United States "would probably enter the war against Germany."

Feb. 28   Henry James, 72, author of *The American* and *Daisy Miller,* internationally acclaimed as "the novelist's novelist," dies in London.

Feb. 29   Child labor legislation is passed in South Carolina, raising the minimum working age in mills, mines and factories, from 12 to 14 years. This represents progress over the Pennsylvania statue of 1848, which set a minimum age for textile workers at 12 years.

Mar. 9   Francisco (Pancho) Villa, rejecting the Government of Mexican President Venustiano Carranza, and angered by U. S. recognition of Carranza, raids the town of Columbus, New Mexico, to demonstrate that he is in charge in northern Mexico. [General John J. Pershing, sent by Wilson to capture Villa, fails in his mission, and President Carranza warns the United States to abstain from invading Mexican territory.]

Mar. 24   The unarmed French steamer *Sussex* with American passengers aboard, is sunk by Germans in the English Channel.

April 11   Richard Harding Davis, 52, war correspondent in six wars and author of romantic novels, dies in Mount Kisco, New York.

April 18   President Wilson issues a last warning (ultimatum) threatening to end relations with Germany if the submarine warfare against merchant craft continues without warning or provision for rescuing passengers.

May 4   Germany agrees to the terms of President Wilson's ultimatum.

June 3   The National Defense Act is passed by Congress. For the first time, this act actually organizes the peacetime land armed forces of the United States, which have been haphazard and arbitrarily interrelated. The three-part division of the Regular Army, Organized Reserves (including a training corps) and National Guard is instituted. From the present strength of about 24,000, the Regular Army is to attain 220,000 in five years; the National Guard is to number 450,000 in that time.

June 7   The Progressive Party proposes to nominate Theodore Roosevelt as its candidate for the Presidency, but he refuses to run and throws his support to Hughes.

June 7-10   The Republican national convention meets in Chicago and nominates Chief Justice Charles Evans Hughes as its candidate for the Presidency. Charles W. Fairbanks, who was President Roosevelt's Vice President, is picked to serve Hughes in that capacity.

June 14-16   The Democratic national convention meets in St. Louis and renominates President Wilson and Vice President Marshall.. The campaign slogan is: "He kept us out of war."

July 2   Henrietta Howland ("Hetty") Green, 81, one of the shrewdest financiers and certainly the richest woman in the United States, dies in New York City, leaving an estate estimated at $100,000,000.

Woodrow Wilson
TWENTY-EIGHTH PRESIDENT   **1913-1921**

Warren G. Harding
TWENTY-NINTH PRESIDENT   1921-1923

Calvin Coolidge
THIRTIETH PRESIDENT   1923-1929

Herbert Hoover
THIRTY-FIRST PRESIDENT 1929-1933

July 11 The Federal Aid Road Act is signed by President Wilson. The measure provides $5,000,000 for the use of states that undertake road-building programs, and it establishes a system of highway classification. Almost 250,000 commercial vehicles and more than 3,000,000 private cars are registered to use public roads.

July 17 The Federal Farm Loan Bank Act is passed by Congress. It establishes a system of 12 land banks and a Federal farm loan board to make funds available to borrowing farmers.

July 22 A bomb is thrown during a Preparedness Day parade in San Francisco, killing 10 persons. [In 1917 labor leader Tom Mooney is sentenced to die for the crime; in 1918 his sentence is commuted to life imprisonment; in 1939 he is pardoned.]

July 22 James Whitcomb Riley, 66, called the "Hoosier poet," dies in Indianapolis.

July 30 German saboteurs explode a munitions dump on Black Tom Island, New Jersey, causing damage of $22,000,000.

Aug. 4 The United States concludes negotiations with Denmark initiated in 1867 by purchasing the Virgin Islands in the West Indies for $25,000,000. (Possession is effective in 1917).

Aug. 25 The Office of National Parks, Buildings, and Reservations is established in the Department of the Interior. [In 1934 this becomes the National Park Service.]

Aug. 29 The Organic Act of the Philippine Islands, sponsored by Representative William A. Jones of Virginia, is passed by Congress. It restates the intention to establish Philippine independence and sets up machinery for self-government, including a responsible elected bicameral legislature.

Sept. 3 The Adamson Act, signed by President Wilson, provides an 8-hour work day for most railroad men, thus averting a nationwide strike called for Sept. 4.

Sept. 7 The United States Shipping Board is formed to acquire merchant ships for sale or charter to U. S. citizens; the Emergency Fleet Corporation is formed and capitalized at $50,000,000 to buy, lease, or operate the ships. The legislation is the result of a crisis in world merchant shipping, because of losses in the war.

Oct. 16 The first birth-control clinic is opened in Brooklyn, New York, by Margaret Sanger, publisher of *Woman Rebel,* and founder of a birth-control organization. [Mrs. Sanger is arrested for "maintaining a public nuisance" and serves a 30-day sentence.]

Nov. 7 In the national elections, President

A Wilson election-campaign truck

Wilson receives 9,127,695 popular votes and 277 electoral votes; Hughes receives 8,533,507 popular and 254 electoral votes. The Democrats control both Houses of Congress.

Nov. 12 Percival Lowell, 61, astronomer and builder of Lowell Observatory at Flagstaff, Arizona, whose studies predicted the discovery of the planet Pluto, dies in Flagstaff.

Nov. 22 Jack London, 40, writer and war correspondent, whose books include *The Call of the Wild,* and the autobiographical *Martin Eden,* kills himself in Glen Ellen, California.

Nov. 29 Outbreaks between warring factions in the Dominican Republic result in proclamation of American military occupation. [The occupation is ended on Oct. 21, 1922.]

Dec. 8 President Wilson signs a treaty between the United States and Canada that protects migratory birds in North America from indiscriminate slaughter, thus internationalizing the provisions of the Lacey Act of 1909 and the Migratory Bird Law of 1913.

Dec. 18 President Wilson follows his reelection by asking the belligerents to state their war aims.

1917 Having won election to a second term, President Woodrow Wilson enters a year of decision from a position of strength. Public opinion is virtually united against Germany and for the cause of the Allied nations, but the President at first hopes to avoid American entry into the war.

Before his second inauguration he tells the Senate that no nation should control another, no one power should be supreme on land or sea, that armaments must be limited, that an international organization must be established to maintain a lasting "peace among equals," which must be a "peace without victory." But three days before this speech is made, Count Johann Heinrich von Bernstorff, the German Ambassador in Washington, is told by his Government that unrestricted submarine warfare is to be resumed, even though this certainly will end American neutrality. After a few more American ships are torpedoed, and after it becomes known that Germany has planned to invade the United States through Mexico, the country is ready to enter combat.

The rest of the year sees a transformation from preparedness to action. A series of enactments by Congress reorganizes the manpower and material resources of the United States, setting numerous precedents. The draft, price-fixing, excess-profits taxes, nationalization of the railway system, diminution of civil liberties—the catalogue of war-related phenomena is impressive. Actual warfare is just around the corner.

Jan. 16   Admiral George Dewey, 79, who defeated the Spanish fleet in the Battle of Manila Bay during the Spanish-American War, dies in Washington, D.C.

Jan. 22   Having received outlines of peace terms from both the Allies and the Central Powers, President Wilson presents his own program to the U. S. Senate.

Jan. 28   President Wilson orders General Pershing to end his pursuit of Pancho Villa. [Pershing withdraws from Mexico on Feb. 5.]

Jan. 29   President Wilson vetoes a bill requiring literacy tests for immigrants, but Congress passes the measure over his veto.

Jan. 31   Germany notifies the United States that unrestricted submarine warfare will be resumed forthwith regardless of the agreement of May 4, 1916.

Feb. 3   The U. S. S. *Housatonic* is sunk by a German submarine. The President immediately informs Congress that the United States has severed diplomatic relations with Germany.

Feb. 5   An immigration act excluding all Asians from the United States is passed by Congress over President Wilson's veto.

Feb. 23   Congress passes the Smith-Hughes Act, initiating a program that commits the Federal Government to provide funds for local job-training education through a Federal Board for Vocational Education.

Mar. 1   The State Department authorizes publication of the so-called Zimmermann telegram, which has been intercepted by the British, decoded, and turned over to the United States. In the communication, the German Minister to Mexico is ordered by German Secretary of State Arthur Zimmerman to attempt to form an alliance between Germany and Mexico if the United States enters the war against Germany, and to invade and conquer Arizona, New Mexico, and Texas.

Mar. 2   The Organic Act for Puerto Rico (the Jones Act) is passed by Congress, making the island an organized but unincorporated territory of the United States. Its people are granted American citizenship and the right to elect local legislators.

Mar. 5   President Wilson is inaugurated for a second term.

Mar. 8   Because of anticipated difficulty in overcoming a filibuster over an impending bill to arm merchant ships, the U.S. Senate adopts the cloture rule, permitting a two-thirds vote of a quorum to terminate unlimited debate (filibuster) on any measure before the body; each Senator is limited to one hour of debate after the rule is invoked.

Mar. 12-13   The United States announces that merchant ships sailing in war zones will be armed. The U. S. Navy then instructs armed ships to fire on submarines.

Mar. 18   Word is received that German submarines have torpedoed three U.S. ships; many American lives were lost on the *Laconia*.

Mar. 20   The Cabinet unanimously advises President Wilson to request Congress to declare war on Germany.

Mar. 31   The United States formally takes

U.S. troops search for Pancho Villa.

President Woodrow Wilson addresses a special session of Congress and asks for a declaration of war on Germany.

Members of the U.S. 107th Infantry advance behind a tank.

General John J. Pershing (left) on his arrival in London

possession of the Virgin Islands from Denmark.

April 2 Jeannette Rankin, Republican of Montana, becomes the first woman to be seated in the House of Representatives.

April 2-6 In a special session, President Wilson asks Congress for a declaration of war against Germany, saying that "the world must be made safe for democracy." Within four days the Senate, by a vote of 82 to 6, and the House of Representatives, 373 to 50, pass the resolution, and on April 6 the President signs it.

April 24 The Liberty Loan Act is passed by Congress to raise funds for the war effort. [Five loan drives from June, 1917, to April, 1919, raise more than $20,000,000,000.]

May 18 The Selective Service Act is passed by Congress after weeks of debate and strong opposition by Republicans. [Under this act and later amendments some 24,200,000 men 21 through 30 years of age are registered and almost 3,000,000 are drafted into military service.]

June 14 General John J. Pershing arrives in Paris to direct the American Expeditionary Force, which is expected to number 1,000,000 men within a year.

June 15 The Espionage Act is passed by Congress. It provides fines of up to $10,000 and prison terms of up to 20 years for persons who hinder the war effort or aid the enemy.

June 26 A token force of U.S. troops arrives in St. Nazaire, France.

July 24 Congress votes to appropriate $640,000,000 for development of military aviation with a program to supply 4,500 aircraft by the spring of 1918.

Aug. 10 The Lever Food and Fuel Control Act is passed by Congress, providing for price-fixing and other controls of output and consumption. Herbert Clark Hoover is named Food Administrator and Harry A. Garfield is named Fuel Administrator. They are for increasing production, reducing waste, persuading the public to buy prudently, and cracking down on speculators.

Oct. 3 Congress passes the War Revenue Act, increasing corporate and personal income taxes and establishing excise, excess-profits, and luxury taxes.

Oct. 6 The Trading with the Enemy Act is passed by Congress, giving the Government control over foreign trade and the authority to censor foreign mail. It also provides for the seizure and administration of German-owned factories to guarantee war production for the United States; and it establishes a War Trade Board with power

Congresswoman Jeanette Rankin

to license imports and exports in order to facilitate American trade and hamper that of the enemy.

Nov. 2 Secretary of State Lansing signs an agreement with Viscount Kikujiro Ishii of Japan, under which the United States agrees that Japan has special interests in China, and Japan promises to respect the independence of China in accordance with the U.S. Open Door Policy.

Nov. 11 New York State amends its constitution to grant women the vote. While several smaller states have adopted women's suffrage, this action in a major state indicates that Federal legislation will soon be successful.

Nov. 13 The Federal Fuel Administration orders that all electric advertising signs be turned off on Thursdays and Sundays as a conservation measure.

Nov. 30 Units of the 42d Division, U.S. Army, begin to arrive in France. Organized from National Guard units of 26 states and the District of Columbia three months ago, it boasts the diversity of its composition under the name of the Rainbow Division.

Dec. 7 War is declared against Austria-Hungary by the United States.

Dec. 18 Congress passes and sends to the states for ratification a proposed amendment to the Constitution prohibiting the making, sale, or transportation of intoxicating beverages within or into the United States.

Dec. 18 The U.S. Railroad Administration is established under Secretary of the Treasury William G. McAdoo, giving the Government control over most U.S. rail trackage. The railroads are to be operated as a unified system, funds are to be made available for improvements, and the owners are to be paid rent equivalent to their average earnings in the previous three-year period.

Dec. 20 Two passenger trains collide near Louisville, Kentucky, causing the death of 46 persons.

1918

Fully committed to war in Europe, the United States undertakes a gigantic effort to regear its economy and enormous resources to the needs of such an undertaking. On the domestic front, faced with the overwhelming requirements of supplying the war effort, President Woodrow Wilson succeeds in winning from Congress legislation that gives him almost unlimited economic power. The President, his hopes of avoiding war dissipated, finds he must also turn to an examination of the politics that will be essential to keep the peace when it has been achieved. He proposes to Congress a program that becomes known as the Fourteen Points. Among these are an end to secret diplomacy through open covenants openly arrived at; freedom of navigation in peace and war; removal of economic barriers; reduction of armaments; adjustment of colonial claims with consideration of the interests of both the controlling government and the people; and, most important of all, a general association of nations to give mutual guarantees of political independence and territorial integrity to great and small states alike. The other points concern the political problems of specific countries and regions of Europe.

Early in the year, Germany has virtually eliminated the Russians and Italians from the war, and thus has troops available to move to the Western front for a massive onslaught to break the Allied lines. The object is to take Paris before the Americans can make a significant contribution to the Allied cause. Beginning on Mar. 21, German forces breach the British and French lines in the Somme and in the following month stage a massive attack in Flanders. Under extraordinary pressure, the Allies succeed in stabilizing their lines, and on April 14 the French General Ferdinand Foch is made supreme commander of all Allied armies. General John J. Pershing is put at Foch's disposal, with the consent of President Wilson. Pershing himself would prefer to retain a separate American army under his personal command. Nevertheless he participates in the effort to hold back the German thrust to cross the Marne, and in the counteroffensive that thrusts the Germans back across that river in July and August. American troops also fight with the British in Belgium, and from the middle of September Pershing has under his command the U.S. 1st Army, which succeeds in driving the Germans back to the Meuse. In October, when the Germans seek to negotiate an end to the war, it is on the basis of the Fourteen Points that President Wilson has proposed in January.

The Allies accept Wilson as their spokesman in the armistice negotiations, and he in turn informs the Germans that they will have to send their representatives to meet with Marshal Foch. The armistice is signed in Foch's railroad car in the Forest of Compiègne on Nov. 11.

Of a total of 4,744,000 Americans who take part in the war, some 116,000 die in service.

Jan. 8 President Wilson addresses Congress on the question of the war and the peace to follow it.

Jan. 10 The House of Representatives adopts a resolution to submit a constitutional amendment providing for Federal women's suffrage.

Feb. 12 Under the program of the Emergency Fleet Corporation to build shipyards and design ships, the first keel, is laid at the Hog Island shipyard at Philadelphia. [The first ship is delivered after the armistice is signed.]

Mar. 4 President Wilson names Bernard Baruch, a Wall Street broker, to take over the faltering War Industries Board and gives him broad powers to coordinate industry.

Mar. 19 Congress enacts legislation advancing the clocks by one hour from the end of March to the end of October, in order to conserve electric energy. The new time system [later called Daylight Saving Time] is effective on Mar. 31.

April 5 The War Finance Corporation is formed, capitalized at $500,000,000 to support war industries through loans and bond sales.

April 8 The National War Labor Board is established to handle labor disputes; it comprises five members each for labor and industry and two co-chairmen representing the public. The

U.S. infantrymen training at Condre-Court, France

U.S. troops in France in action during the Meuse-Argonne offensive

U.S. front-line troops celebrate the signing of the armistice with Germany.

board bars strikes or lockouts but recognizes the right of unions to organize and bargain collectively.

April 10   The Webb-Pomerene Act is passed by Congress to promote export trade by exempting export associations from the antitrust laws.

April 20   The Sabotage Act, directed primarily at the antiwar activities of the Industrial Workers of the World, is passed by Congress.

May 15   The first airmail service in the United States is inaugurated between New York City and Washington, D.C. Pilots of the Army Signal Corps fly the planes. [The Post Office Department takes over the services on Aug. 12.]

May 16   The Sedition Act is passed by Congress, greatly broadening the Espionage Act of 1917 by defining as criminal the direct advocacy of treason and criticism of the Government, conscription, or the American flag.

May 28   The first offensive by American troops in Finance takes place when the strategic town of Cantigny, in the Somme sector, is captured from the Germans and held against several counter-attacks.

May 28   The American Railway Express Company is organized, under Federal supervision, by the merger of Adams, American, Wells-Fargo, Southern, Great Northern, and Western express companies. [Permanent approval of the company is authorized in December, 1920, with capitalization of $40,000,000.]

June 3   The U.S. Supreme Court, in *Hammer* v. *Dagenhart,* rules unconstitutional a Federal law of 1916 that prohibits interstate shipment of products made by child labor.

June 3   The U.S. 2d Division and parts of other divisions join French forces to halt the German advance at Château-Thierry, and about 27,000 U.S. infantry and marines attack the German lines and retake Vaux, Bouresches, and Belleau Wood.

June 8   The War Labor Policies Board is established under the direction of the attorney Felix Frankfurter to coordinate the policies of the numerous other labor boards and agencies.

July 18-Aug. 6   Some 270,000 U.S. troops along with French forces counterattack the Germans between the Aisne and Marne rivers and drive the Germans back across the Marne.

July 30   Joyce Kilmer, 31, whose "Trees" is one of the most widely known poems of the day, is killed in combat in France.

Aug. 17   About 85,000 Americans join French troops in an attack north along the Soissons-Reims line toward the Belgian border.

Aug. 21   British troops reinforced by 108,000 Americans attack in Belgium from Ypres.

September   An epidemic of influenza, moving from Europe, strikes the Eastern states and spreads through 46 states, causing panic among the American people. [Before the epidemic ends in 1919, some 500,000 persons die.]

Sept. 12-20   General Pershing, in full command of 550,000 men of the U.S. 1st Army, launches an attack on the St. Mihiel salient south of Verdun. By Sept. 20th the salient is wiped out and 15,000 enemy soldiers have been captured.

Sept. 14   Eugene V. Debs is sentenced to 10 years in prison for sedition, specifically for advocating pacifism in violation of the Espionage and Sedition acts. [His sentence is commuted in 1921.]

Sept. 21-Nov. 7   Pershing's 1st Army, participating in a major offensive along 200 miles of the front, attacks in the Argonne Forest. By the end of October the Americans have crossed the forest. On Nov. 7, they establish bridgeheads across the Meuse River and cut the railroad that carries German supplies to the front.

Oct. 1   The U.S. Senate votes, 62 to 34, in favor of the amendment (passed by the House in January) to grant suffrage to women. The two-thirds majority required to pass a constitutional amendment is short by 2 votes and the amendment fails to pass.

Oct. 3   Germany notifies President Wilson that it will accept the Fourteen Points as a basis for peace negotiations.

Oct. 13-15   Forest fires sweep a large area of Wisconsin and Minnesota, causing about 1,000 deaths.

Oct. 16   Congress passes a wartime measure barring entry into the United States of aliens who advocate overthrow of the Government by force.

Nov. 2   A subway derailment of five cars of New York City's Brooklyn Rapid Transit kills about 100 persons and injures as many more.

Nov. 5   In the Congressional elections, the Democrats lose 26 seats in the House of Representatives and 6 in the Senate, giving the Republicans control of both Houses.

Nov. 7   Reports of the signing of an armistice in New York newspapers give rise to wild celebrations in the streets. [The report is later found to be erroneous.]

Nov. 11   The armistice with Germany is signed, and Americans again take to the streets in enthusiastic celebrations.

Nov. 18   President Wilson announces that he

will attend the peace conference in Paris.

Nov. 21 President Wilson signs a temporary prohibition act, banning the manufacture and sale of intoxicating liquors, except for export, between June 30, 1919, and the completion of troop demobilization.

Dec. 1 British and American troops begin the occupation of Germany.

Dec. 4 President Wilson sails for France on the *George Washington* to attend the peace conference; he is accompanied by Bernard Baruch and Herbert Hoover. [He arrives at Brest on Dec. 13.]

Officers of the 77th Division stand in front of their shelter in the Argonne Forest.

German prisoners of war at Verdun

1919 **The peace conference opens at Versailles, outside Paris, with** President Wilson speaking for the United States. Neither Germany nor its allies are represented at the conference. The delegates, under strong pressure by Wilson, agree unanimously to make the League of Nations a part of the treaty. When President Wilson sails for home, he takes with him the controversial Covenant of the League of Nations, but the Senate and House committees on foreign relations and many Senators will not consider a treaty that includes the Covenant. Returning to France, Wilson seeks to meet some Senate objections by proposing an amendment to the Covenant that would exempt the United States from some of its provisions. With this example set, each country seeks some special exception from the proposed Fourteen Points in its own national interest. The final treaty is adopted only after severe conflict. On May 7 the treaty, containing the League of Nations Covenant, is submitted to the German delegation, which protests strongly that the terms violate the conditions under which Germany signed the armistice. On June 28, however, the Treaty of Versailles is signed. The German Government ratifies it on July 7; France, Great Britain, Italy, and Japan ratify it in October.

On July 10 the treaty comes before the U.S. Senate. Despite strong objections by numerous Senators, Wilson refuses to accept amendments or reservations. During the summer Senator Henry Cabot Lodge holds extensive public hearings on ratification, and the Senate majority remains adamant against it. Exhausted and ailing, President Wilson tours the United States for a month to seek support for ratification. His physical condition deteriorates, and when he returns to Washington, he suffers a massive stroke, which incapacitates him for two months. On Nov. 6 Senator Lodge offers a resolution for ratification of the treaty with 14 reservations. President Wilson urges his Democratic supporters to defeat the resolution because it provides "for the nullification of the treaty." In the end, Wilson wins a Pyrrhic victory, for the Lodge version is blocked and ratification fails.

Jan. 6 Theodore Roosevelt, 60, the 26th President of the United States, dies at Oyster Bay, New York.

Jan. 29 The 18th Amendment, prohibiting the manufacture or sale of alcoholic beverages is declared ratified. It becomes effective within a year.

Mar. 4 President Wilson's potent political enemy, Senator Henry Cabot Lodge, exhibits a statement signed by 37 Senators asserting that they will not accept the Covenant of the League of Nations in its present form.

Mar. 15-17 The American Legion is founded in Paris by delegates from 1,000 units of the American Expeditionary Force.

April 8 Frank Winfield Woolworth, 67, founder of the Woolworth chain of 5¢ and 10¢ stores, dies in New York City.

May 21 A Curtiss NC-4 Navy seaplane reaches England via Newfoundland, the Azores, and Portugal after a takeoff from Rockaway, New York. This is the first air crossing of the Atlantic Ocean and takes 18 days.

June 28 The Treaty of Versailles, ending World War I, is signed at Versailles, France. It must now be ratified by the governments of the signatories.

July 4 Jack Dempsey wins the world heavyweight boxing championship, knocking out Jess Willard in the third round, in Toledo, Ohio.

July 10 President Wilson presents the Treaty of Versailles to the U.S. Senate for ratification.

Aug. 11 Andrew Carnegie, 83, pioneer in the steel industry and philanthropist, dies in Lenox, Massachusetts.

Aug. 31 At the convention of the Socialist Party in Chicago, the more radical or left-wing faction splits from the party and organizes a movement more sympathetic with the Bolshevik wing of the Russian Social-Democratic Party. [The dissident socialists become the Workers or Communist Party in the 1920's.]

Sept. 9 About three-quarters of the 1,500-man Boston police force strikes. [Governor Calvin Coolidge of Massachusetts mobilizes the State Guard and breaks the strike, stating that "no one has the right to strike against the public safety." All of the strikers are discharged.]

Sept. 22 Some 365,000 workers strike against the U.S. Steel Corporation and other companies that still maintain a 12-hour work day. [The strike, led by William Z. Foster, a left-wing socialist and a founder of the U.S. Communist Party, is broken with the help of military force after almost four months.]

Sept. 25 While speaking in Pueblo, Colorado, in defense of the Versailles Treaty, President Wilson collapses and is forced to return to Washington.

Oct. 28 The National Prohibition Act, or Volstead Act, is passed by Congress over President Wilson's veto. It defines intoxicating beverages as those containing more than ½ of 1 per cent of alcohol and regulates the manufacture and sale of alcohol for industrial, medicinal, and sacramental purposes.

Nov. 19 The U.S. Senate votes on ratification of the Treaty of Versailles. A majority favors accepting most of the parts, but insists on exempting the United States from Article X of Part I, a pledge that member states will defend one another. The majority also insists on affirming that Congress may withdraw the United States from the League. Those Senators who want no part of the treaty, and the Wilson supporters who insist on the entire treaty, together prevent a required two-thirds majority, and the Senate fails to ratify the treaty.

Dec. 22 As anti-Communist hysteria begins to sweep the country, a series of raids is organized by Attorney General A. Mitchell Palmer. [About 250 alien anarchists, Communists, and labor organizers are deported to Russia.]

The Curtiss NC-4 seaplane in flight as it makes the first transatlantic crossing by an aircraft.

1920

The aftermath of the war and the animosities over the conditions under which peace will be established pervade the Presidential campaign. The choices of both the Republican and Democratic parties are arrived at, not in the convention halls, but in the smoke-filled rooms. The only significant minor party candidate, Eugene V. Debs of the Socialist Party, runs for the highest office in the land from behind prison bars and receives a record, for a radical nominee, of almost 920,000 votes. In the contest between the two relatively obscure major candidates, Governor Cox of Ohio remains loyal to Wilson and defends the League of Nations, while Senator Harding stresses a return to "normalcy," thereby giving a new word to the language. In the election, women vote for the first time on a nationwide basis, and a radio audience for the first time hears the results on their home receivers, if they live near Pittsburgh. Harding receives 16,143,407 votes to 9,130,328 for Cox. The electoral vote is equally decisive: 404 to 127. Along with the Presidency, the Republicans win handsomely in Congress, increasing their delegations in both Houses. Clearly the United States is not about to join the League of Nations. A trend toward isolationism is apparent.

The 14th decennial census places the population of the United States at 106,021,537, an increase of almost 15 per cent over that of 1910. The total includes 5,736,000 immigrants. For the first time, the rural population is smaller than the urban. Illiteracy among persons over the age of 10 is 6 per cent, compared with 7.7 in the previous census. The number of states is now 48, an increase of two during the decade: Arizona and New Mexico, both in 1912.

Jan. 2 As the Red scare continues, Federal agents again stage nationwide raids and arrest 2,700 persons. [The raids and arrests continue until May.]

Jan. 16 The Prohibition amendment to the Constitution goes into effect.

Feb. 13 Secretary of State Robert Lansing leaves office at the request of the incapacitated President Wilson, who charges Lansing with holding unauthorized Cabinet meetings during Wilson's illness.

Feb. 20 Robert Edwin Peary, 59, Arctic explorer, first to reach the North Pole (in 1909), dies in Washington, D.C.

Feb. 28 Congress passes the Esch-Cummins (Transportation) Act, returning the railroads to private control. The Interstate Commerce Commission is authorized to require the railroads to establish and maintain rates that yield a "fair return" and the ICC is empowered to set rates, and to establish the Railway Labor Board.

Mar. 19 The question of the Treaty of Versailles again comes to a vote in the U.S. Senate. Again a two-thirds majority cannot be persuaded (the vote is 49 to 35 in favor of the treaty), and ratification fails.

May 5 In Braintree, Massachusetts, Nicola Sacco, a shoemaker in a shoe factory, and Bartolomeo Vanzetti, a fish peddler, both Italian immigrants, are arrested and charged with the murder of a paymaster and a guard during a payroll robbery. [The case becomes a *cause célèbre.*]

May 20 Congress, in a joint resolution, declares an end to the war with Germany and Austria-Hungary. [President Wilson vetoes the resolution.]

June 8-12 The Republican national convention convenes in Chicago. It is keynoted by Senator Henry Cabot Lodge, who tells the delegates: "Mr. Wilson and his dynasty, his heirs and assigns, or anybody that is his, anybody who with bent knee has served his purpose, must be driven from all control of the government and all influence in it." The Republicans have difficulty in choosing between General Leonard Wood of New York and Governor Frank O. Lowden of Illinois. After neither man achieves the required number of votes in nine ballots, Lodge forces an adjournment. A caucus of Senators and party bosses in a hotel room picks Senator Warren Gamaliel Harding of Ohio; on June 12 he is nominated, and Governor Calvin Coolidge of Massachusetts is chosen as his running mate.

June 10 The Water Power Act is passed by the U.S. Congress, creating the Federal Power Commission headed by the secretaries of War, Interior, and Agriculture, and authorized to regulate waterways on public lands and navigable streams and to license the use of dam sites for generation of electric power. [The commission is reorganized as an independent agency in 1930.]

Suffragettes form a victory motorcade to celebrate the ratification of the 19th Amendment.

June 28-July 6 At the Democratic national convention, meeting in San Francisco, former Secretary of the Treasury William G. McAdoo and Attorney General A. Mitchell Palmer are deadlocked for 38 ballots. The party bosses choose Governor James M. Cox of Ohio. Franklin Delano Roosevelt, assistant Secretary of the Navy, is chosen as Cox's running mate.

July 3 William Crawford Gorgas, 65, U.S. Army surgeon who introduced mosquito control to reduce yellow fever and malaria in the building of the Panama Canal, dies in London.

Aug. 26 The 19th Amendment to the Constitution is ratified, giving women the right to vote in national elections regardless of state laws.

Sept. 8 Airmail service between New York and San Francisco is inaugurated.

Nov. 2 The first national radio service begins when Station KDKA in East Pittsburgh, Pennsylvania, broadcasts the Presidential election results. Harding wins by a massive 60.3 per cent of the popular vote.

Nov. 8 Judge Kenesaw Mountain Landis of Chicago is appointed commissioner of baseball. His appointment results from the failure of the previously existing National Commission to properly police organized baseball, as made evident in the "Black Sox" scandal last year, when members of the Chicago team (the White Sox) of the American League conspired to throw the World Series to the Cincinnati National League team.

Dec. 10 President Wilson receives the Nobel Peace Prize for 1919.

Bartolomeo Vanzetti and Nicola Sacco

1921

President Harding's first year in office is marked by the formal conclusion of the war between the United States and Germany and the beginning of an attempt to limit naval armaments. Landmark legislation includes an immigration statute that deliberately selects the ethnic composition of those permitted to enter the country; and the first efficient organization of an executive office to plan and manage the spending of the people's moneys. It is a time of transition, with rising unemployment and falling wages. It requires a strong executive, and some of the President's Cabinet are able men: Secretary of State Charles Evans Hughes, who was himself almost elected President a few years ago; banker-financier Andrew Mellon in charge of the Treasury; and Commerce Secretary Herbert Clark Hoover, who performed wonders in relieving the poor of Europe during the late war. Others are considerably less able, including Harding's campaign manager Harry Daugherty, who becomes Attorney General, and a well-known foe of conservation, Albert B. Fall, who becomes Secretary of the Interior.

Jan. 3   The U.S. Supreme Court rules that the provisions of the Sherman Antitrust Act apply to trade unions, even though the Clayton Act specifies that unions are not per se to be considered as functioning in restraint of trade.

Mar. 2   Champ Clark, 71, Speaker of the U.S. House of Representatives from 1911 to 1919, who served 13 terms in the House, dies in Washington, D.C.

Mar. 4   Warren G. Harding is inaugurated as the 29th President of the United States. In his inaugural address, referring to the League of Nations, he declares, "We seek no part in directing the destinies of the world."

Mar. 24   James Cardinal Gibbons, 86, the first chancellor of the Catholic University in Washington, D.C., dies.

Mar. 29   John Burroughs, 84, nature writer in prose and verse, dies on a trip from California to New York.

April 20   The U.S. Senate ratifies the Thompson-Urrutia Treaty with Colombia, under consideration since 1914. It stipulates that the United States will pay Colombia $25,000,000 for the loss of Panama and will grant Colombian warships free access to the Panama Canal.

May 19   Edward Douglass White, 75, named an Associate Justice of the U.S. Supreme Court in 1894 and Chief Justice in 1910, dies in Washington, D.C.

May 19   The Emergency Quota Act is passed by Congress, limiting immigration to 3 per cent of the 1910 figure from any one country in one year and setting a total limit of 357,803 immigrants per year. The majority of those admitted under the act will be from northern European countries, ending the wave of immigration from southern and eastern Europe.

May 27   An Emergency Tariff Act is passed, raising the duties on agricultural products, wool, and sugar and placing an embargo on German dyestuffs.

May 31   President Harding signs an Executive Order, at the urging of Secretary of the Interior Albert B. Fall, transferring from the Navy Department to the Interior Department administration of the Navy petroleum reserves at Teapot Dome, Wyoming, and Elk Hills and Buena Vista Hills, California.

June 3   The Arkansas River floods as a result of a cloudburst; about 200 persons in Pueblo, Colorado, lose their lives.

June 10   The National Budget and Accounting Act is passed by Congress. It vests responsibility for preparing the budget in the Executive Branch, establishing the Bureau of the Budget under the Treasury Department. Charles G. Dawes is named the first director of the budget.

June 30   William Howard Taft is appointed Chief Justice of the U.S. Supreme Court by President Harding.

July 2   Congress, in a joint resolution, declares an end to the war with Germany and Austria-Hungary, and President Harding signs the resolution. [Separate treaties are signed and ratified in August.]

July 2   Jack Dempsey defends his heavyweight championship against French contender Georges Carpentier at Boyle's 30 Acres in Jersey City, New Jersey. About 80,000 spectators, more than four times the audience that watched Dempsey win the crown two years ago, see the champion knock out Carpentier in the 4th round.

July 14   Nicola Sacco and Bartolomeo Vanzetti are convicted of murder in the slaying of two men at a Massachusetts shoe factory in 1920. [Worldwide protest ensues by persons who

The U.S.S. *Alabama* being bombed in a test to demonstrate the superiority of planes over ships.

believe that the two are convicted only because of their radical beliefs.]

July 21 General William (''Billy'') Mitchell, assistant chief of the Army air service, demonstrates the superiority of massed planes over ships when, in a test, planes sink the former German battleship *Ostfriesland* and the condemned U.S. battleship *Alabama*.

Aug. 9 The Veterans' Bureau is established as an independent agency, absorbing the functions of three existing agencies.

Aug. 15 Congress passes the Packers and Stockyard Act, designed to end price manipulations and monopolies in the meatpacking industry.

Sept. 30 A national conference on unemployment proposes a program to create jobs and warns manufacturers and retailers to reduce prices, after the Department of Labor reports unemployment at 5,000,000 and reveals that drastic wage cuts have been made in many industries.

Oct. 5-13 Radio station WJZ in Newark, New Jersey, broadcasts the first play-by-play description of baseball's World Series when two New York teams, the National League Giants and the American League Yankees, play a so-called ''subway series.'' The Giants win.

Nov. 2 The American Birth Control League is created by the merger of the National Birth Control League and the Voluntary Parenthood League; it is headed by Margaret Sanger.

Nov. 11 The first Armistice Day, declared on Nov. 5 by President Wilson, is solemnized by a burial ceremony held at the Tomb of the Unknown Soldier in Arlington National Cemetery.

Nov. 12-Feb. 6, 1922 The Washington Conference for Limitation of Armaments meets. The participating nations are the United States, Great Britain, France, Italy, Belgium, the Netherlands, China, Japan, and Portugal. Agreements reached include the Pacific Treaty (Dec. 13, 1921), under which the United States, Great Britain, France, and Japan guarantee one another's rights to insular possessions in the Pacific Ocean; two nine-power treaties (Feb. 6, 1922) guaranteeing the territorial integrity and independence of China and reiterating the Open Door principle; and the five-power naval armaments treaty (Feb. 6, 1922) among Great Britain, France, Japan, Italy, and the United States, providing that no new capital ships are to be built by the signatories for 10 years and establishing a ratio of capital ships to be built thereafter.

Dec. 25 President Harding pardons Eugene V. Debs, who is serving a 10-year prison sentence after conviction under the Espionage and Sedition laws.

1922

The second year of President Harding's Administration is one of increasing tariffs and decreasing immigration. Beneath the surface bubbles the oil scandal of Teapot Dome, but the public is virtually unaware of the machinations of the "Ohio gang," with which the President has surrounded himself, in defrauding the American taxpayer.

The year is noteworthy for its cultural events. Poet Thomas Stearns Eliot publishes a five-part work *The Wasteland,* which becomes widely discussed for its style and content. Edna St. Vincent Millay's *The Ballad of the Harp Weaver* appears. [It is awarded the 1923 Pulitzer prize.] E.E. Cummings publishes a war novel, *The Enormous Room.* Sinclair Lewis produces *Babbitt,* a novel whose protagonist lends his name as a generic for the blindly conformist middle-class businessman. De Witt Wallace founds *The Reader's Digest,* a periodical reprinting articles from other publications. In the theater, Eugene O'Neill is represented by *The Hairy Ape,* and the playwriting team of George S. Kaufman and Marc Connelly contribute *To the Ladies. Abie's Irish Rose* begins its New York run. King Oliver's jazz band in Chicago acquires cornetist Louis Armstrong, a native of New Orleans, from his riverboat gigs. A commercially successful color process for motion pictures, Technicolor, is developed by Herbert T. Kalmus.

Feb. 18 The Capper-Volstead Cooperative Act is passed by the U.S. Congress, granting agricultural associations and cooperatives the right to process, handle, and market their goods in interstate commerce and exempting certain associations from the antitrust laws.

Feb. 21 The semidirigible *Roma* explodes after striking high-tension wires at Hampton Roads Army Base in Virginia, killing 34 of the 45-man crew.

Mar. 24 The four-power Pacific Treaty, negotiated by the Washington Conference on Limitation of Arms in 1921, is ratified by the U.S. Senate.

April 1-Sept. 4 Coal miners strike across the country in protest against wage reductions and in support of the union dues check-off system. At Herrin, Illinois, on June 22, several hundred strikers induce nonunion miners to surrender and promise them safe conduct out of town; however, they are ordered to run for their lives instead, and more than 20 are shot dead and others wounded.

April 7 Secretary of the Interior Albert B. Fall, after secret negotiations and without competitive bidding, grants a lease to Harry F. Sinclair's Mammoth Oil Company on the Teapot Dome oil reserves set aside for the U.S. Navy. [During the year Fall also negotiates secret leases on Elk Hills and Buena Vista Hills naval oil reserves with two companies controlled by Edward L. Doheny.]

April 15 Senator John B. Kendrick of Wyoming asks Secretary Fall why the Teapot Dome fields are leased to a private company.

May 12 A meteorite weighing 20 tons falls near Blackstone, Virginia, creating a crater 400 feet square.

May 30 The Lincoln Memorial is dedicated in Washington, D.C. Designed by Henry Bacon with 36 columns representing the states of the Union at the time of President Lincoln's death, the memorial contains a seated statue of Lincoln created by sculptor Daniel Chester French.

July 1-Sept. 13 Railway shopmen strike in protest against wage reductions set by the Railway Labor Board.

Aug. 2 Alexander Graham Bell, 75, inventor of the telephone, dies in Baddeck, Nova Scotia.

Sept. 4 Lieutenant James H. Doolittle, in 21 hours 20 minutes flying time (23 hours 35 minutes total time), flies a DH4B-Liberty 400 from Pablo Beach, Florida, to San Diego, California, a distance of 2,163 miles. It is the first transcontinental flight in less than 24 hours.

Sept. 21 The Fordney-McCumber Tariff Act is passed by Congress, reversing the Underwood Tariff trend of 1913 against high protection. Designed to equalize the cost of U.S. and foreign production, the duties on manufactured products are increased to record levels and even higher tariffs are imposed on farm products than those of the Emergency Tariff Act of 1921.

Sept. 22 The Cable Act is passed by Congress, providing that women will no longer lose their U.S. citizenship if they marry aliens.

Nov. 7 In Congressional elections, the Republicans lose 76 seats in the House of Representatives and 8 seats in the Senate, but retain a majority in both Houses.

Crowds gather for the dedication of the Lincoln Memorial.

The coroner's inquest at Herrin, Illinois to determine the responsibility
for the murder of 20 nonunion miners

1923

In the last months of President Warren G. Harding's Administration, rumors begin to circulate about the extent of theft and graft being perpetrated by some of the President's men. It is being said that Charles R. Forbes has mulcted the Veterans Bureau of some $250,000,000; that Thomas W. Miller, the Alien Property Custodian, has fraudulently returned about $7,000,000 to a German metal firm; and that Gaston B. Means, an agent for the Federal Bureau of Investigation, has paid bribes. Attorney General Harry M. Daugherty comes under fire for taking bribes from violators of Prohibition laws. Secretary of the Interior Albert B. Fall resigns from the Cabinet with the proceeds of the bribes he has received in the Teapot Dome, Elk Hills, and Buena Vista Hills oil lease scandals. Senator Thomas J. Walsh of Montana undertakes an extensive investigation of the most blatant case.

As Vice President, Calvin Coolidge breaks precedent by attending President Harding's Cabinet meetings and fully supports Administration policies, but he is in no way involved with Harding's "Ohio gang." President Harding, perhaps never aware of the full extent of the scandal that is about to break, leaves Washington in the summer on a vacation and speaking tour across the country and to Alaska. As word of events in the capital continues to reach him, his health gives way. Returning to San Francisco, he suffers a heart attack and, on Aug. 2, dies. At 2:30 A.M. on Aug. 3, Vice President Coolidge again breaks precedent, by taking the oath of office as President from his father, a notary public, whom he is visiting in Vermont.

Jan. 10 President Harding orders withdrawal of U.S. occupation troops from Germany.

Mar. 4 Congress passes the Agricultural Credits Act, designed to aid farmer cooperatives by providing for a system of 12 Federal intermediate credit banks to handle agricultural loans exclusively.

Mar. 4 Secretary of the Interior Albert Fall resigns.

April 10 The legislature of Oklahoma, a leader among the states in oil production, passes a proration law. (Proration means that everyone owning a producing well in an oil field will receive his proportional share of the output of the field.) The law has the effect of limiting production of petroleum to proportional refining capacity; its purposes, aside from fair distribution of profit, are to increase prices and eliminate waste in production. [The law becomes a model for other states and for the Federal Governnent.]

Aug. 2 Warren Gamaliel Harding, 57, the 29th President of the United States, dies in San Francisco.

Aug. 3 Calvin Coolidge takes the oath of office as the 30th President of the United States.

Aug. 24 Kate Douglas Wiggin, 66, American educator and novelist best known for the juvenile classic *Rebecca of Sunnybrook Farm*, dies in Harrow, England.

Sept. 15 Ku Klux Klan terrorist activities cause Governor J. C. Walton of Oklahoma to place the state under martial law.

Oct. 25 The U.S. Senate subcommittee to investigate the Teapot Dome scandal holds its first meeting under the chairmanship of Senator Thomas J. Walsh of Montana. [The hearings continue into 1924.]

Oct. 26 Charles Proteus Steinmetz, 58, electrical engineer, discoverer of the law of hysteresis (which makes possible the forecasting of losses of electric power because of magnetism), and owner of patents for more than 200 inventions, dies in Schenectady, New York.

Dec. 6 President Coolidge addresses his first message to Congress, calling for support of a world court but for aloofness from the League of Nations, enforcement of Prohibition, tax reduction, and economy in the Federal Government. The speech is the first official Presidential message to be broadcast on radio.

Dec. 10 Robert Andrews Millikan receives the Nobel Prize in physics for "his work on the elementary electric charge and on the photoelectric effect."

Charles Steinmetz
(1865-1923)

President Harding (5th from right) and
Mrs. Harding (on the platform) arrive in
San Francisco.

Calvin Coolidge is sworn in as President by his
father at the elder Coolidge's home in
Plymouth, Vermont.

The temper of the American people and the moral climate of the country undergo a dramatic reversal with the succession to the Presidency of Calvin Coolidge, a man who values, and for many incarnates, the homely virtues of honesty, hard work, and common sense. A conservative Republican, he is a businessman's President, with little sympathy for reforms of any kind. Untouched by the scandals of Harding's Administration, he does what he can to expose and end them. The country is generally prosperous. Thus the Republican national convention easily selects Coolidge for a full term. The platform calls for lower taxes, higher tariffs, economy, limitation of arms, and international cooperation to keep peace.

The Democratic Party, on the other hand, is seriously divided between its urban and rural segments, largely because of the increasing controversiality of the 18th Amendment. William G. McAdoo is the choice of the rural faction and the recipient of much strength from the Ku Klux Klan and supporters of Prohibition, whereas Governor Alfred E. Smith of New York, a Catholic and an opponent of Prohibition, is backed by the urban element. At the national convention, Smith and McAdoo struggle for 16 days until both withdraw and the convention eventually nominates John W. Davis of West Virginia on the 103d ballot. The Democratic platform calls for competitive tariffs, disarmament, and U.S. entry into the League of Nations.

The lack of a candidate with "progressive" credentials encourages another attempt to form an ad hoc third party, the Progressive Party. The emergence of this party, with the support of the American Federation of Labor, the Farmer-Labor Party, and the Socialist Party, affords Robert M. La Follette another opportunity to seek the Presidency. The Progressive platform stresses labor union freedom, government ownership of water resources and railroads, and child labor legislation.

Jan. 24   General Charles G. Dawes is chosen chairman of the committee of experts of the German Reparations Commission.

Feb. 3   Woodrow Wilson, 68, the 28th President of the United States, dies in Washington, D.C.

Feb. 8   A joint resolution of Congress states that the oil leases and contracts negotiated by former Secretary of the Interior Albert B. Fall are against the public interest, and directs the President to institute suits to cancel them and to prosecute any actions that might be warranted. [The U.S. Supreme Court later rules that the contracts and leases are fraudulent.]

Feb. 12   *Rhapsody in Blue,* a new form of symphonic jazz, is given its first performance in New York City by Paul Whiteman's orchestra, with composer George Gershwin as piano soloist.

Feb. 27   The United States signs a treaty with the Dominican Republic, superseding that of 1907, which permitted U.S. intervention on behalf of stability. [In July U.S. marines are withdrawn, but the right to supervise customs receipts is held by the United States until 1941.]

Mar. 28   President Coolidge demands and receives the resignation of Attorney General Harry M. Daugherty.

Mar. 31   In the Oregon Case, the U.S. Supreme Court declares that a state may not require all children of school age to attend public schools.

April 9-16   The Dawes Plan for German reparations is reported out and accepted by Germany. It is based upon German capacity to pay, and includes a loan to Germany of $200,000,000. The plan is to become effective on Aug. 30, 1924, but its acceptance by Germany immediately reduces the tension resulting from the French-Belgian occupation of the Ruhr because of defaults in reparations payments.

May 19   The Soldiers' Bonus Bill for veterans of the World War [World War I] is passed by the U.S. Congress over President Coolidge's veto.

May 26   The U.S. Congress passes an Immigration Bill, further limiting annual immigration from a given foreign country to 2 per cent of the number of its nationals in the United States in 1890, and completely excluding Japanese immigration.

May 26   Victor Herbert, 65, conductor and composer of popular operettas *(Babes in Toyland, Naughty Marietta),* dies in New York City.

June 2   National statutes limiting the hours and other working conditions of children, having

Democratic Presidential-candidate John W. Davis (left) and Vice-Presidential candidate Charles W. Bryan

been adopted in 1916 and in 1919 and having been found unconstitutional, both Houses of Congress react by passing a joint resolution giving Congress such power through a Constitutional Amendment. The bill is sent to the states for the necessary ratification. [It fails to obtain the necessary two-thirds approval, and dies.]

June 10-12 The Republican convention, meeting in Cleveland, picks President Coolidge to succeed himself. His running mate is the respected financier, General Charles G. Dawes, an untainted Harding appointee as budget director.

June 15 By act of Congress, all native-born American Indians are made citizens of the United States.

June 24-July 29 After interminable balloting, a "dark horse" candidate is picked by the Democratic convention, meeting in New York City. He is Senator John W. Davis of West Virginia.

June 30 Albert B. Fall, Harry F. Sinclair, and Edward L. Doheny are indicted on charges of conspiracy and bribery as a result of the Teapot Dome hearings. [Of these, only Fall is convicted and jailed.]

July 1 The U.S. Congress adopts the Rogers Act under which the diplomatic and consular services are merged and the training of young men as career diplomats is begun.

July 4-18 The League for Progressive Politi-

cal Action, meeting in Cleveland, representing the Farmer-Labor Party, the Nonpartisan League, and other small groupings, but supported by the American Federation of Labor and the Socialist Party, names Senators Robert M. La Follette of Wisconsin and Burton K. Wheeler of Montana to head a third-party ticket in November.

Aug. 24 The Agricultural Credits Act is approved by Congress. It is designed to curtail farm bankruptcies.

Nov. 4 President Coolidge is elected overwhelmingly, receiving 15,718,211 popular votes and 382 electoral votes, against 8,385,283 popular and 136 electoral votes for Davis. The 4,831,289 popular votes for La Follette, more than half the number achieved by the Democrats, are thoroughly concealed by the meager 13 electoral votes (the state of Wisconsin). This outcome demonstrates the virtual impossibility of victory outside even the weakest "second" party.

Nov. 9 Henry Cabot Lodge, 74, U.S. Senator from Massachusetts, who was largely responsible for keeping the United States out of the League of Nations, dies in Cambridge, Massachusetts.

Dec. 13 Samuel Gompers, 74, labor leader and president since 1886 (except in 1895) of the American Federation of Labor, which he helped to found, dies in San Antonio, Texas.

Senator Robert La Follete (left) and Senator Burton K. Wheeler, Presidential and Vice-Presidential candidates of the League for Progressive Political Action

1925

Feeling secure under the upright Administration of President Coolidge, much of the American public enjoys a sense of complacency in what is called the New Era. As a consequence of the President's strongly held tenet that "The business of America is business," big business is booming and the stock market is soaring. Yet industrial wages fail to keep pace with productivity, and the plight of the American farmer is left by Coolidge to cure itself without U.S. Government intervention—a cure that fails to materialize.

Remote from and in contrast to the humdrum tedium of life in official circles, this is a year of rich and varied cultural achievement, seeing the publication of Sinclair Lewis' *Arrowsmith,* Theodore Dreiser's *An American Tragedy,* John Dos Passos' *Manhattan Transfer,* F. Scott Fitzgerald's *The Great Gatsby,* and Ezra Pound's *A Draft of XVI Cantos.*

Jan. 5   Mrs. Nellie Tayloe Ross takes office as governor of Wyoming to complete her late husband's term of office, becoming the first woman governor in the United States.

Jan. 21   George Washington Cable, 80, author of novels of life in New Orleans, especially among the Creole and black population, dies in St. Petersburg, Florida.

Jan. 24   Attorney General Harlan F. Stone is appointed an Associate Justice of the U.S. Supreme Court by President Coolidge.

Jan. 24   The Northeastern states and the Great Lakes region see a total eclipse of the sun for the first time in more than three centuries.

Feb. 2   Relays of dog teams reach Nome, Alaska, with antidiphtheria serum to combat a serious epidemic.

Mar. 4   President Coolidge is inaugurated for a full term, and Charles G. Dawes becomes Vice President. Coolidge states in his inaugural address that the United States has reached "a state of contentment seldom before seen."

Mar. 13   The United States and Cuba sign a treaty under which Cuba's long-standing claim to ownership of the Isle of Pines is acknowledged.

Mar. 13   The governor of Tennessee signs a state law that makes it "unlawful for any teacher in [the state educational system] to teach any theory that denies the story of the divine creation of man as taught in the Bible, and to teach in-

stead that man has descended from a lower order of animals."

Mar. 18   Tornadoes sweep across dozens of towns in Missouri, Illinois, Kentucky, Tennessee, and Indiana, taking about 800 lives.

April 25   John Singer Sargent, 69, portrait painter who later turned to impressionistic watercolors, dies in London.

May 13   The Florida legislature passes a measure requiring daily readings from the Bible in all public schools.

June 18   Robert Marion La Follette, 70, U.S. Senator and a governor of Wisconsin, leader of the Progressive movement, dies in Washington, D.C.

July 10-21   John T. Scopes, arrested in Dayton, Tennessee, is tried on charges of teaching the theory of evolution, contrary to state law. He is defended by Clarence Darrow and Dudley Field Malone. William Jennings Bryan is a member of the prosecution. Millions of newspaper readers in the United States and Europe follow the arguments in the small-town courtroom. Scopes is convicted and fined $100. [The decision is reversed in 1927 by the Tennessee Supreme Court on a technicality. The law is repealed in 1967.]

July 26   William Jennings Bryan, 65, U.S. political leader, advocate of the free-silver movement, and three times an unsuccessful can-

The first dog-team arrives in Nome, Alaska, with anti-diphtheria serum.

Colonel William "Billy" Mitchell (center and in uniform) faces the judges at his court-martial.

Dec. 29   The Board of trustees of Trinity College, in Durham, North Carolina, agrees to adopt the name Duke University in order to receive a $40,000,000 trust fund set up by James Buchanan Duke, recently deceased founder of the American Tobacco Company.

The Scope's trial is moved outdoors because of the extreme heat inside the courtroom.

didate for the Presidency, dies in Dayton, Tennessee.

Sept. 3   The U.S. Army dirigible *Shenandoah* crashes in a storm near Ava, Ohio, killing 14 persons.

Oct. 28-Dec. 17   Colonel William ("Billy") Mitchell is court-martialed on charges of insubordination, having accused the War and Navy departments of "incompetency, criminal negligence, and almost treasonable administration of the national defense." He is found guilty and suspended from rank and duty for five years. [In 1926 he resigns from the service.]

Nov. 14   Because of a severe financial depression in Europe, the United States agrees to a sharp reduction in foreign war debts as well as interest rates on them, but still insists on partial payment.

Dec. 10   Vice President Charles Dawes receives the Nobel Peace Prize for his work on the Dawes Plan for German economic reorganization and reparations payments.

311

1926 Although the 18th Amendment (Prohibition) has been the law of the land for seven years, the "wet-dry" controversy continues to dominate national life. In April General Lincoln C. Andrews, Assistant Secretary of the Treasury in charge of Prohibition enforcement, testifies before the Senate Judiciary Committee that the difficulties of enforcing the provisions of the Volstead Act are staggering. General Andrews informs the committee that during the past year alone 875 of his agents have been dismissed for a variety of Prohibition-related offenses. It is estimated that bootleggers are earning more than $3,500,000,000 annually and that the Government is able to confiscate only about 5 per cent of the illegal alcohol produced. General Andrews further testifies that 172,000 stills have been seized during the past year, but this number probably represents about one tenth of the stills in existence. Temperance groups testify to the committee that, despite the difficulties of enforcement, there is less crime and poverty and the nation is generally better off under Prohibition. President Coolidge promises to continue the struggle to enforce the law and to "put into effect the expressed will of the people as written into the Eighteenth Amendment to the Constitution. . . ." Further, Coolidge budgets $30,000,000 to strengthen all agencies charged with the job of enforcing Prohibition.

January-April   War-debt agreements are reached between the United States and several European countries, including France, Italy, Belgium, Czechoslovakia, Rumania, Estonia, and Latvia. In the case of France it is agreed that the $4,000,000,000 owed to the United States will be repaid over a period of 62 years. Italy, which owes about $1,500,000,000 to the United States, also undertakes to repay its debt over 62 years.

Jan. 1   Two hundred persons are hurt and several are killed when a grandstand collapses at the Tournament of Roses at Pasadena, California.

Jan. 14   The United States and Cuba sign an extradition treaty.

Jan. 19   A special study group appointed by Dr. H. S. Cummings, Surgeon General of the U.S. Public Health Service, announces that it sees no reason to prohibit the burning of ethyl gasoline in automobiles.

Jan. 27   The Senate, by a vote of 76 to 17, approves United States participation in the Permanent Court of International Justice located at The Hague, Netherlands. However, the Senate's approval is qualified by several reservations unacceptable to the Court.

Feb. 28   President Coolidge signs into law a revenue act that reduces income and inheritance taxes and ends certain other taxes, including one on passenger cars.

Mar. 7   The first transatlantic radiotelephone conversation links London and New York.

April 11   Luther Burbank, 77, dies at Santa Rosa, California. A practical horticulturist, Burbank is remembered as the creator of many new plants and vegetables, including the Shasta daisy and the Burbank potato.

May-June   U.S. marines again land in Nicaragua to maintain peace after the outbreak of hostilities between Government and rebel forces.

May 5   Writer Sinclair Lewis refuses to accept the Pulitzer Prize for his novel *Arrowsmith*. He claims that such prizes undermine the writing profession, making writers "safe, polite, obedient, and sterile."

May 8-9   Richard E. Byrd and Floyd Bennett use a three-engine Fokker airplane to make the first flight over the North Pole, covering 1,545 miles, from Spitsbergen to the Pole and back in 15 hours 30 minutes. The flight is made possible by using the Bumstead sun compass, designed by Albert H. Bumstead especially for polar navigation, where ordinary compasses do not function.

June 20   The First International Eucharistic Congress opens in Chicago.

July 2   Congress redesignates the Army Air Service, formed in 1920, as the Army Air Corps.

July 10   Lightning strikes a naval depot at Lake Denmark, New Jersey, causing extensive damage. [Explosions continue for several days and result in 31 deaths.]

July 26   Robert Todd Lincoln, 83, son of Abraham Lincoln, dies. He was Secretary of War in the Garfield and Arthur administrations and Minister to Great Britain for President Benjamin Harrison.

Aug. 5   The first motion picture with a synchronized musical score opens at the Warner Theater in New York City. The picture is *Don Juan,* starring John Barrymore. The sound is produced by a phonograph record.

Aug. 6   Gertrude Ederle, 19, a native of New

York City, becomes the first woman to swim the English Channel. She sets a record for the feat, with a time of 14 hours 31 minutes.

Sept. 18 A hurricane sweeps through Florida and several other Southern states, killing 372 persons and injuring 6,000 more. Property damage is said to exceed $80,000,000.

Sept. 23 Gene Tunney wins the world heavyweight boxing championship by defeating champion Jack Dempsey in a ten-round match at Philadelphia, before 120,000 fight fans.

Oct. 25 The U.S. Supreme Court in *Myers* v. *U.S.* rules that the Tenure of Office Act of 1867 is unconstitutional, thus allowing the President to dismiss Cabinet and other executive officers without the consent of the Senate. This act was passed during the term of President Andrew Johnson to limit his control over the military. Johnson, when impeached and tried for defying the act, claimed that it was unconstitutional.

Grease is spread on Gertrude Ederle's body prior to her cross-channel swim.

Commander Byrd's plane and crew at the North Pole

1927 **This is a Franco-American year, marked by two events** that stir the imagination of millions. In April the French Foreign Minister proposes that his country and the United States offer an example to other nations by forever renouncing war as an instrument of policy, and the U.S. Secretary of State responds by suggesting that other nations be invited to participate in the pacific gesture.

The authors of the Kellogg-Briand Pact find their paperwork eclipsed by the flight of Charles A. Lindbergh, the Lone Eagle, who darts across the Atlantic Ocean in a single-engine monoplane for 33 hours in May. This, the first successful solo flight across the ocean, is greeted at the airfield in Paris by 100,000 wildly cheering Frenchmen, probably the most enthusiastic demonstration for a peacetime hero in history. His own countrymen welcome him home in June with ticker-tape parades in New York, Washington, and other large cities. Congress votes him the Congressional Medal of Honor. President Coolidge awards him the Distinguished Flying Cross.

By making the flight, Lindbergh also wins the Raymond Orteig prize of $25,000 and various other awards estimated in value between $50,000 and $100,000. However, his real goal seems to be to bring the message of aviation to the country. He spends months visiting cities throughout the United States, urging localities to support the construction of airports and the training of pilots.

Jan. 2   The Hoover Commission, appointed by President Coolidge in 1924, announces that a waterway following the St. Lawrence River would be the best route to connect the Great Lakes with the Atlantic Ocean.

Jan. 7   The first commercial telephone service between New York and London is opened.

Feb. 23   Congress passes the Conference Radio Control Bill and it goes to President Coolidge for his signature. The bill sets up the Federal Board of Radio Control [later the Federal Communications Commission].

Mar. 3   The Prohibition Bureau is established as part of the Treasury Department by the Prohibition Reorganization Act.

Mar. 7   The U.S. Supreme Court in *Nixon* v. *Herndon* rules that a Texas law forbidding blacks to vote in primary elections is unconstitutional. The unanimous decision, handed down by Justice Oliver Wendell Holmes, maintains that the law is in violation of the 14th Amendment.

Mar. 29   Major H. O. D. Segrave sets an automobile speed record at Daytona Beach, Florida, by driving a Sunbeam at 203.79 mph over a marked mile, the first time a motor vehicle has exceeded 200 mph on land.

April   More U.S. marines are sent to Nicaragua to control the continuing disturbance there. Henry L. Stimson is sent by President Coolidge to try to negotiate a settlement between the U.S.-supported Government and the rebels.

April 6   French Foreign Minister Aristide Briand suggests that the United States and France agree to renounce war as a means of solving disagreements between the two countries.

April 7   The first public demonstration of television takes place.

April 17   Governor Alfred E. Smith of New York, who plans to run for the Presidency on the Democratic ticket next year, is asked if his ability to carry out the duties of the Presidency would be hampered by his loyalty to the Catholic Church. In an article appearing in the *Atlantic Monthly* he replies: "I recognize no power in the institutions of my Church to interfere with the operations of the Constitution of the United States or the enforcement of the law of the land."

April-May   Unusually heavy rains create the worst flood conditions in the history of the lower Mississippi Valley. Miles of levees are destroyed as the waters of the Mississippi and its tributaries rise 55 feet and more above normal. Twenty

Babe Ruth hits his 60th home run.

thousand square miles are flooded, and in one area of northern Louisiana a huge lake is formed, 300 miles long and 100 miles wide. About 675,000 persons are homeless, and despite adequate warning of the impending flood many hundreds drown. Secretary of Commerce Herbert Hoover declares it the ''greatest peacetime calamity in the history of our country.''

May 20-21   Captain Charles A. Lindbergh, an unknown airmail pilot, takes off from Roosevelt Field near New York City in the *Spirit of St. Louis,* a single-engine monoplane. He flies 3,600 miles for 33 hours 39 minutes at altitudes limited by the weather to 10,000 feet, and finds a throng of 100,000 awaiting him when he lands at Le Bourget Field near Paris.

June 11   Secretary of State Frank B. Kellogg acknowledges the suggestion made by French Foreign Minister Briand on April 6, and suggests that Briand write a draft agreement.

June 20-Aug. 4   The United States, Great Britain, and Japan meet to discuss the possibility of restricting the size of their navies, as suggested by President Coolidge on Feb. 10. Unfortunately France and Italy refuse to attend the conference, which is held in Geneva, and the United States and Great Britain fail to agree on cruiser restrictions, so nothing is accomplished.

June 28-29   Lester Maitland and Albert F. Hegenberger make the first successful flight from California to Hawaii, taking 25 hours 50 minutes to cover the 2,407-mile distance in a Fokker monoplane.

July 29   The first electric respirator [the ''iron lung''] goes into use at Bellevue Hospital in New York City. Its inventors, Drs. Philip Drinker and Louis A. Shaw, say that it can be used in almost any type of respiratory failure.

Aug. 2   Responding to numerous appeals that he stand for election to another term, President Coolidge surprises the nation with the statement: ''I do not choose to run.''

Aug. 27   Sacco and Vanzetti are executed in Massachusetts.

Sept. 14   Isadora Duncan, 49, a major personality in the development of modern dance, dies at Nice, France. Death results from strangulation when a long scarf she is wearing catches in the wheel of the car in which she is riding.

Sept. 27   Babe Ruth hits a record 60th home run of the season at Yankee Stadium in New York City.

Sept. 29   A freak tornado, lasting only five minutes, strikes St. Louis, killing 87 and injuring 1,500. More than 1,000 homes are destroyed.

Lindbergh stands under the wing of his plane, the *Spirit of St Louis,* before taking off on his transatlantic flight.

Oct. 6   The first talking picture, *The Jazz Singer,* starring Al Jolson, opens.

Oct. 10   The U.S. Supreme Court rules that the lease of Teapot Dome oil reserve lands to Mammoth Oil Company is invalid because it was obtained by fraudulent means.

Nov. 13   The first underwater vehicular tunnel opens to traffic. Known as the Holland Tunnel, it was built under the Hudson River between New York City and New Jersey, and has two lanes in each direction. It is 1.8 miles long.

Dec. 17   The U.S. submarine *S-4* sinks after it strikes a Coast Guard destroyer as it surfaces off Provincetown, Massachusetts. Divers attempt in vain to free the men trapped inside, and all 40 members of the crew perish.

Dec. 27   Produced by Florenz Ziegfeld, *Show Boat* opens on Broadway to great critical acclaim. The play is adapted from a book by Edna Ferber, with music by Jerome Kern and libretto by Oscar Hammerstein II. ''Old Man River'' and ''Can't Help Lovin' That Man'' are two of the songs that make the show a success.

Al Jolson in a scene from the "Jazz Singer" (*ca.*) 1927

Despite numerous efforts by prominent Republicans to convince President Coolidge to run for another term, he steadfastly refuses. Secretary of Commerce Herbert Hoover, long thought of as a possible Presidential candidate, gathers a powerful organization and easily wins the Republican nomination at Kansas City in mid-June. The Democrats two weeks later select Alfred E. Smith, a dynamic and respected politican, now in his fourth term as governor of New York. Despite Smith's engaging personality, compared with Hoover's more conservative demeanor, the Democrats face a difficult battle. The Republicans campaign on their record, pointing to the increasing prosperity during the Harding and Coolidge administrations. Their plans call for an end to poverty and "a chicken in every pot, a car in every garage." Depressed farm prices, which might be a Republican vulnerability, are of little help to the Democrats, for Smith's New York City background holds no appeal for the farmers. Smith's Catholic religion and his "wet" stand on the prohibition issue prove embarrassing to his party.

On Nov. 6 the voters choose Hoover by a large margin, giving him 58.22 per cent of the votes cast. Hoover also easily wins most of the electoral vote, with Smith carrying only a portion of the normally Democratic South and a few Eastern states. Charles Curtis is the new Vice President.

Jan. 16-Feb. 20 The Pan-American conference gets under way in Havana, Cuba. An opening-day message by President Coolidge calls for peace and increased cooperation among the nations of the Western Hemisphere. Objections are raised to the 1904 Roosevelt Corollary to the Monroe Doctrine, by which the United States claims great latitude in its right to intervene in the internal affairs of its neighbors.

Feb. 2 A fire in the city of Fall River, Massachusetts, causes $20,000,000 property damage and destroys six banks.

Feb. 6 The United States and France sign an arbitration treaty in Washington, D.C. The date marks the 150th anniversary of the treaty of alliance between the two nations signed in 1778.

Feb. 10 The U.S. Senate, by a vote of 56 to 26, adopts a resolution proposed by Senator Robert La Follette of Wisconsin that holds it to be "unwise, unpatriotic, and fraught with peril to our free institutions" if any President were to depart from the tradition set by President Washington of serving no more than two terms. The resolution is intended to discourage a possible draft of President Coolidge.

Feb. 10 Radiotelephone service between the United States and Germany begins.

Feb. 10 The Bar Association of New York City declares itself against national Prohibition and the Volstead Act.

Feb. 21 Oil millionaire Harry F. Sinclair is found guilty of contempt of court in Washington, D.C., and is sentenced to six months in prison. Henry Mason Day, an executive with the Sinclair Oil Company, admits that he hired the Burns Detective Agency to follow members of the jury in the Teapot Dome conspiracy trial, and is sentenced to four months. William J. Burns and his son, Sherman Burns, owners of a major detective agency, are held in contempt and are given light sentences.

Mar. 9 A proposed "Lame Duck" Amendment to the Constitution, which would advance the inauguration of the President from March to January, is defeated in the House, by a vote of 157 to 209.

Mar. 10 President Coolidge signs the Alien Property Act, which provides $300,000,000 to compensate German nationals and German companies for property seized from them at the outbreak of the war in 1917.

Mar. 11 A Senate committee that has been touring western Pennsylvania to investigate the coal strikes in that region charges the state police with brutality and the mine owners with indifference to the plight of the miners.

Mar. 13 A dam located 40 miles north of Los Angeles collapses, flooding the Santa Clara River valley and leaving 450 dead.

April 21 Harry F. Sinclair is acquitted of conspiring to defraud the Government in the second Teapot Dome trial.

May 3 Congress again passes the McNary-Haugen bill, known as the Surplus Control Act, to alleviate depressed conditions on the farm. The bill, which was passed and vetoed last year, proposes a method by which the Government would buy surplus food products and sell them on the world market. [President Coolidge again vetoes the bill.]

May 15 Congress provides $325,000,000 for flood control in the Mississippi Valley.

May 22 Congress passes the Merchant Marine Act to aid the ailing ship industry by providing subsidized mail contracts and increasing the money available for construction of new ships. The bill also permits the sale of surplus U.S. ships to private companies at very low prices.

May 26 Of a group of 274 men who left Los Angeles on March 4 in an attempt to walk to New York City, 55 complete the journey.

June 12-15 The Republican convention is held at Kansas City. Herbert Hoover is nominated for President and Charles Curtis for Vice President.

June 17-18 Amelia Earhart becomes the first woman to fly the Atlantic as a passenger. Two male pilots operate the Fokker monoplane, which crosses from Newfoundland to Wales.

June 19-20 The United States signs treaties of cooperation, one with Austria and one with Denmark.

June 26-29 The Democratic convention is held at Houston. Alfred E. Smith is nominated for President and Joseph T. Robinson for Vice President.

July 2 Interest rates on short-term loans reach a record high of 10 per cent.

July 29-Aug. 12 The ninth Olympic Games are held in the Netherlands. The United States wins 24 gold, 21 silver, and 17 bronze medals to put it 69 points ahead of its closest rival.

July 30 The first motion pictures in color are demonstrated by George Eastman in Rochester, New York.

Aug. 27 Fifteen nations in Paris sign the Kellogg-Briand peace agreement to outlaw war. [Later 47 more sign.]

Sept. 27 The U.S. Government recognizes the Nationalist Government of China. This Government, under Chiang Kai-shek, is the victor against the Communist contenders for power.

Nov. 6 Herbert Hoover is elected President of the United States, decisively defeating the Democratic candidate, Alfred E. Smith. A moving electric sign built by *The New York Times* in Times Square reports the election returns as they are received.

Nov. 16 The New York Stock Exchange has a record day, with trading volume reaching 6,641,250 shares.

Nov. 19 President-elect Hoover begins a tour of South America aboard the battleship *Maryland*.

Nov. 21 Joseph McKenna, 83, Justice of the U.S. Supreme Court from 1898 to 1925, dies in Washington, D.C.

Dec. 11 A plot to assassinate Hoover by blowing up his train at it travels from Chile to Argentina is thwarted by police in Buenos Aires.

Al Smith waves to the crowd in Madison Square Garden, New York City, after making the last speech of his Presidential campaign.

1929

Shortly after the New York Stock Exchange opens on the morning of Oct. 24, stock prices begin to drop dramatically and the volume of trading breaks all previous records. By 11:30 A.M. panic selling prevails as more and larger blocks of stock are thrown on the market. The ticket tape that reports prices outside the Exchange falls increasingly behind. In the offices of J. P. Morgan and Company, where a group of top investment bankers are meeting, cooler heads prevail. In an effort to reverse the tide, Richard Whitney, vice president of the Exchange, is sent to the floor to purchase millions of dollars worth of key stocks. This action is successful and prices begin to steady.

Activity on the Exchange is relatively stable the next day, but on Oct. 28 prices again tumble. This time the bankers do not try to halt the decline. On Oct. 29 panic selling increases. The ticker tape is two and one-half hours behind and by the end of the day a record 16,410,030 shares have been sold, with a total loss in value of 880 issues estimated by *The New York Times* to exceed $8,000,000,000. Thousands of investors see their fortunes wiped out.

Economists, bankers, and politicians grope to find an explanation. Most believe that the economy is still sound and the market will soon recover. Some say it is merely a momentary psychological aberration. Secretary of the Treasury Andrew Mellon insists that the stock market debacle is an illness that will soon run its course and cure itself. Although there are signs that the problem goes much deeper, most prefer to ignore them. Examination of statistics reveals an increasing unemployment rate during the year prior to the crash and a great decrease in construction activity. Still, most industry continues to prosper throughout the year and the automobile companies produce a record 3,000,000 cars.

Jan. 2   An agreement is signed by the United States and Canada for work on the Niagara River intended to safeguard the beauty of the Falls while also allowing greater use of water for the production of electricity.

Jan. 7   *The Question Mark,* a specially equipped Army plane commanded by Major Carl Spaatz [later General Spaatz], lands at Los Angeles after flying continuously for 150 hours 40 minutes, a record for the longest time in the air.

Jan. 12   An eight-mile tunnel built by the Great Northern Railway through the Cascade Mountains of Washington State is officially opened. The tunnel is the longest built in this country.

Jan. 15   The U.S. Senate, by a vote of 85 to 1, ratifies the Kellogg-Briand Peace Pact.

Jan. 22   Saying that it is almost impossible to find a jury that will convict night-club operators who sell illegal liquor, the Government drops charges against 30 such operators.

Jan. 27   The Senate ratifies a treaty between the United States and Japan aimed at controlling the illegal liquor trade between the two nations.

Feb. 4   Captain Frank Hawks sets a record for transcontinental flight, flying from Los Angeles to New York City in just under 18 hours 22 minutes.

Feb. 4   The Ford Motor Company announces that it has produced the first 1,000,000 engines for its Model A automobile.

Feb. 11   The Dawes Plan of 1924 is restructured by Owen D. Young with the assistance of J. P. Morgan and the Committee on German Reparations in Paris. The new plan, known as the Young Plan, reduces the amount that Germany must pay and provides more time for payment. It also establishes the Bank for International Settlements.

Feb. 11   Thomas A. Edison celebrates his 82d birthday with a party at Fort Myers, Florida, that includes President-elect Herbert Hoover and Henry Ford. Edison announces the discovery of a fast-growing rubber plant that can be harvested in the same manner as wheat.

Feb. 13   President Coolidge signs into law a bill authorizing construction of fifteen 10,000-ton cruisers within the next three years.

Feb. 14   Wearing police uniforms, mobsters in Chicago capture seven members of the Moran gang and, lining them up against a garage wall, use machine guns to kill all seven. [The event is dubbed the St. Valentine's Day Massacre.]

Feb. 16   Edward Doheny's son, who carried the $100,000 Teapot Dome pay-off from Doheny to former Secretary of the Interior Albert B. Fall, is killed by Theodore Plunkett, an assistant to the

Thousands of investors gather in Wall Street on Oct. 29 after the stock-market crash.

319

younger Doheny. Immediately thereafter Plunkett kills himself.

Mar. 4   Herbert Clark Hoover takes the oath of office as the 31st President of the United States.

Mar. 7   John D. Rockefeller, Jr., regains control of Standard Oil Company of Indiana by defeating Chairman of the Board Robert W. Stewart in a proxy fight at the company's annual meeting.

Mar. 8   The United States provides 20 planes, 10,000 rifles, ammunition, and other war supplies to the Mexican Government to assist in controlling a revolt that is erupting in several Mexican states.

Mar. 17   Thirteen passengers are killed when a plane belonging to Colonial Airways crashes as it attempts to make a forced landing at Port Newark Airport. Both the pilot and another man riding in the cockpit are thrown from the plane and saved.

Mar. 22   The U.S. Coast Guard chases the British schooner *I'm Alone* for 200 miles and sinks the ship after it fails to obey a heave-to order in U.S. territorial waters. The ship is suspected of carrying contraband. [Both the British and Canadian governments protest the incident on the grounds that the actual sinking took place in international waters.]

Mar. 25   To demonstrate his interest in governmental economy, President Hoover donates the horses in the White House stable to the U.S. Army.

Mar. 25   A sharp decline in prices on the New York stock market is reversed during the late hours as investors buy up bargain-priced issues. A record 8,246,740 shares are traded.

Mar. 31   Myron T. Herrick, 74, Ambassador to France, dies in Paris.

April 4   New York City Police Commissioner Grover Whalen estimates that there are 32,000 speakeasies in the city and says that Prohibition is the cause of the great increase in crime. He also speaks out against judges who are "soft" on criminals and "hard" on police strongarm methods.

April 5   The Government announces that 190 persons have died as a direct result of enforcing the Prohibition law. Of this number, 55 are Government agents.

April 8   The U.S. Supreme Court upholds the contempt-of-Congress conviction of Harry F. Sinclair in connection with the Teapot Dome scandal. [Sinclair serves three months in jail.]

April 10   A tornado in Arkansas kills 56, injures over 200.

April 16   Congress, convened in extraordinary session to consider proposals for farm relief and tariff changes, hears President Hoover suggest the establishment of a farm board with sufficient funds to assist farms in setting up cooperatives. He also calls for increasing specific tariffs to help certain ailing industries. Hoover also urges that the Immigration Act, effective July 1, be changed to eliminate the national-origins provision.

April 16   Secretary of State Henry Stimson announces that the United States has no intention of recognizing the Government of the Soviet Union.

April 18   Actress and entertainer Helen Morgan is acquitted in a Federal court on a charge of maintaining a common nuisance at her night club by violating the Prohibition law.

April 22   President Hoover, speaking before the Associated Press at New York, asserts that lawlessness is now the chief national concern. He points out that Prohibition-related offenses account for only 8 per cent of all serious crime. [In May he appoints the Commission on Law Enforcement and Crime, known as the Wickersham Commission, to investigate the relationship between Prohibition and crime.]

April 25   Sixty-five persons are killed by tornados in Georgia and South Carolina.

May 4   Opera-singer Marion Talley makes her final performance at Cleveland, Ohio.

May 7   With the apparent defeat of the Mexican rebels, U.S. troops on duty along the U.S.-Mexican border are sent to their home stations.

May 11   Judge G. N. Risjord of Wisconsin rules that a police officer cannot be guilty of destroying private property because he set fire to a shed containing an illegal still, on the grounds that no property right attaches to a site for illegal liquor production.

May 13   Charles Evans Hughes, former U.S. Supreme Court Justice and Secretary of State, is appointed to the World Court at The Hague.

May 15   A fire at a hospital in Cleveland, Ohio, kills 124, including much of the staff. Many deaths are attributed to chemical fumes from burning X-ray film.

May 17   Gangster Al Capone pleads guilty to a charge of carrying a concealed weapon, and is sentenced to a year in prison.

May 27   Colonel Charles Lindbergh marries Miss Anne Spencer Morrow in Englewood, New Jersey. The bride is the daughter of Dwight W. Morrow, U.S. Ambassador to Mexico.

Franklin D. Roosevelt
THIRTY-SECOND PRESIDENT   1933-1945

Battle of Midway

"Sailors of the Air"

U.S. NAVAL AVIATION

FIRST AMERICAN ARMED FORCE
TO SET FOOT IN EUROPE

Good Pay-Valuable Training-Interesting Du
Adventure and the Romance of the Sky

Sailors of the Air

D Day

Harry S. Truman
THIRTY-THIRD PRESIDENT   1945-1953

Dwight D. Eisenhower
THIRTY-FOURTH PRESIDENT   1953-1961

May 27 The U.S. Supreme Court rules that the use of the pocket veto by the President is not unconstitutional. (The pocket veto allows the President to reject a bill that is sent to him within 10 days of the date Congress is to adjourn by neither signing it, nor returning it to Congress.)

June 15 President Hoover signs the Agricultural Marketing Bill. The bill establishes the Federal Farm Relief Board to assist farmers in setting up cooperative organizations, but it does not contain a plan whereby the Government would subsidize the sale of surplus commodities on the world market, as desired by a majority of the Senate.

July 10 The new paper currency, only two-thirds the size of the old, goes into circulation.

July 22-Aug. 1 A series of prison riots occur. At the state prison at Dannemora, New York, 1,300 convicts attack guards and burn the power house and several other structures; 3 prisoners are killed. On July 28 inmates at Auburn, New York, capture the prison arsenal and, using ladders and battering rams, attempt a mass escape; 4 manage to get away. Both riots are blamed on overcrowded conditions. On Aug. 1 a food riot at the Federal prison at Leavenworth, Kansas, leaves 1 convict dead and 3 wounded.

July 30 The *St. Louis Robin*, a monoplane piloted by Forrest O'Brine and Dale Jackson, completes a record endurance flight of over 420 hours, increasing the world record by more than 173 hours.

Sept. 20 A Senate committee opens hearings into the role of William B. Shearer at the naval Disarmament Conference at Geneva in 1927. The committee hears that Shearer was paid $46,750 by three U.S. shipbuilding companies to wreck the chances of the conference.

Sept. 24 Lieutenant James Doolittle makes the first all-instrument plane flight.

Oct. 2 Violence breaks out at Marion, North Carolina, when sheriff's deputies attempt to break up a line of pickets, members of the United Textile Workers, outside the Marion Manufacturing Company; 20 strikers are wounded and 3 are killed.

Oct. 4 British Prime Minister Ramsey MacDonald arrives in New York for an 11-day visit to the United States. He meets with President Hoover and invites the United States to join England, France, Italy, and Japan for a naval conference in London in January, 1930.

Oct. 7 Former Secretary of the Interior Albert B. Fall is tried on a charge of taking a

Albert B. Fall is helped to the courthouse.

$100,000 bribe in return for leasing a portion of the Elk Hills, California, naval oil reserve to Edward L. Doheny. [Found guilty, he is ordered to pay a $100,000 fine and serve one year in prison; after his appeal to the U.S. Supreme Court is rejected in 1931, he serves his sentence.]

Oct. 24-28 The stock market crashes as millions of shares change hands and billions of dollars in value are lost.

Oct. 29 The steamship *Wisconsin* sinks in Lake Michigan with the loss of 9 lives.

Nov. 11 The Ambassador Bridge across the Detroit River, linking the United States and Canada, is dedicated. The $20,000,000 structure between Detroit, Michigan, and Windsor, Ontario, has a main span of 1,850 feet and a width of 47 feet.

Dec. 16 President Hoover signs an income-tax reduction bill that would save taxpayers $160,000,000 on their 1929 Federal taxes.

Dec. 17 An explosion in an Oklahoma coal mine kills 59 miners.

Dec. 24 The Executive Office Building in Washington, D.C., is damaged by fire but most valuable papers are saved.

1930

Most government and business leaders still insist that economic conditions are basically sound. This "prosperity propaganda" contributes to a strong stock market recovery during the first four months of the year, and the Dow-Jones industrial average rises from a low of 198 to 294 during the period. But unemployment, which stood at about 1,500,000 in October 1929, rises to 4,000,000 by spring. Industrial production of almost every type starts to drop as consumers save against an uncertain future and businessmen retrench. Wages hold steady for the first half of the year as President Hoover attempts to convince the business community that their decrease would aggravate the nation's problems.

In May the stock market again declines sharply, and despite brief recoveries the trend for the rest of the year is downward. A terrible drought during the summer months in the Ohio and Mississippi valleys causes much suffering in the area and worsens the already bad farm situation. Increasing bank failures during the latter half of the year culminate in December when the Bank of the United States fails. The Hawley-Smoot Tariff, highest in the country's history, is passed in June and has the effect of increasing the price of imported goods and reducing foreign trade.

By October President Hoover recognizes publicly that there are 4,500,000 unemployed, but he is not willing to concede that the Government should provide direct assistance to the needy, as Senator Robert M. La Follette, Jr., of Wisconsin and Governor Franklin D. Roosevelt of New York, among others, suggest. In December, however, Hoover tells Congress that between $100,000,000 and $150,000,000 should be spent for public works; Congress almost immediately approves.

According to the 15th decennial census, the United States now has a population of 123,202,624. The rate of increase, 16.1 per cent, is in the same range as in the previous decade, and the proportion of urban over rural inhabitants continues to grow.

Jan. 2   The United States and Great Britain sign an accord in which Britain recognizes U.S. ownership of the Turtle Islands, as part of the Philippines, in the Sulu Sea. The convention clarifies the boundary between the Philippines and British North Borneo.

Jan. 10   President Hoover repeats his contention that crime is the most serious problem facing the nation. The Wickersham Commission announces that "criminal law enforcement of the county is entirely inadequate; that Prohibition, automobile theft, white slave traffic. . .have overtaxed the capacity and effectiveness of the national machinery for enforcement."

Feb. 3   Chief Justice of the U.S. Supreme Court William Howard Taft resigns as a result of illness.

Fed. 4   The first educational radio program is broadcast to 1,500,000 school children.

Feb. 10   In Chicago a Federal grand jury indicts 31 corporations and 158 persons on charges of conducting a huge bootleg operation in at least 10 of the largest cities in the country.

Feb. 24   Charles Evans Hughes returns to the U.S. Supreme Court, this time as Chief Justice.

Feb. 24   J. P. Morgan and Co. announce that the group formed to halt the market crash on Oct. 24, 1929, has sold all its shares and is disbanded.

Mar. 4   Former President Calvin Coolidge dedicates a dam named in his honor on the Gila River at Globe, Arizona.

Mar. 8   William Howard Taft, 72, recently resigned as Chief Justice of the Supreme Court, dies in Washington.

Mar. 10   Alcohol poisoning believed to come from adulterated Jamaica ginger strikes hundreds of persons in four Southern States. Symptoms are swollen feet and paralysis of the limbs.

Mar. 22   Edward L. Doheny, accused of having given former Secretary of the Interior Albert B. Fall a $100,000 bribe to obtain a lease on Teapot Dome oil lands, is acquitted. Doheny insists that the money was a loan.

April 6   Captain Frank Hawks completes the first cross-country glider flight, arriving in New York City from San Diego after 8 days. The glider is towed by a biplane on a 500-foot line.

April 21   A fire at the Ohio State Prison in Columbus kills 318 convicts.

April 22   The London Naval Treaty is signed by representatives of the United States, Great Britain, and Japan. The agreement calls for the three countries to maintain naval strength at a ratio of 5-5-3; but an escape provision allows Great Britain to increase its naval strength if it feels endangered by similar increases of France or Italy. France and Italy attend the negotiations but refuse to ratify accords.

May 7   U.S. Circuit Judge John J. Parker, nominated by President Hoover to the U.S. Supreme Court, is rejected by the Senate.

May 11   The Adler Planetarium, the first in the United States, opens in Chicago's Grant Park.

May 20   Owen J. Roberts wins Senate confirmation to the U.S. Supreme Court.

May 26   In the case of *U.S.* v. *James Farrar*, the U.S. Supreme Court rules that those who purchase alcoholic beverages do not violate Federal law or the 18th Amendment.

June 12   Jack Sharkey loses his heavyweight championship to Max Schmeling by fouling in the fourth round in New York City. [A year later a rerun of pictures of the match proves that no foul had been committed.]

June 17   Ignoring the objections of economists, President Hoover signs the Hawley-Smoot Tariff Act, which raises import duties on hundreds of goods to record levels. Hoover contends that the tariff will aid the hard-pressed farmer.

July 3   Congress creates a Veterans' Administration, which absorbs all Federal agencies previously dealing with the affairs of ex-servicemen.

July 13   The Standard Oil Company of New Jersey announces the association of companies that handle 80 per cent of the refining capacity in the country. The association will control a new process which will yield twice as much gasoline from the same amount of crude oil.

July 21   The U.S. Senate ratifies the London Naval Treaty.

Aug. 8   Missouri, Kentucky, West Virginia, Virginia, Illinois, Indiana, Ohio, Arkansas, Louisiana, Tennessee, and Mississippi are the states most severely hit by the drought, the Department of Agriculture reports. There are approximately 1,000,000 farm families in the

Max Schmeling lies on the canvas after being knocked down by Jack Sharkey.

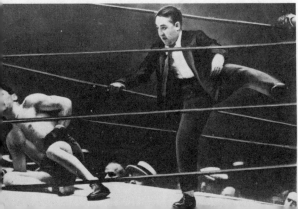

worst-hit area and the Red Cross announces that unemployment and disease are adding to the problems of a diminishing food supply.

Aug. 13   Captain Frank Hawks cuts 2 hours 20 minutes off the transcontinental flight record set by Colonel Charles Lindbergh, flying from Los Angeles to New York in 12 hours 25 minutes.

Sept. 2-3   French airmen Dieudonné Coste and Maurice Bellonte land at Valley Stream Long Island, New York, 37 hours 18 minutes after leaving Paris, the first direct flight from that city to the United States.

Sept. 3   An electric passenger train, designed by inventor Thomas Edison, makes its first run on tracks of the Lackawanna Railroad in New Jersey.

Oct. 8   Secretary of the Navy Charles Adams orders the decommissioning of 46 ships and the reduction of the ranks by 4,800 men to comply with the provisions of the London Naval Treaty.

Nov. 4   In midterm elections, the Democrats gain seats in both Houses and governorships of several states.

Nov. 5   A fire and explosion in an Ohio coal mine kill 79 miners.

Nov. 10   The Public Health Service reports that the nation is experiencing a dramatic upswing in reported cases of infantile paralysis. The first increase, noted in California about two months ago, has spread to most parts of the nation.

Dec. 2   Calling it "the greatest program of waterway, harbor, flood control, public building, highway, and airway improvement," President Hoover asks Congress to approve over $100,000,000 to fight unemployment and stimulate the economy.

Dec. 11   The largest bank failure in the nation's history takes place when the Bank of the United States closes its doors in New York City. Almost 400,000 depositors are affected by the bank's collapse.

Dec. 20   Congress sends the President a bill authorizing expenditure of $116,000,000 on projects to relieve unemployment. The number of unemployed is estimated at 7,000,000.

Dec. 23-26   The Chelsea Bank and Trust Company, with six offices in the New York area, is forced to close by a run started a day earlier. Three days later 20 small banks in six Southern and Midwestern states are closed.

Dec. 28   The state capitol at Bismark, North Dakota, burns down. Loss of property is estimated to exceed $1,000,000.

1931

The nation's economic health, poor in 1930, continues to deteriorate. At least 9,000,000 are unemployed before the year is out. In September U.S. Steel announces that is cutting wages for over 200,000 employes, and other large companies follow. There are 2,294 bank failures during the year, twice that of 1930. The movement of people from farm to city is reversed for the first time; in some industrial cities one out of three workers is unemployed.

As the number of those without jobs grows, private charity is unable to cope with the situation; so the states step in. During the summer, New York Governor Franklin D. Roosevelt sets up the Temporary Emergency Relief Administration with $20,000,000 to be distributed through local governments, and other states quickly adopt similar plans. On the national level President Hoover is reluctant to take such a drastic step as direct Federal aid, but in August he appoints the President's Organization on Unemployment Relief (POUR), whose main activity is to assist private charity to raise money. Later in the year Hoover asks Congress to establish the Reconstruction Finance Corporation (RFC) with a $500,000,000 fund to provide emergency loans to banks and large industries in financial trouble. The move, however, is of no apparent help, either to the unemployed or to the economy.

Jan. 15 President Hoover signs a bill easing the penalties of those caught violating the Prohibition law. Cases involving less than a gallon of liquor are no longer a felony.

Jan. 19 George W. Wickersham, head of the National Commission on Law Observance and Enforcement, states that the country is no longer able effectively to enforce the Prohibition law. Barriers to enforcement are stated to be the high profits in the liquor trade and public apathy or hostility to the law. While the report does not favor repeal of the 18th Amendment, it suggests modifications.

Jan. 21 Congress appropriates $25,000,000 to be used by the American Red Cross to purchase and distribute food. The Red Cross rejects the donation because it expects to receive $10,000,000 from private contributions that will be sufficient for the relief projects it is to carry out.

Feb. 7 Aviator Amelia Earhart marries New York publisher George Putnam at a ceremony at Noank, Connecticut.

Feb. 19-26 Congress passes the Veterans Compensation Act, which permits veterans to borrow up to half the amount of their 1924 bonus certificates at a maximum interest rate of 4½ per cent. A week later President Hoover vetoes the Bill, claiming that it would benefit many veterans who are not in need and would put a heavy burden on the Government's budget. Congress passes the measure over the President's veto.

Feb. 22 As a result of a United States protest, the Turkish Government agrees to supervise the country's opium factories and systematically to reduce exports of the dangerous drug.

Feb. 23 Congress passes a bill to provide funds for government operation of the Muscle Shoals power and fertilizer plants on the Tennessee River, originally built during the Great War [World War I]. President Hoover refuses to sign the bill, stating in his veto message that he is ". . .firmly opposed to the Government entering into any business the main purpose of which is competition with our citizens."

Mar. 3 "The Star-Spangled Banner," the song written by Francis Scott Key during the War of 1812, is officially adopted as the United States national anthem.

Mar. 11-12 A two-day conference of political leaders from both parties who consider themselves progressives takes place in Washington, D.C. On the second day they pass resolutions favoring tariff reduction, increased expenditures for public works, and unemployment insurance.

Mar. 13 The Massachusetts state legislature calls on Congress to start the necessary proceedings for a constitutional convention to consider repeal of the 18th Amendment.

Mar. 20 Casinos in Nevada open their doors as gambling again becomes legal.

May 27 The U.S. Farm Board stops buying wheat futures, and announces that it is ending its stabilization program.

June 17 The railroad industry requests an across-the-board increase in freight charges to meet the competition from other carriers and to strengthen its financial condition.

June 20 President Hoover, in an effort to

bolster the international economic situation, proposes a one-year moratorium on payments of war debts and war reparations.

July 26 The Wickersham Commission reports that the prison system is a disgrace and a failure: costly, brutal, and incapable of rehabilitating convicts. The commission suggests payment of wages to prisoners who work, education, and an increase in the availability of parole.

Aug. 11 The moratorium agreement proposed by President Hoover is signed by 18 countries in London.

September-October The bank panic increases as over 800 banks are closed in two months. Individuals start to hoard gold.

Sept. 22 U.S. Steel announces that, effective Oct. 1, it will cut the wages of 220,000 workers by 10 per cent.

Sept. 29 In Denver a convention of the Episcopal Church liberalizes the church's stand on remarriage, which it has previously forbidden.

Oct. 1 The Pennsylvania, the New York Central, the Baltimore and Ohio, and the Ohio-Nickel Plate railroads agree to consolidate their routes and submit the plan to the Interstate Commerce Commission.

Oct. 4-5 The first nonstop transpacific flight is made by Clyde Pangborn and Hugh Herndon, arriving from Japan at Wenatchee, Washington, in 41 hours 13 minutes.

Oct. 17 Al Capone is found guilty of tax evasion in Federal court at Chicago and gets an 11-year sentence and a $50,000 fine.

Oct. 18 Thomas Alva Edison, 84, dies in West Orange, New Jersey.

Oct. 25 The George Washington Bridge, the first bridge across the Hudson River between New Jersey and New York City, is open to traffic. It is a suspension bridge 4,760 feet long with a main span of 3,500 feet, the world's longest.

Dec. 8 The President's annual message to Congress calls for increased taxation to make up for the deficit of $902,000,000 for the fiscal year 1930-1931. The message also asks Congress to set up an agency to make emergency loans to banks, railroads, and other businesses.

Opening-day ceremonies at the George Washington Bridge

1932 **Although there is great discontent in the country and** in the Republican Party as well, President Herbert Hoover easily manages to win the nomination at the Chicago convention in mid-June. The Republicans blame the nation's troubles on events in Europe, promise that prosperity is "just around the corner," and considerably ease their former policy of supporting strict Prohibition. The Democrats have a more difficult time selecting their candidate when they meet in Chicago later in June, but on the fourth ballot they nominate Franklin D. Roosevelt, the reform-minded governor of New York. The Democratic platform calls for a variety of direct measures, including an expanded public works program, to combat the economic ills that the country is experiencing. In addition the Democrats call for the repeal of the 18th Amendment and the immediate legalization of beer. Roosevelt, in his acceptance speech, promises a "new deal" for all Americans.

The campaign is turbulent, with the Democrats accusing Republicans of inaction, while the Republicans warn that, if the Democrats win, "grass will grow in the streets of 100 cities." Radio is becoming an increasingly important factor in the campaign, as both candidates are heard by millions. Roosevelt's vibrant voice and warm personality, and his appeal to the "forgotten man," come over the air far better than Hoover's serious monotone.

On Nov. 8 Roosevelt is elected President by a plurality somewhat larger than that by which Hoover defeated Alfred E. Smith in 1928, and with 57.4 per cent of the popular vote. In addition the Democrats win decisive control over the Congress by capturing more than 70 per cent of the House and more than 60 per cent of the Senate. As soon as he is elected, Roosevelt selects his advisors, many of them from academic circles, and therefore nicknamed the "brain trust." They include Cordell Hull, Secretary of State; Homer S. Cummings, Attorney General; Harold L. Ickes, Secretary of the Interior; and the first woman Cabinet member, Secretary of Labor Frances Perkins.

Jan. 3 Democratic National Committee Chairman John Raskob announces that a poll he has taken among his supporters indicates the vast majority are in favor of repealing Prohibition.

Jan. 3-6 The Reverend James R. Cox leads a group of 18,000 unemployed men from Pittsburgh to Washington, where they meet with members of Congress and President Hoover. They do not pretend to represent the 13,000,000 in the country who are out of work.

Jan. 12 Oliver Wendell Holmes, 90, resigns after almost 30 years of service on the U.S. Supreme Court.

Jan. 22 The Reconstruction Finance Corporation (RFC) comes into existence with a capital of $500,000,000 and authority to borrow an additional $1,500,000,000 by issuing tax-exempt bonds. Its purpose is to prop up the faltering monetary system by making loans to banks, insurance companies, farm mortgage associations, building and loan associations, and other businesses. President Hoover selects Charles G. Dawes, a noted economist and Vice President under Coolidge, to run the agency.

Jan. 31 Agreement is reached at Chicago between employees and management of most of the country's railroads to lower wages 10 per cent for one year, saving the railroads over $200,000,000.

Feb. 2 Although not a member of the League of Nations, the United States attends an arms limitation conference at Geneva sponsored by the League. President Hoover makes sweeping proposals to reduce armaments, but the meeting ends without the participants having reached any significant agreement.

Feb. 4 The Winter Olympic Games open at Lake Placid, N.Y.

Feb. 27 Congress passes the Glass-Steagall Act, which authorizes the sale of $750,000,000 worth of the Government's huge gold supply and allows the Federal Reserve System more leeway in discounting commercial paper. The purpose of the measure is to counteract the hoarding of gold and to ease credit.

Mar. 1 Charles Lindbergh, Jr., 20 months, is kidnapped from his home at Hopewell, New Jersey.

Mar. 3 The 20th Amendment to the Constitution is sent to the states to be ratified. Known popularly as the Lame Duck Amendment, the measure would reduce the amount of time an outgoing President will serve after the country has elected his successor (as a "lame

Bonus Marchers

"Hunger Marchers" in Washington, D.C.

duck''), by moving the inauguration date from Mar. 4 to Jan. 20. The measure also calls for Congress to convene on Jan. 3.

Mar. 7   Four men are killed and many are wounded as police and firemen battle rioters at a Ford Motor Company plant at Dearborn, Michigan.

Mar. 14   Benjamin N. Cardozo becomes an Associate Justice of the U.S. Supreme Court.

Mar. 20   Several incendiary bombs are exploded in educational facilities in central Illinois. Four persons are killed at the Springfield Public High School.

Mar. 21   Tornadoes in Florida, Georgia, Alabama, Tennessee, and Kentucky kill 360 persons and do considerable property damage.

Mar. 23   The Norris-La Guardia Act is signed by President Hoover. The Act limits the use of injunctions to stop strikes and is favored by organized labor. The act also prohibits ''yellow-dog'' contracts, by which employers, as a condition of employment, require their workers to promise not to join a union.

April 14   The new 14-story state office building at Columbus, Ohio, is seriously damaged by an explosion and fire that leave 8 dead and 40 injured.

May 3   Al Capone begins serving a 10-year sentence for income tax evasion.

May 4   Acting Secretary of State William Castle, Jr., announces that the United States will not recognize any territorial gains made in violation of the Kellogg-Briand Peace Pact.

May 12   The dead body of Charles Lindbergh, Jr., is found six miles from the Lindbergh home.

May 14   Marchers in New York, Detroit, and other large cities parade for 10 hours in favor of the legalization of beer.

May 20-21   Amelia Earhart flies from Newfoundland to Ireland in 13 hours 15 minutes, the first woman to fly solo across the Atlantic. Engine trouble prevents her from reaching her intended destination, Paris.

May 29-July 28   The first veterans of the ''Bonus Army'' arrive in Washington, D.C., with the hope of convincing the Government to approve immediate payment-in-full of their bonuses. Those proposed bonuses are actually prepayments of equities due to the veterans in 1945 under the terms of the 1924 Adjusted Compensation Act. By June approximately 15,000 veterans and 5,000 women and children are camped near the Capitol. On June 15 the House votes to cash the bonuses, but two days

later the Senate turns the measure down. Most of the veterans return home, but approximately 2,000 remain. Finally President Hoover sends Federal troops commanded by General Douglas MacArthur to drive the veterans out. [In 1936 Congress votes to pay the bonus.]

June 14-16   The Republican Party holds its convention at Chicago and renominates President Herbert Hoover and Vice President Charles Curtis.

June 21   Jack Sharkey regains the heavyweight boxing championship from Max Schmeling by decision in the 15th round in New York City.

June 27-July 2   The Democratic Party gathers at Chicago and on the fourth ballot selects Franklin D. Roosevelt, governor of New York, as its Presidential candidate. John Nance Garner of Texas, who turns his delegates over to Roosevelt to break the deadlocked convention, gets the Vice Presidential nomination.

July 11   President Hoover vetoes the Wagner-Garner Bill, passed by Congress two days earlier. The bill would provide for Federal employment agencies in states that do not have their own state employment services.

July 15   With economic conditions continuing to worsen, President Hoover announces that he is taking a 20-per-cent salary cut.

July 18   The United States and Canada sign a treaty to construct the St. Lawrence Seaway to connect the Great Lakes with the Atlantic Ocean and to produce hydroelectric energy. The cost of the project, estimated at $543,000,000, is to be split evenly between the two nations.

July 21   President Hoover signs the Emergency Relief Act, which provides for $300,000,000 in loans to states unable otherwise to raise money for relief purposes. The act also authorizes the Reconstruction Finance Corporation to increase its debt ceiling to $3,000,000,000 and to make loans to state and local governments for the construction of public works.

July 22   The Federal Home Loan Bank Act becomes law, creating 12 regional banks with a capital of $125,000,000 to discount home loans for building and loan associations, savings banks, and insurance companies. President Hoover's hope is that the act will stimulate residential construction, increase employment, and expand home ownership.

July 30   The tenth summer Olympics open in Los Angeles.

Aug. 16   A group called the Farmers Holiday

Association asks farmers to hold back their goods until prices are raised. Many farmers cooperate either by picketing the highways to block delivery trucks or simply by withholding their shipments.

Aug. 31 A total eclipse of the sun is seen over many parts of the northeastern United States.

Sept. 1 Mayor James J. Walker of New York City resigns after several months of investigation into myriad charges of graft and corruption in his administration.

Sept. 9 The steamboat *Observation* explodes and burns in the East River off New York City, killing 70 persons and injuring an equal number.

Oct. 15 The 12 Federal Home Loan Banks begin operations as provided for by the Federal Home Loan Bank Act passed on July 22.

Oct. 31 The Department of Agriculture annual report shows (1) that farm prices are still dropping after three years, despite a brief recovery in July, August, and September; (2) that commodity prices are about 60 per cent lower than they were in the summer of 1929; (3) that

Mayor James Walker of New York City, on the witness stand during an investigation into graft and corruption in his administration

Al Capone is led aboard a train to start his journey to the Federal penitentiary in Atlanta, Georgia.

the average farmer earned about $341 after expenses in 1931, compared with $847 in 1929. The report points out that the prices of the products farmers must purchase are not falling as quickly as the prices they receive for farm products.

Nov. 8 Franklin Delano Roosevelt is elected President of the United States, defeating Herbert Hoover by a margin of over 7,000,000 votes and winning 472 of 531 electoral votes. Congress is heavily Democratic.

Nov. 11 The Tomb of the Unknown Soldier is dedicated at Arlington National Cemetery by Secretary of War Patrick J. Hurley.

Nov. 22 President-elect Roosevelt meets with President Hoover at the White House to discuss the war-debt question. It is virtually the only time the two men discuss policy issues.

Dec. 5 Professor Albert Einstein is granted a visa at the U.S. Consulate at Berlin to enter the United States.

Dec. 27 Radio City Music Hall, the largest theater in the world, opens at Rockefeller Center in New York City.

1933

Between Franklin D. Roosevelt's election on Nov. 8, 1932, and his inauguration on Mar. 4, 1933, conditions in the nation deteriorate. Industrial production drops an additional 12 per cent. By Inauguration Day it is estimated that almost one third of the labor force is out of work; many who have jobs are working for as little as 10 cents an hour. The run on banks becomes acute, as nearly $1,000,000,000 are withdrawn during the two weeks preceding Mar. 4. Many states declare outright bank holidays. Malnutrition is a fact of life in every part of the country, and even starvation appears.

Faced with these conditions, President Roosevelt takes office. During the first "hundred days" with the cooperation of Congress, he puts into effect 15 major pieces of legislation to remedy the nation's many problems. Simultaneously, with encouraging radio speeches ("fireside chats"), he tries and often succeeds in restoring confidence and lifting the nation's morale.

The year contributes many new agencies to enable the executive branch to manipulate the economy: the Agricultural Adjustment Administration, the National Recovery Administration, the Federal Deposit Insurance Corporation, the Civilian Conservation Corps. [The NRA, AAA, and CCC become part of the vocabulary, with only FDIC taking root as an enduring agency.] The Civil Works Administration begins a tradition of providing government work for the jobless. Special bureaus address the needs of home owners (HOLC) and potential home owners (FHA). A pilot project in government power production begins in the South (TVA). A thirsty nation sees the unpopular Prohibition amendment begin to be reversed. A fearful nation, reassured by its President, throngs to Chicago to celebrate a Century of Progress.

Jan. 2   The last U.S. marines in Nicaragua depart for home, ending a long period of U.S. military intervention in that country.

Jan. 4   At a small town in Iowa an agent of the New York Life Insurance Company is threatened by a lynch mob if he does not raise the company's bid at a farm foreclosure sale to cover the $30,000 mortgage on the farm. With company permission, he agrees.

Jan. 5   Calvin Coolidge, 60, former President of the United States, dies at Northhampton, Massachusetts.

Jan. 23   The Department of Industrial Engineering at Columbia University takes over research into "technocracy," a theory that proposes a unit of energy as a basis for establishing prices, and advocates that all economic resources be directed by scientists rather than by businessmen.

Feb. 6   The 20th Amendment, known popularly as the Lame Duck Amendment, is officially declared part of the Constitution.

Feb. 15   An assassin in a crowd at Miami, Florida, fires six shots at President-elect Roosevelt, who is sitting in an open car. A bystander, Mrs. William F. Cross, pushes the assassin's arm up and although the shots hit several others in the party, including Mayor Anton Cermak of Chicago, the President is not injured.

Feb. 20   Congress adopts a resolution to repeal the Prohibition amendment. As a proposed 21st Amendment, it goes to the states for ratification.

Feb. 25   The first U.S. aircraft carrier, the *Ranger,* goes into service.

Mar. 4   Franklin Delano Roosevelt takes the oath of office as President. In his Inaugural Address he states to millions of listeners on the world: ". . .let me assert my firm belief that the only thing we have to fear is fear itself— nameless, unreasoning, unjustified terror which paralyzes needed efforts to convert retreat into advance."

Mar. 5   President Roosevelt calls Congress to convene on Mar. 9 in special session. At the same time, using the 1917 Trading With The Enemy Act, he declares a nationwide bank holiday effective Mar. 6 through Mar. 9, closing virtually every financial institution in the country, including the Federal Reserve. Roosevelt also proclaims an embargo on the export of gold, silver, and currency.

Mar. 6   Mayor Anton Cermak of Chicago dies of wounds received during the attempted assassination of the President on Feb. 15.

Mar. 9   Congress meets and immediately passes the Emergency Banking Relief Act, which gives the Treasury Department power to control

330

Franklin Delano Roosevelt reads his Inaugural Address.

various transactions in currency, credit, and bullion. It also makes it illegal, effective May 1, to own or export gold, and empowers the Treasury Department to regulate the reopening of the banks.

Mar. 10 Earthquakes in the Los Angeles area kill 120 persons, injure many others, and cause over $40,000,000 worth of property damage.

Mar. 12 President Roosevelt addresses the nation in the first of his radio "fireside chats." Addressing his listeners as "My friends," he explains the purpose of the national bank holiday and the measures being taken to deal with the financial crisis.

Mar. 13-Mar. 27 Banks start to reopen, and within two weeks over 75 per cent of all banks, with well over 90 per cent of the nation's banking assets, are operating. During the same period about $1,000,000,000 is redeposited and gold is returned to the U.S. Treasury.

Mar. 14 Tornadoes kill 34 in several small towns in Tennessee.

Mar. 20 President Roosevelt signs the Economy Act, which reduces salaries by up to 15 per cent to save about $100,000,000 a year, and reduces veterans' benefits by a total of $400,000,000 a year.

Mar. 22 The President signs into law a measure to legalize, effective April 17, beer and wine with a maximum alcoholic content of 3.2 per cent by weight. The measure also places a tax of $5 per barrel (31 gallons), which quickly brings in much needed revenue.

Mar. 31 The Civilian Conservation Corps (CCC) is established to provide employment for young men between the ages of 18 and 25 in various projects aimed at conserving or improving the country's natural resources, such as reforestation, soil erosion and flood control, fire prevention, road building, and park and recreational area improvement.

April 4 The U.S. Navy's *Akron,* the biggest dirigible in the world, sinks into the Atlantic Ocean off the New Jersey coast with 72 of the crew of 76 lost.

April 19 President Roosevelt announces that the United States is going off the gold standard and will no longer redeem currency for gold.

April 21 British Prime Minister Ramsay MacDonald arrives for a seven-day visit in the United States.

May 1 Pearl S. Buck resigns from the Presbyterian Board of Foreign Missions at New York City after many years of service. Her second novel, *The Good Earth,* has been on the top of the best-seller list since it was published in 1931.

May 1 The final day for returning illegally held gold to the U.S. Treasury arrives, with an estimated $700,000,000 in gold still in private hands.

May 1-5 Tornadoes and storms rip through portions of Louisiana, Arkansas, Alabama, and South Carolina, killing 99 persons, injuring many, and destroying homes and property.

May 12 The Federal Emergency Relief Administration (FERA) is established and Harry Hopkins of New York is made administrator of the program, which is to distribute $500,000,000 through grants to state and local agencies to relieve the poor and hungry.

May 12 The Agricultural Adjustment Administration (AAA) is established to deal with the problems of low farm prices by controlling surplus crops. This goal is to be accomplished by paying farmers a subsidy when they reduce their production of rice, cotton, tobacco, wheat, corn, dairy products, and hogs. The AAA is to raise money for the subsidies through a tax on food processors.

May 18 Congress establishes the Tennessee Valley Authority (TVA) to run the Muscle Shoals power and nitrate plants on the Tennessee River, built by the Government during the World War. The TVA is also authorized to build additional dams and power plants, develop rural electrification, plan for flood and erosion control, build recreation areas, and help with reforestation. The range of its activities covers seven states and affects 3,000,000 people.

May 27 The Century of Progress Exposition, the second world fair to be held in Chicago, opens its gates. The fair features the achievements of technology; its buildings stress modern architecture.

May 27 Congress passes the Federal Securities Act, which instructs the Federal Trade Commission to police all new stock and bond issues.

June 5 In a joint resolution, Congress supports President Roosevelt's earlier proclamation and takes the country off the gold standard by making all Government and private obligations payable in "lawful money."

June 8 An especially high spring tide causes 200 black whales to wash ashore on the Florida coast.

June 13 The Home Owners Loan Corporation (HOLC) is set up with a capital of

$200,000,000 and authority to raise ten times that amount by issuing bonds. The money is to be used to help nonfarm homeowners escape from high mortgage payments by refinancing all obligations on the home into one long-term, low-payment mortgage.

June 16   The Banking Act of 1933 (The Glass-Steagall Act) is passed, setting up the Federal Deposit Insurance Corporation (FDIC) which guarantees individual accounts in banks up to $5,000.

June 16   The Farm Credit Act becomes law, to assist farmers with loans for production and marketing and for providing refinancing of farm mortgages at favorable terms. The act is administered by the Farm Credit Administration (FCA), set up earlier in the year to handle all Federal legislation pertaining to farm credit.

June 16   The National Industrial Recovery Act (NIRA), is passed with the purpose of improving business activity and providing jobs. Specifically, the act sets up codes of fair practice concerning working conditions, wages, and business practices. These codes are to be enforced by the National Recovery Administration (NRA). Another section of the NIRA gives workers the right to "organize and bargain collectively through representatives of their own choosing." Title II of the NIRA sets up the Public Works Administration (PWA), with the purpose of stimulating the economy through the construction of huge public works projects that require large numbers of workers, such as dams, port facilities, sewage plants, roads, airports, bridges, and hospitals.

June 29   Primo Carnera knocks out Jack Sharkey in the sixth round to become heavyweight champion in New York City.

July 29   Governor Gifford Pinchot calls out the militia to keep order as 27,000 miners go on strike in western Pennsylvania. One striker is killed, but violence is kept to a minimum.

Aug. 1   The Blue Eagle, the sign that a company has agreed to abide by the NRA's codes of business and wages, appears in windows of all types of establishments.

Aug. 5   President Roosevelt sets up the National Labor Board (NLB) headed by Senator Robert F. Wagner to enforce the collective-bargaining provisions of the National Labor Relations Act.

Aug. 17   Secretary of Labor Frances Perkins announces that employment has reached the level of Oct. 1931 and payrolls are running $29,000,000 a week higher than in March. Over

The repeal of Prohibition is celebrated in Boston.

1,000,000 workers have found jobs during the past four months.

Aug. 23   The Government's plan to take 6,000,000 hogs off the market goes into effect in Chicago as the first 30,000 are slaughtered. The animals are to be made into fertilizer or possibly sausage for distribution to those on relief. By purchasing only younger hogs (under 100 pounds) and those about to bear, the Agricultural Adjustment Administration hopes the effort will have a long-term upward effect on prices.

Sept. 13   Marchers numbering 250,000 show their support of the National Industrial Recovery Act by parading in New York City.

Nov. 2   The Mount Wilson Observatory announces that an impending period of sun spots may cause magnetic disturbances, hindering radio, telephone, and telegraph communication.

Nov. 8   The Civil Works Administration (CWA) is set up to create jobs for 4,000,000 workers. Most of the jobs are to be for relatively unskilled workers, who will be paid only the minimum wage.

Nov. 16   The United States and the Soviet Union establish full diplomatic relations.

Dec. 5   Prohibition is repealed as Utah becomes the 36th state to ratify the 21st Amendment to the Constitution.

Dec. 14   At Crescent City, Florida, a school bus is struck by a freight train, killing 10 youngsters and injuring 30.

Dec. 24   Under a decree issued by President Roosevelt, civil rights are restored to 1,500 men who served jail sentences for their opposition to the World War.

333

1934

Economic conditions improve, although not to the extent anticipated by the New Dealers. About 2,500,000 of the unemployed find jobs, and wages begin to rise; but 11,000,000 still need work and the relief rolls are maintained at between 16,000,000 and 18,000,000. Farm prices increase markedly, partly because of the subsidy and crop-limitation efforts of the Agricultural Adjustment Administration, but also because of the worst drought the country has seen, which starts in April and continues through most of the summer. The drought causes dust storms that at times can be seen across half the nation and that convert much of the Great Plains into a Dust Bowl. The stock market turns upward, and industrial production increases slowly.

Congress passes a long list of legislation that almost rivals that of 1933. President Roosevelt takes a variety of measures to inflate the dollar and there is some attempt to lower tariffs. Additional money is pumped into the credit system to aid farmers and home owners. Congress, still generally willing to give President Roosevelt whatever legislation he wants, hands him his first defeat in March by overriding his veto of a bill to raise Government salaries and increase veterans' benefits. Additional "alphabet agencies" are created, such as the Federal Communications Commission (FCC) and the Securities and Exchange Commission (SEC), and other agencies are broadened in scope and given additional appropriations.

This is notably a year in which crime ceases to pay, at least for some renowned practitioners. It sees the end of the careers of Bonnie Parker and Clyde Barrow, of John Dillinger, of Charles Arthur (Pretty Boy) Floyd, and of George (Baby Face) Nelson.

January Dr. Francis E. Townsend establishes Old Age Revolving Pensions Limited, devoted to a plan of providing a $200 a month in government pensions for every retired individual in the country. The Townsend plan is intended to eliminate the widespread poverty of the aged and also to revive the national economy, because each pensioner would be required to spend the $200 within the month during which it is received.

Jan. 1 Floods in Los Angeles kill 40 persons and do extensive damage.

Jan. 7-10 Violence erupts when farmers attempt to stop dairy trucks from delivering milk to Chicago. Thousands of gallons of milk are destroyed in an attempt to raise prices before the embargo is called.

Jan. 8 The U.S. Supreme Court upholds, by a 5-to-4 decision, a Minnesota law that temporarily bans the foreclosure of mortgages.

Jan. 30 The Agricultural Adjustment Act is "so full of holes you could drive eight yoke of oxen through it," announces Judge Alexander Akerman at Tampa, Florida, as he declares the act unconstitutional. The Government plans to take the case to the U.S. Supreme Court. [In 1937 the Supreme Court voids a major section of the act.]

Jan. 30 The Gold Reserve Act gives the President the right to peg the value of the dollar, in relation to gold, at between 50 to 60 cents, and to change the value from time to time as he sees fit. The President immediately devalues the dollar to 59.06 cents.

Jan. 31 The Federal Farm Mortgage Corporation is established to further alleviate the credit problems of farms by providing refinancing of farm debts at favorable terms.

Feb. 8 A fire at the state arsenal at Springfield, Illinois, causes $850,000 damage and destroys vital state records.

Feb. 9 As a result of a Senate investigation into alleged bribes paid by airlines to Government officials to obtain lucrative air mail contracts, President Roosevelt cancels all such contracts, and orders the U.S. Army to carry the mail until the investigation is completed.

Feb. 12 To facilitate foreign trade, and particularly to find markets for U.S. products, President Roosevelt sets up the Export-Import Bank. The bank is authorized to make short- and long-term loans to exporters.

Feb. 16 Gold worth $100,000,000 arrives at New York City, attracted by the devaluation of the dollar at the end of January.

Feb. 20 The Northeast is hit by the worst snowstorm since 1888, causing over 30 deaths.

Feb. 23 Passage of the Crop Loan Act provides $40,000,000 to the Farm Credit Administration to make loans for planting and harvesting.

Mar. 1 Panama refuses to accept a U.S. Government check for $250,000 as rental on the Canal Zone, insisting that payment must be in gold as called for by the 1904 Canal Zone Treaty.

Mar. 5 The U.S. Supreme Court, by a 5-to-4 decision, upholds the right of the states to fix milk prices.

Mar. 12 Earthquakes strike a number of Western states for three hours. Worst hit are northern Utah and southern Idaho.

Mar. 24 The Philippines Independence Bill is passed by Congress. The act provides that, contingent upon ratification by the Philippine legislature, independence will be proclaimed in 1946. [On May 1 the Philippine legislature approves the act.]

Mar. 28 The U.S. Steel and Bethlehem Steel companies agree to raise wages by 10 per cent on April 1, following restoration two weeks earlier of the Ford Company's famous $5 basic daily wage.

April 12 The Senate begins an inquiry headed by Senator Gerald P. Nye into the activities of U.S. weapons makers and financiers who made huge fortunes during the World War.

April 20 A sun spot 16,000 miles wide is observed by astronomers, who predict that it will have tremendous effect on climate and weather.

April 27 An antiwar agreement reached in December 1933, at the seventh Pan-American Conference in Montevideo, Uruguay, is signed by 13 nations, including the United States.

May 18 Six crime-control laws are passed by Congress. One provides the death penalty for interstate kidnappers, the result of publicity surrounding the Lindbergh case. Another measure makes it a Federal crime to interfere with or assault Federal law officers on duty.

May 23 Notorious bank robbers Clyde Barrow, 28, and Bonnie Parker, 23, are gunned down by police on a road in Louisiana.

June 6 In an attempt further to limit abuses in the financial community, the Securities and Exchange Commission (SEC) is established to regulate the stock market.

June 12 The Reciprocal Trade Agreements Act permits the President to lower tariffs against nations that will agree to lower their tariffs against the United States.

June 14 Primo Carnera is knocked out by Max Baer in the 11th round in New York City, and Baer becomes heavyweight champion.

June 19 The Federal Communications Commission (FCC) is set up to regulate tele-

Clyde Barrow   **Bonnie Parker**

graph, cable, and radio communications, previously the responsibility of the Interstate Commerce Commission.

June 25 Harry L. Hopkins, in charge of the Federal Emergency Relief Administration, announces that 16,000,000 Americans are on relief.

June 28 The Federal Housing Administration (FHA) is created to insure loans made by banks and other lending institutions for the construction or improvement of homes and farms.

July 6 Gang leader John Dillinger is shot to death on a street in Chicago by agents of the U.S. Department of Justice.

Aug. 1-15 The United States formally ends its military occupation of Haiti under a treaty signed in 1915. At a ceremony at Port-au-Prince, command of the Haitian army is transferred to Haitian officers. On Aug. 15 the remaining U.S. marines depart.

Sept. 1-Oct. 3 One million members of the United Textile Workers go on strike throughout the United States. Violence breaks out at many plants. On Sept. 21 President Roosevelt asks the strikers to return to work. On Oct. 3 the union agrees to a six-month truce.

Sept. 8 The liner *Morro Castle,* bound from Cuba to New York City with 549 aboard, burns off the New Jersey coast with a loss of more than 120 lives.

Oct. 22 Federal agents discover and kill Charles (Pretty Boy) Floyd at an Ohio farm where he has been hiding out.

Oct. 25 A railroad record is set when a Union Pacific train reaches New York City from Los Angeles in 57 hours.

Nov. 6 Midterm elections increase the Democratic majority in each of the Houses of Congress by about 9 seats.

Nov. 6 Nebraska becomes the first state to adopt a unicameral legislature.

1935 **The efforts of the New Deal to ameliorate the** problems brought about by the collapse of the economy, now identified as a full-scale Depression, begins to be supplemented by a more profound effort to solve long-term problems afflicting the society. In the first days of the year, President Roosevelt tells Congress: "We can eliminate many of the factors that cause economic depression and we can provide the means of mitigating their result. This plan for economic security is at once a measure of prevention and a method of alleviation."

The plan turns out to be legislation, including formulas for social insurance and for strengthening the position of labor as against management. The Social Security Act embodies the former part of the plan. Designed to safeguard Americans against the financial difficulties of old age and unemployment, it provides for equal contributions from worker and employer toward a fund under the control of the Federal Government, from which a retirement pension would be available to every worker at age 65. It also provides for employer-contributed funds to be distributed by the several state governments whenever workers should find themselves temporarily unemployed. Other provisions are in the act to assist the blind, the disabled, and dependent children. As for the management-labor balance, the concept of the right of workers to combine in organizations of their own choosing is clearly stated in the National Industrial Recovery Act of 1933, but enforcement machinery is lacking or inadequate. "We have not weeded out the overprivileged and we have not effectively lifted up the underprivileged," President Roosevelt tells Congress. The National Labor Relations Act, sponsored by Senator Robert F. Wagner of New York (and therefore known as the Wagner Act), sets up the machinery for forming unions with the help and guidance of a National Labor Relations Board (NLRB). It defines specific practices by employers to frustrate unionization as unfair and prohibited, and it provides the impetus for a successful campaign to increase the organized sector of the working population.

Meanwhile the short-term anti-depression activities continue. The work relief program of the Civil Works Administration is taken over by the Works Progress Administration (WPA) and the National Youth Administration (NYA). At the same time the very success of the earlier programs has strengthened the economy to the point where opponents no longer hesitate to raise challenges. One such, brought to the U.S. Supreme Court, overthrows the National Industrial Recovery Act itself. In the area of foreign policy, Congress anticipates the President's possible reaction to the aggressive forces beginning to appear in the Far East and in Europe, and enacts strong neutrality legislation. The "honeymoon" period is about to end.

Jan. 4   President Roosevelt, in his message to Congress, outlines his plans for expanding the New Deal into areas of social reform. One of his chief proposals is a system of social security.

Jan. 24   The passenger liner *Mohawk* and the Norwegian freighter *Talisman* collide off the New Jersey coast, with the loss of 35 lives.

Jan. 26   Floods in Tennessee, Arkansas, and Mississippi kill 27 and cause more than $5,000,000 in property damage.

Jan. 29   Once more the Senate rejects United States membership in the World Court, this time with only seven votes short of the two-thirds majority needed.

Feb. 7   The Department of Justice fingerprints John D. Rockefeller, Jr., in New York City to publicize its campaign for a nationwide fingerprint registration law.

Feb. 12   The recently completed U.S. dirigible *Macon* comes apart and sinks into the Pacific Ocean after encountering a heavy gust of wind, with the loss of two members of the crew.

Feb. 27   A Federal judge in Wilmington, Delaware, rules that the collective-bargaining section of the National Industrial Recovery Act is unconstitutional unless the company involved is engaged in interstate commerce.

April 8   Congress passes the Emergency Relief Appropriation Act, with wide authority under which the President may establish appropriate agencies.

April 11   Terrible dust storms hit the Midwest, destroying crops and causing farm families to abandon their homes.

April 27 In order to stop the massive soil erosion resulting from the drought and dust storms, Congress establishes the Soil Conservation Service within the Department of Agriculture.

May 1 Under the authority granted by Congress on April 8, President Roosevelt sets up the Resettlement Administration (RA) with the responsibility of helping farmers move to better land, relocating poor urban dwellers, and creating low-income housing in suburbs.

May 6 The U.S. Supreme Court rules, 5 to 4, that the Railroad Retirement Act is unconstitutional because Congress does not have the power to regulate the social welfare of workers.

May 6 The Works Progress Administration (WPA) is established by executive order, under the Emergency Relief Appropriation Act of April 8. The purpose of the WPA is to get the Federal Government out of direct aid (leaving this field to the states and municipalities) and into a system of work relief, giving jobs to the unemployed. These jobs are mostly of a simple nature, and 85 per cent of the WPA's budget goes into wages.

May 11 Again acting under authority of the act of April 8, the President establishes the Rural Electrification Administration (REA) to bring electricity to rural areas that are neglected by many power companies as unprofitable. The REA makes extremely favorable construction loans to companies willing to service these areas.

May 22 President Roosevelt addresses a joint session of Congress to explain his veto of the Patman Bonus Bill to pay World War veterans the remainder of their 1924 bonuses. This is the first time a President has appeared in person to veto a bill.

May 27 The U.S. Supreme Court declares that the National Industrial Recovery Act is unconstitutional in its regulation of wages, working conditions, and rules of fair practice unless interstate commerce is involved. Because the specific case before the court is that of a company charged with selling a diseased chicken, the case is referred to as the "sick chicken case."

June 7 The National Resources Committee is set up, also under the act of April 8, to study and suggest plans for appropriate use of the nation's resources, both natural and human.

June 10 In a bold experiment to find a new approach to cure alcoholism, Alcoholics Anonymous is established by four alcoholics.

June 13 In a 15-round heavyweight boxing match in New York City, Jim Braddock gains a decision over Max Baer, and becomes champion.

June 26 The National Youth Administration (NYA) is set up as a unit within the WPA to specialize in providing work for persons between 16 and 25 years of age.

July 5 The National Labor Relations Act is signed into law, providing Government assistance to the organized labor movement.

Aug. 14 The Social Security Act becomes law, instituting a national system of social insurance, including old age pensions.

Aug. 23 The Banking Act of 1935 is passed, restructuring the Federal Reserve System to allow for increased control of banking and credit.

Aug. 28 The President signs the Public Utilities Act, the purpose of which is to eliminate abuses arising from the use of holding companies to monopolize the country's power delivery system. Interstate electric transmission is to be regulated by the Federal Power Commission, interstate gas shipment by the Federal Trade Commission. Finally, the Securities and Exchange Commission is charged with enforcing the financial practices of the public utilities.

Aug. 29 To offset the U.S. Supreme Court's ruling against the Federal Farm Bankruptcy Act of 1934, Congress passes the Farm Mortgage Moratorium Act. This act allows farmers to continue to live on foreclosed property by paying the mortgagee a rental fixed by the courts.

Aug. 31 Congress, reflecting the nation's isolationist mood, passes a neutrality act that prohibits the shipment of U.S. arms to warring nations or the use of U.S. ships to carry such goods.

Sept. 8 Senator Huey P. Long, 42, political strongman of Louisiana, is assassinated at Baton Rouge. Long is best known nationally for his "share-the-wealth" crusade, in which he promised to get the Government to provide a minimum annual income of $5,000 for every family.

Sept. 25 Maxwell Anderson's play *Winterset* opens on Broadway. Written in a poetic form, the play is based on the Sacco-Vanzetti case.

Oct. 10 *Porgy and Bess,* a musical by George Gershwin, based on a novel by Du Bose and Dorothy Heyward, opens on Broadway.

Nov. 9 The Committee for Industrial Organization, using the opportunities offered under the Wagner Act, is set up within the American Federation of Labor to organize workers along vertical lines (by industry rather than by individual employer), a technique that is expected to make possible the unionization of industries.

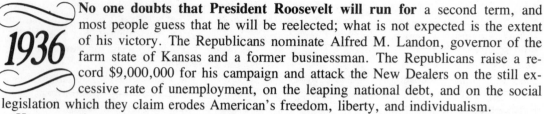

1936 **No one doubts that President Roosevelt will run for** a second term, and most people guess that he will be reelected; what is not expected is the extent of his victory. The Republicans nominate Alfred M. Landon, governor of the farm state of Kansas and a former businessman. The Republicans raise a record $9,000,000 for his campaign and attack the New Dealers on the still excessive rate of unemployment, on the leaping national debt, and on the social legislation which they claim erodes American's freedom, liberty, and individualism.

However, the contrast between 1932 and the present is overwhelming. Although many people are still unemployed, 5,000,000 have returned to work, and real income has increased. Those without jobs have a greater chance of finding some relief. The Democrats point to the record and promise still better things to come. Charges that the Constitution is threatened hold no terror for the man on his way out of the poorhouse.

The vote in November is 27,752,869 for Roosevelt, 16,674,665 for Landon, with Roosevelt carrying every state except Maine and Vermont. (With good grace, Landon parodies a popular slogan by observing, "As Maine goes, so goes Vermont.") The 60.8-per-cent majority is a record since the time of James Monroe. The Democrats also win huge majorities in Congress, capturing 77 per cent of the House and 79 per cent of the Senate. On the state and local levels Democrats win in unprecedented numbers, whether on their own merits, or on Roosevelt's coattails.

Jan. 1   Unemployment insurance begins with a 1-per-cent payroll tax.

Jan. 6   The U.S. Supreme Court, in a 6-to-3 decision, finds the Agricultural Adjustment Act is unconstitutional, on the grounds that the processing tax on food processors, used to support subsidies to farmers, is an unfair enrichment of one group at the expense of another.

Jan. 11-Feb. 3   Auto workers at the General Motors plant in Flint, Michigan, stage the first major sit-down strike in the country. They occupy the plant for several weeks, although the heat and water supply are turned off. Finally, just as the National Guard is about to clear the building, management agrees to recognize the union, the United Automobile Workers, and to negotiate demands.

Jan. 24   President Roosevelt again vetoes the Adjusted Compensation Act, which would give veterans the right to receive full cash payment for their World War bonus certificates. [Congress overrides the veto.]

Jan. 25   Alfred E. Smith, former Democratic governor of New York and 1928 Democratic candidate for President, attacks President Roosevelt as a "socialist" who is patterning the country after the Soviet Union. The charge is addressed to members of the Liberty League, a group of conservatives formed two years ago to fight what they see as the erosion of liberty in New Deal policies.

Feb. 8   Charles Curtis, 76, Vice President under Hoover, dies in Washington, D.C.

Feb. 10   The U.S. Supreme Court declares a 1934 Louisiana tax on newspapers unconstitutional, as a violation of freedom of the press.

Feb. 17   In an 8-to-1 decision the U.S. Supreme Court upholds the activities of the Tennessee Valley Authority.

Feb. 29   Congress passes the Soil Conservation and Domestic Allotment Act to achieve crop limitation, which was ended when the AAA was declared unconstitutional in January. The new act achieves this goal by subsidizing farmers who agree to plant part of their lands with soil-conserving crops, such as alfalfa, rather than with more marketable staples, such as wheat, corn, cr cotton.

March   Heavy rains and melting snow cause severe flooding in much of the Northeast. Water 14 feet high is seen on the streets of Johnstown, Pennsylvania. Several weeks later, when the waters subside, the death toll has risen to 171.

Mar. 2   The United States and Panama sign a treaty by which the United States gives up both the obligation to safeguard the independence of Panama and the right to intervene in that country's internal affairs, even if necessary to maintain order.

Mar. 11   The process by which a Senate committee investigating lobbying activities has obtained copies of telegrams sent by over 1,000 opponents of New Deal measures is declared unconstitutional, as an unreasonable search and seizure, in a District of Columbia court.

Mar. 25   The United States, Britain, and

France agree to limit capital ships to 35,000 tons, with no armament larger than 14-inch guns. Comparable limits are set for aircraft carriers, destroyers, and submarines, but the treaty includes an escape clause for any signatory that feels threatened by war or is actually attacked.

June 1 The U.S. Supreme Court, in a 5-to-4 decision, declares unconstitutional a New York State law that sets a minimum wage of women and children. Seventeen other states have similar laws on the books.

June 9-12 The Republicans meet at Cleveland and nominate Alfred M. Landon for President and Frank Knox for Vice President.

June 14 The 17-year locust reappears in the Northeast with especially heavy concentrations on Long Island.

June 15 The bonus is at last received by mail by more than 3,000,000 former servicemen, as provided for under the Adjusted Compensation Act. The total dollar value of the bonuses exceeds $1,500,000,000.

June 20 The Anti-Price Discrimination Act forbids big companies from setting prices so low that smaller competition, unable to sustain the temporary loss, is driven out of business.

June 23-27 The Democrats hold their convention at Philadelphia and renominate President Roosevelt and Vice President John N. Garner.

June 30 Congress passes the Walsh-Healey Government Contracts Act, which forces all firms doing business with the U.S. Government to conform to a minimum wage, a 40-hour week, and restrictions on the use of child labor.

July 11 The U.S. Department of Agriculture announces that the drought has ruined crops in 336 counties. The Resettlement Administration declares a 12-month moratorium on the repayment of loans made to 30,000 farmers in the worst hit areas.

July 11 The Triborough Bridge connecting the Bronx, Queens, and Manhattan is dedicated. Crossing two rivers, it has a suspension bridge with a main span of 1,300 feet and a vertical lift bridge as well.

Aug. 3 The State Department warns all Americans in Spain to leave that country at once because of the civil war under way for several weeks.

Aug. 5 The American Federation of Labor (AFL) threatens to suspend ten of its unions with over 1,000,000 members if they fail to withdraw from the Committee for Industrial Organization

The Massachusetts delegation leads a demonstration for Landon on the floor of the Republican national convention.

(CIO), which, the AFL contends, is trying to set up an independent, rival organization.

Aug. 9 Newspaperman Lincoln Steffens, 70, dies in California. He was one of the foremost "muckrakers," investigative reporters who exposed the seamy side of urban life.

Aug. 11 At the International Scientific Congress in Copenhagen, Charles Lindbergh displays a pump which he has developed with Dr. Alexis Carrel and which can be used as an artificial heart.

Sept. 25 The United States agrees with France and Great Britain to fix and then maintain the exchange rates between the pound, the franc, and the dollar.

Oct. 9 With the completion of the Boulder Dam [Hoover Dam since 1937] at Boulder City, Nevada, the first generator is turned on, sending electricity 260 miles to Los Angeles. The dam, highest in the country (726 feet) is constructed so that the reservoir it will impound, Lake Mead, will be the world's largest man-made body of water, covering 247 square miles.

Oct. 30 A dock strike on the West Coast brings all shipping to a halt as 39,000 workers walk off the job.

Nov. 3 The Democrats win the election and Roosevelt is reelected President. He has 523 electoral votes to 8 for Alfred M. Landon.

December Sales of Margaret Mitchell's story about the Civil War, *Gone With the Wind,* pass the million mark.

Dec. 25 Newspaper editor Arthur Brisbane, 72, whose sensational "yellow journalism" introduced a new era in editorial style, dies in New York City.

1937 **Frustrated by the fact that seven major New Deal** measures have been declared unconstitutional during the last two years, President Roosevelt decides to remedy the situation. He tells Congress that he does not feel there is a need for a new Constitutional amendment to implement his programs of social welfare, but that there is a need for the cooperation of the judiciary. A month later he reveals his plan: to increase the membership of the U.S. Supreme Court from 9 to 15, adding one new Justice for each present Justice who is past age 70 and refuses to retire.

Even many of Roosevelt's closest supporters are repelled by this plan to "pack" the Supreme Court. The state legislatures of Texas, Maine, Nebraska, and Kansas pass resolutions opposing the measure. The President is accused of trying to "pervert" the Constitution, although that document leaves undefined the number of Justices and historically the number has varied from 6 to 10. The Senate holds hearings on the measure. Chief Justice Charles E. Hughes testifies that the Court is not behind in its work, refuting a justification given by Roosevelt to support his plan. Realizing that the majority of Congress is against his proposal, Roosevelt carries his fight to the people in his "fireside" radio chats.

In the end Roosevelt prevails, although not through an act of Congress. Whatever the reason, the Supreme Court undergoes a marked shift in attitude and during April and May upholds several important New Deal measures, including the National Labor Relations Act, the Social Security Act, and the Farm Mortgage Moratorium Act. Then, in June, the arch-conservative Justice Willis Van Devanter retires, giving the President the opportunity to tip the balance of the Court in a liberal direction by appointing Hugo L. Black to the vacant seat.

The drama of the Court controversy diverts attention, perhaps, from other phenomena that are more significant. The organization of the labor movement proceeds apace, on picket lines and at bargaining tables. Industrial production and even agricultural output rises rapidly, but the unemployed still number more than 7,000,000. In the summer the instability in the economy results in a downswing, for which the new term "recession" is coined. And the instability across the seas, in China and in Spain, begins to have repercussions: a U.S. gunboat sunk in the Yangtze, U.S. volunteers forming an Abraham Lincoln Battalion to fight against General Francisco Franco's insurgents, a more determined legislative stand for isolation.

January-February Floods in the valleys of the Ohio, Mississippi, and Allegheny rivers cause extensive damage with over 900 persons dead and 500,000 homes flooded.

Jan. 8 The United States places an embargo on all shipments of arms to Spain. The action is intended to amend the Neutrality Act of 1936, which prohibits sending arms to nations at war, but does not apply to a civil war such as that taking place in Spain.

Jan. 12 President Roosevelt announces a scheme to add six executives to his staff to keep him better informed of Government activities. He also proposes to establish two new Cabinet posts, a Secretary of Public Works and a Secretary of Social Welfare.

Feb. 1 The Supreme Court refuses to hear an appeal challenging the Social Security Act. [On May 24, the Court upholds the act.]

Feb. 4 The 98-day-old shipping strike on the West Coast is ended as workers accept management's offer of higher wages, an eight-hour day and other measures designed to strengthen the union's position.

Feb. 7 Elihu Root, 92, diplomat and former Senator, dies at New York City. He was Secretary of War for President McKinley and Secretary of State for President Theodore Roosevelt, but he is best remembered for the treaties he negotiated with European countries and Japan, for which work he won the Nobel Peace Prize in 1912.

Feb. 11 A 44-day sit-down strike ends at the General Motors Company at Detroit after management agrees to recognize and bargain with the United Automobile Workers Union, affiliated with the Committee for Industrial Organization (CIO), and to grant workers a five-cent-per-hour increase.

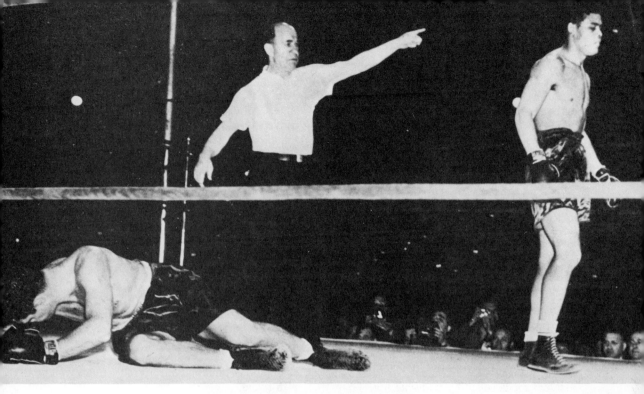

The referee directs Joe Louis to his corner
after he knocks down Jimmy Braddock in the
8th round on June 22.

Crowds gather outside the Chevrolet auto plant
occupied by "sit down" strikers.

Paraders pass the reviewing stand during the
"March for Peace" demonstration in New York City
on August 7, 1937.

Mar. 2   Two of the nation's largest steel companies, U.S. Steel and Carnegie Illinois Steel, faced with the threat of sit-down strikes, agree to recognize the United Steel Workers, another CIO union, and grant a 40-hour week and a wage increase.

Mar. 17   A violent taxi strike erupts in the Loop area of Chicago as drivers wreck cars and slug police while droves of spectators watch from windows.

Mar. 25   An airliner en route from New York to Kansas City crashes in the mountains of Pennsylvania, killing all 13 aboard.

Mar. 29   The U.S. Supreme Court rules that a Washington State minimum wage statute is constitutional, thereby reversing the Court's stand on this issue.

April 12   The U.S. Supreme Court declares that companies that operate on a national basis are subject to regulation under the power of Congress and the National Labor Relations Board, even though individual plants may manufacture goods solely for intrastate use.

April 20   President Roosevelt asks Congress to appropriate $1,500,000,000 for relief for the fiscal year 1937-1938. This amount represents a considerable drop from previous expenditures, and reflects the President's intention to balance the budget.

April 22   The fourth annual peace demonstration, the largest yet, is held in New York City as participants assert that they will "refuse to support the Government of the United States in any war it may conduct."

May 1   Congress passes a second Neutrality Act, which extends the provisions of previously passed measures and adds new provisions, including the "cash-and-carry" clause which specifies that any belligerent nation purchasing certain nonmilitary goods in the United States will have to pay cash for and transport the goods on its own ships.

May 6   The German dirigible *Hindenburg* is destroyed by fire and explosion as it is landing at Lakehurst, New Jersey; 36 of 97 on board are lost. The fire starts when a spark from static electricity ignites some leaking hydrogen.

May 14   A four-month celebration marking the 150th anniversary of the U.S Constitution begins in Philadelphia.

May 18   Willis Van Devanter, 78, oldest Associate Justice of the U.S. Supreme Court, announces his impending retirement. The announcement weakens the President's case for drastic reorganization of the Court.

May 23   John D. Rockefeller, Sr., 97, dies at Ormond Beach, Florida. His name is associated with Standard Oil, the vehicle for one of the largest fortunes ever accumulated, and with the University of Chicago, the chief beneficiary outside the Rockefeller family.

May 27   The longest suspension bridge in the world, across the Golden Gate between San Francisco and Marin County, California, is opened. It has a central span of 4,200 feet, and cost $35,000,000 to build.

May 30   Police fire on steel workers and their families demonstrating near the South Chicago plant of Republic Steel, killing 10 persons. The labor movement describes the event as the Memorial Day Massacre.

June 8   A 60-pound bulb brought from Sumatra to the Bronx Botanical Garden blooms into a single flower eight feet high and four feet in diameter.

June 22   Joe Louis becomes heavyweight champion, knocking out Jim Braddock in the 11th round.

July 2   Aviator Amelia Earhart vanishes on an around-the-world flight with a companion soon after their plane, a Lockheed, leaves New Guinea.

July 11   George Gershwin, 38, one of the country's most beloved composers, dies in Hollywood, California.

July 22   The Bankhead-Jones Farm Tenant Act sets up the Farm Security Adminstration (FSA) to stop the decline in farm ownership by providing low-interest, 40-year mortgages to sharecroppers and others who would ordinarily not be able to afford a farm. The FSA also sets up programs to assist migrant workers.

July 22   The Court reorganization bill dies in Congress.

September   Business activity starts to decline and stock prices drop. The term "recession" is used to distinguish this relatively mild decline from the full-scale depression the country has been battling for several years.

Sept. 1   The U.S. Housing Authority (USHA) is set up to provide low-interest, long-term mortgages to public agencies involved in slum clearance and public housing.

Oct. 1   U.S. Supreme Court Justice Hugo L. Black, appointed in August, asserts in a radio speech that although he did join the Ku Klux Klan 15 years ago, he resigned and has not been a member since.

Oct. 5   President Roosvelt, concerned about the increasing belligerency in other parts of the

The *Hindenburg* in flames at Lakehurst, New Jersey

world, states: "It seems to be unfortunately true that the epidemic of world lawlessness is spreading. When an epidemic of physical disease starts to spread, the community approves and joins in a quarantine of the patients in order to protect the health of the community against the disease." Some isolationists believe that the President is suggesting some type of positive action rather than adherence to the Neutrality Acts.

Nov. 15-Dec. 21   President Roosevelt calls Congress into special session and proposes legislation concerning agriculture, wages and hours, and other matters, but Congress fails to act.

Nov. 27   Garment workers produce *Pins and Needles,* a musical comedy that reflects the themes of the times.

Dec. 12   The U.S. gunboat *Panay* is sunk in Chinese waters by the Japanese air force, with the loss of two Americans. Japan apologizes and offers to pay damages.

1938

The recession that began in mid-1937 continues to worsen. By March the stock market has reached its lowest point in four years and by May the Federal Reserve index of industrial production is down to 76 from 117 the previous August. The number of unemployed has risen by about 2,000,000 in a year. However, by late summer the economy is recovering.

Either the President's leadership or world affairs may account for the upswing. In April, President Roosevelt decides that government action is again necessary, and he asks Congress to finance relief measures and public work projects; and Congress complies in June. In Europe, the German regime of Chancellor Adolf Hitler is active, annexing Austria in March and, with the acquiescence of France and Britain, occupying the Sudetenland in Czechoslovakia in September. In the Far East, Japan's increasing belligerency is highlighted by outright rejection in October of the 38-year old Open Door Policy on China. Although sentiment in the United States is still strongly isolationist, Congress decides to pass a Naval Expansion Act that provides more than $1,000,000,000 to build a "two-ocean" navy. Such spending, combined with armament orders for U.S. firms from war-frightened Europeans, proves effective in turning back the recession.

Jan. 3 President Roosevelt, in his opening message to Congress, stresses the need for military strength, noting that the increasing international tensions may make it necessary for the United States to defend itself.

Jan. 5 U.S. Supreme Court Justice George Sutherland, 75, announces his resignation after 15 years of service.

Jan. 14 A group of top business and labor leaders, including John L. Lewis, meets with President Roosevelt to ask what he plans to do to restore a healthy economy. Concern has been growing since mid-1937, when economic indices again began to slip.

Jan. 17 The American tanker *Nantucket Chief* is seized by Spanish insurgents near the Balearic Islands and its cargo of oil is confiscated.

Jan. 22 Sixteen oil companies and 30 executives are convicted of criminal conspiracy to fix gasoline prices in the Midwest.

Jan. 28 President Roosevelt asks Congress for funds to build a navy capable of protecting both the Atlantic and Pacific oceans.

Jan. 28 The League of Woman Shoppers urges a boycott of silk to pressure Japan into terminating its undeclared war on China. However, representatives of the American Federation of Hosiery Workers protest such a boycott, claiming it will cost their jobs.

Feb. 5 The United States, France, and Great Britain inform Japan that unless it gives assurance that it is not building any ships larger than the 35,000 tons specified in the 1936 London Naval Conference, the three countries will feel free to begin building such ships themselves.

Feb. 6 The Carnegie Foundation for the Advancement of Teaching makes public a report in which it condemns colleges that use unfair competitive methods to attract tuition-paying students.

Feb. 16 In another attempt to curb the problem of farm surpluses and the low prices they create—problems that the recent recession has aggravated—the President asks for and Congress passes a new AAA, the Agricultural Adjustment Act of 1938. The act authorizes the Government to lend money to farmers against surplus crops and to store these crops until they can be sold in a year when production is down and prices up. This system is dubbed the "ever-normal granary," and is intended to benefit not only the farmers but also consumers, who will enjoy stable food prices. Another section of the act sets up the Federal Crop Insurance Corporation (FCIC) to provide insurance against loss of wheat crops.

Mar. 2 Alexander Kerensky, who led the revolution against the Russian Czarist Government in March 1917 and who himself was ousted by the Bolsheviks eight months later, arrives in New York City for a lecture tour.

Mar. 14 The United States is notified by Germany that it is taking over all Austrian diplomatic facilities, inasmuch as Austria is now part of the Third Reich.

April 14 In response to the continuing recession begun in 1937, President Roosevelt asks Congress for $3,000,000,000 to spend on relief and other public works over the next few months.

April 22 Explosions at a mine in Buchanan County, Virginia, kill 45 miners.

May 11 Congress passes a revenue act that

reduces the taxes paid by large corporations and reduces the rates on capital gains. Sponsors of the act claim that it will stimulate business investment and thereby revive the economy. [The act becomes law on May 27, after President Roosevelt refuses either to sign or veto the measure.]

May 17   The Vinson Naval Act, requested by President Roosevelt in January, is passed by Congress. It provides for the construction of a "two-ocean" navy.

May 26   The House Committee on Un-American Activities (HUAC) is set up with Martin Dies, a Texas Democrat, as chairman, to investigate whatever the committee thinks might be an "un-American" group or activity.

June 19   A passenger train from Chicago to Tacoma, Washington, crashes in Montana while crossing a bridge undermined by recent rains. The accident causes 47 deaths and leaves 75 persons seriously injured.

June 22   Joe Louis knocks out contender Max Schmeling in the first round at Yankee Stadium in New York City to retain the heavyweight crown.

June 24   Passage of the Food, Drug, and Cosmetic Act reflects growing consumer awareness during the past several years. The act prohibits a number of abuses, including false advertising claims and misbranding of ingredients.

June 25   The Fair Labor Standards Act sets a minimum wage of 25 cents an hour for workers engaged in interstate commerce and prohibits child labor. As a result of the act, about 800,000 workers receive immediate raises.

June 26   James Weldon Johnson, 67, black author, diplomat, and reformer, dies in an automobile accident in New York. The first black attorney in Florida (in the 1890's), a founder of the National Association for the Advancement of Colored People, he is remembered for his poetry and his contribution to black culture.

July 9   Benjamin N. Cardozo, 68, Associate Justice of the Supreme Court, noted for his many precedent-setting opinions, dies in Port Chester, New York.

Aug. 18   President Roosevelt dedicates the Thousand Islands Bridge across the St. Lawrence River connecting Canada and the United States.

Sept. 15   Thomas Wolfe, 37, author of *Look Homeward, Angel* and other novels, dies in Baltimore.

Sept. 21   A hurricane hits New England and New York State, causing extensive damage and taking 600 lives.

Oct. 30   A radio adaptation of H.G. Wells's *War of the Worlds,* about an invasion from Mars, is narrated by Orson Welles so compellingly that thousands of frantic listeners call the station, the police, and the newspapers in a state of hysteria.

Nov. 8   In midterm elections, Republicans gain 81 seats in the House and 8 in the Senate, but the Democrats retain a majority in both Houses.

Nov. 15   President Roosevelt states that America is deeply shocked by the increase of anti-Semitic activity in Germany and that he cannot "believe such things could occur in a 20th-century civilization."

Nov. 17   A reciprocal trade agreement is signed by the United States, Canada, and Great Britain.

Nov. 18   At its first convention in Pittsburgh, the Congress of Industrial Organizations chooses John L. Lewis of the United Mine Workers as its president. Expelled in October 1937 by the American Federation of Labor, the Committee for Industrial Organization, already having a larger membership than its parent organization and under Lewis's leadership, has changed its name but retains the initials, CIO, by which it is becoming well known.

Max Schmeling hangs on the ropes as he is pummeled by Joe Louis in their championship fight on June 22.

Orson Welles, arms raised, rehearses the *War of the Worlds* broadcast.

1939 **Isolationist sentiment begins to disintegrate as Americans watch in** dismay the spread of fascism across Europe, signaled by the fall of the Spanish Republic in March. Germany moves into Czechoslovakia, claiming that disorder in that country threatens the safety of German nationals. The futility of the policy of appeasement, exemplified by the Munich Pact of September 1938, is evident. Hitler announces the annexation of Memel, Lithuania, a Baltic port near Danzig. At the same time Italy crosses the Adriatic to occupy Albania. Hitler demands access to Danzig across the Polish Corridor, but Britain and France agree to protect Poland if it is attacked. Instead of moving against Poland immediately, Hitler concludes a nonagression treaty in August with the Soviet Union. The pact is revealed as a scheme to divide up Poland between Germany and the Soviet Union, and on Sept. 1 a German blitzkrieg overwhelms Poland. Two days later England and France declare war on Germany. President Roosevelt makes the customary moves in times of international crisis. He asks for legislation to bolster the nation's defenses. He appeals to the belligerents, and together with Congress begins to mobilize forces in favor of those supported by most Americans—the challengers of fascism. Inevitably the war economy begins to improve domestic conditions. With no fanfare, scientists begin to develop new weapons, including a new type of bomb.

Jan. 4   President Roosevelt's opening message to Congress emphasizes the threat to world peace by the growing strength of the totalitarian nations. The next day he asks Congress to approve a defense budget of $1,319,558,000. The money is to be used for air defense, increased naval strength, and improving seacoast fortifications of the continental United States, the Panama Canal, and Hawaii.

Jan. 5   President Roosevelt submits his budget for fiscal year 1939-1940. The $9,000,000,000 budget includes an appropriation of $875,000,000 to carry the Works Progress Administration, now operating at a deficit, through the remainder of the present fiscal year. But Congress grants less than Roosevelt asks, and the WPA cuts back its number of workers.

Jan. 26   Niels Bohr and Enrico Fermi, nuclear physicists, confer in Washington, D.C., on the process of fission, by which a free uranium neutron may be produced capable of initiating a "chain reaction." The matter was brought to Bohr's attention by refugee German scientists, and may have military significance.

Feb. 27   The U.S. Supreme Court rules that the sit-down strike is illegal.

April 3   After a two-year struggle with Congress, Roosevelt succeeds in securing passage of his Administrative Reorganization Act. The act streamlines the Government by consolidating a large number of small agencies into a few large ones. The plan, originally designed by political scientists, gives the President greater feedback on governmental affairs and eliminates duplication of services.

April 15   President Roosevelt seeks reassurance from Hitler and Mussolini that they do not intend to attack additional nations.

April 30-Oct. 31   The New York World's Fair is held in Queens, New York. The theme of the fair is "The World of Tomorrow," and various scientific wonders, including television, are displayed. Twenty-two foreign countries participate; a notable exception is Germany.

May 5-13   The United Mine Workers, led by John L. Lewis of the CIO, shuts down most bituminous coal mines until a contract is reached.

May 5   A Declaration of Union is signed by the three branches of the Methodist Church, uniting 8,000,000 members in one organization.

May 11   A fire in a Chicago grain elevator takes several lives and destroys over 4,000,000 bushels of grain.

May 16   The first food stamp plan goes into effect at Rochester, New York, and soon spreads to many other cities. Stamps permit those on relief to receive free surplus commodities to supplement their regular food budget.

May 23   The U.S. submarine *Squalus* sinks off Portsmouth, New Hampshire, during a practice dive, and settles on mud 240 feet below the surface. Using a specially designed rescue chamber, two Navy divers rescue 33 men, but 26 die, trapped behind a bulkhead in the flooded section of the ship.

June 7-12   King George VI and Queen Elizabeth of Great Britain visit the United States.

June 28   Pan American Airways introduces the first regular passenger plane service between the United States and Euorpe.

June 30   The Emergency Relief Appropriation Act provides almost $1,500,000,000 for the WPA, but the wage is reduced and a limit of 18 consecutive months of work is imposed.

July 25   The Senate ratifies the 1936 treaty with Panama by which the United States relinquishes the right to intervene in that country's internal affairs.

Aug. 2   Congress passes the Hatch Act, which forbids Federal civil service employees from taking part actively in political campaigns for office.

Sept. 3   Reflecting on the hostilities in Europe, President Roosevelt declares: "This nation will remain a neutral nation, but I cannot ask that every American remain neutral in thought as well. . . .Even a neutral cannot be asked to close his mind or close his conscience."

Sept. 8   President Roosevelt declares a state of limited emergency.

Oct. 18   All warring nations are ordered to keep their submarines out of U.S. waters.

Oct. 21   The Advisory Committee on Uranium holds a meeting to consider the possibility of making an atomic bomb. The committee was appointed after Albert Einstein sent a report on Oct. 11 to the President, discussing the findings of Bohr and other nuclear physicists. [The deliberations of the committee and the content of Professor Einstein's letter are not made public until after the detonation of the atomic bombs over Japan.]

The perisphere and trylon, the theme figures of New York's World's Fair

Douglas Fairbanks Sr. (right) and son Douglas, (*ca.*) 1933

Nov. 4   Congress, in a joint resolution during a special session called by President Roosevelt, repeals the arms embargo clause of the Neutrality Act of 1937. The new Neutrality Act allows belligerents to purchase armaments in the United States providing that they pay cash and use their own ships for transportation. This "cash-and-carry" concept is designed to aid the Allies, who alone have the money and control the oceans.

Dec. 11   The U.S. Supreme Court outlaws the use of wiretapping evidence obtained without a warrant.

Dec. 12   Douglas Fairbanks, Sr., 56, one of the country's most popular film actors, dies at Santa Monica, California.

1940

To an increasing extent the President and Congress devote their attention to shoring up the country while the Germans overrun most of Scandinavia, Prime Minister Winston Churchill tells the British people that he has "nothing to offer but blood, toil, tears, and sweat," Dunkerque is evacuated, the Germans enter Paris, the Japanese enter Nanking, and the three-way Axis (Germany, Italy, Japan) becomes a modern sword of Damocles. Yet the constitutional system imposes an obligation on the American people, come prosperity or chaos: an election must be held.

This year the Republicans, encouraged by their victory in the 1938 midterm elections, feel they have a chance to unseat "that man in the White House." To challenge Roosevelt they select Wendell L. Willkie, a man who has never held an elected office, a former Democrat and nonpolitican, a power company executive whose opposition to the Tennessee Valley Authority makes him attractive to business and professional people. Willkie's candidacy is declared shortly before the Republican convention by self-styled "amateur" Republicans.

Willkie runs a brilliant energetic campaign, traveling 30,000 miles and giving 540 speeches in eight weeks. His Midwestern background and his frank, witty demeanor make him highly popular in the farm states. His campaign themes, the dangers of a third Presidential term and the domination of one man, please both Republicans and conservative Democrats. Although Willkie criticizes the methods of the New Deal, he does not dispute its purpose. Nor does he quarrel with Roosevelt's stand of giving all possible support to Britain short of declaring war on Germany.

President Roosevelt at first leaves campaigning to his Vice Presidential choice, Henry Wallace. But indications of Willkie's increasing popularity change the President's mind and during the last days of the campaign he takes to the stump. When the votes are counted, Roosevelt wins by almost 5,000,000, but with only 54.7 per cent of the popular vote, notably lower than in 1932 and 1936. Now the United States has its first third-term President. But it is in his second term that another precedent is broken, for the first peacetime draft is already on the books seven weeks before Election Day.

The rate of population increase has been sharply cut to 7.3 per cent over the decade of 1930-1940, according to the 16th decennial census. The total population is now 132,164,569, and there is only a slight movement from the countryside to the cities.

Jan. 3   President Roosevelt, in his budget message to Congress, asks for $1,800,000,000 for defense.

Jan. 19   William E. Borah, 74, Senator from Idaho since 1906, dies in Washington. A liberal Republican, but a champion of isolation, Borah is remembered for his successful campaign to keep the United States out of the League of Nations and the World Court. He supported some New Deal laws but opposed the draft and the Court-"packing" effort.

Jan. 26   The United States declines to renew its commercial treaty with Japan.

Feb. 9   President Roosevelt sends Under Secretary of State Sumner Welles to study and report on the military situation in Europe. [After meeting with leaders of both the Axis and the Allies, Welles returns to the United States without any concrete peace plan.]

Feb. 26   The Air Defense Command is established to plan air defense of the United States against possible attack.

Mar. 4   Kings Canyon National Park, a 454,000-acre tract of unspoiled California wilderness, is created by an act of Congress.

April 12   A bill to extend the Reciprocal Trade Agreement Act of 1937 for three years is signed by Roosevelt. The bill gives the President the right to continue negotiating mutual tariff reductions with willing nations.

April 20   A microscope that focuses electrons instead of light is displayed by Radio Corporation of America. The device has a magnification potential far greater than that of ordinary microscopes.

April 22   The U.S. Supreme Court declares antipicketing laws of Alabama and California unconstitutional, on the grounds that they violate the First Amendment.

April 29 It is constitutional for the Federal Government to determine minimum wages paid by firms doing government contract work, according to a decision of the U.S. Supreme Court.

May 15 Igor Sikorsky demonstrates the first direct-lift aircraft in the United States, the Vought-Sikorsky helicopter.

May 31 President Roosevelt asks Congress for $1,300,000,000 in supplemental funds for military and naval development. He calls for the building of 50,000 planes annually.

June 3 The United States starts to supply Great Britain with surplus war material, including aircraft.

June 10 Marcus Garvey, 52, one of the most eloquent and controversial black leaders of his time, sometimes called Black Moses because of his effort to lead American Negroes to power in Africa, dies in London.

June 16 Passage of the Pittman Resolution in Congress permits the sale of U.S. arms to the countries of South America.

June 16 Fearing a German takeover of Dutch and French colonial possessions in Latin America, the United States informs the Axis powers that such acts will not be recognized.

June 22 Congress raises the national debt ceiling to a record high of $49,000,000,000.

June 24-28 The Republican Party convention is held in Philadelphia, and Wendell L. Willkie is nominated for President; Senator Charles L. McNary of Oregon is selected as the candidate for the Vice Presidency.

June 28 The Alien Registration Act (Smith Act) requires all foreigners to register and be fingerprinted. It also makes it unlawful to be a member of any organization that advocates the overthrow of the Government by force or violence, or to advocate or conspire to advocate such overthrow.

July 4 An American Negro exposition is held at Chicago to celebrate the 75th anniversary of the Emancipation Proclamation.

July 13 The Department of State and the Department of Justice announce that present immigration statutes do not prohibit unlimited numbers of refugee children from coming to the United States as visitors.

July 15-19 The Democrats hold their convention at Chicago and renominate Franklin D. Roosevelt for a third Presidential term. Secretary of Agriculture Henry A. Wallace is selected as his running mate.

July 20 Presidential campaign expenditures are limited to $3,000,000 and no individual may contribute more than $5,000, under an amendment to the 1939 Hatch Act.

Aug. 29 Color television is demonstrated over the Columbia Broadcasting System station in New York by Peter C. Goldmark.

September The America First Committee is organized to challenge President Roosevelt's policy of intervention in the war.

Sept. 3 In an attempt to strengthen this country's ability to defend its eastern coast, President Roosevelt provides Britain with 50 overage destroyers in exchange for the right to establish naval bases on seven British territories from Newfoundland to British Guiana.

Sept. 4 The United States warns Japan not to attack French Indochina.

Oct. 24 The 40-hour week, a provision of the Wages and Hours Act of 1938, goes into effect as scheduled.

Oct. 25 John L. Lewis, president of the Congress of Industrial Organizations, asks his membership to vote for Willkie, promising to resign if Roosevelt is reelected. [He resigns on Nov. 21.]

Oct. 29 At a ceremony in Washington, D.C., numbers are drawn to select those to be inducted in the first peacetime draft in the United States. As a result of the passage on Sept. 16 of the Selective Service Training and Service Act, more than 16,000,000 men have registered for possible military conscription.

Nov. 5 President Franklin D. Roosevelt is elected to a third term, with 449 electoral votes to 82 for Wendell Willkie.

Nov. 7 The Tacoma Narrows Bridge, the third-longest single-span bridge in the world (2,800 feet), falls into Puget Sound in Washington, four months after its completion. Aerodynamic flaws are blamed for the collapse during a 42-mph windstorm.

Dec. 20 The Office of Production Management (OPM) is established to regulate defense production and to facilitate shipment of war materials to the anti-Axis forces.

Dec. 21 F. Scott Fitzgerald, 44, author of *The Great Gatsby* and spokesman for the "lost generation," dies in Hollywood, California, of a heart attack.

Dec. 29 President Roosevelt supports his policy of giving all possible aid to Britain by asserting "that there is far less chance of the United States getting into war if we do all we can now to support the nations defending themselves against attack."

1941　**The fact of imminent U.S. involvement in the conflict,** which is now clearly World War II, cannot be avoided. Necessary legislation and Executive orders provide what preparedness is possible as the war in Europe intensifies, with the German invasion of the Soviet Union completely changing the war's character. If the United States is not yet involved in the war itself, the President proposes to anticipate the peace, and a sense of history pervades the formulation of the Atlantic Charter in mid-ocean. At home, a new generation of alphabet agencies appears, oriented toward the approaching military crisis—agencies to develop defense production and distribution of war materials, and to manipulate the economy through price and wage controls. Labor makes its final effort to gain an advantage before making peace with management and Government for the duration. Nevertheless, when the "day of infamy" dawns, the nation is horrified.

Jan. 3　The 76th Congress, after a 367-day session, the longest in American history, adjourns.

Jan. 6　President Roosevelt, in his message to the 77th Congress, urges that the United States be an "arsenal of democracy" by supplying arms to all nations fighting the totalitarian aggressors. At this time he also proposes that all peoples should be guaranteed "four freedoms" when the war is over: freedom of speech and expression, freedom of worship, freedom from want, and freedom from fear.

Jan. 8　The President's budget calls for a record $17,500,000,000, of which about 60 per cent is to be earmarked for defense. Roosevelt estimates that deficit spending will run about $9,200,000,000 for the year.

Jan. 27　The United States and Britain hold secret talks in Washington, in which it is decided that, should the United States enter the war on the side of England and Japan enter on the side of Germany, the strategy will be to defeat Germany first.

Jan. 30　The U.S. Government charges several American and German companies, including the Aluminum Company of America, with conspiring to regulate the price and supply of magnesium in the United States and at the same time favoring shipments of the material to Germany.

Feb. 3　The U.S. Supreme Court upholds the Federal Wages and Hours Act. The Court also decides that disputes between labor unions are not regulated by the Sherman Antitrust Act.

Feb. 15　The first B-24 bomber built by Consolidated Aircraft for the British Royal Air Force is completed.

Feb. 16　Harry L. Hopkins returns from Great Britain warning that that nation is in dire need of assistance from the United States.

Feb. 19　President Roosevelt approves a measure that raises the ceiling on the public debt to a record $65,000,000,000.

Feb. 19　Construction of a third set of ship locks is started to enlarge the capacity of the Panama Canal.

Feb. 28　A heavy snowstorm paralyzes much of the East Coast.

Mar. 5　To provide greater security for the Panama Canal, the United States requests and receives permission from Panama to extend its air defense zone around the Canal.

Mar. 8　Sherwood Anderson, 64, author of *Winesburg, Ohio* and other works depicting life in the Midwest, dies in the Canal Zone after becoming ill during a cruise.

Mar. 11-12　The Lend-Lease Act is passed by Congress and signed by President Roosevelt to provide supplies for those nations fighting the Axis powers. Prime Minister Churchill terms the act a "new Magna Carta."

Mar. 17　The National Gallery of Art opens in Washington, D.C.

Mar. 19　An increasing number of strikes in various defense industries, reaching almost crisis proportions, culminates in the formation of the National Defense Mediation Board (NDMB). The purpose of the board is to prevent strikes by helping unions and management negotiate differences.

Mar. 22　The Grand Coulee Dam on the Columbia River begins to produce electricity. The installation, with a potential capacity of 1,974,000 kilowatts, could become the largest hydroelectric plant in the world.

Mar. 28　The U.S. Antarctic Expedition starts home after completing its two-year mission at the South Pole.

Mar. 30　President Roosevelt orders the Coast Guard to seize 2 German, 28 Italian, and 35 German-controlled Danish ships at present in U.S. ports. [On May 15 French ships are also ordered seized.]

Mar. 31-April 28   After the United Mine Workers union fails to reach an agreement with mine operators, 400,000 soft-coal miners strike and, after considerable violence, win a $1-a-day raise.

April 4   The Office of Production Management reports that the United States is now producing airplanes in record numbers: 1,216 completed and delivered in March.

April 9-12   The Danish Minister to Washington, Henrik de Kauffmann, signs a treaty giving the United States the right to protect Greenland and to establish bases there. He is recalled from Washington and the treaty is declared void by the Danish Foreign Office. Nevertheless, U.S. forces are sent to Greenland.

April 11   Anticipating that a wartime economy will involve inflation, the President sets up an agency, the Office of Price Administration (OPA), to plan wage and price controls.

April 16   Steel prices in the United States are fixed at present levels by OPA.

April 17   U.S. auto makers agree to reduce output by 1,000,000 units annually as of Aug. 1, in order to divert production capacity and raw materials into the manufacture of armaments.

April 19   A resolution in the Senate introduced by Robert F. Wagner, Sr., states that U.S. policy favors the "restoration of the Jews in Palestine." The resolution is supported by 68 Senators.

April 21   U.S., British, and Dutch officers meet in Singapore to coordinate military activity in the event of a Japanese attack there.

April 28   Colonel Charles Lindbergh gives up his post with the Army Air Corps Reserve. He explains that he is responding to President Roosevelt's criticism of his isolationist position. (Roosevelt has termed Lindbergh's stance "disloyal.")

April 28   The U.S. Supreme Court decides that black people must be offered train accommodations equal to those offered to white people.

May 9   Utilizing a 15- by 20-foot screen, theater television makes its debut in New York City.

May 20   President Roosevelt ends a two-year experiment of holding Thanksgiving one week before the traditional last Thursday in November.

May 21   The U.S. freighter *Robin Moor* is sunk by a German submarine.

May 27   President Roosevelt declares an unlimited state of national emergency.

May 31   After its 3,180th performance on Broadway, *Tobacco Road* closes.

June 2   Charles Evans Hughes, 79, retires as Chief Justice of the U.S. Supreme Court, effective July 1. [His position is filled by Associate Justice Harlan F. Stone.]

June 2   Lou Gehrig, 38, former first baseman for the New York Yankees, dies of a rare type of paralysis in New York City.

June 14-17   President Roosevelt freezes all German and Italian assets in the United States. On June 16 all German consulates are shut down. The next day Germany moves against the $450,000,000 in U.S. property in that country.

June 16-20   The U.S. Government stops shipment of 250,000 gallons of lubricating oil to Japan because of defense needs in the United States. A few days later all petroleum products are put under export control.

June 22   All Italian consulates in the United States are closed.

June 24   President Roosevelt releases $40,000,000 in credits for the Soviet Union and promises to aid that country, in reaction to the German invasion of the U.S.S.R. on June 22.

June 30   The President establishes the Franklin D. Roosevelt Library at Hyde Park.

July 7   U.S. forces arrive in Iceland to strengthen that country's defenses against possible German occupation.

July 24   The first major agreement between labor and Goverment to modify the right to strike during the national emergency is made between construction unions and the Office of Production Management. [The policy is extended to all war industries on Dec. 15.]

July 26   President Roosevelt impounds all Japanese credits in the United States in retaliation for an agreement by Vichy France to permit Japan to occupy French Indochina. At the same time President Roosevelt puts the Philippine army under the direct command of the United States.

July 30   Harry L. Hopkins, on a secret mission to Moscow, tells Premier Stalin that the U.S. Government will begin sending a large quantity of war material to assist in the fight against Germany.

July 30   President Roosevelt asks for legislation permitting him greater control over prices in order to check inflation.

July 31   The Japanese Government apologizes for the sinking of the U.S. gunboat *Tutuila* and promises to pay damages.

Aug. 3   Listed gasoline rationing goes into effect in the Eastern states as stations stay closed at night.

The U.S.S. *Arizona* burns, following the bombardment by Japanese aircraft, during the attack on Pearl Harbor.

The U.S.S. *Pennsylvania*, the U.S. *Downes*, and the U.S.S. *Cassin* after the bombing of Pearl Harbor

President Franklin D. Roosevelt addresses a joint session of Congress and asks for a declaration of war against Japan.

John Fitzgerald Kennedy
THIRTY-FIFTH PRESIDENT   1961-1963

A military honor guard carries the body of the late President John F. Kennedy from St. Matthews Cathedral following a Pontifical mass. (The funeral cortege proceeded to Arlington National Cemetery and final rights and burial.)

A mule-drawn wagon carries the casket of Dr. Martin Luther King, Jr., to Morehouse College for memorial services.

Dr. Martin Luther King, Jr., arrives in Montgomery, Alabama at the conclusion of the civil rights march from Selma.

Astronauts Neil A. Armstrong, Commander of Apollo 11 (left) and Edwin E. Aldrin, Jr., Lunar Module Pilot, deploy the U.S. flag after their historic landing on the lunar surface.

U. S. troops in Vietnam return from a "search and destroy" mission.

Members of the U.S. First Cavalry Division climb 100 foot ladders to a hovering helicopter near An Khe, Vietnam.

Lyndon B. Johnson
THIRTY-SIXTH PRESIDENT   1963-1969

Aug. 14   President Roosevelt and Prime Minister Churchill meet off the coast of Newfoundland and draw up the Atlantic Charter, containing goals suitable for postwar policy. While the charter is not a treaty and therefore need not be ratified by the Senate, it is, in the words of Churchill, "astonishing" that a neutral nation and a warring nation should join to make such a declaration. [By the end of September, 15 other countries also subscribe to the Atlantic Charter.]

Aug. 18   A new measure that amends the Selective Service Act of 1940 becomes law. It increases the term of service for inductees from 12 to 30 months.

Aug. 19   A $275,000,000 flood-control bill is signed into law by President Roosevelt.

Sept. 4   The American destroyer *Greer* is attacked by a German U-boat, but manages to escape.

Sept. 5-12   In war games in Louisiana, paratroopers (units dropped by parachute) are used for the first time in tactical maneuvers. Most of the credit for these maneuvers, the most elaborate in peacetime history, is attributed to Colonel Dwight D. Eisenhower.

Sept. 9-22   On Sept. 9, two U.S.-owned steamships, the *Montana* and the *Sessa*, are torpedoed in the Atlantic near Iceland. On Sept. 22, the U.S. Government-owned freighter *Pink Star* is sunk in the Iceland area.

Sept. 11   President Roosevelt instructs the Navy to attack any German or Italian submarine or warship entering U.S.-protected waters.

Sept. 11   Charles A. Lindbergh charges that there are three groups forcing the U.S. into war—the British, the Jews, and the Roosevelt Administration.

Sept. 23   A ceremony at the New York World's Fair dedicates a time capsule which is to be opened after 5,000 years. The capsule contains examples of and information about 20th-century civilization.

Oct. 1   A 10-per-cent excise tax on many items, especially luxury goods, goes into effect.

Oct. 24   Arthur Starnes sets a new free-fall parachute record by dropping almost 30,000 feet before pulling his ripcord.

Oct. 29   A dispute between the American Society of Composers, Authors, and Publishers (ASCAP) and the NBC and CBS radio networks ends, increasing the prices paid to ASCAP members and restoring for broadcast use ASCAP-controlled music kept off the radio networks

since Jan. 1.

Nov. 7   As a result of German U-boat attacks on several more U.S. destroyers, Congress passes a bill to repeal certain sections of the 1939 Neutrality Act. U.S. merchant ships may now be armed and carry cargoes to warring nations.

Nov. 10   Great Britain promises that it will declare war on Japan "within the hour" should that nation attack the United States.

Nov. 24   The California Antimigrant Law is ruled unconstitutional by the U.S. Supreme Court. The measure was used in an attempt to keep "Okies," families driven from their homes in the dust-bowl states, from entering California.

Nov. 27   In a move of hemispheric solidarity, Argentina agrees to sell no more tungsten to Japan; all tungsten produced in the next three years will be sold to the United States.

Dec. 7   At about 6 A.M., 190 Japanese warplanes take off from 6 aircraft carriers stationed 275 miles north of the Hawaiian island of Oahu, the site of Pearl Harbor, and the home of the U.S. Pacific fleet. Flying south, the planes are detected by a radar operator about 130 miles before they reach Oahu, but they are assumed to be American Flying Fortresses due in at this time. Arriving at Pearl Harbor about 7:50 A.M., the Japanese pilots find most of the U.S. Pacific fleet anchored, unprotected, and unprepared. Within two hours, 5 of the 8 battleships are in ruins, the others are badly damaged, and some 200 aircraft are destroyed. More than 2,300 soldiers, sailors, and civilians are killed. The Japanese lose 29 of their aircraft and 5 midget submarines on hand to attack any U.S. battleship that might try to escape.

Dec. 8   President Roosevelt addresses a joint session of Congress, describing the attack on Pearl Harbor as "a day which will live in infamy. . . ." The United States declares war on Japan. Various cities on the West Coast are blacked out after Japanese warplanes are erroneously reported in the area.

Dec. 11   Germany and Italy declare war on the United States.

Dec. 12   Japanese forces occupy the U.S. possession of Guam.

Dec. 22   President Roosevelt signs a new Selective Service Act under which all men from 18 to 64 years of age must register, and all men from 20 to 44 may be conscripted.

Dec. 22   A U.S. possession in the Pacific Ocean, Wake Island, is captured by Japan.

As the nation commits itself to the war, men—and a few women—are mobilized into the armed services, the entire population finds a role in production or civil defense or both, and the unemployed are demobilized. In the combat areas, the story is highlighted, in the war with Japan, by the defeat in Manila followed by the resurgence on Guadalcanal; while the infantry enters the European theater by way of North Africa and bombers raid targets in France and Italy. The entire nation adopts daylight-saving time (appropriately renamed "war time") and accepts other controls—of prices, the right to strike, the right to buy—unheard of in peacetime America.

Jan. 1   The Office of Production Management (OPM) orders a ban on the sale of new cars and trucks.

Jan. 1   Twenty-six nations agree at Washington, D.C. to support the aims of the Atlantic Charter, to work for the defeat of the Axis, and to make no individual peace settlement with the Axis.

Jan. 3   After a week of bombing the Philippine capital, Manila, Japanese forces enter the city unopposed. General Douglas MacArthur orders his small contingent of American and Philippine troops to withdraw to Bataan, a small peninsula extending into a bay opposite Manila.

Jan. 12   President Roosevelt establishes the National War Labor Board (NWLB) to settle conflicts between labor and management in order to prevent strikes that would cripple defense production.

Jan. 16   The War Production Board (WPB) takes over from OPM the task of maximizing production of war materials.

Feb. 10   The French passenger liner *Normandie* is destroyed by fire in New York Harbor.

Feb. 12   American artist Grant Wood, 50, dies in Iowa City, Iowa. After a trip to Europe where Grant studied the work of 15th-century Dutch primitives, he achieved fame with *American Gothic,* a portrait of an American farm couple.

March   Both as a result of security precautions and public pressure, the U.S. Government rounds up the Nisei (Americans of Japanese ancestry) living in California and moves them to camps in isolated areas for the duration of the war. The majority of the 110,000 persons so relocated are second- or third-generation Americans. In Hawaii, where they represent about one-third of the population, Nisei are allowed to remain at their homes and jobs.

Mar. 17   General MacArthur arrives in Darwin, Australia, after leaving Bataan under orders from the President, to organize the Allied forces for a counteroffensive against Japan. He promises that he will one day return to the Philippines.

Mar. 27   The U.S. Government gives servicemen free mail privileges.

April 9-May 6   The Japanese take the Bataan Peninsula on April 9. The next day the infamous "Death March" begins as the U.S. and Philippine war prisoners are made to walk 85 miles in six days; suffering from heat, thirst, starvation and exhaustion, thousands die or are killed by Japanese guards; the rest are taken to prison camps. A small unit under General Jonathan Wainwright holds out on the fortress island of Corregidor, at the tip of Bataan, until May 6, after which the Japanese for the first time have full use of Manila Harbor.

April 14   *Social Justice,* a weekly paper published by "Radio Priest" Father Charles Coughlin, is cited as seditious, in violation of the 1917 Espionage Act, and is therefore denied mailing privileges.

April 18   To solve problems created by an excessive demand for labor, the War Manpower Commission is set up to maximize the effectiveness of the nation's available workers.

April 18   Led by General James H. Doolittle, 16 B-25 bombers take off from the aircraft carrier *Hornet,* 800 miles from Japan, and bomb Tokyo and other cities. Most of the raiding bombers came down in mainland China. This is the first offensive against Japan. It causes little material damage, but boosts U.S. morale and brings the war home to the Japanese.

May 5   Sugar rationing starts in the United States.

May 7-8   U.S. naval and air forces intercept a Japanese fleet in the Coral Sea, between Australia and the Solomon Islands. The battle is fought entirely with air power; for the first time in the history of sea warfare, ships in combat do not fire on each other. Five Japanese warships and 2 transports are sunk, 100 planes are shot down, and about 3,000 men are killed. U.S.

354

forces lose 2 warships, 20 aircraft and 500 men. Japanese plans to invade Australia are foiled.

May 14   The Women's Army Auxiliary Corps (WAC) is created by Congress.

May 20   The Office of Civilian Defense (OCD) is set up to train civilians to provide emergency defense within their own localities in case of anticipated air raids.

May 29   Actor John Barrymore, 60, dies at Hollywood.

June   Eight German saboteurs who have landed by submarine in the United States are arrested by the FBI. [Six are condemned to death, the others are given long prison terms.]

June 4-5   Attempting to take Midway Island, 1,200 miles west of Hawaii, the Japanese suffer a severe defeat, losing 7 large ships and 275 planes. The United States loses 2 ships and 100 planes. [This proves to be the critical battle in the Pacific.]

July 22   Gasoline rationing coupons are issued.

Aug. 7   American marines land on Guadalcanal, one of the Solomon Islands, where the Japanese are building an airbase in preparation for an attack on Australia. [The island is completely under U.S. control by Feb. 9, 1943.]

Aug. 12   Prime Minister Churchill and Premier Stalin meet in Moscow with Averell Harriman, representing the United States, to discuss the possibility of relieving pressure on the Russians by opening a second front in Europe.

Aug. 17   U.S. bombers make their first raid on Europe, flying 12 B-17's to rail yards at Rouen, France.

Oct. 2   The first U.S. turbojet plane, an XP-59A, is test-flown by the Bell Aircraft Corporation at Muroc [Edwards AFB], California.

Oct. 9   The United States and Great Britain agree to give up extraterritorial rights in China.

Nov. 3   In midterm elections, the Republicans increase their representation in both the House and the Senate, but the Democrats maintain majorities.

Nov. 8   Operation Torch, planned in July, is implemented as a combined British and U.S. army of 400,000 men, commanded by General Dwight D. Eisenhower, lands in French North Africa at several points.

Nov. 13   The minimum draft age in the United States is lowered from 21 to 18 years of age.

Nov. 28   A fire at the Cocoanut Grove night club in Boston kills 487 persons.

Dec. 4   In the first U.S. air raid on the Italian mainland, 24 B-24's strike Naples.

Dec. 4   After more than 7½ years during which it provided a minimum income for some 8,500,000 unemployed persons and contributed considerably to the material, moral, and cultural welfare of the United States, the Works Progress Administration is closed down. The project cost an estimated $11,000,000,000.

Dec. 21   Anthropologist Franz Boas, 84, dies in New York City. His extensive scientific research refutes theories of racial superiority.

American and Australian wounded soldiers lie on litters in a New Guinea village on Dec. 21, 1942.

1943 **The chiefs of state hold major meetings throughout the year,** in Casablanca in January, in Cairo and Teheran at the year's end. The Allied armed forces rally and begin to take the offensive, with increasing U.S. participation, winning North Africa and Sicily in Europe, more than holding their own in the Pacific. General Dwight D. Eisenhower emerges as the Commander-in-Chief in the European theater. At home, the economy is functioning efficiently. The unions keep their men on the job, except for the miners, whose recalcitrance provokes stiff antistrike legislation.

Jan. 5   George Washington Carver, 78, born a slave in Missouri during the Civil War, who became an outstanding agricultural scientist, dies in Tuskegee, Alabama.

Jan. 5   The U.S. Government announces that American war casualties already exceed 60,000.

Jan. 11   President Roosevelt's proposed budget for fiscal 1943-1944 is $108,903,000,000.

Jan. 12-24   President Roosevelt and Prime Minister Churchill, with their chief military planners, meet in Casablanca, Morocco, to formulate the strategy for the war in Europe. In the end they agree to attack Italy by way of Sicily, with the possibility of later crossing the Channel to invade France. They also agree to continue saturation bombing of Germany and aid to the Soviet Union. At a final conference on Jan. 24, President Roosevelt enunciates the Allied intention to exact "unconditional surrender" of the Axis forces. To head the European theater of operations, General Dwight D. Eisenhower is selected, with Sir Harold Alexander as his deputy.

Jan. 18   The U.S. Supreme Court finds the American Medical Association guilty of antitrust violations in attempting to block the activities of cooperative health groups.

Feb. 9   President Roosevelt declares that all American war plants must operate on a minimum 48-hour week.

Mar. 2-5   A huge Japanese naval force carrying troops and supplies to the east coast of New Guinea is attacked by U.S. and Australian planes. In the ensuing Battle of the Bismarck Sea, the Japanese lose 10 warships, 12 transports, and more than 100 aircraft; 15,000 Japanese troops are drowned.

Mar. 7   The War Manpower Commission drops the 4-H deferment, thus qualifying men 38 to 45 years of age for conscription.

April 8   President Roosevelt orders that all wages, salaries, and prices be frozen at present levels.

April 12   The War Manpower Commission announces that all able-bodied men from 18 to 38 not working for an essential war industry may be inducted by the end of the year.

May 1-2   President Roosevelt authorizes the Government to take over the anthracite coal mines of eastern Pennsylvania that have been closed down by 80,000 striking miners. The next day union leader John L. Lewis sends the miners back to work.

May 11-June 2   U.S. forces land on the Japanese-occupied Aleutian island of Attu and after three weeks of murderous fighting, culminated by a suicidal charge of 1,000 Japanese soldiers, retake the outpost.

May 19   Prime Minister Churchill, in an address to Congress, gives his assurance that, once the Germans are defeated in Europe, Britain will continue to pursue the Pacific operation alongside the United States to a victorious conclusion.

May 22   Admiral Emory S. Land announces that during the first 20 weeks of 1943 the United States has produced 700 ships, about as many as were produced in all of 1942.

May 27   President Roosevelt forbids racial discrimination in any industry working on Government war contracts.

June 4-8   Blacks and Mexican-Americans wearing "zoot" suits are attacked by white servicemen in Los Angeles. Rioting continues until military authorities declare the city off limits.

June 14   The U.S. Supreme Court, in a case involving the West Virginia school system, rules that it is unconstitutional to force school children to salute the flag.

June 25   The Smith-Connally Anti-Strike Act becomes law over President Roosevelt's veto, making it illegal for a union to strike any war industry and giving the Government the right to seize and operate such installations if necessary. Furthermore, unions must give at least a 30-day notice of any intended strike.

July 10-Aug. 17   Preceded by more than 4,000 U.S. paratroopers, the Allied forces invade Sicily, defeat the Italian army, and pursue the German support troops across the Strait of Messina to the Italian mainland.

July 19 U.S. planes bomb Rome, while Mussolini begs Hitler for help. [On July 25 Mussolini resigns and is interned; he is replaced by Marshal Pietro Badoglio as Premier.]

July 19 The "Big Inch," the world's longest pipeline, is dedicated. It carries oil from Texas to Pennsylvania.

Aug. 2 The War Manpower Commission announces that, as of Oct. 1, fathers may be inducted into the military.

Aug. 11-24 President Roosevelt and Prime Minister Churchill meet in Quebec City to discuss the Far Eastern theater of the war, and decide on Lord Louis Mountbatten to lead a military effort to recover Burma.

Aug. 15 American and Canadian forces land at Kiska in the Aleutians but find that the Japanese have abandoned the island. With all the Aleutians back in U.S. control, the threat to Alaska and the West Coast is greatly reduced.

Sept. 9-17 On Sept. 9, one day after the flight of King Victor Emanuel and Premier Badoglio from Rome, and six days after a British force crossed the Strait of Messina, a combined British-U.S. force under General Mark Clark lands at Salerno. After heavy fighting against an entrenched German force, it joins the British armies coming north from the toe of the Italian boot.

Oct. 16 Chicago's first subway train goes into operation.

A doctor examines a wounded soldier in Bougainville.

U.S. Marines hit the water as they leave their LST to take the beach at Cape Gloucester.

Oct. 19-30 U.S. Secretary of State Cordell Hull meets with British Foreign Secretary Anthony Eden and Soviet Foreign Minister Vyacheslav Molotov in Moscow to negotiate the broad principles governing cooperation during and after the war.

Nov. 9 The United Nations Relief and Rehabilitation Administration (UNRRA) is established by 44 nations meeting at Washington, D.C., to provide help for the victims of the war.

Nov. 22-26 Roosevelt, Churchill, and General Chiang Kai-shek meet in Cairo and pledge to fight for the "unconditional surrender" of Japan. It is decided that Japan will be deprived of all the territory it has acquired since 1894.

Nov. 23 After days of heavy fighting, U.S. marines capture Tarawa, a heavily fortified outpost in the Gilbert Islands, which was considered virtually invasion-proof by the Japanese military.

Nov. 28-Dec. 1 The "Big Three"—Roosevelt, Churchill, and Stalin—meet in Teheran, Iran, pledge mutual cooperation, and determine war aims, confirming the agreements reached by their foreign ministers in Moscow in late October.

Dec. 10 Testimony before the House Foreign Affairs Committee reveals that almost 600,000 victims of Nazi persecution have been allowed to enter the United States since 1933.

1944

Whatever national tension is produced by the conduct of the war is confined to the question of the inevitable "second front," that is, the when and where of the offensive against "fortress Europe" by the British-U.S. military. This is resolved before the year is half over, and the sweep to Paris and Brussels is followed with fascination. Equal satisfaction follows the offensive against Japan, including the recapture of Guam and reentry into the Philippines. The productive capacity of the United States is so immense and the money available for spending so abundant that a problem arises concerning ways to channel these forces within the war environment. Inflation appears, rationing is reduced, a G.I. Bill is passed. Somehow, also a Presidential election is held, and President Roosevelt is awarded his fourth term with less controversy than accompanied the seeking of his third. Yet fewer citizens vote, and the victor's share is reduced to 53.3 per cent.

Jan. 6   Ida M. Tarbell, 86, author and editor, dies in Bethel, Connecticut. One of her books, *The History of the Standard Oil Company,* published in 1904, led to investigation of that company by Federal authorities and indirectly to the Sherman Antitrust Act of 1911, which was intended to break up such monopolies.

Jan. 13   A budget just short of $100,000,000,000 for fiscal 1944-1945 is proposed to Congress by President Roosevelt.

Jan. 16   General Eisenhower sets up Supreme Headquarters, Allied Expeditionary Forces (SHAEF) in Britain to plan the proposed invasion of continental Europe.

Jan. 22-May 25   In an attempt to outflank the German defenses in southern Italy, U.S. forces land at Anzio. The Germans quickly surround 50,000 U.S. troops, who withstand a four-month siege of their beachhead, while British, Polish, and French troops try to break through from the vicinity of Cassino. The two Allied forces meet east of Anzio on May 25.

Jan. 31-Feb. 4   U.S. troops land on the Marshall Islands, capturing Roi, Namu, and Kwajalein. [By Feb. 22 all of the Marshalls are in U.S. hands.]

Feb. 29   The Office of Price Administration announces that the U.S. black market is doing business in excess of $1,000,000,000 annually.

Mar. 1   U.S. forces land on the Admiralty Islands, 250 miles northwest of New Guinea. [They secure the islands by mid-April.]

Mar. 1   The Army Air Force reaches a record strength of more than 2,400,000 personnel and almost 80,000 military planes.

April 22   U.S. forces attack Japanese-held New Guinea, capturing the airfields at Hollandia and cutting off 50,000 enemy troops stationed on the eastern half of the island.

May 3   *The Journal of the American Chemical Society* publishes an article revealing development of synthetic quinine, by Drs. Robert Woodward of Harvard and William Doering of Columbia. The article disclosed that there is now a substitute for treating malaria, a problem since the Japanese captured the sole source of natural quinine.

May 8   The first eye bank is established by 19 New York hospitals.

June 4   Nine months after Allied forces land on the Italian mainland, troops of the U.S. Fifth Army enter Rome.

June 6   Shortly after midnight thousands of British and U.S. paratroopers are dropped several miles inland from the Normandy beaches. D-Day is about to dawn. Tons of equipment and 150,000 troops have been gathered in southern England, turning the area into a huge military camp. Germany, too, has prepared for the expected invasion; some 500,000 troops guard 800 miles of coast in Holland, Belgium, and France, and reserves in the rear are set to move to the site of any Allied attack. Workers and soldiers have installed concrete fortifications, mined the waters, and devised obstacles to impede an invasion. During the early morning hours waves of Allied bombers attack rail lines, bridges, roads, in an attempt to cut off the invasion area from the rest of the German army, while Allied ships pound the shore fortifications. Near dawn the main invasion force, carried across the Channel by 5,300 vessels, begins to land on a 60-mile stretch of the Normandy coast. Before the day is out 70,000 Americans have landed on Utah and Omaha beaches, while 83,000 Allied troops have taken Gold, Juno, and Sword beaches to the east. Despite tremendous losses, the invaders cling to the beachheads and push the Germans back.

June 13   The United States and its allies are confronted with a new weapon as the Germans launch their first V-1 rocket against London. The

American troops march down the Champs Elysees
to celebrate the liberation of Paris.

U.S. soldiers wade ashore at Omaha on D Day.

General Douglas MacArthur strides ashore during
the landing on Leyte on Oct. 20, 1944.

American paratroops descend on the Kamiri Strip on Noemfoor Island.

jet-propelled device, dubbed the "buzz bomb," carries a ton of explosives and travels at 350 mph.

June 15-July 9   U.S. marines take Saipan in the Marianas against stubborn Japanese resistance, including the most massive *banzai* (suicide) charge of the war.

June 19-20   The Battle of the Philippine Sea results in a great victory for the Allies, who destroy over 200 Japanese planes, 3 aircraft carriers, and assorted other ships. American losses are slight.

June 22   President Roosevelt signs the Servicemen's Readjustment Act.

June 26-28   Republicans meet in Chicago and nominate Thomas E. Dewey, governor of New York, for President, and John W. Bricker, governor of Ohio, for Vice President.

July 1   Representatives of 44 countries meet for three weeks at Bretton Woods, New Hampshire, and establish the International Monetary Fund and the International Bank for Reconstruction and Development.

July 6   A fire during a performance of Ringling Brothers and Barnum and Bailey Circus at Hartford, Connecticut, kills 167 people and injures many more.

July 17   An ammunition ship at Port Chicago, California, explodes, killing 300 persons.

July 19-20   The Democrats hold their convention in Chicago and renominate Franklin D. Roosevelt for his fourth term as President and Senator Harry S. Truman of Missouri for Vice President.

July 21-Aug. 10   U.S. forces capture Guam at a cost of 1,484 marines and 591 infantrymen killed.

Aug. 1   The U.S. Army is called into Philadelphia to stop a strike in the public transit system. The cause of the strike is the promotion of blacks in compliance with Presidential orders.

Aug. 14   The War Production Board permits limited return to production for a number of specific consumer goods that have been unavailable except on the black market.

Aug. 15   A huge Allied force lands in southern France between Toulon and Cannes.

Aug. 16   In retaliation for Argentina's continued covert aid to the Nazi regime, President Roosevelt orders frozen all Argentine gold assets held in the United States.

Aug. 21-Oct. 9   Representatives of the United States, Great Britian, China, and the Soviet Union gather at Dumbarton Oaks in Washington, D.C., to make plans for an international organization to safeguard world peace. They suggest that the name of the organization, modeled after the League of Nations, be "The United Nations."

Aug. 25   Allied troops enter Paris, liberating the "city of light" after four years of German occupation.

Sept. 4   Brussels and Antwerp, Belgium, are freed from Nazi control.

Sept. 8   The first German V-2 rocket is fired at London. Traveling at supersonic speeds, the missile is impossible to detect or shoot down.

Sept. 11-16   President Roosevelt and Prime Minister Churchill meet in Quebec to continue planning for the defeat of Japan and Germany and to come to a decision on the conduct of postwar occupation.

Sept. 14   A hurricane hits the Northeast coast, killing over 400 persons and causing about $50,000,000 damage.

Oct. 4   Alfred E. Smith, 70, Democratic candidate for President in 1928, dies in New York City.

Oct. 20-Dec. 26   American troops land at Leyte in the Philippines, fulfilling General MacArthur's promise to "return."

Nov. 7   Franklin D. Roosevelt, in his fourth Presidential campaign victory, defeats Thomas E. Dewey, winning 432 electoral votes to 99 for Dewey. Harry S. Truman is the Vice President.

Nov. 24   The first massive bombing raid by B-29's on Japan from the Marianas, rather than from aircraft carriers, opens with an all-out attack on Tokyo.

Dec. 15   The rank of General of the Army is created by Congress to honor Generals Dwight D. Eisenhower, Douglas MacArthur, Henry (Hap) Arnold and George C. Marshall. The new rank is equivalent to that of marshal in other armies.

Dec. 16-26   U.S. forces in the Ardennes Forest of Belgium and Luxembourg are surprised by a fierce German counterattack led by General Karl Rudolf von Rundstedt. Prisoners of war are slaughtered by the Germans, and combined casualties rise to the hundreds of thousands in the winter battle, known as the Battle of the Bulge. Joint ground and air action halt the German offensive.

Dec. 17   The U.S. Army declares that, as of Jan. 2, 1945, Americans of Japanese ancestry will no longer be excluded from the West Coast.

Dec. 31   A railroad accident at Ogden, Utah, kills 48 persons.

The era of the rise and fall of fascism ends with the signing of documents at Reims, by the Germans, and at Tokyo Bay, by the Japanese. The victors confer at Yalta and Potsdam. In all this the United States plays a leading role, but its spokeman changes, for President Roosevelt, who has seen the country through depression and war, dies a few days before the new era spectacularly begins. President Truman is in charge at the opening of the epochal meeting in San Francisco, birthplace of the United Nations, and at the creation of the mushroom cloud over New Mexico, and over Hiroshima and Nagasaki in Japan. For most Americans, demobilization and an end of bloodshed and rationing are evidence that their way of life is vindicated and assured.

Jan. 1   The Federal Bureau of Investigation announces the arrest of two German spies landed in the United States by submarine. [On Feb. 19 they are sentenced to hang.]

Jan. 3   By a vote of 207 to 186, the House of Representatives puts its temporary Committee on Un-American Activities on a permanent basis.

Jan. 9   General MacArthur's troops land on Luzon, main island of the Philippines.

Jan. 15   To conserve needed coal, nationwide restrictions on the use of display lighting are ordered by the War Production Board.

Feb. 4-12   The Big Three—Roosevelt, Churchill, and Stalin—meet at Yalta in the Crimea to discuss the problems of the postwar world. Agreement is reached to form a future world peace-keeping organization, and to assist liberated nations and former Axis satellites to rebuild their economies and create democratic forms of government. The conferees also decide that Germany will be divided into four occupation zones and that it is necessary "to destroy German militarism and Nazism and to ensure that Germany will never again be able to disturb the peace of the world." All war criminals are to be brought to justice, and Germany is to be made to pay reparations for the destruction it has done. Other matters concern the settling of various territorial questions. In a secret agreement, the Soviet Union agrees to declare war on Japan within three months after the defeat of Germany, in return for a variety of concessions in the Far East.

Feb. 7   General MacArthur personally returns to Manila, a few days after its liberation from the Japanese.

Feb. 8-14   Recovering from their setback at the Bulge, the Allies begin their offensive against the German homeland, reaching the Rhine by Feb. 14.

Feb. 19-Mar. 14   Iwo Jima is taken by U.S. troops in one of the most desperate battles of the war. U.S. casualties exceed 20,000, but they are justified by the strategic importance of the island, which is only 750 miles from Tokyo and brings medium bombers within range of all Japan.

Mar. 3   The United States and 19 countries of the Western Hemisphere, after conferring at Mexico City, sign the Act of Chapultepec, promising to protect and respect each other's territory and political rights.

Mar. 7-25   A U.S. armored unit crosses the Rhine River at Remagen. Eighteen days later German combat west of the Rhine ends.

Mar. 21-24   In the most intensive air attack in history, more than 40,000 sorties are made by U.S. and British bombers over German cities in four days.

April 1-July 2   Okinawa in the Ryukyu Islands, 350 miles from Japan's main islands, is captured by U.S. forces. From here it is proposed to attack Japan in force.

April 12   President Roosevelt dies at Warm Springs, Georgia, at the age of 63. Harry S. Truman becomes President.

April 18   Ernie Pyle, 44, America's most popular war correspondent, is killed by a machine-gun bullet on a small island near Iwo Jima.

April 25   A. U.S. Army unit advancing eastward contacts a Soviet force approaching from the west at the Elbe River, dramatizing the collapse of the German defense.

April 25-June 26   Representatives of 50 nations meet at San Francisco to draft the Charter of the United Nations.

April 28-29   A report by an Allied military mission calls the Buchenwald concentration camp an "extermination facility." The next day U.S. forces capture the Dachau concentration camp, freeing 32,000 prisoners.

April 30   Sugar rations in the United States are cut an additional 25 per cent.

April 30   General Mark Clark announces: "The military power of Germany in Italy has

Prime Minister Winston Churchill, President Franklin D. Roosevelt and Premier Joseph Stalin at Yalta

The mushroom cloud formed by the detonation of the atom bomb over Nagasaki

Japanese surrender signatories arrive aboard the U.S.S. *Missouri.*

American servicemen in Paris hold up newspapers announcing the unconditional surrender of Japan.

practically ceased.''

May 4 Berchtesgaden, Hitler's mountain fortress in Bavaria, is taken by U.S. troops, four days after Hitler's suicide in Berlin.

May 4 The U.S. Department of War announces that as soon as Germany surrenders, 2,000,000 troops will be discharged from the Army and 6,000,000 will be sent to fight in the Pacific.

May 6 The U.S. Department of Agriculture estimates that about 1,000,000 tons of food per month must be sent to Europe to feed its population for the near future.

May 7 At a ceremony at General Eisenhower's headquarters in Reims, General Alfred Jodl signs Germany's unconditional surrender to the Allied forces.

May 10 A point system is established to determine which U.S. troops will be first to be demobilized. Points are based on length of service, combat record, and parenthood.

July 1 The first state agency to fight discrimination in employment on the basis of race, creed, color, or national origin is established by New York State.

July 9 Architect Frank Lloyd Wright displays his plans for a new museum in New York City in which the paintings will be exhibited along a many-tiered spiral ramp.

July 16 The theory of the atomic bomb is put to its first practical test by exploding the device atop a steel tower far from human habitation, at Alamogordo, New Mexico. The test is considered satisfactory.

July 17-Aug. 2 President Truman, Prime Minister Churchill followed by Clement Attlee, and Premier Stalin meet at Potsdam, near Berlin, to discuss the demilitarization and denazification of Germany. Terms of the impending occupation of Germany are negotiated, and an ultimatum demanding the unconditional surrender of Japan is prepared. Stalin learns of the atomic bomb test at Alamogordo. The first disagreement appears concerning the postwar borders of Poland.

July 28 The United Nations Charter is ratified by the U.S. Senate.

July 28 A B-25 crashes into the Empire State Building in New York City, striking the structure at the 79th floor.

Aug. 6-14 On Aug. 6 a B-29 flies over Hiroshima and releases an atomic bomb on the city five miles below. With a destructive capacity equal to 20,000 tons (20 kilotons) of TNT, the bomb levels about four square miles of the city, killing about 80,000 persons and injuring many

The U.S. flag is raised on Iwo Jima.

more. Three days later another bomb is dropped on Nagasaki, causing less destruction because the city is more spread out; and on Aug. 14 the Japanese Goverment decrees its surrender to the Allies and transmits the document through neutral embassies.

Aug. 18 Consumer production is given a boost as the War Production Board eliminates 210 production controls.

Sept. 2 General MacArthur and Admiral Nimitz receive the formal surrender of Japan aboard the battleship *Missouri* in Tokyo Bay.

Sept. 11-Oct. 2 Foreign ministers of the Allied nations meet in London to draw up peace treaties with the former Axis powers. Soviet demands for large concessions cause the negotiations to bog down.

Oct. 30 Rationing of shoes comes to an end.

November General George C. Marshall, resigning as chief of staff on Nov. 20, is sent by President Truman to China, on a mission to mediate between the Nationalists, led by Chiang Kai-shek, and the Communists, led by Mao Tsetung.

Dec. 19 President Truman calls upon Congress to unify the Armed Forces under a single chief of staff.

Dec. 21 General George S. Patton, 60, affectionately called ''Old Blood and Guts,'' dies of an automobile accident in Germany. He led U.S. armies in Morocco, Tunisia, Sicily, and Western Europe throughout the war, and was known equally for his courage and his abrasive temper.

1946

After four years of war the United States adapts itself to its first full year of peace. The expected return to an economic depression does not materialize. Unemployment is less than 4 per cent, and about half of those unemployed are former servicemen, each receiving around $20 a week unemployment insurance in the so-called "52-20 club." Annual income by July 1 hits $161,000,000,000, twice that of 1929. Americans go on an unprecedented spending spree, with a demand for consumer goods that far surpasses the capacity of industry, still in the process of reconverting from wartime production. Inflation is rampant. Unions, unable to strike during the war years, do so now on a massive scale: more than 4,500,000 workers engaged in 4,700 walkouts. Government pressure restricts the number of days lost, and pay raises average 18½ cents per hour.

Internationally, Americans realize that the United States can never again be isolationist. The country participates actively in the United Nations. Poverty and starvation in Europe and other parts of the world place a tremendous demand on American generosity. After years of hesitation the Senate finally decides to join the World Court, now a part of the United Nations. It quickly becomes apparent, however, that the cordial relations established with the Soviet Union after 1941 will not continue. Soviet demands make it impossible to reach a common peace agreement with Germany and Japan. The United States finds that it is waging "Cold War."

Jan. 3   President Truman asks that all Americans put pressure on Congress to hasten reconversion from a wartime to a peacetime economy.

Jan. 10   A radar beam from a U.S. Army laboratory at Belmar, New Jersey, is bounced off the moon, returning to earth in 2.4 seconds.

Jan. 12   The Committee for Economic Development announces that industrial reconversion is all but 10-per-cent complete, and the number of unemployed stands at 2,000,000 out of a total labor force of 54,000,000.

Jan. 15   President Truman announces that he will insist that the United States be made the sole trustee of the islands captured from the Japanese by American forces.

Jan. 21   The President, in his state-of-the-union message, asks for legislation to fight inflation, provide full employment, offer food subsidies, and extend his war powers. His proposed budget totals $35,860,000,000.

Jan. 21-Feb. 17   An industry-wide steel strike, involving 750,000 workers, ends with an 18½-cent hourly wage increase and a $5-per-ton increase in the price of steel.

Jan. 26   A jet aircraft, the P-80, sets a non-stop California-to-New York record of 4 hours 13 minutes, averaging 584 mph for the trip.

Mar. 5   In a speech at Westminster College in Fulton, Missouri, former Prime Minister Churchill describes the existence of an "iron curtain" across Europe from the Baltic to the Adriatic, the border of "freedom."

Mar. 11   The Famine Emergency Committee, set up by President Truman, requests that Americans cut down their consumption of wheat products by 40 per cent and fats by 20 per cent to provide more food for export to starving nations.

Mar. 13   Strikes at both General Motors and General Electric end with an 18½-cent hourly pay raise.

Mar. 25   The War Assets Administration (WAA) is set up by Executive order to dispose of surplus Government property.

April 1-May 29   A strike by 400,000 members of the United Mine Workers shuts down coal production. President Truman asserts that the strike is a threat to the national interest. On May 21 he orders the seizure of the mines. On May 29, however, an agreement is reached and the strikers go back to work.

April 22   Harlan F. Stone, 71, Chief Justice of the Supreme Court, dies in Washington, D.C.

April 30   Professor Ernest Orlando Lawrence announces that an atom smasher capable of accelerating electrons to an energy of 300,000,000 volts is being built at the University of California at Berkeley.

April 30   A war-crimes trial for 28 Japanese, including former Premier Hideki Tojo, gets under way in Tokyo.

May 4-5   A riot at Alcatraz prison in San Francisco Bay lasts two days. By the time it is quelled by U.S. marines, 5 persons are killed and 14 injured.

May 14   The Selective Service Act is continued until Sept. 1, but exempts fathers and 18- and 19-year-olds.

May 17-28 President Truman orders the seizure of the railroads when the railway unions refuse to cancel a strike set for May 18. The unions agree to postpone the strike for five days. On May 28 a settlement is reached that gives workers an 18½-cent hourly raise.

May 25 President Truman asks Congress for strong measures to stop strikes in any industry crucial to the national interest. [The House votes, 306 to 13, for such a bill, but it fails in the Senate.]

June 6 Frederick M. Vinson, Secretary of the Treasury, is appointed to the U.S. Supreme Court as Chief Justice.

June 14 Bernard Baruch, U.S. representative in the United Nations, tells the U.N. Atomic Energy Commission that the U.S. would favor an international inspection system to monitor the production of atom bombs.

July 1 A 20-kiloton atom bomb is dropped in a test near the Bikini Atoll in the Pacific, using 73 surplus ships as targets. [On July 25 an underwater bomb is tested in the same area.]

July 4 In a ceremony at Manila, the Philippine Islands is given its full independence from the United States.

July 7 Mother Frances Xavier Cabrini becomes the first U.S. citizen to achieve sainthood. She founded the Missionary Sisters of the Sacred Heart, and was dedicated especially to con-

Police attempt to restrain workers during the Bethlehem Steel strike in Alameda, California.

demned prisoners.

July 27 Author Gertrude Stein, 72, dies in Paris.

Aug. 1 The Atomic Energy Commission, a civilian agency, is given authority by Congress to administer the production and uses of nuclear energy.

Aug. 2 The U.S. Senate accepts the jurisdiction of the World Court, the judicial arm of the United Nations, within limits determined by the United States.

Aug. 8 President Truman signs a bill providing $2,431,708,000 for terminal-leave pay for servicemen.

Nov. 5 In the midterm elections, Republicans make impressive gains, capturing control of both the House and the Senate.

Nov. 20-23 Coal miners again go out on strike, a second time this year. John L. Lewis is fined $10,000 and the United Mine Workers, $3,500,000 for contempt of court in disobeying a no-strike order. Three days later Lewis asks the miners to go back to work.

Dec. 2 The United States and Great Britain agree to merge the economies of their respective German occupation zones, effective Jan. 1, 1947.

Dec. 7 A fire at the Winecoff Hotel in Atlanta, Georgia, kills 119.

Dec. 25 Comedian W. C. Fields, 66, dies in Pasadena, California.

The Texas City explosion, April 16, 1947

1947 **The United States becomes firmly committed to its role** as a superpower. President Truman asks Congress for an appropriation to supply Greece and Turkey with military and economic assistance, on the grounds that "it must be the policy of the United States to support free peoples who are resisting attempted subjugation by armed minorities or by outside pressure" wherever such conditions exist. In plainer language, under the Truman Doctrine the United States must attempt to contain the spread of Communism.

Secretary of State George C. Marshall, speaking at Harvard University, adds an important refinement to the Truman Doctrine. Realizing that political stability and world peace require a speedy "return of normal economic health," the Marshall Plan proposes a massive non-military aid program to assist Europeans to rebuild their countries and their economies, providing that the Europeans take it upon themselves to plan and implement such a recovery program. In response 16 nations meet in Paris and set goals for food and industrial production, power output, and transportation over the coming four years. They submit a request for $22,000,000,000 from the United States to help meet these goals.

Jan. 10 In President Truman's annual budget to Congress, expenses are pegged at just over $37,000,000,000 and revenues somewhat higher. This attempt at balancing the budget results in a slight reduction of the national debt.

Jan. 17 The Federal Reserve Board reduces the margin requirement for the purchase of common stock from 100 per cent to 75 per cent.

Feb. 10 The U.S. Supreme Court rules that it is not unconstitutional for parochial school children to be transported by the public school system.

Feb. 10 Peace treaties are signed in Paris between the Allied nations and five of the Axis powers: Bulgaria, Rumania, Hungary, Italy, and Finland. In the case of the treaty with Finland, the United States is not a signatory, not having been at war with that country.

Feb. 17 The Voice of America begins broadcasting to persons in Soviet-dominated areas.

Mar. 10 Foreign ministers of Great Britain, France, the Soviet Union, and the United States meet in Moscow in another unsuccessful attempt to agree on a peace treaty with Germany. Among the many areas of disagreement is the demand by the Soviet Union for $10,000,000,000 reparations.

Mar. 12 President Truman formulates his doctrine of providing aid to non-Communist nations that seek assistance against Communist aggression.

Mar. 14 The Philippines gives the United States 99-year leases on several military and naval bases.

Mar. 16 President Truman's daughter, Margaret, debuts as a singer with the Detroit Symphony Orchestra.

Mar. 22 President Truman announces a program to check the "loyalty" of all U.S. Government workers.

Mar. 31 Congress terminates the peacetime draft into the armed forces.

April 2 The U.N. Security Council approves a plan to grant the United States sole trusteeship over all islands that were held by Japan under a League of Nations mandate.

April 9-10 A series of eight tornadoes in Texas, Oklahoma, and Kansas kills 167 persons and causes more than $10,000,000 property damage.

April 11 Jackie Robinson becomes the first black man to sign with a major-league baseball team, the Brooklyn Dodgers.

April 16 A ship explosion at Texas City, Texas, kills more than 500 persons and destroys most of the city.

April 19 The U.S. Supreme Court rules that a newspaper may not be held in contempt of court for criticizing a judge.

April 24 Novelist Willa Cather, 71, dies in New York City. Her works celebrate the pioneer spirit of the Great Plains, the Southwest, and French Canada.

June 5 George C. Marshall proposes a plan to assist European economic recovery, partly for humanitarian reasons, partly out of enlightened self-interest.

June 11 The rationing of household sugar ends, the last consumer-rationing program to go.

June 14 Pan American Airways begins the first round-the-world air route.

June 23 Congress overrides President Truman's veto of the Labor Management (Taft-Hartley) Act, which is designed to curb alleged excesses practiced by unions since the passage of the Wagner Act of 1935. Passage of the act ends the closed shop (which has required the hiring of nonunion workers) and provides for a 60-day moratorium before a strike may be called against industries engaged in interstate commerce. Union finances must be made public, unions are forbidden from giving to political campaigns, Communists are forbidden to hold union offices, and jurisdictional strikes are outlawed.

July 5 President Truman announces that during the fiscal year 1946-1947 the United States sent more than 18,000,000 tons of food to the starving throughout the world. He promises to continue the program.

July 18 The Presidential Succession Act becomes law. It interposes the Speaker of the House and then the President pro tem of the Senate in the line of succession to the Presidency, after the Vice President but before the Cabinet members in the previous order of succession.

July 26 After passing both Houses of Congress by a unanimous vote, a measure allowing veterans to cash their terminal-leave bonds is signed by President Truman.

Sept. 17 Anthropologist Ruth Benedict, 61, dies in New York City. *Patterns of Culture,* her best remembered work, has been translated into more than a dozen foreign languages.

Sept. 18 The U.S. Air Force is established as an independent service with status equal to that of the Army and Navy, and all three are

Stalled vehicles on 98th Street between Park and Madison Avenues, following the worst snow storm in New York City's history

Jackie Robinson signs autographs for young fans on his second day as a member of the Brooklyn Dodgers baseball team.

combined to form the National Military Establishment.

Sept. 20 Fiorello La Guardia, 64, former three-term mayor of New York City, dies there.

Oct. 5 President Truman asks Americans to observe meatless Tuesdays and poultryless Thursdays in an effort to provide food for the starving of Europe.

Oct. 14 The rocket-powered research plane XS-1, piloted by Captain Charles E. Yeager, diving from a B-29, breaks the sound barrier at a speed of 650 mph for the first time during a test flight at Muroc [Edwards AFB], California.

Oct. 30 The United States participates in the General Agreement on Tariffs and Trade (GATT) in Geneva, resulting in some tariff reductions but generally leaving the country with a fairly strong import barrier.

Dec. 23 The United States announces it is giving up all military bases in Panama outside the Canal Zone, after the Panama assembly refused to extend a lease on these bases.

Dec. 26-27 About 80 persons die as a result of a huge snowstorm that hits the Northeast. A record 25.8 inches falls on New York City within 20 hours.

Dec. 30 Philosopher Alfred North Whitehead, 86, dies in Cambridge, Massachusetts. He was the author, with Bertrand Russell, of *Principia Mathematica,* a three-volume work on mathematics and logic.

1948

The United States is back to business as usual as the nation prepares for its first election in 16 years that does not have Franklin Roosevelt as a candidate. With Republicans in charge of the 80th Congress, it appears likely to be a Republican year. The convention in Philadelphia nominates Thomas E. Dewey for President on the third ballot and Earl Warren, governor of California, for Vice President. Three weeks later, at the same hall in Philadelphia, President Truman easily wins the Democratic nomination, despite severe doubts about his ability to win in November. A number of conservative Democrats, angered by Truman's stand on civil rights, form a new party, the Dixiecrats, and nominate Governor Strom Thurmond of South Carolina. Another new party, the Progressive, formed by radicals, former Communists, and non-party liberals, nominates Henry Wallace for President.

The public opinion polls until Election Day point to a Dewey victory. It is reasoned that the minor parties will take votes from Truman. Dewey avoids issues and promises honest, capable government. He says that only the Republicans can unify the country and insure world peace. Truman, on the other hand, lambastes the 80th Congress for failure to take measures that he has proposed to stem inflation and help the farmers. He attacks the Taft-Hartley Bill and speaks in favor of civil rights legislation. The Chicago *Tribune* is so certain of a Dewey victory that it prints its post-election news story accordingly. But when the votes are counted, Harry S. Truman is returned to the White House, this time as an elected Chief Executive. Thurmond and Wallace between them secure less than 5 per cent of the vote. Dewey receives 45 per cent. Truman is technically a minority President, by a fraction of a percentage point. But his popular vote exceeds Dewey's by a respectable 2,000,000.

January   President Truman, in his budget to Congress, sets expenditures at $39,670,000,000, a sizable $4,000,000,000 less than expected revenues.

Jan. 12   Oklahoma must provide equal educational facilities for the study of law to black and white students, according to a decision of the U.S. Supreme Court.

Jan. 30   Orville Wright, 76, dies in Dayton, Ohio. He survived his brother, Wilbur, by 36 years, during which the airplane developed from the first biplane to the supersonic experimental and the jet aircraft.

Feb. 2   President Truman asks Congress to pass civil rights legislation that would include abolition of the poll tax, an antilynching measure, and the creation of a commission to study job discrimination.

Mar. 8   The U.S. Supreme Court rules that the use of "released time" as a means whereby public school children, with parental consent, receive religious instruction during school hours and in school buildings is a violation of the separation of Church and State.

Mar. 15-April 12   Coal miners strike over the issue of an old-age pension plan to be paid for by management, and win their demands.

April 2   The Tax Reduction Bill is passed by Congress over President Truman's veto. It provides for a reduction of 10 to 30 per cent in tax rates and an increase to $600 in the personal exemption for taxpayer and each dependent.

April 3   President Truman signs the Economic Cooperation Act, providing $5,600,000,000 for 16 countries participating in the Marshall Plan during the next 15 months. Additional money is also appropriated for military and economic aid to Greece, Turkey, and China.

April 30   Representatives from 21 Western Hemisphere nations sign a charter establishing the Organization of American States (O.A.S.) in Bogotá, Colombia. The Charter proclaims the equality of all members and outlaws the intervention of one state into the internal affairs of another. Members are also pledged to resist outside aggression and to work cooperatively towards social and economic well being.

May 10   The first sliding-wage contract is signed by General Motors and the United Auto Workers, providing for cost-of-living increases.

May 31-June 7   A conference in London of representatives of the United States, Great Britain, France, and the Benelux countries agrees to set up a West German state composed of the British, American, and French zones, under three-power military occupation.

June 3   A telescope with a 200-inch reflector, the largest in the world, is dedicated at Mount Palomar Observatory in California.

June 21-25 Thomas Dewey and Earl Warren are nominated for President and Vice President respectively at the Republican convention in Philadelphia.

June 21-26 The Soviet Union initiates the land and water blockade of Berlin to demonstrate their disapproval of the proposed West German state. Their first move is to halt rail traffic from Berlin to Helmstedt. On June 26 Operation Vittles, an airlift by the U.S. and British air forces, swings into high gear to supply the city with food, coal, and other goods. [By May 1949 the blockade is broken.]

June 24 The Selective Service System is restored in a bill signed by President Truman. All men 18 to 25 years of age must register and, at age 19, may be called to serve for up to 21 months. A peacetime force of just over 2,000,000 is authorized.

June 25 A measure is signed by President Truman which permits immigration into the United States of increased numbers of displaced persons.

July 12-14 The Democrats, in convention in Philadelphia, nominate Harry S. Truman and Alben W. Barkley for President and Vice President respectively.

July 17 Anti-Truman Democrats hold a convention in Birmingham, Alabama, to form the States Rights Party. They nominate Governor Strom Thurmond of South Carolina for the Presidency, and Fielding Wright as the Vice-Presidential candidate.

July 24-27 The newly formed Progressive Party convenes in Philadelphia and names former Vice President Henry Wallace as its Presidential

President Truman holds up the Chicago *Daily Tribune* which announces his defeat by Dewey.

candidate. Glenn Taylor, a Senator from Idaho, is selected as his running mate.

Aug. 4 A five-day filibuster by Southern Senators kills the chance to pass a bill abolishing the poll tax.

Aug. 16 Baseball superstar Babe Ruth, 53, dies in New York City.

Aug. 27 Former Chief Justice of the Supreme Court Charles Evans Hughes, 86, dies at Cape Cod, Massachusetts.

Oct. 1 The U.S. Supreme Court rules unconstitutional a California law that makes miscegenation a crime.

Nov. 2 Harry S. Truman is elected President in his own right by winning 304 electoral votes to 189 for Thomas E. Dewey.

Nov. 10-27 Longshoremen in New York stage a wildcat strike to protest an inadequate wage settlement. The strike, which quickly spreads to other Atlantic ports, ends as a result of efforts by the Federal Mediation and Conciliation Service.

Dec. 16 A commission headed by former President Herbert Hoover reports that, since unification of the armed services under the National Military Establishment in 1947, waste and inefficiency have been reduced, but there is still room for considerable improvement.

Dec. 20 The U.S. Supreme Court rules that it lacks jurisdiction to review the death sentences imposed by an international tribunal in Tokyo on Nov. 12 against former Prime Minister Hideki Tojo and six other Japanese war criminals.

Dec. 29 Secretary of Defense James T. Forrestal announces that the United States is engaged in an "earth satellite vehicle program."

Hideki Tojo (front row center), wartime Prime Minister of Japan, and other defendants at the war crime trials in Tokyo

1949 President Truman's program for a "Fair Deal," as proposed during his campaign, runs into roadblocks in a three-party Congress. While the Democrats have a majority in both the House and Senate, many Southern Democrats find their sympathies more closely aligned with those of the Dixiecrats or Republicans than with the liberal Northern Democrats, especially on civil rights and social issues. An attempt by Administration forces to curtail the use of the Senate filibuster fails in the face of opposition by Dixiecrats and Republicans. Truman's promise to organized labor to modify the Taft-Hartley Act twice meets defeat on the floor of the House, destroyed by the Dixiecrat-Republican coalition with the help of many conservative Democrats. An important bill providing for slum clearance and public housing is enacted, but most of Truman's major reforms are rejected.

The economy weakens early in the year as prices drop rapidly; by the end of February the average household food basket costs some 20 per cent less than a year earlier. Unemployment, however, grows steadily, and with 4,000,000 out of work by summer, critics contend that the country is entering a "Truman recession." Administration economists claim that the trend is a temporary and natural reaction from the overly rapid growth of the past two years. At midyear Truman resumes deficit spending to stem the decline, and by the last quarter the economy appears to be improving.

Jan. 10   In his budget message, President Truman calls for expenditures of $41,858,000,000, of which more than one third is earmarked for military spending.

Jan. 19   Truman signs a bill raising the annual Presidential and Vice-Presidential salaries to $100,000 and $30,000 respectively.

Jan. 20   Harry S. Truman is sworn in as the 33d President of the United States. In his inaugural address Truman makes a major foreign policy statement, accusing the Communists of trying to prevent "world recovery and lasting peace." The speech outlines four points of action, including continued use of the Marshall Plan and further negotiations to establish an Atlantic defense pact. The President puts greatest stress, however, on a proposal to provide technical and scientific assistance to the underdeveloped nations of the world. [This fourth point becomes known as the Point Four Program. From it develops most of the "foreign aid" operations in the form of grants or loans to underdeveloped countries.]

Feb. 2   Responding to a suggestion by Soviet Premier Joseph Stalin that he and Truman hold peace talks somewhere in Eastern Europe, the President rejects a two-power meeting and insists that such talks must include the allies of the United States.

Feb. 8   An unofficial record is set by a six-engine XB-47 which crosses the country from Moses Lake, Washington, to Andrew Air Force Base, Maryland, in 3 hours 46 minutes, with an average speed of 607.2 mph.

Feb. 9   Film star Robert Mitchum is sentenced to 60 days in jail for participating in a marijuana party.

Feb. 19   The Bollingen prize for poetry is awarded to Ezra Pound, who has been confined to a mental hospital since he was judged mentally unfit to stand trial for treason in 1946.

Feb. 24   An altitude record is set for rockets by a WAC Corporal (boosted by a small A-4) which reaches 250 miles above its launching site of White Sands, New Mexico. [The record is not broken until 1956.]

Feb. 25   Reflecting the lower cost of living, an automatic salary cut is taken by workers at General Motors; at the same time the prices of the automobiles they make are reduced.

Mar. 2   The Lady Luck II, a Boeing B-50, piloted by Captain James Gallagher, returns to Carswell Air Force Base, Fort Worth, from which it took off on Feb. 26. This is the first nonstop air circumnavigation of the world, covering 23,452 miles in 94 hours 1 minute.

Mar. 21   Samuel S. McClure, 92, founder of the influential *McClure's Magazine* and the McClure Syndicate, the first newspaper syndicate in the country, dies in New York City.

April 4   Twelve nations, including the United States, sign a pact in Washington, D.C., to establish the North Atlantic Treaty Organization (NATO). [The Treaty is ratified by the U.S. Senate on July 21.] The key purpose of the organization is the mutual defense of all signatories: "An armed attack against one or more . . . shall be considered an attack against them all."

April 14   After 17 months, the so-called "Wilhelmstrasse" trial comes to an end with the conviction of 19 of 21 former Nazi officials. Sentences range from 4 to 25 years. U.S. war crimes tribunals in Europe have now tried 1,873 persons, with 1,569 convictions. The death sentence has been imposed in 459 of these cases.

April 20   Edward C. Kendall of the Mayo Foundation announces the discovery of a chemical he calls cortisone, which appears to be useful in the treatment of rheumatoid arthritis. The chemical is secreted in small quantities by the adrenal gland, but can also be produced in the laboratory.

May 12   Americans rejoice, and Cold War tensions are briefly reduced, as the Soviet Union ends its blockade of the ground and water routes to West Berlin. [The U.S.-British airlift ends July 8, by which time more than 1,500,000 tons of cargo has been transported into the city by plane.]

May 31-July 8   Alger Hiss, a former State Department official, is tried for perjury in a Federal court in New York City. The trial ends with a hung jury.

June 22   Ezzard Charles defeats Joe Walcott in a boxing match in the 15th round in Chicago. The National Boxing Association names Charles world champion because of the retirement of Joe Louis on Mar. 1.

Aug. 9   Psychologist Edward L. Thorndike, 74, dies at Montrose, New York. He is best known for his work in experimental and educational psychology.

Aug. 10   The National Military Establishment—the Departments of the Army, the Navy, and the Air Force—is renamed the Department of Defense.

Aug. 16   A deep-sea record is established as Otis Barton descends 4,500 feet into the Pacific Ocean in a benthoscope.

Aug. 19   The Federal Communications Commission bans the popular giveaway prize shows on radio.

Sept. 7   The Bureau of Reclamation begins construction of the Hungry Horse dam on the South Fork of the Flathead River in Montana. [When completed in 1953 it is the fourth highest dam in the world, 564 feet.]

Sept. 23   Truman announces that the Soviet Union has developed and tested an atomic bomb three years ahead of the time predicted by U.S. scientists.

Oct. 1-Nov. 11   A steel strike shuts down the nation's steel mills in a dispute over who should

The remains of the Eastern airliner after colliding with a P38 fighter plane near Washington's National airport

pay the costs of pensions. Bethlehem Steel Company, the first to settle, agrees to pay $100 monthly to workers at age 65 who have put in 25 years service.

Oct. 26   The minimum wage under the Fair Labor Standards Act is raised from 40 cents to 75 cents per hour.

Nov. 1   A P-38 fighter plane collides with an Eastern Airlines DC-4 near Washington, D.C., killing 55 persons. The crash is the worst in domestic civil aviation.

Nov. 3   Dr. William F. Giauque of the University of California, a specialist in the research of substances at low temperatures, wins the Nobel Prize for chemistry. Dr. Hideki Yukawa, visiting professor at Columbia University, wins the prize for physics for his work in the field of elementary particles.

Nov. 7   General Motors announces a record profit of $500,000,000 for the first nine months of the year.

Dec. 1   After months of strife in the coal industry, John L. Lewis tells the 480,000 members of the United Mine Workers to work only three days per week until new agreements are reached with the mine operators.

1950 The growing tension between the two great political systems of the world finally erupts into open hostility this summer. Although the fighting remains restricted to Korea, Americans are disillusioned about the possibility of detente between the Communist and non-Communist worlds. The existence of the atomic bomb on both sides of the Iron Curtain and dire scientific warnings of the widespread danger of radioactive fallout add to the fear that the country may soon be involved in a far more deadly world war than the one recently ended.

Anti-Communist sentiment increases rapidly. A new Federal law requires all Communists and members of organizations dominated by Communists ("fellow travelers") to register with the Government. A restrictive immigration law makes it virtually impossible for anyone suspected of being associated with a totalitarian regime to enter the country. Led by Senator Joseph McCarthy of Wisconsin, virulent anti-Communists accuse the Government, especially the Department of State, of being "riddled" with Communists and Communist sympathizers who take their orders from the "enemy" in Moscow. A committee set up by the Senate and chaired by Senator Millard Tydings of Maryland finds no evidence to support these charges, but the public, influenced by rumors and reports, tends to believe the worst. Many members of Congress are voted out of office in November for insufficient anti-Communist vigor.

The 1950 decennial census shows that the rate of population growth in 1940-1950 was 14.5 per cent, double that of the preceding decade. The United States now has 150,325,798 inhabitants, three fifths of whom live in urban areas. It is worth noting that California is now the second most populous state, outranking Pennsylvania, Illinois, and Ohio during the past decade.

Jan. 2   A report by the U.S. Department of Commerce shows that for the period from July 1, 1945, to Sept. 30, 1949, the United States spent almost $25,000,000,000 in foreign aid—an annual average of $6,000,000,000.

Jan. 9   In President Truman's budget message for the coming fiscal year, almost one third of the requested $42,400,000,000 for expenditures is again allotted for military spending and $4,700,000,000 is sought for foreign aid

Jan. 15   General of the Air Force Henry H. (Hap) Arnold, 63, who learned to fly from the Wright Brothers and achieved five-star rank in 1944, dies in Sonoma, California.

Jan. 17   Masked gunmen take $2,775,000 from the Brink's garage in Boston, over $1,200,000 of which is in cash.

Jan. 21   Alger Hiss is found guilty by a Federal jury at his second perjury trial. He was accused of lying about his role in passing confidential documents to Whittaker Chambers. Hiss is sentenced to five years in prison.

Feb. 9   At a speaking engagement at Wheeling, West Virginia, Senator Joseph McCarthy announces that he has the names of 205 persons working in the Department of State who are members of the Communist Party. [The majority of a Senate committee investigating these charges brings in a report that they are a hoax.]

Feb. 20   The U.S. Supreme Court rules, 5 to 3, that when police make an arrest they do not need a warrant to search a limited area under the suspect's control.

Feb. 27   A pact signed by the United States and Canada provides for increased utilization of Niagara Falls to produce electricity and for steps to protect the Falls.

Mar. 7   Judith Coplon, accused of passing secret documents to a Soviet spy, is found guilty of conspiracy to commit espionage. [Her conviction is later overturned because evidence was gathered illegally.]

Mar. 17   Scientists at the University of California, Berkeley, announce that they have synthesized a new element, which they name californium.

Mar. 19   Edgar Rice Burroughs, 74, author of the Tarzan series, dies in Los Angeles.

April 1   Dr. Charles Richard Drew, 45, originator of a method to store large amounts of blood plasma in "blood banks," dies as a result of a car accident in North Carolina. In need of blood, he is denied admission to a white-only hospital.

April 10   The U.S. Supreme Court refuses to review contempt convictions against two film writers, thereby upholding the right of Congressional committees to force witnesses to reveal if they are Communists.

April 19 Truman signs an $88,510,000 bill designed to provide economic assistance to the Navajo and Hopi Indians over the next 10 years.

May 8 Secretary of State Dean Acheson announces in Paris that the United States will supply military aid to France, Vietnam, Laos, and Cambodia to assist in the fight against insurgents in French Indochina. It is alleged that the rebels are Communists.

June 5 The U.S. Supreme Court rules that segregation of blacks and whites in railroad dining cars violates the Interstate Commerce Act.

June 24 A Northwest Airlines DC-4 plane explodes and crashes into Lake Michigan, killing 58 persons in the worst civil air disaster in the United States to date.

June 25-30 North Korean forces cross the 38th parallel launching a huge attack against South Korea. On June 27 the United Nations Security Council votes to call upon U.N. members to provide military support to South Korea. Truman, without consulting Congress, authorizes the use of U.S. ground troops and the launching of air attacks against North Korean targets. A naval blockade of the Korean coast is also ordered.

July 13 The Ute Indians are awarded $31,700,000 as compensation for tribal lands taken from them in Colorado and Utah from 1891 to 1938.

July 19 Truman calls for a partial mobilization and asks Congress for $10,000,000,000 for rearmament.

Aug. 1 The island of Guam, an important U.S. military base in the Pacific, is granted civil rule under the administration of the Department of Interior.

Sept. 1 Congress passes the Defense Production Act, giving the President authority to control wages and prices. The measure also provides for the rationing of goods and allocations of scarce materials.

Sept. 15-Oct. 1 After two months of retreat into a tiny corner of South Korea, U.N. forces, under the command of General Douglas MacArthur, launch a massive counterattack. U.S. marines land at Inchon on the eastern coast, while South Koreans land in the west and U.N. troops in the southeastern pocket move against the overextended North Korean lines. Seoul, the capital, in North Korean hands since July 1, is recaptured by Sept. 26 and by Oct. 1 the North Koreans have withdrawn across the 38th parallel.

Sept. 23 The McCarran Internal Security Act becomes law over the President's veto. The measure requires that all members of the Communist Party register with the Justice Department and that all designated Communist-front organizations disclose their finances and membership.

Sept. 27 Ezzard Charles defeats former champion Joe Louis in a 15-round match in New York, thereby confirming his claim to the championship. The match results from the fact that Louis decides to come out of retirement.

Oct. 7-Dec. 31 Despite threats by the Communist Chinese that they will not tolerate American troops north of the 38th parallel, MacArthur sends his forces into North Korea. Truman, reluctant to press too far into North Korea, is persuaded by MacArthur at a meeting on Wake Island on Oct. 15 to allow the general to press on towards the Yalu River, the boundary between North Korea and China. On Nov. 25, with U.N. troops in control of almost all of North Korea, the Chinese launch a massive invasion with over 250,000 men. By the end of December MacArthur's forces have been driven south of the 38th parallel.

Oct. 23 Entertainer Al Jolson, 54, dies in San Francisco. Just before his death he visited Korea to entertain U.S. troops.

Nov. 1 Two Puerto Rican nationalists attempt to assassinate President Truman at Blair House, the President's temporary residence. One assassin is killed, the other captured; the President is not harmed.

Nov. 3 The U.N. General Assembly votes, 52 to 5, to approve a plan submitted by the United States allowing the General Assembly to deal with military aggression should a veto prevent the Security Council from acting.

Nov. 7 Although they do not win control of Congress, Republicans make large gains in the midterm election. They win 30 seats in the House and 5 in the Senate.

Nov. 8 Two jet planes meet for the first time in aerial combat, when a North Korean MiG-15 is shot down by a U.S. Air Force F-80 piloted by Lieutenant Russell J. Brown.

Nov. 29 The National Council of the Churches of Christ is formed, combining 29 churches with a membership of about 32,000,000.

Dec. 16 Truman proclaims a state of national emergency.

Dec. 18 General Dwight D. Eisenhower is appointed Supreme Commander for the Allied Powers, Europe (SACEUR), the military arm of NATO.

1951 U.S. forces in Korea slowly recover from the Communist Chinese onslaught and by the end of March most of Korea south of the 38th parallel is recaptured. But when General Douglas MacArthur announces that the solution to the Korean conflict is to attack Communist China, President Truman, who believes that such a course would lead to war with both China and Russia, relieves MacArthur of his command. MacArthur returns to a hero's welcome, but other military leaders side with the President. Nevertheless, the widespread popular support which President Truman enjoyed a year earlier as the war began is gone for good. As the year continues increasing polarization becomes apparent and a sense of frustration and disappointment sets in. The brief glimmer of hope in July as truce talks begin is gone by December as the negotiations appear to be unproductive.

At home evidence of widespread corruption in the Bureau of Internal Revenue and the Reconstruction Finance Corporation come to light. But the prevailing malaise is occasioned by the fortunes or misfortunes of war and such related phenomena as scarcity of consumer goods and rising prices.

Jan. 6   The Department of State announces that the United States has signed a military aid agreement with Portugal.

Jan. 15   The U.S. Supreme Court rules that a New York City ordinance requiring a police permit for street preachers violates the First Amendment guarantee of freedom of speech and religion.

Jan. 15   President Truman's budget calls for expenditures of $71,594,000,000, of which $41,421,000,000—an amount comparable to last year's total budget—would be allotted to military expenses; the increase is caused by the Korean war. [On April 30 the President submits a budget calling for defense expenditures of $60,679,000,000. On Oct. 12, Congress sets the defense appropriation at just under $57,000,000,000 for the 1951-1952 fiscal year.]

Jan 26   The Economic Stabilization Administration orders a freeze on most wages at the current level and a ceiling on prices of services and commodities based on the period of the last five weeks. [The order is subsequently modified several times to permit a variety of increases.]

Jan. 27-Feb. 6   The Atomic Energy Commission (AEC) sets off a series of five atomic explosions at an Air Force bombing range 45 miles north of Las Vegas, Nevada. Shock waves are felt in Las Vegas and flashes can be seen as far away as San Francisco, 425 air miles distant. The AEC claims that there is no danger from radiation to nearby residents.

Feb. 1   The Senate Banking and Currency subcommittee, headed by Senator J. William Fulbright of Arkansas, begins an investigation into alleged questionable loans made to favored individuals by the Reconstruction Finance Corporation (RFC). [On April 17, the President appoints W. Stuart Symington to head the RFC, with instructions to straighten out the agency.]

Feb. 22   The Atomic Energy Commission and the Air Force announce plans to design an atomic-powered airplane. It is estimated that such a craft will be able to fly around the world 80 times on one pound of atomic fuel.

Feb. 26   The 22d Ammendment to the Constitution becomes effective, prohibiting any President (after the present incumbent) from holding office for more than two terms. If a President serves more than two years of a term to which he was not elected, he may be elected to one full term only.

April 4   The U.S. Senate completes months of debate on the issue of European security with a resolution approving the President's use of ground forces to defend Western Europe.

April 5   Ethel and Julius Rosenberg are sentenced to death in Federal court after having been convicted of conspiring to steal atomic secrets. Accomplice Morton Sobell is given 30 years in prison.

April 11   General MacArthur, who differs with the Commander in Chief on the conduct of the war in Korea, is relieved of his command by Truman and replaced by General Matthew B. Ridgeway.

April 19   MacArthur, addressing a joint session of Congress, reiterates the view that caused his dismissal—that the United States should extend the war into China.

April 25   Truman signs the Servicemen's Indemnity Act, which provides a payment of

**U.S. infantrymen in Korea observe the
Communist-held area (background).**

$10,000 to the survivors of any serviceman who dies or has died on or after June 27, 1950.

April 28   Truman announces that Federal employees may be dismissed and applicants denied employment if there is "reasonable doubt" as to their loyalty.

May 11   Benefits available to World War II veterans are extended to cover those serving in the armed forces since the outbreak of the Korean conflict.

June 4   The U.S. Supreme Court upholds the constitutionality of the 1940 Smith Act, which makes it illegal to advocate or to conspire to advocate the violent overthrow of the U.S. Government. Justices Hugo L. Black and William O. Douglas dissent. The decision is made in upholding the conviction of leaders of the U.S. Communist Party, who were indicted in 1948 for conspiring to advocate seditious acts.

June 15   Truman signs the India Emergency Food Aid Act, which authorizes a loan of $190,000,000 to famine-stricken India for the purchase of food from the United States.

June 19   Selective Service is extended to July 1, 1955, and the minimum induction age is lowered from 19 to 18 years 6 months. All males must register at age 18 and the length of service is extended from 21 to 24 months.

June 23-Dec. 31   When Soviet delegate to the United Nations Jacob Malik suggests a truce in Korea, both sides respond favorably. Talks begin at Kaesong on July 10. Negotiations break down but are resumed again on Oct. 25 at Panmunjom. A tentative truce line for eastern Korea is agreed upon on Nov. 27. As the year ends, however, the talks are stalemated over the issue

of prisoner exchange. [Truce talks continue at Panmunjom during the period of active hostilities until an armistice is agreed on in 1953.]

July 2-19   Floods in Kansas and Missouri kill 41 and leave 200,000 homeless.

July 12   Governor Adlai Stevenson of Illinois calls on the National Guard to maintain order in Cicero, a Chicago suburb, where a race riot has erupted. The riot occurs when a Negro family tries to move into town.

July 18   Joe Walcott makes a comeback and regains the world championship by knocking out Ezzard Charles in the 7th round of a fight in Pittsburgh.

Aug. 14   Newspaper publisher William Randolph Hearst, 88, dies in Beverly Hills, California.

Sept. 1   The United States, Australia, and New Zealand sign a mutual defense agreement, which becomes known as the ANZUS pact.

Sept. 4-8   At a conference in San Francisco, a peace treaty with Japan is signed by 48 nations not including the Soviet Union. Japan's sovereignty and inherent right to self-defense are recognized. The treaty also provides for the withdrawal of occupation forces three months from the date the treaty becomes effective. An incidental feature of the conference is the broadcasting of President Truman's address on Sept. 4 over a television network simultaneously throughout the United States—the first coast-to-coast circuit.

Oct. 19   President Truman signs an act ending the state of war with Germany.

Nov. 15   Edwin M. McMillan and Glenn T. Seaborg win the Nobel Prize in chemistry for their research in the field of synthesizing heavy elements.

Nov. 28-Dec. 31   As a result of continuing investigation into corruption within the Bureau of Internal Revenue, 31 employees are dismissed or asked to resign. On Dec. 5 Charles Oliphant, general counsel of the Bureau, resigns as a result of charges made against him in a House subcommittee.

Dec. 16   The crash of a nonscheduled airplane near Newark, New Jersey, kills 56 persons. This is the third major U.S. airline disaster this year: a United DC-6 claimed 50 lives in a crash in the Rocky Mountains of Colorado on June 30, and 50 persons died in the crash of another United plane, a DC-6B, near Decoto, California, on Aug. 24.

Dec. 20   Electricity is generated from atomic energy at a testing station at Arco, Idaho.

1952

The nation elects its first Republican President since 1928 as General Dwight D. Eisenhower sweeps to victory in November. Sought as a candidate as early as 1947, Eisenhower has resisted entering politics on the principle that "soldiers should stick to soldiering." However, at the urging of Senator Henry Cabot Lodge and a group of other influential Republicans, Eisenhower allows his name to be entered in the New Hampshire primary in March. Despite the fact that he remains in Europe as commander of the NATO forces, Eisenhower is unanimously chosen at the Republican national convention over Senator Robert A. Taft of Ohio, who is backed prior to the convention by the regular party organization. Eisenhower returns to the United States in June to campaign on his own behalf.

The Republicans take the offensive in the campaign, attacking the Democrats for the war in Korea, corruption in government, and a soft-headedness in dealing with Communism. The Democrats are placed on the defensive, with little to say against Eisenhower; their attacks are mainly directed against the Republican Party as represented by the old-line leadership. Eisenhower's overwhelming victory in November is a personal rather than a Republican triumph, for the candidate far outpolls his party. However, it must be admitted that he is aided by war-weariness and the low state of the economy, and to some extent even by the ceaseless accusations on the part of the McCarthyites that the Democrats are "soft on Communism."

Jan. 2   President Truman sends Congress a plan to end corruption in the Bureau of Internal Revenue by replacing the present system of politically appointed collectors with a series of 25 district commissioners under the civil service. [On Mar. 13 Congress endorses the plan.]

Jan. 21   The President's budget calls for expenditures of $85,444,000,000 for the coming fiscal year; slightly over three fourths of the budget is to be spent for "national security."

Feb. 1-April 3   On Feb. 1 Newbold Morris, a liberal New York City Republican, is appointed by Truman to investigate charges of corruption in the Department of Justice. Attorney General Howard McGrath refuses to allow Morris to question employees of the Justice Department, and Morris resigns. As a result Truman forces the resignation of McGrath and names James P. McGranery to replace him. [The investigation is dropped.]

Feb. 27   The United States and Japan sign a treaty providing for U.S. military bases in Japan.

Mar. 3   Puerto Ricans vote to accept a new constitution similar to that of the United States, and redefining the territory as a commonwealth. [On July 3 Truman signs a bill approving the Puerto Rican constitution with slight modifications.]

Mar. 3   The U.S. Supreme Court upholds a New York State law banning public school teachers who are members of subversive organizations.

Mar. 21-22   A series of tornadoes in the Mississippi Valley kills 229 persons and does widespread property damage.

Mar. 27   As of April 25 restaurants will have to display ceiling prices for their services, according to an order by the Office of Price Stabilization.

Mar. 29   Truman announces that under no circumstances will he run for another term.

April 8   Truman seizes the steel mills to prevent a strike by 600,000 steel workers that has been threatening for several months. The President acts under powers granted him by the Defense Production Act of 1950, and his authority as Commander in Chief in time of war. [On June 2 the Supreme Court rules that the President's action is unconstitutional and the steel companies are returned to their owners.]

April 13   The Federal Communications Commission drops its restrictions on new television stations and assigns 2,053 new stations throughout the country.

April 22   An atomic explosion is televised live for the first time at the Nevada testing grounds.

April 26   Two U.S. ships, the aircraft carrier *Wasp* and the destroyer-mine-sweeper *Hobson*, collide in the Atlantic, sinking the *Hobson* with the loss of 176 lives.

May 26   The U.S. Supreme Court extends First Amendment guarantees of freedom of speech and press to the motion picture industry by reversing a New York ban on the movie *The Miracle*.

General Dwight Eisenhower greets a jubilant crowd after winning the Republican Presidential nomination on the first ballot.

June 1   John Dewey, 92, one of the nation's most eminent philosophers and educators, dies in New York City.

June 14   The keel of the first atomic submarine, the U.S.S. *Nautilus*, is dedicated by President Truman at Groton, Connecticut.

June 27   Congress passes the McCarran-Walter Act over the President's veto. The Act continues the national origins quota system, but eliminates the exclusion of Asians. It also tightens provisions for the exclusion of aliens believed to be dangerous to the nation's security, and facilitates the deportation of such immigrants.

July 7   The S.S. *United States*, a 51,000-ton liner, completes the eastward crossing of the Atlantic Ocean, from Ambrose Light to Bishop Head Light, in 3 days 10 hours 40 minutes, an average of 35.6 knots. [This record remains unbroken.]

July 7-11   The Republican Party holds its convention in Chicago. The anticipated contest between Senator Robert Taft and General Dwight D. Eisenhower for the nomination fails to occur; Eisenhower is chosen on the first ballot, unanimously. The choice of Vice President, by acclamation, is Senator Richard M. Nixon of California, who is best known for his role in the successful prosecution of former State Department official Alger Hiss.

July 16   Truman signs the Veterans' Readjustment Assistance Act, also known as the G.I. Bill of Rights. It provides educational and other benefits for those who have served in the armed forces during the Korean War.

July 21-26   At the national convention of the Democratic Party in Chicago, a consensus to nominate Governor Adlai Stevenson of Illinois does not develop until the first two ballots fail to produce an acceptable nominee. Stevenson is the choice of President Truman, but is reluctant to run, and is "drafted." The Southern conservatives in the party are placated by the choice of Senator John Sparkman of Alabama to run for the Vice Presidency.

July 25   The Commonwealth of Puerto Rico is formally established.

Aug. 7   Truman declares Kentucky and Tennessee disaster areas as a result of drought.

Sept. 18-24   In a nationwide television address Vice-Presidential candidate Richard Nixon confirms that he has accepted $18,235 from supporters over the past two years, but claims that this "special fund" was used only to pay political expenses. [Because Nixon also declares he will keep the dog Checkers, a gift from admirers, the speech is popularly called the Checkers Speech.] General Eisenhower supports his running mate, and the Republican National Committee votes to keep Nixon on the ticket.

Sept. 23   Rocky Marciano wins the heavyweight boxing championship from Joe Walcott in Philadelphia by knocking him out in the 13th round.

Sept. 26   George Santayana, 88, philospher and man of letters, dies in Rome.

Oct. 23   The Nobel Prize for medicine is given to Selman A. Waksman as co-discoverer of the miracle drug streptomycin and its effect on tuberculosis.

Nov. 1   A hydrogen bomb of at least 5 megatons is exploded by the U.S. Atomic Energy Commission at the Pacific Proving Grounds.

Nov. 4   Dwight David Eisenhower is elected President with a popular vote of 33,936,234 as compared with 27,314,992 votes for Adlai Stevenson. Eisenhower gets 442 electoral votes to 89 for Stevenson. Republicans gain control of both Houses of Congress, but by a slim margin in each case.

Nov. 6   The Nobel Prize for physics goes to Edward M. Purcell of Harvard University and Felix Bloch of Stanford University for developing a new technique for measuring the magnetic fields of atomic nuclei.

Nov. 29   Keeping a pledge he made on Oct. 24, President-elect Eisenhower travels to Korea for a personal assessment of the war.

1953

Just six months after he takes office, President Eisenhower fulfills his campaign promise to bring the Korean War to an end. Peace is achieved after tiresome negotiations during which almost as much effort is directed at getting factions of the Republican Party and leaders of South Korea to agree on the truce terms as is spent negotiating those terms with the Communists. The Armistice is regarded by some as a form of appeasement, because the dividing line between Communist and non-Communist Korea remains at the 38th parallel, where it was when the costly war began. Even President Eisenhower is cautious about the chances for a lasting peace. Most Americans, while not rejoicing as enthusiastically as they did at the end of World War II, are glad that the fighting is over. Many insist that the country proved to the Communists that the United States would not permit them to conquer territory by force.

In the White House, the President sets a new style. Taking frequent vacations, playing bridge and golf whenever he can find time, Eisenhower is more relaxed than his predecessors. His "staff system," moulded by his military experience, gives his subordinates a greater hand in administering the Government, and to a degree allows the President to act as a man above politics. To the relief of many liberals the new President does not champion such conservative Republican proposals as sale of the TVA to private industry, the ending of foreign aid, cutting taxes, or curtailing the powers of the Department of State. Eisenhower's businesslike approach to government is reflected in the small amount of legislation that does become law, mostly sound measures designed to simplify government operations. The nation seems to approve; an opinion poll taken near the close of the year shows his popularity to be greater than ever.

Jan. 9   President Truman's budget calls for an outlay of $78,587,000,000 during the coming fiscal year. [Expenditures are later cut some $5,200,000,000 by President Eisenhower and even more by Congress. Two thirds is allotted to "national security"; foreign grants absorb about $6,350,000,000.]

Jan. 20   Dwight David Eisenhower is inaugurated as the 34th President of the United States. He delivers a brief speech in which he outlines his foreign policy. Stressing that he hates war, he indicates that he is willing to use force to deter aggression: "In the final choice a soldier's pack is not so heavy a burden as a prisoner's chains."

Jan. 21   The Cabinet of the new Administration is announced. The Secretary of State will be John Foster Dulles, an international lawyer who was chief U.S. negotiator at the Japanese Peace Treaty.

Feb. 6-25   The Government suspends all Federal wage controls and lifts price ceilings on many consumer items, including poultry, eggs, tires, gas, and cigarettes. [All remaining price controls are dropped the following Mar. 12.]

Feb. 16   The Air Force announces that two Soviet-type fighter planes were sighted over Hokkaido, northernmost of Japan's three main islands, and are forced to withdraw by fire from two U.S. jet planes.

Mar. 10   A U.S. Air Force Thunderjet is shot down over the U.S. zone of Germany by two Czechoslovak MiG-15 jets. The pilot of the U.S. craft parachutes to safety. [In response to a U.S. protest, Czechoslovakia admits having shot down the plane, but claims that the pilot violated Czechoslovak airspace.]

Mar. 17-June 4   A series of 11 atomic explosions are conducted in tests at Yucca Flat, Nevada. Automobiles, houses, and military equipment are placed at varying distances from ground zero to discover the destructive capacity of the different devices. In a test on May 25, a one-half-ton atomic projectile is launched from a cannon and explodes 7 miles away.

April 1   Congress establishes the Department of Health, Education, and Welfare, effective April 11, to include the Social Security Administration, the Office of Education, the Food and Drug Administration, and the Office of Vocational Rehabilitation; it also takes over the functions of the Federal Security Agency. On April 11 Oveta Culp Hobby becomes the first Secretary of the new department.

April 18   President Eisenhower announces that he is giving up the Presidential yacht *Williamsburg* as an economy measure.

April 24-25   Senator Wayne Morse of

Oregon sets a record by speaking for 22 hours 26 minutes against a bill that would return title of coastal oil reserves back to the states. [The measure is nevertheless passed, and is signed by President Eisenhower on May 22. It provides that all offshore oil shall belong to the states up to a 3-mile limit in the case of California and Louisiana and a 10½-mile limit in the case of Texas and Florida. Another bill, signed a few months later, provides that oil between these limits and the edge of the continental shelf are under the control of the Federal Government.]

April 27   U.S. military leaders announce that $50,000 and political asylum has been offered to any Communist pilot in the Korean War who defects with a Soviet jet aircraft.

June 2   Films of the coronation of Queen Elizabeth II are flown from England to the United States by special plane and are seen by millions of Americans on television only hours after the event has taken place.

June 8   The U.S. Supreme Court rules that restaurants in Washington, D.C., cannot discriminate against Negroes.

June 8-9   Tornadoes in Michigan, Ohio, and Massachusetts kill 234 persons and do millions of dollars worth of property damage.

June 17   East Berliners riot in an attempt to overthrow their Government. Martial law is declared and Soviet troops are used to prevent further disturbance. [On July 1 Eisenhower announces that he will not intervene militarily in the struggle.]

June 18   A U.S. Air Force transport plane crashes near Tokyo, Japan, killing 129 persons on board.

June 19   Ethel and Julius Rosenberg are executed at Ossining, New York; they are the first U.S. civilians ever to suffer capital punishment for a crime associated with espionage.

June 24   Congress passes a measure to give Pakistan 1,000,000 tons of surplus wheat, as requested by Eisenhower on June 10.

July 27   More than two years after the start of negotiations, an armistice ends the Korean War. Terms of the agreement call for a demilitarized zone near the 38th parallel. There is to be no forced repatriation of prisoners of war, but each prisoner not wishing to return home must be accounted for and must discuss his decision with delegates from his home country. [Thousands of North Korean and Chinese soldiers refuse repatriation, as do a small number of South Koreans and 23 Americans.]

July 30   Eisenhower signs two measures that

Mourners follow the hearse bearing the bodies of Julius and Ethel Rosenberg en route to the cemetery after funeral services in Brooklyn, New York, on June 21.

end the Reconstruction Finance Corporation, established in 1932, and replace it with the Small Business Administration, designed to carry out similar functions on a lesser scale.

July 31   Robert A. Taft, 63, Senator from Ohio and long a leader of the Republican Party, dies in New York City.

Aug. 7   Eisenhower signs a bill authorizing the admission to the country of 214,000 refugees not allowed for by the regular quotas.

Sept. 8   Chief Justice Frederick M. Vinson, 63, dies in Washington, D.C.

Oct. 5   Earl Warren, governor of California, takes the oath as Chief Justice of the Supreme Court. [He is confirmed Mar. 1, 1954.]

Oct. 12   Greece signs an agreement with the United States to permit U.S. military forces to be stationed on Greek territory. A similar agreement was reached with Spain on Sept. 26.

Oct. 14   Eisenhower authorizes the dismissal of any Federal employee who cites the Fifth Amendment to avoid giving testimony at Congressional hearings.

Oct. 30   The 1953 Nobel Peace Prize is awarded to George C. Marshall, who as Secretary of State for President Truman developed the Marshall Plan to assist the European nations to recover from the effects of World War II.

Dec. 16   Air Force Major Charles E. Yeager flies an X-1A airplane, an experimental, rocket-powered research aircraft, at a record speed of 1,650 mph at 90,000 feet altitude.

Senator William F. Knowland from California (left), swears in Richard M. Nixon as Vice President of the United States on Jan. 20.

1954

Americans are sharply divided over the continuing activities of Senator Joseph McCarthy. Having been appointed chairman of the Senate Committee on Government Operations, a post with little power, the Senator appoints himself head of the committee's Permanent Investigating Subcommittee. That group then embarks on an investigation of the U.S. Army, in the course of which an Army dentist is charged with having Communist ties. McCarthy uses the allegation as an opportunity to malign the dentist's superiors, including Secretary of the Army Robert Stevens, charging the Army with a grand conspiracy to coddle Communists. The Army in turn accuses the Senator of allowing his aides to seek special treatment for one of their number who has been drafted. For two months millions of Americans watch on television the charges and countercharges of the McCarthy-Army confrontation as the investigation continues in session. A report issued on Aug. 31 dismisses all of McCarthy's charges against the Army, but supports some of the Army's charges against McCarthy.

The result is not favorable either to McCarthy or the Republican Party. The party loses ground in the November elections, and public opinion polls show that at the end of the year only about one third of those questioned support McCarthy. The Senate asserts a degree of moral leadership by censuring the Senator. [McCarthy remains in the Senate until 1956, but he is increasingly less active.]

Jan. 4   With the nation entering a mild recession, President Eisenhower goes on television to promise that the Government will use "every legitimate means" to prop up the sagging economy.

Jan. 12   Secretary of State John Foster Dulles, addressing the Council of Foreign Relations, propounds a policy of basing the nation's defense not on its capacity to wage a series of small wars, such as Korea, but on "the deterrent of massive retaliatory power." The Secretary asserts that such a policy will result in greater protection at less cost.

Jan. 21   The U.S.S. *Nautilus*, the first atomic-powered submarine, is christened by Mrs.

General Maxwell D. Taylor (standing) and Robert T. Stevens, Secretary of the Army, and Major General Ming Ton Lai of the Chinese Nationalist Army, observe as General Paik Sun Yup signs a receipt certifying that all POW's have been turned over to the Republic of Korea and to the Republic of China.

Dwight D. Eisenhower, at its launching at Groton, Connecticut.

Feb. 10   Secretary of Commerce Sinclair Weeks announces a ban on the sale of Government-owned surplus commodities to Communist countries.

Feb. 16   The U.S. Bureau of the Census announces that over 3,000,000 persons were out of work during January, representing an unemployment rate of 5 per cent. [By April 1 the number of unemployed reaches 3,725,000. In the fall the rate of unemployment again returns to "acceptable" levels.]

Mar. 1   Screaming "Freedom for Puerto Rico," three men and one woman open fire from a spectator gallery in the House of Representatives and wound 5 of the 243 Congressmen present.

Mar. 1   A powerful nuclear explosion at Bikini Atoll in the Pacific Proving Ground continues the series of tests in this area, from which the population has been removed. [It is later discovered that radioactive fallout resulted in serious injury to test personnel and inhabitants of nearby islands, and that the 23 crew members of the Japanese fishing vessel *Fukuryu Maru*, 85 miles from the site, were so seriously affected that all require lengthy hospitalization and one later dies.]

April 3   Secretary of State John F. Dulles meets in secret with a group of Congressional leaders to ask that Congress pass a resolution allowing the President to provide air and sea support for the French forces in Indochina, which are fast being overrun by the Vietminh. When Dulles admits that he has failed to line up any international support for such intervention, his proposal is rejected.

April 5 The U.S. Supreme Court, in *Federal Communications Commission* v. *American Broadcasting Company*, rules that prize shows on radio and television are not violations of the lottery laws.

April 8 At a news conference Eisenhower propounds a "domino theory" of Communist expansion, asserting that allowing one country to fall into Communist hands will lead to the fall of all nearby countries.

May 13 The St. Lawrence Seaway Development Act is signed into law by President Eisenhower. The United States will cooperate with Canada on the St. Lawrence Seaway project in order to open the Great Lakes to ocean-going vessels.

May 17 The U.S. Supreme Court, in *Brown* v. *The Board of Education of Topeka*, rules that racial segregation in public schools is a violation of the 14th Amendment. The unanimous decision asserts that separate facilities are "inherently unequal," and thus reverses an 1896 ruling permitting racial segregation if the facilities provided each race are of equal quality.

June 21 On the final day of a conference at Geneva to reach an agreement on the crisis in East Asia (Korea and Indochina), called by the major powers (Britain, France, the Soviet Union, and the United States) and attended also by Communist China and the Vietminh representative, General Walter B. Smith represents the United States. Following the decisive French defeat by the Vietminh at Dienbienphu on May 8, the conference focuses on a settlement in Indochina, and France and the Vietminh now sign an agreement to withdraw on either side of a "military demarcation line," the 17th parallel, and to maintain a truce pending elections in 1956. The other conferees, except the United States, issue an oral Final Declaration supporting the agreement. General Smith refuses to join in the Final Declaration, but issues a statement concerning the terms agreed on: The United States "will refrain from the threat or use of force to disturb them. . . ."

June 29 The U.S. Atomic Energy Commission votes to remove [permanently] the security clearance of J. Robert Oppenheimer, known as "the father of the atomic bomb." The order states that the scientist has associated with Communists beyond "tolerable limits of pru-

dence." Oppenheimer denies having any Communist sympathies.

July 17 The first jazz festival at Newport, Rhode Island, takes place. Plans call for holding the event annually.

Aug. 17 In response to avowed Communist Chinese policy to conquer Formosa [Taiwan], held by the Nationalist Chinese, President Eisenhower promises that the United States will protect the Nationalists.

Aug. 24 The Communist Control Act becomes law. The Act virtually outlaws the Communist Party and denies certain civil rights to Communists and Communist-front organizations.

Aug. 30 Eisenhower signs the Cole-Hickenlooper Act, which provides that atomic knowledge and fuel may be shared with friendly nations for peaceful purposes. The law also permits the construction of atomic power plants by private industry.

August-October A series of three violent hurricanes hits the east coast of the United States. Hurricane Carol, in the last week of August, costs 60 lives from Cape Hatteras to New England; Hurricane Edna, early in September and mostly in New England, results in 25 deaths; Hurrican Hazel, affecting mainly the Carolina and New Jersey coasts, hits early in October and accounts for 95 fatalities.

Sept. 8 The United States joins with Britain, France, New Zealand, Australia, the Philippines, Thailand, and Pakistan to form the South East Asia Treaty Organization for mutual defense.

Nov. 2 Despite pleas by Eisenhower to elect a Republican Congress, the midterm elections give the Democrats a majority in both Houses.

Nov. 3 Linus Pauling of the California Institute of Technology wins the Nobel Prize for chemistry for his work on molecular bonds.

Nov. 28 Enrico Fermi, 53, physicist and one of the developers of the atomic bomb, dies in Chicago. A Nobel Laureate in physics, he was also awarded the Congressional Medal of Merit and the first $25,000 prize from the Atomic Energy Commission. [This last award is renamed the Fermi Prize.]

Dec. 2 The U.S. Senate votes, 67 to 22, to censure Senator Joseph McCarthy for "conduct that tends to bring the Senate into dishonor and disrepute, to obstruct the constitutional processes of the Senate, and to impair its dignity. . . ."

Dec. 10 U.S. Air Force Colonel John P. Stapp, on a rocket sled at a land speed record of 632 mph, endures an enormous gravitational force (46.2G's).

1955 **Full employment, rising personal income, increased consumer spending, and** rapid business expansion all reflect the prosperity that is overtaking the country. By October about 2,100,000 are still without work—some 1,000,000 fewer than at last year's low point—but those who have work are earning more than ever as the average work week expands. Businessmen, eager to make the most of the boom, prefer to meet organized labor more than half way, and raises of 7 to 8 per cent are common. Many low-paid workers benefit as the Federal minimum wage is raised and extended to cover an additional 2,200,000 individuals.

Americans do not hesitate to spend their new wealth. Personal savings drop to 5.7 per cent of disposable income for the first three quarters of the year, as compared with 7.2 per cent for the same period in 1954. Consumer credit expands rapidly, especially installment credit, which increases by some 20 per cent to reach a level of $26,700,000,000 by September. Half of this money goes to finance new automobiles; a record of 7,920,000 passenger cars are sold. The steel industry reaches a production level of 98.8 per cent of capacity by November and produces about 3,500,000 tons more than during its record year of 1953. The gross national product is more than twice as large as that of 1929.

Jan. 4 Announcement is made that the United States will pay $2,000,000 for injuries to 23 Japanese fishermen while their boat was within the contamination zone of a hydrogen bomb explosion at the Bikini test site in the Pacific last March.

Jan. 17 The President's proposed budget calls for expenditures of $62,408,000,000 for the coming fiscal year, with the expectation of a decreased deficit. [As a result of expanded economic activity, actual receipts are far above those estimated and the budget shows a surplus of $1,626,000,000.]

Jan. 28 Congress passes a resolution to give Eisenhower permission to use U.S. forces to defend Formosa (Taiwan) and the Pescadores from a possible Communist Chinese attack.

Feb. 15 A report issued by the U.S. Atomic Energy Commission states that Americans have been exposed to an amount of radiation equal to that of one chest X-ray as a result of fallout from all nuclear explosions conducted by the United States, the Soviet Union, and Britain.

Mar. 2 Eisenhower signs a bill to raise the salaries of members of Congress, the Vice President, Federal judges, and members of the Department of Justice. [Later in the year two more bills raise the salaries of postal workers and another 1,000,000 Federal employees.]

Mar. 16 Eisenhower states that he may use atomic weapons in the event that the United States is drawn into war.

April 7 Actress Theda Bara, 64, dies in Los Angeles. She appeared in more than 40 silent movies and was one of the period's most famous "vamps."

April 12 After completing extensive tests during 1954, involving about 2,500,000 children, researchers announce that the vaccine developed by Jonas Salk is a safe and effective means of preventing poliomyelitis. Six firms receive licenses to manufacture the drug and a nationwide plan to inoculate all first and second graders is announced.

April 18 Scientist Albert Einstein, 76, dies at Princeton, New Jersey. Best known for his theory of relativity, he also contributed to the development of the atomic bomb, but he advocated disarmament and warned of the dangers of nuclear warfare.

May 31 The U.S. Supreme Court orders that its 1954 decision outlawing segregation in public schools must be implemented within a "reasonable time."

June 6 The United Auto Workers and the Ford Motor Company sign a three-year contract which, aside from a pay boost, provides for payments to laid-off workers to supplement governmental unemployment insurance. The hope of labor leaders is to create a "guaranteed annual wage."

June 15 Congress extends the Reciprocal Trade Agreement for three years.

June 17 The Senate ratifies the Austrian State Treaty which was signed on May 15 in Vienna. The treaty reestablishes Austrian sovereignty and provides for the country's permanent neutrality. The acquiescence of the United States is required because of its status as one of the four occupying powers.

June 30 The military draft is extended for four years.

Albert Einstein
(1879-1955)
This photograph is considered to be the last one
made of the physicist. The occasion was Professor
Einstein's 76th birthday on Mar. 14.

July 11 The United States Air Force
Academy is dedicated at its temporary location,
Lowry Air Force Base in Colorado. [Its permanent site near Colorado Springs is ready in
1958.]

July 18-23 President Eisenhower meets with
Soviet Premier Nikolai Bulganin, British Prime
Minister Anthony Eden, and French Premier
Edgar Faure in Geneva, Switzerland. [Such meetings are henceforth described as summit
conferences.] Eisenhower proposes an "open
skies" policy, in which the United States and the
Soviet Union would permit each other to make
complete and ongoing aerial inspection of each
other's military installations. Disarmament and
the unification of Germany are also discussed.
No important agreements are reached, but international tensions are relaxed.

Aug. 7-21 Heavy rains caused by Hurricane
Diane result in destructive floods along the eastern seaboard from New Jersey to Rhode Island.
Property damage runs to several billion dollars,
and the number of dead is put at 191.

Aug. 9 Eisenhower signs the Reserve Forces
Act of 1955, creating a ready reserve and providing young men with an alternative to the draft.

Aug. 12 Eisenhower signs a measure raising
the Federal minimum wage from 75 cents to
$1.00.

Sept. 7 Government reports indicate that for
the first time more than 65,000,000 Americans
are classified as employed.

Sept. 18 Astronomers of the National Geographic Society and Lowell Observatory report
that an area on Mars about the size of Texas has
turned a blue-green color, possibly the result of
plant life. The announcement gives further credence to theories of extraterrestrial life forms.

Sept. 23-24 Eisenhower suffers a heart attack at Denver, Colorado, after returning from a
four-day fishing trip in the mountains. He is
taken to nearby Fitzsimons Army Hospital for
treatment. [Eisenhower recovers quickly and
leaves Denver on Nov. 11 for his farm at Gettysburg, Pennsylvania. On. Nov. 22 he presides
over a Cabinet meeting.]

Sept. 26 As a result of the President's heart
attack, the stock market suffers its worst one-day
loss in history. Issues on the New York Stock
Exchange show a dollar loss of about
$14,000,000,000. [The market recovers rapidly,
and by October record highs are reached.]

Oct. 18 Scientists at the University of
California, Berkeley, announce that they have artificially created antiprotons, confirming the scientific theory about the existence of antimatter.
An antiproton has the same mass as a proton, but
a negative rather than a positive charge. [It is
subsequently learned that when an antiproton collides with a proton, both are converted instan-
taneously into radiant energy.]

Nov. 1 Dale Carnegie, 66, dies at Forest
Hills, New York. His book *How to Win Friends
and Influence People*, published in 1936, was a
best seller in the field of motivational psychology
and personality development.

Nov. 7 The U.S. Supreme Court extends its
desegregation ruling to public parks, play-
grounds, and public golf courses. The same day
the Court rules that a civilian may not be tried
by court-martial once he has been discharged
from the military.

Nov. 25 The Interstate Commerce Commission orders an end to racial segregation on interstate trains and buses. The order is effective Jan.
10, 1956.

Dec. 5 The American Federation of Labor
and the Congress of Industrial Organizations,
with a combined membership in the United
States and Canada exceeding 16,000,000, merge
to form a single organization retaining the two
names. [The first president of the AFL-CIO is
George Meany.]

Dec. 27 U.S. motor vehicle deaths reach a
record 609 for the Christmas weekend. On an
annual basis automobile fatalities this year run
about 8 per cent above last year's total of
35,586.

1956

The Presidential campaign of 1956 is marked by the question of President Eisenhower's health. Although his doctors report steady recovery from his heart attack of last September, Eisenhower hesitates to declare his candidacy. Finally, on Feb. 29, after extensive medical tests, he announces his intention to run again, stating that his physicians have assured him that he will be healthy and active for at least another 5 to 10 years. In June, however, Eisenhower is again hospitalized, this time with ileitis. After a successful operation and recovery, Eisenhower reaffirms his candidacy. His nomination at the Republican convention in San Francisco is a mere formality. Vice President Nixon is renominated without opposition.

Despite Eisenhower's tremendous appeal, there is no lack of Democrats willing to run against him. Bitterly fought primary campaigns damage and divide the Democratic Party. At the party convention in Chicago on Aug. 16, Adlai E. Stevenson, the party's choice in 1952, is again nominated for President. He wins on the first ballot, overcoming the opposition of former President Truman, who favors Averell Harriman. Tennessee Senator Estes Kefauver is nominated for Vice President. Most Democrats acknowledge that the campaign will be an uphill fight. The economy is still booming, with personal income, production, and business profits all setting record highs. A report at midyear shows that the United States is producing 40 per cent of the world's output with only 6 per cent of the world's population. Many Americans credit President Eisenhower's Administration for the country's happy state of affairs. Further, Eisenhower is the man who got the country out of the Korean War and has kept it out of war since, while at the same time pursuing an aggressive foreign policy to stop the spread of Communism.

The Democrats attack the President on his poor health and on what they term his "do-nothing" record of legislative accomplishment, but their charges are unavailing. The election is a stunning personal victory for Eisenhower, who far outpolls his party. Democrats repeat their 1954 Congressional victory by winning majorities in both the House and Senate, but this is the first time since 1848 that the party winning the Presidency has failed to capture at least one House of Congress.

Jan. 9   In an effort to curtail mounting farm surpluses, President Eisenhower asks Congress to approve a $1,000,000,000 plan to create a "soil bank"—a plan similar to the cultivation control of the 1930's—to compensate farmers for not growing crops.

Jan. 16   Eisenhower's estimated budget for fiscal year 1956-1957 puts expenditures at $65,900,000,000 and revenues at $66,300,000,000, leaving a small surplus of $400,000,000. [Actual figures for the period show an increase in both expenditures and receipts and a surplus of $1,596,000,000.]

Feb. 22   Eisenhower makes available about $1,000,000,000 worth of uranium for research and power plants, half to be distributed to private companies in the United States and the other half to go to friendly nations. The move is part of a U.S. policy to stimulate peaceful uses of atomic energy both at home and abroad. [By June 30 the United States has entered into 36 bilateral agreements with other nations to cooperate on atomic research and plant construction.]

Mar. 7   In an attempt to circumvent the Supreme Court's desegregation ruling, a constitutional convention in Virginia amends that state's laws to permit the use of public funds for tuition to parents who send their children to private, segregated schools. The state has already closed its public schools to prevent integration.

Mar. 12   The U.S. Supreme Court, in *Florida ex. rel. Hawkins* v. *Board of Control,* orders a Florida state university to admit to a professional graduate program a Negro who was denied admission solely on the basis of race. The Court recognizes the university's contention that the desegregation ruling of 1954 allows local school boards reasonable time to solve the segregation problem; however, the Court rules that the situation at the level of professional education is not the same as that of primary and secondary education and the university may not delay in admitting qualified Negroes.

Mar. 20   The longest major strike in two decades ends as 70,000 members of the International Union of Electrical Workers (AFL-CIO)

Richard M. Nixon
THIRTY-SEVENTH PRESIDENT   1969-1974

Gerald R. Ford
THIRTY-EIGHTH PRESIDENT 1974

Jimmy E. Carter
THIRTY-NINTH PRESIDENT 1977-1981

Ronald W. Reagan
FORTIETH PRESIDENT 1981-

return to work at Westinghouse after 156 days.

April 9 The U.S. Supreme Court, in *Slochower* v. *Board of Higher Education of the City of New York*, holds that it is unconstitutional to discharge a public employee merely because he invokes the Fifth Amendment guarantee against self incrimination at hearings where the purpose is other than to inquire into the fitness of the employee for his job. The Court particularly condemns the practice of "impugning a sinister meaning to the exercise of a person's constitutional right under the Fifth Amendment."

April 21 A 10-year-old boy, Leonard Ross, amazes television audiences as he wins the $100,000 top prize on a popular quiz show.

May 21 The first known airborne hydrogen bomb is dropped from a B-52 over Bikini Atoll in the Pacific Proving Ground.

May 23 Congress passes an agricultural act that provides $750,000,000 per year for four years to pay farmers for reducing crop acreage for corn, wheat, peanuts, cotton, tobacco, and rice. [By the end of the year over 12,000,000 acres have been taken out of production.]

June 9 Eisenhower is successfully operated on at Walter Reed Hospital to remove an intestinal obstruction. Physicians announce that the President's postoperative condition is excellent.

June 29 The Federal Aid Highway Act is signed by the President. It authorizes $33,500,000,000 to be spent over the next 13 years for road construction.

July 23 Announcement is made of the completion of a three-month program of atomic tests at the Eniwetok-Bikini test site in the Pacific.

July 25-26 The Italian ocean liner *Andrea Doria* is struck by the Swedish liner *Stockholm* about 60 miles south of Nantucket. The *Andrea Doria* sinks, but the *Stockholm* proceeds to port on her own. Fifty persons are killed in the mishap, but almost 1,650 are saved.

Aug. 11 Artist Jackson Pollock, 44, dies in an automobile accident near his home in East Hampton, New York. His huge canvases, covered with abstract designs, brought him tremendous attention in the art world. He is considered by many as the founder of the abstract expressionist school of art.

Aug. 13-17 The choice of candidates for the Presidential ticket has been made before the Democratic Party delegates to the national convention meet in Chicago. Adlai Stevenson, despite the poorest showing since Alf Landon in terms of popular percentage four years ago, is named on the first ballot. Estes Kefauver, who withdrew his effort to win the Presidential nomination a week ago, wins the Vice-Presidential line over John F. Kennedy on the second ballot.

Aug. 20-23 The Republican national convention, meeting in San Francisco, renominates the incumbents Eisenhower and Nixon by acclamation.

Aug. 25 Researcher Alfred Charles Kinsey, 62, dies in Bloomington, Indiana. His scientific approach to the study of sex, the findings of which are published in *Sexual Behavior in the Human Male* (1948) and *Sexual Behavior in the Human Female* (1953), brought Kinsey both fame and controversy.

Aug. 29 The United States agrees to send India $305,900,000 worth of agricultural surpluses and to pay $54,200,000 towards shipment of the food.

Sept. 14 Announcement is made at the University of California, Berkeley, of the discovery of another new particle, the antineutron.

Oct. 8 New York Yankee baseball player Don Larsen pitches the first perfect game since 1922 and the only no-hitter in a World Series game.

Oct. 18 The Nobel Prize for medicine is awarded to André F. Cournand and Dickinson W. Richards, both of Columbia University, and a German colleague, for developing a technique to chart the inside of the heart.

Nov. 1 Three U.S. scientists, William B. Shockley, Walter H. Brattain, and John Bardeen, are awarded the Nobel Prize for physics for the invention of the transistor.

Nov. 6 President Eisenhower wins reelection by a huge majority, with 35,590,472 votes to 26,022,752 for Stevenson. The electoral vote is 457 to 73. A single elector from Alabama demonstrates his nonconformity by voting for somebody named Jones.

Dec. 13 The U.S. Supreme Court rules unconstitutional a state law of Alabama (one of a category generally called Jim Crow statutes) that requires Negroes to sit in the rear of public transportation vehicles. The suit results from the refusal, on Dec. 1, 1955, of Rosa Parks, an elderly Negro woman, to move to the rear of a bus on Cleveland Avenue in Montgomery, and her consequent arrest. A massive boycott of the bus system of the city followed, under the leadership of the Rev. Martin Luther King, Jr., and the issue finally reached the Supreme Court. [This event is generally considered the first skirmish in a movement for black civil rights that features the next few years, much of it led by King.]

385

1957   **Americans have plenty to be concerned with during the** first eight months of this year. There is nationwide debate over Federal spending, touched off by President Eisenhower's proposal of the biggest peacetime budget in history, totaling almost $72,000,000,000. Republicans and Democrats alike criticize the size of the budget and Congress seeks ways to cut expenditures. Inflation, which reappeared last year, shows no sign of abating, taking its toll on the consumer wallet. Another prominent concern is the danger of radioactive fallout as Americans argue the wisdom of continuing the nuclear testing program. Important as these issues are, they move into the background during the Fall. By then Congress has voted to restore practically every cent it cut from the President's budget. A downturn in the economy has people more concerned over a possible recession than the current inflation. And assurances by the Administration that research has greatly reduced nuclear fallout and that further work in this area is being pursued help to temporarily calm the testing debate.

Later in the year, however, occur two events of such magnitude that they dwarf all other issues of national concern. In September the governor of Arkansas refuses to comply with Federal law and uses force to prevent the integration of Central High School in Little Rock. All eyes focus on this outright defiance of Federal authority. Then, in early October, the Russians launch the first artifical earth satellite and a month later follow it with a second, heavier and more impressive "Sputnik." Americans are shocked to learn that Soviet rocket technology is so advanced, while the United States does not even have a comparable missile in the planning stage. In response to these crises, President Eisenhower sends Federal troops to enforce the law in Little Rock and announces extensive programs to upgrade U.S. rocket technology.

Jan 5   President Eisenhower asks Congress for permission to use U.S. military forces to resist Communist aggression in the Middle East if aid is requested by a threatened nation. [On Mar. 7 a resolution is passed by Congress approving the President's request. The policy becomes known as the Eisenhower Doctrine.]

Jan. 14   Actor Humphrey Bogart, 57, dies in Hollywood, California. Among the more than 50 motion pictures in which he acted were *The Caine Mutiny* and *The African Queen*.

Jan. 16   The Administration's proposed budget for fiscal year 1957-1958 sets expenditures at $71,807,000,000, leaving a healthy surplus of $1,831,000,000. [Actual figures for the year show a deficit of $2,819,000,000, primarily caused by the downturn in the economy and consequent declining revenue. This deficit follows two years of budget surpluses.]

Jan. 18   A record nonstop flight of 24,325 miles around the globe is completed by three Air Force Statofortresses in 45 hours 19 minutes.

Feb. 12   The U.S. Communist Party renounces all ideological control by the Soviet Communists. [The Federal Bureau of Investigation calls this decision a fraud.]

Feb. 15   The population of the United States passes the 170,000,000 mark, according to an estimate by the U.S. Bureau of the Census. The continuing postwar "baby boom" has resulted in a natural population growth of over 2,500,000 annually for the past several years. This figure does not include population increases that result from immigration.

Feb. 25   In its first obscenity opinion the U.S. Supreme Court, in *Butler* v. *Michigan,* rules that a Michigan law banning the sale to the general public of material that might corrupt minors is unconstitutional.

Mar. 11   Admiral Richard E. Byrd, 68, dies in Boston. Byrd is best remembered for having been the first man (with Floyd Bennett) to fly over the North Pole, and for his extensive explorations in the Antarctic.

Mar. 21-24   President Eisenhower and British Prime Minister Harold Macmillan, meeting in Bermuda, announce that the United States will provide Great Britain with guided missiles.

Mar. 26-27   At well-publicized hearings before the U.S. Senate Permanent Investigating Subcommittee, Dave Beck, head of the International Brotherhood of Teamsters, cites the 5th Amendment some 80 times in refusing to answer questions. The subcommittee has been investigating the misuse of union funds for private gain. [On May 20 Beck is expelled from his post on the AFL-CIO executive council. In December he is convicted of embezzlement.]

April 25 Eisenhower announces a study to ascertain if oil imports are undermining national security. [Later in the year the President asks the nation's large importers to voluntarily cut back oil imports by 10 per cent.]

May 2 Senator Joseph R. McCarthy, 47, for several years a controversial political figure, dies in Bethesda, Maryland.

June 3 The U.S. Supreme Court, in *United States* v. *E.I. du Pont de Nemours and Company,* rules that du Pont's acquisition of 23 per cent of General Motors Corporation stock is a violation of the antitrust laws. The Court rules that, although the two companies do not manufacture the same products, competition is restricted by the fact that du Pont is a major supplier to General Motors and can use its 23-per-cent ownership to influence the auto maker's purchasing decisions.

June 5 President Eisenhower responds to critics of continued nuclear testing by claiming that he is relying on the American Academy of Sciences for advice on atomic fallout. The President adds that present tests are designed to find ways of reducing fallout and that a 90-per-cent reduction has already been accomplished.

June 17 The U.S. Supreme Court frees 5 Communists convicted as Smith Act violators and orders new trials for 9 others. As the Court interprets the Smith Act, the prohibited "advocacy" of revolution cannot convict so long as it is abstract; it must have the "capacity to stir listeners to forcible action."

June 27 Hurricane Audrey sweeps out of the Gulf of Mexico and into Texas and Louisiana, creating huge tidal waves and causing 534 deaths.

July 1 The International Geophysical Year officially begins. The 18-month study, involving some 10,000 scientists from 70 countries, is programed to seek greater understanding of the atmosphere, the oceans, the surface and interior of the earth, and outer space.

July 6 Althea Gibson of New York is the first Negro to capture the Wimbledon tennis singles crown for women.

July 16 Marine Corps Major John Glenn, Jr., flies a Navy plane coast-to-coast in a record 3 hours 23 minutes 8 seconds.

July 31 The Distant Early Warning (DEW) radar defense line is operational. Costing $500,000,000, the system stretches from Cape Lisbourne, Alaska, across Canada to Baffin Island.

Aug. 1 The North American Air Defense Command (NORAD) is established by the United States and Canada. [An agreement signed May 12, 1958, formally ratifies NORAD, a binational operation intended to represent NATO defense of North America.]

Aug. 19-20 Major David G. Simons, U.S. Air Force pilot sets a 19½-mile altitude record in a specially equipped balloon.

Sept. 4-25 An integration plan worked out by the Little Rock (Arkansas) Board of Education in compliance with Supreme Court rulings is thwarted by Arkansas Governor Orval Faubus, who sends in the Arkansas National Guard to prevent the first small group of Negro children from entering Central High School. When it becomes apparent that the governor plans to continue his defiance of U.S. law, President Eisenhower federalizes the National Guard and sends the 101st Airborne Division of the Army into Little Rock. A military escort protects the youngsters from a threatening mob to allow them to enter the school.

Sept. 9 President Eisenhower signs the first civil rights bill in 87 years. The bill is primarily designed to assure the voting rights of all Americans.

Oct. 5 American reaction varies from thrill to dismay at the news that the Soviet Union has launched the first artificial earth satellite, known as "Sputnik." [A second Soviet satellite, with a dog on board, is launched on Nov. 3.]

Oct. 17-21 Queen Elizabeth II and her husband, Prince Philip, receive an enthusiastic welcome as they visit the United States.

Oct. 31 Two Chinese-born professors at U.S. universities, Tsung Dao Lee of Columbia and Chen Ning Yang of the Institute for Advanced Study at Princeton, win the Nobel Prize in physics for work in nuclear physics.

Nov. 26 Announcement is made that President Eisenhower has suffered a mild stroke but is recovering rapidly.

Dec. 6 A U.S. rocket carrying a grapefruit-size satellite explodes on launching at Cape Canaveral, Florida.

Dec. 13-19 President Eisenhower attends the meeting of the North Atlantic Treaty Organization in Paris; he is the first U.S. President to visit Paris since Wilson. The American delegation fails to convince their allies to accept missile stockpiles on their territories other than "in principle."

Dec. 18 The first atomic power plant in the United States, at Shippingport, Pennsylvania, begins to produce electric power.

The sense of crisis caused by the successful launching of a Soviet satellite is somewhat relaxed when the United States orbits several satellites of its own and later launches a successful intercontinental ballistic missile (ICBM). One result of the proof of Soviet scientific expertise is a demand for an overhaul of the educational system, and the Federal Government passes its first major educational assistance bill in over a century.

The economy continues to decline, and by June unemployment reaches 7.7 per cent, a record unmatched since the Depression. Business profits also drop to a postwar low. A reversal occurs shortly after midyear, helped in part when Congress approves such antirecession measures as extended unemployment payments, higher social security benefits, and $3,600,000,000 for highway construction and home-loan guarantees.

Internationally, a crisis in the Middle East and the bombing of Quemoy by the Communist Chinese raises fears of World War III. Diplomatic maneuvering however, contains the hazards.

Although short-term problems are solved, Americans remain anxious over the inability of the nuclear powers to achieve a test ban, or even to reach agreement on the holding of a summit conference. Farmers and taxpayers worry about the nation's ever-more-costly agricultural surpluses. Racial tension and the school integration crisis apparently defy workable solutions. Evidence of the nation's mood is seen in November when, despite vigorous campaigning by both President Eisenhower and Vice President Nixon, the Republicans suffer heavy losses in the midterm elections.

Jan. 7   President Eisenhower, reacting to the impact of the successful orbiting of a satellite by the Soviet Union, tells Congress, in his State of the Union Message, that the United States must attain equality with the Soviet Union in satellite and missile development. To implement this, the President asks Congress for a supplementary appropriation of $1,370,000,000 for the current fiscal year.

Jan. 13   The President's budget for fiscal year 1958-1959 forecasts a surplus of $466,000,000, with revenues of $74,400,000,000 and expenditures of $73,934,000,000. [Congress votes new spending programs and receipts fall below expectations, resulting in a record peacetime deficit of $12,427,000,000 for fiscal 1958-1959.]

Jan. 31   The first successful launch of a U.S. earth satellite, Explorer I, takes place at Cape Canaveral, Florida. Weighing 30.8 pounds, the satellite carries instruments to measure cosmic rays and temperature and to detect tiny meteorites. [By the end of July the United States has placed three more satellites into orbit. On Dec. 18 an 8,800-pound Atlas satellite is put into orbit.]

Mar. 1   Pope Pius XII appoints the Archbishop of Chicago, Samuel Cardinal Stritch, to head the Vatican office of the Sacred Congregation for the Propagation of the Faith. The Cardinal is the first American to be appointed to the

Papal Curia. [On May 26 Cardinal Stritch, 70, dies in Rome.]

Mar. 3   In the event that President Eisenhower is disabled, Vice President Nixon will "assume the powers and duties of the office until the disability is ended," according to an agreement between the two leaders announced by the White House.

April 1   In order to cope with the current recession, Eisenhower signs into law a bill appropriating $1,850,000,000 for emergency housing.

April 14   Texas pianist Van Cliburn, 23, wins the first international Tchaikovsky piano competition in Moscow.

April 28-May 15   Vice President Nixon visits eight Latin American countries on a goodwill tour. In Lima, Peru, and again in Caracas, Venezuela, Nixon is jeered by spectators who hurl rocks and eggs and attack the Vice President's official car.

May 30   Ceremonies are held at Arlington Cemetery to inter the bodies of unidentified soldiers of World War II and of the Korean War in the Tomb of the Unknown Soldier, now renamed Tomb of the Unknowns.

June 16   In *Kent* v. *Dulles* the U.S. Supreme Court rules that the Department of State may not refuse to issue a passport to an individual because of his opinions or membership in organizations. In so ruling, the Court indicates that the right to travel is a liberty granted by the Constitution and may not be curtailed without due process.

June 28 The Mackinac Bridge, the second longest suspension bridge in the world (3,800 feet), across Mackinac Straits and joining the Upper and Lower Peninsulas of Michigan, is dedicated.

July 8-11 President Eisenhower visits Canada, confers with Prime Minister John Diefenbaker, and addresses the Canadian Parliament. The President defends U.S. investments in Canada, the use of surplus wheat in the U.S. foreign aid program, and the import quota placed on Canadian oil—three issues which have recently caused bitter feelings in Canada towards the United States.

July 15 At the request of the President of Lebanon, Camille Chamoun, President Eisenhower sends the first contingent of marines and soldiers to that country to protect it against "indirect aggression" from the United Arab Republic and Iraq and the threat of a domestic rebellion. [The 74,300 troops remain until October, by which time the Arab nations have agreed at the United Nations not to interfere in each other's internal affairs.]

July 29 The National Aeronautics and Space Administration (NASA) is established. Its function is to provide civilian control and coordination of space exploration. Research projects primarily military in nature continue to be carried out by the Department of Defense.

Aug. 5 The U.S.S. *Nautilus,* the world's first nuclear submarine, surfaces near Spitsbergen after completing the first transpolar voyage beneath the Arctic ice pack. The journey, lasting 96 hours and covering 1,830 nautical miles, is made possible by the extended cruising range that nuclear power provides.

Aug. 7 Eisenhower signs into law an appropriations bill for defense in the amount of $39,602,827,000.

Aug. 23 Critical of the recent liberal bent of many U.S. Supreme Court decisions on segregation and civil liberties, a meeting of the chief justices of the 48 state supreme courts resolves that the nation's highest tribunal has failed to show "proper judicial restraint" and has threatened the concept of a "government of laws and not of men."

Aug. 23 Congress passes the National Defense Education Act providing more than $1,000,000,000 to improve educational opportunities at all levels. Much of the money goes to provide loans to college and graduate students.

Aug. 27 Physicist and Nobel laureate Ernest O. Lawrence, 57, dies in Palo Alto, California. Lawrence developed the cyclotron, or "atom smasher," which produced atomic materials for the first nuclear bombs and also made possible the transmutation of elements.

Sept. 11 President Eisenhower goes on television and radio to announce that he will use force to protect the Chinese Nationalist-held islands of Matsu and Quemoy, which have recently come under heavy attack from Communist Chinese shore batteries. [On Sept. 30 Secretary of State John F. Dulles states that the United States has no committment to assist the Nationalist Chinese in recapturing the mainland.]

Sept. 12 As a result of the U.S. Supreme Court's refusal to allow a delay in a Little Rock, Arkansas, integration plan, Governor Faubus immediately shuts down all high schools in the city, and classes are given by television.

Sept. 22 Sherman Adams, considered by many to be President Eisenhower's most influential assistant, resigns after months of controversy. Adams has been accused of using his official position to assist an industrialist who has given Adams gifts and provided free hotel accommodations.

Oct. 4 The first scheduled jet airliner to cross the Atlantic, a British Comet IV, makes the flight in 6 hours 12 minutes. [Pan American World Airways begins regular New York-to-Paris flights on Boeing 707's on Oct. 26.]

Oct. 5 A high school in Clinton, Tennessee, integrated since 1956, is wrecked by dynamite.

Oct. 11 A Pioneer rocket is launched from Cape Canaveral and travels almost one-third the distance to the moon before falling back into the earth's atmosphere and burning up.

Oct. 30 The Nobel Prize for medicine is awarded to three Americans—George W. Beadle, Edward L. Tatum, and Joshua Lederburg —for their work in discovering the role of genes.

Nov. 4 Democrats win a decisive victory in the midterm elections, gaining 47 seats in the House and 13 in the Senate.

Nov. 28 An Atlas intercontinental ballistic missile (ICBM) is fired from Cape Canaveral and lands on target 5,500 miles away in the South Atlantic.

Dec. 1 A report issued by the Department of Health, Education and Welfare estimates that school closings to prevent integration have caused the loss of 1,000,000 student days during 1958.

1959

After years of Cold War hostility between the United States and the Soviet Union, it appears possible that the relationship may be improving. The first break occurs in May, when Soviet Premier Khrushchev's six-month deadline for achieving a settlement to the Berlin problem slips by almost unnoticed. In July, Vice President Nixon makes a successful trip to Moscow to open a U.S. exhibition there. A Soviet exhibition in New York attracts much public attention and is visited by President Eisenhower. With the death of John Foster Dulles in the spring, Eisenhower takes a greater role in leading the nation's foreign policy. He ignores the Dulles warning about dealing personally with the Russians, and welcomes Khrushchev to the United States with a cordiality that is apparently reciprocated. The new relationship, reached during a conference at Eisenhower's retreat in the Maryland mountains, is called "the spirit of Camp David."

Jan. 3   Alaska joins the Union as the 49th state. A new flag with seven rows of seven stars each will become the nation's official banner on July 4.

Jan 7   The United States recognizes the new Government of Cuba established after the overthrow of the regime of Fulgencio Batista on Jan. 1. The provisional President is Manuel Urrutia, and the armed forces are led by Fidel Castro.

Jan. 19   The President's budget is sent to Congress. Expenditures are estimated at $77,030,000,000 and revenues at $77,100,000,000, leaving a small surplus of $70,000,000. [Actual figures for fiscal year 1959-1960 show somewhat higher revenues, resulting in a surplus of $1,156,000,000.]

Jan. 21   Cecil B. De Mille, 77, motion picture producer extraordinary, dies in Hollywood.

Jan. 23   Portions of Ohio and Pennsylvania are declared disaster areas as a result of flooding that began on Jan. 21. Floods in the upper Ohio River basin are the worst in over 40 years.

Feb. 2   Virginia public schools are integrated with no disturbances at Norfolk and Arlington, after the state supreme court on Jan. 19 overturns the alternative system of "massive resistance" (during which the public schools were closed).

Feb. 12   The 150th anniversary of Lincoln's birth is marked by an address of poet Carl Sandburg before the U.S. Congress.

Mar. 3   Pioneer 4 is launched on a journey that will carry it past its intended target, the moon, and into an orbit around the sun.

Mar. 30   The U.S. Supreme Court rules that an individual may be tried separately for the same crime in both state and Federal courts without violating the constitutional guarantee against double jeopardy.

April 8-9   The National Aeronautics and Space Administration tells Congress that its space program should place man on the moon by

1969. The next day the first seven candidates for space travel, called astronauts, are designated.

April 9   Frank Lloyd Wright, 89, dies in Phoenix, Arixona. Wright revolutionized modern architecture by emphasizing that structures should blend into their surroundings.

April 15-28   Fidel Castro, now Premier of Cuba, visits the United States on an informal trip. In a speech to newspaper editors, Castro asserts that there are no Communists in his Government.

April 16   The Bolshoi Ballet makes its first American appearance at the Metropolitan Opera House with a performance of *Romeo and Juliet,* in which Galina Ulanova dances the role of Juliet. The event is part of a cultural exchange program with the Soviet Union.

April 22   Christian A. Herter becomes Secretary of State, replacing John Foster Dulles, who has resigned because of illness.

April 25   The St. Lawrence Seaway, connecting the Great Lakes with the Atlantic Ocean, opens. A joint project of the United States and Canada, the system provides a minimum 27-foot-deep channel (as compared with only 14 feet in the old system) and can accommodate ships up to 730 feet in length. [The project is formally opened on June 26 in ceremonies attended by President Eisenhower and Queen Elizabeth II.]

May 24   John Foster Dulles, 71, dies of cancer in Washington, D.C. As Secretary of State, Dulles pursued an aggressive policy sometimes referred to as "brinkmanship."

May 28   Able, a rhesus monkey, and Baker, a squirrel monkey, are shot 300 miles into space aboard a Jupiter rocket and recovered alive.

June 9   The U.S.S. *George Washington,* the first submarine capable of firing a ballistic missile, is launched at Groton, Connecticut. [On Aug. 27 a Polaris missile is actually fired at sea from a test ship.]

June 11   D.H. Lawrence's novel, *Lady Chatterley's Lover,* is barred from the mails by Postmaster General Arthur E. Summerfield. [The ruling is overturned by a Federal court on July 21.]

June 18   Ethel Barrymore, 79, one of the great actresses of the legitimate stage, dies in Hollywood. Her last professional appearance was on a television program in 1956.

June 26   Ingemar Johanson of Sweden wins the heavyweight championship from Floyd Patterson by a knockout in the third round at Yankee Stadium in New York City.

June 29   An exhibit of Soviet culture and technology opens in the Coliseum in New York City. The exhibit stems from a protocol signed in January 1958, providing for a variety of exchanges between the United States and the Soviet Union. [On July 24, a U.S. exhibit opens in Moscow. Both shows attract record crowds during the six weeks they are open.]

July 15-Nov. 7   Halting 87 per cent of the nation's steel production, workers strike for higher pay, improvements in pension and insurance benefits, and, most importantly, changes in work rules. The strike, the longest in the history of the steel industry, is ended by an injunction under the Taft-Hartley law calling for an 80-day cooling-off period. [An agreement is reached and a new contract signed before the injunction expires.]

July 17   Billie Holiday, whose name was originally Eleanora Fagan McKay, 44, dies in New York City. Known to jazz buffs as "Lady Day," many consider her to have been the finest jazz singer of her time.

July 21   The world's first atomic-powered merchant vessel, the N.S. *Savannah,* is launched at Camden, New Jersey.

July 23-Aug. 2   Vice President Richard Nixon visits the Soviet Union to preside at the opening of the U.S. exhibition in Moscow and to confer with Premier Khrushchev. Nixon addresses the Soviet people on television and radio and, in a much publicized incident, he debates Khrushchev on the relative merits of communisn and capitalism. This polemic is dubbed the "kitchen debate" because of its impromptu location in a model kitchen at the U.S. exhibition.

Aug. 8   The first picture of the world from outer space is transmitted from Explorer VI and broadcast on television.

Aug. 21   Hawaii joins the Union as the 50th state. Another new U.S. flag is designed, to become official on July 4, 1960.

Aug. 27-Sept. 7   President Eisenhower visits England, France and West Germany to assure leaders of these countries that the United States will not deal unilaterally with the Soviet Union.

Sept. 10   Congress enacts a public works bill with an appropriation of $1,185,000,000 over the President's veto. This is the first of about 150 vetoes exercised so far by Eisenhower that Congress is able to override.

Sept. 14   The Labor-Management Reporting and Disclosure Act is signed by President Eisenhower. The product of two years of investigation by Congress into labor union corruption, the act attempts to protect union members from racketeering. Among other provisions, unions must make public their finances and must elect officers by secret ballot.

Sept. 15-27   Soviet Premier Khrushchev visits the United States. After addressing the General Assembly of the United Nations where he advocates total disarmament by all nations, he makes a much publicized trip across the United States, visiting supermarkets and farms, but showing disappointment at not being allowed (for "security reasons") to visit Disneyland. Near the end of his trip, Khrushchev confers for two days with Eisenhower at Camp David. It is announced that no new deadlines will be set for the settlement of the Berlin situation and that President Eisenhower will visit the Soviet Union in 1960.

Sept. 23   Eisenhower signs an omnibus housing bill (having vetoed two such bills passed by Congress) under which $650,000,000 will be spent over a six-year period for urban renewal. The total appropriation for housing is estimated to be about $1,000,000,000.

Oct. 16   George C. Marshall, 78, General of the Army, former Secretary of State, and author of the Marshall Plan, dies in Washington, D.C.

Oct. 21   The Guggenheim Museum in New York City, designed by architect Frank Lloyd Wright, is opened.

Nov. 2   Charles Van Doren, questioned about his winning $129,000, on a television quiz show, tells a Congressional committee that he was given the answers in advance. His testimony is the most dramatic yet in the quiz show scandals.

Dec. 3-21   President Eisenhower makes a "peace and goodwill" tour of 11 nations, the most extensive ever made by an American President.

Dec. 4   A mock-up of the Mercury capsule to be used for the first U.S. manned space flight is sent aloft with a 100-pound biopack.

1960

Americans turn their attention to politics as another Presidential election takes place. With Eisenhower out of the running, Democrats are hopeful that they can recapture the Presidency. Although there are some half-dozen Democratic contenders, only Senators John F. Kennedy and Hubert H. Humphrey enter the primaries. When Kennedy wins in West Virginia, where it is thought his Catholic religion will do him the most harm, Humphrey withdraws. Kennedy wins all seven primaries that he enters and when the Democrats meet in July he is nominated on the first ballot. In a surprising move, Kennedy selects Senate Majority leader Lyndon B. Johnson as his running mate. Johnson helps Kennedy win much of the South in the November election.

At the Republican convention in Chicago, Vice President Richard Nixon wins the nomination unopposed. Nixon's only rival, Nelson Rockefeller of New York, has much earlier withdrawn his candidacy when it has become clear that the Republican regulars want Nixon. Henry Cabot Lodge, a former Massachusetts Senator and a strong supporter of Eisenhower, is selected for the second spot.

An intense campaign begins in early September, highlighted by a series of joint news conferences on television, with each candidate answering reporters' questions. Nixon campaigns largely on the Eisenhower record, of which Kennedy is critical. Kennedy promises to "get this country moving" again, using government spending to stimulate economic growth and to aid areas of chronic unemployment. He also makes an issue of the nation's taking second place to the Soviet Union in the space race.

The election is the closest since 1884. Kennedy wins 303 electoral votes to 219 for Nixon, but the difference in popular votes represents only a 0.2-per-cent margin for Kennedy. At 43 Kennedy is both the youngest man ever elected President, and the first Catholic to win the office.

With the addition of Alaska and Hawaii since the last decennial census, the population of the United States is now 179,323,175. The rate of growth during the decade is the highest in half a century, 18.5 per cent; it is noteworthy, however, that the rate of growth in the suburbs, 48 per cent, far outdistances the 7-per-cent rate in the countryside and the 9-per-cent rate in the central cities. California continues to increase its population at a rapid pace, and Los Angeles has replaced Philadelphia as the third most populous city in the country.

Jan. 4   The steelworkers union and the steel industry come to an agreement, 22 days before the end of the cooling-off period imposed by an injunction. This officially ends the strike that began last July 15 and seriously injured the economy until work was resumed last November.

Jan. 18   The President's budget calls for an optimistic surplus of $4,184,000,000, with expenditures of $79,816,000,000 and revenues of $84,000,000,000. [Actual figures for fiscal 1960-1961 show a deficit of $3,856,000,000 as a result of higher spending and lower revenues than anticipated.]

Jan. 19   A new treaty between Japan and the United States is signed that commits both countries to rely on military means for the defense of Japan. [The treaty proves to be so unpopular in Japan that Premier Nobosuke Kishi is forced to resign.]

Jan. 23   The U.S Navy bathyscaphe *Trieste* descends to the bottom of the Mariana Trench in the Pacific Ocean,, a record dive of 35,800 feet.

Feb. 2   At Greensboro, North Carolina, four Negro students defy a whites-only rule and sit at a lunch counter in a variety store. Refused service, the Negroes remain seated in peaceful protest. [The "sit-in" tactic spreads quickly to other cities. On Oct. 17 desegregation of lunch counters in over 100 Southern cities is announced by several large chain stores, including Woolworth and Kress.]

Feb. 18-28   The eighth winter Olympics takes place at Squaw Valley, California, in the Tahoe National Forest.

Feb. 22-Mar. 6   During a 14-day visit to South America, President Eisenhower meets with an enthusiastic reception in many countries, but he is also greeted by anti-U.S. demonstrators.

Feb. 24-May 10   The world's largest submarine, the nuclear-powered U.S.S. *Triton,* circumnavigates the globe almost continuously submerged, completing a voyage of some 41,500 miles in 84 days.

Mar. 11-June 26   Pioneer 5 is placed in orbit around the sun and continues to transmit radio data back to earth up to a record distance of 22,500,000 miles.

Mar. 15-June 27   A 10-nation committee, including delegates from the United States, set up by the United Nations to draw up disarmament plans, meets at Geneva, Switzerland, but adjourns with no agreement.

Mar. 17   A Lockheed Electra turboprop airplane on a flight from Chicago to Miami explodes over Tell City, Indiana; 63 persons are killed.

April 1   The first U.S. weather satellite, Tiros 1, is launched. The satellite carries two small television-type cameras capable of photographing the earth's cloud cover.

April 24   A race riot occurs in Biloxi, Mississippi, when Negroes attempt to end segregation at the city's all-white beaches.

May 1-17   U.S. pilot Francis Gary Powers, flying a U-2 high-altitude plane, is shot down by Soviet missiles near Sverdlovsk, U.S.S.R. Powers is captured and confesses that he was on a photo reconnaissance flight for the U.S. Central Intelligence Agency. On May 16 Soviet Premier Khrushchev, in Paris for a long-awaited summit conference, condemns the flight. When President Eisenhower refuses to apologize to Khrushchev's satisfaction, Khrushchev cancels the talks. Khrushchev also calls off President Eisenhower's planned visit to the Soviet Union, despite Eisenhower's assurance that the spy flights will be discontinued.

May 6   President Eisenhower signs a Civil Rights Act that attempts to overcome some of the shortcomings of the Civil Rights Act of 1957. The most important aspect of the new law is a provision permitting Federal judges to send referees to supervise voter registration in areas of apparent racial discrimination.

May 20   An Atlas ICBM is fired from Cape Canaveral and 55 minutes later arrives a record 9,000 miles away in the Indian Ocean.

June 16   President Eisenhower, visiting Manila as part of a tour of the Far East, cancels his planned stop in Japan when anti-U.S. riots erupt in Tokyo. Demonstrations are directed against the new U.S.-Japanese mutual security treaty which was signed in January [and is ratified by Japan on June 23].

July 6   Growing tension between Cuba and the United States, caused in part by the nationalization of U.S. property in Cuba, results in President Eisenhower's cutting the annual sugar import quota from Cuba to 700,000 tons, effectively ending Cuban sugar sales to the United States this year. [On Oct. 19 an embargo of U.S. exports to Cuba goes into effect.]

July 13-14   John F. Kennedy and Lyndon B. Johnson are nominated for President and Vice President, respectively, at the Democratic convention at Los Angeles.

July 20   A U.S. Polaris missile is launched 1,100 miles from the nuclear-powered submarine *George Washington* 30 feet below the surface of the Atlantic. [The range of the Polaris is extended to 1,300 miles later in the year.]

July 27-28   Vice President Richard Nixon wins the Republican nomination for President at the party's convention in Chicago. Henry Cabot Lodge is nominated for Vice President.

Aug. 4   An X-15 research plane sets a manned-flight speed record of 2,196 mph. [On Aug. 12 the craft sets an altitude record of 136,500 feet.]

Aug. 12   Echo 1, a 100-foot aluminum-coated balloon, is placed in orbit. It is to be used as a reflector for long-range communication signals.

Aug. 23   Oscar Hammerstein II, 65, dies in Doylestown, Pennsylvania. An outstanding lyricist, he wrote the words for many of the nation's favorite songs, including those of the musicals *Oklahoma!, Carousel, South Pacific,* and *The Sound of Music.*

Sept. 24   The aircraft carrier U.S.S. *Enterprise* is launched at Newport News, Virginia. The largest ship in the world, it is powered by eight atomic reactors and will be able to sail 20 times around the world without refueling.

Nov. 8   John F. Kennedy is elected President with a popular vote of 34,221,531. Richard Nixon polls 34,108,474 votes. Democrats maintain their hold of both the House and Senate.

Nov. 28   Author Richard Wright, 52, dies in Paris. His books, including *Native Son* and *Uncle Tom's Children,* portray the problems of Negro life in the United States.

Dec. 16   Two airliners, a United Airlines DC-8 and a Trans World Airline Lockheed Super-Constellation, collide over the New York area, one crashing into a Brooklyn street, the other into Staten Island. With 134 persons killed, the disaster ranks as the worst in commercial aviation.

1961

With a young, vigorous President newly installed in office, Americans wonder what changes will occur. In keeping with campaign pledges, President Kennedy proposes a wide range of domestic programs: increased aid for the aged and jobless, a higher minimum wage, a health insurance program for all Americans, aid to education, a program of water and flood control, improved housing for lower and middle income groups, and a new agricultural policy. [Kennedy succeeds in getting about half of these measures enacted.]

Kennedy and the nation are soon more concerned with the international situation. Near home, an unsuccessful invasion of Cuba in April—a joint effort of the CIA and Cuban exiles—exacerbates an already tense situation. The civil wars in Laos and in the newly independent Congo both threaten to involve the United States in a shooting war. More serious still is the perennial problem of Berlin. Despite a meeting between Kennedy and Soviet Premier Khrushchev in Vienna June 3-4, no agreement is reached. Shortly thereafter, Khrushchev threatens to give the East Germans control of East Berlin and the access routes from West Germany into West Berlin unless the United States recognizes East German sovereignty. Kennedy responds by getting from Congress more funds for defense and ordering partial mobilization. While all these problems concern Americans, their greatest apprehension is aroused by the Soviet resumption of atmospheric testing of nuclear weapons. Suddenly Americans again worry about fallout, strontium 90 poisoning, and the merits of fallout shelters.

Jan. 3-4   The United States breaks off diplomatic relations with Cuba. On the following day the Administration announces that the United States will not permit any change in the status of its naval base at Guantánamo on the southeastern coast of the island.

Jan. 12   President Eisenhower's proposed budget calls for anticipated revenues of $82,000,000,000 and proposed expenditures of $80,865,000,000 to leave a surplus of $1,135,000,000. [On Mar. 24 President Kennedy revises these estimates to provide for a deficit of $2,826,000,000. The actual deficit for 1961-1962 proves to be $6,378,000,000. As it happens, this amount is almost precisely equal to the increase of the defense appropriation in 1961-1962 ($47,654,000,000) over that of the preceding fiscal year.]

Jan. 17   In his farewell address, President Eisenhower warns of a new danger to the nation's well-being, the rise of the "military-industrial complex." Eisenhower states that while such a development is necessary in view of today's world, the "potential for the disastrous rise of misplaced power exists and will persist."

Jan. 20   John F. Kennedy is inaugurated as the 35th President of the United States. In his inaugural address Kennedy challenges his listeners to "ask not what your country can do for you—ask what you can do for your country."

Feb. 23   The National Council of Churches endorses artificial contraceptive techniques as an aid to family planning.

Feb. 24   A three-year test of pay television is authorized by the Federal Communications Commission.

Mar. 1-April 21   President Kennedy, by Executive order, establishes the Peace Corps. Its purpose is to train U.S. volunteers who will supply badly needed skills to underdeveloped nations. Kennedy appoints R. Sargent Shriver as director of the program. [In September Congress passes legislation to make the Peace Corps permanent and appropriates $30,000,000 for its first year. By the end of the year about 500 volunteers are overseas.]

Mar. 29   The right to vote for President and Vice President is given the people of Washington, D.C., as the 23d Amendment to the Constitution is ratified by the 38th state, Kansas. However, residents of the city still do not have a voting representative in Congress. [The formal ratification is proclaimed on April 3.]

April 16-May 17   About 1,500 Cuban exiles, trained and equipped by the U.S. Central Intelligence Agency, invade Cuba's south coast at the Bay of Pigs. After brief success, they are overcome by Castro's forces and surrender. At first the U.S. Government denies its involvement in the affair, but on April 24 President Kennedy accepts "sole responsibility" for the nation's part in the invasion. Castro offers to trade 1,214 prisoners captured during the invasion for 500 bulldozers. [Later, he is willing to make the trade for 1,000 tractors.]

May 4-24   A biracial group sponsored by the

Congress of Racial Equality (CORE) leaves by interstate bus from Washington, D.C., to force integration of bus terminals in the South. The "freedom riders" are met by hostile mobs at Anniston and Birmingham, Alabama, where one bus is burned and several riders are injured. On its arrival at Montgomery, Alabama, the group is again met by violence until U.S. marshals, sent in by Attorney General Robert Kennedy, restore order. At Jackson, Mississippi, the freedom riders are met by local police who arrest 27 on charges of disturbing the peace and resisting police.

May 5 Alan B. Shepard, Jr., is the first American in space during a 15-minute suborbital flight in a capsule, launched from Cape Canaveral by a Redstone rocket. The capsule reaches a height of 116 miles and lands in the Atlantic 302 miles downrange, where Shepard is picked up by a U.S. Marine helicopter. (Three weeks earlier, on April 12, Soviet cosmonaut Yuri Gagarin achieved the first manned orbital flight.)

May 31-June 5 President Kennedy, in a tour of Europe, talks with French President Charles de Gaulle in Paris, with Soviet Premier Nikita Khrushchev in Vienna, and with British Prime Minister Harold Macmillan in London.

June 9 Under the Area Redevelopment Act passed by Congress on April 26, 114 depressed areas in the United States and Puerto Rico are selected for special Federal assistance.

June 19 The U.S. Supreme Court, in *Mapp v. Ohio*, rules 5 to 4 that illegally seized evidence must be excluded from use in state criminal trials.

July 2 Ernest Hemingway, 61, commits suicide at his home in Ketchum, Idaho. One of the nation's most widely read authors, Hemingway is remembered for such novels as *The Sun Also Rises, A Farewell to Arms,* and *The Old Man and the Sea.*

July 24-Aug. 10 Three U.S. airliners are hijacked. Two are forced to fly to Cuba. The third is recaptured by Federal agents after the pilot convinces the hijackers he must land and refuel at El Paso, Texas, before proceeding to Cuba. In response, the Federal Aviation Agency authorizes the arming of airline crews and President Kennedy announces that U.S. agents will fly on some commercial flights.

Aug. 17 Representatives of 19 Latin American nations at a meeting at Punta del Este, Uruguay, declare their support for President Kennedy's Alliance for Progress (proposed on Mar. 13). The United States pledges itself to supply the major portion of the $20,000,000,000 needed over the next 10 years for joint social and economic programs in Latin America.

Sept. 1 The Soviet Union explodes a nuclear bomb in the atmosphere, ending a 34-month interruption of atomic weapons tests by all nuclear powers. On the same day the Geneva test-ban talks, in progress intermittently since 1958, are called off. [President Kennedy condemns the Soviet resumption of testing, but on Sept. 5 he orders underground U.S. nuclear tests, the first of which takes place in Nevada on Sept. 15. The Soviet Union continues its tests through Nov. 4, detonating at least 50 devices, including a hydrogen device of 50 megatons, the most powerful yet exploded.]

Oct. 1 New York Yankee baseball player Roger Maris brings his home run total to 61 in a 162-game season, breaking Babe Ruth's 1927 record of 60 in a 154-game season.

Oct. 19 George von Békésy, Hungarian-born American, wins the Nobel Prize in medicine for his research on the inner ear.

Nov. 2 Nobel Prizes in physics and chemistry are awarded to Robert Hofstadter for his research on atomic nuclei and to Melvin Calvin for identifying chemical reactions during the process of photosynthesis.

Nov. 9 At the greatest speed ever achieved in a manned aircraft, Air Force Major Robert M. White flies an X-15 rocket plane at a peak of 4,093 mph. On Oct. 11, in the same craft, Major White achieved a record altitude of more than 41 miles.

Nov. 16 Samuel T. Rayburn, 79, dies in Bonham, Texas. Rayburn served a record 25 consecutive terms in the House of Representatives (since 1913) and was Speaker of the House since 1940.

Dec. 11 The United States alters its policy of limiting military aid to South Vietnam to money, arms, and advisors, and sends direct military support in the form of two U.S. Army helicopter units. The Government of President Ngo Dinh Diem, in power since 1955, is waging a campaign against Communist-led rebels (Vietcong) and the change in U.S. policy is based on a report made by General Maxwell Taylor urging a strengthening of the U.S. Military Advisory Group of 685 persons in order to help the Diem regime.

Dec. 14 The Office of Emergency Planning, created in the Department of Defense by Executive order on Aug. 1, proposes a $700,000,000 program to build community fallout shelters.

1962 Although both President Kennedy and Soviet Premier Khrushchev begin the year with mutual expressions of hope for better relations, by October the most serious confrontation yet between the two nations has brought the world to the brink of nuclear war. U.S. reconnaissance photos reveal the construction of a missile base on Cuban soil. Kennedy, campaigning in the Midwest on behalf of Democrats up for election in November, returns to Washington, reportedly because of a cold. Two days later, after extensive discussions with his closest advisors, the President informs the country of the situation and of his intention to order a sea blockade of arms shipments to Cuba; at the same time he demands that the Soviet Union remove the missiles and the jet bombers that it has already supplied to Cuba.

Tension grows as Soviet ships approach the blockade line, and each night Americans wonder if they will live to see the morning. Anxiety lessens when the ships apparently follow instructions to sail elsewhere. Two days later Premier Khrushchev informs the President that he will remove the missiles in exchange for a U.S. promise not to invade Cuba. Kennedy agrees, on condition that the bombers also be removed and that the United Nations make on-site inspections to assure that all Soviet offensive weapons have been taken out of Cuba. By the end of the year the missiles and bombers have been removed, but Premier Castro refuses to allow on-site inspection; the no-invasion pledge by the United States is never issued. President Kennedy wins vast prestige for his demonstrated ability to react decisively without triggering nuclear war.

Jan. 3 President Kennedy activates two new U.S. Army divisions in order to release National Guard units called up during the 1962 Berlin Crisis.

Jan. 3 The text of a U.S. statement made on Dec. 6, 1961, to the Inter-American Peace Committee is released, in which Cuba is described as "a bridgehead of Sino-Soviet imperialism and a base for Communist agitation and subversion within the inner defense of the Western Hemisphere." [At the conference of the Organization of American States at Punta del Este, Uruguay, Jan. 22-31, Cuba is excluded from that body.]

Jan. 18 Kennedy submits to Congress a balanced budget, with estimated expenditures of $92,537,000,000 set slightly below expected revenues. [Actual figures for fiscal 1962-1963 show a deficit of $6,233,000,000.]

Jan. 25 Stating that the progress made by the European Economic Community requires a new U.S. trade policy, the President asks Congress to grant him wide powers to negotiate lower tariffs. [On Oct. 4 Congress passes the Trade Expansion Act, giving the President the right to cut U.S. tariffs by 50 per cent (and in some cases more) in making trade agreements with other nations. These agreements may run for a period of up to five years.]

Feb. 10 Francis G. Powers, pilot of the U-2 reconnaissance plane shot down over the U.S.S.R. in 1960, is released by the Soviet Union in exchange for a captured Soviet spy, Rudolph Abel.

Feb. 14 Approximately 80,000,000 persons watching *A Tour of the White House with Mrs. John F. Kennedy,* a 60-minute television documentary, see the Executive Mansion redecorated with furnishings and art from the nation's past.

Feb. 20 Astronaut John H. Glenn, Jr., becomes the first American to orbit the earth. Launched from Cape Canaveral aboard *Friendship 7,* Glenn completes three orbits in 4 hours 56 minutes and lands in the Atlantic east of the Bahamas.

Mar. 1 An American Airlines Boeing 707 jet aircraft crashes into Jamaica Bay in New York City, with a loss of 95 lives.

Mar. 2 President Kennedy announces that Soviet advances in nuclear weaponry will force him to order a resumption of U.S. atmospheric testing unless an adequate test-ban treaty is reached soon with the U.S.S.R. [U.S. testing is resumed on April 25 and continues until Nov. 4, during which 34 tests are reported.]

Mar. 26 The U.S. Supreme Court, in *Baker v. Carr,* rules that discriminatory apportionment of seats in a state legislature may be remedied in Federal court.

April 10-13 The U.S. Steel Corporation raises its prices by $6 a ton ten days after the announcement of a new contract with steel workers that was negotiated with the help of the

White House and is considered noninflationary. President Kennedy describes the action as "a wholly unjustifiable and irresponsible defiance of the public interest." On April 13 Inland Steel announces its decision not to raise prices, leading other steel companies, that initially followed the example of U.S. Steel, to rescind their increases.

April 21-Oct. 21   Century 21, the first U.S. world's fair in 22 years, is held at Seattle, Washington. The theme of the fair is "Man in the Space Age."

May 6   The nuclear submarine *Ethan Allen,* while submerged, fires a Polaris missile with a nuclear warhead that is detonated above the Pacific Ocean 1,400 nautical miles from the ship, in the first test of this operation.

May 24   Astronaut M. Scott Carpenter makes the second U.S. manned orbital flight aboard *Aurora 7.*

June 25   The U.S. Supreme Court, in *Engel* v. *Vitale,* holds 6 to 1 that the reading of a prayer in public schools violates the 1st and 14th Amendments to the Constitution, despite the fact that the prayer in question is nondenominational and participation on the part of students is voluntary. [In 1963 the Court extends the ruling to cover any prayer or Bible reading in public schools.]

July 9   A U.S. nuclear device of 1.25-megaton yield is exploded from a rocket 250 miles in space over the Pacific Ocean. The blast lights up huge portions of the night sky, including Hawaii, 850 miles distant. [It is found that the test increased radiation in the Van Allen Belt and caused three satellites to malfunction. Kennedy announces that future tests will be held at lower altitudes with smaller bombs.]

July 10   Telstar, a communications satellite designed and owned by American Telephone and Telegraph Company, is launched from Cape Canaveral by NASA for a charge of approximately $3,000,000. The satellite is designed to relay both telephone and television signals between the United States and Europe.

Aug. 5   Marilyn Monroe, 36, dies of an overdose of sleeping pills in Hollywood. She starred in 23 motion pictures and became the nation's foremost female sex symbol.

Aug. 14   A U.S. mail truck en route from Cape Cod, Massachusetts, to a Federal Reserve bank in Boston is held up by gangsters carrying submachine guns. They steal $1,551,277, the largest cash plunder in the nation's history.

Aug. 27-Dec. 14   Mariner 2 is launched from Cape Canaveral, travels to within 21,600 miles of the planet Venus, and transmits data back to earth over a distance of 36,000,000 miles.

Sept. 10   The U.S. Supreme Court upholds a lower court ruling that James H. Meredith, a Negro Air Force veteran, be admitted to the University of Mississippi. [When Meredith tries to register he is stopped by the governor of Mississippi, Ross R. Barnett. On Sept. 28 Governor Barnett is found guilty of contempt and ordered to admit Meredith by a U.S. circuit court. On Oct. 1 Meredith is enrolled at the university while Federal marshals and U.S. troops, called in by President Kennedy, attempt to control rioting on campus which has claimed two lives the day before. Meredith continues to attend class escorted by U.S. marshals.]

Oct. 3   Walter M. Schirra, Jr., completes six orbits of the earth aboard *Sigma 7* and lands on target in the Pacific four miles from the recovery ship.

Oct. 18   Geneticist James D. Watson wins a share in the Nobel Prize in medicine for participating with two English biophysicists (his co-laureates) in discovering the configuration of the NDA molecule, which is responsible for the phenomenon of heredity.

Oct. 22-24   President Kennedy, in a nationwide broadcast to the American people, discloses that reconnaissance photographs taken on Oct. 14 show missile sites on Cuban soil capable of accommodating missiles of 2,000-mile range. He announces that he is issuing an "interdiction" against the delivery of such weapons, effective Oct. 24. The warning is directed against Soviet cargo ships approaching Cuba, presumably with missiles aboard. [The ships do not defy the quarantine, and in the next months missiles and missile-carrying aircraft already in Cuba are removed under orders from Premier Khrushchev, terminating what becomes known as the "Cuban missile crisis."]

Oct. 25   Novelist John Steinbeck, author of *Grapes of Wrath, Of Mice and Men,* and other popular and respected works of fiction, is awarded the Nobel Prize in literature.

Nov. 6   Democrats keep control of both Houses of Congress in the midterm elections, picking up four seats in the Senate. Republicans gain two seats in the House.

Nov. 7   Eleanor Roosevelt, 78, dies in New York City. The widow of former President Franklin D. Roosevelt, her extensive humanitarian activity and her role in drafting the U.N. Covenant on Human Rights brought her worldwide recognition.

1963 **President Kennedy's third year in office is distinguished by** a major accomplishment in the field of foreign affairs. He concludes the first formal agreement on a fundamental issue between the United States and the Soviet Union: the termination of the atombomb tests that have caused anxiety not only in their own countries but throughout the world. The willingness of the Cold War antagonists to negotiate is symbolized by the proposed installation of a permanent and reliable medium of communication between them, in the form of a "hot line," to avoid inadvertent disaster.

At home, the most significant events are associated with the increasing pace of the movement to improve the condition of the Negro, at long last under the leadership of the blacks themselves. The huge demonstration in Washington in August is the climax. According to an estimate by the Department of Justice, more than 750 demonstrations have taken place in the 10 weeks following an outbreak of unrest in Birmingham in April and May. Nearly every major city with a sizeable black population has been affected. In the South demonstrators seek integration of restaurants and public facilities, and increased Negro voter registration; elsewhere they demand an end to de facto school segregation and better employment opportunities for blacks. President Kennedy has made it clear that an effective civil rights bill is high on his list of priorities.

Then comes the shocking proof that violence is no respecter of persons. On a sunny street in Dallas, during one of those preelection rites that distinguish American politics—a campaign motorcade—President Kennedy is struck down by an assassin's bullet, and dies soon thereafter. Even the quiet competence with which the Vice President fulfills his ultimate role in that office cannot entirely quell the sense of depression that pervades the American people. Whatever reassurance they have in the remaining weeks of the year stems from the likelihood that President Johnson will respect, as he promises, the goals set by his stricken predecessor.

Jan. 2   Three U.S. helicopter crewmen are killed and 5 helicopters are shot down as they carry South Vietnamese troops in a combat area 30 miles southwest of Saigon.

Jan. 7   U.S. domestic postage rates are raised from 4 to 5 cents for first-class. (They were raised from 3 to 4 cents on Aug. 1, 1958.)

Jan. 8   Leonardo da Vinci's famous portrait, *Mona Lisa*, goes on display at the National Gallery of Art in Washington, D.C. The painting is on loan from the French Government.

Jan. 17   President Kennedy submits a record budget of $98,800,000,000 in expenditures for fiscal 1963-1964, with a projected deficit of $10,000,000,000. [The deficit for fiscal 1963-1964 is reported as $8,226,000,000.]

Jan. 24   President Kennedy asks Congress to cut taxes by approximately $14,000,000,000 in order to stimulate the economy. The President's plan also calls for closing important tax loopholes, which will yield about $4,000,000,000 extra revenue. [Although Kennedy declares that the tax cut is his primary legislative goal, Congress fails to pass the measure this year.]

Jan. 29   Robert Frost, 88, dies in Boston. The winner of four Pulitzer prizes, Frost's use of homespun language and imagery made him one of the nation's favorite poets.

Feb. 25   The U.S. Supreme Court, in *Edwards* v. *South Carolina,* overturns the conviction of 187 Negroes arrested for disturbing the peace during a demonstration in Columbia, South Carolina, on Mar. 2, 1961.

Mar. 18   The U.S. Supreme Court, in *Gideon* v. *Wainwright,* rules that indigent defendants must be offered free legal counsel in all criminal prosecutions.

April 3-May 12   Massive demonstrations protesting racial injustice take place in Birmingham, Alabama, led by Martin Luther King, Jr., president of the Southern Christian Leadership Conference. Use of police dogs and fire hoses to control demonstrators—many of whom are high school students—causes national indignation, and protest demonstrations spread to other cities. By May 4 over 1,000 demonstrators in Birmingham have been arrested, half of them under the age of 18. The White House sends General Burke Marshall to Birmingham to mediate the dispute between Negro and white leaders. On May 8 Kennedy announces that a settlement has been reached whereby the demonstrations are to be suspended in return for "substantial steps" by white business leaders to integrate public facilities and provide greater job opportunity for Negroes. In addition, jailed demonstrators are to be released on signature bonds and an interracial committee is set up to discuss further steps to achieve full integration. However, on May 11 rioting resumes after a Negro leader's home is bombed. Kennedy sends in 3,000 Federal troops to help maintain the peace.

April 5   Agreement is reached by the United States and the Soviet Union to establish a "hot line" between the White House and the Kremlin in the event that a crisis should necessitate instant communication to avoid nuclear war.

April 10   The nuclear-powered submarine U.S.S. *Thresher,* while engaged in a test dive in deep water off Cape Cod, Massachusetts, fails to return to the surface. All 129 men aboard are lost.

May 15-16   U.S. astronaut L. Gordon Cooper orbits the earth 22 times, completing the nation's first manned space flight program, Project Mercury.

June 12   *Cleopatra,* starring Richard Burton and Elizabeth Taylor, opens at the Rivoli Theatre in New York City. Costing almost $35,000,000 to produce, the film is the most expensive ever made.

July 25   The United States, Great Britain, and the Soviet Union sign the long-hoped-for nuclear test-ban treaty at Moscow. The pact bans nuclear testing in the atmosphere, outer space, and in the oceans, but not underground. [The U.S. Senate ratifies the treaty on Sept. 24. By the end of the year 113 nations have indicated their willingness to go along with the treaty, with the notable exceptions of France and Communist China.]

Aug. 28   During a "March on Washington for Jobs and Freedom," 200,000 persons gather in the nation's capital to demonstrate their demand for racial equality. Addressing the crowd,

President John F. Kennedy, Governor Connally, and Mrs. Jacqueline Kennedy stand under the wing of the Presidential plane moments after arriving in Dallas, Texas, on Nov. 22.

Vice President Lyndon B. Johnson takes the oath of office as President aboard the Presidential plane as Mrs. Ladybird Johnson and Mrs. Jacqueline Kennedy look on.

Martin Luther King, Jr., predicts that turmoil in the United States will continue "until the Negro is granted his citizenship rights."

Sept. 15   A Negro Baptist church is bombed in Birmingham, Alabama, killing 4 children and injuring several others.

Oct. 10   Linus Pauling, already the recipient of a Nobel Prize in chemistry, is awarded the 1962 Nobel Prize for peace (after a year's delay) because of his antiwar activities. He has been a vigorous proponent of a test-ban treaty.

Oct. 24   Operation "Big Lift," in which an entire armored division is airlifted from Texas to West Germany, is completed.

Nov. 5   Eugene Paul Wigner, a Hungarian-born American, and Marie Goeppert Mayer, a German-born American, share with a German colleague the Nobel Prize in physics for research in the structure of the nucleus of the atom.

Nov. 22   President John F. Kennedy is struck by two bullets while riding in a motorcade through Dallas, Texas. He is taken to a hospital and pronounced dead shortly after arrival. Later in the day Vice President Lyndon Baines Johnson is sworn in as the 36th President of the United States aboard the plane that is to fly Kennedy's body and the Presidential party back to Washington, D.C. [Johnson declares a one-month period of official mourning while expressions of grief and sympathy pour in to the Kennedy family from around the nation and the world. Kennedy is buried on Nov. 25 at Arlington National Cemetery at a ceremony attended by leaders from 92 countries.]

Nov. 24   Lee Harvey Oswald, the alleged assassin of President Kennedy, is killed while in police custody by a nightclub owner, Jack Ruby. This incident occurs during a television news broadcast and is seen "live" by millions of viewers.

Nov. 29   President Johnson appoints a committee, headed by Chief Justice Earl Warren, to investigate all facts surrounding the assassination.

399

1964 **Congress and President Johnson collaborate throughout the year to** effectuate the legislation that John F. Kennedy was seeking at the time of his assassination. Taxes are lowered, the initial steps are taken in what Johnson calls the War on Poverty, and a civil rights statute is enacted that is hailed as the most thoroughgoing effort yet made to ameliorate the condition of the blacks. Activity continues on the streets, civil rights activists are persecuted and killed, riots occur in several cities; but on the whole the pace of protest diminishes. A number of black leaders sign a moratorium on demonstrations in July, including Martin Luther King, Jr., who becomes a Nobel laureate in October. Nevertheless, as the Presidential elections approach, it is remembered that aspirant Barry Goldwater voted against the Civil Rights bill, and it is noted that Governor George Wallace of Alabama, arch enemy of desegregation, shows unexpected political strength in Wisconsin and Indiana before abandoning the race for the Democratic nomination.

Goldwater, forthright advocate of the right wing, is chosen as the Republican Party's candidate. His supporters contend that, outside of the Northeast, there is a huge silent, conservative group of Americans dissatisfied with the Government's performance since Franklin D. Roosevelt became President in 1933. For moderate Republicans who hope to stop Goldwater's nomination, his only serious rival is Governor Nelson Rockefeller of New York; but Rockefeller's political chances have been damaged by his recent divorce and remarriage. On accepting the nomination, Goldwater asserts that "extremism in the defense of liberty is no vice. . .moderation in the pursuit of justice is no virtue." The statement—with its implication that the end may justify the means—frightens many Americans.

Selection of the Democratic candidate is never in doubt, as President and master politician Lyndon B. Johnson orchestrates every detail of the Democratic convention at Atlantic City. The only question is his selection of a running mate. Democrats who prefer Robert Kennedy are disappointed when the President chooses Senator Hubert H. Humphrey of Minnesota.

In the election, the political left and center support Johnson, but his espousal of the Civil Rights Act has damaged his popularity in some quarters, not only in the South. On the other hand, millions of Republicans cross the party line to help give Johnson the most overwhelming popular victory (61.3 per cent) since records were kept.

Jan. 8 President Johnson tells a joint session of Congress that he is declaring a War on Poverty in the United States and outlines a plan of action that includes special assistance to Appalachia, youth employment legislation, improved unemployment insurance, a domestic Peace Corps (to be called the National Service Corps), and expansion of President Kennedy's area redevelopment program. [On July 21 Johnson puts the cost of the War on Poverty at over $1,000,000,000.] The President proposes a budget for fiscal 1964-1965 limiting expenditures to $97,900,000,000. The actual expenditures are $381,000,000 below this figure, and the deficit for the year, $3,474,000,000, is the lowest in five years.

Jan. 9-17 Riots errupt in the Panama Canal Zone, resulting in the deaths of 4 U.S. soldiers and 21 Panamanians. On Jan. 17 Panama breaks diplomatic relations with the United States. The immediate cause of the riots is a dispute over the flying of the U.S. flag (and not the Panamanian flag) at a high school for U.S. dependents, despite a previous decision that neither flag is to be flown. The basic problem is Panamanian resentment of U.S. sovereignty over the Canal Zone. [Diplomatic relations are resumed on April 4 with an agreement to negotiate differences.]

Jan. 23 The 24th Amendment, outlawing the use of the poll tax to prevent citizens from voting in a Federal election, is ratified by South Dakota, completing approval by the requisite three-quarters of the states.

Jan. 29 The United States orbits a satellite with a payload of 20,000 pounds using a Saturn booster rocket. It is the first time the United States has put into orbit an object heavier than the Soviet Union has.

Feb. 17 The U.S. Supreme Court, in *Westberry* v. *Sanders,* rules 6 to 3 that U.S.

Congressional districts must not vary substantially in population.

Feb. 25 Cassius Clay becomes the heavyweight champion of the world when Sonny Liston refuses to continue to fight in the seventh round at Miami Beach. [Clay then changes his name to Muhammad Ali. His championship is not recognized by the World Boxing Association.]

Mar. 27-28 An earthquake with a magnitude of 8.6 on the Richter scale (one and one-half times more violent than the 1906 San Francisco quake) hits Alaska and sets off tidal waves that reach Oregon and California. Property damage is put at $750,000,000 and 114 deaths are reported.

April 5 General Douglas MacArthur, 84, hero of the U.S. campaign against Japan during World War II, dies in Washington, D.C.

April 22 The New York World's Fair opens on the site of the 1939 fair in Queens. The theme of the fair is "Peace through Understanding." Represented are 66 nations and 23 states, as well as private organizations. [The fair closes on Oct. 17, 1965, after receiving 51,000,000 visitors.]

July 2 The Civil Rights Act of 1964, originally proposed by former President Kennedy and supported by President Johnson, is passed by Congress and signed by the President. The Act outlaws discrimination in public accommodations, sets up an Equal Opportunity Commission to end employment discrimination, authorizes the Department of Justice to file suits to facilitate school integration, outlaws discrimination in federally funded projects, and provides additional voting safeguards.

July 13-17 At the Republican Party convention in San Francisco, Senator Barry M. Goldwater of Arizona is nominated on the first ballot for President, and Representative William E. Miller of New York is selected for Vice President.

July 31 Shortly before crashing on target into the moon, U.S. spacecraft Ranger 7 sends back to earth more than 4,000 photographs, the first close-ups of the lunar surface.

Aug. 7 Following reports that North Vietnamese gunboats have fired on U.S. ships in the Gulf of Tonkin, the U.S. Senate passes a resolution authorizing the President to "take all necessary measures to repel any armed attack against the forces of the United States and to prevent future aggression." [The resolution becomes the basis for unlimited expansion of U.S. participation in the war in Vietnam. Subsequent evidence revealed in a Congressional inquiry casts serious doubts on the authenticity of the facts as originally reported.]

Aug. 11 The motion picture *A Hard Day's Night,* a musical farce by the Beatles, is released in New York. The Beatles, a British rock group, have for more than a year been the favorite performers of most young Americans.

Aug. 24-27 The Democrats meet in Atlantic City, New Jersey, and nominate by acclamation Lyndon B. Johnson for President and Senator Hubert H. Humphrey for Vice President.

Sept. 27 The Warren Commission, set up by President Johnson to investigate all the details of the assassination of former President Kennedy, reports that Kennedy was shot by Lee Harvey Oswald alone. [Critics of the report claim that the commission ignored evidence pointing to the possibility of others' involvement in the crime.]

Oct. 10 Eddie Cantor, 72, star of vaudeville who extended his career into the theatre, motion pictures, radio, and television, dies in Hollywood.

Oct. 14 Civil Rights leader and advocate of nonviolence Martin Luther King, Jr., is awarded the Nobel Peace Prize. He is the youngest (35 years of age) Nobel laureate ever chosen.

Oct. 15 Biochemist Konrad E. Bloch of Harvard University shares with a German colleague the Nobel Prize in medicine for their research on cholesterol.

Oct. 16 Cole Porter, 71, composer of music and lyrics since the late 1920's, dies in Santa Monica, California. His musical comedies, such as *Panama Hattie* and *Kiss Me, Kate,* and a prodigious number of songs ("Night and Day," "Begin the Beguine," "I've Got You Under My Skin" among them) have made Cole Porter a household word.

Oct. 20 Herbert Hoover, 90, the 31st President, dies in New York City.

Oct. 29 An irreplaceable collection of gems, including the 565-carat Star of India sapphire, is stolen from the American Museum of Natural History in New York City.

Oct. 29 Charles H. Townes of Massachusetts Institute of Technology shares with two Soviet colleagues the Nobel Prize in physics for their work in the development of laser devices.

Nov. 3 Lyndon B. Johnson is elected President in his own right by an overwhelming majority. The popular vote is 43,129,484 for Johnson against 27,178,188 for Goldwater. Johnson, with 486 electoral votes, carries all but six states; the 52 votes of Arizona and the deep South are cast for Goldwater.

1965 **Americans become increasingly concerned as the United States extends** its military commitments overseas—in the Dominican Republic and Vietnam—in keeping with its policy of containing the spread of Communism. In February President Johnson orders air strikes against North Vietnamese targets on a regular basis. Greatly increased bombing of Vietcong positions in South Vietnam is also ordered. After April the number of U.S. ground troops grows rapidly; the first Army combat units arrive in June. In July the draft call is doubled to 35,000 men per month. Soon U.S. troops are fighting Communist forces in savage battles. During the year the number of U.S. military personnel increases from 20,000 to 190,000. U.S. combat deaths total 1,404 for the year, as compared to a total of slightly more than 200 in the preceding four years. Congress appropriates several billion dollars for the war. Nevertheless, by the end of the year, the Communists control about the same portion of South Vietnam as they did in January.

In the United States two diverse groups protest the war. Some call for an all-out attack against the North, including the bombing of Hanoi and the use of nuclear weapons if needed. Others feel that the United States should end the bombing and leave the Vietnamese to solve their own problems. This latter group holds demonstrations across the country during October to dramatize its viewpoint. Most Americans, however, support the Government's policy.

Jan. 4 President Johnson delivers a State of the Union address in which he discusses plans for the "Great Society" in such areas as education, housing, health, job-training opportunities, water quality, and medical care for the aged. The President also promises further aid to South Vietnam.

Jan. 20 President Johnson takes the oath of office for his first full term. The office of Vice President is filled for the first time in 14 months when Hubert H. Humphrey is also sworn in.

Jan. 25 The Administration's proposed budget for the fiscal 1965-1966 sets revenues at $94,4000,000,000 and projects a deficit of about $5,300,000,000. [The actual deficit is somewhat less, $2,286,000,000.] The sum of $49,000,000,000 is earmarked for defense. Only $3,380,000,000 is asked for foreign aid.

Feb. 21 Malcolm X, 39, is shot and killed in

New York City. Born Malcolm Little, he changed his name on joining the Black Muslims while serving a robbery sentence from 1946 to 1952, and became one of the foremost black leaders and orators. In 1964 he broke with the Black Muslims, alienated by their creed of black separatism and their unwillingness to participate actively in the current civil rights struggle.

Mar. 7-9 A sheriff's posse and state troopers in Selma, Alabama, using whips, clubs, and tear gas, injure more than 50 Negroes attempting to march to Montgomery in protest against an earlier killing of a Negro. On Mar. 9, 1,500 Negroes led by Martin Luther King, Jr., again attempting to make the march, decide to halt outside the city and accept Federal mediation; however, a Unitarian minister from Massachusetts, James J. Reeb, is severely beaten on the streets of Selma. [Reeb dies of his injuries on Mar. 11. On Mar. 13 President Johnson meets with Alabama Governor George Wallace at the White House and informs Wallace that the brutality in Selma must be stopped.]

Mar. 8 The first combat ground troops of the United States to land in Vietnam are 3,500 marines, who debark at Danang.

Mar. 17 Mrs. Alice Hertz, 72, dies on a Detroit street of burns resulting from self-immolation in protest against the war in Vietnam.

Mar. 21-25 A 54-mile march from Selma to Montgomery, Alabama, finally begins with

President Lyndon B. Johnson, on Oct. 20, points to where the surgeons had operated for removal of gall bladder and kidney stones.

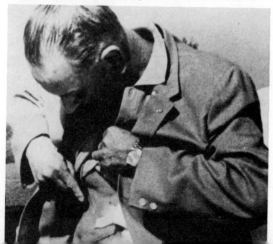

3,200 marchers and finishes with over 25,000. The march takes place after President Johnson federalizes the Alabama National Guard and sends in additional U.S. troops to prevent violence. Led by Martin Luther King, Jr., the march dramatizes the lack of Negro voter registration in Alabama. (In Dallas County, of which Selma is the seat, white voters outnumber Negroes by 28 to 1, although Negroes comprise a majority of the population.) Soon after the march Mrs. Viola Liuzzo is killed by members of the Ku Klux Klan while driving marchers from Montgomery back to Selma. [The alleged killers escape conviction in state court; tried in a Federal court in Montgomery they are found guilty on Dec. 3 of conspiracy to deny a citizen her constitutional rights.]

April 6 Early Bird, the world's first communications satellite capable of being used in commercial operations, is launched from Cape Kennedy (as Cape Canaveral has been called since Thanksgiving Day, 1963).

April 11 Seven states in the Midwest are hit by tornadoes in the worst disaster of its kind in 40 years. The twisters kill 271 persons and injure 5,000.

April 28 President Johnson announces that he is sending 405 U.S. marines to the Dominican Republic to protect Americans and U.S. property endangered as a result of a civil war in that country. [U.S. troops, sent on April 30, eventually are ordered to fight the rebel forces which, according to Johnson, have been taken over by a "band of Communist conspirators." Many dispute this claim, but Johnson, unwilling to risk the success of a second Communist regime in Latin America, sends more troops, reaching a total of 30,000. By Sept. 3, a provisional Government is established acceptable to both sides in the conflict and elections are called for. U.S. troops, who sustain 178 casualties, including 24 dead, are not removed until 1966.]

June 3 Astronaut Edward White leaves his Gemini capsule during a four-day, two-man orbital flight and becomes the first American to "walk in space."

June 7 The U.S. Supreme Court rules that a Connecticut law against the use of contraceptives violates citizens' constitutional rights to privacy.

June 14 A 13-hour Festival of Arts and Humanities is held at the White House.

July 2 Title VII of the 1964 Civil Rights Act goes into effect. It is the first U.S. law aimed at ending discrimination in private employment.

July 14 U.S. Ambassador to the United Na-

tions Adlai Stevenson, 65, Democratic candidate for the Presidency in 1952 and 1956, dies in London.

July 15 After an 8½ month trip over a distance of 134,000,000 miles, Mariner 4 begins sending back pictures of Mars from as close as 7,000 miles to the planet.

July 25 A military jet aircraft transporting marines to Vietnam crashes near Los Angeles, killing all 84 aboard.

July 30 Medicare, a measure to provide the elderly with Federally supported medical and hospital care under the Social Security system, is signed into law by President Johnson.

Aug. 6 Johnson signs the Voting Rights Act, which provides for direct Federal intervention in any district where half or more of the adult population is not registered.

Aug. 12-17 Race riots erupt in the Watts area of Los Angeles, touched off by the arrest of a Negro by white police for drunk driving. The National Guard is called in to help restore order, but 35 persons are killed, many more injured, and extensive property damage done.

Aug. 17 Newspaperman Robert Maury reaches England after a 78-day voyage alone across the Atlantic Ocean in a 13½-foot boat.

Sept. 9 The 11th Cabinet-rank department is established, the Department of Housing and Urban Development. It has jurisdiction over such programs as urban renewal and urban mass transportation.

Sept. 29 Johnson signs a bill establishing the National Foundation on the Arts and the Humanities.

Oct. 4 Pope Paul VI, on a visit to the United States, celebrates a mass in Yankee Stadium and addresses the United Nations on the need for peace in the world.

Oct. 21 Three American scientists receive Nobel Prizes: Robert Burns Woodward, in chemistry, for his work in synthesizing organic compounds; and Richard Phillips Feynmann and Julian Seymour (with a Japanese colleague), in physics, for research in quantum electrodynamics.

Nov. 9-10 An electric power failure in the Northeast affects 30,000,000 persons. The blackout occurs in late afternoon on a workday, and is not remedied until the following morning.

Dec. 15 Two Gemini spacecraft, each with two astronauts aboard, perform a rendezvous in space, coming within six feet of each other. The maneuver demonstrates the feasibility of building an orbiting space station.

An important consideration in 1966 is whether the United States can afford to fight an increasingly expensive war in Vietnam and at the same time support needed domestic programs. In January, with 190,000 troops in Vietnam, President Johnson assures the nation that the United States is strong enough and healthy enough to achieve both goals. But by December troop strength in Vietnam has grown to just under 400,000; the Government is spending more for the war than for its welfare commitments at home, and recently enacted Great Society programs go begging for funds. Moreover, massive government outlays stimulate inflation, pushing prices and interest rates to record highs.

The growth of the war increases dissent. Conservatives, labor leaders, and others continue to support the Administration's Vietnam policy or call for a still larger U.S. effort. But liberals, blacks, students, and many intellectuals—groups that overwhelmingly supported Johnson in 1964—turn from him. Civil rights leaders in particular feel that the war threatens to distract from the struggle for racial equality. In Congress the President is notably less successful than in 1964 and 1965 in securing desired legislation. Voters in the midterm elections give the Republicans a far greater victory than expected—47 new seats in the House and 4 in the Senate.

Jan. 13   Robert C. Weaver is named Secretary of the new Department of Housing and Urban Development, the first Negro to become a Cabinet officer.

Jan. 17   A U.S. B-52 bomber crashes near Palomares, Spain, after colliding with a jet fueler. [Three of the four H-bombs aboard the plane are soon recovered; however, the fourth falls into the sea and is lost until discovered April 7 by a U.S. Navy deep-diving research ship sent to look for the bomb.]

Jan. 24   The President's budget for fiscal 1966-1967 calls for expenditures of $112,800,000,000 and revenues of $111,000,000,000, projecting a deficit of only $1,800,000,000. [A huge excess in defense spending, amounting to more than $12,000,000,000 more than in the preceding year, leaves an actual deficit for 1966-1967 of $9,938,000,000.]

Feb. 6-8   President Johnson and South Vietnam's Premier Nguyen Cao Ky meet in Hawaii to discuss the war.

Mar. 16   Astronauts Neil A. Armstrong and David R. Scott aboard the Gemini 8 spacecraft carry out the first orbital docking maneuver by linking up with an Agena target vehicle launched earlier. A short circuit causes a Gemini maneuvering rocket with a 25-pound thrust to fire continuously, forcing the spacecraft to yaw and spin wildly. After detaching the Agena from the Gemini, which continues to spin, Armstrong stabilizes the craft by deactivating all the other maneuvering jets, which are intended for use on reentry. This requires the astronauts to cancel the remainder of the flight, and return to earth. [Four more two-man Gemini flights and dockings are made during 1966; except for a few minor problems, all are successful. Edwin Aldrin, aboard Gemini 12 launched on Nov. 11, spends 5½ hours outside the spacecraft.]

Mar. 22   James M. Roche, president of General Motors, apologizes before a Senate committee for an investigation ordered by his company into the private life of Ralph Nader. Nader's book, *Unsafe at Any Speed,* published in 1965, is critical of the nation's auto makers for emphasizing style and power at the expense of safety.

Mar. 25   The use of a poll tax in state elections is ruled unconstitutional by the U.S. Supreme Court in *Harper* v. *Virginia Board of Elections.* Elections in Virginia, Texas, Alabama, and Mississippi are affected by the decision.

May 10   An amendment to the California constitution, passed in 1964, that repealed all state fair-housing laws and prevented such laws thereafter, is invalidated by the California supreme court. [In 1967 the U.S. Supreme Court confirms the ruling.]

May 11-16   Students at various universities stage sit-in demonstrations to protest the use of class rank as a factor in determining draft deferments. Students also protest voluntary examinations given to help the Selective Service determine draft eligibility. On May 15, 15,000 persons march on Washington and pledge not to vote for any candidate who supports the Vietnam war.

June 2   The U.S. space program achieves its

first soft landing on the moon with Surveyor 1, which begins transmitting pictures of the lunar surface.

June 6-22 James Meredith, whose enrollment as the first Negro at the University of Mississippi in 1962 set off massive riots, begins a hike from Memphis, Tennessee, to Jackson, Mississippi, a distance of 260 miles, to encourage Negroes to vote. On the second day of his walk he is shot, and though he is not badly hurt, national attention is drawn to the incident. While numerous Negro leaders and others complete the march, an ideological power struggle develops. Newly radicalized blacks, led by Stokely Carmichael, president of the Student Nonviolent Coordinating Committee (SNCC), propound a philosophy of "black power."

June 13 In *Miranda* v. *State of Arizona* the U.S. Supreme Court rules, 5 to 4, that police may not interrogate an individual until he has been informed of his constitutional rights, including the right to remain silent and the right to an attorney.

June 14 The U.S. Supreme Court upholds a portion of the Voting Rights Act of 1965, effectively giving the vote to U.S. citizens who are literate in a language other than English. The decision is particularly applicable to New York City, where the literacy requirement has prevented many Puerto Ricans who are literate in Spanish (but not in English) from voting.

July-August Racial riots erupt throughout the United States, affecting more cities than in 1965. They are less violent than the earlier disorders, and are touched off by minor incidents. Attorney General Nicholas Katzenbach puts the blame on "disease and despair, joblessness and hopelessness, rat-infested housing, and long-impacted cynicism."

July 1 The Medicare program providing medical aid to about 19,000,000 elderly Americans goes into effect.

July 14 Police in Chicago discover the bodies of eight student nurses who have been brutally murdered in the townhouse they share; a ninth victim excapes by hiding beneath a bed. [On July 17, Richard Speck, an ex-convict, is arrested and charged with the crime.]

Aug. 1 Charles J. Whitman, a former marine and presently an architectural student, uses a high-powered rifle to shoot and kill 15 persons from a tower at the University of Texas. He also wounds 31 persons before being shot himself by police.

Aug. 25 The first photograph of the earth as seen from the moon is transmitted by satellite Orbiter 1.

Sept. 6 Margaret Sanger, 83, leader of the birth control movement, dies in Tucson, Arizona.

Oct. 13 Charles B. Huggins and Francis P. Rous share the Nobel Prize for medicine for research into the causes of cancer. Rous showed in 1910 that a virus can cause a particular type of cancer, but his work conflicted with then-current theories and was ignored. Huggins in 1941 demonstrated conclusively the role of hormones in cancer of the prostate.

Oct. 15 A new Cabinet post is created as President Johnson signs legislation to establish the Department of Transportation, which will put the work of some 34 Federal agencies under one roof.

Oct. 17-Nov. 2 President Johnson tours Australia, New Zealand, Malaysia, South Korea, Thailand, and the Philippines, and he pays a surprise visit to U.S. troops in South Vietnam.

Oct. 26 A fire on the aircraft carrier *Oriskany,* operating in the Gulf of Tonkin off Vietnam, takes 43 lives.

Nov. 8 The resurgence of Republicans in both Houses of Congress fails to deprive the President of his Democratic majority there. One of the newly elected Republicans is Edward Brooke, of Massachusetts, the first black Senator since Reconstruction days. Among the new Republican governors (with a net gain in the state houses of eight), the election of former film star Ronald Reagan in California is noteworthy. In the South, where Republican governors are rare, Claude Kirk in Florida and Winthrop Rockefeller in Arkansas are successful. Spiro T. Agnew wins in Maryland against a Democrat who relies unsuccessfully on a "white backlash" for victory.

Nov. 18 Air Force Major William J. Knight sets a record in the X-15 at Edwards AFB in California by achieving a peak speed of 4,233 mph.

Dec. 5 In the first ruling invalidating a state's right to decide on the qualifications of those elected to its legislature, the U.S. Supreme Court orders Georgia to seat Julian Bond, three times elected to the state Assembly. He was denied his seat each time because of his protest against the war in Vietnam.

Dec. 15 Walt Disney, 65, dies in Los Angeles. Creator of the nation's most popular animated movies, Disney is probably best known for his cartoon character Mickey Mouse.

1967 **Two conflicting trends capture the attention of the nation** this year. Race riots of unprecedented scope and intensity affect over 100 cities, including Boston, Tampa, Cincinnati, New York, Philadelphia, Chicago, Minneapolis, Hartford, Washington, New Haven, and Pittsburgh. The worst hit are Newark and Detroit. In these two cities—in a total of 11 days of rioting, looting, and arson—72 persons die, many more are injured, thousands are arrested, and well over $200,000,000 worth of property is destroyed.

While most Americans do not approve of the race riots, they find such events far more comprehensible than the appearance of another phenomenon—groupings of white, young, middle-class Americans (dubbed ''hippies'') who profess to eschew not only violence (typified by the ongoing war) but also the American dream of affluence and power. Instead of rioting, thousands of hippies stream into San Francisco to celebrate peacefully a ''Summer of Love.'' The hippie message, with its rejection of traditional American values, may be more hazardous to established patterns than the rioting blacks, who only want what most Americans already have.

Jan. 5 U.S. trade with Rhodesia is ended by Executive order in accordance with a U.N. resolution passed on Dec. 16, 1966, mandating that member states boycott that country. The economic sanctions were sponsored by Britain and supported by most African nations.

Jan. 8-27 Operation Cedar Falls, the largest offensive to date in the Vietnam war, takes place about 25 miles northwest of Saigon, involving 16,000 U.S. and 14,000 South Vietnamese troops.

Jan. 10 The U.S. Supreme Court rules, in *United States* v. *Lamb*, that citizens who visit countries prohibited by the State Department cannot be subject to criminal prosecution.

Jan. 10 In his State of the Union message President Johnson requests that Congress place a 6-per-cent surcharge on both corporate and individual income taxes to help pay for both the war in Vietnam and domestic programs. [On Aug. 3 he asks for a 10-per-cent surcharge. The latter amount is passed on June 20, 1968.]

Jan. 24 The proposed budget for fiscal 1967-1968, using the system previously used (administrative budget), anticipates on the basis of increased expenditures and revenues a deficit of $8,100,000,000. This sytem, however, is replaced by the more accurate national income budget, which includes in the calculations funds in trust accounts (such as Social Security and Highway Trust). Under this system, the budget anticipates a deficit of $2,100,000,000. [The actual deficit for fiscal 1967-1968, under the new system, is $25,200,000,000.]

Jan. 27 Astronauts Virgil I. Grissom, Edward H. White, and Roger B. Chaffee die in a fire in an Apollo space capsule during a simu-lated launching at Cape Kennedy. [The probable cause of the disaster was faulty wiring, but a better escape mechanism might have saved the astronauts, according to a report issued on April 9.]

Feb. 10 The 25th Amendment to the Constitution becomes effective. In the event of Presidential disability, the Vice President will take over as acting President until the President is able to resume his duties. The Amendment also provides that in the event the office of Vice President is vacant, the President is to select a Vice President who must then be confirmed by a majority of each House of Congress.

Feb. 20 The sale of Leonardo da Vinci's portrait *Ginevra dei Benci* for more than $5,000,000 to the National Gallery of Art in Washington, D.C., is revealed.

Mar. 1 The House of Representatives votes to exclude Adam Clayton Powell of New York from his seat in Congress on the grounds that he misused public funds. [Powell is overwhelmingly reelected on April 11 by his constituents in New York City (Harlem) and again in 1968. On June 18, 1969, the U.S. Supreme Court rules that he

A U.S. Marine patrol approaches abandoned enemy bunkers.

must be seated.]

April 12-14   President Johnson attends a meeting of the heads of state of 18 Latin American countries at Punte del Este, Uruguay, and promises to support the concept of a Latin American common market.

April 15   New York and San Francisco are the scenes of two huge antiwar marches organized by the Spring Mobilization Committee. In New York the number of marchers is estimated as high as 350,000. [On May 13, in a counterdemonstration, some 70,000 persons march down New York's Fifth Avenue to show their support of the U.S. fighting man in Vietnam.]

April 21   Svetlana Alliluyeva, the daughter of Joseph Stalin, finds refuge in the United States.

May 9   Muhammad Ali (Cassius Clay), indicted by a Federal grand jury for refusing to be inducted into the Army, is deprived of his title as world heavyweight champion by the World Boxing Association. [No generally recognized champion succeeds Ali.]

June 12   The U.S. Supreme Court, in *Loving v. Virginia,* unanimously decides that laws against interracial marriage violate the Constitution.

June 23   The Senate, by vote of 92 to 5, censures Senator Thomas J. Dodd of Connecticut for using tax-free campaign money for personal expenses.

June 23-25   President Johnson and Soviet Premier Aleksei Kosygin meet at Glassboro, New Jersey, but accomplish little during their talks. Kosygin is in the United States to attend a U.N. General Assembly meeting on the recent Arab-Israeli war.

July 22   Carl Sandburg, 89, dies at Flat Rock, North Carolina. The winner of many Pulitzer prizes, Sandburg is best remembered for his poetry and his six-volume study of the life of Abraham Lincoln.

July 23-30   Rioters disrupt the city of Detroit and are quelled by the National Guard after 40 persons are killed.

July 29   A fire aboard the 79,900-ton aircraft carrier U.S.S. *Forrestal* off the coast of North Vietnam kills 134 persons and damages some 60 aircraft.

Sept. 4   Michigan Governor George Romney announces that U.S. military and diplomatic officials gave him "the greatest brainwashing anyone can get" when he visited Vietnam in 1965.

Sept. 17   U.S. Air Force bombers hit a bridge in North Vietnam 7 miles below the Chinese border.

Sept. 30   President Johnson signs an appropriation for defense in the amount of $69,936,620,000, the largest sum ever authorized by Congress in one bill.

Oct. 2   Solicitor General Thurgood Marshall, who as an attorney argued and won the landmark 1954 school desegregation case before the U.S. Supreme Court, is sworn in as the first Negro Associate Justice.

Oct. 10   A 63-nation space treaty, signed by both the United States and the Soviet Union, goes into effect. The orbiting of nuclear weapons and territorial claims on the moon and planets are outlawed.

Oct. 18   The Nobel Prize in medicine is awarded to three researchers in the processes that affect the human eye. One of them is Swedish; the other two are Americans: George Wald of Harvard University and Haldan R. Hartline of the Rockefeller Institute for Medical Research.

Oct. 21-22   A protest demonstration of some 50,000 persons opposed to the war in Vietnam is held in Washington, D.C., at the Lincoln Memorial and at the Pentagon.

Oct. 30   Hans Bethe, a German-born American nuclear physicist, who discovered the process by which the sun acquires its energy, wins the Nobel Prize in physics.

Nov. 7   The first blacks to win seats in the state legislatures of Virginia, Mississippi, and Louisiana since Reconstruction are elected. Voters in Cleveland, Ohio and Gary, Indiana, elect black mayors.

Nov. 9   In starting the Apollo program, the second phase of the space effort to reach the moon, the Saturn 5 (carrying an unmanned spacecraft in rehearsal) is launched from Cape Kennedy. The rocket weighs 280,000 pounds and has at least twice the thrust of any booster launched by the Soviet Union.

Nov. 20   According to the official clock in the Census Bureau, the United States now has a population of 200,000,000.

Nov. 29   Secretary of Defense Robert S. McNamara announces that he is leaving his post to become head of the World Bank.

Dec. 2   Francis Cardinal Spellman, 78, Archbishop of New York since 1939, dies in New York City.

Dec. 14   Announcement is made at Stanford University that biochemists have succeeded in creating a synthetic DNA, a molecule that controls heredity in all life forms.

1968

President Johnson announces on television at the end of March his decision not to run for another term; with the country engaged in war overseas and with trouble brewing at home, it would be wrong, he says, for him to devote even "an hour or a day to personal partisan causes. . . ." Unstated is the challenge of Johnson's continued leadership that comes from within his own party, in the persons of two Senators who are contending for the Presidency on only one issue: opposition to the war. Both these Senators Eugene McCarthy of Minnesota and Robert Kennedy of New York, show strength in the primaries and among the antiwar demonstrators. Vice President Hubert Humphrey, who enters the race after the President's withdrawal, participates in no primaries, but with Johnson's help is nominated on the first ballot at the Democratic convention in Chicago in August.

The Republicans, with less fanfare, nominate former Vice President Richard Nixon, whose political career was thought to be ended after his 1960 defeat by President Kennedy, followed by an unsuccessful bid in 1962 for the governorship of California.

Both Humphrey and Nixon are associated with a tough line on Vietnam. Humphrey points to his record as a liberal, but he fails to disassociate himself from the Johnson policy on the war. Trailing Nixon in the polls, Humphrey suddenly picks up strength late in the campaign when he softens his position on the war and President Johnson orders a complete halt to the bombing of North Vietnam. Nixon wins the election, but by an almost insignificant margin: 43.4 per cent to Humphrey's 42.7 per cent of the popular vote. (Wallace receives a surprising 13.5 per cent.)

Not all the events occur in convention halls or at polling booths. If there is any doubt of this, the television watcher knows better, for the demonstrations not only on the streets of Chicago but on campuses all over the country provide competition for the politicians. As if two more major assassinations do not provide enough violence, Americans learn that they have already lost 30,000 young men on Asian battlefields, and the end is not in sight; more than 500,000 U.S. servicemen are still in Vietnam, and the fighting becomes more intense every campaign. It must be admitted, however, that the economy, despite an inflationary trend, seems to be healthy. Employment, pay, savings, and personal consumption have never been higher.

Jan. 2   In an effort to ease the balance-of-payments deficit, President Johnson asks Americans to voluntarily defer for two years pleasure travel outside the Western Hemisphere.

Jan. 19   The draft call for 1968 is estimated at slightly over 300,000 men, up from 230,000 in 1967. [On Feb. 16 most graduate school and occupational deferments are suspended.]

Jan. 21-April 5   A U.S. Marine base at Khesanh, South Vietnam, located just south of the demilitarized zone, is besieged by Communist forces. Supplied only by air, U.S. troops hold the position despite heavy losses until relief comes and the siege is lifted.

Jan. 23   The U.S.S. *Pueblo*, a Navy Intelligence ship, allegedly violates North Korean territorial waters and is captured by the North Korean navy. [The crew, but not the ship, is released in December after the United States signs an apology acceptable to the North Koreans.]

Jan. 29   President Johnson's budget is a record $186,100,000,000. A huge deficit is forecast unless Congress passes a 10-per-cent tax surcharge. [The surcharge is approved and, on June 28, signed into law along with a Federal spending cut.]

Mar. 12   In the Presidential primary in New Hampshire, Senator Eugene McCarthy of Minnesota, a Democratic aspirant for nomination, makes a surprising showing, with 42 per cent of the votes, although write-in votes give President Johnson 48 per cent.

April 4   The Rev. Martin Luther King, Jr., 39, is shot and killed while standing on a motel balcony in Memphis, Tennessee, where he has gone to assist a strike by black sanitation workers. [James Earl Ray is arrested in London on June 8 and charged with the crime. At first he claims he is innocent but at his trial he pleads guilty.]

April 4-6   Riots break out in more than 100 cities as a result of the King assassination. [In

Chicago Mayor Richard J. Daly on April 15 tells his police to "shoot to kill any arsonist—shoot to cripple or maim anyone looting." Riots are brought under control with the aid of Federal troops.]

April 11 Another Civil Rights Act is signed by the President. It makes illegal discrimination in the sale and rental of housing in all but single-family dwellings sold by the owner and apartments of less than four units where one unit is lived in by the owner. The act also makes it a Federal crime to cross a state line to incite a riot.

April 23-30 Students at Columbia University in New York City occupy several campus buildings. Several issues are raised by the students, chiefly the building of a gymnasium on city land without the participation of residents of the neighboring black community (Harlem), and the role taken by the university in conducting research for the Department of Defense. Eventually police are called in to recapture the buildings which the students have "liberated."

May 2-June 24 The Poor People's March on Washington begins under the leadership of the Rev. Ralph Abernathy, who has taken command of the project originally organized by the late Martin Luther King, Jr. Poor people, mostly black, arrive in Washington and camp near the Washington Monument, a site they call "Resurrection City."

June 1 Helen Keller, 87, dies in Westport, Connecticut. Blind, deaf, and mute from the age of 19 months, she learned to speak and read and became a noted author and lecturer.

June 5-6 Senator Robert F. Kennedy, a leading contender for the Democratic Presidential nomination, brother of the assassinated 35th President, is shot after making a victory speech to fellow-Democrats in a Los Angeles hotel. The alleged assailant, Sirhan Sirhan, is arrested on the scene. Kennedy dies 25 hours later.

June 26 Chief Justice of the Supreme Court Earl Warren announces his intention to resign and President Johnson nominates Associate Justice Abe Fortas to succeed him. [The Senate refuses to confirm Fortas, and on Oct. 2 Johnson announces that he will leave the appointment up to the next President.]

Aug. 5-8 The Republican Party, meeting at Miami Beach to name its Presidential ticket, picks Richard M. Nixon on the first ballot on Aug. 8. Nixon selects Maryland Governor Spiro T. Agnew as his running mate.

Aug. 26-29 The Democratic national convention in Chicago is the scene of hectic activity within the amphitheatre itself as the candidates and policy of the party are discussed. Hubert Humphrey is nominated on the first ballot, although he has no record of victories at the primaries. (Humphrey picks Senator Edmund Muskie of Maine to run with him.) The middle-of-the-road plank on the war in Vietnam, favored by Humphrey, easily wins over a halt-the-bombing plank endorsed by McCarthy and (before his death) Robert Kennedy. The scene in the convention hall is challenged, in television coverage, by the scene on the streets of Chicago, where marches and demonstrations take place while the cameras roll. Antiwar protesters, including a group calling themselves the Yippies (for Youth International Party), battle with police. Demonstrators, bystanders, and newsmen are beaten and many police are also injured.

Oct. 3 George Wallace, American Independent Party candidate for President, picks General Curtis LeMay as his running mate. LeMay has indicated his willingness to use nuclear weapons in Vietnam.

Oct. 16 Three Americans are awarded the Nobel Prize in medicine for their research in genetics: Robert W. Holley of the Salk Institute, H. Gobind Khorana of the University of Wisconsin, and Marshall W. Nirenberg of the National Institute of Health.

Oct. 30 The Nobel Prizes in chemistry and in physics are awarded to two Americans. Luis W. Alvarez of the University of California, Berkeley, is cited for "decisive contributions to elementary particle physics." Lars Onsager is credited with the "discovery of the reciprocal relations bearing his name, which are fundamental for the thermodynamics of irreversible processes."

Nov. 5 Republican candidate Richard Nixon is elected President with a popular vote of 31,785,480. Democrat Hubert Humphrey receives 31,275,166 votes and American independent George Wallace gets 9,906,473. The electoral majority for Nixon is more decisive: Nixon, 301; Humphrey, 191; Wallace, 46. Democrats maintain their hold on both Houses of Congress.

Dec. 20 Novelist John Steinbeck, 66, Nobel laureate in 1962, dies in New York City.

Dec. 21-27 Three astronauts aboard Apollo 8 leave earth and orbit the moon 10 times before returning to a safe landing in the Pacific Ocean. The men are the first to view the far side of the moon. Parts of their mission are televised live, and excite great public interest.

1969

This is the year during which one of mankind's apparently impossible dreams comes true: Astronaut Neil Armstrong plants his boot firmly on the soil of the moon and tells 500,000,000 listeners a quarter of a million miles away, "That's one small step for a man, one giant leap for mankind." Now 1969 ranks with 1492 and 1776 as one of the three dates every school child must remember.

As the space age reaches its climax, at least for this decade, events on earth continue to provoke and surprise its inhabitants. A new President is inaugurated, but the slaughter continues in Vietnam. U.S. forces in that country are reduced from 539,000 to 484,000, but hundreds of thousands of antiwar protesters condemn the pace of troop withdrawal in a variety of ways. At the same time, several hundred thousand young people win respect for their manners, however controversial their taste, as they meet in a holiday festival in upper New York State. In a medical report, issued by the U.S. Public Health Service, the American people are told that an "alarming prevalence" of diseases associated with stark poverty exists in the United States. The Department of Health, Education, and Welfare bans the use of cyclamates, a popular artificial sweetener, because of possible carcinogenic qualities detected in laboratory tests. Furthermore, the warning on cigarette packages is changed from "Cigarette smoking may be hazardous to your health" to "Cigarette smoking is dangerous to your health" by Congressional action.

Jan. 14   In his last budget message, President Johnson proposes that expenditures of $195,300,000,000 be appropriated for fiscal 1969-1970, and that the defense expenditure should be raised to $79,000,000,000. The President's salary is raised to $200,000 a year.

Jan. 14   A fire aboard the nuclear-powered U.S.S. *Enterprise* in the Pacific results in the death of 25 crewmen; 85 others are injured.

Jan. 18   Peace talks resume in Paris with all four parties present for the first time: the United States, South Vietnam, North Vietnam, and the National Liberation Front.

Jan. 18-26   Heavy rains create floods and mudslides in southern California, destroying thousands of homes and killing at least 100 persons. [Additional damage is caused on Feb. 23-26 by more rain.]

Jan. 20   Richard Milhous Nixon is inaugurated as the 37th President of the United States. He is the first President in 120 years to contend at his inauguration with a legislature completely controlled by the opposition.

Jan. 28   A blowout in an oil well in the Santa Barbara Channel in California causes hundreds of thousands of gallons of oil to leak into the surrounding waters. [By Feb. 8 the Santa Barbara harbor has been closed and some 40 miles of beaches have been ruined by the oil slick. Further drilling in the area is restricted for several months.]

Feb. 8   After 148 years of publication, *The Saturday Evening Post* brings out its last edition.

Tracing its origin in legend to Benjamin Franklin, the magazine was actually started by Charles Alexander and Samuel Atkinson in 1821, and reached the height of its popularity under the ownership of Cyrus Curtis and the editorship of George Horace Lorimer in the early years of the 20th century. Its circulation reached 4,500,000 in 1954, and is still considerable at its demise, but publication is no longer profitable.

Mar. 28   Dwight David Eisenhower, 78, the 34th President and commander of the Allied forces in World War II, dies in Washington, D.C.

April 2   The longest dock strike in U.S. history ends after 57 days as 43,000 longshoremen go back to work at Atlantic and Gulf ports.

April 7   A unanimous decision by the U.S. Supreme Court declares unconstitutional laws that prohibit the private possession of obscene materials.

May 14   Associate Justice Abe Fortas, who in 1968 was denied the seat of Chief Justice by the Senate, resigns from the Supreme Court amidst public outcry over alleged unethical conduct. Fortas denies any wrongdoing.

June 2   The U.S. destroyer *Frank E. Evans* is cut in half as it is rammed by the Australian aircraft carrier *Melbourne* in the South China Sea during nighttime maneuvers; 74 aboard the destroyer are killed.

June 6   Testimony in a Federal court in Houston, Texas, reveals that the telephones of Martin Luther King, Jr., were tapped despite an order by President Johnson that this measure can only be taken for reasons of "national security" and with the authorization of the Attorney General. [On June 13 it is disclosed in a Federal court in Chicago that the Department of Justice has eavesdropped on suspected subversives without court approval and proposes to continue the practice.]

June 8   President Nixon concludes a meeting with South Vietnamese Premier Thieu on Midway Island with the announcement that 25,000 U.S. troops will be removed from Vietnam by the end of August, to be replaced by South Vietnamese troops. [On Sept. 16 the President announces the withdrawal of an additional 35,000 U.S. troops. This substitution of South Vietnamese for U.S. combat elements is described as "Vietnamization."]

June 9   By a vote of 74 to 3, the U.S. Senate confirms the appointment of Warren E. Burger as Chief Justice of the Supreme Court to fill the post of Earl Warren, who resigned last year but agreed to stay on until a successor could be selected. [Burger replaces Warren on June 23.]

June 22   Judy Garland, 47, popular film singer since her appearance in *The Wizard of Oz* in 1939, dies in London.

July 19   A car driven by Senator Edward Kennedy goes off a bridge on Chappaquiddick Island, Massachusetts, killing Mary Jo Kopechne, a former Robert Kennedy campaign aide. Kennedy escapes unharmed from the car, which lands underwater, but does not report the accident until 10 hours after it occurs. [On July 25 he pleads guilty to leaving the scene of an accident. Public incredulity over the explanation of the accident hurts Kennedy's future Presidential chances.]

July 20-21   Neil Armstrong steps from his lunar module Eagle to become the first man to walk on the surface of the moon, four days after the launching of Apollo 11. Hundreds of millions watch on television as Edwin Aldrin joins Armstrong and the two men set up data-collecting instruments and take samples of moon rock and soil. The following day the astronauts leave the moon and link up with Michael Collins, who has remained aboard the Apollo 11 command ship Columbia in orbit around the moon. The three astronauts then begin the journey back to earth. [They land safely in the Pacific Ocean on July 24. In November the feat is repeated by the three Apollo 12 astronauts.]

July 26-Aug. 3   President Nixon completes a world tour, including visits to five Asian nations. The highlight of Nixon's trip is a final stop at Bucharest, Romania, where he is enthusiastically welcomed.

Aug. 9   The bodies of actress Sharon Tate and four friends are found ritually murdered at her home in Los Angeles. [Police later arrest and charge with the crime an ex-convict and cult leader, Charles Manson.]

Aug. 16-19   More than 300,000 young people rendezvous at the Catskill Mountain village of Bethel, New York, for the Woodstock Music and Art Fair (originally planned for Woodstock, but banned from that town). With inadequate facilities and inclement weather, they spend a memorable four days in the "life style" they admire, listening to music, dancing, smoking marijuana, dressing or undressing as they please. [The goodwill and joyous spirit of the huge gathering wins general admiration, and becomes contemporary legend: the Spirit of Woodstock.]

Aug. 17   Hurricane Camille, the most severe ever to hit the Gulf Coast, wreaks havoc along the Mississippi Gulf shoreline, with tide levels exceeding 30 feet above normal, causing about 150 deaths, and destroying property valued at about $1,000,000,000.

Aug. 24   Soldiers of a light infantry brigade in Vietnam refuse to go into battle as ordered after five days of treacherous fighting and heavy losses. [They are eventually encouraged to continue the fight, and the Army takes no action against them.]

Sept. 10   The state of Alaska receives over $900,000,000 from oil companies in bids for oil and gas leases on the mineral-rich North Slope.

Sept. 24-Dec. 5   Eight men are tried in the Federal district court in Chicago on charges of conspiring to cross state lines to start riots. This is the first case tried under the "incite-to-riot" section of the Civil Rights Act of 1968, and the riot in question in this case occurred at Chicago during the Democratic national convention. Both the judge, Julius Hoffman, and the defendants (the so-called Chicago Eight) and their counsel contribute to the continuous disturbance that features the trial itself. One defendant, Black Panther Bobby Seale, having been denied the right to avail himself of the attorney he prefers, so outrages Judge Hoffman that Seale is forced to sit during part of the trial bound and gagged in the courtroom; after which his case is separated from that of the remaining defendants (now the Chicago Seven) and Seale is sentenced to four years in jail for contempt of court. The case for the prosecution ends on Dec. 5. [The trial continues in 1970.]

Oct. 2 The Atomic Energy Commission explodes a 1.2-megaton hydrogen bomb underground on the island of Amchitka in the Aleutians, despite widespread concern that the test might cause an earthquake.

Oct. 15 Millions of antiwar protesters throughout the nation are involved in a series of activities described by its organizers as a Moratorium to end the war in Vietnam. One activity is the reading aloud, one by one, of the names of young men who have already been killed in what memorialists consider a cause unworthy of Americans. Senators Edward Kennedy, Eugene McCarthy, George McGovern, and Edmund Muskie are among those who participate in a candlelit march around the White House, which the President has already said he would "under no circumstances whatever" allow to influence him.

Oct. 16 The Nobel Prize in medicine is awarded to three Americans for having "set the solid foundation on which modern molecular biology rests." All researchers in viruses, they are Max Delbrück of the California Institute of Technology, Alfred D. Hershey of the Genetics Research Center of the Carnegie Institution, and Salvador E. Luria of the Massachusetts Institute of Technology.

Oct. 30 Murray Gell-Mann of the California Institute of Technology is awarded the Nobel Prize in physics for his classification of elementary particles.

Nov. 15 In the second mass antiwar action of the year, hundreds of thousands of Americans march to demonstrate their anger at the continuation of the war in Vietnam. The "mobilization" is preceded on Oct. 19 by a description by Vice President Agnew of its leaders as "an effete corps of impudent snobs who characterize themselves as intellectuals." At least 250,000 protesters respond to the mobilization in Washington alone, in the largest antiwar demonstration yet to be held.

Nov. 21 Clement F. Haynesworth, nominated by President Nixon as Associate Justice of the U.S. Supreme Court, is not confirmed by the U.S. Senate; the vote is 55 opposed, 45 in favor.

Dec. 28 The American Civil Liberties Union charges that police in nine large cities have been illegally harassing members of the Black Panther Party. Police in many cities have recently raided Panther headquarters and have sometimes been met with armed resistance. The raid in Chicago on Dec. 4, resulting in the death of Black Panther leader Fred Hampton, has aroused considerable anger among blacks, who deny that Hampton or his group resisted the police raiders.

After conducting operations against the enemy, U.S. Marines cross a river near Da Nang, Vietnam, on their way back to their home base.

Relative calm during the early months of the year brings hope that the new decade may bring an end to the turmoil of the late 1960's; that Vietnam and racial discord may be eclipsed by concern for the nation's natural environment. President Nixon himself stresses the need to preserve the environment in his State of the Union message in January, and with his blessing the country peacefully celebrates Earth Day in April. Antiwar dissent is disarmed when Nixon announces plans to withdraw an additional 150,000 troops from Vietnam by the spring of 1971. But when the nation learns that U.S. and South Vietnamese forces have invaded Cambodia, the reaction is swift and sometimes violent. Students in all parts of the country demonstrate against the invasion. Reaction in other areas of society is also apparent. In late May issues on the New York Stock Exchange plunge to an eight-year low. Events begin to cool when President Nixon announces that all U.S. troops have been withdrawn from Cambodia and that the operation is a success. However, it is clear that Vietnam continues to be an issue, and the potential for violent dissent remains.

In the 19th decennial census, it appears that the rate of population growth is again diminishing; this year's census figure of 203,235,298 is 13.3 per cent greater than that of 1960. The nation is now three-fourths urbanized; and one tenth of its people are 65 years of age or over. One eighth of the population is nonwhite; the black population comprises 11.1 per cent of the total. California has overtaken New York as the most populous state.

Jan. 5   Joseph Yablonski, 59, recently defeated candidate for president of the United Mine Workers, is found slain along with his wife and daughter at his home in Clarksville, Pennsylvania. Yablonski was scheduled to testify before a Federal grand jury on alleged union election fraud. [The deaths are later linked to officials of the UMW.]

Jan. 19   President Nixon nominates G. Harrold Carswell as Associate Justice of the Supreme Court. [On April 8 the Senate refuses to confirm Carswell when an investigation reveals his past support of white supremacy. It is the second time that the Senate has failed to confirm a Nixon appointee to the Court.]

Jan. 19   The U.S. Supreme Court, in *Gutknecht* v. *United States,* rules that the Selective Service System may not advance the induction date of an individual who broke the law by leaving his draft card on the steps of a Federal building to protest the nation's Vietnam policy.

Feb. 2   President Nixon's budget for fiscal 1970-1971 is the first to call for spending in excess of $200,000,000,000. A surplus of $1,300,000,000 is projected. [Higher outlays and lower receipts result in an actual deficit of $23,240,000,000.]

Feb. 5   The President seeks an appropriation of $10,000,000,000 to build and improve local waste-treatment facilities.

Feb. 16   Joe Frazier knocks out Jimmy Ellis in the fifth round of a heavyweight championship fight in Madison Square Garden, New York. (Ellis is defending champion as the winner of a "tournament" in 1968 to decide the title holder after Muhammad Ali retired in 1967.)

Feb. 18   The "Chicago Seven" are acquitted of conspiring to incite to riot, charges which grew out of the violence at the 1968 Democratic convention in Chicago. However, five of the seven are convicted on individual counts of crossing state lines to incite a riot. The trial has resulted in numerous contempt citations and much national publicity as the defendants attempted to elaborate their political and social views in order to reach the "big jury out there."

Feb. 25   A branch of the Bank of America is burned during an antiwar protest at the University of California at Santa Barbara.

Mar. 2   A sentence of 10 years in jail is imposed in Houston, Texas, on Timothy Leary, a former educator and present advocate of "mind-expanding" drugs, for the crime of smuggling three ounces of marijuana into the country. [Leary is then taken to California where he is sentenced to another 10-year term, denied bail, and jailed. He escapes on Sept. 12 and finds asylum in Algeria.]

Mar. 11   Mystery writer Erle Stanley Gardner, 80, dies in Temecula, California. He is best known as the creator of the fictional lawyer-hero Perry Mason.

Mar. 17   A U.S. Army panel names 14 officers as responsible for covering up a massacre of civilians at the Vietnamese village of Mylai in 1968. One of the accused is the superintendent of the U.S. Military Academy, General Samuel W. Koster.

April 1-July 29 Contracts are signed by the United Farm Workers and growers representing 85 per cent of California's table-grape production. Agreements come after five years of struggle, including a national boycott of table grapes. [Cesar Chavez, head of the UFW, starts to organize lettuce workers later in the year.]

April 2 Massachusetts enacts a law exempting its citizens from having to fight in an undeclared war. The measure is aimed at the Vietnam conflict, which has never been declared a war by Congress. [On the basis of this state law, an attempt is made in November to bring the issue of the constitutionality of an undeclared war before the U.S. Supreme Court, but by a vote of 6 to 3 the Court refuses to hear proceedings in *Massachusetts* v. *Laird*.]

April 13-17 The third manned moon landing is aborted two days after the launching of Apollo 13, when an oxygen tank in the service module explodes. Unable to turn back at once, the astronauts circle the moon before returning safely to earth.

April 22 "Earth Day" is celebrated around the nation with demonstrations that stress the need for unpolluted water, air, and land.

April 29 Nine days after President Nixon has revealed plans to pull 150,000 U.S. troops out of Vietnam by the spring of 1971. U.S. and South Vietnamese forces begin a major invasion of Cambodia. [All U.S. troops are withdrawn from Cambodia by June 29.]

May 4 National Guardsmen open fire on students at Kent State University in Ohio, killing 4 and wounding many. The students were protesting the extension of the war (although none of those killed appear to have been active protesters). [Throughout the country campus protests again flare up. On May 9 some 100,000 persons hold an antiwar rally in Washington. By May 10 a student strike center at Brandeis University announces that almost 450 institutions of higher learning have either been closed or are experiencing student antiwar strikes. On May 15 a demonstration at predominantly black Jackson State College in Mississippi results in the death of two students when police fire on a crowd.]

May 12 Harry A. Blackmun is confirmed as an Associate Justice of the Supreme Court by a unanimous vote of the U.S. Senate.

May 20 New York City is the scene of a demonstration of some 100,000 persons supporting the President's Vietnam policy.

June 15 The U.S. Supreme Court, in *Welsh* v. *United States,* rules by a vote of 5 to 3 that an individual may qualify for a draft exemption as a conscientious objector despite the fact that his opposition to war is based on moral grounds rather than longheld religious belief.

June 16 Kenneth A. Gibson is elected mayor of Newark, New Jersey, which becomes the first major city in the Northeast to have a black chief executive.

June 19 The U.S. Air Force announces that missiles capable of delivering independently targetable reentry vehicles (MIRV's) have been deployed at Minot, North Dakota.

June 24 The U.S. Senate repeals the 1964 Tonkin Gulf Resolution, which empowered the President to use armed force in Indochina.

July 1 The most liberal abortion legislation in the nation becomes effective in New York State. [By year's end 14 other states have comparable statutes.]

Aug. 7 Judge Harold J. Haley is killed, after he is taken hostage by black militants at Marin County courthouse in San Rafael, California. Two of his abductors and the man who supplied them with guns are also killed. The deaths occur at a shootout with police at a nearby roadblock. [On Aug. 15 one of the black militants involved in the abduction and Angela Davis, a black Communist instructor in philosophy at the University of California (who is charged with owning the guns involved), are charged with kidnapping and murder. On Aug. 16 a warrant for Angela Davis is issued, but she cannot be found until Oct. 13, when she is captured in New York City.]

Aug. 24 Four persons are injured and one is killed when a bomb explodes in the early morning at the Army Mathematics Research Center at the University of Wisconsin in Madison.

Sept. 1 The U.S. Senate defeats, 55 to 39, the first serious attempt to end U.S. involvement in Vietnam, an amendment to a military procurement bill. Under the amendment, proposed by Senators Mark Hatfield of Oregon and George McGovern of South Dakota, withdrawal of U.S. troops by Dec. 31, 1971, would be mandatory. [The last combat ground troops are, in fact, withdrawn on Aug. 11, 1972.]

Sept. 3 Coach Vincent T. Lombardi, 57, who turned the Green Bay Packers into the most formidable team in professional football during the past decade, dies in Washington, D.C.

Sept. 28 John Dos Passos, 74, among the most widely read of American novelists, best known for his trilogy *U.S.A.* published in 1936, dies in Baltimore.

Sept. 29 The New American Bible, translated into English from the original sources by Roman Catholic scholars, is published in Paterson, New Jersey, after 25 years of work. It is intended to take the place held by the Douay version for more than two centuries.

Oct. 15 The Organized Crime Control Act is signed into law. The act permits greater use of wiretapping to fight organized crime, and makes it illegal to finance a legitimate business with money derived from criminal rackets.

Oct. 15 A one-third share of the Nobel Prize in medicine is awarded to Julius Axelrod of the National Institute of Mental Health, for research in the chemistry of nerve transmission.

Oct. 16 The second Nobel Memorial Prize in economic science is awarded to Paul Anthony Samuelson of the Massachusetts Institute of Technology, "for having done more than any other contemporary economist to raise the level of scientific analysis in economic theory."

Oct. 21 Norman E. Borlaug is awarded the Nobel Prize for peace for his work in developing high-yield strains of wheat and rice. [Borlaug asserts that unless population growth can be controlled, his work will merely provide a 30-year delay in the world food crisis.]

Oct. 23 Gary Gabelich sets a land speed record by averaging 622.407 mph in two runs at the Bonneville Salt Flats in Utah, driving the Blue Flame, a rocket-powered vehicle using hydrogen peroxide as a coolant and liquid natural gas as fuel.

Nov. 2 The first defendant to be tried in the case of the mass murder of Vietnamese civilians at Mylai, Staff Sergeant David Mitchell, is acquitted by a court-martial.

Nov. 3 No clear trend is evident in the midterm Federal election results, and both Houses of Congress remain Democratic. The Republicans pick up 2 seats in the Senate and lose 9 in the House. In state elections, however, Democrats make strong gains, increasing by 11 the number of Democratic governors.

Nov. 12 A two-month strike by 400,000 organized auto workers ends with an agreement providing for a 13-per-cent increase the first year and further 3-per-cent increases in each of the next two years. [President Nixon describes these terms as inflationary.]

Dec. 2 The Environmental Protection Agency, consolidating the major pollution-controlling bureaus of the Federal Government,

Apollo 14 astronauts (left to right) Stuart Roosa, Alan Shepard, and Edgar Mitchell

Apollo 13 astronauts (left to right) Fred W. Haise, Jr., John L. Swigert, Jr., and James A. Lovell, Jr., on board the U.S.S. *Iwo Jima* after splash down

which was established on Oct. 2, begins operation under the administration of William D. Ruckelshaus.

Dec. 3 The impeachment of Associate Justice William O. Douglas, proposed by Congressman Gerald Ford of Michigan, is rejected by a House subcommittee.

Dec. 7 Rube Goldberg, 87, cartoonist, whose absurd drawings of technological impossibilities delighted millions, dies in New York City.

Dec. 27 *Hello, Dolly!* closes after 2,844 performances, making it the longest-running musical ever to run on Broadway.

415

1971

The inflation experienced this year, running at almost 5 per cent annually, is unique in the nation's economic history. In the past, inflation was generally associated with full employment and an economy functioning at full capacity, but the current inflation is accompanied by idle productive capacity and 6-per-cent unemployment. Inasmuch as the usual remedy for a lagging economy—an easing of the nation's monetary policy—generally stimulates inflation, this technique is not thought appropriate for the current situation. In its place Nixon announces a temporary freeze on wages, prices, and rents, the first such freeze since the Korean War.

After 90 days, the President announces a postfreeze program of economic controls (Phase 2) that allows certain moderate increases monitored by several committees on wages, prices, and interest and dividends.

Jan. 25　The U.S. Supreme Court, in *Phillips* v. *Martin Marietta,* rules that a company may deny employment to a woman on the grounds that she has young children only if it also denies employment to men on the same basis. The case grew out of the equal-employment provisions of the 1964 Civil Rights Act.

Jan. 29　President Nixon submits a budget request for fiscal 1971-1972 in the amount of $229,200,000,000, with a projected deficit of $11,600,000,000. This deficit is based on an assumed increase in the gross national product to reach the record total of just over one trillion dollars. [The actual deficit for 1971-1972 proves to be $38,783,000,000, the largest since World War II.]

Feb. 5-6　The Apollo 14 astronauts, commanded by Alan B. Shepard, spend almost 10 hours exploring the lunar surface and set up a device for seismographic study.

Feb. 9　Southern California is rocked by a severe earthquake that buckles freeways, causes major damage to almost 1,000 buildings (with total damage in the Los Angeles area estimated at more than $1,000,000,000), and results in 62 deaths.

Feb. 25　President Nixon, in an address to Congress, says that the United States is "prepared to establish a dialogue with Peking." [On April 14, Chinese Premier Chou En-lai tells a visiting U.S. pingpong team that he anticipates that "this beginning of our friendship will certainly meet with the majority support of the two peoples," and on the same day Nixon ends a 20-year embargo on trade with Communist China. On July 15 Nixon announces that he will visit Peking before May 1972 and that plans for the visit have been arranged by his assistant, Henry Kissinger.]

Mar. 1　A bomb explodes in the basement of the U.S. Capitol, causing about $300,000 worth of damage. The blast is preceded by a telephone warning, which includes the statement: "This is in protest of the Nixon involvement in Laos."

Mar. 29　The court-martial of Lieutenant William Calley, Jr., ends with his conviction on charges of murdering 22 civilians during the Mylai massacre in Vietnam during 1968. Calley is sentenced to life in prison. [Nixon orders Calley held in house arrest at his apartment, rather than in the Fort Benning stockade, until appeals are completed, and promises to personally review the case. On Aug. 20 Calley's sentence is reduced to 20 years. In 1974 a U.S. district court overturns Calley's conviction, and he is released.]

April 6　Igor Stravinsky, 88, dies in New York City. Born in Russia, an American citizen since 1945, he became the leading composer in the United States. His works include *The Firebird, Symphony of Psalms, Symphony in C, The Rake's Progress,* and *Abraham and Isaac.*

April 7　President Nixon reveals plans to withdraw an additional 100,000 troops from Vietnam by December. [By the end of the year the U.S. troop level in Vietnam stands at around 180,000.]

April 20　The U.S. Supreme Court, in *Swann* v. *Charlotte-Mecklenburg Board of Education* and several other cases, rules unanimously that busing children is a proper method to achieve desegregation.

April 24-May 5　Some 320,000 persons gather in Washington, D.C., on April 24 to protest the war and the draft, and almost that number stage the largest peace demonstration ever held on the West Coast in San Francisco. During the next two weeks demonstrations continue in Washington. Notable is the large number of participating Vietnam veterans, many of whom turn in their war medals to protest the continued fighting. On May 3 police arrest more

Astronaut Alan B. Shepard, Jr., commander of the Apollo 14, stands beside the deployed United States flag on the moon.

Astronaut David R. Scott, commander of Apollo 15, works the lunar drill on the surface of the moon. The solar wind experiment is in the foreground.

than 7,000 persons during an attempt by demonstrators to disrupt traffic in the capital. These arrests cause controversy because the police use illegal arrest procedures. Those arrested are released under court order unless legally charged with a specific offense.

June 11   Alcatraz Island, occupied for 19 months by Indians, is occupied by Federal marshals; only 10 Indians remain. The purpose of the Indian occupation was to use the island as a cultural center.

June 30   The U.S. Supreme Court, in *New York Times* v. *United States,* rules 6 to 3 that *The New York Times* and the *Washington Post* have the right to publish a secret Pentagon study entitled "History of the U.S. Decision-Making Process on Vietnam Policy," known popularly as the Pentagon Papers.

July 1   The Post Office Department is superseded by the semigovernmental U.S. Postal Service, and the Cabinet position of Postmaster General is abolished. In another reorganization, the Peace Corps and other volunteer agencies are absorbed into a new agency called Action.

July 2   The Commerce Department officially designates the year from Nov. 1, 1969, through October 31, 1970, as a year of recession.

July 6   Louis D. ("Satchmo") Armstrong, 71, a leader of the U.S. jazz movement, dies in New York City.

July 25   President Nixon certifies that the 26th Amendment to the Constitution has been ratified by the required three-fourths of the states. The amendment lowers the voting age from 21 to 18 in federal, state, and local elections.

July 31-Aug. 2   The Apollo 15 astronauts, commanded by David R. Scott, use a battery-powered, four-wheeled "lunar rover" to ride about the moon's surface.

Aug. 2   In a reversal of a long-standing U.S. policy, Secretary of State William P. Rogers announces that the Government will support the admission of Communist China to the United Nations. [The U.N. General Assembly votes on Oct. 25 to admit Communist China; the Assembly also votes to expel the Nationalist Chinese (Taiwan), a move opposed by the United States.]

Aug. 15   President Nixon announces the start of a 90-day freeze of wages, prices, and rents. Reversing previous policy, the President describes the move as temporary and, after appointing a Cost of Living Council to administer the freeze, says he relies on voluntary compliance. In a simultaneous and equally unprecedented move, Nixon declares that the dollar will no longer be convertible into gold.

Sept. 8   The John F. Kennedy Center for the Performing Arts in Washington, D.C., opens with *Mass,* a new work by Leonard Bernstein.

Sept. 13   The four-day occupation of the Attica, New York, state prison by about 1,000 of its inmates ends when over 1,000 heavily armed state police, guards, and sheriff's deputies, with the help of helicopters, storm the cellblock. Thirty-four prisoners and nine of their captives die in the brief battle.

Oct. 14   Earl Sutherland of Vanderbilt University wins the Nobel Prize in medicine for research in hormones.

Oct. 15   Because of his application of the concept of the gross national product as a technique for measuring economic output, Simon Kuznets, formerly of Harvard University, is awarded the Nobel Memorial Prize in economics.

Oct. 21   President Nixon picks William H. Rehnquist and Lewis F. Powell, Jr., as Associate Justices of the Supreme Court to fill the seats of Hugo L. Black and John N. Harlan. [Both appointees are confirmed by the Senate, Powell on Dec. 6 and Rehnquist on Dec. 10, and both are sworn in on Jan. 7, 1972.]

Nov. 13   Mariner 9 becomes the first space probe to orbit another planet as it begins to circle Mars, transmitting pictures back to earth.

Dec. 9   Ralph J. Bunche, 67, former Undersecretary General of the United Nations, whose labors on behalf of peace brought him the Nobel Prize in 1950, dies in New York City. He was the first Negro Nobel laureate.

1972 This is a very good year, according to two signs that the American people have learned to consider reliable. One sign is the landslide election of the incumbent President; the other is a soaring market in stocks. At the end of the year, for the first time, the well-known Dow Jones thermometer of the New York Stock Exchange passes 1,000. President Nixon is completing one term and, having captured more than 60 per cent of the total popular vote and 520 of the 538 electoral votes, is triumphantly preparing for "four more years."

The President's campaign is relatively low key, although some of his men get out of hand, to the extent of entering the Democratic headquarters uninvited in the small hours of the morning with equipment usually reserved for counterespionage. Not too much is made of this infringement on their privacy by the embattled Democrats. The principal thrust of their activity is directed toward the more vocal minorities in the country, who are given a platform for the first time at a Democratic convention. One third of the delegates are women, one third are less than 35 years of age, one seventh are black, and old-line officials who usually dominate such proceedings (including Mayor Daley of Chicago) take back seats or no seats at all. George McGovern easily wins the nomination, once the infighting of the credentials battle ends. The national party membership is not so easily won over as the convention; many evidently desert to Nixon, fearful that the departure from Indochina promised by McGovern will be precipitate and embarrassing. Others misinterpret McGovern's stand on welfare. Still others are disenchanted by the fiasco of picking, then rejecting, Eagleton for the Vice Presidency.

On the positive side, Nixon wins considerable esteem for his reversal of foreign policy and his dramatic and apparently successful overtures toward governments in China and the Soviet Union, nations which he has condemned throughout his political lifetime. He has also redeemed part of his pledge to end the fighting in Indochina, and continues to assure the American people of an honorable ending to what has become a deplorable episode in American history.

Jan. 24 The U.S. Supreme Court rules that laws refusing welfare to those residing in a state less than a year are unconstitutional.

Jan. 24 The budget for fiscal 1972-1973 is set at $243,300,000,000, with a projected deficit of $25,500,000,000; the President emphasizes that this deficit is some $13,500,000,000 less than last year's. This year a new budget formula is introduced, resulting in balances (whether surplus or deficit) that cannot be compared to those in previous years.

Feb. 7 A bill limiting the amount that may be spent for advertising in Federal elections is signed into law by President Nixon. The measure also calls for more complete reporting of the sources of campaign funds.

Feb. 15 John Mitchell resigns as Attorney General in order to manage the Committee for the Reelection of the President (CRP); Nixon names Mitchell's deputy, Richard Kleindienst, to succeed. [Kleindienst is confirmed by the Senate on Feb. 25.]

Feb. 21-27 President Nixon, accompanied by his chief adviser on foreign policy, Henry Kissinger, visits Communist China for a week of discussions with Chinese leaders, ending over two decades of hostility between the United States and the People's Republic of China. At the conclusion of the visit, President Nixon and Chinese Premier Chou En-lai issue a joint communique promising to work for increased contact between the two nations.

Mar. 9 Writer Clifford Irving, his wife, and an assistant, Richard Suskind, are indicted in New York City on charges stemming from a fictitious autobiography of Howard Hughes written by Irving after what he claimed were a long series of interviews with the reclusive tycoon. In fact, the book, which was sold to publishers for $750,000, was based on material already published, one unpublished memoir, and events created by the imaginations of Irving and Suskind. [The three defendants plead guilty on Mar. 13 to various charges and are later given light sentences.]

Mar. 10-12 Some 3,500 delegates at the first National Black Political Convention at Gary, Indiana, set up a National Black Assembly to provide leadership for the black community.

Mar. 17 President Nixon proposes to Congress that it enact legislation to prevent the courts from mandating the use of busing as a means of achieving racial desegregation, and he asks all concerned for a "moratorium" on busing.

Mar. 22 A constitutional amendment to prohibit discrimination based on sex, passed by both Houses of Congress, is sent to the states for ratification.

April 16-27 The Apollo 16 astronauts, commanded by John W. Young, spend three days on the moon. Among other discoveries, they measure a local magnetic field 100 times greater than that predicted by scientists.

May 2 A fire in a silver mine at Kellogg, Idaho, causes the deaths of 91 miners.

May 2 J. Edgar Hoover, 77, director of the Federal Bureau of Investigation since 1924, dies of a heart attack in Washington, D.C.

May 8 The mining of the North Vietnamese port of Haiphong is ordered by President Nixon.

May 14 Okinawa, occupied by the United States since the end of World War II, is returned to Japan.

May 15 Alabama Governor George C. Wallace, campaigning in the Presidential primaries, is shot by a 21-year-old drifter, Arthur Bremer, in Laurel, Maryland. [Bremer is convicted on Aug. 4 and given a 63-year sentence. Wallace appears at the Democratic convention in July, but he decides to withdraw from the Presidential race.]

May 22-28 President Nixon meets with Soviet leaders in Moscow and concludes his visit with agreements limiting both the United States and the Soviet Union to two ABM sites each.

June 4 A jury in San Jose, California, acquits Angela Davis, black militant philosophy instructor at the University of California, charged with murder, kidnapping, and conspiracy to murder and kidnap. The charges were based on indictments following a shootout in a San Rafael courthouse in 1970. In the intervening years the case became a *cause célèbre*.

June 9-10 Heavy rains in the Black Hills of South Dakota create flood conditions in Rapid City and the surrounding area, killing 235 persons and doing $100,000,000 damage.

June 17 James W. McCord, security officer for the Committee to Re-elect the President (CRP), and four other men are arrested in the early morning while breaking into the Democratic National Committee offices in the Watergate building complex in Washington, D.C. Found with the men are cameras and electronic surveillance equipment. [The next day John N. Mitchell, director of CRP, announces that the five men were working strictly on their own. On June 22 and again on Aug. 29 President Nixon assures the nation that no one in his Administration had anything to do with the incident. In the meantime, the Democrats file a $1,000,000 civil suit (later increased to $6,400,000) against CRP and the burglars.]

June 19-23 Hurricane Agnes moves up the Eastern seaboard from Florida. Streets in Elmira, New York, are submerged by 20 feet of water and Wilkes-Barre, Pennsylvania, is largely evacuated. The death toll reaches 134 and well over 100,000 homes are destroyed in the worst flood in recent history.

June 29 The U.S. Supreme Court rules, 5 to 4, that a newsman may be compelled to reveal to a grand jury information obtained in confidence. [Several newsmen are subsequently given contempt sentences based on the Court's decision.]

June 29 In another 5-to-4 decision, the U.S. Supreme Court rules that the death penalty for murder and rape is cruel and unusual punishment and thus violates the 8th and 14th Amendments.

July 10-13 The Democratic Party holds its national convention in Miami Beach. South Dakota Senator George McGovern, an advocate of early withdrawal from Indochina, is nominated on the first ballot. He chooses as his running mate Senator Thomas F. Eagleton of Missouri. [On July 31 Eagleton, whose history as a patient in a psychiatric hospital is revealed after his nomination, resigns from the ticket; on Aug. 5 he is replaced as candidate for Vice President by former Peace Corps administrator R. Sargent Shriver.]

Aug. 3 The U.S. Senate, by a vote of 88 to 2, ratifies the strategic arms limitation treaty (SALT 1) setting the bounds of defense missilery permitted to the United States and the Soviet Union, as agreed at the Moscow summit in May.

Aug. 9 Following an announcement a month earlier of a $750,000,000 grain sale to the Soviet Union, the U.S. Department of Agriculture reports that additional purchases may bring the total value of grain sold to the Soviets to over $1,000,000,000. [The sale causes tremendous controversy as charges are leveled that the U.S.D.A. allowed grain exporters to make huge profits at the expense of farmers by providing the dealers with advance information on the impending purchases.]

Aug. 12 The last U.S. ground troops to leave Vietnam depart from Danang; a 43,500-man support force remains in Vietnam. [This number is reduced to about 16,000 by December. U.S. forces in Thailand, however, reach 50,000.]

Aug. 21-23 At the Republican national convention in Miami Beach, the renomination of President Nixon is achieved almost unanimously; one negative vote is cast by California Representative Pete McCloskey. Vice President Agnew is also renominated with the dissenting vote of only one delegate.

Sept. 1 Bobby Fischer becomes the first American world champion of chess by defeating Boris Spassky of the Soviet Union in a 24-game match at Reykjavik, Iceland.

Sept. 4 California swimmer Mark Spitz sets an Olympic record by becoming the first person to win seven gold medals. He takes first place in four individual events and shares in three relay victories, all of which also set new world records.

Sept. 14 The U.S. Senate votes, again by 88 to 2, to ratify the freezing of the offensive missile strengths of the Soviet Union and the United States as decided at the May summit meeting. It is understood that the Soviet Union has more ICBM's than the United States, but the United States has more units capable of using multiple warheads (MIRV's) and a larger fleet of nuclear bombers.

Sept. 15 The five burglars arrested at the Democratic headquarters in the Watergate complex are indicted, and along with them are indicted former CIA agent E. Howard Hunt and CRP counsel G. Gordon Liddy.

Oct. 12 The Nobel Prize in medicine is shared with a British colleague by Gerald M. Edelman of Rockefeller University, for work in the chemical structure of antibodies.

Oct. 18 Congress overrides a Presidential veto and passes the Water Pollution Act, providing almost $25,000,000,000 over the next three years as part of a program to clean up the nation's waters by 1985.

Oct. 20 President Nixon signs the Revenue Sharing Act, a five-year program by which the Federal Government will share over $30,000,000,000 of its revenues with state and local governments.

Oct. 20 Six more Americans receive Nobel awards in science. The prize in physics goes to three researchers in the field of superconductivity of metals at extremely low temperatures: John

Apollo 17 commander Eugene A. Cernan passes the Lunar Module as he rides the Rover on the surface of the moon.

Bardeen of the University of Illinois (who is the first to receive a second Nobel prize in the same field—he won one in 1956), John R. Schrieffer of the University of Pennsylvania, and Leon M. Cooper of Brown University. The winners of the chemistry prize, who conducted research in enzymes, are Christian E. Anfinson of the National Institutes of Health and Stanford Moore and William H. Stein, both of Rockefeller University.

Oct. 24 Jackie Robinson, 53, the first black man to play major league baseball, dies in Stamford, Connecticut.

Oct. 25 Kenneth J. Arrow of Harvard University shares with a British colleague the Nobel Memorial Prize in economics for major contributions to economic theory.

Oct. 26 Presidential assistant Henry Kissinger, having completed a series of secret talks in Paris with his North Vietnamese counterpart Le Duc Tho, tells the American people that "peace is at hand."

Nov. 7 President Richard M. Nixon is elected to a second term with a popular vote of 47,169,911. Democrat George McGovern receives 29,170,383 votes.

Dec. 7-19 During the visit to the moon of Apollo 17, the last of the Apollo manned moon missions, the astronauts collect rock samples and discover orange and red soil in the lunar surface.

Dec. 18-30 The United States carries out the heaviest bombardment of North Vietnam in the entire war. Fifteen $8,000,000 U.S. B-52's are shot down by the time the bombing is ended on Dec. 30. On the same date it is announced that peace talks will resume on Jan. 8, 1973.

Dec. 26 Harry S. Truman, 88, the 33rd President, dies in Kansas City, Missouri.

420

1973 Except for the good news of a ceasefire in Vietnam in January, the year is distressing for the American people. It is predominantly the year of the unraveling of the Watergate affair. With the opening of the televised hearings of the Senate committee in May begins the disclosure of testimony linking high Government officials with a host of illegal activities: the break-in at the Democratic headquarters last June, the attempt to cover up the origin and responsibility before and after the event, and the illegal or unethical activities designed to discredit political opponents that come to be described as "dirty tricks." For months each revelation seems more incredible than the last, and always the President seeks to convey a sense of his indignation at the perpetrators and his innocence of all involvement. But the burglars begin to talk; members of the official family begin to perjure themselves or tell part of the truth; the existence of essential evidence, planted by the President in his own quarters, becomes known but impossible to come by. One climax is the day in October when Archibald Cox, special prosecutor appointed in May to investigate the scandal, refuses to obey Nixon's command to drop his insistence on receiving the essential tapes. Nixon then orders his Attorney General to dismiss Cox, only to encounter another insubordination. So Cox, Richardson, and his deputy, Ruckelshaus, all become victims of what the press calls "the Saturday night massacre." This event leads directly to an inquiry by the House of Representatives into possible grounds for impeaching the President. Compounding the situation is the plight of Vice President Agnew, symbol to many of law and order, who is forced to resign his office as a felon to escape less acceptable punishment for having taken bribes and falsified his income tax records.

Corruption at the highest levels of Government is accompanied by a record rate of inflation and an energy crisis. Whether the embargo by the Arabs against the consumers of their oil (an indirect result of the Arab-Israeli War) or the machinations of the giant oil companies is responsible for bringing about the energy crisis, the fuel shortage at the end of the year touches everyone who drives a car or depends on motor-borne deliveries; it raises the cost of heating and, indirectly, of hundreds of items, from plastics to fertilizer, that depend on oil. Amid fears of impending recession, the stock market suffers unusually heavy losses.

Jan. 3   As ordered by President Nixon, all airline passengers are screened in an effort to halt the increasing number of hijackers. Most of the 29 incidents of air piracy in North America, last year were carried out for personal gain rather than, as in previous years, for political motives. [During the six months that follow the President's order, no U.S. airplane is hijacked, and the screening process results in the arrest of more than 1,300 persons, many of whom possess illegal weapons.]

Jan. 22   The U.S. Supreme Court rules, 7 to 2, that states may not restrict the right of a woman to have an abortion during the first three months of pregnancy. Guidelines for abortion laws affecting the remaining term of pregnancy are also spelled out.

Jan. 22   Lyndon Baines Johnson, 64, the 36th President, dies of a heart attack while en route from his ranch to a hospital in San Antonio, Texas.

Jan. 22   George Foreman takes the heavyweight crown from Joe Frazier by knocking him down six times in the first two rounds of a fight in Kingston, Jamaica.

Jan. 23   With the signatures of Henry Kissinger and Le Duc Tho, U.S. and North Vietnamese representatives at the Paris negotiations held during the last 19 months, "peace with honor" in Indochina is achieved to the satisfaction of President Nixon. [The formal agreement is signed in Paris by Secretary of State William P. Rogers on Jan. 27.]

Jan. 29   President Nixon asks Congress to accept a budget of $268,700,000,000, including $81,100,000,000 for defense ($4,700,000,000 more than last year), with cuts in the social items.

Jan. 30   The trial of the Watergate defendants, begun on Jan. 8, ends with the conviction of G. Gordon Liddy and James W. McCord for conspiracy, wiretapping, and burglary. E. Howard Hunt and four other defendants pleaded guilty to various charges earlier in the month.

421

Feb. 12   The first group of U.S. prisoners of war is flown from Hanoi to a U.S. base in the Philippines for medical attention and debriefing. A group held by the Vietcong in South Vietnam is also released. [All remaining U.S. prisoners except one are freed by Mar. 29.]

Feb. 12   The Government announces a 10-per-cent devaluation of the dollar (having already devalued it by 8.57 per cent in December 1971). Officially the price of gold is simultaneously increased from $38 to $42.22 per ounce.

Mar. 21   The U.S. Supreme Court, in *San Antonio School District* v. *Rodriguez,* decides 5 to 4 that the use of the property tax by the states to finance education is constitutional.

Mar. 28   James W. McCord charges that John N. Mitchell, director of the Committee to Reelect the President and a former Attorney General, was responsible for the burglary for which he and other Watergate defendants were convicted. He is the first defendant to involve a major political figure in the event.

April 27   Judge William M. Byrne, presiding at the trial of Daniel Ellsberg, reveals that with connivance from the White House two of the convicted Watergate burglars, Liddy and Hunt, broke into the office of Ellsberg's psychiatrist in order to obtain information damaging to Ellsberg.

April 30   Nixon tells the nation that, although he had no part in the Watergate affair, he will take full responsibility for subordinates "who may have done wrong in a cause they deeply believed to be right." The President also promises to see "that the guilty are brought to justice and that such abuses are purged from our political processes. . . ." Nixon announces the resignation of his top assistants, H. R. Haldeman and John D. Ehrlichman, of Presidential counsel John Dean, and of Attorney General Richard Kleindienst; the last of these resigns because some of his close associates may be "involved in conduct violative of the laws of the United States." Secretary of Defense Elliot Richardson is named to succeed Kleindienst, with full authority to appoint a special prosecutor to investigate the Watergate affair. [Richardson names Archibald Cox as the investigator on May 18; the Senate confirms Richardson on May 23.]

May 8   Members of the Oglala Sioux tribe and Federal negotiators reach an agreement to end a siege at Wounded Knee, South Dakota, that began on Feb. 27. The agreement calls for a meeting between tribal leaders and White House representatives to discuss charges that the United States has consistently violated Indian treaty rights, particularly the Treaty of 1868 between the Sioux and the United States. [In September 1974 defendants indicted for their actions at Wounded Knee are dismissed by the court because the Government cannot make a case against them.]

May 11   Judge Byrne dismisses the Government's case against Daniel Ellsberg and Anthony J. Russo, charged with espionage, theft, and conspiracy in providing copies of the Pentagon Papers to the press in 1971. Byrne bases the dismissal on the misconduct by the Government which "precludes the fair, dispassionate resolution of these issues by a jury." Byrne also reveals that the White House offered him a high Government post while litigation was in progress.

May 14-June 22   The $6,000,000,000 Skylab program gets underway with the launching of an 86-ton space station into earth orbit. Shortly after launch a heat and meteoroid shield rips loose, damaging some of the electricity-producing panels and exposing the craft to excessive thermal radiation. A crew of three Skylab astronauts is nevertheless blasted into orbit on May 25 for rendezvous with the space station. Under the shelter of a makeshift sun shield, they restore an electrical system. After a record 28 days in space, the crew returns safely to earth on June 22. [On July 28 a second crew is launched for a 59-day stay aboard Skylab; a final crew is launched on Nov. 16 and remains in space for 84 days.]

May 22   The Governments of the United States and China agree to move toward a relationship with each other by establishing "liaison" offices in Peking and Washington.

May 29   Thomas Bradley wins a runoff election to become the first black mayor of Los Angeles.

June 9   By winning the race at Belmont, Secretariat becomes the first horse in 25 years to be a triple-crown champion.

June 13   President Nixon orders a 60-day freeze on retail prices, acknowledging the inflation has been too rapid under the voluntary controls of Phase 3. [The freeze is partially lifted on July 18, when Nixon announces a new anti-inflation program which he terms Phase 4.]

June 16-25   Soviet leader Leonid I. Brezhnev visits the United States and holds talks with President Nixon. They sign several agreements, including one in which both countries pledge to enter immediate negotiations should it become apparent that they are moving toward nuclear war with one another or with a third nation.

June 21 In five related cases, the U.S. Supreme Court rules, 5 to 4, that local standards must supersede national norms in judging whether a book, moving picture, magazine, or theatrical performance is obscene.

July 1 The President signs an act of Congress under which all U.S. military action in Indochina is to end Aug. 15. [All action is halted on Aug. 15.]

July 16 Alexander P. Butterfield, a former deputy assistant to the President, tells the Senate committee investigating the Watergate affair that Presidential conversations at the White House and at the Executive Office Building have been recorded on tape since March 1971. [Both the Senate committee and Archibald Cox request that the White House provide forthwith tapes relevant to their respective investigations. The President refuses to provide the tapes, citing Executive privilege and the doctrine of separation of powers.]

July 28 An estimated record crowd of 600,000, mostly young people, gather at Watkins Glen, New York, for a 12-hour rock concert.

July 31 In a crash at Boston airport, 88 passengers perish aboard a Delta DC-9.

Aug. 10 Subsidies for farmers who produce cotton, wheat, and feed grains end under a law signed by the President.

Sept. 4 John D. Ehrlichman is indicted in connection with the break-in at the office of Daniel Ellsberg's psychiatrist.

Sept. 21 The Senate confirms the appointment of Presidential assistant Henry Kissinger as Secretary of State.

Oct. 10 Vice President Spiro T. Agnew, accused of having accepted bribes while he was governor of Maryland and as Vice President, pleads no contest on a lesser charge of income tax evasion and resigns his office as a condition of avoiding further prosecution. [Two days later Nixon designates House minority leader Gerald Ford to succeed Agnew.]

Oct. 16 Secretary of State Kissinger shares with his North Vietnamese counterpart Le Duc Tho the Nobel Prize for peace for their effort to bring about peace in Indochina.

Oct. 17 U.S. support for Israel in the recent war with the Arabs results in a ban by Arab oil-producing nations of oil shipments to the United States. [The embargo, which is not lifted until March 1974, aggravates an energy shortage in the United States.]

Oct. 18 The Nobel Memorial Prize in economics is awarded to Wassily Leontief, Russian-born head of the Economic Research Project of Harvard University, for his method of analysis and forecasting of economic phenomena.

Oct. 20 Attorney General Elliot Richardson refuses to dismiss special prosecutor Archibald Cox as directed by the President, and resigns his office, as does his deputy, William D. Ruckelshaus. [Cox is nevertheless dismissed by an acting Attorney General.]

Oct. 23 The Nobel Prize in physics is shared by a British scientist and two American researchers in miniature electronics, Leo Esaki of the International Business Machines Corporation and Ivar Giaever of the General Electric Company.

Nov. 1 Leon Jaworski is appointed as the new Watergate special prosecutor, replacing Cox, and is promised complete freedom to pursue all aspects of the case.

Nov. 7 Congress passes, over the President's veto, a law limiting the authority of the President to commit U.S. troops in combat overseas.

Nov. 16 A measure to permit the building of the Alaska oil pipeline is signed by Nixon.

Nov. 17 During a speech at Disney World in Florida, President Nixon asserts that the "people have got to know whether or not the President is a crook—well, I'm not a crook."

Nov. 25 To help meet the energy shortage, the President requests over a television broadcast that gasoline stations close on Sundays and that Americans observe a 50-mph highway speed limit.

Dec. 6 Gerald R. Ford is sworn in as Vice President, following approval by both Houses of Congress. He is the first to enter the office under the provisions of the 25th Amendment.

President Richard M. Nixon looks on as Gerald R. Ford is sworn in as the 40th Vice President of the United States on Dec. 6.

1974

The resignation of a President of the United States and the smooth transition through constitutional processes to a new Administration are the significant events that set this year apart from all others in American history. Vice President Agnew's fall from grace last year did not seriously disturb the country; an individual manifestation of corruption, it was overshadowed by the "long national nightmare" (in Gerald Ford's words) of Watergate. This year sees the development and, it is hoped, the end of the anguish. For eight months evidence accumulates that an Administration under popular mandate, not a handful of witless "burglars," has been subversive on a grand scale. In the guise of defending national security it was threatening institutions, such as the CIA and the FBI, expressly charged to protect that security. The revelations erode the will to believe a President just because he is President, and convince many that politics is intrinsically dirty. But in the end the guilty are exposed and all except the President are brought to justice. As for Nixon, most Americans agree that his disgrace approximately fits the crime.

Gerald Ford—unelected, but unmarred by Watergate—assumes leadership at a time that overshadows his sparse executive experience. The economy is in peril, with a frightening combination of inflation and recession. The peace vigorously sought by Secretary of State Kissinger is fragile in Indochina and elusive in the Middle East. Ford's hasty grant of a full pardon to Nixon shocks most of the nation. It is followed by the appointment of a Vice President who is known to be competent but who is so suspect on other grounds that a prolonged investigation seems in order; the overwhelming confirmation accorded to Rockefeller, however, is gratifying. Nevertheless, the electorate provides the new President with a new Congress that is predictably incompatible. With the nightmare over, the nation prepares for an uneasy if not a rude awakening.

Jan. 30   President Nixon, in his message to Congress, outlines a 10-point program that includes a health insurance plan, aid to transportation, and the assurance: "There will be no recession." The proposed budget for fiscal 1974-1975 is $304,400,000,000.

Feb. 4   Patricia Hearst, 19, granddaughter of William Randolph Hearst and daughter of San Francisco *Examiner* publisher Randolph Hearst, is kidnapped from her apartment in Berkeley, California. [The Symbionese Liberation Army demands $230,000,000 in food to be distributed to the poor as ransom. A distribution of food worth several millions is made in Oakland, but the SLA considers it inadequate. A recorded message received on April 3 from Patty Hearst indicates that she has been converted to the radical beliefs of her captors. On April 15 she appears in a photograph of a bank holdup as one of the active robbers. On April 24 a Federal warrant for her arrest is issued.]

Feb. 8   The Skylab mission ends with the return to earth of the third 3-man crew of astronauts. This crew was in space for a record 84 days and traveled 34,500,000 miles in 1,214 revolutions around the earth. While in space they tested materials in a weightless environment, observed the sun, and photographed the comet Kohoutek, which approached within 75,000,000 miles of the earth in mid-January.

Feb. 28   The United States resumes diplomatic relations with Egypt, which were disrupted seven years ago.

Mar. 1   Indictments are handed down by a Federal court on a variety of counts for perjury, conspiracy, or obstruction of justice (or a combination of these) against seven Watergate defendants: H.R. Haldeman, John D. Ehrlichman, John N. Mitchell, Robert Mardian, Kenneth Parkinson, Charles W. Colson, and Gordon Strachan. The indicting jury also hands over to the presiding judge, John Sirica, documents indicating the President's involvement in the Watergate affair, but they do not indict Nixon. [He is later described as an "unindicted co-conspirator." Charges against Colson are dropped on June 3, when he pleads guilty to a lesser charge (attempting to obstruct justice in the Ellsberg trial) and agrees to cooperate with the Government; he receives a 1-to-3-year prison sentence and a fine of $5,000 on June 21. Strachan's trial is separated from that of the other five, whose trial begins Oct. 1 and runs through the end of the year. On Jan. 1, 1975, former Attorney General Mitchell, former Presidential aides Haldeman and Ehrlichman, and former Assistant Attorney General Mardian are convicted on all charges; attorney Parkinson is acquitted.]

Mar. 6 An emergency energy bill, passed by Congress, is vetoed by Nixon, who disapproves of its provision for a rollback in crude oil prices. [The Senate fails to override the veto by 8 votes.]

April 3 In a wide belt from Michigan to Georgia, tornadoes cause damage to property worth more than $1,000,000,000, and kill 310 persons.

April 8 Hank Aaron, playing for the Atlanta Braves at Atlanta against the Los Angeles Dodgers, hits the 715th home run of his career, thereby surpassing the long-standing record set by Babe Ruth.

April 11 Tony Boyle, former president of the United Mine Workers, is convicted of the murder in 1969 of Joseph A. Yablonski and his wife and daughter.

April 28 Former Attorney General John N. Mitchell and former Secretary of Commerce Maurice H. Stans are acquitted of charges that they tried to impede an investigation of alleged swindler Robert L. Vesco (now a refugee in Costa Rica) in return for a $200,000 contribution from Vesco to Nixon's campaign fund.

April 30 Nixon releases transcripts of some of the tapes submitted under subpoena to the House Judiciary Committee (which is inquiring into the possibility of impeaching the President). [The contents, even though heavily edited by the White House, shock the nation. On May 7 Republican Senate leader Hugh Scott describes them as "deplorable, disgusting, shabby."]

May 9 Impeachment hearings by the Judiciary Committee of the House of Representatives, under the chairmanship of Peter Rodino of New Jersey, begin. The committee was authorized on Feb. 6, by a vote of 410 to 6, to inquire whether Nixon has committed impeachable offenses. [On July 30 the committee recommends three articles to the full House. On the first article, charging personal misconduct leading to obstruction of justice, the committee vote is 27 to 11; on the second article, charging abuse of power and failure to carry out the Presidential oath of office, the vote is 28 to 10; on the third article, charging defiance of the subpoena power of the committee, the vote is 21 to 17.]

May 16 Richard Kleindienst becomes the first former Attorney General to be convicted of a crime, when he admits he has refused to testify "accurately and fully" before a Congressional committee investigating an antitrust violation. For his guilty plea to a misdemeanor, Kleindienst is spared a possible perjury charge by prosecutor Leon Jaworski. [On June 7 Kleindienst receives a suspended sentence of 30 days and a $100 fine.]

June 12-19 President Nixon tours the Middle East, laying the groundwork for resumption of diplomatic relations with Syria and receiving an enthusiastic welcome in Cairo, a less cordial reception in Israel.

July 9 Earl Warren, 83, for 16 years Chief Justice of the U.S. Supreme Court, dies in Washington, D.C.

July 12 Four defendants charged with conspiring to break in at the office of Daniel Ellsberg's psychiatrist in 1971 are convicted in Federal court. They include John Ehrlichman and G. Gordon Liddy. [Ehrlichman, also convicted of making false statements, is sentenced on July 31 to 20 months to 5 years in jail; Liddy receives a 1-to-3-year sentence concurrent with his years to be served as a Watergate burglar.]

July 13 The Senate Watergate Committee, chaired by Senator Sam Ervin of North Carolina, issues its final report; it contains no charges against individuals, which it considers beyond its mandate, but proposes legislative reforms.

July 24 The U.S. Supreme Court rules, 8 to 0, that President Nixon may not withhold evidence (tapes) in his possession from prosecutor Leon Jaworski; the Court formally rejects the pleas of Executive privilege in this context.

Aug. 2 Former Presidential counsel John Dean, whose testimony against his erstwhile colleagues and the President proves useful to the Government in Watergate prosecutions, is sentenced to 1 to 3 years in prison on his guilty plea to a minor charge of obstructing justice.

Aug. 9 Richard M. Nixon becomes the first President of the United States to resign his office, a step which he has constantly declared unthinkable. It follows his release on Aug. 5 of incriminating tapes that prove he tried, less than a week after the Watergate burglary, to obstruct

President Nixon makes an emotional farewell address to members of his Cabinet and staff in the East Room of the White House on Aug. 9 before his departure for California.

investigation of the event. On Aug. 8 Nixon made his "farewell address" to the nation over television, admitting only to poor judgment. Following Nixon's departure to San Clemente, his California residence, Vice President Gerald R. Ford takes the oath of office as the 38th President of the United States.

Aug. 19   U.S. Ambassador to Cyprus Rodger P. Davies is killed in Nicosia during a demonstration of Greek Cypriotes against the Turks.

Aug. 20   The report of the House Judiciary Committee, recommending the impeachment of Richard Nixon, is accepted by the full House, by a vote of 412 to 3. Committee members who had voted against the articles in July alter their votes in view of the evidence disclosed on Aug. 5, just before the President resigned. [The House considers the issue of impeachment moot under the circumstances.]

Sept. 4   Diplomatic relations between the United States and the Democratic Republic of Germany (East Germany) are established; John Sherman Cooper is named the first U.S. Ambassador to East Berlin.

Sept. 8   President Ford announces that he has unconditionally pardoned Nixon for all crimes against the United States he "has committed or may have committed" while he was President. [In accepting the pardon, Nixon admits to "mistakes and misjudgments," but denies having committed an illegal act. Public reaction to the pardon is unsympathetic.]

Sept. 11   An Eastern Airlines DC-9 crashes near Charlotte, North Carolina, and 69 of the 82 persons aboard perish.

Sept. 12   The integration of Boston's school children by busing, ordered by Federal Judge W. Arthur Garrity in June, meets with violent protest in Irish and Italian sections of the city. [The protest increases in violence; three of the five education officials responsible for implementing the judicial order refuse to comply, are convicted of contempt, and on Dec. 30 are fined and suspended from their capacity to make further decisions on the issue.]

Sept. 16   Ford offers conditional amnesty to deserters and draft evaders on a case-by-case basis.

Oct. 13   Ed Sullivan, 73, personality of television and radio and former newspaper columnist, on whose shows many current stars made their first appearances, dies in New York City.

Oct. 15   The Nobel Prize in physics is awarded to Paul J. Flory of Stanford University for his work in the field of plastics.

Muhammad Ali lands a right to George Foreman during their title bout in Kinshasa, Zaire.

Oct. 30   In a stunning comeback, Muhammad Ali knocks out heavyweight champion George Foreman in the 8th round of a fight in Kinshasa, Zaire, that is seen over television by boxing enthusiasts throughout the world.

Nov. 5   Despite strenuous campaigning on behalf of Republican candidates by President Ford, the long-drawn-out Watergate affair takes its toll in Congressional and gubernatorial contests. In the House of Representatives 290 Democrats—a clear two-thirds ("veto-proof") majority—is elected; in the Senate, Democrats will hold 62 of the 100 seats. The state houses will accommodate 36 Democratic governors (including those of New York and California), 4 more than in 1974. A notable "first" is Governor Ella Grasso of Connecticut; unlike earlier woman governors, former Representative Grasso is elected on her own record rather than that of an ineligible or deceased husband.

Dec. 19   Former New York Governor Nelson A. Rockefeller, long a contender for Presidential office and President Ford's choice for Vice President under the provisions of the 25th Amendment, is confirmed by a majority vote of both Houses of Congress. The confirmations follow protracted investigation into Rockefeller's sources and uses of colossal wealth. For the first time in its history, the United States has an unelected President and Vice President.

Dec. 26   Jack Benny, 80, top-rated comedian of radio in the 1940's and of television in the 1950's, dies in Beverly Hills, California.

U.S. President Gerald Ford and Soviet leader, Leonid Brezhnev at Vladivostok after Ford's arrival on Nov. 23 for their two-day meeting

1975

The mood of the year can be defined as one of uneasy relief. The trauma of Watergate, symbolically terminated by President Ford's pardon for his predecessor, lingers on for less fortunate culprits who await their sentences or prepare to pay or appeal their penalties. The trauma of a long and futile war, which abruptly and ingloriously ceases this year, has an epilogue in the Gulf of Siam and a heritage of Vietnamese refugees who contribute the latest ethnic strain to the American population. The more familiar threat of recession, signaled by rising unemployment, is met by diverse Executive and Legislative programs, leading to a spate of vetoes, some of which are overridden.

In the international arena, the United States signs a declaration in Helsinki that purports to recognize realities in Eastern Europe but has the side-effect of tarnishing the concept of détente. Congressional incursions into foreign policy provide an excuse for cancellation of a major trade pact by the Soviet Union and for Turkish reconsideration of its options as a NATO member. Nevertheless, in the end, American grain once more flows into Soviet silos and American arms again replenish Turkish arsenals.

President Ford ends the first half of his appointive Administration and prepares to present himself for an elective term. He is seriously challenged by Republicans from the right, and from the center and left by a bevy of Democrats contending for the opportunity to unseat the most vulnerable Republican within recent history.

Jan. 5 Vice President Nelson Rockefeller is named by President Ford to head an eight-member commission to investigate charges that the CIA was involved in domestic spy activities, contrary to its charter.

Jan. 8 Three major Watergate convicts—former White House counsel John Dean, former personal Presidential attorney Herbert Kalmbach, and Jeb Magruder, former deputy administrator of the Committee to Reelect the President—are released by order of Judge John Sirica after brief incarceration.

Jan. 13 President Ford, reversing his previous position that inflation is a graver danger to the national economy than recession, proposes an antirecession program that includes massive income tax rebates combined with a high tax on oil and natural gas to mitigate the energy crisis.

Jan. 14 Secretary of State Henry Kissinger announces that the Soviet Union refuses to accept a provision of the recently passed Trade Reform Bill that makes trade concessions to the Soviet Union contingent on more liberal Soviet emigration policies. The Soviet decision nullifies a trade pact negotiated in 1972.

Jan. 21 The U.S. Supreme Court, in *Taylor* v. *Louisiana,* rules that states may not deny to women the opportunity to serve on juries.

Jan. 22 In a major reversal of a 50-year-old rule that allowed committee chairmen to be selected on a basis of seniority of service, the Democratic majority of the House of Representatives removes from the chairmanship of their respective committees Wright Patman of Banking and Currency, W. R. Poage of Agriculture, and F. Edward Hébert of Armed Services. This move follows the forced resignation, on personal grounds, of Wilbur Mills of Ways and Means.

Jan. 24 Historic Fraunces Tavern in New York City, the site of George Washington's farewell to his fellow-officers on Dec. 4, 1783, is bombed by Puerto Rican nationalists; 4 persons die and 44 are hurt in the blast, but the structure is not seriously damaged.

Feb. 3 President Ford asks Congress for $349,400,000,000 for fiscal 1975-1976, anticipating a deficit of $51,500,000,000, about half again as large as the estimated deficit for 1974-1975.

Feb. 4 The Menominee Indians of Wisconsin end a 35-day occupation of the novitiate of the

H. R. Haldeman (right), former President Nixon's top White House aide, on his way to receive his sentence from Judge Sirica on Feb. 21

Alexian Brothers at Gresham when they are assured that the facility, now unused, will be transferred to the tribe to be converted to a hospital.

Feb. 18   Holding that the President cannot freeze funds appropriated by Congress, the U.S. Supreme Court requires the release of $6,000,000,000 impounded by President Nixon. The funds had been earmarked for the use of the states and local communities in 1972 for water-pollution control and President Nixon had been overridden after vetoing the measure.

Feb. 21   Federal Judge John Sirica sentences former Attorney General John Mitchell and former Presidential aides John Ehrlichman and H. R. Haldeman to prison for having conspired to obstruct justice and associated crimes.

Feb. 25   Elijah Muhammad, 77, leader for 40 years of the Nation of Islam (also known as the Black Muslims), dies in Chicago.

Feb. 27   A subcommittee of the House of Representatives is informed by Attorney General Edward Levi that the late FBI director J. Edgar Hoover kept secret files on the activities of Presidents of the United States, members of Congress, and other political personages, and that their contents were improperly used.

Mar. 1   The Bicentennial Era, to run through Dec. 31, 1976, officially opens.

Leslie's Retreat, an event that occurred in Salem, Massachusetts 200 years ago, is reenacted on Mar. 2, 1975 by Colonel Vincent J. R. Kehoe, playing the role of British troop commander Colonel Thomas Leslie, and Reverend Robert Cummings, playing the role of Dr. Thomas Barnard, Jr., the Salem parson who negotiated the compromise that permitted Colonel Leslie and his troops, who were searching for Colonials' ammunition stores, to retreat and avoid a bloody confrontation with the local townspeople.

Mar. 7   The U.S. Senate revises its rule, dating from 1949, under which a two-thirds vote of the entire body is required to end a filibuster. Under the new rule, 60 instead of the former 67—three fifths of the membership—can terminate debate by voting for cloture.

Mar. 12   Maurice H. Stans, former Secretary of Commerce and principal fund-raiser for former President Nixon's reelection campaign in 1972, pleads guilty to five misdemeanor charges of violating campaign laws. [On May 14 he is sentenced to a fine of $5,000.]

Mar. 17   Under a ruling of the U.S. Supreme Court, rights to mineral deposits on the continental shelf off the Atlantic coast beyond the three-mile limit are assigned to the Federal Government rather than to the governments of the coastal states.

Mar. 26   President Ford signs legislation appropriating $3,700,000,000 for foreign aid for fiscal 1975-1976, about $2,300,000,000 less than he had requested.

Mar. 29   The largest tax cut in U.S. history becomes law when President Ford approves a bill that will decrease the Federal tax revenues by $22,800,000,000.

Mar. 31   With the official termination of the "clemency" program instituted by the Ford Administration on behalf of deserters and draft evaders of the war in Indochina, 22,500 out of 124,000 eligibles are recorded as having applied for remission of their offenses.

Apr. 1   The Consolidated Rail Corporation (Conrail), a 15,000-mile system comprising the former Penn Central, Erie Lackawanna, Reading, Central of New Jersey, Lehigh Valley, Ann Arbor, and Lehigh and Hudson River lines, initiates service intended to revive rail traffic with the help of about $6,400,000,000 in Federal funds.

Apr. 4   A. U.S. Air Force C-5, carrying some 300 Vietnamese children and their caretakers on a "rescue mission" to the United States, crashes on the runway in Saigon, killing at least 200 persons. [By Apr. 14, about 1,400 Vietnamese children are evacuated by air for adoption in the United States.]

Apr. 17   Former Secretary of the Treasury John B. Connally, Jr., is acquitted on charges of having accepted bribes from milk producers in exchange for recommending price advantages on their behalf.

Apr. 29   Eight days after the resignation of President Nguyen Van Thieu of South Vietnam, and with the Communist forces in position to enter Saigon, President Ford orders the complete evacuation of Americans from Vietnam. [Largely with the use of helicopters about 400 Americans and some 4,500 Vietnamese refugees are carried to safety just as the North Vietnamese and Provisional Revolutionary Government complete their total occupation of South Vietnam.]

May 7 Declaring the ''Vietnam Era'' officially closed after more than a decade of recognized warfare, President Ford sets this as the terminal date for service-connected benefits to be granted to veterans of the Indochina war.

May 7 The Strategic Arms Limitation Talks (SALT 2) initiated in November 1972 and most recently in session in Geneva since Jan. 31, 1975, again recess in a stalemate as U.S. and Soviet delegates fail to concretize the general areas of agreement reached in November 1974 at Vladivostok by President Ford and party leader Leonid Brezhnev.

May 12-15 The U.S. merchant ship *Mayaguez,* with a crew of 39, is seized by Cambodian armed forces in the waters off Tang Island (claimed by Cambodia). The crew are removed from the ship and taken to the Cambodian port of Sihanoukville; then, on May 14, both ship and crew are separately released. Meanwhile, about 1,100 U.S. marines are dispatched to a Thai base (without Thai approval), from which they bomb Cambodian gunboats and installations on the Cambodian mainland, and land 100 marines on Tang Island by helicopter. [It is subsequently disputed whether the release of the *Mayaguez* and her unharmed crew was known to authorities by the time Tang was assaulted.] A total of 41 American and an unknown number of Cambodian lives are lost in the action on Tang and in related episodes.

May 14 Congress sets a budget deficit for fiscal 1975-1976 of $68,800,000, based on proposed expenditures of $367,000,000,000. Both amounts exceed those set by President Ford in his budget message of Feb. 3.

May 17 The Academy Award of 1957 for the script of the screenplay *The Brave One* is transferred from ''Roland Rich'' to Dalton Trumbo, who used the pen name of Rich during the McCarthy era when an industry blacklist prevented him from openly earning his living as a writer.

May 27 The Alaska Supreme Court legalizes the home use of marijuana.

May 28-June 3 In his first Presidential visit to Europe, Gerald Ford not only attends a summit meeting of NATO in Brussels but also meets individually with presidents Valéry Giscard d'Es-

taing of France and Anwar Sadat of Egypt and with premiers Vasco dos Santos Gonçalves of Portugal, Suleyman Demirel of Turkey, and Constantine Caramanlis of Greece.

May 29 Union farm workers of California are granted the rights under state law to elect representatives for collective bargaining, to strike for contract terms, and to engage in limited boycotts.

June 6 A record rate of unemployment in the United States for the period since World War II, 9.2 per cent, is reported for May by the Labor Department.

June 10 New York City, on the brink of bankruptcy, surrenders much of its financial autonomy to a special state agency, the Municipal Assistance Corporation (popularly called ''Big Mac'').

June 16 Oregon becomes the first state to forbid the use, beginning in March 1977, of aerosols containing chlorofluorocarbon propellants.

June 17 The 14 islands of the Marianas group in the Pacific Ocean, other than Guam (already U.S. territory), vote in plebiscite to seek commonwealth status under the United States, ending their status as a U.S. trust territory. [Be-

The flag is raised over the recovered *Mayaguez*.

fore the desired status is achieved, it is necessary for Congress to ratify the plebiscite petition and for the United Nations, as mandating authority, to give its consent. The House approves the change in July 1975, followed by the Senate in February 1976.]

June 24 A Boeing 727 aircraft on a flight from New Orleans crashes at Kennedy International Airport in New York City during a storm, with a loss of 113 lives. This is the greatest number of fatalities suffered on a single plane over the U.S. mainland.

June 26 Two agents of the FBI, allegedly intent on arresting members of the American Indian Movement on the Oglala (Sioux) Pine Ridge reservation in South Dakota, are shot dead. [Within three days 300 FBI agents are deployed throughout the reservation to apprehend suspects.]

June 30 The U.S. Supreme Court rules, 6 to 3, that a defendant in a criminal case may conduct his or her own defense rather than accept the services of a court-appointed attorney.

July 3 The New York State Bar association disbars John N. Mitchell. This is the first time a former U.S. Attorney General has been denied the right to practice law.

July 16 Secretary of State Henry Kissinger confirms that President Ford followed his advice to avoid antagonizing Soviet authorities when he failed to invite Soviet dissident Aleksandr Solzhenitsyn to the White House. [On July 21 Solzhenitsyn declines an informal invitation to visit the Executive Mansion.]

July 17 U.S. astronaut Thomas P. Stafford and Soviet cosmonaut Aleksei Leonov, commanding respectively the Apollo and Soyuz spaceships about 150 miles above the Atlantic Ocean, shake hands to symbolize the successful completion of the first joint mission in space undertaken by the two countries. The ships were launched on July 15. [The Soyuz returns to Kazakhstan on July 21 and the Apollo splashes down in the Pacific Ocean on July 24.]

July 22 The U.S. Congress restores full citizenship to General Robert E. Lee, Confederate commander during the Civil War. The action occurs 111 years after Lee signed the oath of allegiance to the Union as required, and six years after the signature, which had been mislaid, was discovered in the National Archives.

July 29 Overriding the President's veto, the U.S. Senate enacts a bill, three days after similar action by the House of Representatives, granting $2,000,000,000 over a three-year period to the

Handshake in space between Apollo commander Stafford and Soviet cosmonaut Leonov aboard orbiting modules

states for a variety of health programs.

July 31 James R. Hoffa, former teamsters' union chief, is reported missing under conditions that indicate foul play. [An FBI investigation fails to lead to any clue concerning Hoffa's fate.]

Aug. 1 The postwar borders of Eastern Europe are formally accepted by the United States and more than 30 other countries at a conference at Helsinki, Finland, that appears to signify the ending of the Cold War and to manifest the spirit of détente.

Aug. 5 Alger Hiss, despite his conviction in 1950 for perjury, for which he was sentenced to prison for five years, is reinstated by the state bar of Massachusetts, which describes him as intellectually and morally fit to practice law.

Aug. 11 Ambassador Daniel P. Moynihan casts the U.S. veto in the UN Security Council against the admission to the world organization of South Vietnam and North Vietnam.

Aug. 21 The United States modifies its trade embargo against Cuba to the extent of permitting foreign subsidiaries of U.S. firms to deal with the Castro regime.

September Two attempts to assassinate President Ford in California fail. The first, on Sept.

6 in Sacramento, is foiled by the seizure of Lynette Alice Fromme before she is able to fire a gun she has pointed at the President. The second, on Sept. 22, fails when an onlooker in a crowd welcoming the President to downtown San Francisco deflects a shot fired at him by Sara Jane Moore. [Both Fromme and Moore are sentenced to life imprisonment, on Dec. 17, 1975, and on Jan. 15, 1976, respectively.]

Sept. 4   The shuttle diplomacy of Secretary of State Henry Kissinger in the Middle East is successfully concluded in a pact between Egypt and Israel that involves modification of the Is-raeli occupation of the Sinai area and relaxation of Egypt's ban against Israeli shipping in the Suez Canal.

Sept. 7   A week of violent protest against the busing of children to maintain racial balance between the schools of inner-city and suburban Louisville, Ky., ends after the state national guard provides protection to the beleaguered children. Heavy property damage and the arrest of hundreds of persons preceded the calling of the guard.

Sept. 14   Mother Elizabeth Bayley Seton, who died in 1821 after devoting her life to

Lynette Fromme is led away from the site of her attempted assassination of President Ford.

President Gerald Ford, surrounded by his entourage, moments after surviving an assassination attempt by Lynette Fromme

Police rush to apprehend the woman [Sara Jane Moore] who fired a shot at President Ford.

Sara Jane Moore leaves court on Oct. 30 after a hearing to determine the custody of her nine-year old son.

Catholic education, particularly in the order of Sisters of Charity, becomes the first saint born in the United States.

Sept. 18   Patricia Hearst and two of her alleged captors are seized by FBI agents in San Francisco, ending a 19-month search for the heiress, who is accused of armed robbery. [After a trial lasting from January to March 1976, Hearst is convicted and on Sept. 24, 1976, she is sentenced to seven years in prison.]

Sept. 19   Air Force Technical Sergeant Leonard Matlevich, holder of the bronze star, is declared unfit for service on the grounds of homosexual practices, which he voluntarily revealed. [On Oct. 22 he is given an honorable discharge from the Air Force.]

Sept. 28   The provisions of an omnibus military bill passed by Congress include authorization of an additional $800,000,000 for the de-velopment of a B-1 bomber and for the admission in 1976 of women to the three service academies at West Point, Annapolis, and Colorado Springs.

Oct. 2-3   Congress lifts an arms embargo imposed against Turkey on Feb. 5 on the grounds that Turkey used U.S.-provided weapons in its occupation of part of Cyprus in 1975. On June 17 the embargo had been denounced by Turkey as a unilateral violation of agreements. In May the U.S. Senate voted to end the embargo, but in July the House of Representatives voted to maintain it. On July 26 the Turks repossessed most of the U.S. bases in Turkey. The pressure to lift the ban mounted in response to this action, which was believed to threaten the North Atlantic Treaty Organization.

Oct. 16-17   Three U.S. scientists receive shares of Nobel Prize awards. James Rainwater

Patricia Hearst (right) and Emily Harris clench fists as they leave San Francisco's Federal Building on Sept. 18 after their arraignment.

of Columbia University receives one third of the prize in physics for describing the structure of the atomic nucleus; and Dr. David Baltimore of the Center for Cancer Research at the Massachusetts Institute of Technology and Dr. Howard Martin Temin of the University of Wisconsin are each awarded one third of the prize in medicine for their discoveries in the field of tumor virology.

Oct. 20   An agreement to sell between 6,000,000 and 8,000,000 tons of wheat and corn annually to the Soviet Union, beginning Oct. 1, 1976, is announced by the White House. It is reported that 10,300,000 tons of grain have been sold so far this year.

Nov. 12   U.S. Supreme Court Associate Justice William O. Douglas retires because of poor health after a record 36 years of service on the Court.

Dec. 1-5   In the course of a visit to eastern Asia, President Ford confers with Chairman Mao Tse-tung in Peking, with President Suharto of Indonesia, and with President Ferdinand Marcos of the Philippines.

Dec. 15   A U.S. District Court requires the production for inspection by the Securities and Exchange Commission of documents relating to secret payments of bribes to foreign officials on the part of the Lockheed Aircraft Corporation. Payments over a five-year period in the amount of $22,000,000 have been admitted, but the company refuses to disclose the names of those whom it has bribed, a refusal supported by Secretary of State Henry Kissinger. [During 1976 the Dutch Parliament identifies Prince Bernhard, consort of Queen Juliana, as a Lockheed beneficiary; and former Premier Kakeui Tanaka of Japan is indicted for accepting bribes.]

Dec. 29   A bomb in the baggage area of New York's LaGuardia Airport explodes, killing 11 persons and injuring 75 others in a holiday travel crowd.

Chairman Mao shakes hands with President Ford, continuing the amicable relationship established in 1972 during the Nixon Administration.

1976

The Bicentennial commemoration is often colorful and has more diversity than depth. Perhaps it comes too soon after Indochina and Watergate to permit an appropriate display of enthusiasm. The spirit of '76 in the 20th century cannot echo that of the 18th century.

The economic slump continues, although somewhat muted in the last quarter of the year. The rate of unemployment remains intolerably high, but the rate of inflation is brought to single-digit level. The Executive and Legislative branches continue to parry—enact, veto, override—like protagonists in an ill-organized political tournament.

The Presidential election is the feature of the year. The foreplay includes an unprecedented series of primaries, from which emerges a Democratic champion, Jimmy Carter, who was not seriously mentioned last year, when pundits were projecting fratricidal disarray for the party almost shattered in 1972. Irritation at the shenanigans in Washington favors this Southern contender who is neither a lawyer nor a minion of the military-industrial complex, and the professional politicians wilt before his resolute challenge. In the Republican camp, on the other hand, virulent fratricide appears as the party's right wing rallies behind former California Governor Ronald Reagan, and almost deprives the incumbent President of the long-sought chance to test his standing with the electorate.

An interminable campaign, marked by primaries, caucuses, and unenlightening "debates," and a degree of financial moderation mandated by post-Watergate legislation, leads to the closest election (in electoral votes) since the Wilson-Hughes contest of 1916. Carter is the first manifest beneficiary of the civil rights movement on a Presidential level. This spokesman of the New South can succeed only with the support of black constituents, South and North. In fact the bare majority that elects Carter comprises a coalition of the Democratic machines and organized labor together with unorganized wage-earners, the black and brown minorities, the poor, and the young.

The election is relatively kind to incumbents in the House of Representatives, but a number of senior Senators will not return to the Hill: involuntarily, including Indiana's Vance Hartke, Frank Moss of Utah, Joseph Montoya of New Mexico, and Wyoming's Gale McGee; or out of choice and full of years, such as Mike Mansfield of Montana, Hugh Scott of Pennsylvania, John Pastore of Rhode Island, Philip Hart of Michigan, Roman Hruska of Nebraska; and for reasons more imperative Walter Mondale of Minnesota, the Vice-President-elect. As for incumbent Gerald Ford, he loses his first election in the course of first seeking the Presidency. The year ends with a lame duck in the White House, an ambitious peanut farmer turning to pastures awesomely larger, and a restive nation entering its third century, as it entered its first, facing an inscrutable future.

Jan. 2   Ten Democrats and two Republicans contending for the Presidency this year qualify for Federal matching funds derived from the income-tax checkoff authorized by the Federal Finance Campaign Law of Oct. 15, 1974, and receive their initial stipends.

Jan. 9   The State Department affirms a correlation between the aid available to foreign countries and the support for U.S. foreign policy demonstrated by beneficiaries in their United Nations votes.

Jan. 10   A fire and explosion in a hotel in Fremont, Neb., 30 miles northwest of Omaha, result in death for 18 and injury for 60 persons, most of them elderly.

Jan. 19   Daniel and Philip Berrigan, radical Catholic priests, begin to serve a month in prison as punishment for having protested against nuclear proliferation by digging a pit on Nov. 26, 1975, in the White House lawn.

Jan. 21   Allowing for an anticipated deficit of $43,000,000,000, President Ford asks Congress for a budget for fiscal 1976-1977 (beginning Oct. 1, 1976) of $394,200,000,000. The quarter between July 1 and Sept. 30 is to be "transitional," that is, not assigned to any fiscal year. A balanced budget within three years is envisioned.

Jan. 23   Paul Robeson, 77, black singer, actor, and champion of civil rights, dies in Philadelphia.

Jan. 29   The House of Representatives votes,

246 to 124, not to publish in full the report of its Intelligence Committee headed by Otis G. Pike of New York. Much of the contents of the report have already been leaked to the media and made public. [Television correspondent Daniel Schorr receives a copy of the report and releases it to the New York City weekly newspaper *Village Voice,* where it appears on Feb. 11 and Feb. 18. Schorr is suspended from his job by the Columbia Broadcasting Company on Feb. 23. He refuses, citing the 1st Amendment, to disclose his source to a committee of the House. On Sept. 22 the House committee decides to refrain from pressing the issue against Schorr.]

Jan. 30 Ruling on the Federal Finance Campaign Law of Oct. 15, 1974, the U.S. Supreme Court upholds its provisions concerning disclosure of contributions, limitations of contributions in certain categories, and the use of matching funds earmarked on income-tax forms.

Feb. 8 The heaviest subatomic particle yet identified, with six times the mass of a proton, is discovered by Leon Lederman and a team of scientists at the Fermi National Accelerator Laboratory in Batavia, N.Y., and designated as the upsilon.

Feb. 10 President Ford signs a defense appropriation of $112,300,000,000 for a 15-month period (fiscal 1975-1976 together with the following ''transitional'' quarter). The bill includes a ban, of which the President disapproves, against aid to all factions engaged in the civil war in Angola.

Feb. 24 In the first primary of the Bicentennial year election, incumbent Gerald Ford outpoints challenger Ronald Reagan among New Hampshire Republicans by a ratio of 51 to 49, while the Democrats give underdog Jimmy Carter, former governor of Georgia, a 29 per cent plurality over contenders Morris Udall, Birch Bayh, Fred Harris, Sargent Shriver, and (on write-ins) Hubert Humphrey. Other announced Democratic contenders Henry Jackson and George Wallace abstain from this contest.

Mar. 9-11 Two explosions in a coal mine in Oven Fork, southeastern Kentucky, kill 26 miners and inspectors.

Mar. 27 The first 4.6 miles of the projected 100-mile Washington, D.C., Metro (subway) are opened to passengers, with 1982 the expected time of completion.

Mar. 30 Legislation funding Conrail with more than $2,000,000,000 over a three-year period is signed by President Ford.

Mar. 30 The U.S. Supreme Court upholds a Virginia state law that prohibits homosexual acts between consenting adults, even in private.

Apr. 5 Howard Hughes, 70, legendary billionaire industrialist, aviator, movie maker, and man of mystery, dies on his plane en route from Acapulco, Mexico, to Houston.

Apr. 13 Secretary of State Henry Kissinger tells a gathering of newspaper editors that any political success by Communists in Western European countries would adversely affect U.S. policies toward the countries concerned.

The overturned bus that carried 28 school children to their death near San Jose, Calif., on May 21

Apr. 17 Mary Margaret McBride, 76, also known as Martha Deane, radio talk-show personality from 1934 to 1954, dies in West Shokan, N.Y.

Apr. 20 The U.S. Supreme Court decides, 8 to 0, that a metropolitan area (city plus suburbs) rather than its city area alone is under certain conditions the appropriate entity for determining the location of low-income housing.

Apr. 27 On a flight from Providence, R.I., a Boeing 727 jet plane crashes at the airport at Charlotte Amalie, U.S. Virgin Islands, killing 37 of the 88 passengers and crew aboard.

May 5 According to the Internal Revenue Service, five persons each reporting adjusted gross income of more than $1,000,000 and 239 others with incomes of more than $200,000 were able to avoid paying Federal income taxes in 1974 (the latest year for which such information is available). The total of 244 such tax-exempt incomes compares with 80 three years earlier.

May 8 A 39-day strike of municipal workers in San Francisco precipitated by a proposed pay cut and a ballot proposition considered antilabor by the union is called off when the proposition is withdrawn and a commission is set up to arbitrate the money issues.

May 13 Congress sets a budget target for fiscal 1976-1977 at $413,000,000,000 for expenditures, with an anticipated deficit of $50,800,000,000. This estimate is based on $11,200,000,000 in revenues not included by President Ford, and favors social programs to a greater extent than does the President's proposed budget.

May 21 Near San Jose, Calif., a bus carrying students of the Yuba City High School choir swerves off an elevated superhighway and lands upside down 30 feet below, killing 28 of the passengers.

May 24 The first supersonic Concordes to fly between Europe and the United States touch down at Dulles International Airport near Washington, D.C., after flights of just under four hours from London and Paris, initiating a 16-month test of their tolerability in accordance with a ruling made on Feb. 4 by Transportation Secretary William T. Coleman, Jr.

May 24 Consumer interests are encouraged by a U.S. Supreme Court ruling that invalidates state laws prohibiting the advertising by pharmacies of the prices of drugs.

May 28 The United States and the Soviet Union sign a treaty in Washington on the use of underground nuclear weapons, supplementing a similar treaty of July 1974.

June 2 After the recess of an unproductive session that lasted from Jan. 28 to May 5, the Strategic Arms Limitation Talks (SALT 2) are resumed in Geneva to define the disposition of nuclear weapons to be included in Soviet and American armament programs. [On Nov. 20 the talks are formally adjourned, to be resumed after Jan. 20, 1977, when the Carter Administration succeeds that of President Ford.]

June 4 A turboprop jet Electra crashes immediately after takeoff on Guam, killing 46 persons.

June 5 Eleven persons and some 13,000 cattle are killed and property estimated at more than $1,000,000,000 in hundreds of square miles of Idaho's Snake River valley is devastated when the 300-foot-high, seven-month-old dam across the Teton River bursts, releasing 80,000,000,000 gallons of impounded water.

June 6 J. Paul Getty, 83, Texas oil magnate believed to be the world's richest person, dies at Sutton Place, Surrey, England.

June 9 James A. Farley, 88, Democratic Party national committee chairman from 1933 to 1940, and during those years a staunch supporter of the Administration of Franklin D. Roosevelt, dies in New York City.

June 16 U.S. Ambassador to Lebanon Fran-

The waters released by the bursting of the Teton Dam make canals out of the streets of Rexburg, Idaho.

cis E. Meloy, Jr., is shot to death in his car on a Beirut street while en route to confer with Lebanese President-elect Elias Sarkis.

June 27-28 Dorado Beach, Puerto Rico, is the site of a summit meeting of the seven leading noncommunist industrial powers (the United States, Canada, France, Great Britain, Italy, Japan, and West Germany), at which an agreement is reached to diminish the rate of economic expansion in order to solve the major problems of unemployment and inflation.

June 29 A resolution of the United Nations Security Council demanding the withdrawal of Israeli armed forces from Arab territory by June 1, 1977, is defeated by the sole negative vote of the United States.

June 30 President Ford signs a bill authorizing the expenditure of $6,000,000,000 and the appropriation of $5,929,000,000 on foreign military aid in fiscal 1975-1976 and the following quarter.

June 30 Karl Thomas, who was trying to cross the Atlantic Ocean solo in a helium-filled balloon, is rescued from the sea by a Soviet ship about 300 miles south of Nova Scotia, after a four-day flight from Lakehurst, N.J.

July 2 According to a decision of the U.S. Supreme Court upholding state laws that prescribe capital punishment, the death penalty is not "cruel and unusual" punishment in the sense prohibited by the 8th amendment to the Constitution, unless the penalty is arbitrarily or wantonly imposed. This ruling takes into account state laws that have been enacted since June 29, 1972, with the intent of modifying or redefining the imposition of capital punishment to conform to the Court decision of that date.

July 4 On the 200th birthday of the United States, a variety of celebrations observe the occasion more or less appropriately. The Declaration of Independence is read aloud to a throng in Washington, D.C.; a landing pad to welcome interplanetary visitors is rolled out at Lake City, Pa.; historic events that occurred throughout two centuries are re-enacted at many locations; an international parade of sailing ships, designated Op Sail, is reviewed by about 6,000,000 landlubbers on both banks of the Hudson River above New York Harbor.

July 6 The U.S. Court of Appeals upholds a ban on Red Dye No. 2, the most used coloring agent for many consumer products, as dangerous to health.

July 8 The Appellate Division of the New York State Supreme Court disbars former Presi-

Standing in front of Independence Hall and under the statue of George Washington, President Gerald Ford and Mayor Frank Rizzo of Philadelphia take the Pledge of Allegiance on July 4.

The U.S. Coast Guard plays its part in the spectacular Operation Sail that marked the Bicentennial in New York.

437

Congresswoman Barbara Jordan laughs with Democratic Party Chairman Robert Strauss after he introduces Jordan to the Democratic national convention on July 12.

Mrs. Coretta King, widow of the late Dr. Martin Luther King, Jr., is introduced to the Democratic national convention by Minnesota Governor Wendell Anderson.

Jimmy Carter acknowledges the cheers of the Democratic convention that made him its candidate for President.

dent Nixon from practicing law in the state, on the basis of evidence that he had obstructed justice and committed associated offenses.

July 9 According to a report of the National Institute of Drug Abuse, in the year beginning Apr. 1, 1974, alcohol and Valium (a tranquilizer) were the most pathogenic drugs used in the United States, followed by opiates and barbiturates.

July 10 In accordance with the decision of a military tribunal in Angola on June 28, four captured white mercenaries, including one American, who participated in the recently concluded civil war are executed by a firing squad.

July 14-15 Former Georgia Governor Jimmy Carter crosses the finish line on the first ballot at the Democratic national convention in New York City, overtaking career politicians Henry Jackson and Edward Muskie and neighboring Governor George Wallace, who long commanded the allegiance of Southern Democrats. With his own delegate strength virtually assured after participating in 30 of the 31 primaries, Carter interviews a group of finalists for the Vice-Presidential post before picking Minnesota Senator Walter F. Mondale to share his campaign.

July 15-16 A school bus carrying 26 children of Chowchilla, Calif., and its driver is hijacked and the passengers are transferred to vans and hidden in a quarry while police and the Federal Bureau of Investigation search for them for 29 hours. The victims dig their own way out of the buried van and reach rescuers unharmed. [Within two weeks three suspects, all young men of affluent California families, are apprehended.]

July 20 Viking 1 becomes the first spaceship to land on the planet Mars. [It soon sends photographs, showing the landscape, and analyses of the "soil" by radio to the earth, but leaves unanswered the question as to whether life exists on Mars. On Sept. 3, Viking 2 lands a second vehicle about 4,600 miles from the first, and again reports are transmitted through space by radio.]

July 22 Congress overrides President Ford's veto of a public works bill authorizing the expenditure of $3,950,000,000 for fiscal 1976-1977.

July 23 Lazslo Toth, holding dual Yugoslav and U.S. citizenship and imprisoned in Yugoslavia as a spy since August 1975, is returned to the United States almost two months after he was granted a pardon by President Tito.

July 27 With the casualties of the civil war

The rolling Martian landscape is the background for the flag-bedecked housing of Viking 1's power system.

A view of the surface of Mars taken by Viking 1 showing (lower left) the housing containing the surface sampler scoop

Viking 2's first picture on the surface of Mars

439

Presidential candidate Ronald Reagan waves to an enthusiastic crowd on his arrival on Aug. 15 in Kansas City.

President and Mrs. Ford in Kansas City on Aug. 15 wave to a crowd at the Crown Center Hotel.

Senator Robert Dole waves to a standing ovation before delivering his acceptance speech as the Republican Party's Vice-Presidential candidate.

in Lebanon mounting, the U.S. Navy evacuates 308 persons, including 160 Americans, from Beirut; and President Ford thanks the Palestine Liberation Organization, hitherto unrecognized by the United States, for its cooperation in the action.

July 27-Aug. 5   Among participants in the Pennsylvania state convention of the American Legion last week, almost 175 fall seriously ill of a disease that results in 23 fatalities during this period. [By the end of August the death toll reaches 28, and the disease is not yet identified.]

July 29   The House of Representatives reprimands Democratic Senator Robert F. Sikes of Florida for having voted to give advantages to two firms in which he owned undisclosed stocks, thereby violating House ethics.

July 31   Following a 10-inch rainfall in 1½ hours over the Front Range of the Colorado Rockies, a flash flood sweeps down the canyon of the Big Thompson River in Larimer County, destroying habitations and communities from Estes Park to Loveland and killing between 100 and 200 persons while about 1,000 others are evacuated by air.

Aug. 18   Two U.S. officers of a crew trimming a tree in the demilitarized zone of Korea are hacked to death by North Korean soldiers. [Following a brief spate of sabre-rattling, the United Nations and North Korea commands agree on Sept. 26 to institute security arrangements that would obviate further such incidents.]

Aug. 18-19   At the Republican national convention in Kansas City, Mo., President Ford defeats challenger Ronald Reagan, former governor of California, by a vote of 1,187 to 1,070 on the first ballot for the Presidential nomination. Ford names Robert Dole, U.S. Senator from Kansas, as his running mate.

Aug. 23   Secretary of the Army Martin R. Hoffman tells a Senate committee that any cadet expelled or forced to resign from the U.S. Military Academy at West Point, as a consequence of having participated in a massive cheating practice or its cover-up, may be offered a chance to return to the school.

Aug. 23   California enacts a model land-use law, approved by Governor Edmund J. Brown, Jr., that sets up a commission of private and public officials to control virtually all development in a coastal zone extending from three miles offshore to between 1,000 yards and five miles (depending on topography) inland.

Aug. 28   Two U.S. Air Force jet transports flying from McGuire Air Force Base in New Jersey crash in separate accidents, in England and in Greenland, with a combined loss of 38 lives.

Aug. 28 The normal functioning of an artificially constructed bacterial gene implanted in a living cell is reported by the Massachusetts Institute of Technology, whose Dr. Har Gobind Khorana has developed a controversial technique known as genetic engineering.

Aug. 28-29 After 130 days without producing rubber tires, the Goodyear and Firestone corporations grant wage increases to their employees and reopen their factories, but the strike of rubber workers in other major plants continues.

Sept. 1 Wayne Hays, former chairman of the powerful House Administration Committee, resigns after 28 years as a Democratic representative from Ohio. His disgrace was caused by his conduct in retaining his mistress on the public payroll as his secretary.

Sept. 8 Lt. William J. Calley, Jr., convicted in 1971 of complicity in the Mylai massacre of 1968, announces that he favors amnesty for those who evaded the draft for military service in Vietnam.

Sept. 9 Viktor I. Belenko, a Soviet airman who landed a MIG-25 in Japan on Sept. 6 for the purpose of defecting, is flown to the United States as a refugee.

Sept. 10-13 In the first skyjacking over U.S. soil in four years, Croatian nationalists force a Boeing 707 carrying 92 passengers to divert from its projected New York-Chicago course by crossing the Atlantic and landing in Paris. There the skyjackers and their hostages learn that a New York City policeman was killed when a bomb planted in Grand Central Station, New York, by the Croatians exploded before it could be detonated. The Croatians, having gained the publicity they sought, surrender to the French police and are returned to New York on Sept. 13 for Federal and local arraignment.

Sept. 14 An F-14 Tomcat U.S. Navy fighter plane, equipped with special electronic gear and a Phoenix air-to-air missile, slides into the North Atlantic northwest of the Orkney Islands from the deck of the U.S. carrier *John F. Kennedy* during maneuvers. [During an unsuccessful effort in October to raise the plane from about 1,900 feet below the surface of the sea, the missile is recovered; and the Tomcat itself is retrieved in November.]

Sept. 15 Double-decked buses appear on select New York City routes for the first time since 1954.

Sept. 15-16 The ordination of women as priests in the Episcopal Church is approved at a convention in Minneapolis.

Sept. 17 A spacecraft named *Enterprise* (after the spaceship of the popular television program "Star Trek") is rolled out in a NASA ceremony at Palmsdale, Calif. Capable of transporting 60,000 pounds of payload to a site on an earth orbit at an altitude of about 100 miles, the craft is intended to be employed as a reusable shuttle to haul equipment and personnel, such as repair crews, observers, or scientists, to and from satellites in orbit.

Sept. 20 The Department of Health, Education, and Welfare receives a report that recommends the phasing out of a program reported as having aided about 650,000 Cuban refugees over a period of 15 years.

Sept. 22 Orlando Letelier, a former Chilean cabinet minister and ambassador to the United States (in the administration of President Salvador Allende), is killed when a bomb explodes in his car on a street in Washington, D.C.

Sept. 22 President Ford signs a defense appropriation bill for $104,343,835,000 for fiscal 1976-1977, about $14,000,000,000 more than the amount appropriated in the previous fiscal year. The bill provides for procurement of the controversial B-1 bombers, but only $87,000,000 (out of a total allotment for the bombers of $1,000,000,000) can be spent before Feb. 1, 1977, following the inauguration of the President elected this November.

Sept. 23 The first of three so-called debates between Presidential candidates Republican Gerald Ford and Democrat Jimmy Carter reaches an audience estimated at about 90,000,000 per-

The contenders for the Presidency, Jimmy Carter and Gerald Ford, during a pause in their first TV debate

sons. [None of the "debates"—which are actually expanded double press conferences under a rigid format televised for 1½ hours of prime time—is manifestly "won" by either candidate; the third, on Oct. 23, proves the most interesting.]

Sept. 24   After a week during which Secretary of State Henry Kissinger meets with a succession of African leaders (the presidents of four black African countries—but not those of Angola or Mozambique—and the prime ministers of South Africa and Rhodesia) to formulate a technique to abort the impending racial war in southern Africa, he submits a plan originally offered in March by British Prime Minister James Callaghan, providing for a transition over a two-year period to black (majority) rule in Rhodesia.

Sept. 25   The U.S. Bureau of the Census reports a rise in the percentage of Americans below the official "poverty line" from 11.1 per cent in 1973 to 12.3 per cent in 1975; in 1959, the first year of such an estimate, 22.4 per cent were so recorded.

Sept. 28   Congress approves foreign aid for fiscal 1976-1977 in the amount of $5,100,000,000, more than half of which is allotted to countries of the Middle East.

Sept. 29-30   President Ford vetoes an appropriation for fiscal 1976-1977 of $56,600,000,000 in the Labor-HEW and Related Agencies Bill passed by Congress. Congress overrides the veto by a substantial margin in both Houses. This is the 12th time a Ford veto has been overridden, and assures the implementation of a wide range of social service programs that would otherwise be blighted.

Sept. 30   California becomes the first state to legalize formulations such as "living wills" by which the terminally ill may authorize their physicians to withdraw life-sustaining devices or procedures.

Oct. 1   The first of 147,000,000 proposed doses of swine flu vaccine, to prevent a possible outbreak of a pandemic disease that made its first appearance on Feb. 19 in Fort Dix, N.J., are administered in Indianapolis and in the state of Massachusetts.

Oct. 8   Under a new directive from President Ford, following up a statement he made in yesterday's second "debate" with Jimmy Carter over network television, the Commerce Department announces that it will publish the names of U.S. firms that receive requests to submit to or observe the Arab boycott against Israel, and also the intention of the firms to comply or refuse to comply with such requests.

Oct. 10   Ending the second attempt this year to cross the Atlantic Ocean solo in a balloon, Ed Yost is rescued from the sea by a German freighter less than 600 miles west of Portugal. He was aloft for almost 107 hours and covered about 2,500 miles in the balloon since leaving Maine, both records.

Oct. 12   A national contract between the Ford Motor Company and its 165,000 auto workers is approved, ending a four-week strike. The terms include pay increases and enough additional days off to make possible an eventual four-day week.

Oct. 14   The Nobel Memorial Prize in economics is awarded to an anti-Keynsian professor at the University of Chicago, Milton Friedman, whose concept of "monetarism" holds that the key to a sound economy is the coordination of the money supply with the real rate of economic growth. The Nobel Prize in medicine is shared by two American specialists in the study of infectious diseases, Dr. Baruch S. Blumberg of the University of Pennsylvania and Dr. D. Carleton Gajdusek of the National Institute for Neurological Diseases at Bethesda, Md.

Oct. 15   A U.S.-owned cargo ship of Panamanian registry, the *Sylvia L. Ossa,* with a crew of 37, is lost with no report of having sent an SOS, some 200 miles west of Bermuda. This is the latest disappearance in an area known as the "Bermuda Triangle," where countless ships and planes have unaccountably vanished over the years.

Oct. 15   An agreement between the United States and Cuba reached in February 1973, which effectively ended a series of more than 100 plane hijackings to Cuba, is renounced by Premier Fidel Castro, to take effect Apr. 15, 1977. Castro justifies his move by claiming that the Central Intelligence Agency was involved in the destruction by bombing of a Cuban plane in flight over the Caribbean Sea on Oct. 6, with a loss of 73 lives.

Oct. 18   The Nobel Prize in physics is shared by two American scientists working in the field of elementary particles, Burton Richter of Stanford University and Samuel C.C. Ting of the Massachusetts Institute of Technology. William M. Lipscomb of Harvard University, a specialist in research on boranes, is awarded the Nobel Prize in chemistry.

Oct. 20   Only 18 persons survive when an auto ferry with a passenger capacity of 140 is hit and immediately sunk by a tanker in the Mississippi River about 30 miles above New Orleans. Most of the dead are carried to the river bottom within their cars. [A subsequent autopsy indicates that the pilot of the ferry was intoxicated.]

Oct. 21   Saul Bellow, Canadian-born U.S. citizen, wins the Nobel Prize in literature for his ability to combine "human understanding" and "subtle analysis of contemporary culture" in his novels. With this award, the entire group of Nobel awards goes to Americans, the first time any country has monopolized all categories in any year.

Oct. 24   A fire set in a social club in a Puerto Rican district of New York City by an arsonist kills 25 persons and injures 24 others.

Oct. 25   Clarence Norris, the only survivor among the nine black adolescents who were falsely accused of raping two white girls in a freight car rolling through Alabama in 1931, and whose trial as the "Scottsboro Boys" became a *cause célèbre,* is pardoned by Governor George Wallace. Norris, who was for five years a prisoner on death row and was incarcerated 17 years before breaking parole, is thus exonerated and free at age 64 for the first time since he was 19.

Oct. 26   With the United States as the sole abstainer, the General Assembly of the United Nations votes to mandate the total ostracism of Transkei, the tribal homeland of the Xhosa people that was granted independence today by the republic of South Africa.

Nov. 2   Jimmy Carter, with 51 per cent of the popular vote, is elected 39th President of the United States. The electoral vote is 297 for Carter, 241 for President Ford. The composition of the 95th Congress will be almost identical to that of the 94th, in partisan terms, and the preponderance of Democrats in both Houses assures Carter of a level of legislative support unavailable to President Ford.

Nov. 11   Alexander Calder, 78, sculptor best known for his "mobiles"—sculptures in motion—but also admired for massive "stabiles" that ornament public places throughout the world, dies in New York City.

Nov. 11   The United States subscribes to a "concensus" resolution in the United Nations Security Council that deplores the Israeli occupation of Arab territories. This is the first "unfriendly" vote toward Israel registered by the United States in recent years, and is the target of a protest of Premier Itzhak Rabin.

Nov. 12   Diplomats from the United States and the Socialist Republic of Vietnam meet on a secondary ambassadorial level in Paris, the first official contact between the two nations. [On Nov. 15 the United States nevertheless vetoes, for the third time, the effort by the Hanoi government to become a member of the United Nations.]

Dec. 1   The United States, by failing to veto the application for United Nations membership by Angola (as it had done in June), allows the Security Council to welcome the African country as the 146th member of the organization.

Dec. 3   The first proposed member of the Carter Cabinet is announced as Cyrus R. Vance for Secretary of State. Vance was Deputy Secretary of Defense in the Johnson Administration.

Jimmy Carter and wife Rosalynn wave to supporters on the morning of Nov. 3.

President-elect Jimmy Carter and Rosalynn Carter welcome Joan Mondale and Vice President-elect Mondale.

President-elect Jimmy Carter holds his first news conference on Nov. 4 at the train depot in Plains, Ga.

An aura of uncertainty surrounds most Americans as the year gets under-
way. Democrat Jimmy Carter, relatively unknown outside his home state of
1977 Georgia, is about to occupy the White House after a Republican presence of
eight years. Carter's promises of energy independence, pursuit of human rights,
and curtailment of unemployment all sound good, but the mood is one of "wait
and see."

Generally, the stock market performs poorly throughout the year. President Carter's
optimism is reflected initially in market improvement, but the "honeymoon" is soon over and
Carter's promises are not enough to halt the gradual decline in buying.

The worldwide arms buildup continues during 1977. President Carter decides that the U.S.
will not employ the B-1 bomber in its arsenal and opts instead for an air-launched cruise
missile capable of deploying nuclear warheads.

In its continuing quest for energy independence, the U.S. finally moves the first crude oil
through the Alaska pipeline. An extremely cold winter, the depletion of natural gas supplies in
some areas of the country, and the creation of a Cabinet-level Department of Energy all add to
the energy-oriented news of the year.

The world of entertainment is hit especially hard by death among its members. Joan
Crawford (69), Alfred Lunt (84), Groucho Marx (86), and Ethel Waters (80) all die during the
year as well as writers James Jones (55) and MacKinlay Kantor (73). On the national scene
former U.S. Supreme Court Justice Tom C. Clark (77) and Senator John MacClellan (81) also
die.

There is good news, however. America's farmers once again prove to the world that U. S.
agricultural output exceeds that of any other nation. Despite the erratic weather, total farm
output is up over 3 percent from 1976, while per capita consumption is down slightly.

Jan. 1 Jacqueline Means becomes the first
woman to be ordained a priest in the Episcopal
Church in the United States.

Jan. 17 Gary Gilmore, a self-admitted mur-
derer of a hotel clerk, becomes the first person in
ten years to be executed in the U.S.A. Execution
is by rifle squad in the Utah State Prison.

Jan. 20 Jimmy Carter, the first person from
the Deep South since the Civil War to be elected
President of the U.S., promises a "new beginning" in his inaugural address.

Jan. 21 In his first full day as president,
Jimmy Carter grants unconditional pardon to
most Vietnam War draft evaders.

Feb. 2 President Carter signs into law an
emergency natural gas bill which will allow surplus gas supplies to be shared with areas suffering
shortages.

Mar. 9-11 An obscure Islamic sect of Blacks
known as the Hanafi Muslims takes over the International Headquarters of b'Nai b'Rith in Washington, D.C. During the 38 hours of suspense,
150 people are held hostage, and a radio reporter
is killed. [All twelve Muslims are later convicted
on a variety of crimes and sentenced to prison
terms ranging from 24 to 132 years.]

April 4 A Southern Airlines DC-9, flying in
adverse weather conditions, crashes near Atlanta,
killing 62 passengers and eight people on the
ground.

April 19 The U.S. Supreme Court rules that
constitutional rights are not violated in cases involving the spanking of children in school.

May 23 President Carter signs a bill calling
for a $5 billion tax cut for low- and middle-income
families.

May 28 A fire in a posh night-club in South-
gate, Kentucky, kills 164 people.

June 6 The U.S. Supreme Court hands down
a ruling that convicted killers of police officers
need not be given mandatory death penalties.

June 11 Seattle Slew wins the Belmont
Stakes, making him the tenth horse in American
history to win the coveted "triple crown."

June 13 James Earl Ray, the convicted assassin of Dr. Martin Luther King, is captured after
escaping three days ago from a maximum security
prison in Tennessee.

June 16 Wernher Von Braun, the guiding
force of America's space program, dies at the age
of 65 in Alexandria, Virginia.

July 13 An American helicopter which had
accidentally strayed into North Korea is shot
down, killing three GIs and wounding one.

July 13–14 Thunderstorms in the New York
City area cause a power failure which lasts in

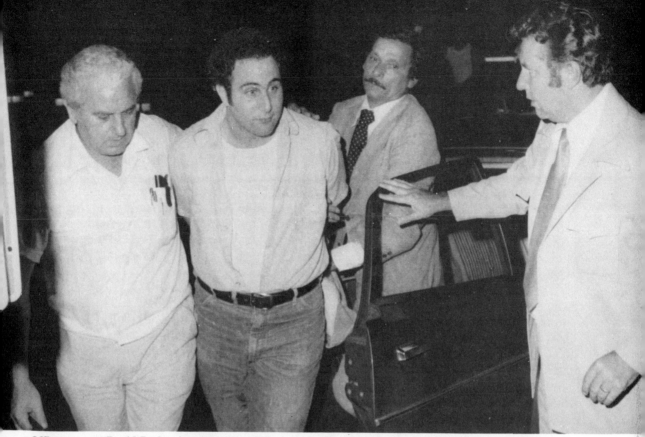

Officers escort David Berkowitz, center, to police headquarters in New York after he was arrested in Yonkers, N.Y. as the primary suspect in the "Son of Sam" killings.

some places up to 25 hours. Nine million residents are affected. Massive looting occurs in the confusion and 3,700 offenders are arrested.

Aug. 4 President Carter signs a bill creating a new Cabinet post, the Department of Energy. James R. Schlesinger will serve as secretary.

Aug. 10 Yonkers, New York, police arrest David Berkowitz, alleged to be the "Son of Sam" killer. Responsible for the death of six persons and the wounding of seven others, Berkowitz tells authorities that he is compelled to kill.

Aug. 12 The space orbiter *Enterprise* makes its first solo flight from atop a modified Boeing 747.

Aug. 16 Elvis Presley, the "king of rock and roll" who shocked the world in the mid-1950s with his fast-moving, hip-shaking music, dies at the age of 42 at Graceland, his palatial home in Memphis.

Sept. 7 Amid great controversy, the U.S. and Panama sign treaties in Washington, D.C., which will relinquish American control over the Panama Canal by the year 2000 and which will guarantee its neutrality. [Panama ratifies the treaties in October 1977. The U.S. Senate, after considerable debate, ratifies them in March and April 1978.]

Sept. 21 President Carter's director of the

Office of Management and Budget, fellow Georgian Bert Lance, resigns amid accusations of improper conduct as a banker in private life.

Sept. 30 The remains of 21 American servicemen who were killed during the Vietnam conflict are returned to U.S. authorities.

Oct. 4 Federal Judge John J. Sirica reduces the prison sentences of Watergate figures H. R. Haldeman, John Mitchell, and John Ehrlichman.

Oct. 14 Singer Bing Crosby, known for his popular rendition of "White Christmas" among other songs, dies at age 73 while playing golf in Madrid, Spain.

Nov. 1 President Carter signs a bill which increases the minimum wage from $2.65 to $2.90 an hour, to be effective on January 1, 1978. Annual increases will boost the minimum wage to $3.35 an hour by January 1, 1981.

Nov. 12 Ernest N. Morial, a Black judge, becomes the first of his race to be elected mayor of New Orleans.

Dec. 25 Charlie Chaplin, the controversial film star, dies in Switzerland at the age of 88. Barred from the U.S. since 1952 because of his liberal slant during the Cold War, he returned in 1972 and received a triumphal welcome.

445

1978

As the year opens, Americans are increasingly concerned with inflation. Before the year is out, prices will rise by more than 9 percent, cutting the buying power of the dollar to 50 percent of its 1967 value. Alfred E. Kahn is appointed by President Carter to become the administration's number one inflation fighter in an effort to boost the growing credibility gap between government and the people. In November President Carter announces drastic measures, including a one percent increase in the Federal Reserve interest rate. The effect is short-lived, and by year-end it appears that the inflation problem is going to be ever present.

The Panama Canal treaties provide new fuel for the flames of American politics. The treaties' advocates maintain that the return of the canal to Panama is the only just thing to do, while their enemies point out that the waterway was built with American ingenuity and with American dollars. The defense of our country is seriously jeopardized if these treaties pass, they maintain. After considerable debate in the U.S. Senate, both treaties are ratified and the U.S. pledges to return the canal to Panama on the last day of 1999.

The year ends with the chilling news from South America that over 900 U.S. citizens were executed or committed suicide as part of a massive ritual of the Peoples' Temple religious group. This sect, led by the Reverend Jim Jones, a power seeking, fanatical cult leader, is based in California, but Jones has led a large number of his flock to the jungles of Guyana where a communal village named Jonestown is settled. "If we can't live in peace, let's die in peace," Jones admonishes his followers after a California congressman and four associates investigating Jonestown are murdered at the local airport.

Death claims writer Hal Borland (77), boxer Gene Tunney (80), and actors Gig Young (60), Charles Boyer (79), and Will Geer (76), as well as Charlie McCarthy's creator, Edgar Bergen (75).

Americans are still energy conscious, and 1978 proves to be a year of considerable research into fossil energy alternatives such as solar generated power for heating homes and water.

Jan. 13   Hubert Horatio Humphrey, Vice President of the U.S. from 1965 to 1969 and a presidential hopeful in 1968 and 1972, dies at the age of 66.

Jan. 16   The National Aeronautics and Space Administration (NASA) recruits 35 new astronauts for its space program, including six women and three Blacks.

Jan. 19   Jimmy Carter delivers his first State of the Union address, declaring that "Government cannot solve our problems."

Feb. 6   The New England and Middle Atlantic states are hit by severe snowstorms, the worst in decades. Some areas are paralyzed for three days and receive upwards of 50 inches of snow.

Mar. 16   The U.S. Senate ratifies one of the two Panama Canal treaties signed by the U.S. and Panama in September 1977. This one, the "Treaty Concerning the Permanent Neutrality and Operation of the Panama Canal," guarantees the neutrality of the canal in war and peace and will allow both the U.S. and Panama to defend that neutrality.

Mar. 24   A new contract is ratified by the United Mine Workers, allowing 165,000 union members to return to work after 110 days, the longest miners' strike in American history.

April 6   A bill which provides for an increase in the mandatory retirement age from 65 to 70 is signed by President Carter amid considerable controversy.

April 14   The New York Stock Exchange records its heaviest day of trading in history with 52.58 million shares of stock sold.

April 18   The second Panama Canal treaty, providing for the absolute takeover of the canal by Panama on Dec. 31, 1999, is ratified by the U.S. Senate.

May 15   The U.S. Senate gives its approval to President Carter's plan to sell fighter planes to Israel and to its adversaries, Egypt and Saudi Arabia.

May 29   The price of a first class stamp is raised by the U.S. Postal Service to 15 cents from 13 cents.

June 1   An official announcement is made that listening devices have been found in the chimney at the U.S. Embassy in Moscow. The U.S.S.R. vigorously denies responsibility, charging that the equipment is actually American, placed there to monitor Soviet radio-telephone transmissions.

June 6 The Jarvis-Gann amendment to the California constitution, better known as "Proposition 13," is approved by a vast majority of the state's voters. Proposition 13, seen as a peoples' backlash to higher taxes, limits California property to be taxed at only one percent of its assessed value.

June 10 Affirmed becomes the second horse in two years to capture the "triple crown" by winning at Belmont.

June 11 Forty-eight hours after the Church of Jesus Christ of Latter Day Saints (Mormons) denounces its 148-year-old exclusion of Blacks from its priesthood, Joseph Freeman, Jr., a Black, is ordained a priest in that church.

June 15 Elizabeth Halaby, a 26-year-old American woman, marries King Hussein of Jordan and is proclaimed queen of that country.

June 28 Allan P. Bakke, a white engineer, is allowed entry into the University of California Medical School by the U.S. Supreme Court after he was initially refused admission. Bakke's suit claims "reverse discrimination," and the high court rules that fixed racial quotas are unconstitutional.

Aug. 17 Three New Mexico businessmen succeed in being the first to cross the Atlantic Ocean in a balloon. The 3,100-mile crossing from Maine to France takes 5 days, 17 hours, and 6 minutes.

Aug. 22 The U.S. Congress passes an amendment providing for voting representation in Congress by Washington, D.C., voters. The amendment must be ratified by 38 states within seven years before it can become effective.

Sept. 17 Egyptian President Anwar el-Sadat and Israeli Prime Minister Menachem Begin end a 13-day meeting with President Carter at Camp David. The meeting, held at Carter's invitation, was to set the stage for seeking "a framework for peace in the Middle East." [The Dec. 17 target date for reaching a peace treaty is not met and the Camp David accords pass into history.]

Oct. 6 The U.S. Senate votes to extend the time period for ratification of the Equal Rights Amendment by 39 months—until June 1982. [Ratification of the ERA by the required number of states does not occur by this delayed date, either.]

Oct. 13 President Carter signs into law the Civil Service Reform Act of 1978, abolishing the U.S. Civil Service Commission. This is the first civil service reform measure to be enacted since the creation of the commission in 1883.

Nov. 7 The Democrats retain strong majorities in both houses of Congress and among this nation's governors in mid-term elections.

Nov. 8 Norman Rockwell, best remembered for his homespun paintings on the covers of *The Saturday Evening Post,* dies in Stockbridge, Mass., at the age of 84.

Nov. 18 California Congressman Leo Ryan and four associates are killed at the Jonestown, Guyana, airport by followers of the Rev. Jim Jones, the leader of a jungle-resident religious cult. Jones and over 900 members of his "church" commit mass murder/suicide shortly thereafter.

Nov. 27 The mayor of San Francisco, George Moscone, and a city supervisor, Harvey Milk, are assassinated in City Hall by a disgruntled ex-supervisor, Daniel White.

Dec. 15 The United States and China announce that the two countries will establish diplomatic relations on the following Jan. 1. The new accord demands that the U.S. break its formal ties with Nationalist China, a prerequisite which infuriates U.S. conservatives.

Dec. 30 The House Assassinations Committee announces that President John F. Kennedy and Martin Luther King were both probably killed "as a result of a conspiracy."

California Congressman Leo J. Ryan rests after he was attacked by followers of the Reverend Jim Jones at Jonestown. Shortly afterwards, the Congressman was murdered in an ambush at the airport.

447

1979 The U.S. government starts the new year off on the very first day by opening formal relations with China. Normalization of policy between the two giant countries was begun in 1972 by President Richard Nixon when he visited mainland China. Treaties signed in December 1978 brought the reality closer. China's fear of the Soviet-Vietnamese alliance and its urgency to break out of its shell into the midstream of technology and self-sufficiency have pushed it toward its goal of United States friendship, while America sees the 950 million inhabitants of China in a crucial role in any future worldwide conflict.

While it is a luxury to dream of world peace, it is still a distant commodity. The SALT talks waiver back and forth throughout the year. The proponents see the treaties as being a first step to worldwide disarmament, while the opponents point out that they are flagrantly one-sided in favor of the U.S.S.R.

The thin line between war and peace is evident in the latter part of the year when the U.S. Embassy in Tehran, Iran, is captured by revolutionaries. Many American citizens, most of them employees of the Embassy, are held hostage in a "diplomatic" move that shocks the entire world. Despite efforts from various sources, Iran remains adamant throughout the remainder of the year and holds the hostages as virtual prisoners of the state.

The U.S. loses to death many of its beloved people: the composer Richard Rodgers (77); actress Joan Blondell (70); actor George Brent (75); cartoonist Al Capp (70); baseball player Thurmon Munson (32); poet Allen Tate (79); motion picture producer Darryl Zanuck (77); and Charlie Smith, claimed to be the oldest person in the U.S. (137).

Jan. 1 In accordance with the agreement made on Dec. 15, 1978, the U.S. establishes formal relations with China.

Jan. 11 The Surgeon-General of the United States releases conclusive information that cancer, heart disease, and other maladies are caused by cigarette smoking.

Jan. 22 President Carter submits a budget to Congress calling for revenues of $502.6 billion and expenditures of over $531 billion.

Jan. 26 Nelson A. Rockefeller, Vice President of the U.S. from 1974 to 1977 and presidential hopeful in 1960, 1964, and 1968, dies in New York City at the age of 70.

Feb. 5 Demands for higher price supports are voiced by over 3,000 farmers who drive their tractors into Washington, D.C., as a sign of solidarity.

Mar. 5 The U.S. spacecraft, *Voyager I*, sends back to earth photos of the first extensive close-up exploration of Jupiter.

Mar. 26 The 31-year state of war that has existed between Egypt and Israel is ended as Egyptian President Anwar el-Sadát and Israeli Prime Minister Menachem Begin sign a peace treaty in Washington, D.C., with President Carter as a witness.

Mar. 28 The cooling system on the Three Mile Island, Pennsylvania, nuclear power plant breaks down, causing great fear and alarm in the area over a potential threat to the population's safety. Over 400,000 gallons of radioactive wastewater are dumped into the Susquehanna River.

April 3 Jane Byrne, the former consumer affairs commissioner of Chicago, is elected mayor by the largest margin ever recorded in the city's mayoral race, becoming the first woman to serve in that role.

May 18 Damages amounting to $10.5 million are awarded to the estate of Karen Silkwood in a negligence case against the Kerr-McGee Corporation. Silkwood's suit claimed that while she was employed as a lab technician at the company's plutonium plant in Oklahoma in 1974, she was contaminated by radiation.

May 25 In the first of what appears to be a series of accidents involving the DC-10 jetliner, 273 passengers aboard an American Airlines flight from Chicago die when the plane crashes after losing an engine.

June 11 John Wayne, star of over 200 films and the archetypical American cowboy, dies in Los Angeles at the age of 72.

July 10 Arthur Fiedler, conductor of the Boston Pops Orchestra for over 50 years, dies in Brookline, Massachusetts at the age of 84.

July 10 President Carter proclaims a 78° Fahrenheit minimum on the temperatures allowable by air conditioning in public, commercial, and government buildings.

July 18 The London market reports that the price of gold rises to over $300 per ounce.

July 31 The Chrysler Corporation, the nation's third largest automobile manufacturer, discloses losses of over $207 million for the second quarter.

Aug. 13 Mayor Frank Rizzo and several civic and police officials of Philadelphia are sued by the U.S. Justice Department on charges of "severe" police brutality. [The major elements of the suit are dropped Oct. 30 by a U.S. District judge.]

Aug. 31 Between two and three thousand Soviet combat-ready troops are stationed in Cuba, according to a report released by the U.S. State Department.

Sept. 1 After a 3 billion mile journey lasting over six years, the U.S. spacecraft *Pioneer II* passes within 13,000 miles of Saturn, giving observers on earth the first closeup photos ever taken of the planet.

Sept. 7 President Carter approves the $33 billion dollar deployment of the new long-range MX missile at underground sites in the American West.

Oct. 1 The U.S. relinquishes control over the Panama Canal Zone, in accordance with previously signed treaties.

Oct. 16 More than 400 commuters are injured in Philadelphia as three trains collide.

Oct. 21 The U.S. and Mexico reach a joint agreement allowing Mexican natural gas to be sold to American companies.

Oct. 24 The Shah of Iran, who had fled his country in January, undergoes gallbladder surgery in a New York hospital. [The Shah departs the U.S. for Panama Dec. 16.]

Nov. 1 Mamie Eisenhower, widow of Dwight Eisenhower, 34th President of the U.S., dies of a massive stroke in Washington, D.C., at the age of 82.

Nov. 3 At an anti-Ku Klux Klan rally in Greensboro, N.C., five Communist Workers Party members are killed.

Nov. 4 Amid continuing and growing animosity toward the U.S., a group of Muslim students take over the American Embassy in Tehran, holding as hostages some 90 people including 63 U.S. citizens.

Nov. 10 In a fruitless attempt to get the upper hand in the Iranian hostage crisis, President Carter announces that all Iranian students who have entered the U.S. illegally will be immediately deported.

Dec. 9 Archbishop Fulton J. Sheen, one of the most influential Catholic spokesmen in America, dies in New York City at the age of 84.

Dec. 19 After the U.S. House of Representatives gives its approval Dec. 18, the U.S. Senate approves a $1.5 billion loan guarantee to the Chrysler Corporation.

Dec. 26 New York gold prices climb to over $500 per ounce for the first time.

Egypt's President Anwar Sadat, left, President Jimmy Carter, and Israeli Prime Minister Menachem Begin listen to the national anthems of their respective countries during peace treaty ceremonies at the White House.

1980 This year begins for most Americans with a grave concern for the plight of the 52 hostages still in Iran. Illegally held in Tehran since early November 1979, there apparently has been no progress to free them through diplomatic channels. As the year progresses, an attempt is sanctioned by the administration to free the hostages forcibly, but the mission fails when mechanical difficulty in the desert spoils the plan. As the year ends, there is no release date in sight; in fact the Iranian government flaunts its upper hand by offering to release the Americans in return for a multi-billion-dollar payment.

The year is an election year so Jimmy Carter is in trouble, and Ronald Reagan, the ex-governor of California and a political opposite of Carter, handily wins the November election by capturing 51 percent of the popular vote.

Interest rates continue to climb toward unrealistic levels as the year progresses, reaching an all-time high of 21.5 percent in late December. The estimated annual inflation rate hovers at 12.4 percent. The budget deficit by year-end will almost double to $60 billion from its earlier prediction. The unemployment rate varies from 7 to 8 percent, while real spendable income of those who do work drops 6.5 percent by September from the previous 12 months.

Hundreds of American athletes are disappointed by the U.S. decision to boycott the Moscow Olympics. But American performance in the winter games proves satisfactory, particularly in ice hockey, where the American team upsets the U.S.S.R. by a score of 4 to 3 in the first Olympic defeat for the Russians since 1964.

Alice Roosevelt Longworth (96), Jimmy Durante (86), Alfred Hitchcock (80), Mae West (86), Kentucky colonel Harland Sanders (90), and NASA's "Shorty" Powers (57) all succumb to death this year.

Jan. 4　In an effort to force pressure upon the U.S.S.R. to withdraw its troops from Afghanistan, President Carter announces a ban on the sale of U.S. grain to the Soviets.

Jan. 10　George Meany, who masterminded the union of the American Federation of Labor and the Congress of Industrial Organizations into a single, all-powerful group, dies in Washington, D.C., at the age of 85.

Jan. 19　Supreme Court Justice William O. Douglas, who sat on the bench of the country's highest court longer than any other person, dies in Washington, D.C., at the age of 81.

Jan. 23　In his annual State of the Union message, President Carter promises "military force" to repel any attack in the Persian Gulf area.

Feb. 3　Ending one of the nation's most brutal prison riots, New Mexico authorities recapture the state prison at Santa Fe. Thirty-three people are killed and 89 are wounded before the ordeal is over.

Feb. 24　The XIII Winter Olympics come to an end in Lake Placid, N.Y. The U.S. captures 12 medals, including five golds for Eric Heiden.

Mar. 27　Mount St. Helens begins to emit steam in what proves to be the first of a series of dramatic eruptions.

April 2　Several large U.S. banks announce the increase in the prime lending rate to 20 percent.

April 7　The U.S. severs diplomatic relations with Iran, as that government remains adamant over its refusal to take away from the so-called "students" responsibility for the welfare of the hostages.

April 16　The Carter administration admits that the country "has probably entered a period of recession."

April 25　Eight U.S. servicemen are killed when an abortive attempt is made to rescue the hostages in Iran.

April 29　Senator Edmund S. Muskie (D–ME), a one-time presidential aspirant, is named the new Secretary of State in the Carter Cabinet.

May 9　Part of the Sunshine Skyway Bridge across Tampa Bay collapses as it is rammed by a 35,000-ton freighter. Thirty-five people are killed.

May 18　Mount St. Helens, the volcano in Washington which has been in the news since March with its minor eruptions, finally "blows its top," killing 22 people and destroying 122 square miles of the surrounding territory.

May 19　Over 1,000 people are arrested and at least 18 are killed as a three-day-long race riot ends in Miami.

450

Mount St. Helens belches smoke and debris 60,000 feet into the air as it begins its most devastating eruption in mid-May.

June 16 In the case of Diamond v. Chakrabarty, the U.S. Supreme Court rules, 5–4, that biological organisms can be patented under federal law.

June 20 The Carter administration announces that most of the 15,000 Haitian and 114,000 Cuban "boat people," even though in the U.S. illegally, can stay for at least six months. At the same time it is announced that legislation will be pursued which would make them permanent residents of the U.S.

June 30 In another 5–4 decision, the U.S. Supreme Court rules that neither individual states nor the Federal Government are constitutionally bound to finance abortions for poor women.

July 2 Men born in the years 1960 and 1961 are ordered to register for the draft, pursuant to a proclamation signed today by President Carter.

July 24 Billy Carter, the president's brother, becomes the subject of a U.S. Senate investigating committee looking into his possible activities as a Libyan agent.

Aug. 3 The XXIII Summer Olympics end in Moscow, having been boycotted by the U.S. over the invasion of Afghanistan by the U.S.S.R. in December 1979.

Aug. 14 President Carter and Vice President Mondale are nominated for second terms at the Democratic Convention in New York City.

Sept. 21 As President Carter refuses to participate, other presidential candidates, Ronald Reagan (Republican) and John Anderson (Independent) debate on national television.

Sept. 24 The U.S. Senate approves an earlier executive order allowing 38 tons of enriched uranium to be sold to India.

Oct. 28 President Carter and presidential contender Ronald Reagan finally meet each other in a debate sponsored by the League of Women Voters.

Oct. 29 A federal budget deficit of $59 billion is announced for fiscal year 1980.

Nov. 4 Ronald Reagan defeats incumbent Jimmy Carter in the presidential election. Reagan wins 51 percent of the popular vote to Carter's 41 percent, making Carter the first elected president to be defeated in a subsequent election since Herbert Hoover was not returned to office in 1932.

Nov. 17 An all-white jury in Greensboro, N.C., acquits six Ku Klux Klan and Nazi Party members in the 1979 killing of five Communist Workers Party protestors at an anti-Klan demonstration.

Nov. 21 Eighty-four people are killed and hundreds of others injured as fire sweeps through the spectacular MGM Grand Hotel in Las Vegas.

Dec. 3 Two U.S. Congressmen, Frank Thompson, Jr. (D–N.J.) and John M. Murphy (D–N.Y.), are found guilty of charges related to the controversial undercover "Abscam" operation.

Dec. 8 John Lennon, the 40-year-old member of the Beatles musical group, is shot to death outside his apartment in New York City by a deranged follower.

Dec. 19 The prime rate of interest offered by most major banks rises again, to an unprecedented 21.5 percent.

Dec. 21 A price tag of $24 billion is placed on the heads of the 52 American hostages in Iran. The U.S. denounces the offer as "unreasonable."

Dec. 24 The final results of the 1980 census reveal a U.S. population of 226,504,825.

1981 **Again a new president is in office. Ronald Reagan,** who defeated Jimmy Carter in the November 1980 election, is ideologically the opposite of his predecessor. Promising reduced unemployment, major tax revisions, and a return of America to its premier position in national defense, Reagan ironically is inaugurated on the very day that the hostages in Iran are released.

The country is again shaken by an assassination attempt upon its president. Outside a Washington, D.C., hotel, a lone drifter fires shots into President Reagan's entourage, wounding him, his press secretary, and two others. America loses another friend this year to the assassin's bullet. President Anwar el-Sadat of Egypt is killed by Muslim dissidents during a military parade near Cairo in October.

Two labor disputes disrupt the American scene. The air controllers' strike temporarily disrupts flight service and ends disastrously for the union when strikers are fired. Millions of Americans find themselves seeking other entertainment when the baseball players' strike shuts out this all-American pastime.

Before the year is out President Reagan's economic policies are being severely criticized as damaging to the poor, while leaving the rich unaffected, but the economy is on the upswing as some of the new administration's programs begin to take effect. Sandra Day O'Connor becomes the first woman Supreme Court Justice.

Death claims Roy Wilkins (80), who built the National Association for the Advancement of Colored People into the largest and most influential civil rights organization. Among others who die during the year are dancer Adele Astaire (83); actor Richard Boone (63); anthropologist Carlton Coon (76); labor leader Frank Fitzsimmons (73); and radio personality Lowell Thomas (89).

Jan. 5　For the first time since 1932, the U.S. Congress convenes with different parties in control of each house: The Republicans hold the Senate while the Democrats have control of the House of Representatives.

Jan. 20　After 14 months of captivity, the American hostages being held in Iran are released. The U.S. agrees to repay some $8 billion in Iranian frozen assets, a figure much more than the Iranian government eventually received.

Jan. 20　Ronald Reagan, the former actor and ex-governor of California, is inaugurated as the 40th President of the United States.

Feb. 8　Over 200 people are injured and eight persons die in a fire which destroys 20 floors of the Las Vegas, Nevada, Hilton Hotel.

Feb. 18　A 10 percent cut in individual personal income taxes is called for by President Reagan in his first State of the Union message.

Feb. 27　The federal government guarantees an additional $400 million loan to the Chrysler Corporation after it announces a 1980 loss of $1.71 billion.

Mar. 30　A lone gunman, 25-year-old John Hinckley, wounds President Ronald Reagan in the chest with a single bullet from a .22 caliber handgun. Also wounded in the affair, which takes place outside the Washington Hilton Hotel, are White House Press Secretary James Brady, and two others.

April 8　General Omar N. Bradley, who with 69 years of military service was the U.S. Army's record holder for longevity, dies in New York City at the age of 88.

April 12　Joe Louis, heavyweight champion of the world from 1937 to 1949, who was nicknamed the "Brown Bomber," dies in Las Vegas at the age of 66.

April 14　After a flight lasting for 54½ hours, the U.S. space shuttle *Columbia*, lands successfully in the California desert with John W. Young and Robert L. Crippen the pilots.

April 24　The U.S. grain embargo against the U.S.S.R., imposed when Jimmy Carter was president, is lifted by President Ronald Reagan.

May 1　Sen. Harrison Williams (D–N.J.), after his persistent refusal to give up his Senate seat, is found guilty on nine criminal charges by a federal jury. The charges stemmed from the 1980 "Abscam" scandal.

May 26　Fourteen men are killed as a U.S. Marine jet plane crashes into the aircraft carrier *Nimitz* near the Florida coast.

June 16　After several years of refusal to sell arms to China for fear of further alienating the U.S.S.R., a United States announcement is made in Peking by Secretary of State Alexander Haig that the U.S. has decided in principle to begin such sales.

July 17　Two suspended walkways in the

Hyatt Regency Hotel in Kansas City, Missouri, collapse, killing 111 persons.

July 22 After suffering earlier in the year the largest annual loss ever experienced by an American company, the Chrysler Corporation announces second quarter earnings of over $11 million.

Aug. 3 Approximately 13,000 air traffic controllers walk off their jobs across the United States in a labor dispute. [After ignoring President Reagan's 48-hour back-to-work ultimatum, termination notices are sent to striking workers. Initially "black-listed" from any federal employment, they are allowed Dec. 9 to apply for any federal job except those in the Federal Aviation Administration.]

Aug. 7 *The Washington Star,* one of America's largest newspapers, ceases publication.

Aug. 9 The longest and most expensive strike in American sports ends as major league baseball resumes with the All-Star game. Ticket revenue loss is calculated at $1.25 million daily during the dispute.

Aug. 24 Mark David Chapman is sentenced from 20 years to life in prison after his self-admitted murder of former Beatle John Lennon.

Aug. 25 The U.S. spacecraft, *Voyager II,* passes the planet Saturn and transmits to earth photographs of its moons and rings.

Sept. 25 The first woman ever to sit on the bench of the U.S. Supreme Court, Sandra Day O'Connor, is sworn in by Chief Justice Warren Burger.

Oct. 4 The body in the grave of President John F. Kennedy's assassin, Lee Harvey Oswald, is exhumed and positively identified after doubts are cast on its real identity by a British writer.

Oct. 19 The U.S. celebrates the 200th anniversary of the Battle of Yorktown in which the British were decisively defeated by American troops in the last battle of the Revolutionary War.

Nov. 1 The cost of first class postage is raised to 20 cents per ounce.

Nov. 17 Houston, Texas, elects its first woman mayor, 35-year-old Kathryn Jean Whitmire.

Nov. 23 James Brady, the White House press secretary who was shot eight months earlier in the assassination attempt upon President Reagan, returns home from the hospital.

Dec. 5 The U.S. and Turkey announce plans to improve military cooperation between the two countries.

Dec. 27 Hoagy Carmichael, composer of such favorite songs as "Stardust" and "Georgia on My Mind," dies in California at the age of 82.

A group of elated ex-hostages, accompanied by their families, leave "Freedom One" at Andrews Air Force Base, Maryland, on their way to a welcome home meeting with President Reagan.

1982 **President Reagan has made it clear that his administration** intends to pursue a policy of less federal government involvement in local affairs and a greatly strengthened defense posture, but some of his ideas are not well received. In early summer several hundred thousand people congregate in Central Park in New York City to protest the country's continuing involvement in the development of nuclear arms. Unemployment hits a 42-year record high, a fact that is quick to bring criticism of Reagan's economic philosophies.

The Middle East is rapidly becoming a hot spot in world affairs—even more so than it has been in the past. Following his strong nationalistic leanings, the President sends military supplies and men to Lebanon to assist that tiny country in its disputes with its neighbors. Criticism for these actions is widespread in Congress, the opposers insisting that the U.S. has no business interfering with the domestic affairs of other nations.

Weather makes the news. An abnormal spring in some locales brings horrible storms with devastation of life and property. Spectacular aircraft tragedies in Washington, D.C., and near New Orleans claim over 200 victims. The question of proper maintenance arises from the Washington episode when it is discovered that the aircraft was severely hampered in its takeoff by ice buildup.

Again, the U.S. loses many well-known figures: old time TV host Dave Garroway (69), actors Fernando Lamas (67) and Victor Jory (79), poet Archibald MacLeish (89), sports writer Walter "Red" Smith (76), and General Nathan Twining (84) all die during 1982.

Jan. 5 A Little Rock, Arkansas, federal judge declares a state law requiring balanced teaching of creationism and the theory of evolution to be unconstitutional.

Jan. 8 The American Telephone and Telegraph Company agrees to relinquish its 22 Bell System companies in order to satisfy the anti-trust suit brought against it by the U.S. Justice Department. In doing so, the company loses two-thirds of its total assets.

Jan. 13 A Boeing 737 jetliner, just off the ground from Washington's National Airport, crashes into a Potomac River bridge during the business rush hour. Seventy-eight people die, including four in their cars atop the bridge.

Jan. 26 President Reagan announces in his State of the Union message his plan for local and state government to control federal social programs.

Feb. 6 President Reagan, in his budget message, calls for a reduction of governmental influence in social programs and a strengthening of the nation's defense posture.

Mar. 2 The U.S. Senate passes by a vote of 57 to 37 legislation seeking to eliminate school busing for the purpose of achieving racial integration.

Mar. 4 The Metropolitan Museum of Art receives a $60 million art collection from Mrs. Belle Linsky.

Mar. 11 Sen. Harrison A. Williams, Jr. (D–N.J.) resigns his seat in the Senate following

his conviction on bribery and conspiracy charges in the "Abscam" scandal.

April 1-10 Severe spring weather hits the nation from California to North Carolina. Blizzards dump 16 feet of snow in the Sierras and winds of 148 miles per hour are recorded in North Carolina. At least 46 people die in the aftermath.

April 19 American tourist traffic to Cuba is outlawed. In the future only official travel and that by news reporters, academic researchers, and families seeking reunification will be permitted.

April 22 Melville B. Grosvenor, president of the National Geographic Society, dies in Miami at the age of 80.

May 18 The Rev. Sun Myung Moon, founder of the Unification Church ("Moonies"), is convicted of tax fraud in New York City.

May 28 A disgruntled ex-employee of the IBM Corporation drives his car through the lobby doors of the company's Bethesda, Maryland, offices. He shoots two people and wounds 10 others. He surrenders after seven hours of negotiations.

June 1 The U.S. Supreme Court rules that police be permitted to search automobiles without warrants. "Probable cause" would be all that is necessary to search a car and/or its contents.

June 12 Close to half a million people crowd New York City's Central Park to participate in a massive anti-nuclear arms demonstration.

June 21 John W. Hinckley, Jr., the attacker of President Reagan in March 1981, is found not guilty by reason of insanity.

454

The icy waters of the Potomac River deter rescue workers striving to reach survivors from an Air Florida 737 which crashed into the 14th Street Bridge moments earlier.

June 24 Leaders of the Equal Rights Amendment admit defeat after 10 years of trying to obtain ratification by 38 states.

June 28 San Francisco becomes the first large American city to outlaw the private possession of weapons.

July 9 A Pan Am jetliner crashes near New Orleans, killing 153 persons, including eight on the ground. Amidst the tragedy, an 18-month-old girl is found alive.

Aug. 5 The U.S. House of Representatives rejects by a vote of 204 to 202 a measure calling for an immediate freeze of American and Soviet weapons.

Aug. 6 The Department of Labor announces a 9.8 percent unemployment rate for July, the largest since the end of World War II.

Aug. 14 Thurston B. Morton, former U.S. Senator from Kentucky, dies in Louisville at the age of 74.

Sept. 13 The Interstate Commerce Commission authorizes the merger of the Union Pacific, the Missouri Pacific, and the Western Pacific railroads, creating a single railway system linking large areas of the American West.

Sept. 14 Princess Grace of Monaco, the former American actress Grace Kelly, dies of injuries sustained in an automobile accident in Monaco. She was 52 years old.

Oct. 2 Chicago, Illinois, officials announce that the seventh person known to have used cyanide-filled Tylenol capsules had died. Panic

strikes Chicago and the nation. A reward is offered by the manufacturer as the medicine is removed from stores' shelves.

Oct. 8 The U.S. Labor Department announces another increase in unemployment. During September the rate had climbed to 10.1 percent, the highest figure in 42 years.

Oct. 18 Bess Truman, the widow of President Harry Truman, dies at Independence, Missouri, at the age of 97.

Oct. 19 John Z. DeLorean, chairman of the DeLorean Motor Company, is arrested in Los Angeles and charged with possession of cocaine. The government charges that his involvement in drug trafficking was to raise money for his failing automobile company. [After months of pre-trial publicity, he is acquitted of all charges in late 1984.]

Nov. 4 The U.S. presence in the Middle East increases as the Lebanese Army requests and receives additional military support. Fourteen American Marines begin patrolling the Christian-dominated sector of East Beirut.

Dec. 7 Convicted killer Charlie Brooks becomes the first person in American history to be executed by "lethal injection." The process, involving the entry into the blood stream of three lethal chemicals, is termed by critics as "high-technology death."

Dec. 8 A nuclear arms protestor threatens to blow up the Washington Monument. He is killed by police.

455

1983 This year is one of unusual weather, optimism in the stock market, and tragedy for America abroad. Californians across the Pacific Coast are devastated by tropical storms in January and again in February and March. Floods in the Deep South in April kill 15 people and destroy $625 million in property in Mississippi, Alabama, Tennessee, and Louisiana. An earthquake in California in May causes damages of over $50 million, while the Texas coast is lashed by Hurricane Adelicia in August destroying $1.6 billion of property in the Houston and Galveston areas. Blizzards cause havoc in the Midwest in November, closing the Denver airport, stranding travelers, and killing 56 people throughout the region.

The stock market attempts to make a comeback from its disastrous performance in previous years. Beginning the year with a record Dow Jones average of 1,092.35, it continues its optimism, reaching 1,287.20 in late November, while in January unemployment is announced at its highest since 1941, with a 1982 average of 9.7 percent. However, by October the GNP is up, boasting a growth of 7.9 percent in the third quarter, and unemployment is down to 8.2 percent.

Terrorism abroad is on the minds of most Americans. Attacks on the U.S. Embassy in Beirut in April claim 17 American lives, two more Marines die in a Christian-Muslim conflict in Lebanon in August, and 241 servicemen die in October at the Beirut airport when a terrorist drives an explosive-laden truck into the Marine compound. Eight more Marines are killed in December in another attack on the Beirut airport. Americans are appalled at the lack of security provided to embassies abroad and are told by their government that cutbacks in expenses prohibited more secure measures from being implemented.

Americans lost to death several well-known people, including comedienne Judy Canova (66); Olympic swimming champion and actor Buster Crabbe (75); inventor R. Buckminster Fuller (87); Chicago Bears founder and coach George Halas (88); actor Pat O'Brien (83); actor Raymond Massey (86); and playwright Tennessee Wlliams (71).

Jan. 3 The 98th Congress convenes with 269 Democrats and 165 Republicans in the House of Representatives and 54 Republicans and 46 Democrats in the Senate.

Jan. 7 After five years, the arms embargo on Guatemala is lifted by the Reagan administration because of "significant steps" by the Guatemalan government to eliminate human rights abuse.

Jan. 10 The stock market propels to a record high; the Dow-Jones average closes at 1,092.35

Jan. 16-31 Four separate storms lash the California coast, causing $70 million in damage, killing 11 people, and ruining over 3,000 homes. [In late February, another storm batters the Pacific coast, resulting in $200 million damages and 13 people killed.]

Jan. 17 George C. Wallace, the one-time highly popular independent candidate for the U.S. presidency, wins an unprecedented fourth term as governor of Alabama.

Jan. 31 Protesting higher taxes on diesel fuel and gasoline, thousands of independent truckers call a strike and leave their trucks idle. [The strike ends on February 10 after the truckers receive promises that fuel taxes will be studied.]

Feb. 11 The mid-Atlantic region from New York to Washington, D.C., is paralyzed by a major winter storm. Fifteen people die amid snow accumulations of up to 22 inches.

Feb. 14 The fourth largest banking failure in the U.S. since the Depression is declared as the Tennessee Banking Commission closes the United American Bank in Knoxville.

Feb. 17 A decision to produce subcompact automobiles jointly at a California General Motors plant is agreed upon by GM and the Toyota Motor Company of Japan.

Mar. 23 The first human ever to receive an artificial heart implant, Dr. Barney Clark, dies after all organs, except the heart, fail.

April 12 Chicago voters elect by a 52 percent majority the first Black mayor, U.S. Rep. Harold Washington (D–Ill).

April 18 Seventeen Americans are killed at the Embassy in Beirut as a carbomb explodes outside the building.

April 30 A U.S. Navy C-131 airplane crashes on takeoff from the Jacksonville, Florida, Naval Air Station, killing 15 crew members.

May 18-23 Fifty-nine tornadoees hit the states of Texas, Mississippi, Missouri, Georgia, Tennessee, and Louisiana; 32 persons are killed.

May 28-30 President Reagan hosts the ninth industrial summit at Williamsburg, Virginia. Leaders from France, Britain, Japan, Canada, Italy, West Germany, and other nations attend.

June 17 The stock market again climbs to an all-time high, with the Dow Jones average closing at an unprecedented 1,248.30.

June 18 Dr. Sally K. Ride becomes the first U.S. woman to enter space as she and four male companions perform maneuvers with the space shuttle *Challenger*.

July 21 Ling-Ling, the Giant Panda given to the U.S. by China in 1972, gives birth to the first panda ever born in America. The cub dies three hours later.

July 28 The law allowing the withholding of income tax from interest and dividend payments, originally scheduled to take effect August 5, is repealed in a compromise House–Senate bill.

Aug. 29 A skirmish between Christians and Muslims in Lebanon results in the killing of two U.S. Marines.

Aug. 31 The month of August closes as the hottest on record, with temperatures averaging 4 degrees above normal for much of the country. The summer's heat and drought cause 220 deaths and $10 billion in crop damage.

Sept. 1 A Korean Airlines 747 passenger jet is shot down by Soviet fighter planes over the Sea of Japan, killing 269 people including 61 Americans. The U.S.S.R. initially denies involvement in the incident.

Sept. 1 Sen. Henry Jackson (D–Wash.) dies at the age of 71.

Oct. 22 The Metropolitan Opera celebrates its 100th anniversary, grossing $1.45 million from two concerts given for the occasion.

Oct. 22 While President Reagan is playing golf at the Augusta National Golf Course, a lone intruder crashes his truck through the gates to the resort and takes seven hostages. He demands to talk to the President, then surrenders with no further incident.

Oct. 23 A terrorist, driving a truck loaded with explosives, crashes into the headquarters building of the U.S. Marine compound near the Beirut airport, killing 241 servicemen. Nearby in a similar, almost simultaneous incident, 56 French soldiers are killed.

Oct. 25 In a move to rescue U.S. citizens from the island of Grenada, 1,900 U.S. Marines and paratroopers invade the island along with units from six Caribbean countries.

Nov. 7 A bomb explodes outside the U.S. Capitol office of Senate Minority Leader Robert C. Byrd. There are no injuries.

Nov. 18 The U.S. Senate votes, 71 to 18, in favor of confirming William P. Clark as the new Secretary of the Interior, replacing the controversial James G. Watt, who has served since 1981.

Dec. 4 As Syrian militiamen attack the Beirut airport, eight U.S. Marines are killed. Meanwhile, U.S. fighter planes hit Syrian targets in Lebanon in retaliation for a Syrian attack on an unarmed reconnaissance plane the day before. President Reagan threatens military action against Syria if U.S. positions are attacked.

Dec. 15 The last of the U.S. combat troops leave the island of Grenada.

U. S. Marines take care of their dead comrades in the aftermath of a terrorist-engineered explosion which destroyed the headquarters building of the Marine detachment at the Beirut Airport.

1984 The year brings with it another opportunity for the U.S. to prove itself in the Olympics. It also brings another presidential election in which for the first time a Black is a really serious contender for nomination. However, Jesse Jackson finally throws his support to Democratic challenger Walter Mondale. Setting another precedent is the selection of a woman, Geraldine Ferraro, as the vice-presidential candidate to complete the Democratic ticket facing Republican incumbents Ronald Reagan and George Bush. During the two prime-time presidential debates and one vice-presidential argument, the various candidates hurl charges and counter charges with such fury that no one emerges as a clear-cut debate winner. Pollsters indicate Reagan as a decisive victor at the polls, a prediction which proves accurate as the Nov. 6 election gives the President a decisive win.

America fares better in the Olympics this year than it has in several meetings past. The winter games, especially the ice hockey competition, are somewhat disappointing, but the U.S. attacks the summer events with no holds barred, claiming a record number of medals.

Among those who died in 1984 are Gen. Mark Clark (87); athletes Johnny Weismuller (79) and George Zaharias (76); McDonald's food chain founder Ray Kroc (81); former Sen. Frank Church (59); photographer Ansel Adams (82); writer Irwin Shaw (71); and actors Richard Burton (58), Jackie Coogan (69), Peter Lawford (61), Ethel Merman (76), and Walter Pidgeon (87).

Jan. 5 Texaco Oil Company offers to buy out Getty Oil Company for $9.9 billion. Texaco is the third largest oil company in the U.S., with Getty ranking 14th. If successful, this will be the largest corporate takeover in American history to date.

Jan. 12 Former Secretary of State Henry Kissinger files his "Report of the National Bipartisan Commission on Central America" in which it is recommended that the U.S. supply more aid to that strife-ridden region.

Jan. 15 Eight major Democratic hopefuls for the U.S. presidency gather at Dartmouth College for a nationally televised debate.

Jan. 25 President Reagan delivers his State of the Union address. He emphasizes the improved domestic economy and the positive effects of America's military buildup.

Feb. 7–19 The XIV Winter Olympic Games take place in Sarajevo, Yugoslavia. The U.S. team takes eight medals, including four gold.

Feb. 20 A *Time* magazine poll shows Walter Mondale to be the favorite Democratic presidential candidate by a showing of 50 percent compared to that of his closest contender, John Glenn at 18 percent.

Feb. 24 U.S. Marines in Lebanon complete their withdrawal from that country after a presence of 18 months.

Mar. 28-30 Sixty people are killed in the Carolinas as numerous tornadoes sweep through the Southern Atlantic States. Three thousand residents are left homeless and over 1,000 others are injured. In related storms 250,000 homes are left without electricity in Massachusetts and Connecticut.

May 21 A *Time* magazine survey shows Walter Mondale to be the Democratic Party's front-runner for the presidency with 1,528 delegates compared to Gary Hart's 886 and Jesse Jackson's 303. A total of 1,967 votes is required to win the nomination.

July 16-20 Democrats hold their National Convention in San Francisco with Walter Mondale handily nominated for the presidency. In an unprecedented move, Geraldine Ferraro, a congresswoman from New York, becomes the first woman to win the nomination for vice president.

July 28-Aug. 12 The XXIII Olympiad is held in Los Angeles with athletes from 140 nations attending. Most of the Eastern bloc countries, led by the U.S.S.R., do not participate, but both Rumania and the Republic of China send delegates. The U.S. wins a record number of medals.

Aug. 20-24 Ronald Reagan and George Bush are easily renominated for the presidency and vice presidency respectively at the Republican Convention in Dallas.

Sept. 15 The deadline passes for a new agreement between the United Auto Workers and General Motors. The UAW authorizes workers at 13 GM plants to strike.

Sept. 20 For the third time in 17 months a United States target, this time the Embassy Annex in Beirut, is damaged by terrorist explosives. At least 12 people are killed and 35 are wounded.

Rafer Johnson, an American Gold Medalist in the 1960 Olympics, prepares to light the Olympic flame formally opening the 1984 games.

Oct. 1 Peter V. Ueberroth, the guiding genius behind the success of the 1984 Los Angeles Olympics, becomes the Commissioner of Baseball, succeeding Bowie Kuhn.

Oct. 7 President Reagan and Democratic presidential nominee Walter Mondale hold the first of two presidential debates in Louisville.

Nov. 6 Incumbents Ronald Reagan and George Bush defeat Democrats Walter Mondale and Geraldine Ferraro who carried only Minnesota and the District of Columbia.

Nov. 25 In a Louisville, Kentucky, hospital William Schroeder becomes the world's second recipient of an artificial heart.

Nov. 29 "Miss Baker," the 27-year-old, 14-ounce squirrel monkey who became the first survivor of an American space mission, dies in Huntsville, Alabama.

Dec. 25 Officials of the Utah Power & Light Co. report attempts to seal their fire-gutted mine eight miles north of Orangeville, Utah. Twenty-six men and one woman were trapped when fire erupted Dec. 19. As flames and smoke continued to rage out of control the bodies were sealed in the mine, possibly to become permanently entombed.

Index

Black Hawk, 99, 102, 103
Black Hills, 210, 212
Black Hugo L., 340, 342, 375, 417
Black, James, 125, 204
Blackmun, Harry A., 414
Black Muslims, 402
Black Panther Party, 412
Black Warrior, 144
Blaine, James Gillespie, 213, 219ff., 225, 230, 233
Blair, Francis P., 97, 99, 196
Blanchard, Jean Pierre Francois, 49
Bland-Allison Act, 217
Bland, Richard P., 213
Blennerhossett, Harman, 63
Blizzard of '88, 231
Blondell, Joan, 448
Bloomer, Mrs. Amelia Jenks, 143
Blount, James H., 238
Blount, William, 46, 54
Blunt, James G., 173
Bly, Nellie, 233
Boas, Franz, 355
"Boat people," 451
Bogart, Humphrey, 386
Boggs, Lilburn, 113
Bohr, Niels, 346, 347
Bolivar, Simon, 87, 93
Bonaparte, Napoleon, 59, 66, 68, 74
Bond, Julian, 405
Bonhomme, Richard, 26
Boniface, George C., 157
Bonneville, Benjamin L.E., 102
Bonus march, 328
Bonus (veterans), 337ff.
Boone, Daniel, 21, 85
Boone, Richard, 452
Booth, Edwin, 236
Booth, John Wilkes, 188
Borah, William E., 348
Borden, Gail, 149
Borland, Hal, 446
Boston African Society, 52
"Boston Tea Party," 15
Boucicault, Dion, 156
Bower, Anthony, 143
Bowie, Jim, 108
Boxer Rebellion, 257, 258
Boy Scouts of America, 276
Boyer, Charles, 446
Boyle, Emmet, D., 286
Braddock, Jim, 337, 342
Bradley, Joseph P., 215
Bradley, Omar N., 452
Bradley, Thomas, 422

Brady, James, 452, 453
Bragg, Braxton, 172, 174, 177, 186
Brandeis, Louis D., 288
Brandeis University, 414
Brandywine Creek, 23
Brant, Joseph, 25, 26, 32
Brazil, 71, 88, 90, 184
"Bread riot," 175
Breckenridge, John Cabell, 149, 158, 160, 181
Brent, George, 448
Brezhnev, Leonid I., 422
Briand, Aristide, 314, 315
Bridger, Jim, 87, 91
Bridges (new), 135, 148, 209, 214, 224, 274, 275, 339, 342, 345, 349, 389, *See also* under specific names.
Bright, Jesse D., 133
Brisbane, Arthur, 339
Briscoe v. *Bank of Kentucky,* 112
British Orders in Council, 62, 63, 67, 69, 70
Bristou, Benjamin, 210
Brooke, Edward, 405
Brooke, Fort, 107
Brooklyn Heights, Battle of, 20
Brooks, Charlie, 455
Brooks, James, 206
Brooks, Joseph, 208
Brooks, Preston S., 148
Brown, Benjamin Gratz, 204, 205
Brown, Charles Brockden, 56
Brown, Edmund J., Jr., 440
Brown, Jacob, 74, 127
Brown, John, 149, 152, 154ff.
Brown, Joseph E., 185
Brown, Russell J., 373
Brown v. *Board of Education of Topeka,* 246, 361
Brown, William Wells, 143
Bruce, Blanche Kelso, 210, 251
Bryan, William Jennings, 234, 240, 244ff., 256, 257, 264, 272, 273, 280, 282, 286, 310
Bryant's Minstrels, 155
Byrn Mawr College, 226
Buchanan, James, 108, 124ff., 145, 149, 150ff., 160ff., 196
Buck, Pearl S., 332
Buckner, Simon Bolivar, 246
Buell, Don Carlos, 169, 172
Buena Vista, 302, 304, 306
Buena Vista, Battle of, 131
Buford, Fort, 220

Bulkeley, Morgan G., 212
"Bull Moose" Party, 280, 281
Bullock, William, 175
Bull Run, Battle of, 162, 166, 168, 171
Bulwer, Henry, 136, 137
Bunche, Ralph J., 417
Bunker Hill, 16, 18, 120
Burbank, Luther, 312
Burchard, Samuel Dickinson, 225
Bureau of Labor Statistics, 225
Bureau of Mines, 276
Burger, Warren E., 411
Burgoyne, John, 22, 23
Burlingame, Anson, 196
Burlingame Treaty, 218
Burns, Anthony, 145, 146
Burns, Sherman, 316
Burns, Tommy, 268, 273
Burns, William J., 316
Burnside, Ambrose E., 168, 169, 172ff, 220
Burr, Aaron, 53, 57, 58, 61, 63, 64, 111
Burroughs, Edgar Rice, 372
Burroughs, John, 302
Burton, Richard, 399, 458
Bush, George, 458, 459
Butler, Andrew P., 148
Butler, Anthony, 97
Butler, Benjamin F., 104, 167, 181, 185
Butler, Nicholas Murray, 281
Butler v. *Michigan,* 386
Butler, William O., 132, 133
Butterfield, John, 153
Byrd, Richard E., 312, 386
Byrne, Jane, 448
Byrne, William M., 422

Cable, George Washington, 310
Cabot, George, 75
Cabot, John, 9
Cabrini, Frances Xavier, 365
Calder, Alexander, 443
Calder v. *Bull,* 55
Calhoun, John Caldwell, 69, 78, 79, 82, 83, 91, 95ff., 100, 102ff., 108, 122, 131ff., 136, 137, 162
California, 94, 125ff., 128, 130ff.
Calvert, George (Lord Baltimore), 10
Calvin, Melvin, 395
Cambodia, 373, 413, 414
Camden, Battle of, 28, 29

Cold War, 364, 371, 390
Cole-Hickenlooper Act, 381
Colfax, Schuyler, 196, 204, 205, 206, 226
Collins, Michael, 411
Colombia, 86, 87, 94, 146, 260ff.
Colorado, 153, 164, 185, 213, 219
Colorado River, 261
Colored Methodist Episcopal Church, 201
Colter, John, 64
Columbia Broadcasting System, 349, 353
Columbia River, 62
Columbian Centinel, 79
Columbian College, 86
Columbus, Christopher, 9
Columbus Day, 48
Comanche Indians, 195
Committee for Industrial Organization, 337, 339, 340, 342, 345, 346, 349, 383
Committee for the Reelection of the President (CRP), 418, 419, 420
Committee on Un-American Activities, 361
Common Sense, 18
Communism, 366, 370, 372, 373, 375, 376, 380, 381
Communist Control Act, 381
Communist Party (Workers), 298, 300, 386, 449, 451
"Compact Theory," 55
Compromise of 1833, 104, 119
Compromise of 1850, 136, 141, 143, 144, 149
Comstock, Anthony, 206
Comstock, Henry T.P., 155
Comstock Lode, 155
Concord, 18
Confederate States of America (Confederacy), 162ff., 169ff., 178ff., 195
Confederation Congress, 42
Confiscation Acts, 166, 170
Congress of Racial Equality (CORE), 395
Congressional Medal of Honor, 314
Conkling, Roscoe, 220, 231
Connally, John B., Jr., 428
Connecticut, 25, 28, 30, 35, 42, 46, 85, 119
Connecticut Compromise, 40
Connor, Patrick E., 189, 190

Conscription Act, 174, 177, 178
Constellation, 54, 56
Constitution, 54, 71
Constitution of the Confederacy, 164
Constitution of the United States, 39ff., 44, 46ff., 52, 60, 61, 76, 83, 84, 88, 97, 98, 104, 105, 110, 430ff.
Constitutional Convention, 39, 40, 52
Constitutional Union Party, 157, 158
Continental Army, 18, 34
Continental Congress, 15, 18, 20, 25, 44
Continental Divide, 91
"Continental System," 68
Contract labor, 182, 226
Contrast, The, 44
Convention of 1800, 57
Conway, F.H., 156
Conway, Thomas, 23
Coogan, Jackie, 458
Cook, Frederick Albert, 274
Cooke, Jay, 174, 175, 206
Coolidge, Calvin, 298, 300, 306, 308ff., 312, 314ff., 322, 330
Coon, Carlton, 452
Cooper, James Fenimore, 140
Cooper, L. Gordon, 399
Cooper, Peter, 99, 213, 224
Cooper, Thomas, 95
Coppage v. *Kansas,* 286
Copperhead, 166, 181, 189
Copyright legislation, 100, 236, 284
Corbett, James J., 237, 247, 256
Cornell, Alonzo B., 217
Cornell, Ezra, 209
Cornell University, 209
Cornwallis, Lord, 28, 29ff.
Corregidor, 354
Cortelyou, George B., 262
Cost of Living Council, 417
Cotton cording machinery, 46
Cotton gin, 49, 50
Coughlin, Charles, 354
Council Bluffs, 83
Cournand, André F., 385
Courtship of Miles Standish, 154
Covode Resolution, 196
Cox, Archibald, 421ff.
Cox, James M., 300, 301
Cox, James R., 326

Coxey, Jacob, 240
Crabbe, Buster, 456
Craig v. *Missouri,* 98
Crapsey, Algernon Sidney, 268
Crawford, Joan, 444
Crawford, William, H., 32, 90ff.
Crazy Horse, Chief, 212
Credit Mobilier, 204, 205, 206
Creek Indians, 69, 72ff., 92ff.
"Crime of '73," 206, 213
Crippen, Robert L., 452
Crittenden, George B., 168
Crittenden, John C., 116
Crittenden, John J., 122, 161, 166, 168
Crittenden, William L., 140
Crockett, Davy, 108
Crosby, Bing, 445
Cuba, 134, 140, 142, 144ff., 149, 160, 207, 244, 247, 250ff., 258, 260, 268, 269, 274, 281, 310, 312, 390ff., 396, 397, 449
Cultural exchange program, 390, 391
Cumberland College, 36
Cumberland River, 28
Cumberland Road, 69, 79, 87, 99
Cuming, Thomas B., 145
Cumming, Alfred, 150, 153, 155
Cummings, e.e., 304
Cummings, Homer S., 312, 326
Curtis, Charles, 317, 328, 338
Curtis, Samuel R., 169, 184
Cushing, Caleb, 208
Custer, George A., 210, 212, 213
Cutler, Manasseh, 38
Czechoslovakia, 344, 346, 378

Dade, Major, 107
Daft, Leo, 227
Dahlgren, John A., 177, 178
Daisy Miller, 288
Dakota Territory, 164, 174, 210, 220, 233
Dallas, George M., 122, 124, 127
Daly, Augustin, 195, 199, 201, 202
Dana, Richard Henry, 222
Danbury Hatters Union, 272
Darling, Fort, 170
Darrow, Clarence, 238, 310
Dartmouth College, 82
Davidson Academy, 36

465

Du Pont, Eleuthère Ireneé, 58
Du Pont, Francis, 175
Du Pont, Samuel F., 167
Durand, Asher Brown, 229
Durante, Jimmy, 450
Durfee, Amos, 112, 115
Duryea, Charles, 237, 242, 243
Dust Bowl, 334
Dutch Henry's Crossing, 149

Eads, James Buchanan, 209, 230
Earhart, Amelia, 317, 324, 328, 342
Early, Jubal, 182, 183, 184
Earth Day, 413, 414
Earthquakes, 69, 268, 332, 335, 401, 416
Eastman, George, 317
Eaton, James H., 97, 100
Eaton's Station, 20
Ecuador, 86, 87
Eddy, Mary Baker, 277
Eden, Anthony, 357, 383
Ederle, Gertrude, 312
Edgerton, Sidney, 181
Edison, Thomas Alva, 198, 217ff., 236, 238, 240, 244, 318, 323, 325
Edmunds, George F., 222, 234
Edward, Fort, 22
Edwards v. *South Carolina*, 398
Eggleston, Edward, 202
Ehrlichman, John D., 422ff., 428, 445
Eight-Hour System, 192, 228
Eighteenth Amendment, 293, 298, 300, 308, 312, 323, 324, 437
Eighth Amendment, 419, 437
Einstein, Albert, 329, 347, 382
Eisenhower, Dwight D., 353, 355, 356, 358, 360, 363, 373, 377ff., 410
Eisenhower, Mamie, 449
El Brazilo, Battle of, 129
Electoral College, 61, 90
Electoral Commission, 215
Electoral Count Act, 230
Electoral votes, 44, 53, 57, 58, 66, 71, 78, 85, 91, 92, 96, 103, 111, 123, 133, 149, 158, 160, 180, 184, 197, 212ff., 219, 225, 231, 237, 246, 256, 265, 272, 280, 289, 300, 309, 316, 329, 339, 349, 369, 377, 385, 392, 401.

Electric lamp, 218, 219
Electric locomotive, 224, 323
Eleventh Amendment, 49, 50, 55, 90
Eliot, Thomas Stearns, 304
Elliott, Jesse Duncan, 71
Ellmaker, Amos, 101
Ellsberg, Daniel, 422ff.
Ellsworth, Leavitt Henry, 210
Ely, Eugene, 277
Emancipation Proclamation, 170, 174, 190, 349
Embargo, Act of, 64, 66, 67
Emergency Banking Relief Act, 330
Emergency Fleet Corporation, 289, 294
Emerson, Ralph Waldo, 146, 156
Emmett, Dan, 155
Empire State Building, 363
Empress of China, 35, 36
Enabling Act, 59
Enemy Act, Trading with, 330
Energy crisis, 421, 423, 425
Enforcement Act, 67
English, William H., 152, 219
Eniwetok-Bikini, 385
Enquirer, The Richmond, 122, 174
Environmental Protection Agency, 415
Episcopal Church, 444
Equal Opportunity Commission, 368, 401
Equal Rights Amendment (ERA), 447, 455
Equal Rights Party, 204, 231
Era of Good Feelings, 79, 94
Ericsson, John, 168
Erie Canal, 79, 87, 92
Erskine, David, 67
Ervin, Sam, 425
Esaki, Leo, 423
Espionage Act, 293
Espionage and Sedition Acts, 296, 303
Essex Junto, 61, 67, 75, 162
Estaing, Jean Baptiste d', 25, 27
Eucharistic Congress, First International, 312
European Economic Community, 396
Everett, Edward, 158, 179, 186
Evolution, theory of, 454
Ewing, Thomas, 116, 134
Executive Office Building, 321
Executive privilege, 423, 425
Expedition Act, 262

Explosions, 189, 270, 271, 274, 321, 323. *See also under* Disasters and accidents.
Export-Import Bank, 334

Fairbanks, Charles W., 264, 265, 288
Fairbanks, Douglas, 347
Fairfield, John, 114
Fair Labor Standards Act, 345, 371
Fall, Albert B., 302, 304, 306, 309, 318, 321, 322
Fallen Timbers, Battle of, 50
Fallout shelters, 394, 395
Fannin, James W. Jr., 108
Farm Mortgage Moratorium Act, 337, 340
Farm Security Administration (FSA), 342
Farmer-Labor Party, 308, 309
Farmers' Alliance, 236
Farmers Holiday Association, 328, 329
Farragut, David Glasgow, 74, 168ff., 175, 183
Faubus, Orval, 387, 389
Faure, Edgar, 383
Federal Aviation Agency (FAA), 395
Federal Bureau of Investigation, (FBI), 306, 361
Federal Communications Commission (FCC), 314, 334, 335, 371, 376, 381, 394
Federal Council of Churches of Christ in America, The, 273
Federal Crop Insurance Corporation (FCIC), 344
Federal Deposit Insurance Corp. (FDIC), 330
Federal Farm Mortgage Corporation, 334
Federal Fugitive Slave law, 118
Federal Government, 39, 46, 50, 55, 68, 78, 90, 98, 100, 102, 103, 105. *See also under* specific agency, department and branch names.
Federal Hall, 42, 44
Federal Home Loan Bank Act, 328, 329, 335
Federal Judiciary Act, 44
Federal Power Commission, (FPC), 300, 337
Federal Reserve System, (FRS), 326, 332, 335, 337
Federal Securities Act, 332
Federal Society of Journeymen Cordwainers, 50

Irving, William, 64
Israel, 423
Italy, 256, 298, 346, 350, 351, 353, 356, 366
Iturbide, Augustin de, 86, 87

Jackson, Andrew, 63, 72ff., 79, 80, 82, 85, 87, 91, 92, 96ff., 115, 122, 125
Jackson, Fort, 162, 169
Jackon, Henry, 457
Jackson, Jesse, 458
Jackson State College, 414
Jackson, Thomas J., 166, 168
Jackson, William, 40
James, Henry, 288
James, Jesse W., 222
James, William, 277
Japan, 256, 257, 272, 278, 298, 308, 343, 344, 349ff., 360, 361, 363, 364, 366, 375, 392
Jarvis-Gann Amendment (California Constitution), 447
Jay, John, 25, 32, 35, 37, 38, 42, 45, 50, 52, 97
Jay Treaty, 51ff.
Jefferson Day, 98, 100
Jefferson, Fort, 162, 189
Jefferson, Territory of, 156
Jefferson, Thomas, 18, 20, 21, 35, 36, 38, 40, 44, 47, 48ff., 53, 55, 57, 58ff., 62ff., 66, 67, 76, 82, 94, 162
Jeffries, James J., 255, 256, 266
Jeffries, John, 49
"Jim Crow," 236, 245
"John Brown's Body," 166
Johnson, Andrew, 165, 169, 180ff., 188ff., 211, 213, 228
Johnson, Herschel V., 160
Johnson, Hiram, 281
Johnson, Jack, 273, 286
Johnson, John, 26
Johnson, Joseph E., 166, 168, 169, 179, 181
Johnson, Lyndon B., 393, 398ff., 421
Johnson, Rafer, 459
Johnson, Richard M., 106, 112, 115
Johnston, Albert S., 151, 153, 169
Jolson, Al, 315, 373
Jones, Anson, 123, 125
Jones, James, 444
Jones, Jim, 446
Jones, John Luther (Casey), 256

Jones, John Paul, 22, 26, 48
Jones, William, 79
Jory, Victor, 454

Kalakawa, King, 210
Kalb, Johann de, 28
Kamehameha III, King, 144, 146
Kanagawa, Treaty of, 146
Kansas, 87, 144ff., 163, 164, 210
Kansas-Nebraska Act, 144, 145, 149, 150
Kantor, MacKinlay, 444
Kaskaskia, 25, 81
Kauffmann, Henrik de, 351
Kaufman, George S., 304
Kearney, Denis, 218
Kearny, Stephen Watts, 127ff.
Keene, Laura, 149
Kefauver, Estes, 384, 385
Keller, Helen, 409
Kellogg-Briand Pact, 314, 317, 318, 328
Kendall, Amos, 97
Kendrick, John B., 304
Kennedy, Edward, 411, 412
Kennedy, John F., 385, 392ff
Kennedy, Robert, 395, 400, 408, 409
Kent State University, 414
Kentucky, 21, 25, 32, 41, 48, 55, 57, 84
Kentucky Derby, 211
Kent v. *Dulles,* 388
Kern, Jerome, 315
Kerr-McGee Corporation, 448
Kettering, Charles F., 278
Key, Francis Scott, 75, 324
Khrushchev, Nikita, 390ff.
Kilmer, Joyce, 296
"King, Andrew I," 105
King, Fort, 107
King Kalakaua, 238
King, Jr., Martin Luther, 385, 398ff.
King, Rufus, 42, 61, 66, 78
King, Samuel W., 118
King, William R.D., 141, 143
Kings Mountain, 29
Kingston, 23
Kinsey, Alfred Charles, 385
Kirby-Smith, Edmund, 171
Kirk, Claude, 405
Kiss Me, Kate, 401
Kissinger, Henry, 416, 418, 420ff., 430ff., 458
"Kitchen Cabinet," 97
"Kitchen debate," 391
Kitty Hawk, 263

Klondike, The, 249
Knapp, Isaac, 100
Knight, William J., 405
Knights of Columbus, 222
Knights of Labor, 199, 217, 222, 232, 233, 235
Know-Nothing Party, 125, 145ff.
Knox, Frank, 339
Knox, Henry, 18, 36, 39, 44, 51
Korea, 222, 266, 372ff.
Korean Airlines, 457
Kossuth, Louis, 139
Koven, Reginald de, 234
Kroc, Ray, 458
Ku Klux Klan, 195, 200, 286, 287, 306, 308, 342, 449, 451

Labor Day, 222
Labor, Department of, 231
Labor Unions, 192, 194, 199, 210, 217, 222, 228, 231, 235ff., 356ff., 365ff., 384, 391, 392; strikes, 228, 237, 240, 241, 253, 260, 261, 280ff., 298, 304, 316, 321, 328, 333, 335, 338ff., 346, 351, 356, 360, 364, 366ff., 391. *See also* specific names.
La Branche, Alcee, 112
Lady Chatterley's Lover, 391
Lafayette, Marquis de, 22, 31
Laffite, Jean, 79
La Follette, Robert M., 256, 274, 278, 279, 308ff., 316, 322
La Guardia, Fiorello, 367
Lakes; Champlain, 21ff., 74, 75; Erie, 32, 51, 73, 74, 79; Mead, 339; Michigan, 38; Oneida, 93; Ontario 70; Superior, 119
Lamar, Mirabeau B., 111
Lamas, Fernando, 454
Lamb, William, 186
"Lame Duck" Amendment, 326
Land Act of 1796, 52; of 1800, 57; of 1804, 61
Land, Emory S., 356
Land grants, 62, 117, 120, 170
Landon, Alfred M., 338, 339, 385
Lane, James H., 148
Langdon, John, 44
Langston, John Mercer, 146
Lansing, Robert, 286, 300
Laos, 373, 394, 416
Laramie, Fort, 189
Larkin, Thomas O., 119, 125

472

Muir, John, 285
Mulligan, James, 213
Munson, Thurmon, 448
Murdock, John, 51
Muscle Shoals, 324, 332
Muskie, Edmund, 409, 412, 450
Mussolini, Benito, 346, 356

Nader, Ralph, 404
Nagasaki, 361, 383
Nashborough, Fort, 28
Nashville Journal, 149
Nast, Thomas, 209
Natchez, 55
Nation, Carry (Amelia), 278
National Academy of Design, 93
National Aeronautics and Space Administration (NASA), 389, 390, 397, 446
National Afro-American Council, 255
National Association for the Advancement of Colored People, (NAACP), 345, 452
National Black Political Convention, 418
National Broadcasting Company, 353
National Budget and Accounting Act, 302
National Civil Service Reform League, 230
National Congress of Parents and Teachers (PTA), 247
National Council of the Churches of Christ, 373
National Democrats, 160
National Foundation on the Arts and the Humanities, 403
National Gallery of Art, 350, 398, 406
National Grange, 195, 198, 232
National Guard, 288, 293
National Intelligencer, 122
National Labor Relations Board (NLRB), 336
National Labor Union, 192
National *Negro* Convention, 143
National Progressive Republican League, 278
National Prohibition Party, 199, 204
National Recovery Administration (NRA), 330

National Republican Party, 101, 102, 103, 106
National Union Party, 180, 181, 182
National Wildlife Refuge, 262
National Youth Administration (NYA), 336, 337
Native American Party, 125
Naturalization Act of 1795, 55
Nautilus, U.S.S., 337, 380, 389
Navajo Indians, 373
Navy, Department of, 55
Nazi party, 451
Nebraska, 144ff., 164, 194, 338
Nebraska Relief and Aid Society, 209
Negroes, 42, 46, 47, 51, 53, 60, 78, 86, 87, 96, 101, 102, 114, 116, 118, 153, 170, 177; citizenship, 192, 194ff., first Senator, 200; first Congressman, 201; first governor, 205; civil rights struggles, 202, 204, 219, 224, 234, 235, 245, 251. *See also* under specific names or subjects.
Netherlands, 31, 32, 103, 104
Nevada, 164, 184, 324
Newbold, Charles, 54
Newburgh Addresses, 34, 72
"New Colossus, The," 230
"New Deal," 334, 336, 338, 340, 348
New England Anti-Slavery Society, 102
New England Colored Citizen's Convention, 156
New England Emigrant Aid Company, 144, 148
New Freedom, 282
New Hampshire, 25, 40, 42, 46, 116
New Harmony, 92
New Jersey, 18, 22, 25ff., 36, 38, 44ff., 50, 61
Newlands, Francis G., 260
New Mexico, 128, 132ff., 276, 280
New Orleans, 51, 59ff., 74. 75. 76. 168
New Orleans, Battle of, 75, 76
New Republican Party, 144ff., 158
New York, 20, 21, 24, 30ff., 38, 39, 42, 46, 54, 57, 64; West Point, 24, 26, 29, 59; Saratoga, 23; Elmira, 28; White Plains, 31; Staten Is-

land, 34; Long Island, 20, 34; Sacketts Harbor, 70, 73; Plattsburg, 71; Hudson River 79, 92; Albany, 49, 54, 64; Buffalo, 73, 92
New York *Evening Post,* 58, 266
New York *Herald,* 106, 133
New York Historical Society, 81
New York State Constitutional Convention, 86
New York Stock Exchange, 160, 199, 206, 238, 264, 270, 318, 303, 320ff., 334, 344, 383
New York *Sun,* 104, 205
New York *Times,* 140, 190, 202, 317, 318
New York Times v. *United States,* 417
New York *Tribune,* 116, 166, 189, 237
New York University, 100
New York World's Fair, 346, 368, 401
Nez Perce Indians, 216
Niagara Falls, 318, 372
Niagara, Fort, 71, 73
Niagara River, 71, 72, 113
Nicaragua, 146ff., 91, 274, 312, 314, 330
Nicholls, Robert, 11
Niles Weekly Register, 69
Nilsson, Christine, 201
Nimitz, Chester, 363
Nineteenth Amendment, 301, 406
Nisei, 354
Nixon, Richard M., 377, 384, 388ff., 408ff., 448
Nobel Order of the Knights of Labor, 220
Nobel Prize, 269, 271, 281, 289, 301, 306, 311, 371, 375, 377, 378, 385, 387, 389, 395, 397, 399, 401, 402, 406, 407, 409, 412, 414, 415, 417, 420, 423, 426
Non-Importation Act, 63, 64
Non-Intercourse Act, 67, 68
Norris, George W., 276
Norris-La Guardia Act, 328
North American Air Defense Command (NORAD), 387
North Atlantic Treaty Organization (NATO), 370, 376, 387
North Carolina, 18, 20, 24, 28ff., 32, 35, 44ff., 57, 165
North Castle, 21
North Dakota, 61

Northern Pacific Railroad, 182, 206
North West Company, 66, 80
Northwestern Alliance, 233, 236
Northwest Ordinance, 40, 42, 130
Northwest Territory, 36, 40, 43, 47, 51, 59
Notre Dame, University of, 122
Nova Scotia, 18, 32, 34, 77, 114, 118
Nuclear energy, 380; testing, 386ff., 394; bombs, 389, 395; physics, 387; submarines, 389, 390, 393, 397, 399
Nullification Doctrine of, 96, 98, 100, 102ff.,

O'Brien, Pat, 456
O'Connor, Sandra Day, 452, 453
Octoroon, The, 156
Office of Price Administration, 351, 356
Ogden v. Saunders, 95
Oglala Sioux Indians, 422
Oglethorphe, James, 13
Ohio, 42, 43, 50ff., 59, 60, 69, 78, 79, 92, 112, 115
Ohio Company of Associates, 38, 40, 42, 59
Ohio University, 59
Oil, 200, 278, 357, 379, 387, 389, 410, 411, 421, 423, 425
"Okies," 353
Okinawa, 361
Oklahoma, 66, 105, 232, 234, 268, 270
"Old Black Joe," 160
"Old Folks at Home," 140
"Old Ironsides," 54
"Old Man River," 315
Olive Branch Petition, 16
Oliver, King, 304
Olney, Richard, 242
Olympic Games, 264, 317, 326, 328, 392, 420, 450, 451, 458, 459
Omaha World-Herald, 240
"Omnibus Bill," 136, 137
Oneida, 70
O'Neill, Eugene, 304
Onis, Luis, de, 82
Open Door Policy, 255ff., 264, 293, 303, 344
Operation "Big Lift," 399
Oppenheimer, Robert J., 381

Order of the Knights of St. Crispin, 194
Order of the Patrons of Husbandry, 195
Ordinance of 1785, 36, 40, 59
Ordinance of 1787, 59
Oregon, 63, 80, 82, 90, 105, 120, 124; occupation, 125ff., boundary, 125ff., slavery issue, 130ff., statehood, 155; labor law, 272
O'Riley, Peter, 155
Orleans, Territory of, 61, 63, 68, 70
Osage, Fort, 102
Osage Indians, 66
Osborn v. Bank of the United States, 90
Osceola, 106, 112
Ostend Manifesto, 144ff.
Oswald, Lee Harvey, 453
O'Sullivan, John, 126
"O Susanna," 140
Otis, Elwell S., 255
Ottawa Indians, 36
Our American Cousin, 188
Overland Monthly, 197
Owens, Robert, 92

Pacific Proving Grounds, 377, 380, 385
Packers and Stockyard Act, 303
Paine, Thomas, 18, 22, 48
Pakenham, Edward, 76
Pakenham, Richard, 122, 125, 127
Palma, Tomas Estrada, 260, 268, 269
Palmer, A. Mitchell, 299, 301
Palmer, John M., 246
Palmer, Nathaniel, B., 85
Panama, 87, 93, 94, 263, 335, 338, 347, 350, 357, 367, 400
Panama Canal, 129, 150ff., 256, 259, 260, 262ff., 281, 284, 286, 301, 302, 400, 445ff., 449
Pan American Airways, 346, 366, 367, 389
Pan-American Conference, 316, 335
Panic of 1837, 111, 112; of 1857, 151; of 1873; 207, 270, 272, 318, 325, 330
Paris, Treaty of, 34, 35, 36, 38
Parker, Alton B., 264, 265
Parker, Bonnie, 334, 335
Parkman, Francis, 140

Parks, Rosa, 385
Parsons, Samuel, 38
Patapsco River, 74
Patents, 46, 54, 105, 181, 190, 198, 200, 209, 212, 217, 218, 238, 242, 243, 278
Paterson, William, 40
Patterson, Floyd, 391
Patton, George C., 363
Patuxent River, 74
Paulding, Hiram, 151
Paulding, James K., 64
Pauling, Linus, 381, 399
Paulus, Hook, 26
Payne-Aldrich Tariff Act, 274
Payne, John Howard, 88
Payne's Landing, Treaty of, 102, 105
Payne, Sereno Elisha, 274
Peace Corps, 394, 400, 417
Pearl Harbor, 230, 353
Peary, Robert E., 274, 300
Peel, Robert, 113
Pell's Point, Battle of, 21
Pemberton, John C., 174, 175, 177
Pendelton Act, 224
Pendleton, G., 183
Pennsylvania, 21, 23, 28, 31, 34ff., 39, 40, 46, 48, 52, 54, 96, 97
Pennsylvania Council of Censors, 35
Pennsylvania Packet and Daily Advertiser, 35
Penn, William, 11
Penobscot River, 26
Pensions, 218, 226, 228, 230, 231, 234. See also Veterans.
Pentagon Papers, 417, 422
People's Party, 117, 234, 236, 237, 245
Perkins, Frances, 326
Perkins, Simon, 92
Perry, Matthew Calbreith, 142, 143, 152
Perry, Oliver Hazard, 72, 73
Pershing, John J., 288, 290, 293ff.
Perryville, Battle of, 172
Peru, 111, 116
Peterson, William, 188
Philadelphia, 21ff., 31, 34, 39, 40, 46, 49, 50, 57
Phil Kearney, Fort, 193
Philippines, 250ff., 270, 271, 283ff., 289, 335, 351, 354, 358, 360, 361, 365, 366, 381
Phillips, Wendell, 191, 225

Shay's Rebellion, 38ff., 44
Shearer, William B., 321
Sheen, Fulton J., 449
Shelby, Evan, 26
Shellabarger, Samuel, 191
Shenandoah, 232, 311
Shepard, Alan B. Jr., 395, 416
Shepherd, William, 40
Sheridan, Philip H., 181ff., 187, 189, 210
Sherman Antitrust-Act, 217, 235, 242, 247, 258, 260, 264, 272, 278, 302, 352, 358
Sherman, James S., 272, 281
Sherman, John, 156, 158, 234, 247
Sherman, Roger, 20, 40
Sherman Silver Purchase Act, 217
Sherman, William Thomas, 167, 173, 179ff., 217
Shields, James, 169, 170
Shockley, William B., 385
Show Boat, 315
Shreve, Henry Miller, 79
Shriver, R. Sargent, 394, 419
Sibley, Henry H., 152
"Sick chicken case," 337
Sikorsky, Igor, 349
Silkwood, Karen, 448
Silliman, Benjamin, 80
Silver Democrats, 242
Silver Purchase Act, 234, 235, 238, 240
Silver Republicans, 245
Simms, William Gilmore, 200, 287
Sinclair Harry F., 304, 309, 316, 320
Sinclair, Upton, 268
Singer, Isaac M., 211
Single-tax movement, 249
Sioux Indians, 171ff., 190, 193, 210
Sirhan, Sirhan, 409
Sitting Bull, Chief, 212, 213, 220, 235
Sirica, John, 424, 427ff., 445
Sixteenth Amendment, 282, 283, 435
Sixth Amendment, 212, 434
Slater, Samuel, 46
Slaughterhouse cases, 206, 210
Slavery, 18, 28, 31, 34, 42, 47, 49, 52, 57, 64, 66, 76, 80, 81ff., 90, 91, 95, 101, 102, 106, 108, 112ff., 130ff., 140ff., 150ff., 160ff., 166ff., emancipation, 167, 170ff.;

black regiment, 175, 186
Slidell, John, 124ff., 167
Sloan, John, 272
Sloat, John D., 127
Small Business Administration (SBA), 379
Smith Act, 349, 375, 387
Smith, Alfred E., 308, 314, 316, 317, 338, 360
Smith, Charlie, 448
Smith, Jedediah, 87, 91, 94
Smith, John, 10
Smith, Joseph, 98, 123
Smith, Robert, 67
Smith, Walter "Red," 454
Smith, William, 96
Smithsonian Institution, The, 128
Snake River, 62, 105
Social Democratic Party, 247
Socialist Party, 280, 290, 300, 308, 309
Social Security Act, 336, 337, 340
Society of the Cincinnati, 30, 40, 42
Soil Conservation Service, 337, 338
Son of Sam, 445
Sons of Liberty, 14
Soule, P., 144, 145
South Carolina, 20, 22, 28, 31ff., 42, 47, 103, 161, 162
South Carolina College, 95
South Carolina Exposition and Protest, 96
Southern Alliance, 233, 235
Southern Christian Leadership Conference, 398
South Pass, 91, 94
Southwest Territory, 52
Soviet Union (USSR), 320, 333, 346, 350, 351, 356, 360, 361, 363, 364, 366, 369, 371, 381, 387, 390ff., 407
Space Exploration programs, 380ff.; Pioneer, 390, 393; Tiros, 393; Mercury, 391, 399; Telstar, 397; Mariner, 397, 403, 417, Ranger, 401; Gemini, 403, 404; Surveyor, 405; Apollo and Lunar landing Program, 401, 404ff., 407, 409, 414, 416, 417, 419, 420; Mars, 403, 417; Agena, 404; Skylab 422, 424, space shuttle *Columbia,* 452; *Enterprise,* 445; *Pioneer II,* 449; *Voyager I,* 448;

Voyager II, 453. *See also* specific names of astronauts.
Spain, 34, 51, 52, 54, 57, 59, 63, 80, 85ff., 105, 114, 116, 140, 141, 144, 207, 244, 247, 250, 251, 254, 340, 379
Spangler, Edward, 189
Spanish-American War, 250ff., 258, 259
Spanish Civil War, 339, 340, 344, 346
Sparkman, John, 377
Sparks, Jarod, 92
Sparks, William A.J., 226
Spaulding, Henry Harmon, 111
Specie Circular, 108, 111ff.
Specie Resumption Act, 210, 213, 218
Spectator Papers, 64
Spitz, Mark, 420
"Spoils system," 96, 116, 220, 224, 226, 230
Spooner Act, 260, 262
"Squatter sovereignty," 131
Stalin, Joseph, 355, 361, 363, 370
Stalwarts, 219, 220
Stamp Act, 14
Standard Oil Company, 200, 320, 323
Stanley, Francis E., 254
Stans, Maurice F., 428
Stanton, Elizabeth Cady, 141, 191, 193, 195
Stanton, Frederick P., 151
Stanwix, Fort (Schuyler), 22
Stark, John, 23
Star-Spangled Banner, 75, 324
"State of Deseret," 138
States Rights Party, 369
Statue of Liberty, 225, 226, 229, 230
Steam engine, 50
Steffens, Lincoln, 262, 339
Stein, Gertrude, 365
Steinbeck, John, 397, 409
Steinmetz, Charles Proteus, 306
Stephens, Alexander Hamilton, 163, 186, 190
Stephens, Uriah S., 199
Stevens, Ann Sophia, 160
Stevens, John, 67, 76
Stevens, John F., 238, 266
Stevens, Thaddeus, 191, 197
Stevenson, Adlai E., 237, 257
Stevenson, Adlai, 375, 377, 384, 385, 403

BIG BOOK OF
Whittle Fun